CLASSIC CONFLICTS

WARFARE
AND THE
THIRD REICH

CLASSIC CONFLICTS

WARFARE
AND THE
THIRD REICH

THE RISE AND FALL OF HITLER'S ARMED FORCES

CONSULTANT EDITOR
CHRISTOPHER CHANT

SMITHMARK

A SALAMANDER BOOK

This edition published in 1996 by SMITHMARK Publishers,
a division of U.S. Media Holdings, Inc.,
16 East 32nd Street,
New York, NY 10016

1 3 5 7 9 8 6 4 2

SMITHMARK books are available for bulk purchase for sales
promotion and premium use. For details write or call the manager
of special sales, SMITHMARK Publishers Inc.,
16 East 32nd Street,
New York, NY 10016;
(212) 532-6600

ISBN 0-8317-7289-1

All correspondence concerning the content of this book should be
addressed to Salamander Books Ltd,
129–137 York Way,
London N7 9LG,
England

CREDITS

Designed by DW Design, London
Filmset by SX Composing
Printed in the United States of America

This book was originally published in three illustrated volumes:
Hitler's War Machine, Hitler's Generals and Their Battles
and *Hitler's Luftwaffe.*

14.98

CONTENTS

PART 1
HITLER'S WAR MACHINE

GERMANY IN THE THIRTIES

The Treaty of Versailles, signed in the Hall of Mirrors in the palace of the French Sun King on June 28, 1919, the anniversary of the Sarajevo murders, would, it was fervently hoped by Mankind, banish for ever the spectre of German aggression. Under the Treaty Germany lost 25,000 square miles of territory, six-and-a-half million subjects, over half of them German-speaking, and much valuable industrial potential, particularly in Upper Silesia. In the west Alsace-Lorraine, annexed by victorious Prussia in 1871, was restored to France. As partial compensation for the ravages of war, the industrial Saarland was placed under French administration for 15 years. In the north a plebiscite returned Danish-speaking North Schleswig to Denmark. In the east the triumph of nationalism – a dynamic historical force, largely outside the control of Woodrow Wilson, Lloyd George and Clemenceau, which had already destroyed three giant empires in a matter of weeks before the Peace Conference met – cost Germany much land in Posen, West Prussia and Pomerania.

It was here that the peace settlement was most bitterly resented; the separation of East Prussia from the rest of the Reich by the so-called Polish Corridor and the creation of the anomalous Free State of Danzig under League of Nations control (to guarantee Polish access to port facilities) were in German eyes intolerable impositions to be endured just so long as Germany was weak and despised. Resentment – though less acute – was aroused by the allied powers' refusal to permit the union of Austria and Germany so that when Hitler annexed Austria in 1938 his action could be represented, plausibly enough, as a rectification of a blatant injustice in the application of the self-determination principle. Germany lost all her former colonial possessions, which were taken over by the League of Nations and administered by the victorious powers as mandated territories.

As 'Prussian militarism' was widely regarded as a major cause of the war, Germany was severely restricted in respect of armaments. She was forbidden to have military aircraft, heavy weapons and tanks; the general staff was abolished; conscription was forbidden; and she was allowed a professional army of no more than 100,000 men and 4000 officers. In addition, the Rhineland and a 50-kilometre strip on the right bank was permanently demilitarised and an allied army of occupation stationed there for 15 years. Severe restrictions were imposed on the navy which was limited to 15,000 men, forbidden to have submarines, and allowed a total of 12 cruisers and 24 destroyers. The Kiel Canal was internationalised and coastal defences restricted. Finally, Germany was forced to acknowledge her sole war guilt and was saddled with an unknown burden of reparations. The fact that the German delegation was allowed only 48 hours in which to register objections strengthened the widespread conviction in Germany that the treaty was a '*Diktat*' deriving its validity exclusively from the armed might of the victors.

No major power takes kindly to defeat, especially a country as accustomed to the ostentatious display of power as Imperial Germany. The shock of defeat, revolution and economic dislocation failed to bring about any radical re-appraisal of Germany's foreign policy objectives. The permanent officials who staffed the foreign office in the Wilhelmstrasse and the military establishment in the ministry of defence in the nearby Bendlerstrasse lived on happily in the power-conscious world of 1914 believing as steadfastly as ever in Germany's natural right to dominate Europe. Left to their own devices by successive chancellors and presidents, they set about the uphill task of reversing the verdict of the battlefield as quickly as possible.

Geography made Germany the country of the middle destined to live in constant fear of being 'encircled' and trapped into disastrous two-front wars by envious and powerful neighbours to east and west of her. Subjugation or conquest were the stark strategic alternatives facing her in the twentieth century. No middle way was open to her – or so it seemed to Germany's political and military rulers between 1871 and 1945. The same reasoning was applied to her future as a highly industrialised power. Unless she wished to remain dangerously dependent on foreign countries for the ever-increasing quantities of food and raw materials essential for survival, then the only alternative compatible with 'national independence' was the creation of a *Grossraumwirtschaft* in Central and Eastern Europe, an economically self-sufficient area dominated by Germany and responsive to her economic needs. And in a sense the pre-occupation with *Weltpolitik* at the beginning of the twentieth century was an attempt to correct the precarious balance of diplomatic and economic power in Europe in Germany's favour by transforming her into a broadly-based world power with colonial possessions and a large navy.

Paradoxically enough, the general strategic situation in 1919 was potentially much more favourable for the realisation of these ambitions than ever before in German history. The collapse of Imperial Russia and its replacement by a weak and ostracised

Bolshevik regime removed at a stroke the 'Slav nightmare' that so oppressed Germany's leaders in 1914. Where the mighty Romanov and Habsburg empires once stood, was a mosaic of medium-sized and small states, economically weak, divided by deep suspicions and unlikely in the long run to represent a serious obstacle to German ambitions notwithstanding strenuous French efforts in the 1920s to create a *cordon sanitaire* in the Little Entente and to cultivate the Polish connection. In the west victorious Britain and France were manifestly weakened by the economic price of war and by the withdrawal of America into isolation. French power might be irresistible in the short term as the traumatic experience of the occupation of the Ruhr by French forces in 1923 and the subsequent capitulation of the German government amply demonstrated. But the essential unity of the Bismarckian *Reich* had survived peace treaty and Ruhr invasion; so that once Germany had a sizeable army at her disposal she stood every chance of being able to re-establish her political and economic hegemony in Europe in the long run in the absence of countervailing Russian and American pressure.

Within the narrow constraints of the treaty the foundations of a first-class army were already being laid in the 1920s largely through the efforts of General Hans von Seeckt, the talented and imaginative chief of army command. What the new *Reichswehr* lacked in numbers was more than compensated for by a high level of efficiency and intensive training in the tactics of mobile warfare. The *Blitzkrieg* tactics of 1939-41 with their emphasis on armour and air power were forged twenty years before in the manoeuvres and war games Seeckt made an integral part of officer training. With government connivance, the army successfully evaded many of the disarmament provisions of the treaty. The general staff survived thinly disguised as a *Truppenamt*; through short-term enlistment, cadres for a much larger army were illegally trained; prototypes of heavy weapons forbidden under the treaty were manufactured abroad in Holland and Spain with the help of German industry; and from 1921 onwards, in return for German financial and technical assistance to help build a Russian armaments industry, German pilots and tank crews were trained in Russia. By 1926 when Seeckt resigned, Germany already possessed a great army in miniature which could be transformed into a mass army when the political situation was ripe.

The rehabilitation of German military power was accompanied by corresponding steps in the diplomatic field. At first co-operation between army and foreign office was strictly limited; Seeckt, ever suspicious of the 'frocks', tended to plough his own furrow. But after his resignation the army ceased to pursue an independent line in foreign affairs and accepted the general line laid down by the foreign office largely because senior officers came to realise that Seeckt's hopes of a Russian alliance were exaggerated and that more could be gained out of good relations with the western powers.

For the next few years Germany benefited considerably from the growing feeling in Britain, France and America that Europe needed a stable and prosperous Germany.

France, too, was forced to try the policy of reconciliation with the old enemy if only because the Ruhr episode had shown the futility of trying to extract reparations at bayonet point. With the Dawes Plan of 1924 a more realistic attitude was at last adopted on that question. In 1925 Gustav Stresemann, who bore responsibility for foreign policy between 1924 and 1929, was able to play a significant role in the negotiation of the Locarno Pacts which made Germany a member of a western security agreement. In 1926 the War Guilt clause was conveniently forgotten when she was allowed to join the League of Nations with a permanent seat on the Council. Finally, in 1929, in return for a final reparations settlement, allied troops left the Rhineland five years ahead of schedule. Yet the success, though real enough, was strictly limited; it cannot be denied that the major provisions of the treaty were all intact at the time of Stresemann's death in October 1929. That did not surprise him. For, though widely regarded as an apostle of European reconciliation – he was awarded the Nobel Prize for Peace – Stresemann remained what he had always been: an old fashioned *Machtpolitiker* from the Wilhelminian era with no illusions about the role of force in the international jungle. Only countries with large armies were likely to be respected by other powers and until Germany was again in that enviable position the correct policy in respect of the recovery of Danzig, the Polish Corridor and Upper Silesia and the Anschluss with Austria was 'to finesse and avoid major decisions'.

Three years later the Republic was in its death throes and Hitler's accession to power was a matter of weeks away. The rise of the Nazis is too complex a phenomenon to be investigated here. In general one can say that the great economic crisis which swept through Europe in the early 1930s exposed grave structural weaknesses in the social and political fabric of *Weimar* Germany and favoured the growth of what in good times had been nothing more than a fringe movement destined to permanent opposition. What is of interest in this context is that even before Hitler became chancellor in January 1933 German foreign policy was entering a new and more aggressive phase.

A recrudescence of xenophobic nationalism accompanied the economic crisis in most European countries in the early 1930s as a kind of group reaction to the stimulus of external peril. In Germany mounting nationalist resentment of the Government's record obliged successive chancellors to pursue a bolder policy if only to maintain their quasi-authoritarian regimes. Bruening's abortive attempt to arrange a customs union with Austria in 1931 as the first step towards political Anschluss, and Papen's refusal to return to the Disarmament Conference in 1932 until the German demand for equality of armaments was met reveal a greater readiness than in Stresemann's day to challenge the status quo of 1919. This was also reflected in the growing confidence of the military. At this stage the army was still thinking exclusively in terms of defence against possible Polish aggression. Nevertheless, in April 1930 Wilhelm Groener, the Minister of Defence, issued a directive ordering the army to plan for rapid expansion from ten to twenty-one divisions in a future emergency –

11

in effect a mobilisation plan and as such forbidden by the treaty. So that in one sense Chancellor Hitler, heading an orthodox right-wing cabinet with two other Nazis in it, simply continued and radicalised this new trend in German policy.

The Nazi movement itself expressed in a more extreme form ideas commonplace in right-wing political circles for generations. The Nazis glorified physical violence, accepting the crude Social Darwinian proposition that life is struggle, i.e. they popularised what 'respectable' foreign office officials had believed since the days of Bismarck. Nations, like individuals, struggled for existence and survived only at the expense of the weak; that was Hitler's constant theme from *Mein Kampf* to the last days in the Berlin bunker. War was a natural instrument of policy and within certain limits had a therapeutic value as a purgative of weak elements in a people. Hitler's rabid anti- semitism and his fanatical belief that Germany had a mission to save the Aryan race from the infamous schemes of 'World Jewry' infused a sense of cosmic urgency into traditional nationalist demands for the union of all Germans in one *Reich* and for eastward expansion to obtain 'living space' for the German people. Possibly, too, as many German historians now believe, Hitler envisaged a second phase of expansion in the distant future when a German dominated continent would wrestle with America (and possibly Britain) for Western Mastery. To realise the immediate objectives in Europe, whether by war or intimidation, Germany needed a large army.

The form rearmament took under Hitler was determined by internal and external constraints. For the first 18 months relatively little was done partly because of the overriding need to get Germany back to work again and partly because the form military expansion should take was in dispute. Ernst Roehm, leader of the restless and powerful Brownshirts, pressed for the creation of a peoples' militia under Brownshirt control. Only in February 1934 did Hitler finally decide in favour of a mass army trained and led by professional soldiers. And not until after the Blood Purge of June, which decimated the Brownshirt leadership, did rearmament get under way in earnest.

Rearmament posed serious economic problems for Germany because of her heavy dependence on food and raw material imports. Once the slack in the economy had been taken up by 1935, continued emphasis on rearmament led inevitably to balance of payments difficulties. What is significant is Hitler's refusal to tolerate any substantial depression of living standards as the price of rearmament, for the very good reason that dictatorships are in practice more sensitive than democracies to the mood of the public or what their secret police suppose is the public mood. Gestapo reports revealed much dissatisfaction just below the surface which Nazi leaders feared (probably quite erroneously) would assume serious proportions should economic conditions worsen appreciably. Another consideration that weighed heavily with Hitler was an instinctive feeling that long-term investment in the armaments industry and the general disruption of the peace-time economy consequent upon in-depth rearmament of the 1914-18 variety would endanger his personal rule by placing too much power in the hands of economic overlords.

The alternative strategy of rearmament in breadth fitted the bill exactly. For by restricting war production to a limited sector of the economy it proved possible to combine the production of large quantities of tanks and guns with minimum dislocation of the economy. No undue strain was placed on the people and in addition Hitler was able to build up an impossibly large army in the shortest possible time. The existence of a considerable army would of itself tend to demoralise Germany's small neighbours. And to this end the propaganda machine deliberately exaggerated the extent of rearmament so effectively in practice that only after the war did it become apparent how far Germany had been from total mobilisation in 1939. The fact was that, despite Goering's defiant boast of a choice between 'guns and butter', the Germans continued to have reasonable quantities of both up to 1942.

Finally, rearmament in breadth made military sense in the opinion of at least some of Hitler's generals. If it came to war, a small army with a core of powerful armoured units supported by motorised infantry and trained in *Blitzkrieg* tactics could strike quickly and win decisive battles in a matter of days, always provided of course that the Führer could isolate the victim and guarantee that Germany would not be plunged into a long war which she could not possibly win.

Externally, the progress of rearmament was dependent upon the attitude of the Great Powers towards the Nazi regime. As Hitler expected vigorous reactions from the French he moved cautiously at first, seeking to reassure the powers of his peaceful intentions though not with any great success. What proved decisive was not Hitler's manoeuvres but the feeling in British, Italian and American government circles that it was intolerable for Germany to remain disarmed while other powers – especially France – refused to reduce their arms levels. With the tacit consent of the powers Hitler was able to take Germany out of the Disarmament Conference and the League of Nations in October 1933, a defiant gesture calculated to show the German people that, like preceding chancellors, he intended to pursue an active foreign policy. By the spring of 1934, when France precipitately broke off further disarmament negotiations, it was clear that Hitler's fears of France had been grossly exaggerated and that rearmament could proceed without hindrance from that quarter.

It was the gathering pace of German rearmament that dictated the next move. By the beginning of 1935 the *Reichswehr* had increased in size from 100,000 to 240,000 men (not counting another 200,000 policemen trained outside the army as infantrymen), and military command was already planning a peace-time army of twenty-one divisions. But without conscription it was impossible to produce the reserves that army would need in wartime. The opportunity to put this right presented itself in March 1935 when France increased the period of compulsory service and lowered the age of enlistment to offset the effects of a falling birth-rate. On March 9 Goering had already announced the existence of a German air force, which amounted to some

2000 machines, few of them fit for front line service. As the news met with little adverse reaction in the west, on March 16 Hitler announced the re-introduction of conscription and the creation of a peace-time army of 36 divisions (the army's revised target). The western powers, as expected, confined themselves to verbal protests at this clear breach of treaty.

In March 1936 Hitler re-militarised the Rhineland, his most daring diplomatic move so far. The disunity of the western powers over the Abyssinian affair was too good an opportunity to miss and three battalions were sent into the demilitarised zone as a token of the restoration of complete sovereignty. The re-occupation marked a new and more aggressive phase in German foreign policy. For had France ordered immediate counter measures – as common prudence suggested she ought to have – it would have been quite beyond the military capacity of Germany to have resisted at this stage; in that event the battalions were under orders to stage a fighting withdrawal. Hitler's intuitive judgment – supported by the experience of the last three years - that France would remain passive proved right. Germany derived considerable strategic advantage from the re-occupation. Her exposed western flank could now be protected and work commenced on the famous West Wall. But it was the psychological significance of the French failure to resist that encouraged Hitler most, revealing as it did a deep malaise at the heart of Germany's old foe.

In September 1936 Hitler began to mobilise the Germany economy for war. The Four Year Plan announced by Hitler at the Party Congress was intended to make Germany as self-sufficient as possible in respect of certain raw materials with particular emphasis on petrol and rubber, both essential ingredients of a modern war machine. Of course complete self-sufficiency was not possible within Germany's existing frontiers as Hitler knew full well. Only by expanding eastwards to the Ural mountains could Germany achieve a degree of autarky corresponding to her political ambitions. Meanwhile, the measures adopted in 1936 were more in the nature of a crash programme to prepare the German army for war by 1940. In the summer of 1938, under the pressure of the Czech crisis, the wider aspects of the plan were abandoned in favour of intensified efforts to attain maximum production of gunpowder, high explosives and vital chemicals by – significantly enough – the end of 1939.

Towards the end of 1937 Hitler was growing restless and inclined to accelerate the pace of German expansion. There were good reasons for this. In recent months the strategic situation had changed dramatically in Germany's favour. Italy was now the friend of Germany. The Abyssinian War strained Italy's relations with Britain and France, and close upon its heels came the Italian involvement in the Spanish Civil War. Italy moved closer to the German camp and in November the so-called Berlin-Rome Axis came into being. Hitler could now feel reasonably confident that Italy would be too pre-occupied with Mediterranean problems to intervene – as she had done over Austria in 1934 – should Germany move eastwards.

In the west France was gravely weakened by the collapse of the Locarno system.

Belgium had lapsed into neutrality. Britain, though prepared to aid France in the event of German aggression, made it clear that this promise did not extend to France's allies in Eastern Europe; Poland and the Little Entente were, in effect, left to their own devices whilst the weakness of Russia, ally of France since 1935, was dramatically illustrated by the purges in the summer of 1937 which decimated the top echelons in the Red Army.

Hitler was aware, too, that any military advantage Germany might possess over her opponents would certainly disappear by the mid-1940s when those powers would themselves have rearmed. Possibly he sensed that his regime, rigidly committed to rearmament, could not satisfy the growing social aspirations of a people now back at work; only by intensifying the pace of his foreign policy could he preserve his own dictatorial power, escape the inflationary effects of rearmament and maintain the dynamic of the Nazi state. Therefore, in the autumn of 1937 he decided, as he informed his closest associates at the Hossbach meeting on November 5, that Germany must secure her 'living space' by 1943-5 at the latest, and might seize Austria and Czechoslovakia before that date if favourable circumstances arose.

As a preliminary to a more aggressive policy, Hitler extended his control over the army. So far he had left the army to get on with the task of rearmament without interference. But he had grown increasingly impatient of conservative-minded von Fritsch, commander-in-chief of the army since 1934 and a constant opponent of Hitler's pressure for accelerated rearmament. Early in 1938 a scandal concerning the wife of von Blomberg, the Minister of War, and false charges against Fritsch were pounced upon by Hitler as a pretext to be rid of them both. The pliable von Brauchitsch replaced Fritsch. Blomberg was not replaced; instead Hitler assumed the post of commander-in-chief of the Wehrmacht and appointed the subservient Wilhelm Keitel head of a new planning staff – the *OKW* or armed forces command – immediately responsible to himself. The balance of power in the high command shifted decisively in his favour and a process commenced which ended logically with Hitler's assumption of personal command of the army in 1941.

For some years after Hitler's accession to power army strategy remained defensive in nature. Plan Red, a deployment plan to deal with a possible French attack, was drawn up in 1935. Although Blomberg had been interested in studying at that time the feasibility of attacking Czechoslovakia, not until 1937 was work begun upon Plan Green for a pre-emptive strike at Czechoslovakia and only then in the event of a two-front war. However, by the summer of that year the army was beginning to adopt a more aggressive posture largely because Blomberg, an ardent Nazi, was under Hitler's influence. Already the army was instructed to be ready for the exploitation of favourable circumstances as and when they arose. After the Hossbach meeting pride of place was given by Germany's military leaders to Plan Green. Army and air force leaders were now prepared to launch an attack on Czechoslovakia in peace-time if conditions were favourable, i.e. the army was no longer pursuing a defensive strategy but consciously underwriting Hitler's imperialist plans for living space.

Even so, when Hitler seized Austria in March 1938 it was by accident rather than design. Since July 1934 when an abortive Austrian Nazi coup resulted in the death of the then Chancellor Dollfuss and aroused world opinion against Germany, Hitler handled Austria with kid gloves. By the winter of 1937/8 the Austrian Nazis, like the Sudeten Germans, were growing restless. When Chancellor Schuschnigg visited Hitler in February 1938 to discuss Austria's future, the latter succeeded in driving a hard bargain with the Austrians which went a long way toward the peaceful absorption of Austria in Germany. Hitler was perfectly satisfied, and there the matter would probably have rested had not Schuschnigg tried to upset the arrangement by announcing a plebiscite to allow the Austrians to decide their own future. An angry Hitler, under pressure from the more aggressive Goering, intervened and when he had 'arranged' an invitation from a pro-Nazi chancellor ordered German troops into Austria.

Next day, March 13, Austria became part of the *Reich*. The Great Powers acquiesced in the Anschluss. Neither Britain, France nor Italy was prepared to help Schuschnigg as Hitler knew before his troops marched. Overnight the strategic situation in Central Europe was transformed. Control of historic Vienna gave the Germans a dominant position in the Balkans. In the south Germany now had a common frontier with her friend Italy while in the north Czechoslovakia's strategic position suddenly worsened.

The ease of his victory undoubtedly encouraged Hitler not to wait any longer – as he might have done despite the Hossbach 'timetable' – but to turn his attentions to Czechoslovakia without delay. The 'neutralisation' of this democratic state, king-pin of the anti-German Little Entente and a spearhead in the German flank, was a strategic necessity to give Germany freedom of manoeuvre for eastward expansion. To achieve this end, Hitler relied on a mixture of political and military pressure. The grievances of three-and-a-half million Sudeten Germans against the Prague government were ruthlessly exploited by the local Nazis under strict orders from Berlin to keep the tension at boiling point throughout the summer and so demoralise the Czechs that military intervention in the autumn – a course to which Hitler committed himself in May – would deliver the *coup de grâce*. All the indications were that Britain and France would remain passive spectators while Italy was still too preoccupied with Mediterranean problems to be concerned about a German attack on Czechoslovakia.

Though one cannot entirely discount the possibility that Hitler was bluffing from start to finish and never intended war over Czechoslovakia, the balance of probability strongly supports the view that the military threat to Czechoslovakia was a very real one and that the Germans could have defeated her. Thirty-seven divisions, including three armoured and four motorised, were concentrated around Czechoslovakia in a menacing semi-circle from Austria to Silesia when Chamberlain's unexpected intervention in mid-September upset Hitler's plans. To maximise the surprise element (so vital for the success of Blitzkrieg tactics) the Germans adopted the cunning stratagem of calling up reservists not for war – formal mobilisation would have been a provocative step likely to stretch French and Czech patience to breaking point – but ostensibly for routine autumn manoeuvres. In this way Germany 'mobilised' so effectively that an attack on Czechoslovakia could have been launched without waiting for formal mobilisation orders. Significantly, too, assault divisions were moved into advanced positions at night and heavily camouflaged. An element of bluff entered the picture only in respect of Germany's military preparations in the west where five divisions were stationed to defend the half-completed West Wall which could not, in fact, have been held for more than two to three weeks in the face of a French offensive as Hitler must have realised.

It was precisely this fear of French intervention and the corollary of a two-front war which Germany could not possibly win that explains the mounting opposition in high military circles to Hitler's plans. In so far as Hitler could not guarantee absolutely that war with Czechoslovakia would be strictly localised, his entire policy in the autumn of 1938 amounted to a piece of reckless brinkmanship based on intuitive judgment about western reactions and not on the logistical reality of German military capabilities. On the other hand, Hitler did not allow his primitive desire to smash the Czechs by force to blind him to changes in the tactical situation. Thus, when the Czechs mobilised on September 23 and reports came in of partial mobilisation in France, Hitler was quick to appreciate that the vital surprise element was virtually eliminated from the picture leaving him with no viable alternative but to settle, reluctantly, for the surrender of the Sudetenland at the Munich Conference.

Six months later German troops drove through the snow-covered streets of Prague and completed the destruction of the Czech state. Once again Hitler relied upon a judicious blend of political and military pressure. In the spring of 1939 the Slovaks acted as his Trojan horse; their demands for independence were fostered by the Germans and precipitated a crisis which gave Hitler his chance to intervene – as always – at the 'invitation' of the victim. The army had been alerted to Hitler's intentions as early as October 1938 whilst, significantly, no-one anticipated serious opposition from the western powers. The balance of military power in Central Europe shifted decisively in favour of Germany. The Little Entente was smashed to pieces and Romania and Yugoslavia hastened to make their peace with Hitler. German influence became predominant in the Danubian Basin and exploitation of the economic resources of the area entered a new and more aggressive phase. In the mid-1930s Schacht, Hitler's minister of economics, negotiated barter agreements with the countries of South-eastern Europe in order to acquire the essential raw materials for rearmament. In the late 1930s Goering, the new economic overlord of Germany, was attempting to create a *Grossraumwirtschaft* in the area, reducing Yugoslavia, Romania

17

and Bulgaria to quasi-colonial territories; Germany not only took their grain and ores but was pumping in capital sums to ensure that they produced the raw materials Germany needed.

In June 1939, exactly 20 years since the peace of Versailles had been forced on a resentful people, Germany's position had changed out of all recognition. She was again a power to be reckoned with and every utterance of her leader was studied in minute detail in every European chancellery. For example, pressure from her foreign minister von Ribbentrop was sufficient to make little Lithuania decide hurriedly in March 1939 to hand over the Memelland taken from Germany in 1919. Internally, though political opposition was ruthlessly repressed and the Jews were being systematically persecuted from 1933 onwards, the German people were back at work. Instead of the mass unemployment conditions which plagued western lands material conditions were tolerable and a shortage of labour actually existed in Germany on the eve of war.

Three months later Germany was at war with Poland, Britain and France and Hitler was set on a course which led in the end to the total and utter collapse of Nazi Germany in 1945. How did this come about?

Wars do not have trivial causes. Several factors must combine to produce an inflammatory situation where only a spark is needed to cause the final explosion. Such was the case in August 1939. A crisis existed in German-Polish relations ever since the breakdown of negotiations over the Corridor in March, a failure which signified the end of genuine German attempts to win Poland over as a junior partner for adventures in the east. In this tense situation the British guarantee to Poland on March 31 and the formal alliance in August – suggesting that Britain had reversed the traditional policy of disengagement in Eastern Europe and would now resist Hitler's designs in the east - strengthened his resolve to teach the Poles a lesson. Whether economic pressures played a significant role in the decision to strike at Poland it is difficult to say. Undoubtedly stresses and strains were mounting in Nazi Germany because of the unwise acceleration of rearmament in an already overheated economy, and may well have confirmed Hitler in his decision. That is very far from saying that economic pressures were so intense that Hitler was obliged on that account to go to war. But there were sound military reasons for striking soon. In two or three years, as Hitler often remarked in the winter of 1938/9, Germany's opponents would have a military advantage over her. If war was unavoidable to achieve his aims in the east then better war in 1939 than 1943. In that sense it can certainly be said that Hitler was driven to war ahead of the Hossbach 'timetable'. The parallel with Imperial Germany springs to mind. In the summer of 1914 a not dissimilar 'either-or' situation faced her (or so her leaders supposed); either Germany waited passively until the balance of military power moved inexorably against her and 'encirclement' turned into subjugation; or else she exploited her waning military power to break the ring of 'encirclement' closing round her and re-establish her hegemony in Europe.

Without doubt Germany's armed forces were ready for war with Poland. Instead of the ten divisions of 1920 Germany possessed a peace-time army of 52 divisions to call on, her total mobilised strength was 103 divisions; of these 70 were fit for active service. By 1942 it was estimated that Germany would have sufficient reserves for 150 divisions and would then reach the maximum capacity of her arms-producing industry. Morale was high in the armed forces on the eve of war. In the west the defences had been greatly strengthened and Hitler's generals were much more confident of holding the line (with ten divisions) than at the time of the Czech crisis.

Though air power was primarily a support weapon for the ground forces, Germany's progress was impressive here also. In 1920 she had no military aircraft; in 1939 she possessed about 3000 aircraft including 1180 medium bombers, 771 single-seater fighters and 336 dive bombers. Most of the craft were types first produced in 1936 whereas French and British aircraft were of an older vintage. But once the western powers started to rearm in earnest from 1938 onwards, their aircraft were inevitably equipped with machines of slightly better design and performance than the Germans. From about mid-1939, all things being equal, the balance of air power would begin to move against Germany slowly but surely, another good reason for exploiting the temporary advantage quickly.

Economically, Germany was in a position to wage a short successful war in 1939. It is true that her dependence on foreign supplies of copper, zinc, lead and iron ore was greater in 1939 than ever before. On the other hand, Germany was producing sufficient synthetic rubber (22,000 tons in 1939) to meet current needs; aluminium output was in excess of demand; and though synthetic oil production at 2.8 million tons (all types of fuel) was disappointing and left Germany dependent on Romanian and Yugoslavian supplies she had considerable stocks of diesel oil and petrol. Thanks to Nazi agricultural policy, she was practically self-sufficient in bread, potatoes, milk, sugar and meat. Bearing in mind that Hitler intended to plunder occupied territory and to depress the living standard of the inhabitants to recoup his material losses, it can certainly be maintained that Germany was ready for war.

Not, of course, for a major war. Nor did Hitler intend to wage such a war. He assumed that Britain and France would abandon Poland in the final resort as they had abandoned Czechoslovakia. If there were any lingering doubts in the west these would surely be removed, so he supposed, by the Non-Aggression Pact Ribbentrop signed with Russia on August 23. The western powers were stunned by the news. Their hopes of an alliance with Russia to contain Nazi Germany were dashed; Poland was completely isolated and an attack on her virtually certain unless she capitulated, of which there was no sign. In the short term Hitler was surely right. Britain and France made no serious effort to aid Poland when Germany attacked her on September 1 and she was defeated within a month in the first *Blitzkrieg* of the war. Probably Hitler did not suppose the British and French declarations of war represented more than a fleeting mood, a face-saving device by elderly politicians who would soon see reason once

Germany had defeated Poland. The attack on Poland was not an irredeemable error. The fatal mistakes came later between the summer of 1940 and the summer of 1941; it was the failure to drive Britain out of the war in 1940 and the attack on Russia in 1941 that trapped Germany once more in a two-front war, which it was beyond her military and economic capacity to win.

THE HOME FRONT

On April 21, 1945, the last conference at the Ministry of Propaganda took place. Dr Joseph Goebbels, the Minister, limped into the shuttered, candle-lit room, slightly late; as always, his appearance was dapper, his hair oiled and carefully brushed. German defences on every front had disintegrated; the Russians were closing in on Berlin. Goebbels developed the theme of treason by the old officers' clique at length: Hitler's Germany had been destroyed from the inside. Perhaps the Minister remembered 1918, and the 'stab in the back' excuse for Germany's failure in the war. The Social Democrats, rather than the officers, had then allegedly committed the act of treason. In 1945, there existed no organisation of consequence in Germany, apart from the Nazi party and the army, which could be blamed for the disaster.

The differences between 1918 and 1945 went further. In 1918, Germany itself had escaped comparatively unharmed; the destruction of the war had stopped short of the country's frontiers. In 1945, however, Hitler had issued, on March 19, his destruction order. The German people had failed him; there was no other alternative before Germany than Bolshevism; the Allies were therefore to find a desert in the place of the Third *Reich*. Hitler ordered that:

'1. All military, transport, communications, industrial and supply installations as well as equipment with the *Reich* which the enemy might use for the continuation of his struggle now or in the future must be destroyed.

2. The destruction of all military objects, including transport and communication installations, is the responsibility of the military commando posts; that of all industrial and supply installations as well as other materials is the responsibility of the *Gauleiters* and *Reich* Defence Commissioners. The troops must give the *Gauleiters* and *Reich* Defence Commissioners the necessary assistance for the execution of their work.

3. This order must be made known to all commanders as quickly as possible.'

Even without Hitler's destruction orders, Germany lay in ruins in the spring of 1945; Hitler and Goebbels, who had won control of Berlin from the Communists in the street battles of the early 1930s, were now defending the capital in a last-ditch effort against the Red Army. In the last months of the Third *Reich*, the fortunes of Joseph Goebbels – the Minister for Enlightenment and Propaganda, to give him his full title – and of the skills he represented, stood high. In the second part of his political testament of April 29, 1945, Hitler rewarded Goebbels by appointing him the *Reich* Chancellor – while at the same time, expelling Hermann Goering, and the *Reichsfuehrer SS* and Minister of Interior, Heinrich Himmler, from the party and all other offices.

The National Socialist state was founded and run by the means of a blend of persuasion and coercion – of the carrot and the stick – in a starker and more visible form than other one-party states. Joseph Goebbels and Heinrich Himmler were the leading exponents of the two arts: Goebbels was the persuader; Himmler wielded the stick. Like their chosen instruments of power, their personalities sharply differed. Goebbels was the intellectual: flamboyant in his youth, he toned down his manner and appearance when he assumed Ministerial responsibilities. But there remained something of a showman about him; everything he did was calculated to impress. He had written a novel in his youth; but his main strength lay in the manipulation of words for political purposes. He was good at coining phrases and constructing images. For instance, in terms of Nazi predilections, Goebbels and his propagandists described the Italians as ideologically sound but racially questionable; the English the other way round; of the Austrians Goebbels said that they were not a nation, but a 'hallucination'.

But it was the construction of the Hitler myth that was Goebbels' masterpiece. The Minister of Propaganda, who usually took a very detached view of his art as well as of his performance, perhaps came closest to believing his own propaganda when it concerned Hitler. Goebbels depicted him at first as a representative of a hard-pressed generation – the symbol of the Nazi view of post-war Germany; then as both a superman and a man of the people. Goebbels used quasi-religious imagery; miracle, mission, Messiah were words which occurred frequently. Hitler was the far-sighted planner of Germany's recovery: he was tolerant of other people's foibles; he was, basically, an artist. By the outbreak of the war, the image of Hitler had so many facets to it that it appeared to the great majority of Germans to shine; Hitler as the great military expert emerged in the course of 1939. With one exception, the imagery was purely masculine. On only one occasion, Goebbels wrote of Hitler that 'The whole nation loves him because it feels safe in his hands like a child in the arms of his mother'.

The personality cult of Hitler was the kingpin of Nazi propaganda and, during the war, doubtless made a great contribution to the maintenance of the morale of the nation. One of the last photographs of Hitler shows him, on a bleak early spring day in 1945, reviewing a ragged row of young boys, members of the *Hitlerjugend*. They, together with pensioners and veterans unfit to wage another war, made up the *Volkssturm* – the people's last reserve. Their loyalty to the synthetic image of Hitler, rather than to the Germany lying in ruins around them, probably made it possible for them to wage the unequal struggle.

Goebbels himself, however, hardly ever believed his propaganda. He was too much of an intellectual for that: but he was a very tough kind of intellectual. He remained with Hitler to the last moment; he, as well as his large family, died with their Fuehrer. He had never wavered in his determination to win the war for Germany; he never even winced, in public, when the war was lost. His judgment, especially when he was flushed with fight as a young man, was questionable. On April 13, 1926, for instance. Goebbels wrote in his diary '. . . with Himmler in Landshut; Himmler a good fellow and very intelligent, I like him.'

Himmler was then 26 years old; Goebbels was some three years older. He is the only person on record who described Himmler as 'very intelligent'. Himmler's strength lay elsewhere: in 1926, this may not yet have been apparent. Himmler was the second son of a schoolmaster, who was born, and spent his youth in Bavaria, the stronghold of National Socialism. He married in 1928, a woman seven years older than himself, of Polish origin. She then owned a small nursing home in Berlin: she sold it after her marriage and bought a smallholding outside Munich. Himmler had a diploma in agriculture: his wife reared chickens, while he gave a lot of his time to the Nazi party in Munich. In January 1929, his devotion to the cause was rewarded. He was appointed, by Hitler, the *Reichsfuehrer SS*: in spite of the grand title, he had only some 300 men under his command, and a salary of 200 marks a month. The SS, or *Schutzstaffel*, was originally intended to protect Nazi speakers: but Himmler had other plans for it. He wanted to make the SS into an utterly reliable body of carefully chosen men. He succeeded in doing this, and thereby laid the basis for his future fortune.

Himmler was a dedicated perfectionist: his drab personality and appearance, as well as his hidden conviction, made him a person who was easily underestimated. Those of his colleagues and enemies who made the mistake paid for it dearly. He was far from detached: he was totally committed. He was totally committed to Hitler, though he betrayed the *Fuehrer* in the end, and ran away from Berlin; he was totally committed to his vision of the kind of people the Germans should be. But Himmler was neither an intellectual nor was he very intelligent. He had only his early training in agriculture to fall back on, and his practical experience of breeding chickens: he had to rely heavily on the wisdom, and advice, of others. It was not his habit to exercise discrimination in the choice of his mentors.

In 1929, Walter Darré, who became the Minister of Agriculture in 1933, published the book *Um Blut und Boden*. It expatiated on the essential nobility of the

Nordic peasant, his blood and the soil he tilled, which Darré thought was especially rich and fruitful. He contrasted the Nordic Aryan peasant with the Jews and the Slavs, who according to the author preferred to lurk in the decaying, decadent city streets. Darré was neither saying anything new nor did he say it in a new way. The mood against towns, against all the complexities of modern industrial civilization, was a part and parcel of German populist philosophy. In the nineteenth century, it had spread especially among school-masters; it struck a chord among the Nazi thinkers: Darré, together with Alfred Rosenberg, gave it currency within their party. They stressed the reasons why the German nation was so particularly privileged, and they succeeded in convincing the party that true Nordic Germans had a special claim to racial superiority.

The drab, pedantic person who, together with his wife, believed in efficiency, thrift and herbal cures, really thought that Rosenberg and Darré made an important and valid point, that it amplified the teachings of Hitler, and that he should dedicate his life to its realization. Goebbels, on the other hand, could not take the low quality intellectual outpourings of Rosenberg and Darré, and mocked them whenever the opportunity arose. The image of the blue-eyed, blond giant of the Nordic myth was too much for the black-haired, dark eyed Rhinelander with a club foot.

Nevertheless, by the outbreak of the war, Himmler had all the means of coercion under his control just as Goebbels controlled the instruments of persuasion. They were complementary, though neither the relative positions of their instruments nor of their masters remained static at any given time. In the *Kampfzeit* – the period of struggle after World War I until the *Machtergriefung* when Hitler became the Chancellor in January 1933 – the importance of propaganda was paramount. It helped Hitler to capture power: in the process, the services of Goebbels were indispensable. While Goebbels was helping Hitler to win Berlin and then Germany for the Nazi cause, Himmler was still busy constructing the SS and, with the aid of Reinhardt Heydrich, the SD, the *Sicherheitsdienst*. The best the SS could do was to create incidents of violence which were then exploited by Nazi propaganda.

It was in 1931 – a year of great importance for Himmler – that the foundations of his later empire were laid. Walter Darré then joined Himmler's staff to organize the *Rasse und Siedlungshauptamt*, an office which was set up to establish the racial standards required of good German stock; it was to enquire into extant ethnic groups in Europe which could be claimed for Germany; it was to settle doubts as to the racial status of individuals. In the summer of the same year, Reinhardt Heydrich joined Himmler: his work was to develop the *Sicherheitsdienst*, the Nazi security service. The year ended with the publication of the famous SS marriage code, which legislated for the racial purity of a fast-growing organization. Thousands of young men were joining the SS in 1931, the darkest year of the world economic crisis.

After January 1933 Goebbels still used propaganda to secure maximum popular support for the Nazi party and then for the Nazi state; but from then on it could be reinforced by the coercive machinery of the state. Propaganda therefore had to find its place as one of the instruments for the maintenance of political power, rather than being the main means of achieving it. Broadcasting, the film industry, publishing of every kind passed under Goebbels' control, and their administration, as well as the excitement they offered, somewhat distracted him.

After Hitler came to power, Goebbels was free to address himself to propaganda abroad: but here he ran into all kinds of difficulties. Among these were the diplomats, who did not want to relinquish any of their responsibilities; the poverty of Nazi ideology and its restricted, nationalist appeal; the lack of international experience of the Nazi leaders themselves. Nazi propaganda abroad, unless it was directed at German minorities, was mostly ineffective. On the whole, Goebbels and the art of propaganda entered the war relatively weakened. There had also been a crisis in Goebbels' personal life: he had asked Hitler, in the summer of 1938, to be relieved of his duties. The Minister of Propaganda wanted to divorce his wife, one of the leading Nazi ladies, to marry a young Czech actress, Lida Baarova.

Himmler's rise, on the other hand was less spectacular. It was steady, slow and somewhat stealthy. In 1933, Himmler became the Chief of Munich police; in that year, he set up the first concentration camp in Dachau. The SS was still nominally a part of the SA, and Ernst Roehm was still the chief of staff of the stormtroopers. On June 30, 1934, during the Night of the Long Knives, Himmler and the SS smashed the power of the SA, on Hitler's orders. The SS then came directly under Hitler's command: Himmler thus gained direct access to the *Fuehrer*. In 1934 he also gained control of the Secret Police of the State of Prussia, the dreaded Gestapo. By 1936, Heinrich Himmler had control of all the police forces in Germany.

The war, we shall have on occasion to see, vastly added to Himmler's empire; though Goebbels' powers increased as well during the war, he had to fight hard to find his way back into Hitler's favour. By skilfully using the German minorities in central and eastern Europe, Nazi propaganda, linked with the party organisation, was able to shatter the established order in that area. But after it had achieved its most impressive victories – in the Rhineland, in Austria and in Czechoslovakia – a certain exhaustion appeared in the Nazi propaganda effort. It was also, in the summer of 1939, pursuing too many objectives: it was becoming diffuse, from having once been ruthlessly concentrated.

Hitler always grasped for any instruments which could underpin and extend his power. For some time before the beginning of the war, he had fixed his attention on the army: in the months before the war, Goebbels and his Ministry had to give much of their time and resources to publicity on behalf of the army. After the outbreak of war the Ministry of Propaganda had to hand over some of its functions to the *Abteilung Wehrmachtpropaganda* of the OKW, the High Command. Central direction of the press disappeared after the outbreak of the war and the Propaganda Ministry became largely responsible for disseminating the material fed to it by the army. Though propaganda had to move into a subordinate place in the summer of 1939, the territory in which it operated vastly increased. As one country after another fell, Goebbels gradually became responsible for information media in the whole of occupied Europe.

Propaganda, after all, could not win the war for Hitler; nor could it do much to save Germany from defeat. (The peoples of occupied Europe came into direct contact with the realities of German control: their attitudes were formed by this contact rather than by the outpourings of Nazi-controlled propagandists.) But propaganda could try to keep up the morale of the Germans and in this area it scored some notable points. Indeed it may have helped to make the war last longer. It is difficult precisely to assess the morale of a nation, even using the instruments available at the present: opinion polls, audience research and all the other innovations of social science. But the war took place well before the sampling of public opinion was established in Europe as either a game or a science: though samples were taken, they were either primitive and limited, or totally misleading. On the whole, more and probably better information on the attitudes of the Germans in the war has survived in the files of Himmler's *Sicherheitsdienst* (SD) than anywhere else: the papers of the Propaganda Ministry were severely depleted towards the end of the war. Nevertheless, both Goebbels and Hitler had very sensitive antennae with regard to popular mood; their actions at any given time – often reactions to the mood of the people – are an extremely good indicator of the movements of the German mass psyche during the war.

It had started badly: on the day of the invasion of Poland, or two days later, when Britain and France came into the war, there were no wild scenes of enthusiasm in Berlin, comparable to August 1914. On September 3, 1939, William Shirer, an American correspondent in Berlin, wrote in his diary: 'It has been a lovely September day, the sun shining, the air balmy, the sort of day the Berliner loves to spend in the woods or on the lake nearby. I walked in the streets. On the faces of the people astonishment, depression. Until today they have been going about their business pretty much as usual. There were food cards and soap cards and you could not get any petrol and at night it was difficult stumbling around in the blackout. But the war in the east has seemed a bit far away to them – two moonlight nights and not a single Polish plane over Berlin to bring destruction – and the papers saying that German troops have been advancing all along the line, that the Polish airforce has been destroyed. Last night, I heard Germans talking of the 'Polish thing' lasting but a few weeks, or months at the most. Few believed that Britain and France would move.'

On the same day, a decree was issued which made listening to foreign broadcasts illegal; and Heydrich instructed the *Gestapo* on matters of internal security of the state in wartime. Any attempt, Heydrich wrote, to undermine the unity of the people would be severely punished: anyone who was in doubt as to the final outcome of the war was to be arrested. Imprisonment and fear were meant to maintain the morale of the people: arrests were to be followed immediately by interrogation. Defeatism was to be eradicated by admonition, or worse. Here again, other agencies – in this case the *Gestapo* – were poaching on Goebbels' preserves. Goebbels himself was unhappy about the war: he said that Hitler would 'soon listen to his Generals only and it will be very difficult for me.'

Key reports on the war situation were published in the form of communiqués of the Army High Command: in this process the Ministry of Propaganda played only a small part. And as long as victory followed victory, there was no need for a special propaganda effort: the morale of the nation floated on the waves of military success. A security service report of June 24, 1940, confidently asserted that 'Under the impression of the great political events and under the spell of military success, the whole German nation is displaying an inner unity and a close bond between the front and the homeland which is unprecedented. The soil is no longer fertile for opposition groups. Everyone looks up to the *Fuehrer* in trust and gratitude, and to his armed forces pressing forward from victory to victory.'

Poland had fallen with the greatest of ease; France was defeated; many of the smaller countries of western Europe were occupied. Plans had been made for the invasion of Britain: but here, the general mood of euphoria was broken. On September 4, 1940 – a year after the outbreak of war – Hitler, in another of his *Sportpalast* performances, issued a stern warning to the British. 'If people in England are at the moment highly inquisitive,' Hitler shrieked at one point, 'and ask "Well, why doesn't he come?" I say to them: "Don't worry, he's coming!" One shouldn't go on being so inquisitive.' But in the first year of the war, the Germans had been spoilt: they had come to expect too much of their leader. Early in October 1940, another security report suggested that large sections of the population did not much appreciate what they read in the press and the radio (was that a thrust of the *Sicherheitsdienst* aimed at Goebbels?) and that they were impatient about the coming of the 'big blow' against Britain.

But the blow against Britain never came, and soon Hitler's thoughts started turning elsewhere. By December 18, 1940, his directions for the invasion of Russia had been issued; after postponements, the campaign was finally launched on June 22, 1941. Demands of military secrecy had of course ruled out a preparatory campaign; the Nazi-Soviet Pact of 1939 was still in force when the German army crossed the border into the Soviet Union; the operation against Russia was not expected to last long. The propagandists themselves seemed, at first, to have been taken by surprise: they simply repeated Hitler's arguments on the necessity for action against the Soviet Union, and on the British-Bolshevik conspiracy against Germany.

The first instructions to newspaper editors from the Ministry of Propaganda, on June 22, were therefore hesitant: 'Unfortunately we had been unable to prepare the German nation, as on previous occasions for the forthcoming decisions: this must now be done by the press. It must provide intelligible reasons, because it is politically educated, and the nation is not. We must make it clear that this (the attack on Russia) does not represent a change. Reporting on Russia was banned for months, so that the press would be spared difficulties during the necessary switch (of policy). Now at last we can speak fairly of hypocrisy, by which the Soviets tried to deceive us for many years. The true feelings, which the German nation instinctively entertains towards Bolshevism, must be freed again. Bolshevism has waited for its hour. We have proof that it would have stabbed us in the back at a suitable moment.'

Four days later, on June 26, 1941, the *Sicherheitsdienst* reported that the initial state of shock, noticeable especially among the women, which followed the invasion of Russia, lasted only a few hours. After that, 'as a result of the comprehensive campaign of enlightenment, an attitude of calm and confidence generally spread'. References to Napoleon and the fate of his armies in Russia had been, the SD agents reported, very rare. Nevertheless, 'The events in the east have injected into the population a new degree of bitterness and hate towards England. They are now again longing for the day on which the attack on the island will at last begin.' The theory of British-Bolshevik conspiracy did, after all, prove popular.

Whereas popular reaction to the attack on the Soviet Union was swift and strong, the entry of the United States into the war against Germany failed to make a similar impact. The leaders of the Third *Reich* had learned nothing from the mistakes of their predecessors in World War I: the strategic thinking of the Germans was firmly fixed on Europe, and on the continental landmass; in both wars, the global connections had not much meaning for them. On the occasion of the second entry of America into a European war, an SD report of December 15, 1941, indicated that no-one was very surprised by Germany's declaration of war on America, and that it simply officially confirmed the *status quo*. 'Only among the peasantry were there a very few who reacted with surprise and with a certain anxiety about the addition of another opponent.'

The actions of Hitler did indeed have a certain perversity about them; when attack against one country was frustrated, he turned round and attacked another. The advance on Moscow had run into difficulties and, with it, faith in swift victory through *Blitzkrieg*, war on America was then declared. Until then Goebbels had been marking time, and busied himself with various projects as best he could. He toured armament factories in the Ruhr; received Japanese youth leaders; founded a prestige magazine for intellectuals; interested himself in the sexual needs of foreign workers in Germany. But then, early in 1942, the interests of the Minister of Propaganda acquired a new sense of direction. Hitler apparently asked him to write a report on the subject of defeatism in high places.

There were signs some time before the Stalingrad defeat that the war was turning sour for the Germans. On April 26, 1942, Hitler spoke to the *Reichstag*; after the speech, Goering introduced a new bill giving Hitler full executive legislative and judiciary powers. Reports on the reactions of the public to the event which reached the Ministry of Propaganda were not all favourable. The people were asking why Hitler was given plenary powers, and why he had criticised conditions at home so sharply. There was some concern about the military situation; Hitler had spoken of another winter campaign. As far as the mood of the people was concerned, early in the spring of 1942, there was a touch of chill in the air.

On April 28, 1942, Goebbels wrote in his diary that 'the *Fuehrer's* speech represents, as it were, the cry of a drowning man.' In his public speaking, Goebbels chose a different technique from that of Hitler; from the end of 1942, Goebbels began to conduct a propaganda of deep pessimism. It was modelled on Churchill's 1940 approach, and was designed to mobilise the total resources of the country. On January 4, 1943, he told the departmental heads of his Ministry: 'I myself want to see disappear from my mind and the mind of the Ministry the idea that we cannot lose the war. Of course we can lose the war. The war can be lost by people who will not exert themselves; it will be won by those who try hardest. We must not believe fatalistically in certain victory; we must take a positive view.'

Goebbels appealed to the deepest instincts of the nation: to hate and fear, to the need for self-preservation. On November 12, 1942, for instance, he disclosed that, 'We want our nation to be filled not only with deep love for its community, but also with an infernal hate of all the men and all the forces who attack this community, and who want to destroy it. When somebody objects that this is un-German, then I have to say: an exaggerated objectivity is a fault of the German character.'

An important victory on the eastern front was needed: Stalingrad did not provide it. The defeat was a devastating blow for the morale of the nation. A *Sicherheitsdienst* report of January 28, 1943, suggested that 'At the moment the whole nation is deeply shaken by the impression that the fate of the Sixth Army is already sealed and by concern about the further development of the war situation. Among the many questions arising from the changed situation, people ask above all why Stalingrad was not evacuated or relieved and how it was possible, only a few months ago, to describe the military situation as secure . . . Fearing that an unfavourable end of the war is now possible, many compatriots are seriously thinking about the consequences of defeat.'

Goebbels' second rise to prominence in fact coincided with the fall of the Third *Reich*. He delivered the 'total war' speech in the Berlin *Sportpalast* on February 18, 1943. He said that the situation reminded him of that of the *Kampfzeit*, before the Nazis came into power. As before 1933, the Germans were again hard pressed: again there were wounded men in the halls where Goebbels was speaking. 'Before me sit rows of German wounded from the eastern front who had their arms and legs amputated, men with shattered limbs, men blinded in the war, who had been brought here by their Red Cross nurses, men in the best years of their lives . . .'

A Spartan way of life and a total war effort was Goebbels' offer to the Germans in the first months of 1943. They were to do the fighting, and the whole of occupied Europe would work for them. Goebbels fully committed himself to postponing Germany's defeat, and he may well have succeeded in doing so, against many odds.

The debits included a desolate, uncaring Hitler; a population which itself was going the same way; defeat after defeat. Goebbels knew that he had been beaten at his own game; that the Nazi monopoly of information, not only in occupied Europe, but in Germany itself, had been broken. On May 25, 1943, he recorded in his diary that 'There are reports . . . that many people are again listening to foreign radio stations. The reason for this, of course, is our completely obscure news policy which no longer gives people any insight into the war situation. Also, our reticence regarding Stalingrad and the fate there of our missing soldiers naturally leads the families to listen to Bolshevik radio stations, as these always broadcast the names of German soldiers reported as prisoners.'

Though the means of persuasion may have failed Hitler towards the end of the war, Goebbels, the last remaining pillar of the crumbling Nazi order, never did. The means of coercion went on being used until the bitter end, with increasing brutality. Heinrich Himmler, however, made an attempt to sue for peace, before he escaped out of the beleaguered capital. In Hitler's last testament, we have seen, Himmler was struck out of the list of the heirs of the *Fuehrer's* diminishing powers.

Coercion was used, in the Nazi state, both to punish political opposition and to intimidate the people; it had a number of other uses such as, for instance, the provision of a foreign labour force for Germany's industries. Though Goebbels pursued a more or less unitary information policy in Germany and in the occupied territories, Himmler, on the other hand, offered a number of different security policies. The hand holding the whip was given more freedom of action in eastern than in western Europe. In the East Himmler was not only responsible for the security of the Nazi system; his task was to produce a better and more dominant German race.

He became, in October 1939, 'Commissioner for Strengthening Germandom', with responsibility for resettlement in conquered Poland; in 1943, he was appointed the Minister of the Interior. The last desperate *levée en masse* which Hitler ordered in October 1944, was to be carried out under Himmler's command. Himmler's only failure was his bid to extend, early in 1941, the *Gestapo's* power over the German courts of justice. Otherwise, Himmler's control over both criminal and political police had been established already on the outbreak of the war; he was the master of the *Schutzstaffel* as well as the *Reichssicherheitshauptamt*, the central Security organisation. Himmler's SS came to supplement provincial administration: for every *Gauleiter* in every *Gau*, there was a high SS leader. Himmler even challenged the monopoly of the army to fight for Germany and of industry to supply Germany's economy. The *Waffen*-SS – the armed force of the SS – was formally established in 1940, when it comprised three divisions. By the end of the war, there were 35 *Waffen*-SS divisions. The concentration camps, for which Himmler was also responsible, developed into a great industrial empire during the war.

On the whole, Hitler allowed or encouraged the expansion of Himmler's power. The *Waffen*-SS spiked the army's guns; but, most important, the SS ran the kind of state Hitler needed. Though the legal system was subservient to the Nazi regime, Hitler needed an organisation which would be free of bureaucratic and other restraints. The SS became such an organisation. Though it was independent of the state, it controlled an important organ of the state: the police, including the *Gestapo*. The struggle between Himmler and the Minister of the Interior, Frick, which had taken place in the years 1935 and 1936, ended in Himmler's victory.

The *Reichsfuehrer-SS* therefore controlled the concentration camps as well as the sources of supply for the camps – the police – and a considerable intelligence network. In 1944, his only rival in the intelligence field, Admiral Canaris, was forced to disband his *Abwehr*, thus leaving Himmler the sole master of all security and intelligence operations of the Third *Reich*. At one point, however, Himmler came near to being pushed out of his commanding position. Reinhard Heydrich was made the head of the *Reichssicherheitshauptamt*. It meant that Heydrich came to control the *Gestapo*, the *Kripo* (the criminal police) and the SD, which soon became a state rather than a party organisation. This gave Heydrich direct access to Hitler, and considerable freedom of action. Himmler depended on Heydrich's judgment and intelligence; he was apparently unable to stand his own ground in Heydrich's presence.

In September 1941 Heydrich added another office to those he already held: he became the Acting *Reich* Protector of Bohemia and Moravia. He commuted between Prague and Berlin: the register of telephone calls between Himmler and Heydrich's offices show the degree of dependence of Himmler on Heydrich. But fate was slowly moving towards Heydrich's destruction. It was ironical that Himmler himself had given a reference of good character to Paul Thuemmel, a friend of his youth, and a senior officer in the *Abwehr* based in Prague. Thuemmel was born in Landshut, where Himmler had spent his youth; Himmler knew his parents well and knew Thuemmel as a good Nazi party member. Himmler said so when the *Gestapo* in Prague started making enquiries about Thuemmel. In fact, Thuemmel had been one of the main contacts for the Czechoslovak intelligence services since before the war; he remained in constant touch with them when they moved to London after the outbreak of the war. It was in London that the decision was made by the Czechoslovak government in exile to assassinate Reinhard Heydrich. On May 27, 1942, two British-trained parachutists fatally injured Heydrich on his way to the airport.

Though Himmler cried when he heard the news of Heydrich's death, his only serious rival was in fact eliminated. Himmler could go on administering his empire undisturbed, assisted by subservient men. A few months before his death, Heydrich had attended the Wannsee conference on January 20, 1942, which was to make arrangements for the 'final solution' of the Jewish problem. There, he had staked his own claims. According to the minutes of the conference, 'the Chief of the Security Police and the SD, SS *Obergruppenfuehrer* Heydrich, began by announcing his appointment by the Reichs-Marschall Goering as the agent responsible for the preparation of the final solution of the European Jewish question . . .'

The 'final solution' meant the deportation of the Jews to territories in the east and the destruction of those who were unable to contribute to Germany's war effort. When the war started going badly for the Germans, the Nazi régime asked for far-reaching provisions for tightening their security and for the exploitation of all the resources available to them. Under Adolf Eichmann's command, Oswald Pohl was in charge of the economic administration of the concentration camps. He was a parsimonious man, and a former paymaster captain in the navy. Photographs of the by-products of mass extermination, including mountains of toothbrushes, shaving brushes, spectacles and dentures, which used to belong to the inmates of the camps, bear witness to the neatness and thrift of Pohl's administration, where nothing was ever wasted. He was given the impossible task of making starving and weak men and women work efficiently and operate the whole system of expendable labour.

Early in the spring of 1942 concentration camps – apart from the Jews, they contained members of the anti-Nazi opposition from all over Europe – became forced labour camps. The prisoners were either on hire to war production factories, or were employed by the SS in their own industries. Special extermination camps were built, at the same time: Auschwitz, Birkenau, Belsen, Treblinka. Before the war, the number of detainees – they were members of the German opposition to Hitler – were not above 10,000; in 1939, 25,000 prisoners were being held in the concentration camps and some 100,000 in 1940. On April 30, 1942 the Chief of the SS Office, Economics and Administration, reported that:

'1' At the outbreak of the war there existed the following concentration camps:

(a) Dachau   1939   4000 prisoners, today 8000

(b) Sachsenhausen   1939   6500 prisoners, today 10,000

(c) Buchenwald   1939   5300 prisoners, today 9000

(d) Mauthausen   1939   1500 prisoners, today 5500

(e) Flossernburg   1939   1600 prisoners, today 4700

(f) Ravensbrück   1939   2500 prisoners, today 7500

'2. In the years 1940 to 1942, nine further camps were erected: (a) Auschwitz, (b) Neuengamme, (c) Güsen, (d) Natzweiler, (e) Gross Rosen, (f) Lublin, (g) Niederhagen, (h) Shutthof, (i) Arbeitsdorf.'

Though the formal acceptance of genocide by the Nazi party did not take place before 1941, when it was very closely linked in the mind of Heinrich Himmler with the invasion of Russia, the SS had started gaining its experience with mass murder in 1939. In October that year, Himmler was requested by Hitler to assist in a euthanasia programme for the mentally sick. Two years later, some 60,000 patients in mental asylums throughout Germany had been killed. In August 1941 the experiment was stopped after protests, especially from the churches. In any case, another similar programme was then beginning, this time in the occupied territories in Russia.

Himmler and the SS were to look after 'political' and security administration of the occupied territories in the east and they did so with the assistance of special units, the *Einsatzgruppen*. Otto Ohlendorf, who was in charge of such a group, made the following sworn statement: 'In June 1941, I was appointed by Heinrich Himmler to lead one of the special action groups which were then being formed to accompany the German armies in the Russian campaign . . . Himmler stated that an important part of our task consisted in the extermination of Jews – women, men and children – and of communist functionaries . . . When the German army invaded Russia I was leader of Action Group D in the Southern Sector . . . it liquidated approximately 90,000 men, women and children.'

In November 1945, at the trial of the Nazi war criminals at Nuremburg, the indictment gave the figure of 5,700,000 Jewish victims. Though the figure has been subsequently questioned, it is certain that at least five million Jews were murdered by the SS in the course of the 'final solution'. Again, at Nuremburg, the French prosecution gave the figure of the number of hostages taken from the civilian population and shot by the Germans in revenge for attacks on the occupation forces: the figure was 26,660. In the Soviet Union, at least seven million civilians were killed during the war. It has been impossible to estimate the exact figure of the losses suffered by the civilian population of Europe at the hands of Himmler and his assistants in murder.

Nevertheless, in the mind of Himmler, administration of death and the preservation of life, in the manipulative way of the live-stock breeder, went hand in hand. When the Jews started being evicted from Poland, and Himmler's SS doctors embarked on the euthanasia programme, Himmler issued the *Lebensborn* decree on October 28, 1939, in the belief that 'every war is a drain on the best blood . . . Beyond the bounds of bourgeois laws and customs it will now become the general task, even outside the marriage bond, for German women and girls of good blood, not in frivolity but in deep moral earnestness, to become mothers of children of soldiers going to war . . .' On the one hand, Himmler pledged himself and the SS to look after all children of pure blood, legitimate or bastards, whose fathers died fighting; on the other hand, he ordered the hanging of a Polish farm labourer who had had sexual relations with a German woman.

The *Lebensborn* decree had, however, to be supplemented. On January 30, 1940, Himmler had to correct misunderstandings which the decree had given rise to: 'The worst misunderstanding concerns the paragraph which reads: "Beyond the limits of bourgeois laws and conventions . . ." According to this, as some people misunderstand it, SS men are encouraged to approach the wives of serving soldiers. However incomprehensible such ideas may be to us, we must discuss it. What do those who spread or repeat such opinions think of German women? Even if in a nation of 82 million people some man should approach a married woman from dishonourable motives or human weakness, two parties are needed for seduction . . .'

Finally, on August 15, 1942, the 'SS Order to Last Sons' was issued:

'1. As last sons you have been withdrawn from the frontline by the *Fuehrer*'s orders. This step has been taken because nation and state have an interest in your families not dying out.

'2. It has never been the way of SS men to accept fate and not to contribute anything to change it. It is your duty to ensure as quickly as possible by producing children of good blood that you are no longer last sons.

'3. Endeavour to guarantee in one year the survival of your ancestors and your families so that you may be available once again to fight in the frontline.'

The *Lebensborn* and subsequent orders did not unfortunately make Himmler the laughing-stock of the Third *Reich*. He continued to be obeyed and feared; breeding, race, and associated subjects continued to add ideological zeal to his actions. The ideology of pure race justified the breeding as well as the killing.

When in October 1939 Hitler appointed Himmler *Reich* Commissioner for Strengthening Germandom his first function was to replace Jews and Poles in the eastern provinces, annexed by Germany, by German settlers. Himmler was able to establish his own administration in the occupied territories, and put his theories into practice. On February 6, 1940, General Blaskowitz, commander of the *Ober-Ost* region in former Poland, and by no means a hard opponent of Hitler's regime, wrote that: 'It is misguided to slaughter tens of thousands of Jews and Poles as is happening at present; because, in view of the huge population, neither the concept of the Polish state nor the Jews will be eliminated by doing so. On the contrary, the way in which this slaughter is carried out is causing great damage; it is complicating the problems and making them more dangerous . . .'

The war in eastern Europe opened up new vistas before Himmler and the SS: in an address to SS leaders, Himmler laid down the guidelines for their behaviour in Slav Europe: 'One basic principle must be the absolute rule for the SS man: we must be honest, decent, loyal, comradely to members of our own blood and to nobody else. What happens to a Russian or to a Czech does not interest me in the slightest. What the nations can offer in the way of good blood of our type we will take, if necessary by kidnapping their children and raising them here with us . . . Whether 10,000 Russian females fall down from exhaustion while digging an anti-tank ditch interests me only insofar as the anti-tank ditch for Germany is finished . . . We Germans, who are the only people in the world who have a decent attitude towards animals, will also assume a decent attitude towards the human animals . . .'

Himmler echoed the sentiment, which was expressed in Hitler's 'order of the day' of October 2, 1941: 'this enemy does not consist of soldiers but to a large degree only of beasts'. Hitler had been making a sharp distinction between the war in the west and in the east: when he talked, for instance, to the Commanders-in-Chief of the Armed Forces on ideological warfare a few months before the launching of the campaign against Russia, he described the forthcoming invasion as 'a struggle between two *Weltanschaungen*'. Hitler described Bolshevism as the equivalent of social delinquency; the war as a 'war of extermination'. Bolshevik Commissars and the Communist intelligentsia had to be destroyed: 'In the east toughness now means mildness for the future', Hitler explained to his senior Commanders.

Acute antisemitism and weird racial theories had been Hitler's gift to the Nazi movement from the early days of their association; now, when enormous tracts of territories in the east were under German occupation, eccentric theories were being translated into an appalling practice. Himmler, as we have seen, had come to his disastrous conclusions in the domain of racial theory before Hitler and the Nazi movement came to power; during the war, Himmler was responsible for administering the practice of terror.

The directive on the administration of the 'final solution' of the Jewish problem, or on the activities of the *Einsatzgruppen* in Russia, of course remained largely hidden from public view during the war; the criminality of the regime was known chiefly to those who were taking a part in the crime. It was however reflected in the ideological propaganda during the war. Though Goebbels tended to mock Rosenberg and other theorists of race, the theme concerning the subhumanity of the enemy in the east – of the Slav *Untermensch* – was pushed hard by the Nazi propagandists. Photographs of Red Army prisoners of war were constantly appearing in German newspapers, on posters, in newsreels. They usually contrasted with clean-cut, clean-shaven defenders of western civilisation: the threat from the east was there, for everyone to see.

There were, however, indications that Goebbels was trying to revise the intellectual standards of Nazism. It had long been an anti-intellectual movement: the capture of the masses, the lowest common denominator, and how to appeal to it, were its main concerns. On May 26, 1940, the first number of *Das Reich* appeared in Berlin, under Goebbels' sponsorship. It was intended to appeal to the *denkende* Nazis – to the thoughtful, if not intellectual, members of the movement. In terms of quality journalism, this was as far as Goebbels and the Nazi journalists ever got: it presents a record of their ideas and of their ambitions. The ideas expressed in *Das Reich* were firmly based in the belief of Germany's military supremacy. In the early days of the newspaper, the Germanic Empire was seen as holding sway in the north of Europe, while in the south scope was allowed for the Roman Empire of Mussolini. Europe – the Nazis found it rather difficult to fit France into their scheme – was to be a self-contained economic unit, run on national-socialist lines, capable of resisting blockade and breaking the supremacy of Great Britain.

Until the summer of 1941, however, the Europe of Nazi propaganda had been an elusive image with most of its outlines rather blurred. The campaign against Russia brought the image of *Festung Europa* into a sharper focus: the German press was instructed, for instance, a week after the invasion, that 'Reports from the whole world make it apparent that a rising of the whole of Europe against Bolshevism can be noted . . . Europe marches against the common enemy in a unique solidarity, and it rises, as it were, against the oppressors of all human culture and civilisation. This hour of birth of the new Europe is being accomplished without any demand or pressure from the German side . . .'

Almost all European peoples in fact took some military part in the Russian campaign – Finnish, Hungarian, Slovak and Romanian units were later joined by volunteers from Spain, Belgium, France, Holland and Norway. However insignificant the participation of these groups in Germany's war effort was, the whole of Europe was represented, by Nazi propagandists, as defending itself against the threat of *Judeo-Bolshevismus*. The Jews, who supposedly manipulated the Soviet states, were also described as the 'cement of the alliance between Soviet Russia and the Western Powers.' Somehow, all the ideological lunacies which the Nazis had been, for a long time, gathering from various corners of the European mind, started clicking into place for them in the summer of 1941.

Soon, there was to be an empire in the east; soon, the Germans were to be racially pure and therefore unbeatable; the *apartheid* lines between the Germans on the one hand and the Jews and the Slavs on the other, could now be firmly drawn. The master race was about to prevail: in Europe first, and then in the world. It is impossible to tell how many people really believed in the ideals which were held before them by their Nazi rulers. Military success and then military disaster were the hard currency of propaganda. In the end, it mattered little who believed in Nazi ideology. The master race came to fail Hitler, and he was no longer interested in its fate.

THE ECONOMY

From the day that Hitler came to power at the end of January 1933 there was never a time when the economy of the Third *Reich* was not being directed towards war. Rearmament, by reflating the economy, helped in the solution of some of the immediate problems, such as unemployment; but from the start it was pursued for its own sake. It was to provide the solid base for Hitler's foreign policy, which, to paraphrase a favourite Nazi slogan, was to restore the unity and honour of the *Reich*.

This fundamental aim took precedence even over important elements of Nazi ideology, which before 1933 had proclaimed the intention of the NSDAP to promote the business interests of the small man and the growth of a rural population of peasants and small farmers. Instead, as rearmament got under way, big business flourished, the cities grew and the flight from the land continued. Rearmament, indeed, provided the cement for the uneasy alliance between the NSDAP, big business and the army, which marked the first three or four years of Hitler's reign. Big business made high profits and held down wages; the army expanded and officers enjoyed opportunities for advancement that had not existed since 1919. In 1934 Hitler conciliated their convergent interests by cutting down Roehm, Strasser and others who might have promoted 'the second revolution' at the expense of the traditional elitist elements.

Hitler was only biding his time. By 1935 the unstable triumvirate was beginning to give way under the economic pressures set up by the furious tempo of rearmament, upon which Hitler insisted, and his indifference to the sound economic arguments advanced by Schacht, who in 1934 became Minister of Economics, and Goerdler, who shortly afterwards took over the unenviable function of controlling prices. The core of the problem, which even Schacht's ingenuity could not overcome, lay, as in World War I, in Germany's lack of the raw materials necessary for carrying on war.

In 1939 the *Reich* was dependent upon external suppliers for 45 percent or more of its vital requirements of iron ore and scrap, oil, rubber, lead, copper, chrome, tin, nickel and bauxite; imported supplies of the four last-mentioned accounted for over 90 percent of German needs. Imports of these and other commodities, even though Hitler set his face against stock-piling on the scale requested by the army, imposed an intolerable strain on foreign exchange reserves. The balance of payments could have been eased if Hitler had slowed the pace of rearmament and (as in West Germany after World War II) orientated the economy towards exports; but except during the period of profitable trading relations with the USSR from 1939 to 1941 Hitler's mind always rejected strength through production and exchange in favour of strength through conquest, which in the end destroyed his co-existence with Stalin.

The first major domestic crisis was precipitated in 1935 by a poor harvest, which necessitated use of scarce foreign currency in order to buy grain abroad. The army proposed food rationing, but Hitler refused and in this was strongly supported by his *Gauleiters* (regional leaders); the Nazi dictatorship was designed, so far as possible, to be a popular dictatorship. Even after the outbreak of war, when the coercive power of the regime had been immensely increased, Hitler never forgot that in 1918 it had been the home front that had succumbed in the face of growing privation and (according to the legend of the 'stab in the back', in which the NSDAP passionately believed) had betrayed the front-line soldiers. Hitler rejected not only the army's proposal, but also Schacht's recommendation in favour of diverting a greater proportion of resources into exports; insisting on the absolute priority of rearmament, he appointed Goering in 1936 as Plenipotentiary for the Four Year Plan, instructing him that within four years the army and the national economy must be ready for war. In the event a bare three years elapsed before the invasion of Poland.

Goering's magic formula was autarky; discarding the industrialists' traditional preference for buying in the cheapest market, whether foreign or domestic, he accepted the arguments advanced by I. G. Farben in favour of heavy investment in home production of synthetic oil, aviation spirit and rubber (*Buna*). Ignoring the opposition of Ruhr magnates, who declined to cooperate, he also set up a state-owned corporation to extract low-grade domestic ores. In each case the overriding argument was that the Reich would achieve a greater degree of independence from foreign suppliers, as well as saving foreign exchange. By this time the NSDAP was flexing its muscles and the Corporation Law of 1937 was a clear indication that big business was expected to toe the line. Cartels and price-fixing had largely eliminated free competition; the state had become the principal investor and virtually controlled the capital market. Before war broke out, the Third *Reich* had ceased to be capitalist, in the accepted sense, but had not yet achieved a planned economy; the war forced it to move further in that direction.

Whilst the NSDAP, which now dominated the state, was acquiring a measure of control over big business, Hitler moved to decapitate the third element in the original partnership, namely the army. Late in 1937 he had allowed Blomberg, his War Minister, and Fritsch, the Commander-in-Chief of the army, to catch a glimpse of the full scope of his restless ambition. Neither General displayed any liking for what he saw and early in the following year both were removed as a result of sordid manoeuvres involving Goering and the SS. In the autumn of 1938 General Beck, the army Chief of Staff, appalled by Hitler's aggressive designs against Czechoslovakia, also tendered his resignation. With the concurrent expansion of the military units of the SS (*Waffen*-SS) it became apparent that the *chasse gardée* of military privilege was no longer secure. In due course the army was to lose its cherished right over procuring raw materials and allocating armament contracts.

The Prussian tradition had been that the General Staff was responsible for procurement and production for the Armed Forces. So little foresight had been shown at the beginning of World War I, that the Generals had had to avail themselves of the services of Jewish industrialist, Walther Rathenau, in order to remedy their shortcomings. Nonetheless, the system had the merit of imposing a single channel and eliminating competitive bidding for scarce resources and skilled labour. In 1933, however, Goering asserted his independence, insisting that the speedy expansion of the *Luftwaffe* could only be assured if it entered the market directly to supply its needs. The Navy then followed suit, as did, in due course, the *Waffen*-SS. This system – or rather lack of one – was recognised in 1935 by the *Reich* Defence Law, which provided that the *Wehrmacht* (Armed Forces) should remain in time of war responsible for their own equipment.

Some degree of coordination could still have been imposed, if the Services had been subjected to civilian financial control, as would have been normal in a constitutional state. But the Third *Reich* reversed normal practice; each branch of the Forces, after appealing, if it thought it necessary, to Hitler for special treatment, presented its requests entirely to the Ministry of Finance, which then had to adjust taxation and credit policy, as far as possible, in order to cover the aggregate demand on national resources. Such chaotic procedures could not have continued indefinitely without leading to disaster; but disaster was progressively deferred by Hitler's conquests, which replenished the barrel before the danger level was reached. When war broke out, there was still no systematic allocation of raw materials to meet competing demands, though Hitler from time to time decreed priority for certain sectors of the armaments industry.

The lack of coordination was exacerbated by the fact that by 1938 the *Reich* Cabinet had ceased to meet. A Defence Council had been set up, of which Hitler was nominal Chairman with Goering as his deputy; but this, too, soon ceased to meet and in any case never attempted to exercise control over arms production and distribution. Nor did a Combined Chiefs of Staff Committee come into existence. The defects of this vacuum at the heart of the military machine were aggravated by an unresolved conflict between the *Fuehrer* and his military planners about the strategic aims of the resurgent *Reich* and the means of achieving them. It was Hitler's belief that hegemony in Europe, as a first step to world power, could be won by successively isolating his opponents and defeating them singly in a series of short, sharp wars. Since each of those wars would make significantly different demands upon the *Wehrmacht* as a whole, it followed that the armaments industry had to be flexible, so that manpower and resources could be switched from one sector of production to another to meet changing strategic requirements. This concept, to which the designation *Blitzkrieg* was given (though not by Hitler), was predicated upon armament in breadth; in Hitler's eyes it had the added merit of imposing less strain on the consumer sector of production; the army were to have their guns and the people their butter.

This seemed altogether too optimistic to most of the military planners and especially to General Georg Thomas, who was their principal economic expert from 1934 to 1942, when Hitler silenced his Cassandra-like voice by removing him from his post. Thomas did not believe that Hitler could avoid a confrontation with a coalition of major powers, nor that in a long war of attrition, as World War I had proved to be, the *Reich* could be defended without the full mobilisation of its human and economic potential. This meant austerity on the home front and armament in depth with adequate stock-piling and investment in the railways and other parts of the military infrastructure. Thomas lamented that 'Hitler shut his eyes to the need for fixed, long-range planning . . .' It seemed to him (as it has since seemed to some historians) that Hitler's moves were opportunistic and lacked any inner cohesion. This was to underestimate Hitler's discernment; he had seen from the outset that, as he put it, there was no solidarity in Europe, so that he could divide his opponents. He had also sufficient grasp of modern military technology to know that, whilst the *Wehrmacht's* equipment was one jump ahead of that of its enemies, they could be eliminated in quick, mobile wars, before they could apply the lessons of defeat. At first his judgment was brilliantly vindicated; Austria and Czechoslovakia fell to him without a struggle and he was able to add their undamaged resources to those of the *Reich*. In the autumn of 1939 he added Poland to the list, whilst the Anglo-French forces remained inactive behind their fortifications. Early in 1940 Denmark, Norway, the Low Countries and France were also subdued and became available for economic exploitation.

The machine had been creaking even whilst Hitler was achieving these great successes. The invasion of Poland, brief as it was, led to a munitions crisis; instead of taking steps to rationalise production, Hitler adopted his usual expedient of appointing a Party man to get things done. His choice fell upon Fritz Todt, who had made his name building the strategic roads of the Third *Reich* and in 1938 had been put in charge of construction of the West Wall, taking over from the army which, in Hitler's opinion, lacked a proper sense of urgency. For this purpose Todt set up on para-military lines the Organisation Todt, which Albert Speer inherited. Todt's powers were circumscribed by the fact that Goering, being in charge of the Four Year Plan, was his superior, as well as being the worst offender in the scramble for scarce resources.

Although the *Wehrmacht* was not obliged to place orders with industry through Todt, he managed to impose some economies on them and in March 1940 Hitler made him Minister for Armaments and Munitions. This was the first step towards taking away from the soldiers the right to control their equipment. Todt began the process, which was later greatly extended by Speer, of giving industry and its technical experts a greater share of responsibility for weapon design and development. A Munitions Committee was set up and underpinned by special committees in the various sectors of the armaments industry; this not only tightened links with factory managements, but forced the Services to place their orders with the most efficient firms. Although the latter continued to make substantial profits, their voracity was restrained by 'fixed price' contracts. The state was at last beginning to dominate both big business and the economic operations of the *Wehrmacht*.

In July 1940, when Hitler's power was at its height, he was turning over in his mind the alternatives of invading England or invading the USSR. The very fact that he was able to contemplate these alternatives appeared to vindicate the concept of *Blitzkrieg* and armament in breadth; but by September it was clear to him that deficiencies in Navy and *Luftwaffe* denied sea-borne invasion an even chance of success and his intention to embark on 'Barbarossa' against the USSR became fixed. Hitler and many of his Generals had grown so over-confident that the military problems of following Napoleon's footsteps in the snow did not greatly worry them; but Thomas and others had serious misgivings about the economic implications, since German industry was heavily dependent on the supply of Russian raw materials and on the transit trade, which was also assured by the Russo-German economic agreements of September 1939 and January 1941. In 1940, for example, over 600,000 tons of the total mineral oil imported by the *Reich* came from the USSR, as compared with one million tons from Romania, Germany's other main supplier. In the long term, therefore, the success of Hitler's new venture would turn on his securing the oil wells of the distant Caucasus before these could be destroyed. The immense expanse to be covered by the advancing *Wehrmacht* would also impose great strain on transport, especially as the gauge of the Russian railways differed from the German.

Against these economic counter-arguments, Hitler could point to the vast war booty won by his campaigns and the productive resources of the conquered countries. It is easy to underestimate these, if only because, after the defeat of Nazi Germany, those who collaborated were either silenced, or chose to remain silent; historians and writers of memoirs have therefore tended to concentrate on the resistance to Hitler in occupied Europe. It must in all candour be said that, until 1942 at earliest, apart from scattered and gallant acts of defiance, resistance in Europe did not amount to much. It is true that in occupied France, for example, there was a marked decline in production between 1940 and 1941; but this was mainly because Germany was exploiting the territory by deporting labour, fixing a fictitious exchange rate and imposing massive occupation costs, as well as keeping France short of iron, coal and oil. Later, the French aircraft industry was brought into the *Luftwaffe's* production programme and, after the Anglo-American bombing offensive on the *Reich* had begun to bite, the Germans attempted to increase textile production in France, in order to enable factories in Germany to concentrate on arms and munitions.

The only countries in which virtually no economic collaboration took place were Poland and Yugoslavia (apart from Croatia, where a puppet dictatorship was set up). In Poland the Nazis sought no collaboration, though they impressed slave labour. In Yugoslavia the case was different; Hitler had not at first intended to invade the country, which provided German industry with significant proportions of its intake of tin, lead, copper, aluminium, bauxite and antimony. He reversed this prudent policy after the coup of March 27, 1941, removed the Germanophile Regent and his Government. By April 13 Belgrade was in his hands; but the Bor copper mines were sabotaged and partisan movements, though often in conflict with one another, soon began to interfere with the production that the *Reich* required. In most other countries serious sabotage only started after Hitler's invasion of Russia, when Communists in occupied Europe, most of whom had observed the Comintern's instruction to promote the aims of Stalin's pact with Hitler, at last turned against the latter and became the hard core of resistance in industry. Resistance movements were a sensitive barometer of fluctuating German fortunes and, after the Soviet recapture of Stalingrad in January 1943, the ranks of the various movements were swelled by the prospect of the ultimate triumph of the anti-Hitler coalition.

Hitler, if indeed he foresaw how 'Barbarossa' would aggravate the problem of European security, would have discounted it, because the invasion, which began on June 22, 1941, and incomprehensibly took Stalin by surprise, was confidently expected to end victoriously within a few months. Instead, the bitter Russian winter found the *Wehrmacht* in December still outside the defences of Moscow and Leningrad. Failure to arm in depth worsened their plight; too little warm clothing was available; even if it had been, the railways could not have moved it to the front. Transport deficiencies deprived some factories of coke and coal; others were short of electricity. *Blitzkrieg* had failed and Hitler, with a war of attrition on his hands, was at last forced to take the measures he had so long deferred; the first decrees were issued restricting production of consumer goods and rationalising arms production. The chief beneficiary was not Thomas, whose earlier warnings were resented, nor Todt, who was killed in an air crash early in February 1942, but Speer, who succeeded him.

The achievements of Speer, though he shared in Germany's defeat, deserve comparison with those of Carnot, *l'organisateur de la victoire*. Speer, who was only 36 when he was called upon to fill one of the most vital posts in the *Reich*, had been Hitler's architect and his personal link with the *Fuehrer* remained the foundation of his power until 1944, when it began to weaken. He was more fortunate than his predecessor in that by 1942 Goering was a spent force; but he had to contend with the growing hostility of Himmler, Bormann and most of the *Gauleiters*, who, as *Reich*

Defence Commissioners, were well placed to set regional and Party interests against the national need for efficiency and austerity. Nevertheless, there was still so much slack in the economy after nearly two-and-a-half years of war that striking increases in war production were recorded. Taking production for January-February 1942 as 100, a rise of 53 percent had been achieved by July of that year; 229 percent by July 1943 and 322 percent by July 1944. It was what Speer designated in a speech in the last-mentioned month as 'This armaments miracle'.

Speer soon absorbed Thomas' department of the *Wehrmacht* High Command (OKW) and was then in a stronger position to co-ordinate the demands of all three Services. Partly through his good relations with Field-Marshal Milch of the *Luftwaffe* and Admiral Doenitz, who in 1943 replaced Raeder as Commander-in-Chief of the Navy, Speer restricted the independence of these two Services. He chaired a Committee of Three, including Milch and Paul Koerner, representing the Four Year Plan, which allocated raw materials. As pressure on manpower grew, he also used his authority to prevent the Services from calling up skilled men from vital industries.

Speer never achieved the same control over manpower that he had over industry; in March 1942 Hitler appointed a senior *Gauleiter*, Fritz Sauckel, to be Plenipotentiary for Labour. This division of authority, however inefficient, almost certainly saved Speer at Nuremberg from the death sentence meted out to Sauckel. Sauckel press-ganged labour all over occupied Europe and doled it out at exiguous wages to such firms as Krupp and I. G. Farben. Workers from Poland and Russia were the worst treated; a German witness, giving evidence at Nuremberg about Krupp's camps, observed, 'The food for Eastern workers was completely inadequate. They received 1,000 calories less per day than the minimum for Germans . . .' Whilst imported labour was being exploited in this way, it was not until 1943 that any serious attempt was made to use German female labour; indeed between 1939 and 1941 the number of women in employment actually fell.

The worst exploitation of labour occurred within the economic enclave operated by the SS. The idea of using the labour in concentration camps to enrich the SS and enable it to achieve financial independence from the state originated with Theodor Eicke, who in 1934 became Inspector-General of Camps, as well as Chief of the Death's Head units, which guarded them. It was a major factor in ensuring an ever-growing camp population at a time when political dissidence, except within the army, had ceased to represent a threat to the regime. In 1939 the various camps had about 25,000 inmates, but the war greatly increased the number, on account of Himmler's assumption of control over subject populations in the East. In 1940 the numerous SS firms employing slave labour were organised in a trust under Oswald Pohl, Chief of the Main Office of SS Economic Administration. The largest of the component firms, the German Earth and Stone Works (DEST), branched out into arms production and by 1944 was even producing aircraft. DEST, like other SS operations, entirely escaped Speer's attempts at co-ordination. Their use of labour was notoriously inefficient, as well as offending against every canon of humanity.

Hitler's belated recognition of the implications of a war of attrition faltered in the summer of 1942; but the disaster of Stalingrad fortified his resolve. Speer found an ally in Joseph Goebbels and in mid-January 1943 Hitler signed a decree for the direction of women into war work and the combing out of able-bodied males, many of them holding posts in the massive bureaucracy of the NSDAP. In mid-February 1943 Goebbels hurled at his carefully selected audience in the Sports palace in Berlin his famous rhetorical question: 'Is it total war you want?' There came back the answering roar of well rehearsed assent; but it came too late. By May 1944 nearly 3.3 million men were dead, missing or maimed; sullen foreign labour could not replace them, whatever means of coercion were used. In July 1944 Goebbels was made Plenipotentiary for Total War and at once clashed with Speer: were men to be withdrawn from the *Wehrmacht* to produce arms, as Speer wished, or withdrawn from industry to fight, as Goebbels insisted? The dilemma underlined the fact that the war was lost. Goebbels got his way and in October 1944 the Home Guard (*Volkssturm*) was created; but by then it did not matter.

If lack of manpower played an important part in Germany's defeat, so too did the strategic bombing of the British and American Air Forces, which were able to exploit three fatal defects in the defence of the *Reich*. First, too much vital production was located in the Ruhr and the attempt to disperse it, or bury it underground, was left too late. Secondly, Hitler and Goering, in their savage determination to trade atrocity for atrocity, insisted until early in 1944 on maintaining bomber production, long after Speer and Milch had been pleading on military and economic grounds for concentration on fighters. Thirdly, Hitler's misplaced hopes of a short war led to neglect of research, which was not reversed until February 1941; crucial innovations, such as jet-propelled fighters and rocket-projection (V2), came just too late.

In spite of these errors and a tonnage of Anglo-American bombs rising from 200,000 in 1942 to five times that weight in 1943, war production in Germany continued to rise steeply until mid-1944. Moreover, the belief of Marshal of the RAF Sir Arthur Harris that persistent bombing of German cities would destroy morale proved unfounded; the Germans, in contrast to 1918, fought to the end. The increase in production in 1944 was partly due to a switch to mass production of standardised weapons, instead of an attempt to maintain the qualitative superiority, on which Hitler had earlier insisted; but on any terms it was an astonishing achievement. An authoritative view, expressed after post-war research, was that, 'until the last six months of war the (German) army was never critically short of weapons or shells'. On the other hand, when the U.S. Eighth Air Force concentrated after May 1944 on German oil production, it soon reduced the mobility of the *Wehrmacht*; indeed shortage of aviation spirit in July 1944 came close to grounding the *Luftwaffe* and inhibited training of pilots. By that date the diminishing area of Europe over which the *Reich* exercised control was in any case fatally restricting Hitler's capacity to wage war.

As far as the war effort within the *Reich* itself is concerned, Speer has expressed the view that by 1944 armaments production had reached the maximum level that could be expected of a nation of 70 million people; that this proved inadequate to stave off defeat was due, in his opinion, to the fact that Germany confronted a hostile coalition of far greater economic potential. To this fact was attributable Anglo-American domination of the skies over the dying *Reich*, bringing with it the constant interruption of production, which we have already discussed. To this fact was attributable also the defeats and withdrawals before the Red Army on the Eastern front with the loss of weapons, munitions and vehicles on a scale that could no longer be made good by replacement. Speer concludes, however, that there was another factor determining the German collapse, which could only be ascribed to mistaken policies: 'In the years 1940 and 1941 the chance was lost to develop more efficient weapons; the precipitate introduction after 1942 of new systems of production necessarily caused technical setbacks.'

Therefore, as another captive Nazi leader wrote at Nuremberg, all questions from every side always lead back to Hitler. It was he who at the end of 1939, when the first munitions crisis led to an investigation, remarked that, 'he had no interest in what could be produced after October 1941'. It was he who in the autumn of 1940 decided to invade the USSR before Britain had been defeated. It was he who believed that the USSR could be crushed during the summer and early autumn of 1941 before the latent threat of United States intervention could materialise. It was these misjudgments that proved fatal to the German war effort; they could not be rectified by the organising ability of Speer, nor by the pertinacity and endurance of the German soldier and worker.

These circumstances give a special poignancy to the struggle that developed in the latter part of 1944 between Speer and his *Fuehrer* over the latter's 'scorched earth' policy. Speer, who was prepared privately to admit, at least by August 1944, that the war was lost, wished to preserve enough plant and equipment to permit the survival of the German people. In this endeavour he was backed by the industrialists themselves and even by certain *Gauleiters*, such as Karl Kaufmann of Hamburg. But Hitler, who was, of course, seconded by Bormann, had lost faith in his people even before they lost faith in him; he was no longer interested in their survival once his own power was broken and his evil career at an end. For nearly six months Speer devised ways of circumventing Hitler's vicious orders. When in mid-March 1945 the confrontation finally occurred between the two former friends, Hitler bitterly informed his Minister: 'If the war is to be lost, the nation also will perish. This fate is inevitable. There is no need to consider the basis even of a most primitive existence any longer. On the contrary it is better to destroy even that and to destroy it ourselves. The nation has proved itself weak, and the future belongs to the stronger Eastern nation.'

Hitler's Viking funeral, which followed his suicide on April 30, 1945, was consummated with 180 litres of scarce petrol, which had with difficulty been collected in the area of the besieged Chancellery in Berlin. Three days later a message recorded by Speer was broadcast, appealing to the German people in their own interests to produce food, repair communications and keep famine at bay. It was a message of hope, marking the end of Nazi nihilism. It opened the way for a new era, in which the creative and productive capacities of the German people could again be employed in the cause of prosperity and peace.

DAS HEER

When the terms of the Treaty of Versailles were presented for Germany's acceptance in 1919, the victorious powers intended that never again must Germany have an army capable of waging an aggressive war. The maximum strength of the postwar German Army – the *Reichswehr* – was not to exceed 100,000 men: ten divisions, three of them cavalry and seven infantry. It could not recruit or, much more important, train, by conscription. It must have no heavy guns or tanks. Nor must it import any weapons at all.

But the Treaty could not prevent the wide acceptance of the legend that the defeat of 1918 had not been the fault of the German Army, nor dispel pride in the achievements of that Army between 1914 and 1918. Such anger that did flare out against the Army after the Armistice of 1918 – soldiers and officers being insulted or beaten up for the uniform they wore – belonged to the immediate period of angry disillusionment between 1918 and 1920. The General Staff of the Army survived; and under the direction of Colonel-General Hans von Seeckt the *Reichswehr* began a period of consolidation and training.

The officers and men of the 'hundred thousand army' were taught to regard themselves as *professionals* – a hardcore force of experts, a functioning nucleus working for the future. Almost right from the signing of the Treaty the restrictions of Versailles were quietly and successfully broken. Shooting clubs trained the young civilians in marksmanship. Demobilisation and welfare departments kept the organs of mobilisation alive. And officers were sent on official visits to other countries to keep abreast with the latest military techniques. Perhaps the most important of the latter were the visits made by German 'tank enthusiast' officers such as Heinz Guderian to the Soviet tank training centre at Kazan in Russia.

A typical example of how Germany infringed the weapons restrictions may be given. In the 1920s, a team of designers from Krupp were attached to the Bofors gun company in Sweden. They came back in 1931 with the working design for one of the most famous German weapons of 1939-45: the 88mm anti-aircraft gun, renowned for its devastating punch in the anti-tank role.

But the most influential long-term result of the *Reichswehr* period was the training of an 'army of leaders'. This marked a growing swing away from the old rigidity of *Junker* discipline in the Imperial German Army. It was generally agreed that a new type of fighting man was needed: a soldier who could think for himself. An Army Psychology Research Institute was set up in 1920 with a staff of seven professional psychologists. They had an uphill task in convincing 'old guard' soldiers that their newfangled doctrines were worthy of respect. But the atmosphere remained one of experimentation; and German Army Training Directions for 1931 announced that 'the individual soldier must be educated so that he is able to accomplish his tasks in battle even if left to himself. He must know that he alone is responsible for his acts and failures'. Leadership training moved up to rank with the foremost priorities and psychological criteria were applied to Army Selection Committees. Candidates for Army service before the reintroduction of conscription in 1935 were given rigorous testing in groups of four or five, scrutinised by three psychologists, a medical officer and an Army colonel. The average yearly number of candidates examined on the eve of Hitler's accession to power was in the region of 2500.

Yet there was plenty of resistance to the new ideas. An obvious one was traditional 'class prejudice' against excessive promotion from the ranks. Worst of all was the 'cavalry mentality', which is perhaps the least of the criticisms normally levelled at the German Army. Whether or not massed tanks would be accepted as a revolutionary new battlefield arm was touch and go. After 1945, Panzer virtuoso Heinz Guderian recalled his difficulties in obtaining facilities and materials for tank experiments. In 1931 he was told by the Army Inspector of Transport: 'Believe me, neither of us will ever see German tanks in operation in our lifetime', and General Beck, hailed as one of the best military brains Germany could boast, told him: 'No, no, I don't want anything to do with you people. You go too fast for me.'

The *Reichswehr* period, then, was a blend of old and new with the new predominating. It was a constructive, forward-looking period. And Brigadier Desmond Young has summed it all up by calling the German Army of the period 1920-1933 as 'the reinforcement, the steel frame, on to which the concrete of conscripts could quickly be poured, if and when it became possible to reintroduce conscription'. Ingeniously cutting their coat according to the cloth permitted by the hated limitations of Versailles, the leaders of the German Army worked consciously on the shape of things to come.

The German Army, which prided itself on its obsession with keeping out of politics, was in fact deeply involved with the accession to power of Hitler in January 1933. The President who made Hitler *Reich* Chancellor was the living embodiment of the

Army's tradition: Field-Marshal von Hindenburg. The President's son, an Army colonel, was won over by Hitler and backed the upstart's case. An Army general, Werner von Blomberg, was specially appointed Defence Minister to see to it that the Army would back Hitler. Even the man whom Hitler replaced, Schleicher, was an Army general. Basically, however, the German Army backed Hitler because its leaders could find little comfort elsewhere. Nobody else looked capable of suiting their book.

What the Army commanders wanted from Hitler above all was *reassurance*, and this they got in full measure. They were flattered again and again with Hitler's assurances that they were indeed the official arms-bearers of the *Reich*, and that no 'private army' would be allowed to usurp that role. Both Army and Navy looked the other way when Hitler smashed their biggest worry – Ernst Roehm's brown-shirted SA – having already suspended the constitutional liberties of the German Republic in the name of 'National Security'. Nor were either of them kept long in waiting for the reward for this connivance. Hitler became Chancellor on January 30, 1933. The seven guarantees of individual and civil liberties were suspended on February 28. The Nazi Party was proclaimed the only political party of Germany on July 14. The SA purge – 'the Night of the Long Knives' – occurred on June 30, 1934. Hindenburg died on August 2, 1934, and Hitler proclaimed himself '*Fuehrer*' – President and *Reich* Chancellor – of Germany on the same day. The traditional oath of allegiance to the Head of State was transformed in an oath of allegiance to the *person* of Adolf Hitler and immediately administered. On March 16, 1935, Hitler 'tore up' Versailles, announced conscription and the new German air force – and Blomberg, effective head of the Army, practically went down on his knees to thank the *Fuehrer*.

The Army was staggered by Hitler's announcement of a new conscript Army of 36 divisions – the Army professionals, in their wildest dreams, had never hoped for more than 21. And on May 2, 1935, Army staff planners began work on Hitler's first international move: the military occupation of the Rhineland, demilitarised since the ignominy of 1918.

By the time of the denunciation of Versailles in March 1935, experiments with dummy tanks had come up with impressive results, upon which Hitler seized. With the *Fuehrer* backing the new ideas for mechanised warfare, the expansion of Germany's *Panzer* (armoured) forces began with the creation of the first three Panzer divisions in the same year. A point was made of selecting famous cavalry regiments to form the backbone of the new formations, a cunning retention of the best of the Army's old traditions. Rapid though the Army's growth was after the reintroduction of conscription, it was still dwarfed by the forces of Germany's neighbours when Hitler took the gamble of reoccupying the German Rhineland in March 1936.

This was the move that would set the seal on Germany's repudiation of Versailles and the Army leaders were convinced that Germany's neighbours would not let Hitler get away with it. Hitler believed otherwise, but he was not taking a complete gamble:

he had already seen Mussolini get away with the invasion of Abyssinia in the face of the feeble protests of the League of Nations, while France was obsessed with making the decision to sign a mutual-assistance pact with Stalin. The move into the Rhineland was made at dawn on March 7, 1936. The German forces involved were tiny: one division. The generals were worn to the point of breakdown, particularly Blomberg; the troops were under orders to pull back at once if the French moved against them. After 48 nerve-racking hours it was clear that nothing was going to happen. Hitler had pulled off the first of his 'miracle' coups and his generals had been proved utterly wrong.

Army, Navy and Air Force expansion – all three branches of the *Wehrmacht*, or 'Armed Forces', as the old *Reichswehr* was now termed – continued throughout 1937. At the close of the year an incident occurred which gave Hitler the chance to strengthen his hold over the *Wehrmacht*. On November 5 he informed the armed forces commanders-in-chief that his expansionist policies were aimed at both Austria and Czechoslovakia and that war must be regarded as inevitable. Blomberg and Army C-in-C Fritsch protested – not on moral grounds, but at the prospect of a premature war before the *Wehrmacht* was strong enough. Hitler reacted by sacking them on trumped-up charges. (Blomberg had dug his own professional grave by marrying an ex-prostitute.) The charge of homosexual acts levelled against Fritsch caused an uproar in the German officer corps; they demanded and got a military hearing to clear the name of their former chief. This was done, but Fritsch was not reinstated. Instead Hitler set up the 'Armed Forces High Command' with himself as chief and Keitel as chief-of-staff and, later, Jodl as operations head. And the whole furore was eclipsed by Hitler's opportunist decision to annex Austria.

A snap order went out for the Army to enter Austria on March 12. The Army was totally unprepared and frantic improvisation was needed – particularly in the Panzer divisions, where the main problem was fuel supply. Fortunately for the German Army there was no resistance. Austria was incorporated into the 'Greater German Reich' on the pretext that she had been saved from Communist-inspired internal anarchy. And the German Army absorbed the lessons of the crisis: the need for more balanced deployment and adequate, faster supply.

Hitler's next objective was Czechoslovakia, now surrounded on three sides by German territory. The biggest military worry was the formidable defences in the *Sudetenland*, the frontier territories inhabited by a high percentage of racial Germans. Hitler's initial pretext was that Czechoslovakia must cede these territories to the *Reich*. Czechoslovakia stood firm, and the result was the crisis of September 1938, which France and Britain resolved by abandoning the Czechoslovak cause at Munich. Once again the German Army got a bloodless victory march.

Germany was not the only neighbour of Czechoslovakia with territorial ambitions against that country: Poland and Hungary also helped themselves. For a while war had seemed imminent. General Beck, Army chief-of-staff under Fritsch's successor,

Brauchitsch, had tried to trigger off mass resistance by the Army. He had resigned in protest when no action was forthcoming, but the prevailing mood was one of relief – not only that the *Fuehrer* had got away with it again, but that the German Army would never again have to worry about the military defences in the Sudetenland.

The rump of Czechoslovakia was swallowed in March 1939. The Slovaks were persuaded to set up an 'independent' Slovakia under German patronage; and the German Army marched into Prague on March 15, again on the fake pretext that its victims had asked for German protection. Now the situation was transformed. Germany's eastern frontier was eminently defensible – the digestion of Czechoslovakia had shortened the frontier of the *Reich* by some 700 miles. The excellent weapons of the Czech army were placed at Germany's disposal, together with the arms factories – the *Wehrmacht* received so many Czech tanks that it was able to set about the formation of three new Panzer divisions.

One equally important but less dramatic result of Hitler's aggressive designs on Czechoslovakia was the resignation of Beck as Army Chief-of-Staff. Although hailed as one of the best brains in the Army, he was a vacillator and a reactionary who had never understood the new doctrines of mobile, armoured warfare and had sought to block their development. General Halder, Beck's successor, became respected for his practical approach to the new ideas and the technique of putting them into practice.

Fears in Army circles that a premature war might still explode over Poland were largely dispelled by Hitler's surprise pact with Soviet Russia in August 1939, which effectively sealed off Poland from any practical military aid. There were still worries about the viability of the western defences – Hitler's much-vaunted *Westwall* or 'Siegfried Line' – but discussion on this subject was discouraged by the *Fuehrer's* habit of exploding in rage whenever the subject was raised.

In general, the German Army went to war on September 1, 1939, with the feeling that the *Fuehrer* would pull it off again. Even if the French and British did come to Poland's help, they could do nothing before Poland had been battered into defeat. It was widely believed (as events in fact proved) that the Western Allies would in fact do nothing.

In terms of *matériel* the German Army was still in the process of evolution from the old days of the *Reichswehr* when war came in 1939. Horse-drawn transport and guns predominated; nor had the Army yet said farewell to its last horsed cavalry units. The Panzer formations included the ill-fated 'Light Divisions' and their hitting-power was still in dispute. (The early campaigns of the war proved this inadequate, and the light divisions were used as foundations for new Panzer divisions, of which Germany had six in September 1939.) But the German Army's best card was *mobility*: not only from the six Panzer and four light divisions, but from the four motorised divisions as well. The basic infantry and artillery weapons were sound and the supply machine had been vastly improved.

Another vital advantage possessed by the German Army in September 1939 was the speed of mobilisation. This, when coupled to the strategic advantage of commencing hostilities, proved decisive in the early days of the Polish campaign.

In more general terms, suffice it to say that since Hitler's arrival in January 1933, the German Army had been built up from the ten divisions permitted by Versailles to 53, shielded and assisted by the best air force in Europe.

The immense victories won by the German Army from the invasion of Poland in September 1939 to the Battle of Moscow in December 1941 are deceptive. They give the impression of having been won by an impeccably-functioning machine, unleashed on its enemies according to a series of detailed plans. This is not so. The Army owed its triumphs as much to the disunity, timidity, and material inadequacy of its enemies as it did to the German High Command.

Technical advantages, admittedly, reaped full dividends in Poland, where deep armoured thrusts could not be threatened by strong armoured countermoves. It was found that the idea of using the *Luftwaffe*'s dive-bombers as 'flying artillery' for the advancing ground troops worked well. But there was constant bickering between the German infantry and Panzer generals about the true role of the Panzers: should the latter cut loose on their own, or stay and help the infantry grind down the surrounded pockets of enemy troops? It is also easy to forget that Poland was conquered by the Red Army (which invaded on September 17) as well as by the *Wehrmacht*, which limited German Army operations to the western two-thirds of the country.

Yet there was adequate proof that the German Army owned impressive reserves of flexibility, as when the unexpected Polish counter-attack across the Bzura river was brilliantly handled by General von Rundstedt's southern army group.

Despite Hitler's initial enthusiasm for the idea, there could be no question of an immediate assault in the West in 1939. Deployment would take too long, and ammunition stocks had to be built up. In addition the Army staff plan for the attack ('Plan Yellow') was little more than an unimaginative rehash of the notorious 'Schlieffen Plan' of 1914. Hitler was not happy about it. Nor was Rundstedt's staff officer Manstein, whose repeated suggestions for a central breakthrough at Sedan on the Meuse and a thrust to the Channel were sat on by Brauchitsch and Halder. Not until January 1940 did Hitler hear of the idea and accept it at once. But before Manstein's plan of attack in the West could be tried, Hitler had made the snap decision to reduce Denmark and Norway.

This was ideal from the Navy's point of view: it was a maddening distraction for Brauchitsch and Halder, who were kept in the dark until the last minute. The entire plan ('Exercise Weser') depended on the Navy landing a division at the key ports of Norway simultaneously; they would then push inland and link up. Again, there were snags. The landings at Oslo were initially repulsed; British and French landings threatened the German beach-head at Trondheim; General Dietl's mountain troops were flung out of Narvik by another Allied landing. The day was saved by the *Luftwaffe*, which made it impossible for the British and French warships to supply the

Allied troops ashore; and by the speed with which the German troops landed in the south pushed north.

Before the Allies pulled out of Norway in the first week of June – but not before the German hold on southern and central Norway was secured – the bulk of the German Army, 136 divisions strong, attacked in the West. Once again, results were spectacular. The youngest arm of the *Wehrmacht*, the airborne and parachute troops, took a mere 24 hours to capture 'the strongest fort in the world', Belgium's Fort Eben-Emael on the Albert Canal. The Panzer divisions – seven concentrated in one *Panzergruppe* under General von Kleist – tore through the centre of the Allied line at Sedan and plunged west to the Channel, sealing off the French and British troops which had advanced into Belgium, all according to plan. Once again, there were near-fatal mistakes. At Rotterdam, a crass breakdown in air-ground communications resulted in the razing of the city centre while surrender talks were under way. At The Hague, the airborne attacking forces were totally beaten, badly mauled, and flung off their objectives. The scorching pace of the *Panzergruppe*'s advance across the Meuse panicked senior commanders through Kleist, Halder and Brauchitsch, right up to Hitler himself. The advance only went as fast as it did because of the brilliant insubordination of Guderian with his Panzer corps. He interpreted the cautious orders he received in the light of the situation at the front, and as a result got to the Channel in five days. As in Poland, an unexpected Allied move required prompt and unorthodox handling: at Arras on May 21, a British tank attack was halted by General Rommel's 7th Panzer Division (the first time that the 88mm AA gun was used against tanks).

The decision of Hitler and Rundstedt not to charge on to Dunkirk has been fiercely criticised. Rundstedt argued that the battle of France had still to be fought, and that it would be folly to send Panzer divisions into a head-on clash on unsuitable ground. Thus the British forces were allowed to escape – but the Panzer divisions, now regrouped into three new *Panzergruppen*, were largely intact when the final assault on France began on June 10. The French fought superbly on the line of the Somme and the Aisne, but there was nothing behind their front once the *Panzergruppen* had ripped it open. By June 22 the French had sued for, and signed, an armistice, by which time German spearheads were not only on the Swiss frontier but as far south as Lyons and the approaches to Bordeaux. Hostilities finally ended on June 25.

Between May 10 and June 25, 1940, the German Army had utterly destroyed the Anglo-French military line-up in the West and had occupied Holland, Belgium, Luxembourg, and northern France. But it had cost the Army 27,074 killed, 111,034 wounded, and 18,234 missing – and as the Dutch, Belgian, and French armistices resulted in the immediate release of German prisoners, most of those 'missing' were dead. With Britain resolved to fight on under Churchill, the hollowness of this great victory became apparent, for Britain could not be invaded. The German Navy had taken savage losses during the Norwegian campaign; the German airborne forces had suffered equally badly in the West. And when the *Luftwaffe* failed to win the certainty of an unopposed crossing in the skies over Britain, the war went on.

Thwarted in the West, Hitler turned to the gigantic gamble of ending the war by smashing Soviet Russia. The great invasion – 'Operation Barbarossa' – was scheduled for the early summer of 1941, but in April Hitler had to send large numbers of German troops into the Balkans. Mussolini's ill-advised war with Greece had proved a disaster; Yugoslavia had repudiated the Axis. Yugoslavia and Greece were reduced with little trouble and Crete was taken by German airborne troops – but the latter suffered so heavily that never again in the war was the German airborne arm able to mount such a powerful operation.

With the German invasion of Russia on June 22, 1941, it was seen how much had been learned from previous campaigns. *Luftwaffe* support was superb. Panzer advances were unprecedented. Such huge 'bags' of prisoners were taken that two-thirds of the pre-war Red Army strength had been wiped out by December. But the Red Army fought on. It got reinforcements from the Far East, from Siberia – crack troops, well-equipped for the Russian winter. On December 6 the Russians counter-attacked and drove the German forces back from the gates of Moscow. For the first time, the German Army of the Third *Reich* was forced to fight for its life.

What had gone wrong? The basic viewpoint of the German generals was the plaint that nothing kept them out of Moscow except for Hitler and the cloying mud of the Russian autumn. But this argument does not seem good enough.

Nor, basically, was the 'Barbarossa' plan itself adequate: three army groups, North, Centre, and South, were to advance along the respective axes of Leningrad, Moscow, and Kiev and destroy the Red Army as far west as possible. But two elementary flaws eroded 'Barbarossa'. The first was the *size* of Russia, which enlarged the battle-tried *Blitzkrieg* format until it went out of focus. It was impossible for the *Luftwaffe* to wipe out, or break up, the Soviet armies to the East – not to mention in Siberia – and pre-vent them from entering the battle. The huge distances covered exhausted the men and sent the vital Panzers to the repair workshops by the hundred from wear and tear alone. Apart from the solitary Minsk/Smolensk/Moscow 'motorway' metalled roads were non-existent and dissolved in mud when rained on; and the Russian railways had to be painfully converted to the German gauge. These factors alone made it inevitable that the German advance must run out of steam sooner or later. The further East the Army went the wider it was dispersed, the harder it became for it to concentrate in emergency, and the more easy it became for the Red Army to gain local superiority in repeated spoiling attacks. Above all, where was the German advance to *stop*? The much-vaunted 'A-A' (Archangel-Astrakhan) Line was no answer, for it had no naturally-defensible features. And there were certainly none along a front connecting Leningrad, Moscow, and the Black Sea.

The advance was to be on a broad front, and this raised the delicate question of co-operation between the army groups. There could be no irrevocable objectives for each army group commander, for it would be impossible to forecast precisely where the biggest enemy masses would polarise once the front line had been driven deep into Russia. Thus, if events made it advisable for Army Group Centre to help Army Group North, swift orders from the top and wholehearted co-operation on the part of the army group commanders must be the order of the day. Neither materialised once the campaign had been launched.

Five key generals stood out as recalcitrants of one kind or another, each pulling in different directions. Bock, commanding Army Group Centre, secretly longed to be hailed by German posterity as the Captor of Moscow and the Arch-Hammer of the Bolshevik Horde – but during the crucial months of 'Barbarossa' his conscience was nagged by officers on his staff who belonged to the anti-Hitler underground movement and wanted a field-marshal to take the lead in a *putsch*. Subordinate to Bock were two arch-rivals: the petulant Kluge and the impetuous Guderian. Kluge always complained that Guderian's Panzers, dashing on into the blue, left Kluge's infantry without adequate support; Guderian, subordinate to Kluge, chafed at all restrictions. Then came the important duo, Halder and Brauchitsch, at the head of OKH – impotent because, by June 22, 1941, it was crystal clear that the reins would not be left in the hands of OKH. And all five knew that Hitler's unpredictable 'intuition' would get its own way in any case.

It has long been commonplace to heap all the blame on Hitler for ordering the Ukraine to be cleaned up before the decisive drive on Moscow, which meant that the latter was launched too late. It would be more just to blame him for not bringing his generals sharply to heel – for allowing them, in effect, to waste two and a half vital weeks. This period of vacillation was caused by the uncertainties thrown up by conferences at Novy Borisov (July 27) and Lotzen (August 23). The Lotzen conference was the decisive one – Moscow or the Ukraine? Halder and Bock had 'passed the buck' to Guderian, who had the job of persuading Hitler to push for Moscow at once; Brauchitsch, by now almost totally unnerved, forbade Guderian even to mention Moscow to Hitler; Guderian disobeyed, but found himself isolated, watching the other officers nodding sycophantically while Hitler announced that his generals knew nothing about the economic aspects of war – the Ukraine must come first.

As the events moved to their crisis before Moscow and the first terrible winter frosts set in, the omens were already clear to see. On paper, the German Army had achieved its original brief: it had destroyed the estimated strength of the Red Army, but more and more Russian divisions were encountered. The Russian T-34 had been a hideous surprise to German tank crews and anti-tank gunners; one of the best tanks of the war, it, too, was threatening to achieve dominance of the battlefield. And fatuous over-confidence at OKW meant that when the first frosts came to wither the German Army on the Eastern Front, its winter equipment was still stuck in Warsaw station. The cold, not the Red Army, was the main foe of the Germans during the Battle of Moscow.

But they stood, and the man responsible was Hitler. He sacked every general who counselled strategic retreat. He did more – he took over command of the Army from Brauchitsch and kept it until the end in Berlin. He ordered that every inch of ground must be held, that the men must die where they stood. Digging-in was impossible in the intense cold and the men died by the thousand – but their comrades were still holding an intact front when Stalin's ill-co-ordinated offence petered out in March 1942.

Since September 1939 the German Army had won the greatest victories in its history. They were all meaningless, in that they had all been pursued to end the war – and they had failed to do so. Now Britain had an ally which the German Army could never escape. Two-thirds of Hitler's *Wehrmacht* had fallen on Soviet Russia and seized it by the throat. But after Moscow it could never dare let go – or flee.

When the diminutive *Afrika Korps* under General Erwin Rommel was originally sent to Libya in February 1941, the sole idea was to preserve Tripoli for Mussolini after a disastrous series of Italian defeats in the Western Desert. The build-up for 'Barbarossa' was the obsession of the German High Command; and the original forces scraped together for the *Afrika Korps* – 5th Light Division and 15th Panzer Division – would not be up to full strength until May 1941. Then, it was hoped, Rommel might try a limited attack to recover western Cyrenaica.

Rommel's lightning string of victories two months before he was even supposed to start appalled OKW and OKH. It was impossible to reinforce him – even to supply him properly. The shaken British later put it about that the *Afrika Korps* were an élite of supermen trained in hot-houses for the desert. This was not so. The German soldier did not take to the desert as did the British. The *Afrika Korps* – the German hard core of what became Rommel's German-Italian *Panzerarmee Afrika* – ate badly compared to the British 8th Army (British Army bully-beef was a prized German spoil of battle, which gives one some idea of how bad German rations were). Health was a major problem, chief villain being amoebic dysentery. Rommel himself was invalided out, chronically ill, as the crisis in North Africa approached in early autumn 1942.

The German psychological and material advantages over the 8th Army were, however, vital. First was Rommel himself, who became a bogeyman to the British desert soldier. His three major bungles – the first attack and siege of Tobruk, his throwing-away of victory at Sidi Rezegh in November-December 1941, and his attack at El Alamein in July 1942 – went almost unnoticed at the time. He was flexible, unpredictable and a born leader of men. His retreat from Alamein to Tunisia was a masterpiece.

Next came weapons: the battle-tried Panzers were more than a match for the Allies until the 8th Army received American Grants and Shermans in 1942. Mechanically reliable, their tracks did not fall off at the least excuse. Rommel's enthusiastic use of the 88mm AA gun as a tank-killer was another brainwave. A more lowly German advantage was the 'jerry-can' – the ultra-practical metal liquid container which never leaked and from which every drop could be poured. This was vital because of the chronic Axis supply problem in North Africa, with Malta lying squarely across the supply-lines from Sicily and Italy. Fuel was Rommel's bugbear: the further away he got from his base in Tripolitania after winning a victory, the harder it was to supply him.

Twice, however, Rommel was helped in that the British had to pull out desert-wise troops to send elsewhere. This aided Rommel in his first offensive (March-April 1941, when Wavell was obsessed with reinforcing Greece) and his second (January 1942, when the Japanese offensive in the Far East again drew off British troops from the desert theatre).

By mid-April 1941 Rommel had overrun Cyrenaica and was besieging Tobruk. 'Barbarossa' still lay two months in the future and Halder at OKH thought Rommel had gone mad. Tobruk was still holding out in May and June, when Rommel beat off two clumsy British attacks on his frontier positions. In November 1941, after initial successes against the 8th Army's first serious attempt to relieve Tobruk, Rommel mishandled the battle and had to retreat into Tripolitania to avert the destruction of his forces. He recoiled brilliantly in January-February 1942, reaching Gazala. In May-June 1942 he broke the 8th Army at Gazala and took Tobruk at last. There he was supposed to stop while Malta was taken – but in a brainstorm of opportunism Hitler and Mussolini backed Rommel's pleas for an immediate invasion of Egypt, which was halted at Alamein in early July.

At last, Hitler was willing to take Africa seriously. It was too late. Anglo-American landings in Algeria coincided with Rommel's defeat by the vastly superior 8th Army at Alamein. German troops were poured into Tunisia to keep a bridge-head open for Rommel's retreating *Panzerarmee*. By February 1943 the vice had closed. After a last throw – a counter-attack against the Americans at Kasserine, which met with initial success – the Axis forces in Tunisia were thrown on the defensive. Rommel, sick again, was withdrawn from Africa before the final débâcle on May 12, 13, 1943 – but a quarter of a million German troops had been ripped from the strength of the German Army.

The Army lost in North Africa largely because Rommel's victories raised the theatre to high-priority status at a time when little or nothing could be done to reinforce the Axis forces there. Thus Rommel's victories in Africa proved as empty as the earlier victories in France and western Russia. Worse – the more victories Rommel won, the further his troops advanced, the weaker their position became. The German Army troops under Rommel created the legend of the *Afrika Korps* and fought superbly. But that legend was all they had to show for their magnificent efforts.

In the first days of February 1943 the German summer offensive of 1942 reached its disastrous end with the annihilation of the 6th Army, trapped at Stalingrad on the Volga since November 23, 1942. Russia's retaliatory second winter offensive snatched back all the territorial gains won by the German Army since June 28 and pushed it back behind its start-line. Brilliant manoeuvres by General Manstein stabilised the front, leaving a westward-bulging salient around Kursk; but the loss of the 6th Army deprived the Army in Russia of its strongest single field force. Then came the second disaster of Tunis. Together, the two defeats lowered the German Army's fighting strength by around half a million men.

Nevertheless, strenuous efforts by Guderian and Speer had started the re-equipment of the Panzer divisions with Panther and Tiger tanks, and Hitler was determined to launch a third summer offensive. Thus there were no reserves at all to spare when the Allies launched their assault on southern Europe by invading Sicily on July 10. At this time Mussolini was still in the saddle and Italy still in the war; the defence of the island was predominantly left to the Italian Army. Field-Marshal Kesselring, C-in-C southern Europe, reinforced the shaky Italian garrison with two German divisions, whose tenacious fighting did much to delay the Allied advance. Both were evacuated to the Italian mainland to join the German garrison already assembling there under Kesselring's direction. His dispositions were aided by Hitler's determination to secure Italy with German troops, which had been effected in the nick of time by the moment when Mussolini's successor, Badoglio, took Italy out of the war and Eisenhower's forces invaded on July 10.

Kesselring's second piece of luck was that the Allies decided not to 'go for broke' and strike direct for Rome.

Instead their follow-up force landed at Salerno on September 3, hours after the 16th Panzer Division had moved into the area to disarm the local Italian troops. The narrowness of the Salerno battle (September 9-17) was an immense shot in the arm for the German defenders of central Italy. As the shaken Allies joined up and prepared to continue their advance, they were faced not only by a determined enemy and the foulest Italian autumn known for years, but by every natural feature of the Italian peninsula (mountain ranges, foothills, and water-courses), all of which favoured the German troops.

These features were exploited to the maximum by the Germans in the brilliant defensive battle at Monte Cassino (December 1943-May 1944). Once again the endurance and flexibility of the German troops was constantly underestimated by the Allied commanders. The German successes were won by small units of paratroops and Panzer Grenadiers (as the old motorised divisions had been styled since 1942) working in close co-operation even when temporarily isolated.

Kesselring's men held firm even when the Allies made a surprise landing behind their front at Anzio-Nettuno in January 1944. With another brilliant piece of improvisation, Kesselring held the Anzio front with a scattering of cooks, clerks, and other rear-echelon forces scraped together and thrown into the sector. The Cassino line was eventually breached by French colonial mountain troops, and the confused German defenders were faced with engulfment. Again, Kesselring's determination not to give up averted total disaster and a fighting retreat was made to the more northerly 'Gothic

Line' – a chain of positions most of which had not been completed. Again, the German forces were helped by the drawing-off of Allied forces to be sent to other theatres. As the winter of 1944 approached, Kesselring was still holding a firm front in northern Italy south of the River Po; his opponent, General Alexander, was forced to sit down and plan another set-piece assault.

This was launched on April 9, by which time Kesselring had been called to take command on the crumbling Western Front; his continued presence in Italy would have made little difference. The energy and ingenuity of the Allied attack - particularly the amphibious assault across Lake Commachio – unseamed the German front, and the withdrawal across the Po was a shambles. Undercover surrender negotiations between the SS chief in Italy and the American Office of Strategic Services brought forward the inevitable surrender of the German troops on the 'southern front' – Austria and Italy, about a million men all told – on May 2, 1945.

If any single campaign justified the aims of the German Army training of the *Reichswehr* period – the production of the 'thinking fighting man' who could operate effectively in small units – it was the Italian campaign. Time and again the Allies were stopped, not only by their own mistakes and miscalculations, but by the resilience and endurance of the German soldier. A propaganda myth was fostered by the Allies that the German troops in Italy were fanatical Nazis. This was not so – they were the proverbial collection of 'odds and sods', but one held together by a common professionalism.

The Stalingrad disaster was due to three main factors. First, the Russians were learning fast not to throw away vast numbers of men by ordering them to risk encirclement. Second, the German strategy ordered by Hitler was a mess - neither one thing nor another, a fatal halving of the German Army's available resources. When it resulted in the unexpected encirclement of the 6th Army at Stalingrad, Hitler's obstinate insistence that the latter must hold its ground sealed its death sentence.

Stalingrad could have been 'snatched' in August by a powerful drive, but the power, in the form of the 4th Panzer Army, was not to hand: it was wasting its time pulling back from the Don crossings in the south, where it was not needed and should never have been sent. Stalingrad could have fallen to a sophisticated series of concentric attacks in September, but the heads-down 'sledge-hammer' attacks of the German commander Paulus (in his first independent command) were immensely wasteful and resulted in a grinding battle of attrition in which the Russians were able to hold their own. Meanwhile, the down-at-heel Italian and Romanian divisions on the 6th Army's flanks were marked down as the targets for the counter-offensive which Zhukov was preparing.

Nor had Hitler's obsession – the oilfields of the Kuban and the Caucasus - been attained. Kleist's 1st Panzer Army found that the further it got the tougher it had to fight, over increasingly bad going. By the end of October 1942 the Germans had been halted in the High Caucasus and along the line of the Terek river.

The resultant disaster at Stalingrad was partly due to previous defensive battles brilliantly won by the German Army – at Demyansk and at Kholm during the Moscow counter-offensive. There, large bodies of surrounded German forces had successfully beaten off the Russians until relieved. But Stalingrad was a different matter: the 6th Army was the biggest single unit fielded by the Germans on the south-east front – about 300,000. The men trapped in Stalingrad died or went into captivity because of the appalling weaknesses in the High Command which Hitler had created. Paulus and his staff said they could hold if adequately supplied by air; Goering said they could be; Hitler chose to believe both; the supply and combat officers who knew the real position were sat on when they protested.

The 6th Army achieved one thing in their hopeless struggle: they pinned down *seven* Russian armies which would otherwise have been thrown into the gap in the German front. This gap was brilliantly sealed by Manstein's series of armoured counter-attacks in February-March 1943, which recovered Kharkov but left a westward-pointing salient in the front around Orel and Kursk.

Manstein's successes had the same fateful effect as the earlier airlifts at Demyansk and Kursk: they produced over-confidence. Hitler was convinced that a fresh offensive, this time with the new tanks which were being rushed to the Panzer forces, would finally reap success. He played down the hideous truth of the Russian tank strength, the knowledge that the Kursk salient was the strongest sector of the Russian line, and awareness that the new German armour was not fully battle-worthy. These three factors resulted in the titanic armoured battles on the northern and southern flanks of the Kursk salient (July 4-13), which ended any chance of forming a strong German reserve on the Eastern Front and placed the German armies there on the defensive for the rest of the war.

'Barbarossa' had ducked realities from the beginning. No final strategic objective made sense – the only one mentioned had been the meaningless 'A-A' Line. Also under-estimated was the supply problem: the further the German armies marched, the wider their front became, and the logistic problem of an orthodox campaign was first squared, then cubed. On the other hand, the first three years of the campaign in Russia showed how the magnificent fighting qualities of the German Army could restore an apparently hopeless position. Kursk wasted all that; it was little more than a desperate squandering of the last handful of chips in a single throw.

In attack and defence, the burden fell on the German infantry – inevitably. This had been the case ever since Moscow. Conversely, the German Army had learned much about the Red Army's cardinal weaknesses – wooden adherence to the letter of orders, a comfortable tendency to panic when surprised. But the weight and pace of the Russian pursuit in the summer and autumn of 1943 prevented the Germans from conducting that military dream, 'an ordered tactical retreat' to the hoped-for bastion of the Dniepr river. And it was on the Dniepr that the German Army learned another lesson – the virtual impossibility of eliminating Russian river bridgeheads once established and reinforced. The long retreat to the very ruins of Berlin had begun.

'What can you do? Make peace, you fools! What else can you do?' That was Rundstedt's testy response to a panicky Keitel on July 1, 1944. That, too, was the situation plain and simple, and it did not take a seasoned professional like Rundstedt to see it. But, six months before, that was not the case. Germany could have struggled on with a fair chance of fighting the Allies to a standstill, if only a temporary one.

The crucial conundrum was the problem of what would happen when the Allies launched their invasion in the West – the inevitable recipe for Germany's defeat. It was Jodl, of all people, who had already come up with the daring plan to pull right back to the eastern frontier of the *Reich*, thus halving the breadth of the Eastern Front, and sending the troops thus released to buttress the garrisons along the Channel coast. With Rommel just beginning his bid to make the invasion coast impregnable – and given a couple more months he would probably have done it – this could, on paper, have taken the impossibility out of the situation and given the *Reich* a fighting chance.

Hitler, inevitably would have none of this. He held to his obsession of holding every inch of ground, however useless. Thus the German Army in the East was doomed to the terrible battles in White Russia of June-July 1944, which carried the Red Army on to the Vistula and had destroyed the Eastern Army Group Centre by the time the British and Americans finally ground down the threadbare forces in Normandy and broke out, eastwards to the Seine. The jaws of the Allied vice had begun their inexorable closing which was to end in May 1945 with Germany squeezed in half.

The 'Generals' Plot' of July 1944, which all but killed Hitler, was in fact the work of a tiny body of determined activists motivated by the mistaken belief that the Allies would be happy to negotiate with them once Hitler was removed from the scene. And the reaction of the Army majority – officers and men – was one of outraged betrayal of their efforts in the field. Even Guderian consented to sit in judgment on his fellow officers after the failure of the plot. This was an individual decision significant in itself.

For the German Army, the tragedy was that, by the time of the Normandy landings, it had never been better equipped. Its infantry had anti-tank rocket missiles (*Panzerfaust* and *Panzerschreck*) and heavy tanks which only the Anglo-American hybrid Sherman 'Firefly' with its 17-pounder gun, and the Russian JS-2 and JS-3, could tackle with confidence. Production of weapons had never been higher – but it was too late. The Allied air offensive, at last turned against Germany's bifold Achilles' heel – oil and the transport system – was beginning to bite.

Nevertheless, the Allied landslide advances in both East and West during the high summer of 1944 did peter out from sheer exhaustion and made an autumn and winter campaign inevitable. By now it was a question of nothing more or less than the defence of the *Reich*, which again could have been protracted. But the armoured striking force which Hitler managed to assemble during autumn 1944 was squandered in the Ardennes sideshow in the West, removing the last high-quality reserves which could have intervened in the terrible Russian offensive of January-February 1945. This carried the Red Army forward to the Oder, while the British and Americans were still grinding away at the Siegfried Line in the West.

Two additional factors attenuated the German Army still further during the defence of the *Reich*: the need to detail forces in the south-east to buttress the flagging morale of Hungary, and Hitler's new obsession: 'Fortress' defence. This boiled down to declaring every large town a 'fortress' and throwing away troop concentrations in futile defence. There were also 18 useless divisions trapped in Courland, which Hitler refused to evacuate.

The Western floodgate collapsed first, when the British and Americans cracked the Rhine barrier in March and surrounded the Ruhr, complete with German C-in-C West, Model. The Ruhr pocket was the biggest 'bag' ever made: 317,000 POWs were eventually taken, by which time Zhukov and Koniev had launched the final drive on Berlin from the Oder. Even then, outnumbered by well over two to one in men and aircraft, and four to one in tanks and guns, General Gotthard Heinrici stopped Zhukov in his tracks for over 48 hours before being surrounded from north and south. With forces that in the 'glory days' of 1940 and 1941 would have been considered a pitiful rabble, the German Army made the Russians pay dearly for their final victory. Between April 16 and May 8, 1945, the Russians lost about 300,000 men killed, wounded, or missing.

For having achieved so much, endured so much, and held for so long against such odds, the German Army of the Hitler era stands unique in military history. It lost because it was asked to do the impossible. It should never have been set to tackle the tasks it did. It is the job of strategists to see that their armies are not asked to do the impossible.

Hitler's armies started the war with one mighty advantage over those of their enemies. Unlike the latter, whose armed services had been eroded to the verge of impotence by cheese-paring peacetime governments in the 1920s and 1930s, the German Army was very well equipped for war in 1939.

It was not, however, a picture of modern warfare incarnate. Horsed transport (especially as gun tractors) was still vital, and even as late as the invasion of Russia the German Army still boasted an entire cavalry division. Nor was it a picture of impeccable organisation – like every army, the German Army of World War II had plenty of brainchildren which died in infancy, taking an unnecessary amount of good soldiers' lives with them. But all in all the 'guns or butter' motivation of Hitler's Germany had done an excellent job for the German armed forces.

To start at grass roots, with infantry weapons, provides a good example. Standard infantry rifle in 1939 was the time-tested Mauser '98k, a worthy opponent to the British Lee Enfield .303. The '98k with its lower rate of fire was not, *per se*, an inferior weapon: it existed because the German Army had very definite ideas on the correct rate of fire to achieve accuracy. (German recruits were taught to fire their five deliberate rounds and take a deep breath, rather than work up to the British standby of 'fifteen rounds rapid'.) But this did not mean that high fire-power was discounted. The German Army had some of the best automatic weapons of the war. These included the famous (but often wrongly-named) 'Schmeisser' – *Maschinenpistole* MP38, and its immediate successor, the MP40. This was the standard German sub-machine-gun of the war and over a million were produced. Later came the *Sturmgewehr* StG44, a short automatic rifle.

As far as machine-guns were concerned, a totally new format emerged with the lightweight MG34 and MG42, two more classic weapons with amazing rates of fire – the MG42's cyclic rate of fire was 20 rounds per second, and the gun when firing was said to sound like tearing calico.

In artillery, too, the German soldier was well served with conservative models. Massive siege guns appeared – *Moerser Karl* (60cm) and *Kanone Dora* were among the most famous. They did score successes, such as the cracking of the Soviet armoured turrets at Sebastopol; but they were given a crazed over-importance by Hitler, who once flabbergasted Guderian by wanting to use them against tanks!

Armoured warfare in World War II triggered off the inevitable escalation-race between armour-cracking guns and shell-resistant armour, and until the *Panzerjaeger* ('tank-hunting') crews ran into the Russian T-34 the 35mm Pak gun with which the German Army went to war was adequate. The armour race then produced the Pak 50 and the Pak 75, but long before these two made their battlefield debuts the Luftwaffe's 88mm AA gun had been pressed into service as the ultimate tank-killer. Despite its tall scaffold-like silhouette (unless dug in, in a static position), the '88' was found to be a match for any Allied tank.

The two-year 'glory days' period of the Panzer division had the Pzkw Mks III and IV as the twin mainstays. Both were comparatively small machines, mechanically reliable (they had not been designed with the appalling distances of Russia in mind). The Allies had nothing to beat them, although the British 'Matilda' with its massive shell could survive them, lumbering along at a valiant but totally inadequate eight miles an hour on its London bus engine. The best advantage the Germans had was that the Panzer virtuosos never bothered with producing 'infantry' tanks intended to co-operate with the foot-sloggers. But Russia changed all previous Panzer specifications – or to be precise, the T-34 tank did. Now more speed was needed, more armour, sloped as much as possible, and a bigger gun. The result was the superb Panther (Pzkw V) with its 75mm gun; and the two classic German 'heavies', the Tiger I and Tiger II with 88mm guns.

One of the biggest surprises about the German war machine is the time it took to get it organised, which explains why Panther and Tiger were not really ready for the massive tank collision at Kursk in July 1943. Hitler's influence, however, was a baneful one, and in some ways epitomises his whole record as German supreme warlord. He had been right in wanting the 50mm 'long' gun for the Mk III; the Army Ordnance office had flouted him and given him the 'short' 50, with its lower hitting-power. Hitler never forgave this. What made matters worse was his gradual departure from reality. He insisted that a tank be developed for street fighting. The 88mm *Elefant* was a useless concept because this turretless assault-gun was an infantry sup-port weapon and needed machine-guns for infantry fighting. *Elefant* had none. Hitler's obsession with size produced the design for *Maus*, 188 tons of sluggish juggernaut which was to be armed with a 128mm turret gun with a co-axial 75! (It never got past mock-up stage, but far too much time was wasted on it.) Then there was *Stuermtiger*, a Tiger hull packing a 15 inch rocket mortar – a battlefield White Elephant if ever there was one.

One field in which the German Army blazed a trail was in that of rocket missiles. In Russia the German soldier learned of the horrifying effects of mass bombardment by rocket missiles – the dreaded *Katyusha* or 'Stalin's organ', as the Germans sardoni-cally called it. By early 1943 the German Army had its own six-barrelled rocket mortar – *Nebelwerfer* or 'smoke-thrower', a nerve-shaker in its own right although it was too top-heavy to permit a simultaneous discharge of all six rockets. By 1944 and 1945 experiments were being made to emulate the mobile Katyushas by mounting racks of rocket missiles on half-tracks. By this time, too, the first infantry bazookas had appeared with the recoilless *Panzerfaust* and *Panzerschreck* missile projectors. These prompted unorthodox counter-measures – Russian tanks smashing into Berlin in April 1945 mounted bed-springs on their frontal armour to detonate the hollow-charge missiles away from the armour.

In the field, the German soldier was basically well served, with disastrous excep-tions. The most famous of these occurred during the first campaign in Russia, when over-confidence at the top failed to get the Army's winter uniforms up to the front in time for the battle of Moscow. There was plenty of bureaucratic insubordination in the German Army, but it never seemed to work on the side of the German soldier. The story of the frozen *Gluehwein* solemnly dropped into the Stalingrad pocket was an absurdity, but a justified one. (Soldiers freezing to death before Moscow while the good citizens of the Reich donated their spare fur coats to be sent to the front were ready to believe stories like that.)

The German Army was a *European* army, and in the one theatre outside Europe in which it performed – North Africa – its essential services did not do well. The orig-inal tropical kit issued to the *Afrika Korps* included a massive solar topee. Much more serious was the failure of the Germans to *adapt* to the desert. They were never really happy there and both food and medical services left much to be desired. Rommel himself had to go on sick leave on the eve of Alamein with amoebic dysentery. Food was monotonous and deficient in vitamins: British Army field-baked bread and tinned 'bully' were prized spoils of battle. Field medicine, however, was certainly up to standard, although no army of World War II ever reached the sophistication of the

American system. (Patton's 3rd Army set the record, with 90 percent hospital admissions and only 2 percent mortality of that total.) The German medical services even functioned during the Stalingrad tragedy – as long as the aircraft kept coming.

To sum up, we must return to the blunt fact that Germany was not fully 'geared up' to total war until 1944 and it was inevitable that the Army should suffer from this. What the men had to work with was good. But the experts back in the Reich, let alone factory production, could never match the ruthless speed with which the Russians or Americans latched on to a good idea, ironed out the essential teething troubles, and rushed the product into action. It was, in a way, inevitable that as far as material was concerned the Allied story between 1941 and mid-1942 was 'too little, too late'. From then onwards the boot was on the other foot. It was easy to put the whole blame on Hitler, and to say that if he wanted to wage total war he should have prepared for it. He had his experts and they let him down far more often than is frequently admitted. None of this detracts from the achievements of the fighting men who had to suffer in consequence.

DIE WAFFEN-SS

The SS (*Schuetzstaffeln*) followed the SA (*Sturmabteilung*) as the second – and, to start with, emphatically smaller – of the 'private armies' of the Nazi movement. The SS leader Heinrich Himmler had been a *protégé* of Gregor Strasser, Hitler's greatest rival for the leadership of the Party; and until 1934 Himmler remained, at least in theory, subordinate to Ernst Roehm, boss of the SA.

The SS, which Himmler took over in 1929, had as its immediate aim the provision of a bodyguard to Hitler, who soon saw the advantages of having to hand a more tightly-knit force than the SA. Finally, in June 1934, Hitler used the SS to eliminate Roehm and the other SA leaders in the 'Night of the Long Knives'. Himmler then began to expand the SS to fill the power vacuum – and to provide Hitler with an executive arm beyond the control either of the law or of the state. At the same time, strenuous efforts were made to invest the SS with spurious honours as the visible expression of the Nazi ideal.

The *Waffen*-SS (or 'armed SS') was as old as the Nazi state. It came into being as the 'SS *Leibstandarte* Adolf Hitler' (Adolf Hitler's lifeguards) in 1933, an outfit destined to become the first field unit of the *Waffen*-SS. It is not hard to see why Hitler encouraged the formation of SS military units – he profoundly distrusted the 'old boy' mentality of the traditional German Army officer caste and knew very well that it was the only institution in Germany which could turn against him. He wanted his own Praetorian guard; and if it made the regular German army look slack and inferior by comparison, so much the better.

After the hard-core *Leibstandarte* came the formation of *Verfuegungstruppen* or 'armed reserve troops' throughout the *Reich*. These were described as 'exclusively at the service of the *Fuehrer*, for special tasks in peace and war'. Selection standards were high – originally candidates were failed if they had fillings in their teeth. Standards of drill, training, and turnout were perfectionist – one in three SS men applying for a walking-out pass would be turned down because of some minute fault in his dress or bearing.

There were applicants in plenty, for any new élite unit attracts recruits with a multitude of motives. Many regular Army officers transferred to the *Waffen*-SS (it should be remembered that the official term did not begin to be used until the 1940 campaign) because promotion was faster.

In addition to the SS-VT units there were the *Totenkopfverbaende* or 'Death's Head units', originally raised as concentration camp guards, for use against any civil strife in the event of Germany going to war.

By 1940 four regiments had been raised: *Leibstandarte, Deutschland, Germania,* and *Der Fuehrer*, most of which had taken part in the occupations of Austria, the Sudetenland, and Prague, and were gradually becoming accepted as part of the military machine. There were also four *Totenkopf* units, the regiments being given provincial names: *Oberbayern, Brandenburg, Thuringen*, and the Austrian *Ostmark*. Typical of the regional formation of *Waffen*-SS units in the year 1939 was *Heimwehr Danzig*, raised in that city as the Nazi programme of threats and demands against Poland increased in tempo. As its name suggests, it was a hardcore Nazi vigilante outfit, used to police the city and beat up recalcitrant Poles.

The army's situation was intricate. Its leaders had backed Hitler's accession to power because Hitler had promised them that the brown-shirted SA would not be permitted to challenge the army for the title of official arms-bearers of the Reich. These new SS regiments were doing just that, but as every officer and man in the Army had sworn personal allegiance to Adolf Hitler it was not good for the conscience to worry about them. It was easier to regard the SS regiments as 'Asphalt soldiers', very pretty on the parade-ground, but basically amateurs who could not shape up if ever they were to be exposed to combat.

The *Waffen*-SS units which received their baptism of fire in Poland were the *Leibstandarte* and *Verfuegungstruppe* regiments, well corseted by regular Army units to which they were subordinate. For all their much-vaunted training with live ammunition and balancing of live grenades on helmets, the *Waffen*-SS troops put up a generally mediocre performance and suffered proportionately heavy loss. Had the German High Command possessed any sane structure, the decision must certainly have been made to break up the *Waffen*-SS formations and post the men to Army units. Instead a highly complicated series of orders up-graded and re-formed the battered regiments to divisional status – and even more of them were planned.

Leibstandarte, surprisingly enough, was merely retained as a strengthened motorised infantry regiment; but a new division was formed from the *Totenkopfverbaende* and was christened *Totenkopf*. Another division was raised from the police forces of the Reich: *Polizei*. The latter SS unit was the first noticeable breach in the original perfectionist standards of recruiting – but more soon followed.

Inevitably, the members of the imitation movements which were to be found among Germany's neighbours – and imminent victims – were soon regarded as suitable recruiting material. These included the followers of future collaborationists Quisling (Norway), Degrelle (Belgium) and Mussert (Holland), who formed the first non-German *Waffen*-SS unit. This was the *Nordland* regiment, formed in 1940 and soon followed by *Westland*.

Two further modifications of the *Waffen*-SS 'order of battle' in 1940 improved upon these beginnings. *Nordland* and *Westland* were merged with the *Germania* regiment to form the *Germania* Division. This was subsequently re-christened *Wiking*, while the *Verfuegungsdivision* was re-christened *Das Reich*.

The campaign in the West did two things for the *Waffen*-SS: it confirmed its title and established a reputation for efficiency, but at the same time put an enduring black mark on its reputation for atrocity. The culprits were the men of *Totenkopf* who massacred surrendered British POWs at Le Paradis, triggering off a ripple of uneasy protest from regular Army commanders that was never translated into punitive action. And more expansion was promised. Addressing *Leibstandarte* officers in September 1940, Himmler announced: 'We must attract all the Nordic blood in the world to us so that never again will it fight against us.'

It remained to be seen what definitions would be drawn for 'Nordic blood', and just how much of it would in fact be attracted. A mixture of opportunism and desperation helped make an utter nonsense of the original Nazi definitions of what made a worthwhile citizen – and potential soldier – of the *Reich*. Germany never lacked for direct allies down to the end of the war – Italians, Hungarians, Romanians. But the racial creed of the *Waffen*-SS had originally stood above foreign integration. As Hitler's Germany strengthened its grip on Europe, the categories of German citizens (*Reichsdeutsch*) and ethnic Germans (*Volksdeutsch*) were increased by the addition of 'honorary Germans' – and for this latter category the sky was the limit.

A total of about 6000 Norwegians and Danes served in the *Waffen*-SS under a bewildering kaleidoscope of titles. *Freikorps* – foreign legions – were raised in addition to the *Wiking* Division. In early 1943 the Scandinavian troops were merged in a reborn *Nordland* Division which was finally immolated in the battle of Berlin. These, at least, were recognisable 'Nordics', and so were the volunteers from Holland, which was granted the status of being closest by blood to Germany herself. The Dutch produced a record crop of SS volunteers – the figure has been set as high as 50,000. What was finally described as the *Nederland* Division ended up trapped in Courland, and only a few survivors were evacuated. The Belgians, led by Léon Degrelle, produced two paper divisions: *Langemarck* and *Wallonie*, both of which were ground to pieces on the Eastern Front.

The campaign in the East produced the most promising crop of foreign recruits, starting with the Baltic States, in particular Latvia and Estonia. By the spring of 1943,

22,000 had volunteered and were formed into three divisions – two Latvian and one Estonian. Their survivors, too, ended up in the Courland pocket. Down in the occupied Balkans Himmler made strenuous efforts to recruit Balkan Muslims disenchanted by the Yugoslav state, officially dismembered by the conquest of April 1941. Three divisions reached paper strength: the Muslim *Handschar*, the Albanian *Skanderbeg*, and the Croat *Kama*. After blotting their copybook by mutinying under training, the Muslims were set to deal with Tito's partisans. Their successes in this field were negligible and their main achievement was the massacre of Yugoslav civilians.

In Russia proper the Ukraine and the Cossack lands of the Don and Kuban were also fruitful recruiting-grounds until the true nature of German occupation made its mark. Some 100,000 anti-Communist Ukrainians volunteered, were formed into the 14th Galician Division, and virtually wiped out in their first (and last) battle: the Tarnov-Brody pocket in June 1944. Several Cossack units were raised, but none of them achieved any military successes, although they were encountered by the Allies as far afield as France and northern Italy.

Perhaps least effective of all were the attempts made to recruit from Allied POWs. The Indian independence leader Subhas Chandra Bose tried to raise an Indian nationalist army from POWs taken in North Africa, but never attracted more than 2000. Recruitment among the French produced the volunteer *Sturmbrigade 'Charlemagne'*, subsequently elevated to divisional status but never up to actual brigade strength. *Charlemagne*, too, was wiped out in the Berlin battle. And most ignominious of all was the failure to form a British SS unit, the *Britisches Freikorps* or 'Legion of St George'. These military drop-outs never made up more than two platoons, and caused their German patrons constant headaches by their insatiable demands for loose women and drink. Here indeed was a case of pure propaganda winning out over military practicability.

For their failure to make more out of the available recruits (particularly in the East) the Germans could blame lack of time and their own atrocious behaviour to conquered populations. Both were key ingredients in the destruction of Germany and her SS.

By the middle of 1941 the overall strength of the *Waffen*-SS was six divisions, of which the majority were manned by native Germans. A year later, in the fearful battles of the Eastern Front, they had more than won their spurs. All six had suffered heavily and *Leibstandarte*, *Das Reich*, *Totenkopf* and *Wiking* were withdrawn to be re-equipped with the newest weapons and restored to strength. Nos 1, 2, 3, 5, 9, 10 and 12 were to be raised to the status of full Panzer divisions. They formed the élite striking force with which Manstein restored the Eastern Front during the Stalingrad crisis. But by this time Hitler had come to the decision that more must be raised.

Hohenstaufen and *Frundsberg* were the next German SS divisions raised, followed by *Hitler Jugend*, one of the most frightening combat units of the war: recruited from the 1926 class of dedicated young Nazis.

The first time that *Waffen*-SS Panzer divisions were used as a unified bloc was during the superb Manstein counter-offensive of February-March 1943, which recovered Kharkov. From then on Hitler used his SS divisions as a mobile 'fire-brigade' and rushed them mercilessly about the map of Europe. They were sent to France. They were rushed back to Russia. They served in northern Italy. The record was put up by the most renowned of them all, *Leibstandarte*, which oscillated between East and West seven times, each time being required to throw in a major attack immediately upon arrival. Between Kursk and the Normandy landings *Waffen*-SS divisions were constantly in action, carrying out this emergency role. And during this time Hitler, thanks to his growing distrust of the regular Army generals, came to develop an exaggerated respect for the indifferent military skills of the SS generals – Dietrich, Steiner, Meyer.

Perhaps the most crucial of these 'fire-brigade' battles was the containment of the British and Canadians at Caen in June-July 1944, where the seven *Waffen*-SS divisions employed fought themselves to virtual destruction. Here, too, the *Waffen*-SS added to its atrocity dossier with the Oradour massacre (*Das Reich*) and the slaughter of 64 Allied POWs (*Hitler Jugend*). The latter atrocity could not be cancelled out by the superhuman efforts made by *Hitler Jugend* in keeping open the Falaise Gap for the escape of their defeated comrades.

The last major event in the *Waffen*-SS story was the Ardennes offensive of December 1944, which saw the first attack by a full-blooded SS Panzer Army (the 6th) spearheaded by *Leibstandarte*. Superbly equipped with the 'King Tiger' heavy tanks, *Leibstandarte* nevertheless got itself bogged down on the northern flank of the 'Bulge' which was hammered into the Allied front. The furthest advance was made in the centre by regular Army troops – and *Leibstandarte* was the culprit for the infamous murder of 86 American POWs at Malmedy.

It should be remembered that by the last months of the war Hitler had lost all confidence in every single fighting arm of the *Wehrmacht* – including the *Waffen*-SS. When he ordered *Leibstandarte* to remove their armbands as a punishment for failing to bring off an impossible attack, the reaction was one of bewilderment, resentment and fury. It was to this that the original concept of the *Waffen*-SS as the Nazi Praetorian Guard had come.

The men of these superb divisions had an *esprit de corps* second to none, however reluctantly this must be granted. Their achievements were frequently remarkable. The most dedicated men in their ranks fought as super-patriots, members of a unique comradeship. But their survivors today owe their Jekyll-and-Hyde reputation to the fact that the evil that they did lived after them.

One of the most frightening aspects of the *Waffen*-SS is the fascination which it still has for military collectors and modellers. The glamour which that service undoubtedly had for the Germans of Hitler's day has by no means been dissipated by the passage of time. Nor can it be claimed that the survival of this interest stems purely from the detached academic motives of the military historian. There is something else. But what?

Muddled thinking is one of the clearest guidelines to the Nazi mentality, and we have seen how this came to affect the composition of the *Waffen*-SS. The propaganda slogan 'Join us in the Crusade Against Bolshevism' came late in the day, and this is hard for many to accept. Indeed, many *Waffen*-SS veterans go so far as to insist that they were the prototype of the United Nations and NATO multi-national armies. One fact that is obvious is that the origins of the force lay in the desire of Hitler to have at his disposal an iron guard which owed allegiance to nothing and nobody but himself, and that the deliberate efforts to build up this hard core into a Nazi field army woefully dissipated the resources of Nazi Germany's war effort. It is impossible to create a *corps d'élite* overnight: time is needed for that, and once Hitler had made his decision to bring on a war in Europe in 1939, time was the one thing he did not have. Nevertheless, by 1943 the German divisions of the *Waffen*-SS *did* regard themselves as a *corps d'élite* and by the end of the war could claim, with justification, that their efforts in the field had made them one.

Certainly the story of the *Waffen*-SS reflects the dehumanising effect of World War II. It was *impossible* for Nazi Germany to produce a combat arm that could claim to emerge from the whole mess with an unspotted record. To coin a phrase, it might be said that the entire Nazi system was 'self-soiling'. The 12 years of Hitler's Reich offered scope for, and fulfilment to, Germans motivated by genuine ideals of patriotism, public service, and self respect. But the institutions of brute force which upheld Hitler's *Reich* – of which the *Waffen*-SS was clearly one – offered not only scope and fulfilment but rapid promotion to the thugs and brutes who alone could do the dirty work without going mad. Hence regular Army combat units fighting at the front could voice their contempt for, and disgust with, the murderous thugs of the *Einsatzkommados* in their rear. *Waffen*-SS commanders, too, could and did pride themselves on their military honour – while belonging to a force which was capable of Oradour, Malmedy, Le Paradis, and other atrocities. The comic-opera characteristics of the worst of the foreign SS units might be the object of general mirth among 'real German soldiers' but it all stemmed from the same source.

The *Waffen*-SS can claim one justification for its mottled reputation: the dehumanising influence of war. By 1944 those soldiers which had survived Moscow, Stalingrad, Kursk, and a score of other murderous battles were not as other men. But in the case of the *Waffen*-SS, with its self-imposed standards of ruthless efficiency, of being the best soldiers in the world bar none, this dehumanisation was all too often carried beyond all acceptance.And none of the military glamour with which the *Waffen*-SS is still invested today can change the fundamental misdirection of so much dedication and sacrifice.

DIE KRIEGSMARINE

On November 21, 1918, one of the most important and unprecedented events in the history of sea power took place when the German High Seas Fleet steamed into the Firth of Forth and voluntarily surrendered to the Royal Navy. Restricted throughout World War I to the North Sea and Baltic by Germany's unfavourable geographical position, unable to match the superior strength of the British fleet, hampered by a divided command structure and internal dissensions, and always overshadowed by the army, the German surface navy had never been able to carry out the role envisaged for it by its creator, Admiral von Tirpitz. Now, to fulfil one of the demands of the armistice settlement, it was being forced to give itself up without a fight to its old enemy. Although Germany had built up its fleet to be the second largest in the world, it appeared that it was abandoning any further claim to be a sea power.

Exactly seven months later, however, on June 21, 1919, that same High Seas Fleet scuttled itself without the permission of its British captors in the anchorage of Scapa Flow. By this action Admiral von Reuter and his crews had not only prevented the victorious Allies from laying hands upon first-class German warships, but they had also redeemed the honour of the navy and provided a symbol of resistance for the rest of the service. Out of the watery consummation at Scapa Flow there would arise, Phoenix-like, a restored German fleet at some future date. Certainly, none of the naval leaders in the post-1919 years, Trotha, Behncke, Zenker and the rest, ever believed that the humiliating surrender meant anything other than a temporary defeat or that the navy's size would always remain the 'treaty fleet' of eight old, pre-Dreadnought battleships and some smaller vessels. As early as 1921 the first tentative steps were taken to revive operational planning; as one officer put it, even if they had no fighting navy, 'at least we must prepare ourselves *theoretically* for war'. Like the rest of the German nation during the 1920s and early 1930s, the navy's attitude was essentially a revanchist and expansionist one, hidden only by a thin crust of deference to the Versailles settlement and to Weimar democracy. Only in the decision of 1928 to begin building the *Deutschland*-class of so-called 'pocket-battleships' (*Panzerschiffe*) was there any sign given to the outside world of this feeling in the navy: for such vessels, with their high speed and long cruising range, were clearly designed for commerce-raiding on the high seas and not for the restricted waters of the Baltic. It symbolised the ambitious ideas of such naval writers as Vice-Admiral Wolfgang Wegener, who argued that only by breaking out to the Atlantic trade-routes through the occupation of Scandinavia and Iceland could Germany overcome her unfavourable geographical position and thus defeat Great Britain in a future war. Nevertheless, the German navy was still very small when Adolf Hitler came to power in 1933.

In the years following 1928 the service was commanded by Admiral Erich Raeder, who had made his name as Hipper's Chief of Staff in the battle-cruiser actions of World War I and who had also written the German official naval history of the overseas surface raiders. A cautious, stable and systematic officer, Raeder was not the sort of person to take dramatic decisions or to urge the swift build-up of the fleet in order to fight Britain and France; Wegener's ideas were acknowledged by the Commander-in-Chief but the latter preferred to concentrate his energies upon the slow but steady warship construction programme and upon improving the organisation of the navy. Besides, no great change could take place in German naval policy without the backing of the *Fuehrer*.

Hitler's attitude towards the navy depended largely upon his attitude towards Britain. At the back of his mind, he had always planned that Germany should become a great *world* power in the future; but he also firmly believed that it would be possible to achieve an alliance with London during the early stages of Germany's recovery, provided that he gave assurances that Berlin would not re-assume the pre-1914 policy of naval and colonial expansion. After 1935 or so, however, Hitler's doubts about the likelihood and desirability of an English alliance increased in reaction to what he considered to be the obstructionism of the British government. This latter development now forced him to compress his step-by-step programme of expansion and to contemplate a war with the sea-powers by the mid-1940s. Thus the Czech crisis of 1938 gave the impetus to his decision to permit the navy's famous 'Plan Z' – the construction of an enormous surface fleet for trans-Atlantic warfare – even though the greater part of Germany's rearmament measures still had to be devoted to the army and the *Luftwaffe* in order to implement his more immediate aims on land. No-one could doubt that, with a future fleet of 13 battleships, four aircraft-carriers, 33 cruisers and 250 U-boats, all of modern design, Germany would be in a position by 1944 to challenge Britain, and possibly the United States, for mastery of the high seas.

As it happened, however, war between Germany and the western Allies came five years too early even for Hitler's compressed programme, since the *Fuehrer* had never believed that Britain and France would go to war over Poland in 1939 and was amazed when they did so. As events were soon to show, Germany was strong enough on land and in the air to gain easy victories in the first nine months of the war – but the conflict had broken out far too soon for Raeder, just as it had done for Tirpitz in 1914. In addition, Germany laboured under the same crucial geographical disadvantage as it had done in the previous war: its overseas shipping, and the ability of its fleet to reach the Atlantic, were both at the mercy of Britain, which lay athwart the two exits from the North Sea. So long as this strategical inferiority remained, Germany's naval effort was bound to suffer; only by turning Britain's flank, or by achieving numerical superiority, could the disadvantage be overcome.

The second of the alternatives, numerical superiority, was quite out of the question in 1939. At the outbreak of war the German fleet consisted of the battlecruisers *Scharnhorst* and *Gneisenau*, fine, fast vessels, each with nine 11-inch guns, but probably still too weak to engage in a toe-to-toe fight with 15-inch gunned British capital ships; the 'pocket-battleships' *Deutschland, Lützow* and *Graf Spee*, brilliantly-designed long-range raiders but once again no match for a battleship; the heavy cruisers *Admiral Hipper* and *Blücher*, six light cruisers; 34 destroyers and torpedo-boats; and 57 submarines. Against this the British could deploy 15 battleships and battlecruisers, six aircraft-carriers, 59 cruisers, hundreds of escort vessels and 38 submarines, while the French navy consisted of seven battleships and battlecruisers, two aircraft-carriers, 19 cruisers and a large number of destroyers and submarines. Admittedly, many of the British vessels were old and slow, and the Allies had to station squadrons in various parts of the globe for the defence of their extra-European trade and other interests. Yet the odds were overwhelmingly tilted against the German navy, and Raeder recognised on the first day of the war that it would now be futile to pursue the 'Plan-Z' building programme. Apart from the two *Bismarck*-class battleships and the heavy cruiser *Prinz Eugen*, work on all other large vessels, including the aircraft-carrier *Graf Zeppelin*, was suspended.

Because the German surface navy was in no position to challenge its enemies for command of the sea, the early part of the war was – like the land campaign – a 'Phoney War', broken only by the occasional sortie of a German raider. The *Deutschland* cruised without much success in North Atlantic waters in the first two months of the war, and the *Scharnhorst* and *Gneisenau* overwhelmed the British auxiliary cruiser *Rawalpindi* in late November but failed to destroy the convoy it was escorting.

Only with the cruise of the pocket-battleship *Graf Spee*, commanded by Captain Hans Langsdorff, was Raeder's strategy of disrupting Allied naval communications and tying down far larger enemy forces put to real effect. Langsdorff was able to steam around the Indian and South Atlantic oceans unhampered for the first three months of the war, but in December 1939 he was brought to action by the British cruisers *Exeter, Ajax* and *Achilles* in the famous 'Battle of the River Plate'. Although the superior 11-inch shells of the *Graff Spee* damaged the *Exeter* so severely that the latter had to retire from the battle, the German vessel was also hit repeatedly, causing Langsdorff to enter the neutral port of Montevideo to secure repairs. Four days later, fearing that his ship would be overwhelmed by fresh British forces, he had her scuttled in the Plate estuary. By this action, he had not only relieved the Royal Navy of an immediate threat to Allied shipping routes but he had also obscured the important diversionary effects of the commerce-raiding strategy. For example, in October 1939 the British Admiralty had had to direct nine battleships and battlecruisers, five air-craft-carriers and many smaller warships to the protection of trade against the depre-dations of the *Graf Spee* and *Deutschland*. Yet, because Germany possessed so few powerful raiders, and because Hitler feared the loss of further 'big ships', this strategy was never fully exploited.

In the spring and early summer of 1940, however, the strategical handicap under which Germany was operating was removed by the lightning attacks upon Denmark, Norway, the Netherlands, Belgium and France. Within two months of the beginning of these thrusts to the north and to the west, the Germans had broken free from Britain's grip upon the North Sea and had achieved Admiral Wegener's old dream – access to the Atlantic. From the deep fiords of Norway, from the well-developed ports of Britanny, German warships could now steam directly out to the high seas. Moreover, in knocking France out of the war the *Wehrmacht* had effected an enor-mous shift in the naval balance of power; indeed, the British were so alarmed that the French navy would become, not neutral, but actually hostile, that they ruthlessly sought to eliminate it by their attacks upon it in Oran and Dakar in July 1940. To crown it all, Mussolini, with the jackal's sense of timing, now entered the war, thereby forcing the British Admiralty to divert more warships to the Mediterranean theatre.

Yet, despite the defection of France and the entry of Italy, the surface units of the German navy were still inferior to the forces which the Royal Navy retained in North Atlantic waters. Furthermore, the occupation of Norway had not been achieved with-out heavy losses to Raeder's minuscule fleet. The heavy cruiser *Blücher* had been sunk by Norwegian defence forces off Oslo; the light cruiser *Karlsruhe* was damaged by a British submarine and eventually had to be sunk by her own escorts; her sister-ship, the *Königsberg*, achieved distinction by being the first major warship to be sunk by enemy aircraft; ten destroyers were wiped out in the Narvik fiord battles; and many other warships including the *Scharnhorst, Gneisenau, Lützow* (formerly the *Deutschland*) and *Hipper* were damaged. By the summer of 1940, when Hitler and his advisors were discussing the prospects for an invasion of England, there was virtu-ally no German surface navy at all. But thanks to the failure of the *Luftwaffe* to achieve aerial superiority over the RAF, this embarrassing fact was of little relevance.

All this meant that, although Germany was now placed in a strategical position more favourable for naval warfare than at any other time in her history, she simply lacked the strength to fight her enemy in a full fleet battle. Thus the history of the surface war was to remain one of occasional sorties by major warships, which disturbed the Allied trade routes and caused alarm in London but nevertheless did not represent a persistent and determined challenge to the Royal Navy's predominance. Looking at the broader strategical pattern of the war, one might conclude that the most important role of the German fleet had been to pin down in home waters so many major warships of the Royal Navy which were desperately needed elsewhere, in the Mediterranean and especially in the Far East. This does not mean, however, that the various cruises of German vessels lacked interest and excitement, or that they could be regarded by the British as mere 'pin-pricks'. The story of the *Bismarck* in particular was to show how dangerous a sortie by Raeder's ships could be.

Along with the German strategy to interrupt Allied trade through the cruises of their large, conventional warships went plans to use their 'secret raiders' for the same purpose. These vessels were designed so as to look like normal merchantmen, but they concealed behind their innocent exterior a set of guns, torpedo-tubes and other offensive equipment. Their task was not to engage Allied warships – they were not powerful enough for that – but to attack individual merchantmen on the high seas, thereby spreading alarm and upsetting Allied commerce. Well before the outbreak of war the German Naval Staff had made preparations for these raiders – and the larger warships – to be refuelled and rearmed by supply ships at a series of secret oceanic meeting-places, and by early 1940 the first of the disguised vessels had broken out. Most of them headed for the South Atlantic and Indian oceans, where they could prey upon shipping with less risk of being engaged by hostile warships. Individual vessels, such as the *Atlantis* and the *Pinguin*, achieved great successes in capturing or sinking enemy merchantmen; the *Thor* actually sank one and disabled two other British auxiliary cruisers; and the *Kormoran* sank the Australian cruiser *Sydney* although its own crew was also forced to abandon ship. In fact, these raiders sank a total of 133 ships of 829,644 tons, almost twice the tonnage sunk by the conventional warship raiders.

Nevertheless, their strategical importance was not all that great, if only because they preyed upon individual ships and not convoys, and because they represented no threat to Britain's command of the sea. Moreover, they enjoyed their greatest spell of success in the period 1940-1941, when the Royal Navy was hardest pressed. With the growth of Allied air and sea power, and with fewer secret raiders sent out from Germany, this campaign began to peter out. Several of them managed to return home, but the rest were sought out and overwhelmed one by one: the *Atlantis* by the cruiser *Devonshire*, the *Python* by the cruiser *Dorsetshire*, the *Kormoran* by the cruiser *Sydney*, the *Pinguin* by the cruiser *Cornwall*, the *Komet* by British destroyers. With the improvement in aerial reconnaissance and ship identification procedures, and with the tightening of the British blockade in European waters, the end of this type of commerce-raiding was in sight. By late 1943 only the raider *Michel* was at sea, and she was sunk soon after by an American submarine in the Pacific.

The first of the voyages after the fall of France undertaken by a major warship was that of the *Admiral Scheer*, which broke through the Denmark Strait into the North Atlantic in November 1940 and overwhelmed five merchantmen of a British convoy and its escorting auxiliary cruiser *Jervis Bay*. The German warship then proceeded to undertake the longest and most successful cruise of all, returning home only in late March 1941. The superb cruising qualities of these diesel-engined pocket battleships were merely emphasised once again by the two less noteworthy sorties of the turbine-driven heavy cruiser *Hipper* at the same time.

Meanwhile, in January 1941 the *Scharnhorst* and *Gneisenau* had been sent into the Atlantic, the first German capital ships to do so in wartime. In terms of sinkings, their achievement was not great, if only because they had the habit of encountering convoys which were being escorted by 15-inch gunned British battleships. Nevertheless, they disrupted the crucial Atlantic convoy system, took enemy attention from the *Scheer* and *Hipper*, and heightened the feeling on both sides that the surface 'Battle of the Atlantic' was reaching its peak. For, waiting in the wings was the new battleship *Bismarck*, boasting a massive armoured protection, long range and high speed, a displacement of 53,000 tons, and eight 15-inch guns. If this mammoth warship, more formidable than any single British capital ship, was to be joined by the *Scharnhorst*, *Gneisenau*, *Scheer*, *Hipper* and the new heavy cruiser *Prinz Eugen*, the British would be hard pressed to maintain their command of the sea; or, at least, they could only do so by abandoning the Mediterranean to their foes, which would accomplish another of Hitler and Raeder's aims.

Yet such a combination could not be assembled. The *Scharnhorst* and *Gneisenau* needed repairs in Brest, the *Scheer* and *Hipper* were undergoing refits; and the pressure was upon the navy to take decisive action. On May 21, 1941, therefore, the *Bismarck* and *Prinz Eugen*, under the overall command of Admiral Guenther Luetjens, refuelled in a Bergen fiord before setting off into the Atlantic via the Denmark Strait. Despite the stormy and foggy weather, they were picked up by radar-equipped British cruisers, which alerted the Home Fleet and led its nearest heavy force, the old battle-cruiser *Hood* and brand-new battleship *Prince of Wales*, towards the German raiders. The encounter which followed is one of the most famous in the annals of naval history. Casting aside the advantage of his superior fire-power, the British Admiral Holland approached the German squadron obliquely, firing with only the front turrets and exposing his ships to the careful, steady salvoes of the well-trained German gunners. Within five minutes of the opening of the battle, the *Hood* blew up, the victim of enemy shells plunging vertically through her weakly-armoured deck. No more serious blow was made by German warships to the Royal Navy during the whole of World War II than this swift sinking of 'the mighty *Hood*'.

At this point Luetjens made what in retrospect was clearly his greatest mistake:

instead of returning to Norwegian waters, and perhaps even polishing off the damaged and retreating *Prince of Wales* on the way, he elected to carry on with his original plan to disrupt the Atlantic convoys. Had he retraced his route, he might have been able to take out as well the *Bismarck*'s new sister-ship, the *Tirpitz*, within a few months. Instead, he plunged ahead, despite the fact that he was still being shadowed by British cruisers, that other heavy units of the Royal Navy would be directed towards him, and that two shells from the *Prince of Wales* had damaged the *Bismarck*, affecting its speed and fuel reserves. On the next day, Luetjens released the *Prinz Eugen* for independent raiding and turned the *Bismarck* towards the French port of St Nazaire, the only one outside Germany in which he could obtain repairs. This decisions brought him even closer into the Royal Navy's net, as the shadowing by cruisers and attack by ancient Swordfish torpedo planes from the carrier *Victorious* indicated.

Then followed a series of mistakes on both sides which served only to increase the tension and to make the story of the *Bismarck* 'chase' such an epic. On the night of May 24/25, the German ship escaped the radar net of the shadowing British cruiser; yet, unaware of this, Luetjens sent a long radio message to Raeder on the following day, which gave away his position once again. Even so, faulty calculations by the British Admiralty sent all the Royal Navy's warships rushing northwards towards the Iceland-Faeroes passage just when they were only 100 miles from the *Bismarck*, which was then able to steam undisturbed towards St Nazaire! By the time this error had been discovered and contact had again been made with the German battleship by a Catalina flying-boat, many of the British vessels were short of fuel and nearly all were many miles behind her: only the Gibraltar-based 'Force Z' centred on the carrier *Ark Royal*, had the chance to intercept. Yet the carrier's Swordfish planes made a false torpedo attack, upon the cruiser *Sheffield*, which at least revealed the faultiness of the magnetic detectors and allowed these to be changed before the second aerial assault, this time upon the *Bismarck* itself. With the final torpedo of all, a fatal hit was made which jammed the battleships' rudders. Thereafter, the *Bismarck* could only circle hopelessly, fight off destroyer attacks and await the arrival of superior British forces. At 1040 on May 27, 1941, she was scuttled by her own crew after she had been blasted for hours by gun and torpedo fire.

The sinking of the *Hood* had given the German navy its greatest victory; that of the *Bismarck* its greatest defeat, and not just in terms of one fine ship and its crew. For the loss of Germany's great battleship also symbolised a turning-point for the entire surface navy, which henceforward ceased to contend North Atlantic waters. The decision was Hitler's alone, and greatly resented by Raeder; the latter, however, was never able to influence the Fuehrer very much. In part, this was due to Hitler's own character and background, which had little connection with the sea. Like the Kaiser before him, Hitler feared to lose his big ships: 'On land, I am a hero; at sea, I am a coward', he once told Raeder. The U-boats, he felt, could interrupt Allied commerce just as well as battleships, with no risk to Germany's prestige from the sinking of a major vessel. Furthermore, with Hitler concentrating more and more of his attention upon the campaigns in Russia, with the army and the *Luftwaffe* striving to increase their own influence at the expense of the navy's – the assignment of control of all land-based aircraft to Goering in early 1942, and the cutting of the navy's oil quotas are examples here – Raeder was less and less important in the formulation of what one may term German 'grand strategy'.

On the other hand, the future of capital ships had clearly been called into question by new technological developments in any case. The existence of long-range reconnaissance aircraft, which had reported the *Bismarck*'s departure from Bergen and spotted her in mid-Atlantic; of radar devices, which had allowed the British cruisers to shadow for so long; and of aircraft-carriers, which could reach out to cripple or even sink an opposing naval force, not 20, but 200 miles away: all this signalled the end of the heavy-gunned capital ship, and the battles in Pacific waters only confirmed it. Even when the German battleships were in harbour, they were in constant danger from Bomber Command's raids. For all these reasons, then, it was decided to pull back to German and Norwegian bases the *Scharnhorst*, *Gneisenau* and *Prinz Eugen*, which were resting at Brest. Yet the so-called 'Channel Dash' of February 11–13, 1942, which gave Hitler a great propaganda victory by revealing that German warships could burst through the Straits of Dover without the British being able to prevent them, was nevertheless a strategic retreat. The Royal Navy could now abandon its battleship escort of important Atlantic convoys and deploy those vessels elsewhere, for example.

After the spring of 1942, therefore, the German surface fleet was restricted to operations in one area only, apart from the Baltic – the waters off Norway, where more and more of the heavy units were stationed to deter an Allied invasion. However, the first sortie made led to the ignominious encounter of the *Lützow*, *Hipper* and six destroyers with a far weaker British force, which was escorting an Arctic convoy in late December 1942. The news of this failure, coming as it did in the midst of the battle for Stalingrad, confirmed all of Hitler's old prejudices against the surface navy – and this despite the fact that the *Fuehrer* himself had been chiefly responsible for the orders which so restricted the German warships. In January 1943 he ordered the scrapping of all major vessels and the transfer of their armaments to strengthen Norway's land defences, which in turn provoked Raeder to hand in his resignation. No doubt the latter's constant criticism of the 'Barbarossa' operation, which had after all been the chief reason why Hitler had reduced the navy's priority in armament procurement and production in 1940, played a role in the Grand Admiral's dismissal. His successor, Admiral Karl Doenitz, was – symbolically enough – head of the German U-boat arm: we will examine his role in that arena shortly. Doenitz was soon able to achieve a far better relationship with Hitler and to rescue the big ships from their fate; yet they never fully recovered their place in German naval strategy. Their main task, in Hitler's eyes, was to augment Norway's defences against invasion; their main achievement, so far as the Allies were concerned, was to pose a constant threat to the Arctic convoys and to tie up major fleet units in home waters. Hence the many attempts, by midget-submarines, by carrier aircraft and by heavy bombers, to put the chief danger, the battleship *Tirpitz*, out of action; hence, too, the attack upon St Nazaire, which possessed the only dry-dock in France which could house the ship.

In December 1943 the last great surface action of the war took place in European waters when the battlecruiser *Scharnhorst*, seeking to disrupt an Arctic convoy, was itself surprised by superior forces. Aircraft played no part in this battle but the improved British radar allowed the battleship *Duke of York* to pick out its weaker opponent in the darkness and to blast it to pieces. This left the *Tirpitz* as the only active unit, which stimulated the British into more and more attacks upon the lone battleship throughout 1944. Eventually, on November 12 of that year, Lancaster bombers managed to drop several 12,000-lb bombs through her decks, causing her to topple over and sink in Tromsö Fiord. Virtually all the other large warships were now serving as stationary gun-platforms or training-vessels by this time, and coming under increasing attack from the Allied strategic bombing campaign. The *Gneisenau* had already been paid off following bomb damage in 1942, and the *Lützow, Scheer* and *Hipper* suffered a similar fate in 1945. Only the *Prinz Eugen* of the larger German warships survived intact to the end. If the story of the German surface fleet in World War II is one of disappointments, unfulfilled hopes and eventual rejection by its own national leader, the same cannot be said for the U-boat arm. Here, too, there was a precedent in World War I, where the High Seas Fleet had been inactive for most of that conflict whereas the German submarines nearly brought Britain to her knees in 1917. Even during the *Weimar* period the navy had secretly kept up its interest in sub-marines, and under Hitler the service was openly built up. At first the U-boats were small, short-range vessels and even at the outbreak of war only 22 were ocean-going, but more important than this was the aggressive tradition of the submarine branch, the ease with which these boats could be constructed compared with, say, a battleship, Germany's technological strength and the leadership of Doenitz. The latter, who had two years of experience with submarines in World War I, carefully guarded his service in the early years of its growth and established an important place for it in Hitler's mind. This was partly because of the Fuehrer's distrust of the large surface ships and his wish for quick successes, which he believed the U-boats could give him; and partly because Doenitz attracted him more than the formal and distant Raeder. When Doenitz became Commander-in-Chief of the navy in January 1943, for example, he quickly saw the importance of being frequently with the *Fuehrer* if he was to ward off the machinations of Goering and to ensure that sea power was accorded a proper place in German strategy. And finally, of course, there was the undeniable fact that the U-boats *were* achieving many successes and often seemed close to bringing the com-merce of the Allies across the Atlantic to a halt.

With the outbreak of war, the U-boat arm received an unexpected boost, since it was clearly in a position to expand more rapidly than the surface navy, whose building programme was drastically curtailed. Immediately, the submarine construction rate was raised from 20 to 30 boats a month, most of them being the medium-size VII C type of 770 tons. Even so, it would be difficult for the U-boats to have a great influence upon the early stages of the war, not only because of the small number of vessels ready for sea and the inevitable problems of hasty expansion, but also because Doenitz and his crews had to learn from experience what developments had occurred in the Royal Navy's anti-submarine tactics in the inter-war years.

From the very beginning of the war, the British revealed that they were going to take the U-boat menace seriously, even though they were too confident about their ability to detect submarines. Although there were to be many exceptions, they hoped to gather Allied ships into convoys and to escort them across the sea. The problems facing the British Admiralty here were enormous, for they had to provide cover for literally thousands of merchantmen with quite inadequate escort forces; and, as the U-boats increased the range of their operations, this protection had to be extended from the coastal and Atlantic convoys to ones in more distant waters. Furthermore, although the U-boats were the usual – and by far the most lethal – enemy to Allied shipping, attacks from German aircraft or even surface vessels had also to be provided against.

Thus the overall characteristics of the struggle to control the sea-lanes, especially the broad Atlantic highway across which the food, raw materials and armaments for Britain's war effort had to be brought, were relatively simple. It was a long, hard, drawn-out battle, with success to be measured not in some lightning campaign but in the monthly tables of Allied merchant vessels and German submarines sunk in innumerable small engagements; it was a battle fought chiefly around the convoys, everything depending upon whether the U-boats could overwhelm the escorting forces and sink sufficient ships to bring Britain to her knees; and it was, therefore, a war not just of two opposing navies but of two opposing technologies. Could the Asdic, the underwater detecting device, pick up the U-boats before they surfaced, and would the newer radar sets be available to allow the Allies to 'see' at night?; would the panoply of escorts be able to fight off a whole 'wolf-pack' of U-boats?; would the Germans' use of long-range bombers to spot and attack convoys be successfully countered by Allied fighters and anti-submarine patrols by Coastal Command?; would the new 'schnorkel' device permit the U-boats to attack with impunity?; finally, would the Allies, and especially the Americans, be able to replace the merchant shipping as swiftly as it was being sunk?

The early stages of the U-boat war were naturally low-keyed, as both sides struggled to change their organisation from a peacetime to a wartime basis. The smaller submarines were employed in laying mines around British harbours, an activity which not only led to many sinkings but also to the diversion of British escort vessels to mine clearance duties. The larger U-boats, for their part, achieved fame not so much by the extent of their sinkings but by a few individual successes. In September 1939 the U-29 sank the aircraft-carrier *Courageous*, and in mid-October the U-47 under Lieutenant-Commander Guenther Prien daringly penetrated the defences of the main British naval base at Scapa Flow and sank the battleship *Royal Oak*, a deed which gave an immense boost to the submarine service. Yet the sinking of the liner *Athenia* in the previous month revealed that the old problems of keeping to the international conventions on submarine warfare and of maintaining good relations with neutral states were still to be overcome. However, Raeder was soon able to persuade a more cautious Hitler to agree to unrestricted U-boat warfare around Britain, a decision aided by the arming of British merchantmen and by the American neutrality proclamations. By 1940 the campaign was one with 'no holds barred' on either side.

By the end of 1939 114 Allied merchantmen totalling 420,000 tons had been sunk by U-boats, a figure which the British and French merchant marines could clearly take in their stride; after all, the British merchant marine totalled over 21 million tons. Moreover, in March 1940 a shortage of raw materials and Hitler's desire to increase land armaments led to the reduction in the submarine construction, the first of many alterations which would occur as a result of external forces. Finally, all available U-boats were diverted from commercial warfare to the Norwegian campaign, where they experienced many frustrating torpedo failures. Yet, when the smoke had cleared from Hitler's *Blitzkrieg* campaigns, the U-boat arm discovered to its joy that the strategical picture had been amazingly transformed: for the use of French and, to a lesser extent, Norwegian bases for the submarines and the long-range 'Condor' aircraft meant that the campaign against British shipping could now reach much further into the Atlantic – to 25° West, whereas the British at this time could usually only provide escorts up to about 15° West. In June 1940, the first month of this changed situation, Allied ship losses to U-boats were 58 vessels of 284,000 tons and in October they reached 63 vessels of 350,000 tons, figures which provoked the British Admiralty to divert many more warships from anti-invasion duties into commerce protection.

Despite these successes, the U-boats were still not achieving what had been hoped from them. This was partly due to their small numbers (in February 1941 the total of ocean-going U-boats was as low as 21); partly to their diversion into the Mediterranean, to operate against British warships there; and partly to the rough weather of the oncoming winter months. In addition, the British were now launching more and more corvettes, ubiquitous escort vessels which were smaller (and therefore far cheaper) than destroyers; and they were also aided by the increasingly 'un-neutral' acts of the United States in 1940 and 1941, especially the transfer to the Royal Navy of 50 old destroyers and the provision of anti-submarine protection to all shipping in an ever-extending western hemisphere 'security zone'. The Canadians, too, were providing increased naval aerial protection for the important convoys which sailed from Halifax.

Of all these factors, the first was recognised by Doenitz as being the key one. He had earlier estimated that he would require 300 U-boats to cut the British convoy system across the globe, yet at times he had an operational strength of only a tenth of that figure. His plans, to use the submarines in packs and to launch attacks from the surface of the sea, where the Asdic device could not function, were always restricted by the lack of adequate forces: only when Speer assumed responsibility for U-boat production did the situation change. In the twelve months December 1940–November 1941, the U-boats sank 1,726,000 tons of Allied merchant vessels in the North Atlantic alone, but it was noticeable that about two-thirds of these had *not* been in convoy and that German aircraft were causing even greater damage – at least until the British introduced the new escort carriers to deal with that particular menace. These figures suggested that Germany was failing to achieve its main aim, that of disrupting the Allied convoys, and that more attention would have to be paid to that problem.

The real climax of the U-boat campaign came in the years 1942 and 1943, for obvious reasons. By then, both sides had appreciated the nature and importance of the struggle and were throwing all their resources into it; by then, too, it was apparent that only the U-boat arm of the German navy could influence the outcome of the maritime war; and finally, everyone realised that, with the German attack upon Russia now held, the defeat of Hitler's *Reich* was inevitable provided that the massive flow of goods and men from the USA could proceed uninterrupted across the Atlantic. With the American entry into the war at the end of 1941, the German need to cut the sea-routes had greatly increased.

The early months of 1942 were memorable ones for the U-boats, not so much in the North Atlantic, but along the American seaboard, where there were few convoys or other forms of protection for merchant shipping: nearly 500,000 tons of shipping, much of it consisting of oil tankers, was sunk by the end of March, and the figures only began to drop when the US Navy instituted counter-measures in the early summer months. By that time, however, the German submarine production plan was taking effect and Doenitz was deploying almost 150 boats all over the globe, with many sinkings being achieved in the Caribbean and South Atlantic. And in the most vital area of all, the North Atlantic, he now had sufficient of the larger U-boats to form them into strong 'wolf-packs' and to send them against the convoys in the region known as the 'air gap' – those 600 or so miles in mid-ocean for which aerial support could be provided neither from Canada, Iceland nor the United Kingdom. In the last six months of 1942, sinkings by U-boats rose rapidly, so that by the end of the year submarines had sunk 1160 merchantmen of 6,266,000 tons, whilst sinkings by other services raised this to 1664 ships of 7,790,000 tons. Even the immense Allied shipbuilding efforts could not keep pace with these figures, and Britain's stocks of food, oil and other raw materials were very low indeed. More worrying still was the fact that many vessels were being lost in convoy and that more and more U-boats were being made ready for the fray. Not surprisingly, Allied leaders meeting at Casablanca in January 1943 considered that these developments were seriously affecting all their other plans. A drastic counter-offensive was imperative.

After a certain 'lull' in the stormy winter months, the U-boat offensive was resumed in full earnest, 108 merchant ships of 627,000 tons being sunk in March 1943 alone. Many of these casualties occurred when a 'pack' of 38 U-boats tore into two Allied convoys in the mid-Atlantic air gap. However, the battle then took a sudden and decisive turn: the counter-attack planned by the new British Commander-in-Chief, Western Approaches, Admiral Sir Max Horton, had begun. Support groups, each usually consisting of an escort carrier and fast frigates and destroyers, ranged around the convoys, picking off the U-boats as they moved in to attack; very-long-range Liberator bombers closed the air gap and prevented the wolf-packs from coordinating their assaults in advance; improved radar, depth-charges and other devices increased the Allies' chances of both spotting and sinking their enemy; and Coastal Command's patrols in the Bay of Biscay with aircraft equipped with improved radar and 'Leigh Light' searchlights took a very heavy toll of returning and out-going U-boats. Between March and November 1943 204 U-boats were sunk, with great depletions in the ranks of the skilled submariners, so that as early as May of that year Doenitz was forced to recall his fleets from the North Atlantic until new measures against the improved Allied detection and sinking devices could be devised.

The new measures Doenitz had in mind were the revolutionary 'schnorkel' – type submarines, which allowed the boats to charge their batteries at periscope depth; other types – such as the XXI and the 'Walter' hydrogen peroxide/diesel type – which were faster and much more efficient than the existing U-boats; new radar devices; and the acoustically-guided torpedo. However, all of these developments had suffered from the decision to concentrate upon the production of standard types, upon the increasing lack of raw materials in German industry and upon the prior claims of other services. Pulling back the U-boats from the North Atlantic could hardly be a short-term measure, therefore, yet whenever a fresh attempt was made to rupture the convoy system further losses were suffered: in the first three months of 1944 only three merchant ships were sunk in the North Atlantic, yet 36 U-boats did not return to base. And the signs were that convoy defences were stiffening up in other areas also. At this, Doenitz cancelled all further operations against convoys until the newer submarines were ready, and many U-boats were diverted instead to anti-invasion work.

By the time of the D-Day landings, many of the boats had been fitted with 'schnorkel' devices; but, although this reduced their losses, the Allied command of the sea and air was so firm that the sinkings by German submarines were kept to a minimum. With the seizure of Brittany, the U-boats were deprived of many of their best ports and had instead to be based upon Norway. Moreover, the strategic bombing campaign – and in particular the minelaying in the Baltic – was disrupting U-boat trials and training, thus throwing Doenitz's planned counter-offensive ever more behind schedule. All this explains why, although the submarine fleet reached its peak strength, of 463 boats, only in March of 1945, it was unable to influence the closing stages of the war. Just as the newer types, which were far harder to detect and which travelled much faster under water, were setting out to challenge the Allied command of the sea once again, Germany itself was being overrun by the armies of her enemies.

If Doenitz's 'last fling' had failed, there is no doubt that the U-boat threat had been the greatest ever posed to the western Allies. They had sunk 14,300,000 tons of merchant shipping, 6,840,000 tons of it in the North Atlantic, and they had also disposed of 175 Allied warships – in all cases, the majority being British. They themselves lost 785 of the 1162 U-boats built and commissioned during the war, and once again it had been British forces involved on the great majority of occasions. The entire campaign had been a lengthy, relentless fight to the death, for upon its outcome lay so much else. Churchill put it best when he wrote: 'Battles might be won or lost, territories might be gained or quitted, but dominating all our power to carry on the war, or even to keep ourselves alive, lay our mastery of the ocean routes . . . The only thing that ever really frightened me during the war was the U-boat peril.'

Although the campaigns of the German surface fleet and of the U-boats during World War II appear so different in character, the reasons for the eventual failure of both are the same. To a large extent, it was a case of 'too little, too late'. The war had begun at least five years too soon for Raeder's 'Plan Z' and as a consequence his few big ships were never able to do more than to disturb temporarily the British command of the sea. The U-boats proved to be a far more serious peril but even they were always too few in number to achieve a real dislocation of the convoy routes. As far as Hitler and the German High Command was concerned, World War II was primarily a land affair; and the navy did not even take second place, for Goering was always able to secure priority for the claims of the *Luftwaffe*. Raeder, and even Doenitz after him, always had to struggle to make Hitler realise what was at stake – and what success they obtained in this respect was all too often temporary.

Even if the German Navy had been accorded a higher priority in defence allocations, however, it is debatable whether the final result would have been much different. The plain fact was that, in taking on Britain, Russia and especially the United States, Germany had bitten off more than she could chew: even by 1942 its armaments expenditure was down to 25 percent of that of the Allies. The superiority of the Anglo-American surface fleets, and even more the radar devices, improved depth charges, long-range anti-submarine aircraft, escort carriers, and the flocks of corvettes, frigates and destroyers which contributed to the defeat of the U-boat were the outward sign of this ever-increasing industrial and technological dominance. When examined in this light, the final question might well be, not 'Why did the German navy fail?', but rather, 'How did it achieve so much against such heavy odds?'.

SCIENCE AND TECHNOLOGY

The Third *Reich* has too often been portrayed as a ruthlessly efficient centralised state, in which all effort during the years 1939-1945 was geared towards the requirements of total war. Reality, however, was somewhat different. The actual course of events proved not that totalitarian nations are necessarily best equipped to deal with the problems of modern war, but quite the opposite. One of the best examples lies in the scientific and research field, for here it was the Democracies who achieved the indispensable co-ordination between requirement and research, between political direction and science, and not Germany. In contrast, her programme was characterised by chaos rather than by determined organisation. Her lack of any central planning which could co-ordinate the various centres of technological effort was to ensure that the Germans, despite their many achievements, ultimately failed to produce any war-winning weapon.

During the war there were three main groups of research, each completely 0independent of the other. Firstly there were the *Wehrmacht* establishments, divided upon service lines; the *Heereswaffenamt* (Army Weapons Office); *Marinewaffenamt*, and the Air Ministry *Technischesamt* (Technical Office) – which were responsible for the development, testing and procuring of weapons, and the translating of the requirements of the armed forces into technical specifications for industry. The idea was sound, but only in the case of the Army did it work well. For the *Luftwaffe*, with its fatal preoccupation with its tactical rôle and the failures of its planners, the arrangement left much to be desired, and the relationship between Air Ministry and industry too often lacked harmony and understanding – as exemplified by the personal enmity between Field-Marshal Milch, the deputy head of the *Luftwaffe* and sometime head of the technical office, and Willi Messerschmidt, the renowned aircraft designer and manufacturer. Rivalries between the services impeded any proper exchange of information, as did the obsessive desire for secrecy.

Any idea of forming a central office of the *Wehrmacht* High Command to co-ordinate all research effort was opposed not only by the individual services, but also by industry, owing to the fear that direct interference would hamper its freedom of action and development – a view held by Hitler who reversed his decision to set up such an institution on the same day as it was made.

Secondly, there was the very important private sector of industrial research conducted by such companies as Heinkel, Messerschmidt, Krupp, I.G. Farben, Zeiss and Siemens. These firms undertook work for themselves in order to present to the *Wehrmacht* armaments which had already been tried and tested. The Navy, especially, relied on research undertaken by private enterprise. But again there was no interchange of information, this time owing to the restrictions and competition of private enterprise. Also the very existence of the large and expensively equipped private enterprise research centres had the effect of discouraging the *Wehrmacht* from setting up its own establishments.

Thirdly, there were the University research centres and the thirty or so institutes of the Kaiser Wilhelm *Gesellschaft*, which were all linked to the *Reich* Research Council, a body with a grand title but little power of direction. Once again there was no worthwhile liaison with the other groups. Finally, some mention must be made of the smaller research bodies such as those under the auspices of the Ministry of Posts (which did valuable work, among other areas, in the nuclear field and also succeeded in 'unscrambling' supposedly secret telephone conversations, including WSC-FDR conversations after 1942, according to General Gehlen).

The Germans had not learnt from their unhappy experience in World War I that centralisation and direction of research was vital. Just as there was no central agency, nor was there a single scientific adviser to Hitler; the *Reich* Minister for Science, Education and Public Affairs, Dr Bernard Rust, never even attempted this rôle. Rust was a weak leader of little mental agility, whose attitude towards scientists was indicated soon after his appointment when he declared the 'scientists are charlatans, devoid of original ideas'. According to a contemporary joke, a Rust was 'the standard unit of measurement for the minimum time elapsing between the passing of a decree and its cancellation'. In many ways he typifies the Third *Reich*'s curiously ambivalent attitude towards scientists and researchers. On the one hand relatively high salaries were paid to researchers, and the traditional German respect for practical attainment still proved valuable. But on the other there was the anti-intellectualism of the National Socialists which manifested itself in a general disregard for scientists and their views among the nation's leaders. When war broke out Rust made little effort to ensure that scientific and technical personnel were directed to jobs in which they could be of most use to the national effort, and later on some 10,000 had to be released from the *Wehrmacht* in order to use their skills according to their ability.

This unfortunate inefficiency in the organisation of research was not peculiar to Germany – the Allies suffered too. But this lamentable situation was further compounded by the special factors to which science in the Third *Reich* was alone subjected. Foremost among these was the policy carried out by the National Socialists towards the Jews and other 'antisocial' elements. Although the numbers of Jews expelled or imprisoned during the Thirties constituted a relatively small proportion of Germany's scientists (at most 12 percent), the repercussions were particularly grave. Rust once addressed himself to a leading mathematician and asked, 'Is it really true, Professor, that your Institute suffered much from the departure of the Jews and their friends?', to which the reply was, 'Suffered? No, it hasn't suffered, Herr Minister, it just doesn't exist any more.' Not only were the Jews themselves rejected, but so was their work. Certain methods of physics were branded 'Jewish physics', and the Germans espoused them as 'White Jews'; while in the search for the atomic bomb Germany laboured under the disadvantage of not only losing Einstein (he had left for the United States at the beginning of the persecution) but also losing his valuable theory of relativity – since it had been declared invalid by the National Socialist theorists.

As a corollary to this, there was a small but growing and influential number of German scientists who, realising the intellectual and moral enormity of Hitler's *Reich*, sought to retain their positions but at the same time undertake no work which would significantly help the war effort.

Two other factors must also be considered when evaluating the success or otherwise of Germany's research. First was the Third *Reich*'s isolation from the world of international research, especially during the war, and the consequent loss of all the advantages that the exchange of scientific knowledge between friendly nations brings. Niels Bohr, the eminent Danish physicist, was the most important of many scientists who refused to work with the Germans and who gave their very considerable services to the Allies (who also had the benefit of the many exiled German Jew researchers). The second factor was the strong but mistaken belief of Germany's rulers that the war would be a short one and that costly scientific research, especially if long-term, would be of little or no benefit and therefore would not justify any great effort spent on it. As a result the necessary determination for expensive and long-term research was not forthcoming until too late.

But despite such disadvantages the scientists and technicians of the Third *Reich* were able to undertake a range of research projects unrivalled by the Allies. Their expertise and imagination was particularly impressive. For example, the use of air as a weapon was something that particularly interested German scientists. A 'wind cannon' was developed which fired a 'bolt of air under great pressure from a weapon standing some 30 ft high with a sloping barrel 50 ft long. During tests it was shown that the cannon could smash a board one inch thick over a range of 200 yds. Intended as an anti-aircraft gun, the prototype proved unsuccessful. Also developed was a 'hurricane cannon' which attempted to produce artificial vortices in the air which would cause the destruction of enemy aircraft by throwing them out of co-ordination. Success of a kind was at last achieved, but the weapon was never used operationally. Thirdly, air pressure was used in the 'sound cannon' – two large parabolic reflectors of different size which were attached on to the front of a combustion tube fed with an oxy-methane mixture. This projected a beam of intensive sound energy which would, it was thought, kill a man within a minute under a distance of 60 yds and severely incapacitate him at up to 300 yds. Tests were instituted but the project did not develop.

Pressure was also the prime idea behind the development of the *Hochdruckpumpe*, the high pressure pump gun which was intended to bombard such distant and important targets as London, Antwerp and Luxemburg. It was no less than 150 ft long and fired an 8 ft projectile by means of successively firing a number of charges which were contained in paired lateral projections along the tube. By such means the missile was ejected at a speed of 4800 ft per second – sufficient to carry it 85 miles. However, allied air activity and the faults innate in the construction of the gun (usually one of the component sections would explode during firing) ensured that this weapon was of no practical use to the German war effort.

Much intensive work was carried out upon guns and ballistics. An arrow projectile – a shell stabilised not as was usual by its spin but by special lateral fins – was a significant development used against the Russians (it was considered too secret to be used against the western Allies). Hollow explosive charges, shell clusters and the use of concrete as a shell housing were other developments.

Contrary to popular belief, the Germans were as far advanced in radar technology at the beginning of the war as the British. In 1938 they had invented the 'Freya' radar set, a mobile piece of equipment operating on the decimetre wave which could determine distance but not height. Far better was the 'Wuerzburg' radar, which came into production at the beginning of the war. It used an ultra-short wave length of 53 cm and could achieve excellent results, reading the location, course and altitude of aircraft with very great accuracy up to a distance of 25 miles. With its range of up to 90 miles the 'Freya' served as the early warning radar, while the 'Wuerzburg' gave the precision necessary for anti-aircraft guns and interceptors. In an Allied field the Germans did well with the 'X apparatus', a radio-direction beam invention which brought bombers directly over their targets at night, and which signalled the moment to release bombs. It was not effectively jammed until 1941. The 'Lichtenstein' was an airborne radar for use with night fighters, and was used operationally for the first time on August 9, 1941. However, it could have been in use as early as the spring of 1940, when it was first required, had it not been rejected earlier by the *Luftwaffe* authorities. As it was, it was not until mid-1942 that the set's difficulties were finally overcome.

Up to 1942, then, the electronic warfare of the German Air Force was as advanced as the British, it's greatest failing lying not with the quality of the equipment but with the system of use (co-ordination between radar, central control, and aircraft was not developed until late 1942). But by this time it was apparent that the Germans were lagging behind considerably. Goering gave the reason: 'I have long been aware of the fact that there is nothing the British do not have. Whatever equipment we have, the enemy can jam it without so much as a by your leave . . . Gentlemen, It's not man-power you have too little of, it's brain power in your brain boxes to make the in-ventions we need.' This, however, was only part of the story, for lack of official interest and direction contributed in the main to the unfortunate state of affairs which mani-fested itself so dramatically in 1943. At that time, during the Battle of Hamburg, the RAF dropped thousands upon thousands of strips of silver paper which resulted in paralysing the radar system. Known as 'Window', the Germans had been aware of its effect since mid-1942, but had failed to seek a counter-measure due to official lethargy.

This short-sightedness had also been responsible for the rejection in 1938 of Dr Esau's research in the field of radar. He had then found the 4.4mm wave, but this was only later developed into the 'Heidelberg' radar set towards the end of 1944 – far too late. This was a considerable improvement upon the 'Giant Wuerzburg' then in service (a 40 mile range), and reached as far as 240 miles. In other words, the *Luftwaffe* could have had a radar which was able to detect the take-off of Allied bombers in Norfolk early in the war. The realisation by the High Command that the war in the air over Germany would be won by such inventions came too late, although the six new radar systems developed between July and December 1943 is evidence of the drive that was initiated. But even then, German research was severely behind that of the Allies, due in no small way to the fact that before the war amateur radio enthusi-asts had been banned, the authorities thereby cutting off thousands of small inven-tors. In the end Germans were forced to copy captured Allied equipment – for example the so-called '*Rotterdamgeraet*' for use in detecting submarines.

In the field of marine development, research was almost automatically confined to the submarine, since this was the only area where Germany, after 1940, could hope to defeat Great Britain. The U-boats of 1939 were in many respects similar to those that had been in operation in 1918, for although their range had been increased, their underwater speed and limited capacity to move below the surface were much the same (only some six knots for a few hours at a time). Owing to a lack of oxygen underwater, a U-boat had to run its engines by means of electric power and therefore had contin-ually to surface to recharge its batteries (during which time it would be powered by its diesel engines). This made the U-boat a diving boat rather than an underwater ves-sel and consequently this not only limited its operations but also ensured that it was extremely vulnerable to air detection which had reached dangerous proportions by 1942. German research was to solve this problem with supreme success, but too late.

The only improvement which saw operational service was the schnorkel. It was an old concept, being essentially an air pipe which could be extended like a periscope above the surface of the sea in order to supply the U-boat and its engines with the necessary oxygen. By the end of 1943 all German submarines had been fitted with the schnorkel. However, while it considerably reduced the danger from aircraft, it did not eliminate it, and, just as important, it did nothing to increase the U-boats' underwater speed.

Of far greater importance was the development of an entirely new, indeed revolutionary, engine designed by Professor Walter. The first experiments took place in 1940. A closed circuit turbine was substituted for the diesel-electric combination, and the oxygen source was switched from the surface air to the decomposition, induced by a catalyst, of hydrogen peroxide in the fuel Ingolin. Thus Walter's invention, coupled with a redesigned hull, enabled the new Type XVII U-boats to operate at high speeds totally submerged for long periods. In July 1943 the approval for construction of the Type XVII was given, and the first four were supplied at the end of 1944. During trials they reached an underwater speed of 21 knots. An improved, larger version was immediately embarked upon but never completed. In July 1943 the approval for the construction of the Type XXI was also given. This was regarded as a stop-gap until the Walter submarine could be brought into service; it had a conventional engine with increased battery capacity and capable of an underwater speed of 17.5 knots. 120 were completed but, like the Type XVII, they were not to see action. One interesting feature in the production of these U-boats was the brilliant way in which the German technologists overcame all the manufacturing difficulties posed by congested and vulnerable shipyards. The various parts of the submarines were built in inland factories, transported to the coast and there assembled quickly. Thus, whereas the old types of U-boats had taken eleven and a half months in drydock to build, prefabrication meant that the new types took only two months. This timesaving was to have a notable effect in the future.

But, despite the submarine revolution which had taken place in the Third *Reich*, the new developments came too late to exert any influence upon the war. As Speer recalls: 'At the time, Doenitz and I often asked ourselves why we had not begun building the new type of U-boat earlier. For no technical innovations were employed; the engineering principles had been known for years. The new boats, so the experts assured us, would have revolutionised submarine warfare.' So they would have. Had the Third *Reich*'s leaders placed more emphasis upon marine warfare earlier, research might well have meant the introduction in sufficient numbers of these new U-boats which, in turn, would have ensured for Germany the all-vital supremacy of the Atlantic.

Before Hitler's acquisition of power Germany had the great advantage of having the cradle of nuclear science within its borders – at the University of Goettingen. It took the National Socialists only a few weeks in the Spring of 1933 to destroy this ancient foundation as a centre of research. The University was never to recover from the expulsion or forced resignation, mentioned earlier, of numbers of 'politically -

unreliable' and Jewish professors and scholars. Nor was German nuclear physics.

The German nuclear research and the search for the ultimate war winner – the atomic bomb reveals the folly of allowing scientists to determine their own aims and progress during wartime. It is clear that the ultimate Allied supremacy in this field was no foregone conclusion. Indeed it was a German, Dr Otto Hahn, who in 1938 found that if uranium atoms were bombarded with neutrons, atomic energy would result. But with the exception of one man, Professor von Ardenne, the men involved in research did not envisage the possibility of an atomic bomb during the war and therefore failed to fire their political masters with the necessary enthusiasm for its development.

Von Ardenne, who worked in the *Reichspost* laboratory, had his ideas dismissed as those of a dilettante by men such as von Weizsacker, a leading physicist. Another, Werner Heisenberg, the head of the Kaiser Wilhelm Institute atomic research laboratory, while he envisaged that an atomic bomb would be 'about as big as a pineapple', nevertheless succeeded in impressing upon Speer and others the virtual impossibility of producing such a weapon in Germany. Heisenberg, who was never a Nazi, has claimed that he exaggerated the problems in order to discourage the authorities from trying to acquire the bomb. Speer was put off by the modest demands for money and material made by Heisenberg which had led him to believe that the atom bomb development would have no significance in the war effort. Others such as Esau, the first Plenipotentiary to Goering for Nuclear Physics and titular head of the atomic energy project, even went so far as to attempt to prevent any idea of the possibility of manufacturing such a bomb from leaking out, fearful that they might be ordered to make one and suffer unpleasant consequences in the event of failure. Also, as an Allied report suggested in 1945: 'German science is not without guile, and took advantage of the lack of understanding of science by those in authority to engage in interesting scientific research, under the guise of war work, that could not possibly help the war effort'. The characters of the scientists, too, could serve against purposeful development of the A-bomb; Esau, for example, had little drive, and Gerlach, his successor, even less, both being stolid workers with little vision.

Another disadvantage for the development of the German A-bomb was the dominance of theory over practice which caused a divorce between the physicists and the engineering industry and denied the Germans any significant material achievements in the nuclear field. Heisenberg and his men preferred to build up a solid theoretical basis rather than progress through trial and error, and therefore there was no immediate urgency to get the uranium pile 'critical' – an indispensable step in the progress towards a bomb.

German nuclear research, then, was left almost entirely in the hands of the scientists. Owing to the contributions of men such as Einstein, Hitler referred to nuclear physics as 'Jewish physics', and this attitude coloured the whole approach towards development. While the Allies put a prodigious effort into the project, the German leadership, believing the war would be over before any results were produced, failed to give it anything like the resources it needed. There was no effective central agency, no purposeful direction and no proper organisation. While the Germans were ahead in some respects before 1942, the complete failure of their scientists to gain recognition and support from the government meant that little further progress was achieved. Perhaps Germany had never had the necessary economic resources to produce such a revolutionary weapon, and certainly the purely practical mistake which caused the German physicists to use heavy water instead of graphite as a 'breaking substance' in the reactor, ensured that failure would be definite.

Of all the end-products of the Third *Reich*'s research, it is the rockets which not only have fired the imagination of all who have read about them, but also, and far more important, have served as the basis of a vast post-war development – a development which has taken man to the moon. In the field of rocketry, wartime Germany was supreme. But there was no guarantee that this, too, would not suffer the usual debilities inherent in the *Reich*'s research – the initial paucity of interest and resources, the lack of central direction and the abundant variety of projects which resulted in the dissipation of effort.

In the early 1930s rocket research had been undertaken by such pioneers as Oberth and Winkler, and had interested the Army to a point where they placed Captain (later Major-General) Dr Walter Dornberger in charge of secret weapons' development. He was assisted by Dr Werner von Braun, the man who more than any other was responsible for Germany's lead in this field (he also supervised the post war US rocket programme). In 1933 the A1 was developed (the forerunner of the V2), followed by the A2 in 1934, which flew to a height of 6500 ft and the A3 in 1937 (a large rocket standing 21 ft tall, weighing 16,500 pounds and powered by a liquid fuel LOX/ethanol motor).

However Dornberger was given only limited resources for this highly experimental and expensive work. By 1939 his staff consisted of only some 300 men, and the High Command proved reluctant to allocate scarce raw materials to a project which might well not be operational until after the war was over. The *Luftwaffe*, too, was suspicious of the Army's rocketry and gave no help. After the Battle of Britain the programme was given a higher priority – one leading contemporary expert reckoned that in the early war years perhaps one third of all German scientists worked upon the rocket development in some way (fuel, navigation, tele-communications etc) – but this still was not enough. It was only after the successful firing of the A4 rocket on October 3, 1942, that the situation changed – though somewhat late. With a rocket reaching a range of nearly 120 miles and an altitude of some 50 miles, the attitude of Germany's leadership altered considerably. Now, with a war-winning weapon within his grasp, Hitler gave the project the backing it should have had from the start. Money and equipment was injected into the programme, and the rocket centre at Peenemuende was enlarged (its ultimate cost was £50 million), eventually housing over 2000 scientists. A committee was even instituted to co-ordinate development on the rocket (in fact it became something of a hindrance, headed as it was by an expert not in rocketry but in locomotives!). But even with all this it took a further nine months from the first successful firing for the project to be given top priority in the German armaments programme. Ominously the A4 was designated *Vergeltungswaffe* 2 – V2 – (Vengeance Weapon).

The V2 project survived the RAF attacks on Peenemuende in August 1943 and while further development work was carried out in Upper Austria, an underground production line was set up in the Harz mountains. This meant that the programme was set back by a number of months and time was of the essence for Hitler's Germany. The V2 which was ready for operational firing by mid-1944 was a considerable improvement on the first A4. It was capable of a range of over 200 miles carrying a load of 1650 pounds of high explosive. Standing 46 ft tall it weighed over 12½ tons at launch (nine tons of which was fuel). Manufacturing time was cut down from 19,000 man hours in 1943 to only 4000 in 1945 (each V2 contained over 30,000 parts).

The other major German rocket weapon was the Fi103 (designated V1), the *Luftwaffe*'s flying bomb. Launched by catapult, the V1 was powered by a petrol-fuel pulse-jet motor which was extremely simple in design and manufacture. The V1 was in essence a small pilotless aircraft 27 ft long weighing 2 tons and carrying 1870 lbs of high explosive in its nose. After launch it reached a height of between 1000 and 7000 ft and proceeded at a cruising speed of 400 mph over a maximum range of 180 miles (later extended to 250 miles). Distance and direction were predetermined by means of a propeller mechanism which, once it had completed a specific number of revolutions, would cut the engine thus causing the V1 to dive steeply towards its target.

In many ways the V1 and V2 were rivals. Both performed much the same function in considerably different ways. The V1 was both simple and cheap to make, taking only about 280 man hours to manufacture. It cost between 1500 and 10,000 marks as against the 75,000 of the V2 and took but a part of the 200,000 skilled workers and the 1000 tons of aluminium a month of the larger rocket. Their warheads were both around a ton in weight. The V1 however had several disadvantages. Its launching pads were easily destroyed by enemy air action, whereas the V2 was mobile; its relatively slow speed and height allowed it to be shot down or even trapped by barrage balloons, whereas the V2 was supersonic and neither seen nor heard until its impact (the V1, however, did tie down a significant proportion of Britain's air defences); Lastly, the V1 was not only inaccurate, but also it could not be depended upon to detonate – neither, as it turned out, could the V2.

There was inevitably much rivalry between the Army and the *Luftwaffe*, each service championing its own weapon to the exclusion of the other – the Army especially was reluctant to abandon or even to economise its seven-year old rocket programme. Faced with a difficult choice between the two, the High Command decided upon a middle course by continuing with both weapons, concentrating on neither.

The first Fi103 flight took place in December 1942, and in the middle of 1943 the weapon was placed in full production. Owing to an inability to fulfil the schedule, combined with Allied bombing of the launching areas, the *Luftwaffe* opened its V1 offensive on June 13, 1944, six months later than planned. A total of 105,000 were directed at England, most of them at London, but only one fifth of them ever reached their targets; 2419 fell on London and 30 on Portsmouth, while 3957 were shot down. About 1600 of these V1s were launched from modified He111 bombers. The casualties caused were 6184 dead and 17,981 were injured. Aimed against Antwerp the V1 proved itself to be even less reliable – of the 5000 fired only 211 ever exploded upon the city.

The V2 offensive opened on September 6, 1944; two were fired at Paris, but both failed in flight. On September 8 the attack on England began, but the Army's much-vaunted secret weapon proved to be no better than the *Luftwaffe*'s. Of the 4000 odd V2s fired, less than 1500 ever reached the country, causing 2500 deaths. Another 2050 came down over Brussels, Antwerp and Liége. The rocket's weaknesses soon became only too apparent. Its design still had many faults – faults which could on occasions cause it to explode on the launch pad or in descent, or which might send it violently off course. Its payload, also, was far too small, while its speed on impact (over 3500 mph) caused it to dig itself into the ground before exploding; and it thus expended most of its force upon making a deep hole.

The rocket offensive was not a serious threat to the British war effort as a whole, owing to the weaknesses of the weapons and the late timing of its advent. However the nature of the V campaign was particularly unpleasant for the inhabitants of the South of England and did cause the government to draw up plans for the evacuation of London (something not done even during the Blitz). This is an indication of the potential that lay in Hitler's rockets.

Other rocket developments abounded, illustrating both German ingenuity and the diffusion of effort which marked the *Reich*'s research. This was in no small measure due to the keen conflict of interest between the Army and the *Luftwaffe*, and it resulted not only in a lack of co-operation in research but also in a series of policies which took no account of Germany's real and pressing military needs. By 1943 it had become painfully apparent that what the *Reich* needed was not terror weapons but an effective anti-aircraft system – which could be provided by rockets (a new 'secret' weapon to smash the hard-won Allied air supremacy). But the Army concentrated on the former to the detriment of the latter – the *Luftwaffe*'s requirement. Thus even as late as January 1945 there were 2210 scientists and engineers working on the never completed A4-B and A9/A10, (considerably heavier versions of the V2), while only 335 were members of the C2 'Waterfall' and 'Typhoon' anti-aircraft programmes. Advocating the development of 'Waterfall' in mid-1943 a leading German authority wrote: '. . . every expert, every worker, and every man-hour devoted to the speeding of this programme will yield results proportionately far more effective for winning the war than the same resources invested in any other programme. Delaying such a programme can mean the difference between victory and defeat'. After the war Speer wrote: 'To this day I think that this rocket ('Waterfall'), in conjunction with jet fighters, would have beaten back the Western Allies' air offensive . . . Instead gigantic effort and expense went into developing and manufacturing long-range rockets which proved to be, when they were at last ready for use . . . an almost total failure. Our most expensive project was also our most foolish one.'

The 'terror weapons' programme concentrated primarily upon two extensions of the A4. One was the A4-B, a winged version of the A4 which was designed to glide to its target after the engine had cut out, thus significantly increasing its range. This had reached test-flight stage by January 1945. The other was the impressive A9/A10 which had resulted from the A4-B tests. It was designed to enable Germany to bombard the USA. (This was a requirement which had previously led to the 'Laffarenz Project' – a special container with three V2's which would be towed across the Atlantic by a Type XXI U-boat to within range of the American seaboard. There the containers would be brought into an upright position, the rockets fuelled from the submarine and fired.)

Work was being concentrated upon this rocket towards the end of 1944, but the war ended before it reached prototype stage. It was to have a range of some 3000 miles, and consisted of two stages – the A10 booster rocket and the A9 second stage (this being a streamlined, winged version of the A4) and as such it would have been almost twice the size of the V2. The A10 booster would take the rocket 110 miles up into the stratosphere where it would separate and descend to the earth by means of special parachutes, and there be recovered and used again. The A9 would continue up to an altitude of some 217 miles, and then descend to 28 miles. There the air would be dense enough for the wing controls to operate, and the rocket would glide down on to its target - hopefully somewhere in the USA.

The *Rheinbote* (Rhine Messenger), manufactured by Rheinmetall, was the only other ground-to-ground rocket to be used operationally. It was a four-stage missile, the first two of which separated six miles after launch, the others remaining with the warhead. Powered by solid fuel, it had a range of 136 miles. It was an accurate rocket whose chief weakness lay in its extremely light warhead – only 88 pounds. At least 220 were successfully fired at Antwerp but little damage resulted.

There were several ground-to-air rockets but none were used operationally. The *Feuerlilie* F25 was first flown in 1943 but cancelled the following year. It was six feet tall and flew at subsonic speeds for three miles. Its successor, the F55, was 16 ft tall, flew faster than the speed of sound, and had a range of roughly six miles. It consisted of two stages, one powered by solid – and the other by liquid fuel. First tested in mid-1944, the war came to an end before much more could be accomplished. The '*Hecht*' – an 8 ft tall 'flying bomb' type of anti-aircraft missile which was launched from a ramp – was only developed to the prototype stage.

The '*Enzian*' was a highly powerful missile based on the Me163 Komet aircraft – an unmanned version made of plastic wood and powered by 4 booster rockets. Its warhead was 660 pounds of high explosive fired by a proximity fuse. Sixty were completed but none saw service. Likewise the Hs117 '*Schmetterling*' was based upon another operational weapon – the Hs293 glider bomb. The design was unwisely rejected in 1941 and resurrected in 1943 – too late to iron out all its teething troubles before the war ended. It had a range of 33,000 ft, a warhead of 50 pounds and was guided to its target by means of a radio transmitter which fed impulses to its servo-controlled fins. Had this weapon been used it would have proved itself effective against the high-flying Allied bomber formations.

The '*Rheintochter*' (Rhine daughter) R1 was a missile designed to be used with two radars (known as the Rheinland system), one of which traced the aircraft while the other guided the rocket to the target. The R1 was in two stages, the booster separating over a mile up and the main rocket continuing to 20,000 ft. It was 20 ft tall and carried a 250 pound warhead. Eighty were fired and the rocket had all the appearance of becoming a successful and much needed weapon. But promising though the project was it had not reached completion by May 1945. There were also an R2 and an R3.

Lastly the C2 '*Wasserfall*' (Waterfall) must be considered. Its design was based upon the A4, but its physical appearance was shorter and slimmer with four stub wings above its middle. It stood 26 ft tall, possessed an effective range of 17 miles and carried a warhead of 675 pounds. It was highly sophisticated and the final version was intended to have an infra-red homing device and a self-contained guidance system. Of the 45 test firings only 12 were successful and much work remained to be done at the close of the war. Developed from the 'Wasserfall' was the '*Taifun*' (Typhoon) barrage rocket. It was only six ft tall and, having no guidance system, was designed merely to keep the Allied bombers at bay. It, too, only reached the development stage.

There were also several rockets designed to be fired from aircraft. The BV143 and BV246 were anti-ship missiles which were intended to be dropped from aircraft to within 10 ft of the surface of the sea and then fly, wavehopping to their targets, guided by a number of differing homing devices. The 143 was 20 ft long and had a range of 10 miles, while the 246 was only 11 ft long with a slightly greater range. However good the idea might have been on paper it did not work out well in practice, and the project was scrapped. The SD1400 'Fritz X' was a similar weapon. There were several versions, all radio-controlled, 15 ft long, and carrying a 3300 pound warhead. The aimer situated in the aircraft could direct the 'Fritz' by means of a joy-stick control and a bright tracking flare situated in the missile's tail. It was not a particularly efficient weapon but it did achieve the famous sinking of the battleship *Roma*. Its successor was the X4, a 6⅔ ft long missile guided by pulses sent along a wire unspooled from the wing tip (there was a similar weapon intended for land use, the X7). Also a number of glide bombs were designed by Henschel. The Hs293, the world's first guided missile, was in many ways a miniature aircraft, 12 ft long, carrying a 1100 pound warhead. It was radio controlled and relied on its rocket motor and its gliding capabilities to reach the target. It was used mainly against lightly-armed ships and merchantmen, and in this rôle was relatively successful. The Hs294 was designed to shed its wings at the end of its journey and continue as an acoustic-homing torpedo to its target. Other Henschel projects were begun but never completed.

Germany's researchers also utilised rocket propulsion in their aircraft designs. Most notable was the Messerschmidt 163 'Komet', which was an audacious concept and incorporated some remarkable design innovations. It was a short, stubby, delta-shaped plane powered by a liquid-fuelled rocket motor at its rear. Upon take-off its undercarriage dropped off to allow the proper aerodynamic forces to come into play around its structure and landing was done on skids. The Me163 flew well, reached a top speed of 593 mph, and could climb at over 10,000 ft per minute. The first test flight took place in May 1941 and the first production Me163 entered the *Luftwaffe* three years later. But despite its promise, the aircraft did not do well in combat. This was owing to a combination of its high speed and poor armament.By the end only 279 'Komets' had been produced, manufacture ending in February 1945.

An improved design resulted in the Me263. Although it never reached test flight stage it was a plane of evident good qualities. Its projected maximum speed was 620 mph, and its rate of climb was 49,000 ft in only three minutes.

Lastly, there also existed the Bachem 8-349 A1 '*Natter*' (Adder), a novel answer to the problem posed by the Allied bombers. It was a rocket powered aeroplane of the simplest and cheapest design which was launched vertically and which was heavily armed with rockets. It was to be sent right into the Allied bomber formations at a maximum speed of some 500 mph and, after having shot down as many aircraft as possible, the pilot would bale out. He and the *Natter* would then be recovered. Work began in late 1944, but none were ever used against the Allies, and the only manned test flight ended in complete failure.

Just as in rocketry, Germany led the world in jet aircraft research. But the saga of the development of the Reich's jets has been considered by historians as one of the great 'might-have-beens' of the war, as a lost opportunity which sealed the fate of the *Luftwaffe* and gave to the Allies undisputed mastery of the skies over Germany. For many it is the 'cause célèbre' of faulty planning, official apathy and downright ignorance adversely affecting promising research. But was this so?

Certainly at the beginning, Germany's leaders failed to grasp the immense signif-icance of the jet engine. It was indeed a German, Professor Ernst Heinkel, who was the first man to take steps to overcome the limitations of the conventional driven air-craft. On August 27, 1939 his He178, the world's first jet aircraft, took to the air and eight weeks later, in front of senior *Luftwaffe* personnel, it reached a speed of 510 mph. But this failed to impress the officials, included amongst whom was General

Udet, the influential chief of aircraft procurement and supply. He remained sceptical of the military value of this revolutionary development till his suicide in November 1941. Thus no official support was given to jet research in these vital early years, and Heinkel was left to continue research on his own. To his credit he did so undaunted, and in April 1941 his He280 twin engine jet prototype flew for the first time.

By the spring of 1942, Heinkel believed that the He280, which had a maximum speed of 497 mph, was ready for series production, but the *Luftwaffe* High Command did not agree. Further tests continued and, fitted with two Jumo 004's, the He280 reached 509 mph. But in March 1943 Heinkel was ordered to discontinue work on the plane, the *Luftwaffe* having decided to concentrate on the Me262. It has been argued that this was a lost opportunity for an early introduction of a jet aircraft into service. However in many ways, especially in range, the He280 was inferior to the Me262, and production delay would have ensued from its turbo-jets.

At his own expense and initiative, Professor Willy Messerschmidt began research into his Me262 at the end of 1938, and it was not until March 1940 that the *Luftwaffe* gave him a development contract for three prototypes. On June 18, 1942, the plane made its first jet powered flight, and successful tests continued until well into the next year. But still the *Luftwaffe* High Command failed to grasp the full implications of the weapon. Even Udet's successor, Erhard Milch displayed little enthusiasm at first, and even as late as October 1942 the *Luftwaffe* considered preparations for series production of the plane to be premature.

However in mid-1943 the situation changed. Firstly the General of the Fighter Arm, Adolf Galland, flew the Me262 and pronounced it a 'tremendous stroke of fortune for us', then Hermann Göring saw, and was impressed by the jet and finally, in June, it was decided to release the plane for series production 'because of its superior speed as well as its many other qualities'. Even then, the *Luftwaffe* envisaged the production of only 60 a month from May 1944. This, however, was optimistic, and a certain amount of continued official apathy and scepticism resulted in the following response from the head of the Fighter Staff, Otto Saur: '. . . we deserve to be soundly reproached . . . We simply assumed that we would have a goodly number of machines available for rigorous testing by January or February; we assumed that we would produce at least 30-40 during March, 60 per month by May, and soon thereafter 75-80 per month. It is now June and we do not have one single machine [in operational service]. We have only ourselves to blame – we were incapable of finding the necessary resources, incapable of concentrating our efforts, and incapable of approaching the problem with the energy and determination warranted by its vital importance.'

All this is true. There was indeed bad planning (as exemplified by Hitler's misguided order that the Me262 be developed as a jet bomber and not as a jet fighter) and inexcusable apathy, but these factors did not in fact delay the jet's introduction. Even if Hitler himself had been at the production line in order to speed the project along, the Me262 would not have been ready any sooner than it was. For of all the components which went to make up the plane, none were more important than the jet engines. Work on these (the Junkers 044 turbine) had begun in late 1939 and was continued until June 1944 when they were put into series production. Tests and modifications to such a revolutionary engine must of necessity take a long time, and the Jumo 004 was no exception. Even by mid 1944 it was still considered insufficiently developed, and certainly it was not until then that the engine was advanced enough to go on to the production line. Because of this, it is the consensus of opinion of all those who worked on the project that the Me262 was introduced into service as soon as was practicable. Therefore any amount of enthusiasm on the part of Germany's leaders could not have materially affected the outcome. The Me262 was simply too late.

However, German research had managed to produce the first jet aircraft to see combat, and thus claims a unique position in aviation history. The Me262 itself was a good aircraft. Its maximum speed was 540 mph which far exceeded that of contemporary conventional aircraft, as did its weight of fire. It was a tragedy for the *Luftwaffe* that only 200 Me262s (out of 2000 produced) ever fired their guns in anger.

Another remarkable development was the Heinkel 162, the Peoples' Fighter (*Volksjaeger*), which was conceived, designed and flown within three months – surely the shortest time ever for any plane. The order for a simple and cheaply produced yet effective jet fighter was given to Heinkel in September 1944; in December the first prototype was flown successfully and in February 1945 the He162 was in series production. A monthly output of 2000 machines was aimed at. There were to be no half-measures here.

The configuration of the He162 was remarkably similar to that of the V1 flying bomb. Its back-mounted turbo-jet, while it made for ease of production, caused the plane to be somewhat unstable around its longitudinal axis and therefore in need of careful handling by the pilot. Its maximum speed was 562 mph.

Whatever potential the He162 might have had as a 'miracle plane' flown by legions of semi-trained Hitler Youth pilots (as such it would have probably been suicidal) which would sweep the Allies from the skies of Germany (Goering's original idea), it was too late to see action. Only 120 had been accepted by the *Luftwaffe* by the end of the war.

The only other jet propelled plane to enter into service was the Arado 234 'Blitz', the first operational jet bomber. Work on the planes began in late 1940, the first prototype was flown in June 1943, and the first Ar234 entered into service a little over a year later. It proved itself to be a fairly handy aircraft, but only 210 were ever completed. Powered by two Jumo 004 engines, its maximum speed was 461 mph and it could carry a 3300 lb bomb load. The Ar234's most noted action was the bombing of the Remagen bridge.

Other plans for jet aircraft abounded. Perhaps the most ambitious was the Junkers 287, which was designed to possess higher speeds than any Allied fighter interceptor.

A radically new design was the end-result, for the Ju287-VI had swept-forward wings built into a He177A airframe, and was powered by four Jumo 004 engines, two under the wings and two either side and below the cockpit. The prototype reached a maximum speed of 404 mph. More impressive was the designer's estimated figures for the projected V3 version, which, powered by six turbojets, would reach a top speed of 537 mph.

The *Blohm und Voss* P202 was a projected jet powered by two Jumo 004s which had wings which swivelled on the centre line of the fuselage over an angle of 35°. The left wing would lead in the configuration during high speed flight. Another, the Messerschmidt P1102 project, was a swing-wing bomber powered by three turbo-jets. The Junkers EF09 was a jet vertical takeoff fighter, as was the Focke-Wulf *Triebfluegel* which was to have multi-directional jets. Such was the inventiveness of the Third *Reich*'s researchers.

NAZI POLITICAL WARFARE

Political warfare (or psychological warfare in American parlance) is a term coined during World War II for direct assault by non-military means on the morale of the enemy. Its main weapons are sabotage, subversion and propaganda of different kinds. It employs non-military means in the sense that large formations of army, navy or air force personnel are not involved. It does not however exclude commando raids, irregular warfare, support of guerrilla or partisan bands, the fomentation of discontent, mutiny or rebellion among the forces or civilian population of the enemy and his allies. It can be used in time of peace as well as in time of war. It can aim at a *coup d'état* which will overturn an inimical government as much as at a rebellion or civil war. It was an essential part of the technique by which Hitler acquired Austria and the Sudetenland in 1938, occupied Prague and the Memelland in 1939 and fomented conflict with Poland over the Free City of Danzig, just as it was a part of his military victory over Poland and his conquest of Norway, Denmark, the Netherlands, Belgium, France and Jugoslavia. He does not appear to have used it against Greece and only to a limited extent against Britain in 1940-41, and then unsuccessfully in the Middle East. He used it against the United States and the Soviet Union, with very limited success in the first case, while in the second he refused to avail himself of the real weapons at his disposal despite the urging of his military advisers; he did use it however as part of the means by which he secured the support of Finnish, Baltic, Slovak, Romanian, Hungarian, Italian and Spanish forces on the Eastern Front.

From this it will be clear that an account of Hitler's use of political warfare must be to some extent an account of the entire German effort in World War II and its antecedents, something we have altogether too little space for here. What is needed however is a little more analysis of the nature of Nazi political warfare, some account of its particular institutions and weapons and an estimate of the reasons for its success or failure.

When Hitler came to power on January 30, 1933, he inherited a military machine that had accustomed itself to the idea of political warfare from World War I, and had developed a number of the necessary institutions. A considerable effort had gone into subversive work against Germany's enemies during World War I, especially against Czarist Russia and the British Empire in the Middle East and in Ireland. German clandestine subsidies had encouraged the subject nationalities of the Russian empire from Finland and the Baltic republics through Poland and the Cossacks of the Ukraine to the Georgians of the Caucasus. A German mission had been active among the tribes of Iran attempting to turn them against the British-owned oil wells of Abadan. Contacts had been made with the tribes of Afghanistan and the Ottoman Empire had been encouraged in its attempts to raise a Holy War against Britain and France. When the first Russian revolution came in March 1917 Germany had smuggled Lenin and his closest followers from their exile in Switzerland to St Petersburg and German money had kept the Bolshevik cause going in its blackest moments in the summer of that year. Germany had backed Sir Roger Casement in his attempts to raise an army among the Irish prisoners of war and a German submarine had ferried him to Ireland.

In propaganda and the acquisition of clandestine information however the Germans had been a long way second to Britain. British propaganda was credited with a large part of the responsibility for the American entry into the war and with the collapse of morale on the home front in the Austro-Hungarian and German empires. And Germany was a long way second to Britain in the effective use of espionage and intelligence gathering generally.

The vast bulk of this political warfare had been carried out by the German foreign ministry and by the appropriate sections of the army and navy. After the collapse of Germany and the concurrent collapse of the Ukrainian and Don Cossack states in the face of the Red Army, the only parts of this clandestine warfare apparatus that were kept in being were the military intelligence contacts with the Ukrainian and Cossack exiles, and the similar contacts established during the war with Flemish nationalists in Belgium and with Bretons in France. At the same time the terms of the Treaty of Versailles opened a whole new area of clandestine activity in its creation of large German and other discontented minorities throughout eastern Europe. German minorities existed in Eupen-Malmédy in Belgium, in the Italian South Tyrol, in northern and central Yugoslavia, in the now Romanian province of Transylvania, in the Czech Sudeten provinces, in Polish Silesia and the Corridor, in the League of Nations territories of the Saar and Danzig, in Lithuanian Memel, in South African South West Africa and in Danish Schleswig. In all these territories strong nationalist economic pressures were to develop to bear down and destroy the economic institutions of these German minorities, to break the cohesion of the German communities and to force their members off the land. In the mid 1920s therefore, the Foreign Ministry developed an undercover financial network to plump German money into these agencies and keep them alive and flourishing.

During the 1920s also the various German intelligence agencies were rationalised and combined. As Hitler was taking power this process was just ending. Official propaganda was concentrated in the hands of the press and political archive sections of the Foreign Ministry, whence a ceaseless campaign was waged against the War Guilt clauses of Versailles. Here too the work of a number of private 'grey propaganda' agencies, such as the *Wirtschaftspolitische Gesellschaft* (Economic Political Association) was co-ordinated. Clandestine intelligence gathering and the machinery for subversion and sabotage was concentrated in the *Abwehr*, a joint military naval intelligence service under the Ministry of Defence. Interception and cryptography was concentrated in a new agency, the *Forschungsamt* (Research Office), which, in order to keep it out of the hands of the extreme Nazis, was attached to Goering's staff in the newly created German air ministry.

To this existing machinery Hitler brought five new elements: first, personal charismatic leadership to replace impersonal patriotism as a centre for nationalist sentiment; second, an enormously strong belief in the importance of propaganda; third, contact with a network of extreme German nationalists and Nazis among the German minorities abroad; fourth, an equally strong pull on right wing anti-Bolshevist and anti-semitic movements, especially in the non-Catholic or ex-Catholic areas of Europe, coupled with a special appeal to those extreme nationalist movements who also thought of themselves as 'Aryan'; fifth, a contempt for officialdom and a method of government that encouraged the proliferation of differing and rival agencies of a party character, which he used or threw to one side according to their own effectiveness in particular cases.

This last element is the explanation for the difficulty one has in always elucidating what the main line in German propaganda or political warfare was at any one time. Thus in 1933 propaganda abroad was officially taken away from the Foreign Ministry and put into the hands of Goebbels' newly founded Ministry of Propaganda. In practice however the organisation of measures to win support abroad for Germany, the distribution of propaganda materials, the use of money to secure outlets for German views and so on continued in most cases to be organised by the German embassies abroad, to some of which, though by no means all, attachés sent from the Ministry of Propaganda were attached, while in others the critical figure was the press attaché reporting to the press department of the Foreign Ministry. As the SS strength grew, so it began to intervene in propaganda activities abroad, while under von Ribbentrop, who became Foreign Minister in 1938, a very large part of the responsibility for propaganda abroad was officially recovered by the Foreign Ministry.

In much the same way the conduct of subversive activities against specific governments became disputed between a number of different agencies. Where support was given to local Nazi or crypto-Nazi parties, it might be given from the German Embassy, as was, for example, the clandestine financing of Konrad Henlein's Sudeten German party in Czechoslovakia. It could be given through various Nazi party organisations of which the *Auslandsorganisation* (Foreign Organisation) of the Nazi Party was the official body. It could be placed in the hands of some *ad hoc* representative of Hitler's own staff, as the organisation and control of pressure on the Austrian government was placed in the hands, firstly of Theo Habicht as Gauleiter for Austria, and later of Wilhelm Keppler. It could be assumed by the SS whose *Volksdeutsche Mittelstelle* (Liaison Office for German Minorities abroad) was charged with the fomentation of trouble in the rump of Czechoslovakia after Munich. It might remain in the hands of the Army High Command or the *Abwehr* as, for example, the recruitment of 'free Russian forces' after 1941 was lodged with the Army while relations with Flemish or Breton nationalists remained with the *Abwehr*.

The outbreak of World War II complicated matters still further by multiplying the number of intelligence agencies. Ribbentrop's Foreign Ministry, the separate German armed services, the SS and even the Post Office (which succeeded in 'unscrambling' Churchill's coded transatlantic telephone conversations with President Roosevelt and giving advance warning of Italy's capitulation to the Allies) all entered the decipherment and interception business. The position of the *Abwehr* was challenged and its rôle finally taken over in most respects by the *Sicherheitsdienst* (the Security Service) of the SS, metamorphosed as it were under Himmler into the *Reichssicherheitshauptamt* (the Reich Security Main Office). Walther Schellenberg was the driving force in this enterprise, once he had made his reputation by kidnapping the heads of the British Secret Service in the Netherlands across the Dutch frontier at Venlo in November 1939.

Theoretically the various Nazi organisations had entirely separate rôles. The *Aussenpolitisches Amt der NSDAP* (the Foreign Policy Office of the Nazi Party) advised on and conducted party foreign policy, and relations between the party and foreign political figures. Its head was Alfred Rosenberg, the Baltic German, who was regarded as the party's main philosopher. The *Auslandsorganisation* (AO) controlled, organised and supervised all Nazi party organisation among German citizens abroad, with branches from San Francisco to Shanghai. Relations with German minorities abroad were the responsibility of the *Verein des Deutschtums im Ausland* (Union for Germans Abroad) until its supercession by the *Volksdeutsche Mittelstelle* in 1937. Advice on foreign policy and a part in negotiation with foreign statesmen conducted by the office of the Fuehrer and of his deputy was conducted by Joachim von Ribbentrop and his *Dienstelle von Ribbentrop* (Office Ribbentrop) up to 1938 and his appointment as Foreign Minister.

In practice, of course, where a particular office succeeded in taking an initiative successfully, there it tended to stick irrespective of any theoretical disqualification;

distinctions between the party, the offices of the party leader and his deputy and the official organs of the state became difficult to maintain when the party was the state, its leader the Chancellor and head of state. Thus is was Rosenberg who acted as the intermediary between Hitler and Vidkun Quisling, the Norwegian leader whose treasonable actions played so large a part in the occupation of Norway. It was von Ribbentrop who negotiated the Anglo-German Naval Agreement and the anti-Comintern pact with Japan; the original Axis agreements with Italy were the reply of the Foreign Ministry. Relations with General Franco, leader of the insurgent Spanish nationalist military and subsequently *El Caudillo*, were conducted in part through the AO, the head of whose branch in Spanish Morocco intervened at the opening of the Spanish Civil War to secure German arms and aircraft for Franco's forces and partly through Admiral Canares, head of the *Abwehr*, whose Spanish political connections dated back to the 1914-18 war.

Political warfare and subversion played a large part in Hitler's successful expansion of power before 1939. In the case of Austria, the initial phase which culminated in the abortive coup of July 1934 in which a group of Austrian Nazis attempted to seize power in Vienna and assassinated the Austrian Chancellor, Engelbert Dolfuss, was led by Theo Habicht, appointed *Gauleiter* (Provincial Leader) of Austria in 1933. He organised violent radio propaganda attacks by the German radio in Munich against the Austrian government. He incited members of the Austrian Nazi party to sabotage attacks, mainly with bombs, against offices of the Austrian provincial governments and the principal Austrian political party. He organised an Austrian stormtroop legion among those who sought refuge in Germany once the Austrian police had got on to their terrorist activities. He certainly had a hand in the coup. With its failure his rôle came to an end. A press truce and a Gentlemen's Agreement between Germany and Austria were signed in 1936.

The second phase which was to end with the annexation of Austria under threat of invasion in March 1938 involved pressure on the new Austrian Chancellor to take into his government representatives of the so-called neutral opposition, that is ultra right wing Austrian political figures who lacked any overt Nazi connections but were in fact last-ditch supporters of an Austrian union with Germany and Hitler. The strategy involved keeping the Austrian Nazis under strict discipline and control, the job given to Hitler's personal representative, Wilhelm Keppler. It was the discovery by the Austrian police that the Austrian Nazis resentment of Keppler's control had led to their drafting plans for another coup which led to the series of events which ended in the replacement of Schusnigg by the crypto-Nazi Seyss-Inquart, under extreme military threats from Berlin, the inviting in of German troops and Hitler's proclamation of Austria's annexation to Germany.

The course of pressure on Czechoslovakia which resulted in the Munich conference of September 1938 was much more carefully organised at first. Henlein was ordered to advance demands for autonomy for the Sudeten Germany minority in

Czechoslovakia that would be too severe for the Czech government to concede. In his initial planning Hitler saw Henlein's rôle as the creation of a dispute which he, Hitler, could utilize to provide an occasion which, together with a carefully organised incident (the assassination of the German minister in Prague was discussed), would provide an excuse for the conquest of all Czechoslovakia in a sudden all out military attack. In the event, his handling of the situation was inept, his own propaganda assaults on the Czech government so violent that, driven by the imperative desire to avoid war, the British premier, Neville Chamberlain, aided and abetted by Mussolini, compelled the Czechs to cede the Sudetenland to him at the Munich conference. His desire for war was thwarted and he was forced to organise a second political campaign against the Czechoslovak state by inciting the Slovak and Ruthene separatists and the German minority. As an exercise in political warfare it was ineptly handled, and Hitler was forced, as against Austria, to substitute open military threat for clandestine political warfare. Under threat the Czech president was forced to invite the Fuehrer to make the Czech provinces a German protectorate, and the Slovak leaders forced to ask for independence under German leadership. The unhappy Ruthenes were abandoned to the mercies of Hungary who annexed the Ruthene areas after a day of independence.

Against Poland the campaign was more carefully orchestrated. Hitler made serious and lengthy efforts to persuade the Polish government to meet his desires in the matter of Danzig and the Polish Corridor, ignoring a prolonged and savage campaign against the German minority in western Poland. When Polish intransigence thwarted his hope of negotiation, pressure began through the newspapers of the German country areas bordering on Poland who were for the first time freed of censorship to write of Polish persecution of the German minority. Thereafter Hitler employed three means of pressure. Trouble was incited among the German minority in Poland by agents of Himmler's SD. The government of the Free City of Danzig, which was completely Nazi, were incited into a conflict with Poland over the Polish customs inspectors in Danzig. And as the final stage in the preparations for attack on Poland an SD unit faked a 'Polish' attack on the German radio station at Gleiwitz, complete with corpses (of concentration camp inmates) in Polish uniform. This was intended to provide the occasion for the German assault on Poland, originally timed for four o'clock in the morning on August 26, 1939. Hitler countermanded his orders for the attack too late to prevent the 'incident' from being staged. In the meantime Hitler's own speeches and the German press raged over Polish 'atrocities' against the German minority in Poland and the German Foreign Ministry produced a White Book of diplomatic correspondence, much of it faked, on these atrocities to follow with the declaration of war.

In the German assault on Poland itself *Abwehr* units played their part ahead of the main German forces in sabotage and guerrilla activities, some in civilian clothes, some in Polish uniforms. One unit acted on August 25, before the countermanding orders could be issued, occupying the Jablonka pass in Southern Poland and holding out for some days against the Polish frontier troops. Others acted to prevent Polish 'scorched earth' measures being applied in Polish Silesia's industrial and mining areas. One unit organised among the German minority even captured the town of Kattowitz from the Poles before the regular German troops arrived.

The conquest of Poland was followed by a new intrusion by the German Foreign Ministry into the field of political warfare. In this case the action was led by a special section formed in the archive department of the Foreign Ministry. This had first intervened as a force in German propaganda against the War Guilt clauses of the Treaty of Versailles in the 1920s, pioneering the selective publication of diplomatic documents with the enormous series, *Die internationale Politik der Europaeische Maechte,* and allowing selected foreign historians known to be sympathetically disposed to Germany access to files from which material casting doubt on the German case had, unbeknownst to them, been carefully removed. It now developed a unit under Dr Fritz Berber, head of the once independent German Institute for Foreign Policy, to screen the captured archives of the Czechoslovak and Polish governments and to publish white books showing or purporting to show the war guilt of the conquered and the support they enjoyed from allegedly neutral governments such as that of the United States. Their activities were later extended to Belgian, Norwegian and French archives. Their two most successful publications were the so-called second *Polish White Book* which threw allegations against Roosevelt and his diplomatists and the *Secret Archives of the French General Staff* which published material on French military schemes to bomb Russian oil fields from bases in Turkey. Other damaging material on Czech subsidies of British and French journalists passed largely unnoticed in the later years of the war.

The German military conquest of Poland, Norway and the Netherlands gave rise to an enormous mythology about the German 'fifth column', a phrase dating from a remark allegedly made by the Spanish nationalist general Mola in the early days of the Spanish Civil War. He had, he was alleged to have said, four columns marching on Madrid, held by Spanish Republican forces. But the real assault would be opened by the fifth column which, so he was alleged to have continued, was already in Madrid, spies, saboteurs, defeatists, a Trojan Horse already within the city's walls. The phrase was made enormous use of by Spanish left-wing Republican propaganda to justify counter-measures against alleged pro-Franco sympathisers. In the circumstances of 1940, with the sudden overwhelming collapse of all western Europe, save only Britain, the overwhelming power and universal presence of the Nazi fifth column, spies, saboteurs, sympathisers, special operations troops caught the public imagination with contagious collective hysteria. The typical fifth columnist was pictured either as a German agent planted years before Hitler came to power or as a parachutist disguised as a civilian, usually as a nun. The British interned all enemy aliens above the age of 16, the overwhelming majority of them being Jewish refugees from Nazism, and rounded up those who had supported the various British Nazi and Fascist organisations. The Americans panicked themselves with the chimaera of a Nazi conspiracy spreading its tentacles like an octopus from the Niagara border to Patagonia.

The facts were rather different. Despite the Norwegian Major Quisling's role in inciting Hitler's attention towards Norway, no Norwegian traitors took any part in the German attack on Norway. Some *Abwehr* units in disguise operated in central Norway, perhaps 100 in all. No fifth column played any part in the German conquest of the Netherlands, though in the initial assault on the Dutch frontier, *Abwehr* units in Dutch uniform in some cases had limited success in seizing bridges over strategic water barriers. Parachutists played a more important rôle, but in German uniform, not in disguise. The dropping of dummy parachutists in German uniform was practised both in the Netherlands and in Belgium to add to the demoralisation of the opposing forces and to distract them into searching the rear areas rather than making ready to meet the main German assault. The usual rôle was played by small numbers of *Abwehr* units. In the case of Britain, the United States and Latin America there was no fifth column whatever. The British had eliminated or taken over the entire German espionage network in Britain. In America the pro-Nazi movements were minute and the Nazi '*Bund*' movement organised among German citizens was a total failure. The *Abwehr* were under orders to refrain from sabotage in America until after America's entry into the war. And Latin America ?

In the German attack on Jugoslavia, fifth column and political warfare measures were more effective. The main target of the German political warfare campaign was the Croats, long opposed to Serbian domination of the state. They failed to support the leading political figure in Croatia, Dr Matchek, who instead of fomenting rebellion called on Croatian reservists to obey orders for mobilisation. But Veesenmayer of the Foreign Ministry encouraged the Croat extremist, Pavelic, to proclaim an independent Croatia as soon as the German attack started. Some Croatian units refused to fight. Others even attacked Yugoslav army command posts. German minority members played an active military rôle as in Poland. *Abwehr* units seized crucial positions, bridges and airfields.

At this point it is worth pausing to see how the German political warfare machine had developed during the first two years of warfare. At the tactical level this was governed very much by the development of Himmler's empire, *Reichssicherheitshauptamt*, *Sicherheitsdienst* and SS, by the side of the Army High Command with its *Abwehr*, field security police, radio interception and field radio propaganda units. As an intelligence gathering organisation *outside* German occupied territory, the *Abwehr* was only intermittently competent. As an organisation of special operations, its special unit the *Lehrregiment* Brandenburg had a long list of successes. Even here it was about to be challenged by the SS leader, Otto Skorzeny, the man who was to lead the rescue of Mussolini. At the field radio propaganda level the Army High Command had scored notable success with the radio campaign against French troops during the

Phoney War period, broadcasting in French from stations just across the border. These certainly played a part in the progressive collapse of French army morale even before the German *Blitzkrieg* started. The 'black' radio stations, which pretended to be organs of resistance groups within the enemy like the 'New British Broadcasting Company' or the bogus Russian Leninist station run by the German ex-Communists, Thaelmann, Kaspar and Albrecht, came under the Ministry of Propaganda and had only limited success.

At the strategic level control of political warfare was disputed between the Ministry of Propaganda, the *RHSA*, the Foreign Ministry and the Army High Command. Goebbels retained control over his Ministry, over the media of press, radio and film to the bitter end. The carefully orchestrated attacks of the German press, the foreign language radio broadcasts of, for example, William Joyce, 'Lord Haw Haw', and the Americans, Kaltenbach and Chandler, the superb exploitation of the discovery of the bodies of the Polish officers, murdered at Katyn, which destroyed relations between Russia and the Polish exile government in London, were all Goebbels' work. The Foreign Ministry was responsible for the not altogether ineffective encouragement of isolationism in the United States in 1940 and the employment of George Sylvester Viereck, who played so effective a part in encouraging the activities of the America First Committee. Substantial funds were placed at his disposal.

The Foreign Ministry was equally responsible for the whole mobilisation of right-wing European political leadership behind Hitler's banner in the crusade against 'Bolshevism', the anti-Comintern Pact. They used this treaty organisation, which, since its original signature between Germany and Japan and Italy's accession in November 1937, had been moribund even before the signature of the Nazi-Soviet non-aggression pact of August 1939, as the agency first for binding Hitler's European allies to Germany and then for recruiting their armies to fight alongside the *Wehrmacht* against Russia. Between November 1940 and March 1941 Hungary, Romania, Slovakia and Bulgaria were forced to adhere to the anti-Comintern pact and it was the agreement of the Regent, Prince Paul, of Jugoslavia to follow their example which provoked the overthrow of his government and the seizure of power by the young King Peter in March 1941. When Hitler's forces invaded Russia in June 1941 they were accompanied by Romanians, Hungarians and Slovaks, together with divisions from Spain and Italy and volunteers from Vichy France, from Belgian and Dutch Fascists. The SS in pursuit of the same ideal recruited from Scandinavia, the Netherlands, and from the inhabitants of the independent Baltic republics annexed by the Soviet Union in 1940, Latvians, Estonians and Lithuanians as well as from Bosnia, Albania and the Ukrainian minority in Galicia.

The invasion of Russia presented Germany's political warfare experts with their biggest challenge. It is fair to say that they failed it entirely for all the reasons that made the Nazi German war machine so incompetent a military force at the level of high strategy and so obstinate and difficult an enemy on the ground. Political warfare in

Russia was governed overall by Hitler. This gave it from the beginning two major weaknesses. Hitler was determined (indeed it was an article of faith with him) to create a German Empire in the East. All who lived there whether Russian, Ukrainians, Cossacks, Georgians, Adzhars, Armenians, Kazaks, Kalmucks, Kughiz, Svanetians, Azerbajanis, Tadjiks, Tartars, Turkestanis, Uzbecks, Ingush, Ossetes, Karachai, Chechens, Balkar-Kamarden or Daghestanis were Slavs in his eyes, fit only to be serfs and bondmen to the new master-race. 'Only the German may bear arms', he declared.

Hitler's second weakness was that political warfare of the kind he had practised between 1935 and 1939-40 was in his eyes a substitute for real force, only to be used when real force was lacking. In 1941-42, he felt more than strong enough to destroy Soviet Russia. It was only after the defeats at Stalingrad and Kursk marked the end of his chances (if not his hopes) of conquering Russia that he began to yield to the urgings of those who wanted to recruit allies for Germany either among Russia's satellite peoples or among Russian anti-Stalinists themselves. Russia was to be stripped of every educated man and every trained official. The courts were to be left behind. It was a war of extermination. Thus ran his address to his generals on March 30, 1941.

The opening phases of the German attack on Russia were greeted by mass surrenders of Soviet troops on a scale which led one eyewitness to call it the second Russian revolution. Between July and December 1941 nearly four million Soviet soldiers surrendered. By the end of the war more than five and a half million prisoners had been taken on the eastern front. Nearly four million of those died in German captivity, the majority of starvation and typhus within six months of their initial capture in the campaigns of 1941. Of the remainder some 80,000 donned some kind of German uniform, rendering themselves liable in 1945 to forced repatriation to the Soviet Labour camps if nothing more, and for many their fate was indeed a lot worse.

Political warfare in Russia was the responsibility of several conflicting agencies. In theory everything in occupied Russia came under Alfred Rosenberg's *Ostministerium* (Ministry of the East) save for the war areas which were under the High Command of the Army, propaganda (disputed between Ribbentrop's Foreign Ministry and Goebbels' Propaganda Ministry), economics which came into dispute between Goering and Sauckel (the plenipotentiary for labour recruitment), and political purges (the SS). In practice Ribbentrop's Foreign Ministry was soon excluded and Goebbels' energies occupied by propaganda *per se* rather than by political warfare in Russia. The real contest lay between Rosenberg, the SS and the High Command of the Army.

All three found themselves faced with the same pair of dilemmas. To do anything they had to fight the policy of extermination and exploitation practised by the SD special commandoes, Sauckel's forced Labour Recruitment measures and the RHSA's treatment of Soviet prisoners of war even after their removal for forced labour purposes to Germany in 1942. To make any positive move they had to decide whether to back the Russians who were still the most numerous and to go hard headed for a

Free Russia movement, a kind of Rapallo in exile, or to back the satellite races against Russian nationalism. The two policies were largely exclusive. The Germans tried both.

Support for the subject nationalities came from the beginning from Rosenberg and the *Ostministerium* encouraged as German forces approached the Caucasus and the Caspian by the Foreign Ministry's hopes of enlisting Turkish interest in the Turkic tribes of the Trans-Caspian. For most of 1942 a similar policy was followed by the Army Command which raised battalions of Moslem volunteers originally to be used on sabotage special duties under the *Abwehr* as early as October 1941. In April 1942 so called national legions were raised. In July Army Group B advancing through the area of the Don Cossacks found Cossack units deserting wholesale, and survivors of the Cossack anti-Soviet republic of 1917-18 emerging from hiding to join them. In the rear of Army Group A a self governing Cossack district was set up and a limited autonomy promised. When the German army began its headlong retreat from these areas, after the Stalingrad débâcle, they were accompanied by over 70,000 Cossack fighting men. Rather similar accidents brought thousands of Kuban Cossacks, Kalmucks and mountaineers from the Caucasus back with the German retreat from the Caucasus, 220,000 in all. To these had to be added a further 35,000 from the Crimean Tartars.

While this was going on the German armed forces in central and northern Russia had been steadily recruiting Russian prisoners of war and deserters as military auxiliaries, drivers, orderlies, stretcher bearers, labourers, interpreters etc. In November 1941 there may have been as many as 200,000 of these. In December 1941, when large scale Partisan warfare began behind the German lines in White Russia, the rear area commanders recruited battalions of these auxiliaries into an anti-partisan militia. The first so-called Russian People's Army was set up under a turncoat Soviet official in a self-governing county near Briansk in 1941. This emboldened the Central Army Group to propose in October 1941 that Smolensk be made the self governing capital of the German occupied area and the centre of recruitment for anti-Soviet forces but Hitler quashed the idea.

The policy which was to lead eventually to the creation of the Russian Freedom Army under General Vlassov began in the *Wehrmacht* propaganda section and had to be fought against Hitler's opposition all the way. Vlassov himself was one of the six Soviet army commanders under Marshal Zhukov defending Moscow in the winter of 1941-42. He fell into German hands as the result of the failure of an attack designed to relieve Leningrad in January 1942, Vlassov having been sent by Stalin to act as deputy to the general commanding the whole Leningrad front and as supervisor of the attack. The attack failed as Vlassov had prophesied, the army making it was cut off by the Germans and Vlassov preferred to stay with his troops which held out until June 1942 rather than return to face Stalin's wrath. He fell into German hands after hiding in disguise for a fortnight and almost immediately proposed a Russian liberation movement, threatening that it would have to lean on Britain and America if Germany would not back it.

The subsequent history of the Vlassov movement is tragic and bloody. Vlassov did not achieve his full aims until November 1944, five months after D Day. Many of the volunteer units had by then been sent to man the coastal fortifications of France against the British and Americans. Indeed the first prisoners of war from those units were already being handed over to Soviet control that very month. Others, including the Cossacks were used in Jugoslavia and Italy where a Kalmuck unit found itself fighting a unit of American-born Japanese, surely the oddest of the war's many grim ironies. By this date the SS had embraced the idea of a Russian Freedom Army, something Himmler had previously denounced, though the military SS had recruited SS Divisions from the minorities for anti-partisan warfare, especially among the Ukrainians. In April 1944, impressed by the success Army-inspired Russian Freedom propaganda was having even then in provoking desertions from the Red Army, Himmler adopted for his own the idea of a pan-European anti-Bolshevik crusade. By September 1944, now in command of the Russian Reserve Army, Himmler was persuaded to meet Vlassov, to authorise the setting up of an all-Russian free government and the combining of all the various free Russian units, plus the various other non-Russian battalions, brigades etc. into a Russian liberation army to consist originally of two divisions. A grand committee for the liberation of the Peoples of Russia was set up in Prague in November 1944. Two divisions were slowly raised, some 50,000 in all from the 800,000 Russian citizens in German uniform. Their only effective action was the part they played in combination with the Czech resistance in 'liberating' Prague from the retreating German troops, a last vain desperate attempt to work their passage back into the good graces of the western allies whom, bemused by Goebbels' propaganda, they believed to be on the verge of war against their Soviet allies. Like the Turcomen and Cossack troops who had retained their separate existence and all the other Soviet citizens found under German control, whether soldiers, prisoners of war, slave labourers or concentration camp inmates, they were duly handed back to Soviet custody, and in the case of the leaders, Vlassov himself included, to execution. Only those who had fought in the Ukrainian SS division escaped repatriation by persuading their British captors that they were Poles.

The failure of German political warfare in Russia to break the hold Stalin maintained on Soviet loyalties, even that Stalin who had terrorised the peasantry of western Russia in the collectivisation programme in the early 1930s and broken the Army leadership in the purges, is always held to be the most flagrant example of the stupidity and wickedness shown in Hitler's management of Germany's war effort. But his propagandists had very little success with their anti-Bolshevik campaign for a European crusade against Bolshevism in Europe. Germany's war aims, as Hitler propounded them, and as Himmler, Speer, Sauckel, Goering and others put them into practice, rested too clearly on the dehumanisation and exploitation of all non-

Germans and gave the lie too clearly to the propaganda of Goebbels and the pan-European dreams of the SS theorists. One cannot reasonably expect the alliance and loyalty of those whom one's minions are all too clearly treating as subject peoples. It is the measure of the effectiveness of German political warfare, divided, contradictory, racialist, incompetent as it was, and of the fears aroused by the Stalinist system that so many thousands of ordinary men and women preferred to serve Nazism against Soviet Russia even under the looming shadow of defeat. In the end however Nazi political warfare failed because Germany's armies were defeated. Political warfare can aid the victorious; but it is very rare for it to turn defeat into victory.

HITLER

Until fairly recently it was fashionable to dismiss Hitler as a mere dilettante in military affairs, the opinionated corporal of the 1914-18 War quite out of his depth as a supreme commander, and a carpet-biting maniac to boot who pulled Germany down to total defeat through his insanely irrational conduct of the war. This unfavourable verdict owed a great deal to the memoirs of certain German generals who rushed into print after the war eager to blame the deceased *Fuehrer* for all that had gone wrong after 1942 whilst claiming full credit on behalf of the army for the earlier successes.

With the return of much captured material to German archives a more accurate and historically credible picture of Hitler the war leader is at last beginning to emerge. It is clear that he did possess at least some of the qualities one expects to find in a supreme commander. Far from being an incorrigible ignoramus, he was in reality exceptionally well informed about and passionately interested in military matters. He had, for example, an astonishing knowledge of weaponry – which he constantly paraded to impress his audience; and he took a lively interest in the development of new weapons – it was Hitler who appreciated the potential significance of armoured and motorised units and pressed for their expansion at a time when most generals were still highly sceptical of *Blitzkrieg* tactics. When war came he soon displayed an exceptional grasp of military strategy and a keen eye for operational possibilities which greatly impressed even those generals who were hostile to the Nazis and contemptuous of the 'Bohemian corporal'. At his daily military conferences Hitler did not rant and rave all the time as is often supposed. On the contrary; he normally displayed a thorough acquaintance with the immediate tactical situation and argued cogently and persuasively most of the time. Only when all else failed did he fall back on his celebrated 'intuition' and bring further discussion to an abrupt end. Nor can it be denied that he showed remarkable devotion to duty and dogged perseverance in the conduct of the war, a side of his personality too often obscured by the familiar picture of the indolent coffee-house Bohemian who shied away from regular work.

On the other hand, when the tide turned against Germany after 1942 Hitler's weaknesses as a war leader were quickly revealed. The stubborn streak in his character grew more pronounced as he insisted more and more on 'National Socialist fanaticism' as the answer to a deteriorating strategic situation. Permission to retreat in the face of superior enemy forces was not ordinarily granted by a supreme commander who insisted vehemently and with monotonous regularity that will power could and must close the yawning credibility gap between Germany's imperialist ambitions and the capacity of her armed forces to realise these. An elastic defence system was rendered utterly impossible because Hitler saw defeatism and cowardice in every attempt to withdraw to new positions. Towards the end of the war he became neurotically suspicious of his closest military advisers sensing that they did not share his 'National Socialist' resolve to fight on until 'five minutes after midnight'. Though his quarrels with generals and staff officers have been somewhat exaggerated in the past – one must remember that his reaction varied considerably depending on the individual – there is no doubt that after the July Plot of 1944 Hitler's relations with his advisers were extremely strained – not that it mattered much to the course of the war by then.

After the crucial changes in army command in February 1938 Hitler began at last to exert decisive influence over military strategy. At his insistence stronger emphasis was laid on the build-up of armoured and motorised divisions. During the Munich Crisis he was deeply involved in the detailed preparations for the attack on Czechoslovakia. In the spring of 1939 it was Hitler who took the initiative in ordering plans to be drawn up for the attack on Poland. And on the very eve of war Hitler personally addressed the commanding generals at the Berghof on the objectives of the Polish campaign. But once Germany was at war in September 1939, though Hitler visited the front line daily, he did not interfere in the conduct of operations.

If the generals inferred from this that Hitler would recede gracefully into the background and allow them to determine the grand strategy of the war as Hindenburg and Ludendorff had done before them, they were very quickly disillusioned. On October 9 Hitler ordered plans to be drawn up for an attack on France and the Low Countries in November. The generals were profoundly shocked. They had been perfectly content to remain on the defensive in the west until the 'phoney war' petered out – for they supposed that Britain and France would soon acquiesce in the *fait accompli* and allow Germany to remain master of Eastern Europe. Hitler would have none of it. As *Fuehrer* he claimed the right to determine politico-military strategy. Logically this was an inevitable extension of the totalitarian principle to the military sphere. But in a more profound sense it signified Hitler's resolve to set out on a revolutionary grand strategy which called for the defeat of the west and war against Russia to achieve the imperialist ambitions he had nurtured since the mid-1920s.

In fact the attack in the west did not take place in the autumn of 1939 for several reasons. The generals argued against a new campaign before the army had recovered from the Polish war. Weather reports were adverse. And, finally, a staff officer carrying campaign plans crash-landed in Belgium making postponement of the operation mandatory. Quite certainly Hitler's mounting frustration in the winter of 1939-40 deepened his instinctive dislike of the socially exclusive officer corps and fed his suspicions that behind their technical objections lay a lack of confidence in his judgment and an unmartial desire to avoid further military engagements.

For Germany one good thing came out of the dark winter months: time to reconsider the plan of attack. Drafted hastily and without conviction in October by General Franz Halder, chief of the general staff, the original plan was to attack through Belgium, roll back the Anglo-French armies and secure bases for an air and sea attack on Britain. With time on their hands the high command, army command and Hitler all started to criticise this unimaginative repetition of the Schlieffen Plan of pre-World-War-I days certain to lead to the same kind of slogging match between equally balanced armies in Northern France. The alternative strategy, the so-called 'Scythe Cut' operation which led to the most spectacular German victory since Sedan, owed at least something to Hitler's nose for tactical possibilities. He sensed, instinctively perhaps, that the Halder Plan would not do. While he was searching around for an alternative, Lieutenant General Erich von Manstein, the brilliant young chief of staff of army group A, managed to catch the *Fuehrer*'s ear with a new plan. The gist of it was to lure the Anglo-French armies into Belgium and Holland by a feint attack in the north and make the main thrust through the wooded Ardennes and across the Meuse towards the Channel ports. Hitler was attracted by the element of surprise and audacity not to say risk in the new plan and finally ordered its adoption.

Before the attack in the west took place Hitler's attention was diverted to Scandinavia. Since the beginning of the war Admiral Erich Raeder, commander-in-chief of the navy, had tried to interest Hitler in the acquisition of Norwegian bases from which to attack the British fleet. This was in effect part of a wider anti-British strategy advocated by naval command since the days of *Tirpitz* and supported by the foreign office. In place of Hitler's anti-French, anti-Russian and pro-British strategy Raeder and Ribbentrop took Germany back to the early years of the century when William II had tried (in vain) to unite the whole of Europe against Britain. At first Hitler showed little interest. Then in January 1940, frustrated by delays in the west and itching for action, he authorised plans for an attack. This would probably have been delayed had it not been for strong – and well founded – rumours that an Anglo-French force was ready to embark for Norway in an attempt to assist the Finns in their last desperate struggle against Russia. Recognising the potential threat to vital Swedish ore supplies on which the German steel industry was still heavily dependent, Hitler decided to attack. On April 9 just 24 hours before British destroyers commenced to mine Norwegian waters, Hitler invaded Denmark and Norway. By the end of the month, after initial setbacks in Norway, both countries were firmly in German hands.

On May 10 'Plan Yellow', the offensive in the west, commenced with Hitler supervising the campaign from a field headquarters at Munstereifel. Everything went according to plan. Von Bock's attack in the north drew the Anglo-French armies into the Low Countries while von Rundstedt's armour, thrusting through the Ardennes forest, had crossed the Meuse by May 14. On May 15 the Dutch armies surrendered. So swift was the advance that Hitler could not believe his good fortune. Fearing a counter-attack from the French armies in the south – a not unreasonable anxiety – he ordered Rundstedt's armour to halt on May 16 until the infantry caught up. However, a young corps commander and fervent advocate of dynamic *Blitzkrieg* tactics, General Heinz Guderian, pressed ahead under cover of 'forward reconnaissance' and in defiance of Hitler's orders. On May 20 Guderian had reached Abbeville dragging the German army after him. Thanks to his initiative the risky gamble had succeeded and Hitler quickly ordered the advance to continue.

Four days later a new crisis arose this time with more serious long-term consequences for Germany. The British had been driven back to the coast and German armour was poised for a last victorious thrust when the cautious Rundstedt suddenly halted the advance on May 24 with Hitler's approval. The *Fuehrer* together with Jodl and Keitel believed that Rundstedt was right not to risk his tanks in the unfavourable Flanders terrain when they would be needed to deal with the 65 French divisions still in the field. Goering's intervention was another factor. Anxious to have the honour of finishing off the British, he probably persuaded Hitler that it was politically wiser to let the *Luftwaffe* have the credit for this rather than Bock and Rundstedt. The 48-hour delay before Hitler ordered the advance to continue on May 26 turned out disastrously for Goering. Bad weather grounded his aircraft and when they did take to the air the British Spitfires proved a match for the Messerschmidt 109s. Meanwhile the British had re-organised their perimeter defences and were able to evacuate 200,000 British and 130,000 French and Belgian troops from Dunkirk. On June 5, the day that port fell, a major German offensive was launched along the Somme. Twelve days later the French sued for an armistice which was signed on May 22 at Compiègne in the railway carriage where the Germans signed their armistice 22 years previously.

Germany was now indisputable master of Europe and the *Fuehrer* was accorded a hero's welcome on his return to Berlin. His reputation stood at its height – the sycophantic Keitel dubbed him the 'greatest commander of all time'. Characteristically, Hitler claimed all the credit for the spectacular victory; without his flair 'Scythe Cut' would not have been adopted and without his drive the campaign would never have been launched. Henceforth he was persuaded that the infallibility of which he had been long convinced in the political realm extended to military strategy as well. And by and large his generals swallowed their reservations and followed him eagerly – as long as he was winning.

By comparison the 'miracle of Dunkirk' was very small beer. Everyone in Berlin assumed that Britain would accept the inevitable and surrender gracefully. Significantly, Hitler's thoughts were already turning to the acquisition of Lebensraum in the east. For a time he toyed with the possibility of launching a *Blitzkrieg* in the east in the autumn of 1940. In the end he decided reluctantly but rightly that insufficient time remained that year to conquer Russia and postponed the operation until the spring of 1941.

The provisional decision to attack Russia made it all the more essential to eliminate Britain from the war quickly and so nip in the bud any danger of a two-front war situation developing. Thus after Britain's peremptory rejection, on July 22, of Hitler's recent peace offer, the Fuehrer decided, reluctantly perhaps, to attempt an invasion of Britain in the early autumn.

From the start there were grave doubts on the German side about the feasibility of this risky amphibious operation. The army doubted the capacity of the navy to provide adequate cover against the powerful British fleet. And naval command, conscious of severe losses during the Norwegian campaign, shared these doubts. Only Goering remained confident that he could dominate the skies over Britain and so fulfil the essential pre-condition for an invasion.

On August 13, 'Eagle Day', Goering's *Luftwaffe* commenced a major offensive striking at British airfields and radar installations and sought to destroy the RAF in air battles. Whether the attacks would have succeeded had they been pressed home relentlessly it is impossible to say. Whatever chance there might have been of victory – and it was probably slim – was thrown away when Goering suddenly switched the *Luftwaffe* to the bombing of London on September 7 probably in retaliation for an Allied air attack on Berlin. The climax of the Battle of Britain came on September 15, a date long to be remembered in British history, when 60 German aircraft – representing half the total bomber force over London that day – were shot down at the cost of 26 British fighters. By the end of the month Hitler had postponed 'Operation Sealion' until the spring; British sea and air power was obviously unbroken and turbulent weather was in the offing. This was, in fact, the end of the entire enterprise. Looking back at this critical stage in the war it does not seem that any special blame attaches to Hitler either for the failure to attack Britain earlier in the summer when Fighter Command was desperately weak or for the failure of the *Luftwaffe* to achieve air mastery over the island. Hitler's advisers shared at least as much of the responsibility for these mistakes.

What then could be done to drive Britain out of the war? For a time Hitler toyed with the peripheral strategy advocated by the navy, the essence of which was to undermine Britain by striking at sensitive points such as Gibraltar and Suez on her lines of communications with her empire. However, this strategy proved no more successful partly because Hitler did not pursue it with his customary ruthlessness and partly because the pawns did not behave as expected. Thus, when General Franco, much impressed by Britain's continued resistance, finally refused to bring Spain into the war Hitler swallowed the rebuff and made no attempt to seize Gibraltar – the key to the Western Mediterranean. By the end of 1940 his plans were upset by the Italians retreating in disorder in North Africa and in deep trouble in Greece which they had attacked in October much to Hitler's annoyance. To help them German troops under General Erwin Rommel were sent to Libya early in 1941. They succeeded, temporarily, in redressing the balance and pushed the British back to the Egyptian borders. But lasting victory was denied the Germans basically because Hitler, unlike Churchill, failed to grasp the importance of the Mediterranean theatre of war. No serious attempt was made to seize Malta – the key to the Eastern Mediterranean. Nor did Hitler concentrate all his efforts on driving the British right out of the Middle East, as Raeder's staff constantly urged him to. Had he done so the Anglo-American landings in Italy in 1943 would scarcely have been possible. All Hitler achieved by committing men and materials to North African campaigns was the dissipation of his own forces. This failure undoubtedly represents a major strategic error on Hitler's part.

Long before Rommel's troops landed in Africa Hitler had decided to give absolute priority to eastward expansion. In November 1940 Molotov made it brutally plain during vital conversations in Berlin that the Soviet Union intended in future to concentrate on the Balkans and had no interest whatsoever in diversionary schemes in the Middle East to destroy the British Empire. Any lingering hope Ribbentrop may have had of including Moscow in a vast anti-British front stretching from Madrid to Tokyo was dead. The stiffening Russian attitude and evidence that their armies were being modernised probably convinced Hitler that the attack on Russia must go ahead even though Britain remained undefeated. Nor did he leave out of his calculations the strong possibility that the Americans would enter the war by 1942. Time was again running out for Germany as Hitler saw it; either she took steps to control the whole of Europe to the Urals while the military balance was in her favour, or she would one day be destroyed by Russia and America combining against her. The risks of waiting appeared infinitely greater than the risk of attacking in the east before the war in the west was over. He even persuaded himself that war in the east was the key to all his problems; Britain, deprived of her last potential ally in Europe, would have to surrender because once Russia was defeated the Americans would face a much greater threat in the Pacific from Japan and would be unable to come to Britain's assistance. If Britain still did not give in then Raeder's plan for a drive through the Middle East toward India might well be adopted. On December 18 Hitler finally decided to attack Russia in the spring of 1941.

The attack was not launched in the spring because of Balkan complications. Continuing Italian difficulties in Greece plus the British occupation of Crete made it imperative for Germany to intervene and remove this growing threat to her flank.

Hitler was also anxious to bring Yugoslavia completely within the Axis sphere of influence to safeguard raw material supplies and to prevent Yugoslavian airfields being used to bomb the vital Romanian oil fields. Early in April the last of the successful *Blitzkriege* was launched against Greece and Yugoslavia. By the end of the month both countries were completely crushed; Italy had been rescued from her folly; Crete was in German hands; and Germany's flank was secured for Operation Barbarossa.

It is easy enough to blame Hitler for the fatal mistake of attacking Russia. As Germany had no reasonable grounds for expecting a Russian attack, Hitler obviously bears massive responsibility for this act of aggression. Yet in the initial stages his generals were as confident as Hitler that the Russian armies could be easily defeated. No-one appreciated the colossal scale of the logistical problems to be faced in the interior of Russia. And as little information was available about the Russian armies, their strength was grossly underestimated. It was deceptively easy to believe that the Fuehrer was right as always when he told Jodl that 'they had only to kick in the door and the whole rotten structure will come crashing down'.

On June 22 three armies led respectively by von Leeb in the north, von Bock in the centre and von Rundstedt in the south, 3,000,000 men in all, swept deep into the heart of Russia on a thousand-mile front carrying all before them; hundreds of thousands of prisoners were taken and in many areas the Germans were hailed as liberators. But attempts to envelope and annihilate the Russian armies first at Bialystok-Minsk and then at Smolensk failed; the simple fact was that the German infantry, being largely unmechanised, was unable to move quickly enough over rain-soaked tracks and could not seal off the escape route of the encircled Russians in time. These failures convinced army command that priority must be given to an assault on Moscow where it was supposed that the Russians would concentrate their forces in defence of the capital city thereby offering the Germans one last chance of annihilating the Russians before the onset of winter. To their dismay Hitler refused to modify the original plan. Full of contempt for the 'fossilised and out-of-date theories' of his general staff, he insisted that Moscow could wait. More important on economic and political grounds was the capture of Leningrad; this would cut the Russians off from the Baltic, protect German imports of Swedish ore and enable contact to be made with the Finns. Similarly in the south the wheat of the Ukraine and the oil of the Caucasus remained essential objectives for Germany's economic survival. After weeks of argument Hitler finally overruled army command on August 21. Bock was ordered to halt the advance on Moscow and Guderian's armour was switched from the central to the southern front to help Rundstedt wipe out the Russian armies in the Kiev region.

It is by no means certain that Hitler was wrong to have his own way. Although Leningrad was not taken, the Kiev encirclement was a great success; 665,000 prisoners were taken; Rundstedt occupied the Ukraine and most of the Crimea; and the road to Moscow was open. Hitler now agreed to attack the city. But he insisted that the drive on Leningrad continue and even ordered Rundstedt to advance to the Caucasus simultaneously – an early example of Hitler's irrational optimism which led to a fatal dispersal of German effort at a crucial moment when Russian resistance around Moscow was hardening. Early in October Bock's offensive netted 600,000 prisoners and brought him within 40 miles of Moscow. Then a series of misfortunes intervened. In mid-October rain and fantastic mud slowed down the advance. Snow was now falling and the cold spell caught the Germans without winter equipment. On December 1 Bock attacked Moscow; next day a reconnaissance battalion from von Kluge's Fourth Army was within sight of the Kremlin but had to withdraw hastily. By December 5 Bock was halted all round the perimeter of Moscow and unable to take the city. Twenty-four hours later at twelve minutes past five on the morning of December 6 General Zhukov hurled one hundred divisions at the German positions and the *Blitzkrieg* era came to an abrupt end.

The Germans faced an unprecedentedly grave situation. If Hitler's constant interference had brought the Germans to this plight – and the arguments are by no means all on one side – it cannot be denied that he was equal to the occasion. If he ever had a 'finest hour' this was it. On December 19, after dismissing a number of generals including Bock and Guderian, Hitler took over as commander-in-chief from Brauchitsch and declared his intention of training the army in a 'National Socialist way'. That way was to order the troops to stand fast at all costs. A wise and courageous decision as it turned out for under the hammer blows of Zhukov's offensive a retreat could easily have become a rout as happened to Napoleon's Grand Army a century before. By March the Russian offensive had ground to a halt.

That does not alter the fact that by the spring of 1942 Germany had lost in Russia 200,000 men killed and 700,000 wounded and than an enemy confidently assumed to be at death's door was still very much alive. Furthermore on December 11, 1941, Hitler added a formidable enemy to the list when he declared war on the United States following the Japanese attack on Pearl Harbor. No doubt American intervention was inevitable sooner or later, and Hitler cannot really be blamed for supporting his Tripartite Pact partner. The fundamental error had been his encouragement of Japanese aggression in the Pacific area in the first place when he should have been persuading Japan to join him in the attack on Russia. As a direct result of that blunder Stalin had been able to switch troops from the Far East to the European front at a critical stage in the war. Looked at in retrospect it is clear that once America, Russia and Britain were banded together against Germany controlling between them vast resources in manpower and materials then Hitler had in effect lost the war. Even when Germany mobilised her economy for total war in 1943-4 there was still virtually no hope of victory trapped as she was in a two-front war. All the same, defeat would not have ended in the utter catastrophe of 1945 had it not been for Hitler's misconduct of the war.

Reference has been made already to Hitler's failure to recognise the importance of the Mediterranean theatre of war. Hence Rommel's new offensive in the summer of 1942 which took him to within 65 miles of Alexandria could not then alter the course of the war. Meanwhile in Russia a new offensive was launched in July on the southern front with the aim of securing the oil of the Caucasus. Elated by early successes, Hitler promptly changed the plan of campaign and attempted to take both Stalingrad and the Caucasus simultaneously, an undertaking quite beyond the capacity of his forces. Already the northern flank of the Sixth Army stretching along the Don from Voronezh to Stalingrad was dangerously overextended and held by unreliable satellite troops, so desperate was Germany's manpower shortage. Attempts to draw Hitler's attention to the mounting danger of a Russian counter-attack likely to cut off von Kleist's forces in the Caucasus only produced great outbursts of rage from the Fuehrer, who stubbornly insisted that the Russians were 'finished'.

Worse followed. Having persuaded himself that the capture of Stalingrad, the 'Mecca of communism', would have enormous prestige value, he recklessly committed the Sixth Army to a war of attrition in this sector. When the inevitable Russian counter-attack came on November 19, 1942, 20 divisions were trapped at Stalingrad. Turning a deaf ear to all entreaties that he abandon an untenable position, he ordered the Sixth Army to stand fast. No doubt he was influenced to some extent by news of the Egyptian situation; General Montgomery was driving Rommel out of Egypt while in the latter's rear an Anglo-American force had landed in Algeria. Once again Hitler was let down by Goering who boasted that he could supply the beleaguered Germans in Stalingrad indefinitely but was unable to do so owing to atrocious weather conditions and shortage of aircraft. In the end, on January 31, von Paulus surrendered. 108,000 men were taken prisoner, few of them ever returning to Germany. For this disaster Hitler's stubborn refusal to face the facts was wholly to blame. It would have been a still greater disaster had not General Kurt Zeitzler, Hitler's new chief of staff, persuaded him to allow the withdrawal of the Caucasus forces before they, too, were cut off. The Stalingrad catastrophe was the beginning of the end for Germany. In May the Axis forces in North Africa including 125,000 Germans finally surrendered. On July 5 the last German offensive in Russia ('Operation Citadel') was launched on the Kursk salient. Within days Hitler's extravagant hopes of decisive victory were dashed and from now on the Germans were forced back slowly but surely towards their own frontiers. On July 10 Anglo-American forces landed in Sicily. True, when they landed in Italy on September 3 Hitler was still able to hold two-thirds of the country, largely because of the dilatory tactics of the invaders. For some months the Anglo-Americans were pinned down in Central Italy by 25 German divisions sorely needed elsewhere. By the summer of 1943 the allies were getting the upper hand in the Battle of the Atlantic, Hitler's 'first line of defence in the west', while in the air Allied bombers pounded remorselessly at German cities. Despite all the portents of disaster, Hitler's determination to fight on 'until the clock strikes thirteen' never wavered. Now a sick man sustained by massive drug injections, he simply ignored the brutal facts, withdrawing more and more into an inner sanctuary where will power and fanaticism bridged the yawning chasm between dream and reality. Where Mussolini – and Goebbels too – would have tried to disengage in the east to cut down the odds, Hitler rejected Soviet peace feelers out of hand in the summer of 1943 and adhered tenaciously to a path certain to end in disaster.

Even so he never quite lost hope that victory might still be won by some miraculous turn of events, just as his hero Frederick the Great had been rescued in his hour of need. Thus he welcomed the long-awaited Allied landing in Europe, confident that the invaders would suffer a crushing defeat as at Dieppe in 1942. Then at last Germany's fortunes would change. The 59 divisions tied up in the west would be switched eastwards bringing the Russians to their knees; new-type submarines would force the Allies once more onto the defensive in the Atlantic; and flying bombs and rockets raining down on British cities would break the nerve of the civilian population.

With a flash of the old intuition Hitler predicted, correctly, a landing in Normandy and strengthened that sector – but not sufficiently to tip the balance against an invader. That apart, he committed many grave errors during the fighting in the west. He interfered in the conduct of individual battles generally exerting a degree of control from a distant headquarters incompatible with military efficiency and initiative. And as always he refused to withdraw his forces – to the line of the Seine – when it was abundantly clear that the landings had succeeded. The inevitable happened when the Americans broke out of their bridgehead; part of the German forces was trapped first in the Mortain-Falaise pocket and later at the Seine crossing; the operations cost Germany 500,000 men and most of their equipment. As for the much-vaunted war-winning V1s and V2s, they came too late in the day. The launching sites were systematically bombed and eventually overrun by Allied forces before too much damage was caused.

Only the Allied failure to sweep into defenceless Germany in the late summer of 1944 saved Hitler. This afforded him a breathing space much like that enjoyed by Imperial Germany in the winter of 1917/18 when the eastern front collapsed and Ludendorff was able to launch one last offensive in the west.

By this time Hitler was well aware that the war could not be won. What he hoped to do at this late stage was exploit signs of disagreement in the grand coalition. If he could convince the western powers that Germany still had a sting in her tail might they not be ready to make peace with him and even join with him in a crusade against bolshevism? Such fantastic optimism is a shattering revelation of the extent to which he was out of touch with reality. Yet what alternative had he? Army command agreed that an offensive in the west was tactically correct however risky the undertaking. The only difference of opinion was about objectives. The over-ambitious *Fuehrer* dreamt of splitting the Anglo-American forces and seizing Antwerp whereas his more sober advisers thought they would be lucky to take Liége. Hitler had his way in the end. But without air power and with only 32 divisions at his disposal he had no hope of reaching Antwerp and could certainly not have stayed there had he, by a miracle, got there. As usual, tight control of tactics worked out in great detail at Hitler's headquarters impeded the commanders in the field. Only because of fierce German resistance plus good leadership and favourable terrain did the Germans escape encirclement.

The Ardennes failure represented Germany's last throw. When the Russians launched their last great offensive in March 1945 they smashed through the German lines – stabilised by the end of 1944 – because Germany was without reserves. Not that she could have avoided defeat; for by this time her economy was in total disarray. But the line might possibly have been held further east with reserves – that is the real indictment of the Ardennes offensive.

Hitler who had so often exhorted his troops to stand fast deserted his own post in April 1945 by putting a bullet through his head in the Berlin bunker. Characteristically he continued to the very end to blame his 'cowardly' generals for letting him down. Obviously his personal responsibility for plunging Germany into a struggle she could not win is a great one. Yet others through miscalculation had done that before him. What Hitler lacked was the greatness of character and breadth of vision which would have led him to break off a hopeless struggle against impossible odds in the interest of the nation's survival. In other words the real indictment of Hitler the war leader is that for all his talk he did not really believe that Germany mattered more than he did and so was prepared to sacrifice the German people needlessly on the altar of his own ambitions.

PART 2
HITLER'S GENERALS
AND THEIR BATTLES

THE GERMAN ARMY AND THE NAZI PARTY, 1932–9

The history of the relationship between the Nazi party and the *Reichswehr*, as the army of the Weimar Republic was named, in the late 1920s and early 1930s is a strange one, marked throughout by a multitude of ambivalent attitudes. On the one hand, many of the *Reichswehr*'s officer's were of aristocratic lineage, and possessed an inherited disdain for the 'jumped-up corporal' Adolf Hitler who sought to take over the running of Germany; they also, moreover, distrusted anything that smacked of socialism, and feared the power of Hitler's private army, the *Sturmabteilung* or SA, under its repulsive and boorish commander, Ernst Roehm. On the other hand, many of the younger officers of the *Reichswehr* saw the advantages of a Nazi accession to power. The restrictions and conditions of service imposed upon the *Reichswehr* by the Treaty of Versailles in 1919 meant that the lot of the junior officers was a sad one: 'The actual purpose of the Reichswehr as a citadel of the military idea and as the basic nucleus of the future war of liberation pales. The need of earning bread becomes all important. Soldiers turn into officials, officers become candidates for pensions. What remains is a police troop. People know nothing of the tragedy of the four words: "Twelve years as subalterns".' Thus younger officers, disaffected by the stultifying round of training with inadequate resources and the appallingly slow rate of promotion, saw the opportunities that the Nazis represented, and attempted to spread its doctrines through the officer corps. The words above were written by a lieutenant serving a gaol sentence in 1930 for such illegal activities.

The attitudes of senior officers also reflected much the same feeling. The high command, in the Bendlerstrasse in Berlin, were basically against the Nazis as a threat to Germany's political stability and their own positions in the politico-military establishment. Many of the slightly lower ranking generals, however, commanding

Wehrkreise (military districts) and divisions, were attracted by the Nazi idea, seeing in it advancement for themselves and for the army. Chief amongst this latter group was Lieutenant-General Werner Eduard Fritz von Blomberg, commander of *Wehrkreis* I in East Prussia between 1930 and 1933, and head of the German military delegation to the Disarmament Conference in Geneva from 1932. Chief of the faction opposed to the Nazis were General Kurt von Schleicher, the *Reichswehrminister* or Minister of Defence from July 1932, and General Kurt Freiherr von Hammerstein-Equord, the *Chef der Heeresleitung* or Commander-in-Chief of the Army from October 1930.

The aged president of Germany, Field Marshal Paul von Beneckendorff und Hindenburg, was faced by almost insuperable problems in late 1932. The Nazis had decided that the time was ripe for their bid for absolute power, and had succeeded in toppling the government by means of a crippling transport strike in uneasy conjunction with the Communist party, the Nazis' sworn enemies. The new government accepted by Hindenburg had as its *Kanzler* (Chancellor or Prime Minister) Schleicher, who attempted to split the Nazi party into two manageable halves by offering the posts of Vice-Chancellor and Minister-President of Prussia to Gregor Strasser, the head of the party's political organisation and the only possible rival to Hitler as head of the Nazis. Strasser urged that Schleicher's offer should be accepted to avoid the possibility of further elections for a new *Reichstag* assembly, which might lose the Nazis some seats. Hitler refused, and Strasser quit the party. Schleicher's miscalculation had thus left Hitler in an even stronger position, especially as Schleicher's government was only a minority one, and must resign as the Chancellor could not form a coalition.

The only two possibilities as successors to Schleicher were Hitler and Franz von Papen, an ex-chancellor. Schleicher devoted his last days in office to ensuring the succession of the one he considered the right man. And although he would have preferred Papen, as did Hindenburg, his choice was forced to fall upon Hitler. The reasons for this were twofold: he thought that accession to power would mellow Hitler's more objectionable traits and policies, especially as he expected to be appointed *Reichswehrminister*, a position in which he could keep a check on Hitler; the second reason was a military one. The transport strike of the previous November and December had taught the *Reichswehr* an important lesson in its limitations. Poland was known to be prepared to launch a pre-emptive war against Germany should the opportunity arise, and so forces had to be concentrated to meet such a threat. This left an insufficient number of men to run the strike-bound transport system and cope with any armed resistance the strikers might offer, collectively or individually. Thus the government crisis of January 1933 offered Schleicher no choice. The Polish threat still persisted, and were Papen offered the chancellorship, there was every likelihood of Hitler and the Nazi party starting an armed revolt. The *Reichswehr* would not be able to cope with this, and therefore Schleicher decided that *faux de mieux* Hitler would have to be the next chancellor. Hitler was informed of Schleicher's *volte-face* by

Hammerstein, but did not at first believe it, and set preparations to deal with an army *Putsch* or coup in hand.

■ Accession to power

The results are well known. On 30 January 1933 Hitler became the new chancellor of Germany, and the Nazi *Machtuebernahme* or assumption of power was accomplished. That the army was centrally involved is now evident, with all its disastrous consequences. Schleicher's folly in January 1933 was compounded, moreover, by his naive and totally erroneous belief that even had his assessment of Hitler turned out to be wrong, the army could then remove the new chancellor. And although the army had not had to use force to ensure Hitler's advancement to the chancellorship, Hitler himself later that year conceded that 'if the army had not stood on our side, we should not be standing here today'. Schleicher began to sense how badly he had miscalculated when Blomberg rather than himself was appointed *Reichswehrminister* in the new government.

Hitler's dealings with the *Reichswehr* were at first circumspect and grateful. The new chancellor thanked the army for its help in his rise to power, and led it to believe that it would continue in its traditional position in the German state, with considerable growth once the political climate was right. All these were just what the generals wished to hear. Hitler was also careful in his international position. He played along at the Geneva conference, insisting that Germany be treated as a major power, and only pulled out of the conference when it urged definite levels of disarmament. This again pleased the generals. Finally he abolished the rights of civil courts over military personnel, and also abolished the system, dating back to the military councils of the immediate postwar months of 1919, of elected representatives of the enlisted men, with all its overtones of socialism.

Although the appointment to key positions of outright Nazis such as Blomberg had not met with the wholehearted approval of the army and the president, this had been counterbalanced by the appointment of highly respected men such as Lieutenant-General Ludwig Beck (to the position of *Chef des Truppenamts* or Chief of the General Staff in October 1933). But the question of Hammerstein's replacement as commander-in-chief on his retirement in February 1934 proved a clearer indication of what lay ahead. Hitler, and of course Blomberg, wished this appointment to go to the Nazi Colonel Walther von Reichenau, who had been head of the *Reichswehr* Ministerial Office since February 1933. This proposal met with violent opposition within the army and from Hindenburg, and despite Blomberg's threat to resign unless Reichenau was appointed, the position went to Lieutenant-General Werner Thomas Ludwig Freiherr von Fritsch. Reichenau had to be content with promotion to Major-General and the control of the Armed Forces Office, as the enlarged Ministerial Office was named.

The only chance that the army ever had to remove Hitler was in the early years of his rule, but the complacency engendered by its minor success in the Reichenau affair and its apparent victory in the purging of the SA caused the army to let its chances slip by without action. The purging of the SA was the direct result of the ambitions of Ernst Roehm to advance both the organisation and himself in the new Germany. He was disgusted by Hitler's dalliance with the army when it had long been his ambition to absorb it into the SA, which would then become Germany's major armed force. Hitler was aware of Roehm's ambitions, and wished to halt them. The problem was how to do so without offending the army and Hindenburg. In an effort to gain time, and to placate Roehm, Hitler invited the latter to join the cabinet. Once in the cabinet, however, Roehm produced his plan for the integration of the army and SA, presumably under his own leadership. The army was appalled, and even Blomberg and Reichenau would have nothing to do with the scheme. Blomberg in particular, who had been attempting to woo Hitler away from the SA to the army, now redoubled his efforts, and some time late in June 1934 told Hitler that unless he took steps to clear up the SA problem, Hindenburg might declare martial law and ask the army to do so. Blomberg then stated that if Hitler took immediate steps to set the party's house in order, the army would not interfere. This offer, combined with the importuning of *Reichsfuehrer*-SS Heinrich Himmler and Hermann Goering, both of whom had for some time been very concerned with Roehm's ambitions, finally decided Hitler to act.

The orders went out to Himmler's SS units, and the results are well known. On 30 June 1934, variously known as the 'Blood Purge' and the 'Night of the Long Knives', Roehm and most of his senior colleagues were murdered by SS troopers. Himmler also took the opportunity to dispose of other 'hostile' elements, such as General von Schleicher and Gregor Strasser. Hindenburg, who was to die in little more than a month, was misinformed of the occasion and raised no objection; the army, with a few exceptions, was well pleased with the elimination of the SA as a real threat to its armed supremacy. Yet the army's compliance in what was only a large-scale series of political murders marked the real beginning of its decline from the high moral standards on which it had always prided itself. From this time onwards Hitler was consistently able to dominate his generals.

On 1 August 1934 President Hindenburg died, and Hitler immediately amalgamated the offices of President and Chancellor in himself as *Fuehrer und Reichskanzler*. And then there occurred a quite extraordinary event. Apparently without urging from Hitler, on 2 August every officer and man of the *Reichswehr* swore the following oath: 'I swear by God this sacred oath, that I will yield unconditional obedience to the *Fuehrer* of the German *Reich* and *Volk*, Adolf Hitler, the Supreme Commander of the *Wehrmacht*, and, as a brave soldier, will be ready at any time to lay down my life for this oath.' The event presumably took place on the instigation of Blomberg, to elicit a suitable reply from the new *Fuehrer*. This was forthcoming on the 20th of the same month, when Hitler wrote to Blomberg, thanking him for the oath and continuing:

'. . . so will I at all times regard it as my highest duty to intercede on behalf of the stability and inviolability of the *Wehrmacht*, in fulfilment of the testament of the late Field-Marshal [Hindenburg]; and, in accordance with my own desire, to fix the army as the sole bearer of arms in the nation.' Thus for a promise of its sovereignty, which the SS was already violating, the leaders of the army sold themselves and their men by oath to a man, rather than to the state. It was an oath that was to drag them and their state down to total ruin by 1945.

As he was consolidating his position as supreme ruler of Germany, Hitler was already increasing the size of the armed forces, in direct opposition to the terms of the Treaty of Versailles. Serious expansion began with the German withdrawal from the disarmament conference in Geneva in October 1933, and during 1934 the basis of an additional 24 divisions was set up, the replacement of cavalry by armoured forces was given Hitler's enthusiastic support, and a start was made in building up the small, and totally illegal, *Luftwaffe*. Although the generals had doubts about the speed with which the army was to be increased, they were on the whole pleased that at last they would have the money and the scope to exercise their long-cherished plans to expand the army into the greatest army in the world. Yet Hitler was not satisfied with his current expansion plans, and in March 1935 he announced to a shocked Europe that Germany would no longer be bound by the military terms of the Treaty of Versailles. At the same time he announced that universal conscription was to be introduced, to produce a peacetime strength of 36 divisions, and that Germany had a powerful air force in the form of the *Luftwaffe*. The Western powers, who had imposed the '*Diktat*' of Versailles on a defeated Germany only 16 years before, did precisely nothing to try to prevent the rearming of Germany.

■ Army problems

Although it was easy for Hitler to announce a vast increase in the size of the army, it was difficult for the generals to implement this quickly. One of the main reasons for this was the acute shortage of officers. It is often claimed that the expansion of the German army in the 1930s was easy, as the 100,000 men of the *Reichswehr*, all long-service men, were an ideal cadre for growth. This is only partially true, however, for the reason that whilst a great many of the *Reichswehr*'s men could profitably be promoted, it was usually to non-commissioned rank. And here the German army of the Nazi period excelled, for its NCOs were experienced and well-trained men. The position was also quite good at the other end of the scale, with the senior commanders. Although the Great German General Staff had been forbidden by the Treaty of Versailles, it continued to operate under the *nom de guerre* of the *Truppenamt* or Troop Department. Thus there was a continuity of senior command, together with its doctrines, practices and experience, which could undertake the limited expansion needed of it with facility.

The position was radically different with junior- and middle-ranking officers, however. The *Reichswehr* had had some 4,000 officers, of whom 450 were medical or veterinary officers. Of the remaining 3,550, some 500 were transferred to the newly-revealed *Luftwaffe*, leaving only 3,050 officers for an army that was to grow to 52 divisions by 1939. Many NCOs were commissioned, and 1,000 policemen trained in military methods were drafted, but the army still had to find and train over 25,000 more officers in the six years up to the beginning of World War II. That it did so, and also produced a large number of first-class junior commanders, is a great tribute to the efforts of the senior commanders and the abilities of the junior commanders. This great expansion is also the reason for the comparative youth of German commanders up to battalion level, and why a young officer who would have commanded only a company in the British and American armies might command a battalion or even regiment in the German army.

There was also another side to the greatly increased need for young officers. With opportunities for promotion being so open, ambitious young men tried to ensure their swift advancement by adopting Nazism. This had little significance at first, but as more Nazi sympathisers reached the middle ranks, there emerged a tendency for pro-Nazi officers to be given promotions in ever greater numbers, with the concomitant problems of commanders having reached their positions on political, rather than military, merit. At the same time, officers who had the temerity to reveal themselves as opponents of the Nazi régime received little or no promotion, any military ability they may have had not withstanding.

The influx of so many new officers, many of them with very dubious backgrounds, helped to break down the cohesive strength of the German officer corps, making it less likely that any action against Hitler could have been undertaken. At the same time the growth of the army with conscripts, most of whom were Nazis or Nazi sympathisers, meant that even had the officer corps decided to take action against Hitler, the men might well have refused to follow them. The Nazis' hold on the conscripted men was also strengthened by weekly indoctrination sessions.

Hitler, ever an astute judge of character, was very careful in how quickly he forced the army along. Although the generals had been taken aback by the size of the army Hitler desired they had gone along with him; the same applied to the large-scale introduction of armoured forces in homogeneous units; and they had even acquiesced in the matter of the ratio of 'tooth' to 'tail' forces, in which Hitler had held out for greater 'tooth' fighting units and smaller 'tail' logistics and communications units than was customary. But Hitler realised that he would have to tread carefully about when he committed his new army to action for the first time, as most army officers considered that the efficiency of the army had been adversely affected by an expansion well over the triple one normally considered the maximum. Fritsch had exemplified the generals' opinions when he issued dire warnings of what might have happened had other states decided to deal with Germany in 1934 after the abortive *Putsch* in Vienna.

■ Hitler's spur

The army, Hitler decided, would take more pushing in 1936, and he decided to re-occupy the Rhineland, which had been demilitarised by the Treaty of Locarno in 1925. The *Fuehrer* gave his generals only five days in which to plan the operation, which they did after great protests. Virtually the whole of the army had to be used for the operation, which took place on 7 March 1936. The generals were ready for an immediate withdrawal in the event of French or British armed intervention, as Germany could not deploy any reserves. Yet Hitler stood firm, France and Britain did nothing, and the operation was a total success. In purely military terms the generals had been right, but Hitler's amazing intuitive combination of political and military opportunism had prevailed. For the first time in 'combat', the *Fuehrer* had showed himself the 'strategic superior' of his staff generals, and his moral ascendency over his 'pusillanimous' commanders continued to grow, as did his belief in his *schlafwandlerische Sicherheit* or sleepwalker's assurance when it came to matters relating to foreign affairs.

Hitler's next venture was the despatch of small forces, with an assortment of the latest German equipment, to help the Nationalist cause of General Francisco Franco against the Republicans in the Spanish Civil War. Once again the generals complained that the despatch of all the equipment left the forces at home with great shortages, with dire results should any military action have to be undertaken. But Hitler insisted, and in the event was proved right. His forces greatly aided Franco, and at the same time learned much of vital importance both about the equipment and about tactics. That some incorrect conclusions were also drawn was the fault of the generals, not of Hitler.

Despite the fears of his commanders, all went well, and Hitler turned his thoughts to his next conquest. There were still grave problems with the expansion of the army, not least of which was Hitler's insistence that no sooner had a formation reached a high level of efficiency than it should be divided into two, each half going to form the cadre of a new division. Thus although the army continued to grow swiftly, there was no efficient and inviolate nucleus that could fight at a moment's notice should the need arise. Fears about Germany's strategic position were also raised at this time, January 1937, by General Ludwig Beck, *Chef des Generalstabs des Heeres* or Chief of the Army General Staff since July 1935. The nation, Beck pointed out, was surrounded by potential enemies who might, individually or collectively, cut off Germany's access to a great number of essential raw materials and foodstuffs. Although Germany had made great strides under the leadership of Hitler, Beck continued, there were virtually no stockpiles of basic foodstuffs for animals and humans, nor were there stockpiles of the strategic materials for war, such as oil, rubber, tungsten, copper, tin, platinum, nickel, iron ore, chemicals etc. Beck was absolutely right, and the closing years of the war were to prove it. Germany's civilians starved, and her armed forces were immobilised for lack of fuel, tires to run on, and shortages of high-quality explosives.

■ Strategic visions

Hitler was not overly concerned, however, and in November 1937 he confided his strategic plans to his senior military and political subordinates: 'The aim of German policy is to make secure and to preserve the racial community and to enlarge it. It is, therefore, a matter of living space [*Lebensraum*]', which was to be acquired by force in central and eastern Europe. First of all Austria and Czechoslovakia had to be taken over, and it was his 'unalterable resolve to solve the problem of Germany's space by 1943–1945 at the latest'. To say that his audience was dumbfounded would be an understatement. Even Goering objected to the plan, but Hitler was determined that now all should obey him. He had already decided that there must be a showdown with the army, and this may have prompted the timing of the meeting, recorded for posterity by Colonel Friedrich Hossbach, the *Fuehrer*'s military adjutant and later an army commander on the Eastern Front.

Hitler was strengthened in his resolve to have it out with the army once and for all by the campaign of slanders being waged against Fritsch by Himmler and his subordinate Reinhardt Heydrich, the head of the *Sicherheitsdienst* or SS Security Service. The two SS men constantly urged it upon Hitler that the completely apolitical Fritsch was the leader of a group of army generals plotting to overthrow Hitler. This, combined with a memorandum submitted by army chaplains, with Fritsch's approval, condemning the Nazi perversion of Christianity, so infuriated Hitler that he resolved to deal with his high command.

The army unwittingly played into the *Fuehrer*'s hands. Blomberg, who had reached the rank of Field-Marshal in April 1936 had recently married for a second time in January 1938. It was now revealed that the *Frau Generalfeldmarschall* had been convicted for prostitution and for posing for obscene photographs. Beck persuaded Fritsch that Blomberg would have to be dismissed from his post as Minister of Defence. Fritsch thereupon approached Hitler and persuaded him that Blomberg had to be sacked. But who was to replace Blomberg? The obvious answer was Fritsch, but here Himmler and Heydrich appeared, like two *diaboli ex machina*, and informed Hitler that Fritsch was a homosexual, 'proving' it by producing a paid informer. Fritsch resigned on the spot. Hitler had thus rid himself of what he imagined were two troublemakers. But how was the army high command now to be reorganised? The answer was revealed on 4 February, when the retirements of Blomberg and Fritsch were announced. (Fritsch, it is worth noting, was subsequently cleared of all the allegations against him by a special army court of inquiry.) General Wilhelm Keitel, the head of the *Wehrmachtsamt* or Armed Forces Department, had been authorised to canvas candidates. He finally settled on General Walther von Brauchitsch, the commander of Army Group 4, who promised to try to bring the army into closer line with Nazi ideology. Brauchitsch took up his position as Commander-in-Chief of the Army or *Oberbefehlshaber des Heeres* with the rank of Colonel-General.

Of more far-reaching significance was the announcement that Hitler himself was to take over Blomberg's functions: 'Henceforth I will personally exercise immediate command over the whole armed forces. The former *Wehrmachtsamt* in the War Ministry becomes the *Oberkommando der Wehrmacht* (High Command of the Armed Forces), and comes immediately under my command as my military staff.' Salt was rubbed into the army's wounds caused by the final assumption of supreme power by the *Fuehrer* and the effective downgrading of the general staff, by the appointment to the head of the OKW of the nonentity Keitel, with promotion to Colonel-General in October. The army's last chance of freeing itself and Germany from Hitler had passed. If Fritsch had called upon the army to support him in January, there is every chance that a large portion of it may have done so. But now the chance had been lost, as Fritsch himself admitted in June 1938. As Hitler explored the possibilities of his new office, Brauchitsch set energetically to work to remove from important positions any potentially seditious officers.

The Germany army, which for centuries had been a power unto itself, and virtually a state within a state, had at last lost its autonomy, and was now merely another adjunct of the Nazi state. John Wheeler-Bennett puts it neatly in his *Nemesis of Power*: Hitler 'had outmanoeuvred, defeated, humiliated and dragooned the Germany army'. And this was only the beginning.

Two weeks after delivering his strategic appreciation to his commanders in November 1937, Hitler was visited by Lord Halifax, Nevile Chamberlain's Foreign Secretary. From what Halifax had to say about the need for a peaceful solution to Europe's problems, Hitler realised that British military strength no longer lay between him and his immediate objectives. He therefore speeded up his plans. First Austria was to be joined with Germany by an *Anschluss* or union. In February 1938 Hitler told the Austrian chancellor, Kurt von Schuschnigg, that unless the Austrian Nazi party were legalised and given a major share in power immediately, the German army would invade Austria to implement Hitler's conditions. After a series of delaying moves, during which Hitler ordered his armies to be prepared to march on 9 March, Schuschnigg resigned on the 11th, being replaced by Dr. Arthur Seyss-Inquart, the Austrian Nazi leader, who immediately sent out a pre-arranged telegram asking for German help. The generals had feared that the occupation would be chaotic, and they were very nearly right, the armoured formations in particular running into grave difficulties. Beck, now extremely worried about the subservient rôle of the army in German policies, had objected strongly to the whole venture, and Hitler determined that he would have to be replaced. But before he could do so, Beck resigned, totally embittered about the army's refusal to assume what he thought were its true responsibilities: 'If . . . [the generals'] advice and warnings are not listened to, then they have the right and the duty before their people and before history to resign their commands. If they all act with a determined will, the execution of an act of war becomes impossible. In this way they save the fatherland from the worst possible fate, from destruction.

'Any soldier who holds a leading position and at the same time limits his duty and task to his military charge, without being conscious of his supreme responsibility to the nation, shows lack of greatness and of understanding of his task.'

■ Another victim

Beck resigned on 18 August 1938, and was succeeded as Army Chief-of-Staff by General Franz Halder on 1 September. Halder had acquired an intense aversion for Hitler's ideas in the 'Blood Purge' of 1934, and at first followed Beck's policies of trying to moderate Hitler's progress towards war. But the West's capitulation to Hitler at Munich partially converted him to Hitler's opinions, and thereafter he mellowed towards Hitler quite considerably.

The *Fuehrer*'s next target was Czechoslovakia, starting with the Sudetenland. He demanded that these German-speaking areas be handed over to Germany; and despite Czech protests that with help from France and Great Britain they could handle the German army severely, Edouard Daladier and Nevile Chamberlain meekly handed Germany this important strategic frontier region of Czechoslovakia at Munich in September 1938. Hitler had told his generals to be prepared to invade Czechoslovakia if necessary, and the latter, although complying with the orders, had very grave reservations about the German army's ability to deal with the formidable Czech border defences, a miniature 'Maginot Line', but a far more powerful and well-planned one than the French *bête noire*. The loss of the Sudetenland sealed the fate of Czechoslovakia, and with it was lost a potentially able ally of the Western powers – and all for Hitler's assurance that it was his 'last territorial demand in Europe', so ensuring Chamberlain's devout wish for 'peace in our time'.

Yet Hitler was already thinking ahead. In May 1939, only two months after the occupation of the rump of Czechoslovakia on 15 March by German troops, Hitler informed his generals of his intentions of invading Poland, which might bring France and Great Britain finally to war, in turn necessitating the seizure of Belgium and Holland to prevent the British and French from occupying them. And on the eve of the signing of the Russo-German Non-Aggression Pact in Moscow on 23 August, Hitler told his generals that Russia would inevitably have to be crushed. There were no strenuous protests, just weary acceptance that the *Fuehrer*'s will be done. The German officer corps, and in particular its generals, had been emasculated by Hitler and had abandoned any attempts to control the type of war it would have to fight. All that was left was to fight an unwanted war as best it could – and its best, as will be seen, was very good.

THE REGALIA AND UNIFORMS OF HITLER'S GENERALS

The dress and equipment of Germany's generals reflect in some respects the fortunes of war of their armies. In the prewar and early war years they rode in recognisable staff cars or command vehicles and wore striking red-striped breeches and riding boots. By the end of the war they travelled in little *Kubelwagen* jeeps clad in the functional uniforms issued to the men at the front. In 1939 the basic uniform of an officer of the rank of *Generalmajor* or above consisted of a greeny-grey tunic with four pleated pockets and a stand and fall collar. He wore darker grey breeches and high black boots. A grey cap, trimmed with gold piping, had a gold chin strap cord and a shiny black peak.

A feature which distinguished all officers from men was a brown belt with a twin-claw buckle. Generals had the national emblem woven in gold thread on their tunic, gold oak-leaves on a red background on their collars, and twisted gold and silver cord epaulettes with a series of silver 'pips' or stars up to the crossed batons of a *Generalfeldmarschall*. An exception to this rule were the six general officers who held the honorary rank of regimental '*Chef*' or Colonel-in-Chief. Rundstedt, who was the *Chef* of 18 *Infanterie-Regiment*, wore the epaulettes of *Generalfeldmarschall* and the parade-quality collar patches of an infantry officer.

The theatres and units with which generals served affected their dress and uniforms. In 1940 Eduard Dietl, the popular commander of the 3rd Mountain Division at Narvik, wore the long baggy trousers and heavily studded boots of the mountain troops. In place of the issue cap he wore the distinctive *Bergmuetze* with the *Edelweiss* badge on the left side.

A year later, in North Africa, the Germans adopted a uniform designed by the Tropical Institute in Berlin. Though the extremes of temperature at night meant that they needed greatcoats, or the fine-grain grey leather coats that officers were permitted to buy, all *Afrika Korps* personnel wore the comfortable open-neck tunic when the weather was hot. Rommel favoured his grey European service cap, though generals like Thoma and Ravenstein wore the characteristic *Afrika Korps* cotton drill cap, edged with gold piping.

The savage winters of Russia meant that officers and men alike adopted the extemporised cold-weather uniforms worn in the first winter campaign. The issue greatcoat was trimmed with fur and reinforced with leather, or entire coats were made of sheepskin. In place of their caps they wore heavy fur or felt caps with ear-flaps. Later in the war, when the two-piece reversible quilted winter uniform became available, this was worn by all ranks.

One of the privileges of rank enjoyed by senior officers was the freedom to wear their own style of an issued uniform. Rommel had his own tropical uniform, which later became an accepted style of dress for the Mediterranean. Lieutenant-General Count von Schwerin wore a tailored M1944 battledress style blouse and long trousers, with the addition of general's epaulettes and collar patches and re-styled pockets.

When wearing camouflaged uniforms the Army, like the Waffen-SS, had a range of special rank insignia. For generals these consisted of a series of yellow stripes on a black background surmounted by crossed oak-leaves and acorns. These stripes were sewn to the upper sleeves of the camouflaged smocks or jackets.

■ Few medals

Waffen-SS officers, however, had an entirely different system of collar patch insignia, though their epaulettes were almost identical to those of the Army. An SS *Oberfuerhrer* or Brigadier-General had two stylised oak-leaves on his collar, whilst an *Oberstgruppenfuehrer* or Colonel-General had three oak-leaves and three pips.

Unlike the Army, the SS had been wearing camouflaged uniforms since the beginning of the war. Many of their senior officers were younger than men of equivalent rank in the Army, and in the spirit of the *Waffen*-SS affected an aggressive style in neat camouflaged uniforms and battered service caps or helmets with camouflaged covers.

The German attitude to medals and awards may seem unusual to some readers. There was only one true campaign medal, the 'Frozen Meat Medal', for men who had served on the Eastern Front during the winter of 1941–1942. When awards were given for campaigns they took the form of cuff-titles or arm-shields. The cuff-titles included ones for the attack on Crete and the campaign in North Africa, whilst those for the defence of Metz in 1944 and of Kurland in 1945 were designed but never issued.

The arm-shields, in white or yellow metal, began with one awarded to troops who served at Narvik in 1940, but the majority were awarded for operations on the Eastern Front, including Kholm in 1942, the Crimea in 1941–1942, and the Kuban in 1943. There was also a range of pin-backed badges awarded to men who had been wounded or participated in infantry, tank, or 'General Assault' attacks. Many of these were worn by generals who, liking to be up with their lead units to exercise personal control of the battle, had become involved in tank or infantry actions.

Among the decorations for valour were the range of Iron Cross medals. Originally instituted in 1813 by King Friedrich Wilhelm of Prussia, they were renewed in all the subsequent European wars. Though they were intended to be a 'Decoration for Merit in front of the enemy' they came to be awarded to generals who had conducted successful operations, and later as diplomatic sweeteners to officers in Axis armies. The Iron Cross, with the exception of two special awards, reached its zenith with the Knight's Cross with Oak-Leaves, Swords and Brilliants, while at the bottom was the Iron Cross, Second Class. Generals who had won the Iron Cross in World War I were entitled to wear a bar when they won it in World War II. It consisted of a pin-backed badge of an eagle and swastika, with the date 1939 at the base. Generals like Rommel and Bock, who had won the premier award of World War I, the *Pour le Mérité*, wore this neck decoration in addition to their Knight's Cross.

■ Batons and pennants

The Field-Marshal's baton produced by The Third Reich was a massive, ornate object similar to those awarded to Napoleon's marshals over 100 years earlier. Understandably, it was used only at the most formal occasions; for everyday use men like Rundstedt used an *Interimstab*, a lightweight staff similar to a British RSM's stick. Topped in silver and lacquered black, it had a tassel in the German national colours of black, white, and red.

In the early years of the war generals openly displayed their car pennants, rather like a general's stars on American or British vehicles. These pennants were metal flags which denoted a headquarters group or commanding officer. They could also be detached and displayed like a British Army Tactical Sign. The HQ symbol for an army group was a rectangular flag divided into quarters of red and black with a white border; the army HQ symbol was similar, but without the border. A corps HQ had a rectangular flag, with four triangular sections, whilst a division had a triangular pennon with red, white, and black bands. During the days when Germany had air superiority many vehicles, including staff cars, had swastika flags draped over their bonnets. When captured vehicles were used, they were boldly marked with the national emblem of a black cross with a white border.

The German vehicles used by senior officers ranged from converted half-tracks, tanks or armoured cars, the heavy Horch 4 × 4 Kfz 21 convertible *Kommandeurwagen* and the medium 4 × 4 Kfz 15 Horch and Opel, down to the jeep-type Porsche and Volkswagen *leichte Personenkraftwagen*.

■ Personal transport

Whilst Germany was on the offensive her generals needed large, fast vehicles which could carry the staff and communications equipment, allowing them to keep in touch with the changing battlefield. Photographs show Guderian in a half-track packed with radio equipment and signallers, whilst Rommel used a Fieseler *Storch* liaison aircraft in North Africa.

As Germany's fortunes turned, however, partisans and ground-attack aircraft made it essential that her generals become more anonymous. In Italy in 1944, General von Senger und Etterlin recalled: 'Every time I drove to the front now, I had to pass through a guerrilla-infested district. Normally I drove in the little Volkswagen and displayed no general's insignia of rank – no peaked cap, no gold or red flags . . .'

Many generals had a more informal attitude to their transport than their opposite numbers from Britain or the United States. *Oberstgruppenfuehrer* Paul Hausser hitched a lift on a half-truck during the fighting around Khar'kov, whilst Rommel did forward reconnaissance in an unarmoured soft-top vehicle and used a captured British armoured command vehicle, called '*Mamut*', to provide him with a mobile communications base.

THE MILITARY CONSPIRACY AGAINST HITLER

Why did the German generals of World War II choose to be led to destruction by Adolf Hitler, instead of pulling him down and putting him on trial for his crimes? This obvious question does not have a single answer; but certainly a major reason why the generals shunned such a decision was that it would have been a clear act of treason against the man who had raised Germany (and, in the process, themselves) to unprecedented heights of power and military glory.

This was the most popular excuse put up by the generals when they were interrogated and tried after Germany's defeat. Another obvious – and fair – claim was that a coup against Hitler would certainly have been against the wish of the German people, whose morale did not crack even when the Allied mass air-raids began in 1942. After all, down to November 1942 Germany was winning victory after victory, and those victories (like the *Fuehrer's* bloodless triumphs in the prewar years) were all very much to the credit – and interest – of the army.

But it was all very well for the German generals to plead conscience as a bar to acting against Hitler: they also knew quite enough about the atrocities and repression which kept Hitler's 'New Order' in being. Instead of agreeing that those atrocities disgraced both Germany and the German army, and that no oath of allegiance to the man on whose authority they were committed could be considered binding, they looked the other way. The most the Army High Command (OKH) ever did by way of protest was to ask that 'house-cleaning' by the *Gestapo* and SS murder squads should not begin until the army had pulled out. The generals, in fact, did not want to get their hands dirty; and they always preferred to fall back on the comforting claim that the army must stay out of politics.

142

Initially, however, there were indeed no reasons for the generals to conspire against Hitler: the promises he had made to the army were more than adequately kept. They thought they were using him; but in fact they never got the chance.

On 2 August 1934, when Hitler's new combined rôle as *Fuehrer* and Reich Chancellor was announced, every officer and ranker in Germany took the fateful oath of allegiance to their new overlord quoted in the first chapter.

The wording was perfectly clear – unambiguous in every respect. It was meant to be. For every German soldier who took that oath – and it was done by means of mass, repeat-after-me parades all over Germany – any future criticism of Hitler, let alone any attempt to tamper with his authority, was treason pure and simple in the legal meaning of the word. And the oath of loyalty of 1934 overshadowed the story of the military resistance to Hitler from beginning to end.

■ Moral ascendancy

But the generals were not unwilling to oust Hitler merely because they were afraid of committing treason. One of the *Fuehrer*'s first acts was the carefully stage-managed proclamation that the restrictions imposed on Germany's armed forces by the victors of World War I no longer existed. On 16 March 1935 conscription was announced together with the open secret of the new German air force, the *Luftwaffe*, and the expansion of the German army to 36 divisions – 15 more than the general staff had considered reasonable. This public 'breaking the shackles of Versailles' also had an immense effect on the morale of the generals. Hitler had made soldiering an honourable calling once more in Germany, and had kept his word to foster the development of the German armed forces.

Then came a third factor: the repeated successes of Hitler in strengthening the *Reich*, expanding its territories to unprecedented extents while making its frontiers progressively easier to defend: the Rhineland was reoccupied by German troops – March 1936; Austria was annexed by the Reich – March 1938; the Czech Sudetenland, peopled largely by racial Germans, was ripped away from Czechoslovakia (together with that country's most powerful defences) by the international agreement at Munich – September 1938; and what was left of the Czech heartland was occupied as a 'Protectorate' – March 1939. On every one of these occasions the generals forecast armed intervention by Germany's neighbours and total defeat, while Hitler's assurances that the German troops would march in unmolested were proved triumphantly correct. Never in her history had Germany achieved so much without going to war – another potent reason for the generals to back Hitler with enthusiasm. But there was another side to the coin. Every stage of this territorial aggrandisement had indeed been a nerve-racking gamble before it became apparent that Germany would get away with it again; and it was during this three-year period – March 1936 to March 1939 – that the generals' resistance to Hitler made its first tentative and completely unsuccessful stirrings.

On 5 november 1937, in a long and rambling monologue, Hitler told Blomberg, Fritsch and Raeder that his expansionist plans for Germany must make another European war inevitable in time. Blomberg, Fritsch and Foreign Secretary Neurath protested, and Hitler reacted by the early sacking of all three. The excuse for the dismissal of Blomberg was comparatively easy to find, for the general made the mistake of marrying a former prostitute. But a monstrous frame-up was engineered for Fritsch, the charge being that he had disgraced the officer corps by indulging in homosexual relations – an utter lie that incensed the officer corps, which had the highest respect for Fritsch. The generals demanded a court of inquiry to exonerate Fritsch. But before they got their verdict of 'Not Guilty' the triumph of the Austrian *Anschluss* reduced the trial to secondary importance. Fritsch was completely cleared of the charge but the army never got its commander back. After getting rid of Blomberg and Fritsch, Hitler strengthened his own hand by setting up the OKW, the *Oberkommando der Wehrmacht* (Armed Forces High Command) with himself as C-in-C and the pliant General Wilhelm Keitel as chief-of-staff. The new commander for the army was General Walther von Brauchitsch, newly married to a fanatical Nazi.

General Ludwig Beck, army chief-of-staff, was retained in his post, however; and it was Beck who decided that the army must act against Hitler if the risks the *Fuehrer* was courting should lead to war.

Convinced that Hitler's obsession with the reduction of Czechoslovakia had in fact made war inevitable, Beck resigned in August 1938. He had hoped that this act would trigger off a wave of protest in the army high command, but was utterly mistaken. Nevertheless, Beck had succeeded in engineering an embryonic conspiracy of army generals. Beck's successor, Franz Halder, was also prepared to act against Hitler in the last resort. So were the following: Erwin von Witzleben, C-in-C Berlin Military District; Erich Hoepner, Panzer commander; and Erwin von Stulpnaegel, Army Quartermaster-General. But the plan they considered to arrest and try Hitler rather than go to war over Czechoslovakia came to nothing when Hitler won his greatest-ever bloodless conquest at Munich. The conspirators did not have to act – and they had the nerve to blame this on Nevile Chamberlain!

■ Constant delays

Within six months the renewed danger of war – this time over Poland – caused further heart-searchings among the generals. These were again largely dispelled by Hitler's astonishing diplomatic coup in concluding a non-aggression pact with Stalin's Russia. This totally isolated Poland and gave the *Wehrmacht* the best possible chance of smashing the Polish army in a knock-out campaign. It was never the fear of war which caused the generals to think of dealing with Hitler: it was the thought of war coming before Germany was strong enough to win. As it was, fuel and ammunition stocks were dangerously low for Germany at the outbreak of World War II and the *Wehrmacht* could certainly not have fought an all-out war on two fronts.

Germany was spared this, however, by the total inability and strategic unwillingness of Britain and France to attack on the Western Front in September 1939. By the end of the first three weeks of the war the Polish army had been shattered and the campaign was over in all but name. Even before Warsaw finally capitulated on 28 September units were being pulled back for the redeployment for the decisive battle in the West.

Hitler's initial determination to attack in the West in November 1939 – which the army high command considered a military impossibility – sparked off the so-called 'Zossen Conspiracy', named after the headquarters of the army. Here everything turned on Halder's efforts to get Brauchitsch to stand up to Hitler, and Brauchitsch was a broken reed. His nerves were not up to the strain of confronting Hitler, and he also suffered from heart trouble. When he finally screwed up the courage to try and persuade Hitler to call off the offensive, on 5 November, he limited himself to warning of bad weather and shaky troop morale. This sent Hitler off into an explosion of rage, after which Brauchitsch returned to his HQ on the verge of total nervous collapse. Within 48 hours, however, Hitler postponed the offensive and the immediate crisis was over.

After the early wilting of the 'Zossen Conspiracy', the only part played by Brauchitsch and Halder inhibiting Hitler's plans was an indirect one inspired by professional stuffiness. The chief-of-staff of General von Rundstedt, commanding Army Group 'Centre' in the West, was General Erich von Manstein, who was convinced that the existing plan could only result in undecisive deadlock along the line of the Somme. He came up with a revolutionary plan to smash the centre of the Allied front, drive to the Channel, and isolate the Belgian, British and French armies in Flanders; and forwarded repeated memoranda on the subject to Halder and Brauchitsch at OKH. The latter, however, sat on Manstein's idea and refused to send it on to Hitler via OKW. Only at the end of January 1940 did a chance visit to Rundstedt's HQ by the *Fuehrer*'s aide, Colonel Schmundt, reveal Manstein's ideas to Hitler, who adopted them with enthusiasm.

For his part, Hitler showed the greatest astuteness in turning Brauchitsch's feeble excuses against the generals and shortening their leash still further. On 23 November 1939 he harangued all general staff officers and many senior commanding officers in the Reich Chancellery in Berlin. Harping on how he had always confounded his critics by proving to have been right, he accused the generals of being lacking in fighting spirit. By thus impugning their loyalty and professional competence, Hitler played very cleverly on the generals' consciences. The basic oath of allegiance, the accusation of not being up to the job – these were potent weapons. And the result was that the generals flung themselves into the tasks which faced them in 1940 without a flicker of further opposition – not even when the invasion of Britain was called off and the conquest of Soviet Russia was mooted as the master-stroke which would win the war. Moreover, with each campaign another factor being to inhibit the generals who still had doubts: the belief that it would surely be treasonable to turn against the head of the German state, not so much because of the oath of allegiance but because enemies of the Reich still remained in the field. Halder in particular found this a decisive stumbling-block. And so the Russian campaign began on 22 June 1941 – the gamble by which the German army – and only the army – could win the war for Germany. In both the planning and execution of the initial attack, the dedication of the generals was unanimous.

Cracks appeared in this unanimity before the Russian war reached its first great turning-point at Moscow in December 1941. Hitler had laid it down that the niceties of war were to be denied the Russians. Prisoners of war were not to be treated according to the provisions of the Geneva Convention. And the notorious 'Commissar Order' made it the duty of the advancing army to shoot all officials of the Communist Party on capture. (Brauchitsch and Halder eased their consciences by passing this order down the chain of command with the rider that it was only to be carried out 'provided the morale and discipline of the troops are not endangered thereby'.) The generals had taken this barbarous brief without a murmur of protest. But once in Russia, despite the smashing initial victories – it was the most successful campaign the *Wehrmacht* had ever fought – they were soon forced to accept that they were faced by an enemy who did not know that he was beaten, and had space and numbers – not to mention superior tanks – on his side. And in Russia, during summer 1941, the conspiracy against Hitler stirred anew.

Chief-of-staff to Field Marshall von Bock, C-in-C Army Group 'Centre' on the Moscow axis of the Eastern Front, was Major-General Henning von Tresckow, who began to approach junior officers and brother generals he suspected of favouring Hitler's removal. He met with uneasy non-cooperation from the men who mattered: the army group and field army commanders. Bock's reaction: 'I do not allow the *Fuehrer* to be attacked!' Brauchitsch himself was approached. His reaction: 'If you persist in seeing me I shall have to place you under arrest.' Yet the key field-marshals and generals approached by the conspirators, while refusing point-blank to commit themselves, made no move at all to denounce their 'treasonable' subordinates. With no absolute guarantee of decisive backing by their chiefs, the conspirators were reduced to temporary impotence.

Meanwhile, the civilian conspirators in the Reich – foremost among them ex-ambassador Ulrich von Hassel – had hopes of winning over the army commanders in the West: Field-Marshal von Witzleben (C-in-C West) and General von Falkenhausen (C-in-C Belgium). Witzleben had promised to support the 'Halder Conspiracy' at the time of Munich and he still favoured Hitler's removal. But early in 1942 he took a brief sick leave to have his piles operated on, and while he was away Hitler replaced him with Field-Marshal von Rundstedt, who had been removed from the command of Army Group 'South' in Russia in December 1941. Witzleben's embarrassing complaint was speedily put to rights – but he was not much use to the conspirators, with no troops at his command and placed on the retired list. It was on this grotesque note that 1942 opened for the conspirators, who had by now adopted ex-army chief-of-staff Beck as their figurehead and provisional head of a German state should the army ever act and purge the Reich government of Nazi domination.

The slump in conspiratorial activity within the army ended dramatically with the disasters of the winter of 1942–43 and the equally disastrous spring of 1943. Stalingrad, El Alamein, the loss of all Libya and the retreat into Tunisia, the Anglo-American landings in French North Africa, and the apparent collapse of the Eastern Front shored up by brilliant improvisation (but for how long?); and the surrender of 91,000 soldiers at Stalingrad in February and of another 250,000 in Tunisia – here with a a vengeance was the writing on the wall, rammed home by the announcement of the Allied policy of 'unconditional surrender' to be demanded from the Axis. And by the approach of the summer of 1943 two invaluable German officers had been rendered ripe for conspiracy by the course of events: a brilliant staff officer, Colonel von Stauffenberg, badly wounded in Tunisia and painfully recovering in hospital; and the incomparable Rommel himself, sickened and disillusioned by Hitler's callous abandonment of his *Panzerarmee Afrika.*

■ New blood needed

Tresckow took up the running again in Russia. For months he had been goading the conscience of another key general Field-Marshal von Kluge, who had received substantial sums of money from the *Fuehrer*; but Kluge remained uneasily on the fence. And there was a new focus of resistance in Berlin: the HQ of the *Ersatzheer*, the Reserve Army, where General Olbricht was Chief of Supplies – and a close colleague of Tresckow's. And in Hitler's own HQ at Rastenburg in East Prussia there was General Stieff, an administrative officer who acted as explosives-keeper for the conspirators' bombs.

The Tresckow/Stieff partnership got off the mark with an abortive assassination attempt (which they code-named 'Flash') on 13 March 1943. Tresckow's aide Schlabrendorff asked a junior officer in Hitler's entourage to carry a present of 'brandy' back on Hitler's plane and hand it to Stieff. The idea was to blow up Hitler in the air, making it look like an accident. The bomb was duly taken aboard Hitler's plane, which took off on schedule – but nothing happened. The *Fuehrer* arrived back at Rastenburg safely. With incredible courage Schlabrendorff telephoned the bearer that a mistake had been made and that he would be arriving with the right package. He retrieved the bomb and investigated: the time-fuse had worked but a faulty detonator had saved Hitler's life.

After the failure of 'Flash' came the equally abortive suicide attempts, made by brave young officers who volunteered to get near Hitler with bombs in their pockets. This came to nothing because of the total unpredictability of Hitler's day-to-day timetable, which made it impossible for the volunteers to put any accurate setting on the time-fuses of their bombs.

By January 1944 the state of the army conspiracy was roughly as follows. The Reserve Army members possessed a plan to take over Berlin and the other key cities of Germany, placing all Nazi officers under arrest – a plan, ironically enough, approved by Hitler himself! 'Valkyrie' was its codename, and the pretext was the supposed danger posed by the millions of foreign workers in Germany staging a revolt. At their posts on the Eastern Front, Tresckow, Schlabrendorff and their colleagues continued their activities unmolested, as did Stieff at OKW. A vital recruit to the conspiracy was General Fellgiebel, a communications officer, whose rôle would be to see to it that OKW was cut off from the rest of Germany when the right moment came. Rommel was being sounded out as to whether or not he was prepared to join the conspiracy and by the end of February he had made up his mind to do so. Most important of all was the sense of optimism and determination generated by Stauffenberg, who was back in harness after convalescing from his wounds, as chief-of-staff first to Olbricht and then to General Fromm, C-in-C Reserve Army. In the latter job Stauffenberg had regular access to the presence of Hitler himself.

The spring and early summer of 1944 were wasted by the conspirators' deluded belief that they could negotiate a separate peace with the British and Americans, give up their conquests in the West, and concentrate their energies against Russia alone. Undercover negotiations via Allen Dulles, head of the Central Intelligence Agency, in Switzerland disillusioned them. And the invasion of Normandy on 6 June 1944 made them realise that the hour had finally come. In Stauffenberg, they had the man to meet the hour.

Within a week it was obvious that Rommel and Rundstedt, the German commanders in the West, were not going to push the Allies back into the sea; the Western Front was a reality. On 20 June the great Russian summer offensive broke upon Army Group 'Centre' in the East. Then, on 4 and 5 July, two key civilian conspirators, Adolf Reichwein and Julius Leber, were arrested by the *Gestapo*. It was vital to act before the full extent of the conspiracy was revealed by their torture; and Stauffenberg was the only man for the job. But the obsession with eliminating Himmler and Goering along with Hitler forced Stauffenberg on two occasions – 11 and 15 July – to abandon his plan of leaving a fused briefcase bomb in Hitler's presence, simply because conditions were not right for the killing of all three. On Stauffenberg's own insistence it was agreed that he should make another attempt to blow up Hitler on his next summons to OKW; and on 19 July he was summoned to report at Rastenburg for a conference on the 20th.

The results of the 'Twentieth of July' are well known. Stauffenberg's bomb exploded within six feet of Hitler but did not kill him. Stauffenberg bluffed himself out of the Rastenburg complex and set off for Berlin. Fellgiebel passed word to Olbricht that the bomb had gone off and then set about sabotaging Rastenburg's communications – but the plotters in Berlin decided to wait for Stauffenberg's return and personal confirmation of Hitler's death. Three vital hours were wasted before Stauffenberg desperately began to make up for lost time – too late. Prompt and effective countermeasures rounded up the Berlin plotters and the coup was over.

It was only the last of a long line of plots, but it failed for the same reason that wrecked them all: the refusal of the key generals to commit themselves until they knew for sure that Hitler was dead. Muddled concepts of duty and a refusal to hazard all that had been gained under Hitler – both for themselves and, to be fair, for Germany – blurred their reasoning. At the time of the 'July Plot' German armies stood everywhere on foreign soil (as at the time of the 1918 armistice) and the frontiers of the Reich were not menaced until the autumn.

This narrow-minded selfishness, this uneasiness at anything that threatened the traditional apolitical mystique of the German officer corps, lay at the root of the German generals failure to their country between 1933 and 1945. Originally they thought they could use Hitler; the fact that he could reduce the vast majority of them to putty in his hands was a traumatic shock from which they never recovered. As with the entire population of Germany under the Nazis, it was so much easier to don mental blinkers and plunge oneself in one's job.

Thus some of the most shaming documents of World War II are those German army memoranda and communications requesting that the army should not get its hands dirty with the by-products of genocide which their conquests, as they knew perfectly well, unleashed. But it is only marginally more shaming than the story of their conspiracies. Success in the latter could only have been achieved by detailed planning and cool, decisive action, and their combined talents in that direction made them the best-trained and organised band of potential conspirators in Nazi Germany. For in the last analysis, detailed planning and decisive action are a general's daily bread.

THE WESTERN FRONT
THE CAMPAIGNS IN FRANCE AND THE LOW COUNTRIES

Although Hitler had been of the opinion that Great Britain and France would not come to the aid of Poland by declaring war in September 1939, he reacted with typical swiftness to their declaration by demanding plans for an invasion of France from his high command. An invasion was originally planned for the end of 1939, but the weather intervened to prevent this taking place. Other plans, all based on a modification of the World War I Schlieffen Plan, were then devised for 1940. Various delays ensued, giving General Erich von Manstein the opportunity to go over the heads of his immediate superiors to recommend another plan to Hitler. The revised Schlieffen plan, so Manstein thought, was too obvious a move, and the Allies would have prepared a means of countering it. Rather than use this simple right-hook through Belgium, along the French north coast and then down past the west of Paris, Manstein urged a far more daring plan, based on the mass use of the Panzer forces available.

In Manstein's plan, which Hitler adopted with enthusiasm over the lingering doubts of his high command, powerful armoured forces would strike right through the weakly defended Allied centre in the Ardennes and launch a short left-hook up to the French coast near Calais. This would cut the Allied armies in half, allowing the pocket trapped on the coast to be mopped up by Army Groups 'A' and 'B' before the rest of France was overrun by the combined forces of Army Groups 'A', 'B' and 'C'. It was a courageous plan, making full use of surprise and the advantages of speed and firepower that the massed armoured formations would enjoy.

The Allies, on the other hand, had as Manstein feared considered the overwhelming possibility of another Schlieffen Plan, and had deployed their forces accordingly. As Belgium and Holland were still neutral, the bulk of the British and French forces were based in northern France, to which the Maginot defence line did not extend. This costly, and in the event entirely useless, static line defended France from Longuyon, just west of southern Luxembourg, down to the Swiss frontier. Once Germany moved west into Belgium, as was almost certain, the Allied forces in the north were to move forward into positions along the River Dyle to check a 'Schlieffen' move.

■ Three army groups

The German armies were deployed in three major concentrations. In the north, opposite Holland and northern Belgium, was General Fedor von Bock's Army Group 'B', of 26½ infantry and three Panzer divisions, in two armies. In the centre, from Aachen to the south of Luxembourg, was General Gerd von Rundstedt's Army Group 'A', of 35½ infantry, three motorised and seven Panzer divisions, in three armies together with *Panzergruppe* 'von Kleist'. In the south, between southern Luxembourg and Switzerland, was General Ritter von Leeb's Army Group 'C', of 19 infantry divisions, in two armies. Reserves totalled 42 infantry divisions. Overall command was exercised by Hitler himself through Brauchitsch, the commander-in-chief of the army, and Keitel, the chief-of-staff. The centre-piece of the German offensive was to be the armoured punch of Hoepner's XVI Panzer Corps (6th Army of Army Group 'B'), Hoth's XV Panzer Corps (4th Army of Army Group 'A'), and Reinhardt's XLI and Guderian's XIX Panzer Corps (*Panzergruppe* 'von Kleist' of 12th Army of Army Group 'A').

The Allied armies were also poised in three major concentrations. In the north, as far south as central Luxembourg, was General Gaston Billotte's 1st Army Group, of 36 infantry, two motorised, and three light mechanised divisions, in five armies including the nine-division British Expeditionary Force. In the centre, between central Luxembourg and Strasbourg, was General Gaston Pretélat's 2nd Army Group, of 36 infantry (including one British) divisions, in three armies. In the south, from Strasbourg to the Swiss frontier, was General Henri Besson's 3rd Army Group, of 14 infantry divisions in one army. Allied reserves in France consisted of 19 infantry and three armoured divisions.

In addition to the Allied forces were those of neutral Belgium and Holland, who both threw in their lots with the Allies once they were invaded. Belgium could field 18 infantry divisions, with another four infantry divisions in reserve; Holland could supply eight infantry divisions, with two infantry divisions in reserve.

■ Fewer men

Germany's forces totalled some 2½ million men, with 2,574 tanks and nearly 2,750 aircraft. France and Great Britain had forces totalling some 2 million men, 3,609 tanks, and some 1,700 aircraft. The slight disparity in numbers of men was of little importance, but that in aircraft was. It enabled the *Luftwaffe* to dominate the skies above the German advance and provide the ground forces with excellent tactical support. The difference in tank numbers, however, was of crucial importance. Although the Germans had fewer vehicles, these were grouped into homogeneous formations, and had been carefully rehearsed in the doctrines and tactics of deep-penetration tank warfare. The Allies on the other hand had only three homogeneous armoured formations, and for these no adequate tactical theories had been evolved. The rest of the Allied tank strength was scattered amongst the field units to provide local infantry support. This was all the more tragic for the Allies as many of their tanks were qualitatively superior to the German vehicles, with better armour and heavier armament. The Dutch and Belgian armies fielded 400,000 and 600,000 men respectively under General H. G. Winkelman and King Léopold III.

The German offensive broke on 10 May with major efforts by Army Groups 'A' and 'B' into Belgium and Holland. The infantry advances into both countries were preceded by special attacks: parachute drops around Rotterdam and The Hague in Holland, to create havoc in the country and seize vital airfields; and a glider-borne attack on Fort Eben-Emael, the linch-pin of the Belgian defence line along the Albert Canal and River Meuse. With Eben-Emael neutralised, the German forces swept through the Belgian defences, which would otherwise have hampered them considerably. Isolated Belgian and Dutch pockets fought on bravely, but the very speed and strength of the German advance, coupled with the panic-stricken streams of civilian refugees fleeing from the German bombing, so confused matters that little co-ordinated defence could be offered to the Germans. Although the British and French had implemented their Dyle plan and moved forward into Belgium and western Holland, there was little that could be done. Holland was effectively beaten by the 14th, and Belgium by the day after.

■ Ardennes triumph

The real drama of the German offensive was taking place further south, however, in the Ardennes. Here the German Panzer forces swept through the wooded hills, which had been considered impassable to armour, and poured into the Meuse valley, where only inferior-grade French troops were stationed. XV and XIX Panzer Corps secured bridgeheads across the Meuse at Dinant and Sedan respectively, followed the next day by XLI Panzer Corps at Montherme. The move had to come as a complete surprise to the Allies, but what followed surprised them even more. Leaving their infantry units to follow as quickly as they could, the Panzer divisions set off in a mad rush to the English Channel coast, supported by the *Luftwaffe*. The Panzer columns' surest defence was the complete surprise of the Allies. The German armour raced through Cambrai and Arras on the 18th, and by the 20th had reached Abbeville and the coast at Noyelles. By the 25th Boulogne had fallen, and with the arrival of the German infantry, the Allied armies in the north were completely cut off by the 'Panzer corridor'. By the 21st, the corridor's southern flank had been established along the line of the Rivers Somme and Aisne.

The Allied armies in the north had realised quickly the import of the German armoured advance – not only were they cut off, but also completely outflanked on their right. Immediately they fell back, but it was already too late. A small armoured force under Colonel C. de Gaulle had attempted to cut the Panzer corridor without anything but some good tactical successes between 17 and 19 May, but now a more ambitious scheme was evolved by General Maxime Weygand, who had taken over supreme command from General Maurice Gamelin on 19 May. French armour was to strike north across the River Somme past Albert to link up with a British thrust coming south from Arras. Scheduled for 21 May, only the British half of the pincer materialised, and although it made good progress in its attempt to cut the corridor, it was doomed without its French counterpart.

In the north the Germans were now gradually squeezing the Allied pocket back towards the Channel ports in a series of concerted armoured and infantry assaults. By the 25th the position was very difficult, and despite Hitler's order that the Panzers were to advance no further, the surrender of Belgium on the 28th meant that the position in the Dunkirk beach-head was no longer tenable. Plans to evacuate the troops trapped in the beach-head to England were immediately implemented, and carried out with great courage and ability. By the time the evacuation was completed on 4 June, leaving the Germans in control of the Low Countries and France as far south as the River Somme, the navies of France and Great Britain, helped by some hundreds of small craft, had lifted some 338,000 men off the beaches around Dunkirk.

The Germans could now turn their attention to the rest of France. Despite a determined and very able defence of the River Somme line, the Germans broke through to the line formed by the Rivers Seine and Oise by the 12th, after starting their renewed offensive on the 5th. The French decided not to fight for Paris, which the Germans entered on the 14th. By now the French were beginning to break, and on 13 June the Germans poured over the Seine-Oise line, driving the French before them. On 10 June Italy had entered the war and invaded southern France, with risible results. The French armies were now in full retreat, and the Germans pressed on in a relentless pursuit south of Paris. Army Group 'B' passed through Rouen and then branched out to the west to take Brest on the 19th, and to the south-west to take Nantes and Saumur on the same date, reaching Royan on the 25th. By the 27th German troops had reached St Jean-de-Luz near the Spanish frontier. The troops of Army Group 'A' fanned out through Paris and Reims to take Tours, Orléans, Vichy on the 20th and Lyons by the same day. Other elements of Army Group 'A' swept the remnants of the French armies back against the Maginot Line, where they were trapped by Army Group 'C' and surrendered on the 22nd.

■ Pétain takes over

Paul Reynaud was succeeded as prime minister by Marshal Henri Pétain on 17 June, and the latter immediately sued for armistice terms, which were granted on the 21st. Hostilities between France on the one hand, and Germany and Italy on the other, ceased on the 25th, and France was partitioned into the Occupied and Unoccupied, or Vichy, Zones. French losses had been enormous, but they had inflicted very heavy casualties on the Germans as well. Nevertheless, the Germans had fought an excellent campaign, and further ironed out the lingering problems of their armoured theories. It is worth noting, however, that the Germans still had, and continued to have until the end of the war, problems with the different speeds attainable by the armour and their supporting infantry, a large proportion of which was still dependent on horse transport.

In 1944 the Allies were at long last ready to invade France and fight Germany into defeat on mainland northern Europe. A variety of plans had been devised for landings in northern France between 1942 and 1944, but finally it had been decided to land in Normandy rather than in the Pas-de-Calais. Careful security planning kept the Germans in ignorance of the landing area, although both Rommel and Hitler suspected that it was to be Normandy. The Allied plan finally adopted called for assault landings by Lieutenant-General Omar Bradley's US 1st Army and Lieutenant-General Sir Miles Dempsey's British 2nd Army, both elements of General Sir Bernard Montgomery's 21st Army Group, on beaches between the Caen area and the Cotentin peninsula. The naval forces escorting the landing forces were to be commanded by Admiral Sir Bertram Ramsay, and the air forces by Air-Marshal Sir Trafford Leigh Mallory. Overall Allied commander was General Dwight D. Eisenhower, with Air Chief-Marshal Sir Arthur Tedder as his deputy. The Allied armies totalled some one million men, in 45 divisions.

The German defence, under the theatre command of Rundstedt, was entrusted to Field-Marshal Erwin Rommel's Army Group 'B', with 30 infantry, two parachute and seven armoured divisions. Further south Blaskowitz's Army Group 'G' in southern France had 13 infantry and three armoured divisions to halt any invasion of the area. The Germans, although fairly strong numerically, were inferior troops compared with those who had conquered France in 1940, and their lack of air support meant that movement was restricted to nights. The Allies were able completely to dominate the skies over France during the reconquest of north-western Europe, and destroy German transport and armour whenever it appeared in daylight. Two final items put nails into the Germans' coffin. The armoured reserve that might have thrown back the Allies on the first day of the invasion was held too far back, against Rommel's wishes, and could only be used with Hitler's express authority; and the 'Atlantic Wall', so beloved of German propaganda, was a mere fiction in the Normandy area.

The Allied invasion began on 6 June, and after some desperate moments in the American sector, a good lodgement had been secured by the 10th. By the 30th the

Cotentin peninsula had been cleared, and Cherbourg was about to become the Allied main port. The British had run into determined opposition in and around Caen, however, and it was not until 20 July, after extremely heavy fighting, that the area was cleared. German defence was still strong, and the Allies were penned into their bridgehead. On 25 July, however, the US 1st Army broke out past St Lô after an exceptional heavy bombing attack had pulverised the German defences. By the 30th the Americans were in Avranches, and the German containment of the Normandy beachhead was unseamed.

■ Falaise Gap

The Allied forces were now reorganised into the 12th Army Group under Bradley, with the US 1st and 3rd Armies, commanded by Lieutenant-Generals Courtney Hodges and George Patton respectively; and the 21st Army Group under Montgomery, with the British 2nd and Canadian 1st Armies under Dempsey and Lieutenant-General Henry Crerar respectively. After the break-out to Avranches, Patton's forces fanned out to the west, into Brittany, and south and east towards Orléans and Paris. The British also broke out, past Falaise, closing the German pocket there just too late to trap considerable German armoured forces. Rundstedt had been replaced early in July as supreme commander in the west by Kluge, and when Rommel was injured on 17 July, Kluge also took over command of Army Group 'B'. But there was nothing Kluge could do to halt the Allied forces now sweeping, with overwhelming air support, towards Paris. Despite Hitler's orders that the French capital should be destroyed, it was not, and when the Allied forces arrived in the city on 25 August they found it in the hands of the French resistance. Kluge was now sacked, shortly afterwards committing suicide, his place as head of Army Group 'B' being taken by Model.

Meanwhile in the south the US/French forces of Lieutenant-General Alexander Patch's 7th Army had landed between Cannes and Toulon on 15 August, and in a remarkably swift advance swept up the Rhône valley to make contact with French forces of the 12th Army Group north of Dijon on 12 September. Most of the forces of Blaskowitz's 1st and 19th Armies managed to slip through to the east before the Allied armies joined up, however. Patch's forces, which later became part of the 6th Army Group under Lieutenant-General Jacob Devers, continued to press north into the Vosges area.

Further north the 12th and 21st Army Groups had advanced over the River Seine and had reached the *Westwall* or Siegfried Line between Aachen and Trier by 15 September, British forces having liberated Brussels on the 3rd of the month and Antwerp on the 4th. There now occurred the bold venture to seize the bridges over the River Rhine at Arnhem. The ground forces that were to have moved up to the positions seized by the British and Polish paratroops on 17 September could not advance fast enough, and the unexpectedly strong German forces in the area crushed the paratroops' positions by the 25th September. It was, however, a bold Allied operation, and perhaps deserved better success.

The Allies continued to press their advantages, and by 15 December had cleared the Germans from the Metz-Strasbourg corner of France with the exception of the Colmar pocket, had advanced into Holland as far north as the River Maas, and had broken through the Siegfried Line around Aachen.

Hitler's last throw in the West came as a complete surprise to the Allies. In this final major offensive Model's Army Group 'B' launched an attack through the Ardennes, with the aim of cutting through the Allies to Antwerp. But the scope of the offensive, which started on 16 December, was too great for the Germans. Fuel for the tanks began to run out, and the Allies failed to crumble away, as Hitler had expected. The Germans had shot their bolt by 24 December, and nothing was left to stop the Allies when they counter-attacked. The Germans had been driven back beyond their start lines by 7 February 1945.

On this date the Allies launched their major offensive towards the River Rhine, which they reached in a month of very heavy fighting. The Americans managed to secure a bridge across the river at Remagen, and quickly built up a formidable bridgehead against desperate German resistance. Another bridgehead was secured by the British east of Wesel. By the 27th the Allies had cleared the east bank of the River Rhine between Nijmegen to Mannheim, and were poised for the final advance into Germany to link up with the Russians from the east.

■ Ruhr pocket

At the end of March the Allies fanned out into Germany, a huge pocket being formed in the Ruhr industrial region. The British and Canadians advanced into northern Germany, reaching Hamburg on 3 May. The Americans moved east and south-east, reaching the River Elbe on 24 April and Česke Budejovice in Czechoslovakia by 7 May. The French and Americans moved south-east into Austria, reaching Linz on 5 May. By agreement amongst the political leaders, Berlin was the Russian prize, and the Allies halted along the line of the Elbe.

In 1944 and 1945 the Germans had stood less chance against the Allies than had been the case (the other way round) in 1940. Yet they fought with their normal tenacity and courage against overwhelming odds to check the Allied advance. That they managed to hold out for so long was a considerable feat.

FIELD-MARSHAL EWALD VON KLEIST

'If this Panzer Group had advanced on a single road its tail would have stretched right back to Koenigsberg in East Prussia, when its head was at Trier.' So said General Kleist in a conversation with Liddell Hart after the war. The magnitude of the German operation on the Belgian right flank can be gauged by the fact that by 10 May 1940 the Germans had massed 45½ divisions, including seven Panzer and three motorised along the 100-mile frontier. Whilst the men of Army Group 'B' were fighting in Belgium and Holland, the three armies of Army Group 'A' were filtering through the Ardennes and Luxembourg. They were deployed into three waves, armoured divisions in the first two and motorised infantry in the third. Behind them, in columns stretching back to the Rhine, came the infantry, marching through the dust of the Panzers singing the songs of the wars their fathers and grandfathers had fought against the French.

■ Drive to the Meuse

The country chosen for what was at the time the greatest concentration of tanks in the war had been described by some military experts as impassable for armour. The Ardennes region had few good roads, was heavily wooded with dense conifers, was intersected by steep valleys with streams and narrow bridges and had patches of marshland. Ideal defensive country – providing it was defended. General Blumentritt recalled afterwards that 'we met no resistance in Luxembourg, and only slight resistance in Belgian Luxembourg – from the *Chasseurs Ardennais* and French cavalry divisions. It was weak opposition, and easily brushed aside.

Had the French or Belgians been able to fly over the area they would have seen an awesome traffic jam grinding along every track and road that was practicable – with infantry using forest footpaths and lanes. However, the *Luftwaffe* provided air cover against reconnaissance and would later give bomber support at the critical Meuse crossing.

Two days after they had crossed the Belgian border the advanced guards of *Panzergruppe* 'Kleist' reached the Meuse and occupied the town of Sedan. The river in this area is about 60 yards wide, unfordable, and fairly fast flowing. The banks consist of a series of gentle wooded hills, sloping down to the river and affording good fields of fire on either side. To the north, between Mézières and Givet, the valley becomes steeper, with entrenched meanders. The Meuse sector was defended by two French armies, the 2nd and the 9th. They held a mixture of field fortifications and fixed concrete emplacements. The latter, however, were far from finished, lacking doors and armoured shutters over the embrasures.

The French 2nd Army, which held the Sedan-Mézières sector, was under the command of General Huntziger. It included two 'Series B' divisions, the 55th and the 71st, which consisted of men who were overaged, undertrained and inadequately armed.

The 9th Army, commanded by General Corap and covering the Mézières-Namur sector, contained similarly discouraging material. Of its seven infantry divisions, four were reservist and two of these, the 53rd and 61st Infantry Divisions, were 'Series B', while the 102nd Infantry was a 'Fortress' regular division.

Kleist, whose Panzer group consisted of XLI Panzer Corps under Reinhardt and XIX Panzer Corps under Guderian, decided that he would force the Meuse crossings on 13 May. On that morning the men of the 1st Rifle Regiment of the 1st Panzer Division, who were to spearhead Guderian's central thrust at Sedan, were worried. 'The French artillery was alert and the slightest movement attracted fire. The German artillery was held up on congested roads, and could not get into position in time, and neither the engineers nor the bulk of their equipment had reached the river.'

However, by ill fortune or bad planning Corap and Huntziger had positioned in a line from Monthermé to Sedan their three poorest divisions, the 61st, 51st and 71st Infantry Divisions. Against these men, with their inadequate training and poor equipment, Kleist would send Reinhardt's 6th and 8th Panzer Divisions and Guderian's 2nd, 1st and 10th Panzer Divisions.

On the left flank Guderian planned to put his troops over the Meuse at 1500 hours in three separate attacks. The 2nd Panzer Division on the right would cross at Doncherry. In the centre the 1st Panzer Division would assault Glaire, at the foot of a meander of the Meuse. The 1st would receive the greatest support from artillery and assault pioneers, and would be the chief recipient of potent assistance from the *Luftwaffe*. The 10th Panzer Division would cross south of Sedan and secure the high ground on the west bank of the Meuse above Pont Maugis.

Reinhardt had a tougher objective than Guderian. The river at Monthermé was more of a natural barrier, and the men of the French 102nd Infantry had been in position since the beginning of the war. Moreover, Reinhardt could not count on receiving the same volume of air support as Guderian.

Guderian had told his men that they would have 'the whole of the Luftwaffe' supporting their crossing – it was an exaggeration, but not far from the truth. They had the whole of *Fliegerkorps* I under Lieutenant-General Bruno Loerzer and *Fliegerkorps* VIII under Major-General Wolfram von Richthofen, a total of nearly 1,500 aircraft.

The effect of these attacks on the French troops covering the Meuse was terrifying. They pulverised the bunkers, overturned exposed gun positions and kept the men blinded by smoke and dust. Besides this, few men wanted to look over the parpapets of their positions, preferring to keep under cover. Meanwhile light and heavy flak guns were being moved down to the river to engage the French bunkers with direct fire.

■ River crossing

At 1500 hours the assault went in. During the afternoon's fighting the men of the 2nd Panzer Division exceeded the expectations of Kleist and Guderian, for their division had been slowed down on its approach march through the Ardennes. The French held the south bank in a line of heavily reinforced bunkers about 500 yards apart and 300 yards from the river. Covered by direct fire from tanks which had driven down to the river, however, German assault pioneers managed to get a foothold on the far bank by the evening, and throughout the night more men were ferried across.

In the centre the men of the élite *Grossdeutschland* Regiment and the 1st Rifle Regiment made rapid progress. Lieutenant-Colonel Balck of the 1st Rifle Regiment realised that it was essential that they capture a firm bridgehead, and by sunset on the 13th he had thrust three miles over the river to a ridge designated his objective. Without tank or artillery support he pushed a further three miles in the dark to a position south-west of the village of Chéhéry. In the middle of the crossings Guderian landed on the south bank of the Meuse and met Balck, who welcomed this front-line conference, but could not resist greeting his superior with 'Joy riding in canoes on the Meuse is forbidden!' – words used by Guderian during an exercise on the Moselle. Guderian had felt that the attitude of the younger officers had been too light-hearted at that time. 'I now realised that they had judged the situation correctly,' he commented.

To the south the 10th Panzer Division suffered many casualties in the first wave of its crossings, for it was under fire from flanking guns undamaged by the Stuka attack. Some units were pinned down on the north bank and withdrawn at nightfall, but individual detachments, notably the men of the assault pioneers, made a lodgement on the far bank and hung on, destroying French bunkers with their demolition charges.

■ Success – just

Down the river at Monthermé the men of Reinhardt's XLI Panzer Corps had one of the least successful crossings. They had scrambled down the steep rocks on the right bank to find the river shrouded in smoke. It was silent. The first pneumatic assault boat was launched, but as soon as it was exposed a machine gun opened up killing and wounding its crew. Tanks destroyed the bunker, but the stream carried the assault boats away from their launching point and wedged them in the spans of the demolished bridge at Monthermé. Here the engineers discovered that they were under cover and began to build an extemporised foot-bridge. By night fall the remainder of a rifle battalion had crossed the river and dug a defensive position.

Panzergruppe 'Kleist' had achieved its first objective – the culmination of staff wargames, air-ground liaison, numerous night marches in the wooded borders of Germany and infantry assault crossings of the Lahn and Moselle. They were over the Meuse – just.

COLONEL-GENERAL HEINZ GUDERIAN

'*Soldiers of the XIX Army Corps!*

'*For 17 days we have been fighting in Belgium and France. We have covered a good 400 miles since crossing the German border: we have reached the Channel Coast and the Atlantic Ocean. On the way here you have thrust through the Belgian fortifications, forced a passage of the Meuse, broken the Maginot Line extension in the memorable Battle of Sedan, captured the important heights of Stonne and then without a halt, fought your way through St Quentin and Péronne to the lower Somme at Amiens and Abbeville. You have set the crown on your achievements by the capture of the Channel Coast and of the fortresses at Boulogne and Calais.*

'*I asked you to go without sleep for 48 hours. You have gone for 17 days. I compelled you to accept risks to your flanks and rear. You never faltered.*

'*With masterly self-confidence and believing in the fulfilment of your mission, you carried out every order with devotion.*

'*Germany is proud of her Panzer divisions and I am happy to be your commander.*

'*We remember our fallen comrades with honour and respect, sure in the knowledge that their sacrifice was not in vain.*

'*Now we shall arm ourselves for new deeds.*

'*For Germany and for our leader, Adolf Hitler!*

signed, GUDERIAN'

Thus on 26 May 1940 General Heinz Guderian summed up the achievements of his men in an order of the day. There were greater victories to come (the corps was to thrust to the outskirts of Dunkirk), and by the end of World War II its commander was to rise to be Chief of the General Staff. However, as the climax of imaginative planning, good staff work and the application of the new doctrines or armoured penetration, the breakthrough at Sedan, and the drive to the Channel stand unrivalled.

The seven armoured and three motorised divisions (and their 35½ supporting infantry divisions) in Army Group 'A' had worked through the Ardennes and crossed the Meuse at Sedan and Monthermé. The men of Guderian's XIX Panzer Corps were installed in a bridgehead about five miles deep. While the infantry paused, awaiting the counterattack they felt must come, the engineers worked quickly to construct pontoon bridges to allow tanks and heavy weapons to cross the river.

The French had planned a two-pronged counterattack, but only one was ready on time. The 213th Infantry Regiment and the 7th Tank Battalion attacked the 1st Panzer Division near Chéhéry. It gained a temporary advantage, was held by a mixed defence of flak and anti-tank guns, and then for the loss of nearly half its tanks (light F. C. M. marks with 37-mm guns) it was crushed by the German armour.

There were to be other attacks by French armour, but each time they ran into Guderian's tanks and guns. In failing to attack the German infantry on the afternoon and night of the 13th–14th, when they were exposed on the south bank of the Meuse, the French were now to pay very heavily.

Feeling free to start the drive to the sea Guderian gave General Kirchner of 1st Panzer Division the dramatic order: 'For the right wheel, road map Rethel!' His forces were now to cross the Ardennes canal and break through what remained of the French defences.

■ Counterattack

During the 14th the Allies had attempted to destroy the German bridges at Sedan with air attacks. Their light bombers (Fairey Battles, Bréguets, Amiots and LeOs) braved the German flak and fighter screens. When they penetrated this defence their light bombs caused little damage, and even this was easily repaired. By the end of the day the Allies had lost nearly 90 aircraft. The RAF official history states that 'no higher rate of loss in an operation of comparable size had ever been experienced by the Royal Air Force'.

Despite these attacks, the lead elements of Guderian's forces pressed westwards. Colonel Balck had captured a crossing over the River Bar and the Ardennes canal near Omicourt. From this point to the River Somme at St Quentin it was rolling open farmland – perfect tank country. The 1st and 2nd Panzer Divisions began to move up.

On the south flank, the critical area of the whole breakout, Guderian had placed the élite *Grossdeutschland* Regiment. It was against them that the French deployed a company of heavy Char B tanks of the 3rd Armoured Division and a battalion of light H-39 tanks. Throughout 15 May the tanks of the 10th Panzer Division and the anti-tank guns of the *Grossdeutschland* Regiment fought the 3rd Armoured and 3rd Motorised Divisions. While other Frenchmen were scattering or surrendering these

162

tank crews showed a courage and *élan* of an earlier generation. By the end of the day the regimental commander of *Grossdeutschland* reported that his men had been forced out of Stonne and were 'in a state of complete physical exhaustion and hardly fit for combat'.

At 1730 the French launched their last and strongest counterattack towards the village of Chéhéry. Like so many of their attacks it had been delayed, and when it went in it was in insufficient strength. The tank crews fought bravely, but the attack was called off before it had achieved anything. The French had missed their last opportunity. On the following day fresh German units arrived and Stonne was recaptured. The south flank was secure.

Now nothing but new orders could stop Guderian. On 15 May Kleist had a 'fit of nerves' and ordered Guderian to halt so that infantry could catch up with him and so cover his south and south-east flanks. By the values of World War I these were sound tactics. But Guderian was fighting a new war and winning it because his adversaries were still thinking in World War I terms and time-scales. Guderian contacted the chief-of-staff of the *Panzergruppe*, Colonel Zeitzler, and then Kleist himself. After a heated exchange he received permission to advance for a further 24 hours.

Having regained his freedom Guderian drove to the front on 16 May to see the 1st Panzer Division. Here he met Colonel Balck, standing dust-covered and red-eyed in the blazing main street of the village of Bouvellemont. Earlier one of Balck's officers had said that the men were overtired and an attack on the village would not succeed. Balck picked up his walking stick and strode off with the reply: 'In that case I'll take the place on my own.'

Morale was soaring as the troops moved deeper into France. Guderian encountered tank crews of the 1st Panzer Division who shouted; 'Well done, old boy' and 'Did you see him? That was Heinz *der Rascher* (hurrying Heinz)'. 'All this was indicative,' comments Guderian.

At Montcornet he met General Kempf. Their two staffs worked out routes for the three Panzer divisions which were now roaring through the town. The two generals fixed the routes for their units (Guderian's 2nd and 1st Panzer, and Kempf's 6th Panzer, XLI Corps) and ordered that the advance go on 'until the last drop of petrol was used up'. By now the point sections had reached Marle and Dercy, 40 miles from their morning's start line and 22 miles from Sedan.

But now on the 17th, just as the battle was developing as Manstein had planned, Guderian, who was making it possible, received a message from *Panzergruppe*. He was to halt the advance and report to Kleist. The meeting was stormy, Kleist claiming that Guderian had disobeyed orders. Shocked and surprised, Guderian asked to be relieved of his command. Happily for the Germans they were not to lose their tank expert. Kleist accepted the resignation, but on behalf of Colonel-General von Rundstedt, head of Army Group 'A', Colonel-General List explained at the halt order came from OKW. List, commander of the 12th Army, understood the reasons for pressing on and authorised Guderian to carry out a 'reconnaissance in force'. The corps headquarters, however, must remain where it was so that OKW could keep in contact.

■ Enter de Gaulle

Welcoming the freedom implicit in these new orders Guderian left his corps headquarters at Soize and moved on with the tanks. His advanced headquarters were linked by telephone so that OKW and OKH monitoring units could not intercept any radio traffic between his two headquarters.

The delay had been frustrating for Guderian, but for his tank crews the 17th was a welcome break. There was time to get some sleep, service the tanks and allow supplies to catch up. It was also the day on which the French proposed mounting two counterattacks from the north and south on Guderian's 'Panzer corridor'. Only the attack from the south materialised on time, however.

The man chosen to lead the French 4th Armoured Division in this attack was Colonel Charles de Gaulle. His forces consisted of two battalions of obsolete R-35 tanks and one battalion of Char B tanks. Despite this his tanks fought their way to Montcornet 'destroying everything which had had no time to flee'.

It was a nasty moment, but again the Germans demonstrated that they could react quickly and extemporise a defence before collecting tanks for a counterattack. Using light flak units and some tanks which were returning from workshops, junior officers halted the French. One wrote afterwards: Here the lack of fighting spirit of the enemy became abundantly clear to us; German tanks against so weak a defence would certainly not have turned round.'

Whilst the drama of armoured attack and counterattack was being fought on the flanks and point, and whilst the generals argued and planned, the German infantry debouched from the Ardennes and marched over the pontoon bridges at Sedan. The Panzer corridor was now getting its infantry lining, and the fears of the more conventionally minded officers at the OKW were put to rest.

Guderian remained as far ahead as his telephone link would allow him. On the 19th his corps began to cross the World War I battlefield of the Somme. Rivers like the Somme, Aisne and Serre were an asset for the Germans – for covered by a screen of reconnaissance troops, anti-tank units and combat engineers they protected the south flank of the corridor.

■ Amiens falls

On the 19th de Gaulle attempted another attack. There was one disturbing moment when tanks from the 4th Armoured Division came within a few miles of Guderian's headquarters. It was protected only by some 2-cm flak guns, but Guderian dismissed the danger as 'a few uncomfortable hours until at last the threatening visitors moved off'.

A day earlier the German 2nd Panzer Division had captured St Quentin, whilst the 1st, after covering 30 miles in a morning, captured some bridges over the Somme. This was no longer war but a 'live firing exercise'. Guderian could have used the words of General George Patton in 1944, that he was 'touring on the continent with an army'.

By the evening of 19 May Guderian's XIX Panzer Corps had reached a line Cambrai-Péronne-Ham. The corps headquarters were moved forward to Marle and received full freedom of movement, without authorisation to move on to Amiens as from the 20th.

The following morning Guderian visited the 10th Panzer Division at Péronne, where they had taken over from the 1st Panzer Division. Here he heard that the impetuous Colonel Balck, who had taken command of the 1st Panzer Brigade when its commander, Colonel Nedtwig, had collapsed from exhaustion, had offended his successor, Colonel Landgraf. When taken to task for leaving Péronne so that he could be in on the assault on Amiens, Balck had cheerfully replied: 'If we lose it you can always take it again. I had to capture it in the first place, didn't I?'

Amiens was German by noon on the 20th and with it they held a bridgehead over the Somme four miles deep. Returning to Albert, Guderian encountered the 2nd Panzer Division, which 'was almost out of fuel and therefore proposed to stop where it was, but was soon disillusioned'. By adjusting available fuel stocks he gave them enough to reach Abbeville by 1900 hours. Tough with himself, Guderian was equally demanding of his men. He writes: 'One must always distrust the report of troop commanders: "We have no fuel". Generally they have. But if they become tired they lack fuel.'

During the night of the 19th/20th a reconnaissance unit of the 2nd Panzer Division passed through Noyelles. These tired, sweaty, dust-covered young men were the first Germans to reach the Channel. They were the men who had turned Hitler's dreams and Manstein's plans into reality.

XIX Panzer Corps had achieved its prime objective of cutting off the Allied armies in northern France and Belgium. Now it awaited orders. It waited for a day on the Somme. Visiting his units Guderian asked the tank crews how they had enjoyed the operations. An Austrian serving in the 2nd Panzer Division gave him a tough professional reply: 'Not bad, but we wasted two whole days.' 'Unfortunately,' comments Guderian 'he was right.'

FIELD-MARSHAL GERD VON RUNDSTEDT

Dignified and aristocratic in outlook with a tall, spare frame, Field-Marshal Gerd von Rundstedt was already an old man at the outbreak of World War II. He had always been wary of the British, and with America's entry into the war, the risk of an Allied invasion of the European continent increased.

Hitler persuaded Rundstedt to come out of retirement and take up the position of Commander-in-Chief West to meet this threat. Once again, Rundstedt obeyed the call to duty and took up command at St Germaine, France, in March 1942.

The task of defending Western Europe was a formidable one. The years 1942–43 were spent by the Western staff trying to forecast where the Allies might launch their attack. The possibilities for an invasion zone seemed endless – the Western theatre of operations stretched from Norway along the coast of Europe to Spain and along the Mediterranean to Greece.

During 1942, the German losses in the East were so devastating that from early 1943, no offensive policy could be envisaged for the West, and the planners concentrated on strategic defence. Great reliance was placed on the Atlantic Wall, a line of static fortifications on or near the coast, to halt the invasion. In parts of Normandy, the Pas de Calais and Holland, the fortifications were quite strong, but elsewhere the Wall was practically non-existent. The technicalities of the Wall were entrusted to the Todt Organisation, and Rundstedt was not consulted. A fortress system was organised, a strongly defended fortress being constructed every so many miles along the defence line, whilst the lines linking these fortresses were extremely weak. Crack divisions were stationed in the fortresses, but these came under Hitler's direct command. Rundstedt was very unhappy about the defence system, and considered it would probably hold an invasion for 24 hours at the most. Moreover, once

166

the Allies had breached the main defence line, what good were the fortresses facing the sea?

Not enough men

Rundstedt also complained about the manpower allotted to him. On his arrival in 1942, only 30 divisions were stationed in France and the Low Countries, but with the increasing threat of invasion, the number was increased by D-Day to 60 divisions,shared between four army commands. Field-Marshal Rommel, commander of Army Group 'B', controlled the 7th and the 15th Armies, whilst Colonel-General Blaskowitz, commander of Army Group 'G' had the 1st and 19th Armies under orders. Rommel's army group was responsible for the defence of the Channel coast, the 15th Army being deployed along the coast from Holland to the River Seine, and the 7th stationed between the Seine and the Loire rivers. The southern front, from the Loire to the Alps, was entrusted to Blaskowitz. Rundstedt was supreme commander.

By the end of March 1944, it was thought that the landings would probably take place on the beaches of northern France. German agents in Britain confirmed that the invasion was to be launched from southern England. But to where in northern France? And how should the threat be met? Rommel, new to the West in November 1943 as commander of Army Group 'B', and Rundstedt were to argue over these questions. The overall situation demanded that the Allies be beaten swiftly in the West so that Hitler could send much needed reinforcements to the Eastern Front. Defences were therefore stepped up in the West, but unfortunately without a unified command structure. Rundstedt could not give orders to the German naval forces, or to the anti-aircraft corps. Naval and army gunners could not reach agreement over the coastal batteries, the setting up of obstacles, and anti-aircraft defences.

In June 1944, Rundstedt supposedly commanded two army groups ('B' and 'G') with between them 15 corps totalling 42 infantry, three parachute, three *Luftwaffe* field, 10 Panzer and one *Panzergrenadier* divisions. But he had only tactical control over the *Luftwaffe* units, the *Waffen* SS divisions and I SS Panzer Corps. He had no authority over appointments or discipline. Such a command structure was to lead to inevitable delays when the Allies landed.

The wrong target

Rundstedt considered that the Allies would cross the Channel via the shortest sea-route and land in the Pas de Calais, which was also the quickest way to the Ruhr and industrial Germany. The V1 and V2 sites were in this area, too. The staff officers in Berlin thought the attack would be launched further west than this – between the Somme and Seine rivers. Coastal defences here and in the Pas de Calais were accordingly built up. Rommel and Hitler, however, decided that the landings were most likely to take place on the beaches of Normandy, as the Pas de Calais would appear to the enemy to be very strongly defended. Rommel immediately set to work to set up effective coastal defences in this region but, unfortunately for the Germans, his efforts were curtailed by a shortage of resources and labour. Most of the workers of the Todt Organisation had been drawn off to Germany by this time to repair air-raid damage. The scope of the planned defences was too extensive for the German troops to achieve much on their own, and both they and the movement of supplies were hampered by the raids of the Allied air forces. Thus, on D-Day, both the underwater obstructions and the coastal fortifications were incomplete. Rommel complained that this state of affairs need not have happened, and blamed Rundstedt for placing too much reliance on mobile defence.

With regard to the strategy to be adopted in the event of an enemy landing, while they agreed that they must defeat the invaders in the shortest possible time, Rundstedt and Rommel held differing opinions concerning the deployment of *Panzergruppe* 'West', Rundstedt's armoured reserve. These forces – 2nd Panzer, 21st Panzer, 103rd Panzer *Lehr*, 116th Panzer, 1st SS '*Leibstandarte Adolf Hitler*' Panzer, 12th SS '*Hitlerjugend*' Panzer and 17th SS '*Goetz von Berlichingen*' *Panzergrenadier* Divisions – came under the command of General Geyr von Schweppenburg, who naturally wanted to keep the force concentrated. Rundstedt agreed with this, as did Guderian, but he was wary of committing all his reserves without first being quite sure of the Allies' intentions. He did not want to commit them to what might be a divisionary feint. Rundstedt's plan was therefore to hold back his strong armoured force approximately 30 miles from the coast and, when he was certain about what was happening, release the reserve in a powerful counter-offensive against the Allied bridgehead. Rundstedt was also doubtful of Germany's ability to prevent a landing, as there were so many miles of coastline to cover.

Rommel's experiences in Africa had led him to hold a different opinion on the best way of blocking an invasion by an enemy with superior air power. He saw a seaborne attack as being weak at the moment of landing, but increasing in momentum and strength afterwards. He therefore thought it best to hurl the armour against the Allies as they were landing and so exploit their initial weakness. The invasion would thus collapse on the very first day. Rommel had assessed correctly the danger of the Allies' superior air power, which would be able to harass any large-scale movement of German troops after the invasion. The armour must be immediately available to aid the coastal defenders as the Allies landed. But only three Panzer divisions were under Rommel's direct control.

Rundstedt's ideas should have prevailed as he was the senior commander. Rommel, however, had influence with Hitler and was therefore able to 'dilute' Rundstedt's orders. On 20 March Hitler gave Rommel permission to take over *Panzergruppe* 'West', but no orders followed from OKW and von Geyr absolutely refused to deploy his force as Rommel wished. He thought Rommel was trying to cover everything and would in all probability defend nothing when the time came. He complained of Rundstedt's hesitation in overruling Rommel. It may be that Rundstedt was coming round to Rommel's plan, but at this time, also, Rundstedt was an old man and suffering severe mental and physical fatigue. Von Geyr went himself to see Hitler to protest about Rommel's forward plan, and Hitler consequently ordered that four Panzer divisions, including '*Hitlerjugend*' and Panzer *Lehr*, were to form the OKW reserve and were not to be moved without his permission. This meant that Rommel's plan was considerably weakened and Rundstedt had fewer reserves to call on.

On D-Day, then, the armour was neither deployed near the beaches nor concentrated ready for a decisive counterattack. The infantry divisions were stretched thinly along the coast from Holland to Marseilles and only in the Pas de Calais did Rundstedt succeed in producing a second layer of infantry. Hitler would not create enough reserves from other theatres, and vetoed Rommel's suggestion that the troops from the southern front be brought up so that they would be in a position to counterattack.

Seven of the 11 Panzer divisions were placed north of the Loire, with the remaining four acting as a reserve for the south and south-west coasts. Rommel stationed his armour as near to the coast as possible, while Rundstedt kept his further back. On 23 April, Rommel vainly requested Hitler to allow him to move the Panzer *Lehr* Division to between the Orne and the Vire rivers and to deploy the '*Hitlerjugend*' Division near St Lô, and to reinforce this sector with more anti-aircraft batteries.

On 5 June, Rommel left France to attend his wife's birthday celebrations in Germany. Everything looked quiet, but just before midnight, it was discovered that the BBC was broadcasting a large number of messages to the French Resistance. The 15th Army east of the Seine was alerted, but Lieutenant-General Speidel, deputising for Rommel, did not alert the 7th Army in Normandy. As Allied paratroops landed in Normandy after midnight, feverish activity at Rundstedt's headquarters tried to determine whether this signalled the start of the invasion, or whether it was merely a diversion. British and American secret agents had employed many tricks to mislead the German generals and signals experts as to the landing site. An entire 'ghost' army had been assembled which led many to believe the main attack would be launched elsewhere.

At 0400 hours Rundstedt decided the landings must be dealt with. Off the five selected landing points, six battleships had appeared, together with 23 cruisers, 105 destroyers, 495 coastal craft and numerous frigates. Under the cover of this great armada, a force of 6,480 transports, landing craft and special-purpose vehicles landed the invasion forces with their amphibious tanks. As Rundstedt decided his forces must counterattack, the infantry divisions in the bunkers along the coast were unable to resist the naval, air and land assault and surrendered in their thousands. The underwater obstacles were swept away by the first wave of attacking infantry. The Allied air forces flew over 10,500 sorties on 6 June, and dropped nearly 12,000 tons of bombs on the German defences, which was as much as was dropped on Hamburg in the whole of 1943.

Early in the day, Rundstedt urgently requested that OKW release the armour reserve, but he received the answer from Jodl that they were not yet convinced that this was the main invasion and that a second landing east of the Seine river was imminent. Rundstedt finally obtained the release of I SS Panzer Corps at 1600 hours, but the armour took two days to reach the invasion zone as a result of air attack and broken bridges. By that time the Allies were firmly established in their bridgeheads. Had Rommel not been absent, perhaps the tanks would have been available earlier, as he had more influence at OKW than Rundstedt.

However, the 21st Panzer, 1st 'Leibstandarte' SS Panzer and Panzer Lehr Divisions constituted a striking force of approximately 600 tanks, together with the best troops in France. They should have been able to deliver at least a counter-blow to be reckoned with, but they never achieved the co-ordination for a counter-offensive. None of the armour reached the coast before the afternoon of 6 June, when it was already too late to push the Allies back into the sea. After the Panzers arrived, they were frittered away in desperate attempts to plug the gaping holes in the Atlantic Wall, where the infantry had been smashed. In the first days after the landing, the Germans lost 10,000 prisoners and 150 tanks. Reinforcements did not get through. By 8 June, the Anglo-Americans had a continuous front between the Dives and St Marcouf. The German forces were dazed and weary and could only wait for help.

In the second week, Rundstedt no longer feared a second landing east of the Seine. Hitler's headquarters still expected such a landing and Hitler was reluctant to move troops from Calais to Normandy to be redeployed as Rundstedt wished. In desperation, Rommel and Rundstedt tried to make Hitler see reason. They wanted to withdraw from Caen, leave the infantry to hold the line of the Orne river and pull out the armoured divisions to reorganise for a powerful counter-offensive against the Americans in the Cherbourg peninsula. Hitler ordered that all troops must remain where they stood. He was still hoping it was possible to drive the Allies back. Hitler brushed aside Rundstedt's objections and said that the new V weapons would soon take effect, but he would not hear of using them against the Allies on the beaches.

At the end of June, Rommel and Rundstedt again appealed to Hitler who reiterated his order for no withdrawal. Rundstedt said he could not carry on without a free hand and was then dismissed, to be replaced by Field-Marshal von Kluge.

COLONEL-GENERAL SEPP DIETRICH

Physically 'Sepp' Dietrich did not look the part of a German general. Squat, thick-necked and with the battered face of a bouncer, he also lacked the mental attributes of the rank to which he had been elevated. Rundstedt had called him 'decent but stupid'. *Obergruppenfuehrer* Bittrich had been less generous: 'I once spent an hour and a half trying to explain a situation to Sepp Dietrich with the aid of a map. It was quite useless. He understood nothing at all.'

It was on the broad shoulders of this man, however, that Hitler had laid the responsibility of commanding the 6th SS *Panzerarmee* in the surprise attack in December 1944 that was to be known as 'The Battle of the Bulge' by the Allies and Operation '*Herbstnebel*' (Autumn Fog) by the Germans. Of the units involved his was to launch the *Schwerpunkt*, the main weight, of the offensive. With him would go the 5th *Panzerarmee* under General Hasso von Manteuffel in the centre and to the south the 7th Army under General Brandenberger would cover their flank.

The 6th SS *Panzerarmee* consisted of LXVII Corps under General Hitzfeld, with the 272nd, and 326th *Volksgrenadier* Divisions; I SS Panzer Corps under General Priess with the 277th and 12th *Volksgrenadier*, 3rd Parachute, 3rd *Panzergrenadier*, and 1st and 12th SS Panzer Divisions; and II SS Panzer Corps under General Bittrich with the 2nd and 9th SS Panzer Divisions. Dietrich's *Waffen*-SS Panzer divisions had been brought up to strength for the offensive with 640 Panther and Pzkw IV tanks. In addition he had some powerful Tiger II tanks with their potent L/71 8.8-cm gun.

The choice of the *Waffen*-SS to bear the main weight of the attack did not mean that the men of the army were no longer effective soldiers, but rather that after the July Bomb Plot of 1944, the army had fallen out of favour. It was ironic, therefore, that two army generals proposed a '*kleine Loesung*', a 'small solution' which would have had a far greater chance of success than Hitler's grandiose scheme.

While the *Fuehrer* envisaged a punch which would reach as far as Antwerp and cut off the Allied armies allowing them no Dunkirk evacuation, Model and Hasso von Manteuffel proposed a more modest and more practical operation. They suggested that 'the 15th Army, with a strong right flank, would deliver an attack north of Aachen, towards Maastricht. The 6th *Panzerarmee* would attack south of Aachen, and cut in behind that place with the eventual objective of establishing a bridgehead over the Meuse in the Liège area. The main aim here was to fix the Allies' attention. The 5th *Panzerarmee* would strike from the Eifel through the Ardennes towards Namur, with the aim of gaining a bridgehead there. The armies would then turn and roll up the Allied position along the Meuse. If opposition seemed to be collapsing, they could exploit their success by an advance towards Antwerp, but otherwise they could limit their risks.' This plan, as explained after the war to Liddell Hart by Manteuffel, was within the capabilities of the forces available and had it succeeded would have destroyed 20 Allied divisions.

Surprisingly, Hitler listened to the proposals without interrupting, but at the end rejected them. He did not want a sortie to gain time and stave off defeat for a few extra weeks or months, he wanted a major victory. Of all the generals involved Dietrich was probably the one who could be trusted to obey his orders with unquestioning loyalty – however ambitious those orders might be.

Hitler's plan envisaged reaching the Meuse in 48 hours. Here Dietrich would cross the river north of Liège and drive for Antwerp via St Truiden and Aarschot. Manteuffel would go for Brussels. Their south flank would be covered by the 7th Army pivoting on Echternach, while paratroops under Lieutenant-Colonel von der Heydte would be dropped to block the northern roads. In addition teams of German soldiers dressed as Americans in captured vehicles, under the command of *Sturmbannfuehrer* Otto Skorzeny, were to infiltrate the American lines, sow confusion and capture bridge over the Meuse.

On the Allied side there was an optimism which was heightened by the lack of intelligence available about the German forces facing them. The Germans were now on their home ground and so there were no friendly civilians to bear information to the Allies about troop concentrations. In fact General Bradley's intelligence summary for 12 December said 'It is now certain that attrition is steadily sapping the strength of the German forces on the Western Front.'

Snow had been falling in the Ardennes for a week and the men of the 6th SS *Panzerarmee* were kitted out in a mixture of waterproof cold-weather clothing, camouflaged smocks and jackets. The carried belts of ammunition, entrenching tools and stick grenades, and some were equipped with the modern StG 44 assault rifle. In their ears rang the words of Field-Marshal von Rundstedt, Commander-in-Chief West: 'Soldiers of the Western Front, your great hour has struck. At this moment the veil which has been hiding so many preparations has been lifted at last.'

■ Early success

Even before dawn had broken on that heavily overcast 16 December, men of the 6th SS *Panzerarmee* were beginning to advance. At 0530 hours a soldier of the 1st SS Panzer Division had turned to his officer, grinned, and said: '*Auf wiedersehen, Herr Leutnant, seh dich in Amerika!*' or 'Cheerio, Lieutenant, see you in America!' Morale was very high. Dietrich had decided to commit his infantry first, and to hold back his armour to exploit the first successes. On his right he came up against the American 2nd and 99th Divisions of V Corps under Major-General Leonard Gerow. The 2nd Division was a veteran unit which overcame its surprise quite quickly, but the 99th, which had never been in action before and, moreover, been on the receiving end, took longer to recover. However, despite attacks by the I SS Panzer Corps the Americans hung on to the Elsenborn ridge. To the south elements of I SS and II SS Panzer Corps brushed aside a screen of the 14th Armoured Division and streamed through the Losheim gap. This opened up the Stavelot road and turned the flank of the 106th Division.

While these attacks were in progress, von der Heydte was giving a condensed briefing to his officers whose paratroops were to cover the Eupen-Malmedy road. Although these 1,200 men were a scratch force, of whom only about 300 were experienced paratroops, they managed to sow confusion and concern among the Americans. The drop on the night of the 16th/17th was hopelessly scattered, and some of the lumbering Ju 52s came under fire from their own men, who automatically assumed that any aircraft was Allied. Von der Heydte later recalled that Dietrich was 'obviously drunk' when he briefed him.

German newsreels of the period show SS men and paratroops advancing along roads blocked with abandoned and burning American Jeeps and half-tracks, and indeed there was an exhilaration in the opening days which had not been felt since the 'glorious days' of May 1940. Suddenly the enemy was on the run, and the sky, covered with low cloud, was no longer filled with enemy aircraft.

However, in isolated positions the Americans showed a resource and courage that saved themselves and their units. At Buetgenbach an artillery unit hung on and prevented the outflanking of the 2nd and 99th Divisions. A company of the 51st Engineer Combat Battalion halted the advance of *Kampfgruppe* 'Peiper' when it demolished the bridge at Trois-Ponts across the Salm. Peiper was forced to return via Ambléve to find another bridge at Werbomont. Here he was again confronted by determined engineers, men of the 291st Battalion who blew up the bridge. Like Hitler, the man who launched the attack, the Ardennes offensive was bogging down into 'a corporal's war'.

Dietrich, with the tactical sense of a battering ram, continued to attack the Elsenborn ridge. Gerow, however, had been able to reinforce the position with a first class unit, the 1st Division, and the young men and boys of the 12th '*Hitlerjugend*' SS Panzer Division were halted around Buetgenbach.

The aggressive *Obersturmbannfuehrer* Jochen Peiper of the '*Leibstandarte Adolf Hitler*'Division led his *Kampfgruppe* to the little town of Stavelot, which he captured on the 17th. Two days later it was recaptured, and Peiper, isolated, fought for five days in the wooded valley of the Amblève. Then, out of fuel, he was forced to withdraw after destroying all his equipment, including his Tiger II tanks.

Meanwhile Manteuffel was making better progress because it was more difficult for the Americans to reinforce their units in the south. Seeking to exploit this success both Model and Rundstedt urged Hitler to transfer II SS Panzer Corps from the 6th to the 5th *Panzerarmee*. They were refused categorically since this would have been an admission that the Nazi Party soldiers and officers of the *Waffen*-SS were inferior to their *Wehrmacht* counterparts.

■ The Allies recover

By now, however, the Allies were beginning to adjust their dispositions: to the north Montgomery, who had taken temporary command, moved XXX Corps down to the Meuse to cover the American 1st Army. To the south Patton's 3rd Army swung north and on 22 December launched a strong attack up the road from Arlon to Bastogne. As Patton gleefully described it, 'this time the Kraut's stuck his head in a meatgrinder. And this time I've got hold of the handle.'

'About 25 December I saw that it would now be impossible for us to attempt a crossing of the Meuse,' said von Manteuffel. He fought for another week, but now his men were trapped in their own salient. On the 23rd the weather had improved and the Allies had been able to enjoy air dropped supplies, while the Germans were subject to strikes by ground-attack fighters.

As they pulled back from their salient the Germans left behind them the last of their pool of tanks and half-tracks. Some had been destroyed by resolute GIs armed with infantry anti-tank weapons, some had been split apart by aircraft rockets and cannon fire, but many had been abandoned when they ran out of fuel. For Dietrich's 6th SS *Panzerarmee* it was a tragic irony that on the 19th they had come within about a quarter of a mile at Andrimont near Stavelot of a fuel dump containing 2,500,000 gallons.

With the failure of his forces to make any progress in the north and the squeezing out of Manteuffel in the south, Dietrich was forced to withdraw. He had never been happy with the plan, and after the war told Milton Shulman: 'All I had to do was cross a river, capture Brussels and then go on and take the port of Antwerp. And all this in December, January and February, the worst three months of the year, through the Ardennes where snow was waist deep and there wasn't room to deploy four tanks abreast, let alone six armoured divisions; when it didn't get light until eight in the morning and was dark again at four in the afternoon and my tanks can't fight at night; with divisions that had just been reformed and were composed chiefly of raw untrained recruits; and at Christmas time.' 'The crack in Dietrich's voice when he reached this last obstacle,' recalls Shulman, 'made it sound like the most heart-break-ing one of all.'

The Ardennes operation left behind 76,890 American casualties and 81,834 German, and though American losses in tanks and aircraft were greater, 733 to 324 and 592 to 320, the German losses were now almost irreplaceable. The Battle of the Bulge also left an atmosphere of bitterness between the Allies and also within the German camp. After the war Rundstedt asserted that Dietrich sent few reports during the operation, 'and what I did receive was generally a pack of lies. If the SS had any problems they reported them directly to the *Fuehrer*, who would then make them known to Model.'

Despite this Dietrich was not a bad officer; he simply lacked the training and experience to command an army. Goering said of him: 'He had at the most the ability to command a division.'

ANALYSIS – GERMAN GENERALSHIP IN THE WEST

In 1940 the Germans had 2,600 tanks whilst the Anglo-French allies had 3,600; moreover, many of the German tanks had thinner armour and lighter guns than those of their adversaries. Despite this, their 136 divisions defeated the 137 divisions of four nations and sent the British Expeditionary Force back across the Channel from the beaches of Dunkirk. In the months that followed May 1940 the Western world tried to understand what had enabled the Germans to score such a decisive victory.

The reasons for the German successes were simply, good training, air superiority (1,490 bombers and 1,260 fighters against 1,690 first-line combat aircraft) and the concentrated use of armour into fast moving spearheads.

An Italian journalist called it 'Lightning War', and '*Blitzkrieg*' became the name for these deep-penetration tactics. The Germans launched their marching infantry on the Low Countries to draw off the Allied mobile units. These spoiling attacks diverted Anglo-French attention from the discreet approach march by the armoured units through Luxembourg and the Ardennes. French reservist units in positions on the Meuse became the target of concentrated aerial attack, and their inadequate positions were pounded to destruction. Through the gap that had been punched the Germans poured their tanks and armoured infantry in a wild drive across northern France to the sea – cutting off the Anglo-French forces in France and Belgium.

■ Ground–air liaison

Since they could not bring up heavy artillery at the speed of their tanks, the Germans used dive-bombers as flying artillery. The Stukas and marching infantry could finish off pockets of resistance that had been bypassed by the Panzer columns. The French, who had fought stubbornly during the bulk of World War I, were ill-prepared for a war of movement. Their communications systems were grossly inadequate for assessing a situation which was changing hourly; their tanks, though good, were spread along the front in small formations; and they had obsolescent aircraft and few anti-tank guns. There was also the important factor of morale – the men of 1940 were not the hardened peasant classes of 1914 burning with a desire to revenge the defeats of the Franco-Prussian War. The long cold winter of the 'Phoney War' (another journalist's creation) of 1939 had sapped the will of many soldiers. The government, unwilling to incur anything like the awesome casualties of World War I, had embarked on no real offensive actions when the bulk of German forces were in action in Poland. Though the British Expeditionary Force kept itself busy with many of the mindless chores that only the services can invent, they were at least busy; the French troops, however, sat in the Maginot Line and its pill-box extensions along the Belgian border. Their officers went on long weekends in Paris and the soldiers failed to practise the skills they had learned as conscripts.

In 1940 the French had been immobilised by ruptured communications and supply lines, and by orders which arrived too late to affect a constantly changing situation. In 1944, despite five years experience of war, the Germans found themselves in much the same situation. It was only the training and discipline of their soldiers, and the fact that they could trade space for time which prevented their collapse. In 1940 a Panzer column had only to drive 200 or 300 miles and it had captured enough towns and territory to make further resistance pointless in countries as small as Holland or Belgium, whilst France was cut off from her industries in the north-east.

Air power was again a major factor in the fighting in 1944, but the Germans had one disadvantage which never beset the Allies even at the nadir of their fortunes. The overall commander of the *Wehrmacht* was Adolf Hitler, a man who in 1940 had demonstrated a surprising grasp of the tactical possibilities of paratroops and glider-borne infantry, and who had supported Manstein's novel reverse Schlieffen plan. However, by 1944 the *Fuehrer* was a prematurely old man, with a brain addled by the crude medication of his personal physician, Dr Morell. Hitler insisted that no ground was to be given up, and also that he direct operations, even those of a very local nature involving quite small forces.

After the war Rundstedt said that the Ardennes offensive 'was planned in all its details, including formations involved, time schedules, objectives and so on, by the *Fuehrer* and his staff. All counter-proposals were rejected. Under such circumstances, there could be little faith in its success. Even during the attack the Supreme Command conducted the operations by means of liaison officers and direct wireless orders to the armies involved.'

■ Over-control

Earlier, in the counter-attack on the American break-out at St Lô in July 1944 Hitler had taken personal control. Blumentritt recalls: 'OKW settled the precise divisions which were to be used and which were therefore to be taken out of the line as soon as possible. The exact limits of the sector in which the attack was to take place were laid down, as well as the routes to be taken and even the villages the troops were to pass through. These plans were all made in Berlin on large-scale maps and the opinions of the commanding generals in France were neither asked for nor encouraged.'

Problems of tactical doctrine were not confined to the misty heights of the Eagle's Nest in Obersalzburg. Rommel and Rundstedt disagreed about the way the defence of the French coastline should be conducted in the event of the Allied invasion. Rundstedt, with a wealth of experience of mobile war in the East, proposed the conventional tactic of letting the Allies get a lodgement, and then moving in with his tanks to crush them against their beach-head. There were precedents for this concept: Anzio had been a near disaster for the Allies. Rommel, however, had been able to appreciate the enemy's growing air power and knew that movement by day would be impossible – even for single vehicles, as he himself discovered when he narrowly escaped death when his car was shot up by fighters soon after the invasion. Rommel maintained that the invasion must be stopped on the beaches – he had the precedent of the abortive Anglo-Canadian raid on Dieppe. Inevitably the two commanders temporised and resources were split, the armour (which could only be used after it had received clearance from Hitler) was held in reserve inland and lost heavily in its approach march to the beach-heads. The Allies were able to get ashore in reasonable order and the only place where Rommel's theory was vindicated was at Omaha beach where due to a series of disastrous coincidences the German defences were largely undamaged and manned by a fresh unit.

■ No new *matériel*

In 1944 and 1945 the Germans were also low in vital raw materials, fuel and men. In 1940 their tank crews were highly trained: some had seen action in Spain, and most were blooded in Poland. They were cross-trained so that a driver could serve as a gunner, or a radio-operator as a driver, if one of the crew became a casualty. In 1944 their Panzer divisions had been worn down in the East, and while there were still some exceptional crews like that of *Hauptsturmfuehrer* Wittman's Tiger, the average age and training of many crews had now decreased. Part of the problem was that the Allied air attacks on German's petrochemical industry had reduced her stocks of fuel so that little could be used for training. Indeed one of the main local objectives of the troops engaged in the Ardennes offensive was the capture of American fuel stocks. It was this lack of fuel that crippled many of the heavily armoured and armed tanks that were produced in the latter part of the war. But it was not only the tank crews that suffered in quality. The changes in Germany's fortunes was more noticeable in her infantry. The Atlantic Wall, which propaganda films showed as a massive concrete barrier garrisoned by alert young soldiers and tough veterans, was a fraud. While in the Pas de Calais a wide range of emplacements had been built, elsewhere the bulk of the defences were still incomplete.

Some of the soldiers were elderly members of 'Stomach and Ear' or 'White Bread' Battalions, units formed largely of men with disorders which required special diets or medication. Divisions which had been exhausted and used up on the Eastern Front were rotated back to France and the West for rest and refitting. Until the summer of 1944 the West, with the exception of Italy, remained a soft posting, while the East became increasingly a one-way journey.

The Germans won in the West in 1940 because they were able to assemble their tanks under a friendly sky. Their opposition could not afford to lose ground, but was inadequately equipped both in tactical doctrine and *matériel* to defend it. The Germans lost in 1944 for almost the same reasons: they no longer controlled the skies, their men were physically unfit and insufficiently trained, but their chief disadvantage was that they were tied by inflexible orders from Hitler.

THE EASTERN FRONT, JUNE 1941–FEBRUARY 1943

THE CAMPAIGN IN RUSSIA, FROM MINSK TO STALINGRAD

At the time of its inception in June 1941, Germany's invasion of Soviet Russia was the largest military undertaking ever attempted, and was exceeded in scope later in the war only by the Russian riposte from the middle of 1943. Operation '*Barbarossa*', as the German invasion was code-named, was the logical conclusion of a major portion of Hitler's racial, political and economic thinking. Russia must be dismembered so that the 'Slavid sub-humans' might be put in their correct place as underlings of the master-race, so that communism might be stamped out as a threat to national-socialism, and so that the German race might possess the necessary *Lebensraum* or living space in the east, together with its enormous potential in foodstuffs and industrial raw materials, not to mention oil. As always, this last item was well to the front of all Hitler's thinking.

The need to invade Russia had always been with Hitler, and although he had declared that a two-front war was anathema to him, planning for '*Barbarossa*' began in December 1940, before Great Britain had been driven into defeat. The idea of an invasion filled the German general staff with foreboding, but detailed planning progressed through a series of basic plans until the definitive version, for implementation in May 1941, emerged. As a result of Hitler's last-minute insistence on the conquest of Yugoslavia and Greece, the launch-date of the offensive had to be put back from 25 May to 22 June; the month's delay was to have disastrous consequences for the German invaders late in 1941.

The final plan called for a major drive into western Russia in three prongs, each formed by a complete army group. In the north, starting from East Prussia, Field-Marshal Ritter von Leeb's Army Group 'North' of two armies and Hoepner's 4th *Panzergruppe* was to advance through the Baltic states and take Leningrad, the spiritual capital of communism. (On Leeb's northern flank, Mannerheim's Finnish forces would drive south towards Leningrad through Karelia, and Falkenhorst's Army of Norway, with some Finnish troops, would seize the Murmansk-Leningrad railway.) In the centre, starting from northern Poland, Field-Marshal Fedor von Bock's Army Group 'Centre' of two armies with Guderian's 2nd and Hoth's 3rd *Panzergruppen* was to advance on Moscow, the administrative hub of the communist world. In the south, starting from southern Poland and from Rumania, Field-Marshal Gerd von Rundstedt's Army Group 'South' of four armies and Kleist's 1st *Panzergruppe* was to advance on Kiev and the River Dnieper to destroy all Russian forces between the Pripet marshes and the Black Sea. Thus the main strategic moves were decided. So were the tactics – similar to those employed against the west in 1940, with the armoured forces encircling the Russian armies in vast, fast-moving pincers, and the following infantry mopping up, leaving the armour to press on again. What had not been fixed, however, was the grand strategic objective of the campaign. This mattered little to the fighting troops, as they had their objectives, but it reflected on the lack of thought by Hitler and his staff generals. All that was envisaged was that once Moscow had fallen, the Russians would capitulate, and the Germans could consolidate on a line running basically from Astrakhan on the Caspian Sea to Archangel in the Arctic. No thought was given to the fact that Russia might not capitulate, but fight on from the enormous tracts of land that lay beyond Hitler's immediate objectives. This lack of concrete, objective planning was to bedevil the 162 German and satellite divisions involved in the invasion.

■ Too far forward

To meet any invasion from the west, the Russian armies defending the German, Polish, Hungarian and Rumanian frontiers were divided into three major groupings, designated by the Russians as Fronts. In Western terminology these would be called army groups. In the north was Colonel General F. I. Kuznetsov's North-West Front of 24 divisions defending the Baltic states and the approaches to Leningrad. In the centre was Marshal Semyon Timoshenko's Western Front of 38 divisions defending the area between the southern border of Lithuania and the Pripet marshes. In the south was Marshal Semyon Budenny's South-West Front of 72 divisions defending the area between the Pripet marshes and the Black Sea. These forces were well supplied with *matériel*, although much of it except the artillery was obsolescent. Although the Russians deployed about the same number of men in the forward areas as the Germans were to use, the tactical disposition of the forces was poor, being too far forward, with insufficient reserves echeloned in depth to check German breakthroughs. Russian leadership was also poor, many formations having lost their leaders in the purges of the late 1930s. The new leaders had been pushed up the ladder of command very quickly, and many lacked the skills and abilities to command large formations in the type of mobile warfare that was to take place between June and

November 1941. Russia's great strengths, however, lay in the size of the nation, and the enormity of the manpower resources she could call upon. And although the major portions of the Red Army were deployed in western Russia to meet the invasion, there were still powerful forces in reserve behind Moscow and in Siberia. The nature of the state, with its all-powerful communist control, also meant that the national effort could be devoted to the war to the exclusion of all else. This last, combined with the stubborn defence of the ordinary soldiers, was to prove Russia's salvation.

The German offensive opened on 22 June, and immediately achieved enormous success. The Russians had been taken completely by surprise and were driven back in disarray. Although some units fought with great determination, the general collapse of the Russian forces left such units to be surrounded and annihilated. Russian losses in *matériel* were extremely heavy, especially in aircraft, guns and tanks. It is perhaps worth noting here that the Russians had known of the obsolence of much of their *matériel*, and several new types of aircraft and tank were being rushed into production. The destruction of the obsolete *matériel* was therefore something of an advantage to the Russians, forcing them to accelerate further the introduction of new weapons. One of these, the T-34 medium tank, was to prove a superlative weapon, and a considerable shock to the Germans.

In the first weeks of the campaign, the German pushed on victoriously along the whole length of the 2,000-mile front. But the nature of Russia gradually led to the slowing down of the advance: as they pushed on the troops became increasingly exhausted by the sheer length of their marches, vehicles and tanks began to wear out in the heat and poor conditions under which they had to operate, and the shape of Russia, widening towards the east, diluted the concentration of troops along the front. Nevertheless, the Germans scored some remarkable victories; by mid-July Army Group 'Centre' had trapped a Russian pocket around Minsk, capturing nearly 330,000 men, 2,500 tanks and 1,500 guns; driving on from Minsk, the two *Panzergruppen* of Army Group 'Centre' then trapped in Smolensk another 310,000 men, 3,200 tanks and 3,000 guns by 5 August. Although the German supply services at this time were under the utmost strain to keep up with the front-line forces, they were just managing to do so, and the strategic objectives of the campaign looked attainable before the onset of winter. But now Hitler made a major blunder.

■ **Different speeds**
Army Group 'Centre', principally by virtue of its two *Panzergruppen*, was advancing faster than either Army Group 'North' or Army Group 'South'. Hitler became increasingly worried about this, as these latter groups were to seize the all-important Ukraine and open up the way to the oil-producing Caucasus, and to take Leningrad respectively. He therefore removed the two *Panzergruppen* and one army from Army Group 'Centre' despite Bock's objections, to strengthen the two flank army groups. At first the changes in strategic direction proved useful. Army Group 'South', with the

aid of Guderian's armour, trapped some 665,000 Russians in the Kiev pocket. Kiev itself fell on 20 September. In the north Leeb's army group moved on towards Leningrad, investing the city in October, whilst Rundstedt's forces reached the River Don on 15 October, threatening the major cities of Kharkov and Rostov. By this time the autumn rains had started, and the German advance lost further momentum. At this point Hitler once again changed his mind about the campaign's strategic objectives, reinstating Moscow as the primary target. The forces taken from Army Group 'Centre' were now given back, and Bock was ordered to take Moscow at all costs. The army group pressed on, and trapped another vast horde of Russians, 650,000-strong, in a pocket at Vyazma between 30 September and 7 October. By 20 October Army Group 'Centre' had reached Mozhaisk, only 40 miles from Moscow.

But by now the German armies had all but shot their bolt. They had advanced deep into Russia against strong opposition, and most units, both infantry and armour, were down to below half strength in men and equipment. The autumn rains, which were to turn into the winter snows of one of the coldest winters in living memory, also hampered the German advance. No provision had been made for winter clothing, it having been anticipated that the campaign would be over by this time, and the men were beginning to suffer the torments of the cold. Russian resistance, moreover, was strengthening as reserves from the east were called in and the lessons of the early days of the campaign were absorbed. Finally, in General Georgi Zhukov, newly appointed to command the defence of Moscow, the Russians had placed in high command one of the greatest generals to serve any nation during World War II. All along the front Russian defences were beginning to hold, and in the south the Russians had even launched a major counter-offensive, driving the Germans back from Rostov on 15 November. Hitler began to lose patience with his commanders and Rundstedt was replaced by General W. von Reichenau on 1 December. In the north Leeb was making no further progress against Leningrad, and in the centre Bock, later replaced by Kluge as commander of Army Group 'Centre', pushed slowly on towards Moscow, getting within 25 miles of the city by 5 December. Hitler now decided on a wholesale reshuffle of his high command. Leeb was replaced by General von Kuechler; General von Brauchitsch was sacked as commander-in-chief of the army, Hitler himself taking over this position and controlling operations in the East by radio; and the OKH under Halder was restricted to Eastern Front operations, responsibility for other theatres being allocated to an enlarged OKW under Keitel.

But now it was the turn of the Russians. Despite the appalling difficulties of the Russian situation before Moscow, Zhukov had managed to prepare a counter-offensive, which broke upon the Germans on 6 December. The main strength of the counter-offensive lay with the fresh divisions called in from Siberia after reports from the spy Richard Sorge in Tokyo that the Japanese had no plans to invade Russia from the east. The Russian offensive broke upon the stunned Germans at Kalinin, north of Moscow; at Tula, south of Moscow; and at Izyum, in the Ukraine. The German generals, shaken by the very fact and scope of the Russian stroke, were all for falling back to defence lines that could be improvised in their rear. Hitler, however, would hear no suggestion of retreat. He feared that in such climatic conditions a retreat might become a rout, and ordered the armies to hold on where they were at any cost. Although they were pushed back slowly, the Germans did manage to hold on near their furthest advances until the Russians called off the offensive. Never was one of Hitler's decisions more justified. He had saved the German armies in the East from almost certain rout in this instance. But the unfortunate consequence was that Hitler acquired an unshakable belief in the need to hold ground at any cost. This was to prove disastrous to the Germans in later years, when orderly retreat might have saved vast numbers of men.

■ Balance of losses

Thus finished the first stage of the German campaign in Russia. Russia herself had lost some three million men, and the Germans 800,000. But whereas the Russians could replace their losses, the Germans could not. And although the Russians had lost vast amounts of *matériel*, they were able to replace it with more modern equipment, produced by the factories that had been moved back from western Russia to behind to Urals in the weeks that their troops had gained by their huge losses. At the same time the Russian commanders had learned how to fight the right type of warfare. Poor commanders had been weeded out, and the new generation of able officers had moved in to teach the new lessons to their men.

The Russian counter-offensive continued against determined German defence until the end of February, making some progress everywhere except around Leningrad and in Finland. The spring thaw, with its attendant mud, halted operations in March, by which time both sides were exhausted. The Germans were the first to recover. On 8 Mary 1942 their reinforced armies went over to the offensive, in an effort to recover the losses to the Russian winter offensive. Considerable advances were made, the Russians suffered heavy casualties, and once again revealing themselves to be tactically inferior to the Germans. In the far south of the German front, the 11th Army (Manstein), swept through that part of the Crimea it had not cleared the previous year and laid siege to Sevastopol. The clearing of the Crimea cost the Russians 150,000 men, and the loss of Sevastopol on 2 July another 100,000.

These offensives had only been preliminaries to the main summer offensive, which started on 28 June. Under the command of Bock, who had taken over from Reichenau in January, Army Group 'South' drove eastwards from Kursk to take Voronezh on the River Don on 6 July. In the command reshuffle that followed this victory, Army Group 'South' was divided into Army Group 'A' in the south of the sector, under General W. von List, and Army Group 'B' in the north of the sector, under General M. F. von Weichs. These two army groups were to co-operate in clearing the River Don and River Donets valleys, take Rostov and then Stalingrad, and finally swing south to take the oil-producing areas of the Caucasus. But on 13 July Hitler once again changed his mind, again for the worse. Instead of the concerted drive by the two army groups, which stood a good chance of success the *Fuehrer* decided that each of the groups should undertake half the offensive independently: Army Group 'B' would head for Stalingrad, and Army Group 'A' for the Caucasus. In fact neither of the two groups was strong enough for the task entrusted to it. Apart from the logistic difficulties raised by the new plan, there was also the strategic disadvantage that the further each group advanced, the greater would be the gap between the two forces, inviting the Russians to take either one or both in flank.

The new two-prong offensive started immediately, with some success. Army Group 'B' moved south-east on Stalingrad, but its lack of resources allowed most of the Russian forces which would otherwise have been destroyed to escape to the east and fight again. The advance was still making good progress when Hitler decided to reallocate Hoth's 4th *Panzerarmee* to Army Group 'A', which was making only limited advances in the Caucasus. Despite the loss of most of its armoured forces Army Group 'B', in the form of General F. Paulus' 6th Army, reached the River Volga above Stalingrad on 23 August.

■ Stalingrad

In the south Army Group 'A' had at first also made good progress, taking Rostov on 23 July and pressing on towards the Caspian Sea. Reinforced by the 4th *Panzerarmee*, Army Group 'A' at one time got to within 75 miles of the Caspian. But then the 4th *Panzerarmee* was once again moved back to help in the struggle for Stalingrad, and the understrength army group was left to struggle on hopelessly. At the same time the theatre reserve, Manstein's 11th Army, was shipped off to Leningrad in the far north. Halder and List, who had dared voice objections to the moves, were both sacked. Hitler himself took over command of Army Group 'A' by radio.

The 4th *Panzerarmee* had been given back to Army Group 'B' as the latter's progress towards Stalingrad had slowed to a halt. With the help of the armoured force, the attack once again got under way, and the Germans reached Stalingrad. The Russians were determined to hold the city, and perhaps the fiercest house-to-house battle of the war swiftly developed, the Germans gradually inching forward with great casualties against fanatical resistance. The Russians, meanwhile, were preparing their own counterstroke. This broke on 19 November, once the temperature had fallen far enough to make tankable ice out of the autumn mud that had made movement so difficult for the last month. Under the command of Zhukov, the Russians launched a massive pincer movement, making full use of the gap between Army Groups 'A' and 'B'. The Germans were completely overwhelmed by the size and ferocity of the Russian attack, and Army Group 'B' fell back, leaving the 6th Army cut off in Stalingrad. Weichs urged Paulus to fight his way out, but Hitler insisted that the 6th Army hold on to Stalingrad whilst a relief force fought its way through. Meanwhile,

Goering assured Hitler, his *Luftwaffe* could keep the beleaguered garrison supplied. This proved a completely idle boast. The counterstroke was organised by Manstein, who managed to get within 35 miles of Stalingrad on 19 December. Manstein urged Paulus to fight his way out to the relief force, but again Paulus listened to Hitler and refused to do so. It was now only a matter of time before the city fell to the Russians. Paulus and his men fought on with extraordinary courage and determination, but their lack of fuel and food, combined with another hard winter, gradually took their toll. On 2 February 1943, Paulus surrendered with 93,00 men. In all, Hitler's ill-advised bifurcated summer offensive had cost the Germans 300,000 men and 1,000 tanks, all of which Germany could not adequately replace.

In the Caucasus Army Group 'A', now under the command of Kleist, had not been able to progress, and the Russians had finally been able to drive it back. With the end in Stalingrad Army Group 'B' ceased to exist, being replaced by Manstein's Army Group 'Don', formed in November 1942. Army Group 'A' had fallen back at the end of 1942, the 1st *Panzerarmee* joining Army Group 'Don' and the rest of the group forming a defensive line between the Black Sea and the Sea of Azov. All along the southern part of the Russo-German front the Soviet forces were putting great pressure on the Germans and their satellites whilst preparing their own major offensive.

The advance into the Caucasus and the taking of Stalingrad marked the high-water point of the German war against Russia, and the defeat of the 6th Army in Stalingrad the beginning of the ebb. Although the Germans tried to wrest the strategic offensive away from the Russians at the Battle of Kursk in July 1943, from the moment of Paulus' capitulation in Stalingrad it can fairly be said that the Germans could not prevail over the Russians in the East.

FIELD-MARSHAL GÜNTHER HANS VON KLUGE

Operation '*Barbarossa*' was the code-name for the German invasion of Russia, which was to be a three-pronged advance, aiming at Leningrad in the north, Moscow in the middle and the Caucasus in the south. The ultimate objective was to occupy within the shortest possible time practically the whole of eastern Europe from Archangel to Astrakhan. The Germans would ultimately fail in this objective, but the first weeks of the invasion were to prove absolutely disastrous for the Russians – they lost thousands of tanks, many planes and hundreds of thousands of troops taken prisoner.

The Russians were not psychologically or technically prepared for the German attack launched on 22 June 1941. Some formations were hardly at paper strength and many units were away from their positions on summer training exercises. Stationed near the Russo-German border were the forces of the Western District under the command of General D. G. Pavlov and comprising the 3rd, 4th and 10th Armies. After the outbreak of hostilities, this became known as the West Front. Pavlov's forces were deployed almost wholly in the Bialystok salient in a line running south from the Latvian frontier to Voldava on the fringe of the Pripet marshes.

On 22 June Pavlov's forces are thought to have consisted of six mechanised corps, one cavalry corps and 24 rifle divisions divided between the three armies, with further mechanised and a cavalry corps in reserve. It is difficult to be certain of the exact forces, as secrecy still covers some aspects of Russia's participation in the war. The Red Army had a large number of tanks, but most of these were obsolete and a shortage of spare parts meant that a great many of them were not operational. The new tanks, KV and T-34, were not yet available, although they would prove a match for the Germans later. The production rate of guns, mortars and automatic weapons was very slow, with the production of ammunition lagging even further behind. Radio equipment was also in short supply and functioned poorly. The vast majority of army planes were obsolete.

Another serious deficiency was the absence of motorised transport. A very large number of guns were therefore drawn by horses or tractors.

■ Many objectives

Very few Russian officers had had direct experience of warfare and many had only lately been drafted to replace the thousands of officers purged during 1937–38. The training of tank and air crews had been badly neglected.

The German army on the Soviet frontier was divided up into three main army groups – 'North', 'Centre' and 'South'. We are concerned with Army Group 'Centre' under the command of Field-Marshal von Bock, which was stationed in northern and central Poland between Lublin and Suwalki and comprising the 4th and 9th Armies and 2nd and 3rd *Panzergruppen*. Altogether, Army Group 'Centre' totalled 49 divisions including six motorised, nine Panzer and one cavalry divisions. In addition, Field-Marshal Kesselring's *Luftlotte* 2 was assigned to Bock, a powerful force with approximately 1,000 planes. The mission entrusted to Army Group 'Centre' was to encircle and then to destroy the enemy in Belorussia by way of two deep thrusts, one in the north from the area of Suwalki and one further south along the northern edge of the Pripet marshes from brest-Litovsk. The 9th Army, under Colonel-General Strauss with General Hoth's 3rd *Panzergruppe* was to make the northern thrust, while Field-Marshal Guenther von Kluge's 4th Army of 21 infantry divisions with General Guderian's 2nd *Panzergruppe* comprising five Panzer, one cavalry and three motorised infantry divisions would execute the southern pincer movement. Both the *Panzergruppen* were under control of the infantry commanders.

The two Panzer groups were to drive east-wards and join at Minsk, the Belorussian capital, lying some 250 miles from the Russo-German frontier. Part of the infantry was to follow the Panzers to Minsk, whilst the rest was to make two shorter enveloping thrusts to the north and south of Bialystok, meeting at a point on the Bialystok-Minsk road about 100 miles from the frontier. The enemy would therefore be trapped inside two pockets, one inside the other, and was to be destroyed before the advance resumed to Smolensk.

■ A good start

Bock, however, disagreed with the order that the pincers should be closed at Minsk. He thought the primary objective should be Smolensk. He requested Brauchitsch and Halder at OKH to change the plan, but he had heard nothing definite when the offensive started, and so Guderian and Hoth set off on their armoured advances to the east uncertain of their first objective.

On the night of 19/20 June, the German armoured forces began arriving in the forests about three miles from the River Bug (which formed the frontier) in preparation for the invasion. Surprise was to be a very important factor and so the Germans were careful to hide themselves before battle commenced. Hitler's HQ was sited in the thick forest near Rastenburg in East Prussia.

Because he thought the Germans would not break the Nazi-Soviet Non-Aggression Pact, Stalin refused to belief there was anything sinister about the German troop movements. Stalin was in a difficult position here – if he took any preparatory measures, for example moving his troops on the border to defensive combat positions, this might give Hitler the 'evidence' for a German invasion, on the grounds that Russia had broken the non-aggression pact. Stalin stuck to this even though information concerning the invasion was received in Moscow, and, in the event, never was an army so ill-prepared to meet an invasion as was the Red Army on the eve of Operation 'Barbarossa'.

On 22 June, Kesselring's *Luftlotte* 2 started a sustained and intensive bombing campaign of all Russian ground movements and cleared the skies of Russian planes. On this day alone, the Soviet Union lost 2,000 planes. The German planes attacked roads, grounded planes, tanks and fuel stores as well. German assault parties crossed land frontiers, achieving surprise almost everywhere, making a special effort to destroy Soviet communications and to isolate units from their staffs.

General Hermann Hoth and his 3rd *Panzergruppe* got off to a good start on their northern pincer movement. They travelled quickly through the forests of Augustow on the frontier. The left wing of the *Panzergruppe* cut the Russian 11th Army in two, captured Kaunas, the bridges of the Niemen intact and the city of Vilnyus on 24 June. A counterattack by Soviet 11th Army's XII Mechanised Corps broke down, thus freeing the tanks to swing south and on towards Minsk. The right wing of the 3rd *Panzergruppe* drove back the Russian 3rd Army (General Kuznetsov) which had evacuated Grodno, and cut through its XI Mechanised Corps on its way to Lida and Volkovisk.

Further west, the Russian 10th Army was already threatened with encirclement. The *Luftwaffe* caught its VI Mechanised Corps in the open trying to counterattack. Its lines of retreat were being steadily narrowed and on 25 June, the 10th Army received permission to withdraw, but by this time Guderian had reached the outskirts of Minsk.

On 22 June the infantry of the German 4th Army attacked into Brest Litovsk while Guderian's Panzers bypassed the fortress, with XXIV Panzer Corps crossing the River Bug to the south of the town and XLVII Panzer Corps to the north. Some of the armour forded the 13-foot river by underwater wading – a technique developed for the proposed invasion of England. Brest Litovsk was the scene of much bloody fighting and the town held out until 29 June, causing heavy casualties to the German 45th Division. Meanwhile, Guderian's Panzer thrust went as planned, his rate of advance proving quite spectacular. He was troubled only by XIV Mechanised Corps of the Soviet 4th Army, which engaged the 18th Panzer Division of the left-flanking XLVII Panzer Corps in battle near Pruzhany. The country here was well suited to armoured warfare. By 26 June, Slutsk, 60 miles due south of Minsk, had been taken by XXIV Panzer Corps, although the Russians trying to break out of Bialystok fired heavily on its left flank.

The Russians apparently did not see the threat of the pincers closing at Minsk. They were in a state of utter confusion and shock. Pavlov's West Front, deployed close to the frontier in the Bialystok salient, seemed to be just waiting to be trapped. When Pavlov did see the danger to the forward elements of his 3rd and 10th Armies from the shorter pincer movement by the German infantry, he ordered all the army and front reserves forward, thus leaving the Minsk area practically undefended and making the task of the German armour that much easier.

The Russians stood and fought bravely where they were, encountering the Germans head-on. There was no co-ordinated defence, partly because of the breakdown in communications. Defence arrangements were left to the initiative of the local commanders and the tenacity of the forward troops, who held on grimly in the under-manned and incomplete fortifications. In the early days of the invasion, there were no orders or directions except the standing order to attack the enemy whenever and wherever he was encountered.

■ Russian failure

A two-day armoured and cavalry counter-offensive by VI and XI Mechanised Corps started on 24 June, under General Boldin, the Deputy Commander of the Western Front. The Russians attacked from the area of Grodno to north-east of Bialystok, against the infantry of the German 9th Army, which was moving south-east in the shorter pincer movement. This was beaten off easily, however, by German infantry and anti-tank gunners, and Soviet losses were heavy. On 26 June, Hoth's 3rd *Panzergruppe* arrived 18 miles north of Minsk, and Guderian received orders to turn north with the majority of his force and join Hoth and so close the pocket. Guderian's rightflanking XXIV Corps was permitted to continue its drive to the east towards Bobruysk on the River Berezina and on to the Dniepr.

Whether the Panzers should wait at Minsk for the infantry or continue their fantastic easterly thrust was a cause of great friction. Guderian, a tank expert, had absorbed the teaching of Liddell Hart on the importance of speed, mobility and firepower. He saw the tank as a separate arm, not part of the infantry. His commander, Kluge, held the opposite view. He disliked seeing the tanks so far ahead and would rather use them to contain the Russian pockets, waiting to advance further until the encirclement battle was completed. Guderian considered containing the enemy pockets to be the infantry's task, and that the armour must be mobile. For tanks to be stationary was to be vulnerable.

Kluge, therefore, was happy that the pincers were to close on Minsk, whereas

Guderian felt frustrated that his advance was slowed down. He and Kluge argued over the formations Guderian filtered off from the pocket and sent on to the Dniepr. Kluge's counter-order conveniently got lost. Hitler agreed with Kluge and was worried whether the pincers should close before Minsk, at Novogrodek, so that the thousands of Russians already trapped at Bialystok should not escape, but he was persuaded that Minsk as the objective would result in even more Russians trapped. And so the pocket was sealed on 28 June after Guderian's tanks had been involved in a sharp clash with the Russian 13th (Reinforcement) Army.

Guderian's drive to Minsk has been called one of the most spectacular marches in history.

Inside this trap 20 Soviet divisions were encircled. By nightfall on 28 June, the marching infantry of the German 9th and 4th Armies had joined up and closed the smaller pocket. Thus the Bialystok pocket was completely cut off from the larger Novogrodek pocket to the east. As a result of this catastrophe, Pavlov was recalled and shot.

By 3 July, the enemy in the Bialystok pocket had surrendered, and by 9 July, 328,000 Russian prisoners were 'in the bag' and at least 2,500 Soviet tanks had been knocked out or captured, together with 1,500 guns.

Kluge was probably right in maintaining that the pocket should be closed at Minsk. Had the Panzers raced on to Smolensk, the infantry would have been way behind and would have been hard-pressed to seal off such a gigantic pocket. Kluge and Guderian did not get on at all, and the fact that no explicit written orders for the conduct of the operation were provided only made relations between them worse.

FIELD-MARSHAL FEDOR VON BOCK

'**M**oscow is merely a geographical concept,' Hitler had said at the beginning of Operation *'Barbarossa'*. He ordered that the main thrusts should be on Leningrad, 'the cradle of the Revolution', and on Kiev. Only after they had been isolated or destroyed would the men of Army Group 'Centre' drive for the Soviet capital. Yet before Kiev had been taken on 15 September, or Leningrad completely encircled on 8 September, Hitler ordered that units be switched to Army Group 'Centre' for its final drive. It seemed a logical move since Moscow was not only the capital of Russia, but also its communications hub and an emotional focus for the Soviet armies. By attacking Moscow Army Group 'Centre' would also be able to destroy the bulk of Russian forces which were sure to be concentrated in front of the capital.

■ Double pincer

The attack on Moscow, which bore the code-name 'Typhoon', could not be launched until 2 October for the Germans had to collect their forces. Bock's Army Group 'Centre' was reinforced to a strength of 78 divisions, with 7 Panzer and 4 motorised divisions in addition to the 7 and 5 of these divisions already in the group. On paper it looked a very powerful force, but by now these units were hardly up to strength. The tanks had been operating across the dusty tracks of European Russia, and not only had they been moving from west to east, but units like Guderian's 2nd *Panzerarmee* had had to travel north by road from the Ukraine and Hoepner's 3rd *Panzergruppe* had had to drive down from the Leningrad front. The dust and heat, and the very poor condition of the roads had worn out the engines of many of the German tanks, and the inadequate communications with the west, based largely on a few overstretched railway lines, meant that insufficient spares had reached the front. The marching infantry, though footsore and dusty, were still reasonably up to strength.

Using a by now well-tried tactic, Bock was going to envelop the Russian forces opposite him in a double pincer movement. The Russian forces, according to German intelligence, were the Bryansk Front under General Eremenko and the West Front under General Konev which between them contained 14 armies of 77 divisions, including six armoured and six cavalry.

Guderian opened the offensive in the south with his *Panzerarmee* and the men of the 2nd Army, on 30 September. In two days he drove 90 miles and captured Orel. XLVII Panzer Corps, following in his dust, swung north and captured Bryansk, linking up with units of the 2nd Army. The Germans surrounded two pockets to the north and south of the city, and though these surrendered on 25 October, strong elements of the northern pocket, composed of the Soviet 50th Army, managed to slip eastwards through the woodland and marshes.

On 20 October the 4th Army and 4th *Panzergruppe*, concentrated near Roslavl, struck the left wing of Konev's West Front. A day later Hoepner's tanks swung north-east and punched through the 'Vyazma Defence Line'. While this thrust was in progress the 9th Army and 3rd *Panzergruppe* had started a drive to the east and south. On 18th October XL Panzer Corps of the 4th *Panzergruppe*, under General Stumme, linked up with advanced units of LVI Panzer Corps of the 3rd *Panzergruppe*, under General Schaal. They had captured the important rail link of Vyazma, and cut the Moscow highway, but more than this, they had encircled parts of four Soviet armies. Between them the Germans estimated that the Vyazma and Bryansk pockets had yielded 663,000 prisoners from 67 infantry divisions, six cavalry divisions and various armoured units, as well as 1,242 tanks and 5,412 guns. With the able support of his energetic subordinates Bock had scored a resounding victory – and moreover with their static defence plan the Russians had done much to contribute to their own defeat. On 7 October Russia's Marshal Zhukov was to recall that 'all roads to Moscow were in essence open'. However, a day earlier Guderian had noted in his war diary that the Germans had experienced the first snowfall of winter. The dusty roads had turned to a deep soft mud and the Panzers had churned to a temporary halt – it was an ominous foretaste of the rigours of a Russian winter.

■ Renewed attack

When Zhukov arrived Bock had become temporarily bogged down in the reduction of the Vyazma/Bryansk pockets, chiefly because the *rasputitsa* had set in. The *rasputitsa*, or 'season of bad roads', comes twice in Russia: in autumn and spring when the early snows and rain, or the melting snow of winter turn the dirt tracks of central Russia into rivers of mud.

On 14 October, however, the Germans got under way again and Hoth's 3rd *Panzergruppe* broke through the screening forces to the north and reached the 'Sea of Moscow', a reservoir 70 miles to the north-west of Moscow. When the news reached the capital, civilian morale plunged, and between 16 and 20 October, in the words of the official Soviet historian Samsonov, 'there were those who spread panic, abandoned their places of work and fled hastily from the city. There were traitors who took advantage of the situation to pillage Soviet property and to try to sap the strength of the Soviet state.'

Bock and Zhukov were now fighting a race with the winter. Bock did not realise as clearly as his Russian opponent what a Russian winter could mean, but he knew that time was running out. Now generals like Rundstedt and Leeb wanted to call a halt to the operations, but Bock, Brauchitsch and Halder argued that superior will-power would carry their troops to Moscow. Blumentritt recalls a conference of chiefs-of-staff which took place on 12 November at Orsha: the chiefs-of-staff of Army Groups 'North' and 'South' were against continuing the attacks, but 'the Chief-of-Staff of Army "Centre", von Greiffenberg, took a more indefinite line, pointing out the risks but not expressing opposition to an advance. He was in a difficult position. Field-Marshal von Bock was a very capable soldier, but ambitious, and his eyes were focused on Moscow, which seemed so near.'

Whatever their views, the men of Army Group 'Centre' received their marching orders from Hitler. After protests from Kluge, they were ordered not to attempt to encircle Moscow and cut its railway links to the east, but were to occupy the capital. Blumentritt said that they were ordered to blow up the Kremlin 'to signalise the overthrow of Bolshevism'.

The final advance began on 16 November. The ground was now hard with winter frosts, and some units had difficulty retrieving their vehicles, which were frozen into the mud. To make up for the losses and wastage in his units Bock regrouped them. The 4th *Panzergruppe* was moved towards the 3rd *Panzergruppe*, which was now commanded by Reinhardt. However, this meant that Kluge's 4th Army, now weak in armour, had a broader front than before. To the south Guderian and his 2nd *Panzerarmee* were out on their own.

Whatever their generals might think, the men were determined to reach Moscow. 'They could see the flashes of the AA guns over Moscow at night, and it fired their imagination – the city seemed so near. They also felt that they would find shelter from the bitter weather.' By now the Russian winter was beginning to tell on the men of Army Group 'Centre'. Dressed as they were in the lightweight uniforms that they had been wearing at the beginning of the Russian campaign, many men went down with frostbite. Guderian noted that on 17 November there were 400 cases in each regiment of the 112th Division. Oil was beginning to thicken up, the grease on shells had to be chipped off before each would fit the breach, without anti-freeze tank engines had to be kept running – or fires lit beneath the engine to make them start – and the German artificial rubber called *Buna* became friable or as rigid as wood.

■ The final check

Despite the resistance of nature and the Russians, Bock displayed, in Keitel's words, 'incredible energy' and his men fought hard. It was to the north that they came within reach of the city. Here the Russians were trying to consolidate their defences on the Volga Canal and the Sea of Moscow. The 9th Army broke through and on 27 November the 3rd *Panzergruppe* linked up with it on a line south of Dmitrov. A day later men of the 7th Panzer Division established a bridgehead across the canal, but were driven back by a Russian counter-attack.

Bock's attack was reaching its high water mark: at Krasnaya Polyana the tanks of the 3rd *Panzergruppe* were only 18 miles from Moscow, while the 4th Army was a mere 25 miles from the city. To the south Guderian had actually reached a point east of Moscow. His 2nd *Panzerarmee*, having isolated the industrial town of Tula where resistance had proved too strong, was now at Mikhaylov nearly 40 miles to the east, while his northern units were 69 miles from Moscow. On 30 November motorcycle patrols of the 62nd Panzer Engineer Battalion, part of the 2nd Panzer Division, reached Khimki, a small river port five miles from Moscow. They returned from their reconnaissance, but not before they had added to the alarm in the city. A combat group of the 2nd Panzer Division under Lieutenant-Colonel Decker reached the town of Ozeretskoye and were able to stand at the terminus stop of the Moscow tram system. At Gorki men of the 2nd Battalion, 304th Rifle Regiment, were 19 miles from the Kremlin, or 12 miles from the suburbs of Moscow, while an assault party of the 38th Panzer Engineer Battalion demolished the station at Lobnya to prevent it being used for tactical resupply – they were just ten miles from the city.

But now even Bock realised that his men could go on no longer. And writing to Halder on 1 December he said: 'The idea that the enemy facing the Army Group was on the point of collapse was, as the fighting of the last fortnight shows, a pipe dream. To remain outside the gates of Moscow, where the rail and road systems connect with almost the whole of eastern Russia, means heavy defensive fighting for us against an enemy vastly superior in numbers. Further offensive action therefore seems to be senseless and aimless, especially as the time is coming very near when the physical strength of the troops will be completely exhausted.'

■ Total exhaustion

In fact many of the men of Army Group 'Centre' had already reached their 'limit of strategic consumption'. Frostbite was now a more deadly enemy than the Russians, though Soviet forces were showing a determination which reflected the firm leadership that Stalin was exercising by telephone from his office in the Kremlin, and which Zhukov was transmitting to his subordinates.

On 4 December Kluge ordered his 4th Army to cease any further attacks and to go onto the defensive. Guderian adopted the same tactics a day later. After the war Zhukov explained that Bock overestimated the capabilities of the forces he employed for the final attack on Moscow: 'To gamble entirely on Panzer formations in the given situation, proved in practice to be erroneous, as they became worn out, suffered heavy casualties, and lost their ability to break through.'

However, it was the well-tried tactics of pincer attacks which rebounded on the Germans: 'The German command failed to arrange for a pinning-down attack in the centre of our front, even though it had adequate forces to do so. This made it possible for us to transfer all reserves, from the central sectors to the flanks of the Front, to fight the enemy assault groups. Their heavy losses, their unpreparedness for fighting in winter conditions, and the fierceness of the Soviet opposition had a sharp effect upon German battle-worthiness.'

The attack on Moscow marks the high point of German operations in World War II. In 1942 they were to drive to Stalingrad and the Caucasus, but though this was spectacular, it would never yield results to compare with the capture of Moscow. By failing to destroy the Soviet capital in the first year of the war in the East they had jeopardised their chances of ever gaining complete victory.

FIELD-MARSHAL WILHELM RITTER VON LEEB

Although Hitler was at fault with his grand strategy for '*Barbarossa*', his planning was sound. He stipulated that Leningrad should be captured before German forces united to thrust deeper into Russia to capture Moscow. The capture of Leningrad appealed to him on political as well as strategic grounds. It was the birthplace of the Bolshevik revolution and bore the name of its originator. However, the elimination of Leningrad would also secure Hitler's left flank and commit the Finns deeper into the war. Communications would be quicker through the Baltic rather than by the vulnerable road and rail links of north and central Russia, and the Red Army would lose the support of Leningrad's considerable arms and engineering industry.

Army Group 'North' was allotted the task of taking the city. Leeb, its commander, had two armies, the 18th and the 16th under Kuechler and Busche, and the 4th *Panzergruppe* under Hoepner, in all a force of 23 infantry divisions and three Panzer divisions.

Opposite him was the Russian North-West Front under Kuznetsov, which consisted of the 8th and 11th Armies totalling 20 infantry divisions and two mechanised corps. They had the advantage of defending an area of low-lying coastal plains with rivers, marshes, woodlands and lakes, impassable to the narrow-tracked German tanks, and disturbingly new territory for German infantry.

Realising that this terrain lent little freedom of movement for major encircling actions, Leeb arranged his forces for a concentrated thrust for Leningrad. The 4th *Panzergruppe* was the meat of a sandwich composed of the 18th Army to the north and the 16th to the south. Whilst the infantry secured the flanks and mopped up Russian forces paralysed by the armoured thrust, the *Panzergruppe* would drive in an almost straight line for Leningrad.

The Germans were lucky to have secured a bridgehead over the River Niemen even before they went to war. Hitler's annexation of the city of Memel gave them nearly 100 miles of the right bank, and a handy jumping off point.

■ Baltic advance

At 0300 hours on 22 June, Army Group 'North' started crossing into Russian-occupied Lithuania. The *Panzergruppe* which came under Leeb's personal control had been assigned the primary objective of securing a bridgehead over the River Dvina, the broadest river on the north-east Baltic coast. Though the German forces encountered few effective fixed defences they were surprised by the numbers of Russian troops who had been moved into Lithuania and Latvia since their annexation in 1940.

On 26 June the Germans captured two bridges over the Dvina at Daugavpils. The 150-mile drive from East Prussia to the Dvina had taken the *Panzergruppe* a mere four days. Now that LVI Panzer Corps had secured bridges at Daugavpils, XLI Panzer Corps struck downstream and captured bridges at Jekabpils. On their right the infantry blocked the Russian escape route from Kurland by securing the river around Riga.

On parallel courses the two Panzer corps now drove for the 'Stalin Line' near Ostrov. This was the old Russian/Estonian border and had been fortified before 1940. XLI Panzer Corps punched through the line and swung north to Ostrov. It was counter-attacked after it had captured the town, and in heavy fighting against Russian KV-1 and KV-2 tanks was saved only by the intervention of the heavy field howitzers of the 73rd Artillery Regiment.

Five days after the capture of Ostrov, the town of Pskov fell to XLI Panzer Corps on 9 July. A day later LVI Panzer Corps joined in a massed attack along the whole front. It had broken through the Stalin Line on 6 July and thrust through to Opochka on the Velikaya river. Now, south of Lake Ilmen the full *Panzergruppe* met heavy resistance. Leeb was faced with a problem: the main strength of the Soviet forces seemed to be on the right flank – just where he had been instructed to put his main weight. Ignoring the OKW edict he began switching the 1st and 6th Panzer Divisions and the 36th Motorised Infantry Division to a position north of Luga. They moved off on 13 July through difficult swampland and woods.

Despite this 100-mile forced march, an advanced unit of the 6th Panzer Division took the little town of Porechye on 14 July, while to the south the 1st Panzer Division established a bridgehead over the Luga river at Sabsk. The men of Leeb's army group were now a mere 70 miles from Leningrad, just a two days' march.

Then, inexplicably, OKW ordered a halt for three weeks. Hitler and his staff gave up the opportunity to capture Leningrad by a direct coup in favour of encirclement by an outflanking movement on the right. This decision gave the Russians a break similar to that enjoyed by the BEF at Dunkirk when Hitler ordered that his Panzers should not move in to clear the beach-head. Leeb could see that it was tactically unsound to put his main weight on the right, and that with his forces on the left he could not only drive for Leningrad but also seal off the Russian forces retreating up the Baltic coast. He had received his orders, however, and unlike some of his more adventurous colleagues he was unwilling to circumvent them.

While Reinhardt's XLI Panzer Corps paused on the Luga, Manstein's LVI Panzer Corps became entangled in heavy fighting around Shimsk west of Lake Ilmen. On 8 August the whole *Panzergruppe* was able to resume the offensive, but this time they were up against fixed defences which had been built by impressed civilian labourers. It took them nearly a week to break out from the northern Luga defences, while Manstein's Panzer division remained stuck in the well-defended lines around the town of Luga.

Having broken through in the north, Hoepner again pleaded with Leeb to give him some forces to cover his left flank – two divisions, perhaps even one, would be enough he said. This time Leeb agreed to detach the 3rd Motorised Infantry Division from LVI Panzer Corps and place it under Reinhardt's command. Once again it seemed that Leningrad was within reach of the men of Army Group 'North'.

■ Counterattack

Then on 12 August the Russians intervened. On the right flank, south of Lake Ilmen and along the River Lovat, the 126th, 30th and 290th Infantry Divisions had been involved in heavy fighting, breaking into the Russian fixed defences. It was against these forces that Marshal Voroshilov launched a counterattack through the gap between Lake Seliger and Lake Ilmen, which had been formed by the division between Army Group 'North' and 'Centre'. He pushed eight rifle divisions, one cavalry corps and an armoured corps through, hoping that these forces could swing round to cut off the Germans from their communications and lift the pressure on Leningrad.

On 19 August, however, four days after he had received his first order to break off fighting and move south-east, Manstein led the 3rd Motorised Infantry Division and the SS Division '*Totenkopf*' in a counterattack on the Russian incursion. They struck the exposed left flank of the Russian forces, who were pressing against Lake Ilmen. Paralysed by this unforeseen German reaction and attacked by the infantry they had trapped against the lake the Russian forces fell apart. They left behind them 246 guns and the first intact multiple rocket-launcher, the 'Stalin Organ'.

Although the Germans had won a victory at Lake Ilmen, the Russians did not give up the pressure, and Manstein's Panzer corps remained in that area to deal with these attacks.

About the time that Manstein was moving his forces south, German infantry were fighting to capture the ancient city of Novgorod. In their operations they were greatly aided by the capture of a marked map of the Russian units deployed in the area, and also by a Karelian engineer who possessed detailed plans of the fixed defences of the city. Novgorod was captured on the 16th and the German forces pressed on to capture a railway bridge over the River Volkhov near Chudovo.

At Luga the Russians still hung on, though their position had been bypassed to the south by the German thrust to Novgorod. However, in order to reach Leningrad on a practicable road, the Germans had to eliminate the Luga position. They had tried frontal assault and this had proved too expensive, so on 13 August XXVIII Corps began its attacks to the east of the town. It took a week before the corps reached the River Oredezh. The corps crossed the river and became involved in fierce Soviet counterattacks. Indeed, it was not until 3 September that the metalled road beyond Luga was declared secure and the Luga pockets had been destroyed. The Germans captured 600 guns, 316 tanks and 21,000 prisoners.

While this fighting was going on to the south, Leeb received pleas from Hoepner that the 4th *Panzergruppe* should be given more support in its drive on Leningrad. It had lost Manstein's LVI Panzer Corps and needed men to cover its northern flank against the Russian troops retreating along the coast from the Baltic states. Though he received some units to cover the flank, the 8th Panzer Division was drawn southward into the fighting around Luga. Advancing slowly, Hoepner reached a point 25 miles from Leningrad on 21 August. he could not move faster even though there was only limited opposition to his front, for now he had only the 1st and 6th Panzer Divisions and the 11th Panzer Regiment. On 16 August the 1st Panzer Division had reported that besides two weakened infantry battalions in armoured carriers, it had only 44 serviceable tanks.

Leeb eventually agreed to give Hoepner the infantry support he so badly needed. On 17 August he instructed Colonel-General Kuechler of the 18th Army to destroy the Russian 8th Army in Estonia and then move from the Baltic coast to Narva. At the same time he also ordered to capture the coastal defences along the southern coast of the Gulf of Finland. This elaborate order meant that the men were tied up in unnecessary assaults on fixed defences when they were desperately needed before Leningrad. The positions they attacked could have been starved out after the capture of the city. It did, however, give Kuechler, Leeb's friend, a chance to collect a little of the glamour that had been the preserve of the fast moving Panzers – but doling out favours does not win battles and every delay meant that the Russians were able to strengthen their city. It was only by September that all the necessary forces were echeloned up to the Leningrad lines.

■ **Assault tactics**
The attack began on 8/9 September and ran into belts of fixed fortifications which had been built by women and children from the city. The Russians had taken every opportunity that German delays had given them, and now the city was surrounded

by concentric belts of fortifications which reached right into the streets. The first belt was 25 miles from Leningrad and the second a mere 15 miles.

The Russian defenders received a demonstration of thorough German assault tactics. Dive-bombing by the Stukas of Richthofen's *Fliegerkorps* VIII, attacks by pioneers and infantry and breakthroughs by tanks after the tank-traps and defences had been neutralised. Around midday on 11 September a German tank commander reported: 'I can see St Petersburg and the Sea.'

Four days later men of the 209th Infantry Regiment were a mere six miles from the city centre. They captured a tram carrying workers to their factory in Leningrad. On the 16th German infantry captured Pushkin, the one-time summer residence of the Tsar.

On the first day of the attack two combat groups under Colonels Count Schwerin and Harry Hoppe, with the reinforced 76th and 424th Infantry Regiments, had attacked the Russian industrial settlements at Schluesselburg without Stuka support after they had cleared the eight industrial settlements outside the town. With its capture the Germans had sealed off Leningrad from the Russian hinterland – the only contact the Russians would have would be via Lake Ladoga. Now the time seemed ripe for the last attack which would be the culmination of all the German efforts; but Hitler had other plans.

On 12 September he had informed the German commanders that Leningrad was not to be attacked but surrounded and starved out. Everyone said that it would capitulate before the winter frosts. It was not Hitler's first mistake, but it was one of his worst for it lost him two cities: Leningrad and Moscow. Leeb's reluctance to go beyond his orders and take risks and the determination of the people of Leningrad not to be starved into submission meant that the city fell neither to a *coup de main* nor to slow starvation.

COLONEL-GENERAL ERICH HOEPNER

'Victory', goes an Italian proverb, 'has many fathers; but defeat is an orphan.' It was Hitler's attempt to foist the responsibility for the German defeat at Moscow on any one but himself that led to a purge of his generals. Besides retiring Rundstedt, Guderian and Brauchitsch, he had Colonel-General Hoepner dishonourably discharged, deprived of the right to wear uniform, draw his pension, live in the house that had been allocated to him and even to wear the medals he had won.

Hoepner's 4th *Panzergruppe*, along with Hoth's 3rd *Panzergruppe*, had as we have seen made the closest penetration to Moscow, and on 5 December had halted, exhausted, in an arc from the Volga Canal through Krasnaya Polyana to Istra. Totally unequipped for winter war, their vehicles and weapons seized up in the severe cold, and men were forced either to pack out their uniforms with paper for insulation, or wear layers of clothes like old tramps. Many took to wearing the clothes of dead or captured Russians so that only their national insignia distinguished them from their enemies.

A day after the Germans had been forced to a halt, the Russians under General Zhukov launched a counter-offensive which caught their enemies badly off balance. Stalin had received information from a spy in Tokyo, Richard Sorge, that though the Japanese had plans for major operations in the Far East, these were not to be directed against the Soviet Union. Trusting his security services, and working on the assumption that if Russia lost the war on her western borders, she would be unlikely to retain her Far Eastern provinces, Stalin ordered that his Siberian troops be sent west. These men were fresh, well-equipped and inured to severe weather. They came from an army which had a reputation and experience similar to the British Indian Army, in that they were independent and battle-wise after border clashes and fights with the Japanese Manchurian Army.

The Germans had been meeting units from this army as they approached Moscow, but it was not until 5/6 December that they began to realise the full quality of their opposition. The clashes on the front line, however, were almost as fierce as the arguments between the generals of Army Group 'Centre'. On 3 December, Hoepner had taken Kluge to task for the failure of his 4th Army to make any progress in their three-day attack on the Nara. Hoepner had reached a point 19 miles from the Kremlin and, feeling his men deserved more support from the 4th Army, suggested that both the 3rd and 4th *Panzergruppen* should be withdrawn from their 30-mile-deep salient in order to straigntem the line. In the meantime, he said, he and his men would take three days rest while OKW made up its mind about what exactly it was trying to do.

Kluge, who had the nickname of '*der kluge Hans*' or 'clever Hans', had earned it not only for his military ability but also his skill in surviving the political and emotional hazards of serving under Hitler. Hoepner's comments about his superiors, and such dangerous phrases as 'civilian leadership' were being noted by Kluge.

Dangerously frank, Hoepner sent a report to Kluge on 5 December in which he complained that the Ministry of Propaganda was incorrectly calling the Russians demoralised, defeated and without courage – in fact, he said, they were fighting very well. He estimated that there were 19 rifle, four cavalry and 12 armoured units in front of the 4th *Panzergruppe*. Whilst some of these units had suffered severe losses, the Germans were nevertheless outnumbered. Moreover, he added that whilst his men were still in their summer-weight denims, the Russians were now appearing in excellent fur caps, felt boots, and quilted trousers and tunics. While the Germans were forced to scrape hollows in the snow, the Russians operated from prepared covered positions.

A day later, under the full shock of Zhukov's counter-offensive, Hoepner received an order from Kluge's 4th Army that he could withdraw from his salient back to the line of the Istra. As Hoepner commented, however, whoever drafted the order had absolutely no understanding of general staff work. He had orders to withdraw, but the 3rd *Panzergruppe* under Reinhardt, which was not under Kluge's command, had received no instructions. It would be out on a very dangerous limb if Hoepner withdrew. When Reinhardt did receive his orders from Army Group 'Centre', he found that he was being attacked on his right flank and rear. Hoepner delivered a sharp protest to Kluge, and on 8 December the 3rd *Panzergruppe* was put under his command for easier command and control.

The *Stavka* was surprised by the speed of the German withdrawal, but as the German author Paul Carell explains, 'the German *Wehrmacht* had never learned the principles and methods of retreat. The German soldier regarded retreat not as a special type of operation, to be bent to his will, but as a disaster imposed by the enemy upon him.

'Even in *Reichswehr* days the practising of withdrawals had been looked upon askance. Somewhat contemptuously it used to be said; One does not practice withdrawals; it merely teaches the men to run away.

'Later, after 1936, even elastic resistance was deleted from the training programme. "Attack" and "holding" were the only two techniques taught to the German soldier. As far as fighting retreats were concerned, the *Wehrmacht* went into the war unprepared.'

Pressed by the Russians, Hoepner reached his stop line at Istra on 12 December. He had lost a lot of equipment, including half his artillery, since it had been immobilised because of the death of horses or the lack of working prime-movers. In spite of this he was encouraged by reports that the men were still in good spirits and he had been able to move the 2nd Panzer Division into reserve now that the line had been shortened.

However, when he examined his position Hoepner realised that he could no longer defend it, for on his left Reinhardt was still in difficulties and his flank was in danger of envelopment. Hoepner decided that he would have to pull back to the River Ruza. On 20 December the 3rd and 4th *Panzergruppen* reached the line Ruza-Volokolamsk-Lama.

Two days earlier Hoepner had received Hitler's controversial 'stand and fight' order. On 24 December the commander of the 4th *Panzergruppe* drafted a reply, explaining simply that a static defence was beyond the capabilities of his men. They were without the equipment, weapons and logistic support, there were too few of them and those that were available were hungry and frozen. The Russians, however, were well-equipped and numerous, so it was doubtful if they could be worn down in a battle of attrition. Reasonable as this report sounds to a post-war reader, it was the sort of truth that was unacceptable to Hitler.

Hoepner's men remained relatively undisturbed until 3 January when Hitler ordered that they were to assume responsibility for part of the front held by the 4th Army. They were to close the breach made by the Russians at Maloyaroslavets.

Not only did Hitler give orders that were near impossible, but he even gave instructions as to how they were to be carried out. Neither the orders nor the instructions bore any relation to the reality of fighting in the East. Although Hoepner's front was secure, his flanks were under attack. To the left, 40 miles to the west, the 9th Army was still withdrawing, while to the right was the Borovsk-Maloyaroslavets gap which Hitler had ordered him to close.

Following Hitler's orders Kluge transferred XX Corps on the north shoulder of the gap from the 4th Army to the 4th *Panzergruppe*. Hitler explained that it was a quite simple operation: Hoepner had merely to stand fast and at the same time thin out his troops to provide a mobile reserve to plug the gap. He explained that the 5th Panzer Division could be moved from the northern flank down to the south and employed as the mobile reserve to attack into the gap.

The men on the ground, however, said that it was impossible. Hoepner spoke with the commanders of XLVI Panzer Corps and the 5th Panzer Division, and they both said that it could not be done in the time allowed. Not only were the road conditions bad, but they did not have enough fuel to move 100 miles. The only possibility would be to withdraw to the 'Winter Line' running from Rzhev to Gzhatsk and Yukhnov. This would allow the 5th Panzer Division to move south – but all this would take time.

Making the best of what was available, Hoepner counterattacked with a small force. He was not allowed to use XX Corps since it was defending ground and Hitler had ordered that there be no further withdrawal. So it sat unused on the shoulder of the gap as Hoepner's modest reserves were swamped by the Russians.

Since the angry exchanges early in December, relations between Kluge and Hoepner had been very cool. They communicated by telephone or by aides, but never met face to face.

On 1 January Hoepner had sent a formal request that the 4th *Panzergruppe* should withdraw towards Gzhatsk starting about 5 or 6 January. He waited a week without a reply, and by then the Russians pressing through the Maloyaroslavets gap had begun to cut off and outflank XX Corps.

On 8 January there were a series of telephone calls between Hoepner and Kluge. The commander of Army Group 'Centre' even suggested that not just XX Corps but the whole of the 4th *Panzergruppe* might be able to withdraw to the 'Winter Line', but he gave no firm orders since they could only come from Hitler.

By the afternoon Hoepner was desperate. He tried to telephone Halder, but only contacted an aide who said that Halder would ring back. The call never came and Hoepner on his own responsibility gave XX Corps the order to withdraw.

Kluge did not hear of the move until the evening. He had a choice; either he could order that XX Corps move back to their position which was still being held by a rearguard, or he could endorse the order and support Hoepner. True to his nickname he managed to do neither. He rang Hoepner, upbraided him and reminded him that he had been warned of the consequences of disobeying the *Fuehrer's* order.

The events of this day are still unclear. Some authorities say that Kluge had in fact given Hoepner the go ahead to withdraw, but realising how this would be received at the OKW covered himself with these warnings to Hoepner and then rang Hitler and reported to him the angry remarks that Hoepner had uttered about civilian leadership. Whatever the truth, Kluge broke the news to Hitler in tones that were guaranteed to fire the dictator's anger.

Though Hitler ordered that Hoepner be dishonourably discharged 'with all the legal consequences that it entailed' these orders were softened either by the intervention of Schmundt or by the judgements of the army lawyers who were ordered to investigate this unjust order. Hoepner lived in retirement, and even after his execution for his part in the July Plot his widow continued to draw a pension.

ANALYSIS – GERMAN GENERALSHIP IN THE EAST, FROM MINSK TO STALINGRAD

The five-month campaign waged against Soviet Russia by the armies of Germany between June and November 1941 is one of the most extraordinary military feats ever performed. Even the fact that it was launched with insufficient resources, too late and against an enemy whose capabilities had been completely misjudged cannot detract from the achievements of the *Wehrmacht*, especially the army and the air force.

Whilst on the part of the ordinary troops the campaign was a triumph of determination and endurance against the enemy, terrain and climate, for the generals the campaign produced other difficulties. Some of these were caused by the enemy, and others by their own high command, in particular Hitler himself. Problems with the enemy were only to be expected. Problems with their own high command were not.

Although the Russian armies always seemed to be on the point of disintegration, with whole formations breaking and fleeing, and hundreds of thousands of demoralised troops being captured in the vast German pockets, there always seemed to be something preventing the wholesale dissolution of the Red Army, and always more troops forthcoming to try to plug the gaps torn in their defence lines by the German Panzer troops. For all that he was poorly trained and poorly equipped, and often led by officers of mediocre quality, the Russian soldier showed right from the outset of the campaign the qualities that have earned him admiration in every campaign fought by Russia in recent history: a dogged determination, enormous physical resiliency, and the ability to make do with very little food and shelter. Yet in this campaign the Russian soldier fought to greater effect as he was better led than previously. Admittedly there had been terrible catastrophes at the beginning of the campaign, largely attributable to bad leadership; but combat had sorted out the worst of these offenders, and the other had been disposed of by an implacable Stalin. The senior commanders left quickly adapted themselves to the new conditions and began to fight back with increasing ability and confidence. Russia was still in dire straits, but with the emergence of men such as Zhukov, Konev, Malinovsky and Rokossovsky some light could be seen on the horizon.

■ Decimated command

There were two reasons for the initial poverty of the Russian senior command. Firstly, the purges carried out by Stalin in the late 1930s had emasculated the officer corps from the level of divisional commander upwards. To fill the gap junior officers had been promoted early in their careers, and whilst all were politically re-liable, their military abilities were not necessarily of the same order. Moreover, those who were able had had little time to get to know their formations and improve their efficiency. The second reason for the Russian officer corps' inefficiency was the result of misappreciations of the lessons of the Spanish Civil War, the border struggles with the Japanese in Siberia, and the 'Winter War' against Finland. The most important of these misconceptions had led to the breaking up of the homogeneous armoured formations built up in the early 1930s in favour of penny packets attached as support weapons to infantry formations. Some indication of this latter concept's disadvantages were gained in the Winter War, but little had been done to revise the older arrangement. The lesson was hammered home by the success of the German armoured formations, and Stalin immediately took steps to reintroduce armoured corps into the Red army on a large scale.

Compared with the Red Army, the German army was well off in its officers, for although the army had been expanded enormously in the middle and late 1930s, with some trouble in finding adequate officer material, this problem had by now been solved. Most of the officers had combat experience in Poland, Denmark and Norway, the West, or the Balkans, and the senior commanders knew how to get the best out of their men. Combat tactics and doctrines had been tested, and the commanders from divisional level upwards developed considerable tactical flexibility. This last was a factor that amazed Allied commanders throughout World War II.

This is not to say that the Germans did not have their problems. The Panzer divisions, for example, were at low strength. This was because Hitler had divided each of the Panzer divisions involved in the campaign in the West to produce more armoured divisions. Thus each of the Panzer divisions involved in the Russian campaign of 1941 had only about half the strength of its 1940 counterpart. In addition to this, much of the German army was still dependent on horse transport, which posed considerable difficulties in Russia – the horses used were well bred European ones, ill-suited to the extremes of the Russian climate.

■ Time or space?

The most important single factor in the Russian campaign, however, was time. The Germans did not have enough of it – Hitler's adventure in the Balkans had cost 'Barbarossa' a vital month, for the Germans considered that they had to win the war by the onset of winter. They did not have the resources to fight a prolonged two-front war, and all was gambled on a swift, knock-out blow on Russia. The result in the short term was near disaster, for no winter clothing had been provided for the men, the animals perished in the extreme cold, and vehicles seized up for lack of proper oils for the low temperatures of winter. The Russians also needed time, but for a different reason. They had to evacuate the industries of western Russia to new sites behind the Urals, safe from German attack or air assault, and they had also to build up the defences of cities such as Moscow and Leningrad, as well as bring up reserves from deep inside Russia. To gain the time for these two objectives, Stalin was prepared to pay with space and lives: his forces would hold on until they were all but annihilated, and then fall back to another position. The Russians were thus able to save their industrial capacity, and thereby the war, at the cost of about 1½ million dead and wounded and 1½ million prisoners.

What finally lost the first stage of the Russian campaign for the Germans were Hitler's two changes of mind, first to make Leningrad and the Ukraine, instead of Moscow, the primary objective, and then exactly the opposite decision. It is interesting to speculate on what might have happened had Hitler not made these two decisions. Without Hitler's insistence the generals would not have contemplated invasion of Russia, but once the decision had been made, it was these same generals, who could have won his campaign for him, who were deprived of the chance to do by others of Hitler's decisions.

■ High standards

The German field commanders were also hampered by the complete inadequacy of the German high command. The staff generals through whom the orders should have come and who would thus have been able to moderate the worst of Hitler's excesses, were so much nonentities that men such as Bock, Leeb, Guderian and Hoepner had to deal with Hitler directly. They could not convince the *Fuehrer* of the sense of their military ideas, and so such men resigned or were sacked, to the detriment of the army's fighting efficiency. The same problem was also prevalent in 1942 and 1943, before the more courageous of the generals evolved the method of agreeing with Hitler and doing what they themselves saw fit.

What of Germany's performance against Russia in 1941 and 1942? Firstly, the abilities of the ordinary fighting men must be mentioned as being quite superb under the most trying and difficult of conditions. The generals fall into two categories: those who had to deal with strategy, and therefore with Hitler, and those who dealt with tactics, and therefore had little occasion to deal with Hitler. The former performed creditably, although their success would have been greater had they been able to stand up to the *Fuehrer* with the aid of an efficient staff. The latter performed extremely well, showing great flexibility and speed of reaction, acting quickly as the situation demanded, without waiting for orders from higher up. It was these men, divisional and corps commanders in 1941, that were to prove so useful to Germany's defence in the desperate days of 1944 and 1945.

THE MEDITERRANEAN FRONTS
THE CAMPAIGNS IN NORTH AFRICA AND
ITALY

The German commitment of land forces to the North African theatre was an emergency measure prompted by Italy's expulsion from eastern Libya and the likelihood of the British capture of Tripoli in 1941. The redeployment of the *Wehrmacht* for the invasion of Soviet Russia had been ordered, and the sudden crisis created by the defeat of Mussolini's forces in Libya was a thorough nuisance. A small mechanised force, with a stiffening of armour, was scraped together, in all an under-strength corps: the 5th Light Division and 15th Panzer Division, whose final disem-barkation at Tripoli was scheduled for the end of May. This purely German armoured force became known as the *Afrika Korps*, and its commander was Lieutenant-General Erwin Rommel, who after his brilliant career in France with the 7th Panzer Division was scheduled for a Panzer corps command.

Rommel arrived in Tripoli in mid-February and immediately deduced that there was every chance of bundling the British out of El Agheila and Benghazi. Although specifically ordered not to undertake any offensive until the end of May, he decided to use his own initiative and see how the British reacted to a series of limited attacks. By 25 March he had prodded the British out of their advanced positions and taken their advanced base at El Agheila. And on the 31st he set in motion a three-pronged advance into Cyrenaica which completely surprised the British, weakened as they were by the withdrawal of their best armoured forces for the Greek campaign. This, his first offensive in Africa, is still a classic of how an energetically-driven armoured thrust can set off a chain-reaction of disorganisation on the other side. On 7 April the three slim German prongs met at Mechili. Rommel had not only taken western Cyrenaica but Generals O'Connor, Neame, Gambier-Parry, Combe, and Rimington, all snapped up in the whirling advance. Only the narrowest of escapes prevented

Rommel from capturing his opponent, Wavell, who also had the defence of Greece to worry about during April 1941.

The Australian General Morshead's success in defending Tobruk ended Rommel's first run of luck. Precipitate attacks on the western sector of the perimeter caused needless losses to Rommel's scanty forces and consolidated the defence. By 2 May he had to accept the need for a prolonged siege. Meanwhile his superiors at OKH thought he had run amok. Halder considered Rommel's version of soldiering chaotic and wasteful, and he sent out General Paulus (destined for disaster at Stalingrad) to rein him in. Paulus relayed firm orders that Rommel was not to advance further to the east (his outposts stood on the Egyptian frontier, commanding the vital Halfaya Pass on the Sollum escarpment) until his lines of communication had been made good and Tobruk captured.

■ Legendary general

At the end of May a tentative British attack, Operation 'Brevity', pushed Rommel's forces out of their frontier positions for a time, but prompt counter-moves by the 5th Light and 15th Panzer (now arrived) Divisions recovered Capuzzo, Sollum and Halfaya. Fortifying Halfaya Pass with dug-in 8.8-cm AA guns, Rommel prepared for the inevitable British counter-offensive to relieve Tobruk. Churchill had rushed a tank-supply convoy ('Tiger') through the Mediterranean and nagged Wavell until the latter was forced to attack prematurely – with tanks that were not 'broken-in' to desert warfare and also inferior on most counts to the German machines. Operation 'Battleaxe', Wavell's attack, showed Rommel at his best in a defensive rôle. The clash lasted three days (15–18 June), in which Rommel kept concentrated, blunted the clumsy British attacks with his minefields and anti-tank guns, and forced back the British armour by hooking repeatedly at its flanks. Churchill replaced Wavell with Auchinleck on 22 June; and the next months saw both Auchinleck and Rommel preparing for new offensives, Rommel to take Tobruk, Auchinleck to relieve it and recover Cyrenaica.

By 18 November 1941, the date of Auchinleck's offensive, entrusted to the 8th Army under General Cunningham and code-named Operation 'Crusader', Rommel was already a legend. This was due not to the Nazi propaganda machine but to the British whom he had so roughly handled. Whether invoked with the blackest invective or with grudging admiration, Rommel's name was fast becoming synonymous with British dis-comfiture in the desert. Auchinleck, recognising this, took pains to issue a general order urging the men of the 8th Army to think more of 'the enemy' or 'the Germans' and less of bogeyman Rommel. No other German general of World War II had such a high (if indirect) compliment paid him by an opponent. And no other German general had a commando raid launched for his assassination. On the eve of 'Crusader' the gallant but totally misconceived 'Keyes Raid' landed far behind the German lines to kill Rommel in what was believed to be his HQ – but he was not even there.

Despite his charisma, Rommel had to account 'Crusader' a defeat. Totally surprised at the outset, he rapidly concentrated the *Afrika Korps* and halted the British armoured thrust towards Tobruk, smashing the 5th South African Brigade. The battle became centred around the Sidi Rezegh airfield outside the Tobruk perimeter to the south-east, with the British getting the worst of it all along the line. Then on 24 November Rommel made a snap decision to slice across the 8th Army's rear areas with the *Afrika Korps* to try to panic his opponent into calling off the attack. It would have been called brilliant if it had worked – but while Rommel was out of touch with his HQ, raising havoc in the British rear areas along the Egyptian frontier, the New Zealand Division kept going and joined hands with the Tobruk garrison. Rommel had to race back to the westward and try to reimpose the siege. The ensuing fighting so depleted his forces that by 7 December he had to abandon the battle for Tobruk and withdraw to the west. Determined to preserve what was left of the *Afrika Korps* as a fighting force, he overrode belated and ill-founded Italian objections and pulled right back to El Agheila. By 28 December he had brought the pursuing 8th Army to a definite halt. One of the hardest decisions he had had to make was to abandon the German garrisons on the Egyptian frontier, the last of which surrendered on 17 January.

Two factors combined to make Rommel's discomfiture a matter of only a few days. The first was the new crisis in the Far East, created by Japan's entry into the war on 7 December, forcing the British, once again, to pull vital forces out of the North African theatre. And the second was the timely arrival in Libya of German tank reinforcements – 45 on 19 December and 55 on 5 January. He immediately decided to repeat his former ploy of upsetting the British deployment in western Cyrenaica. By this time his bi-national force had been raised to the status of *Panzergruppe Afrika* and was on the eve of additional preferment to that of *Panzerarmee*. Far more important was its recent reinforcement coupled with the weakening of 8th Army, which was still out of breath after the closing stages of 'Crusader'.

Rommel's second offensive (21 January–5 February 1942) bundled the 8th Army out of western Cyrenaica and pushed it back to a north–south axis hinged on Gazala on the coast. Both sides then began a mutual build-up for the decisive battle. There was another and far more crucial reason for the lull in the land fighting. The *Panzerarmee* and 8th Army both depended on seaborne supplies. Rommel's supply-lines were far shorter, but they had the British-held island of Malta commanding them. If Malta could be neutralised, or better still conquered, no further obstacle would remain to impede the Axis in North Africa. Logically, both Rommel and his colleague Field-Marshal Kesselring (German C-in-C South) agreed that the fall of Malta must precede an all-out offensive in North Africa. But this would be to ignore the activities of the British. By the end of April 1942 (when the attacks on Malta had reached their peak and Kesselring had concluded, prematurely, that the island had indeed been neutralised), Rommel was becoming uneasy about the pace of the 8th

Army's build-up. The result was the compromise directive which authorised 'Theseus' (Rommel's offensive to take Tobruk) to precede 'Hercules' (Kesselring's airborne invasion of Malta). And on 26 May Rommel attacked the 8th Army's defensive positions in the open desert south of Gazala.

Rommel had set himself an impossibly optimistic deadline, planning for the defeat of the British armour on Day One, the smashing of the British infantry on Day Two, and the decisive assault on Tobruk on Day Three. He wheeled the *Afrika Korps* round the southern extremity of the Gazala line into the rear of the 8th Army's static defences only to find himself trapped. Only the piecemeal armoured tactics of the 8th Army commander, General Ritchie, saved him from disaster. Supplies for the trapped *Afrika Korps* (now a subsidiary formation of the *Panzerarmee*) were forced through in the nick of time on 1 June, hours before the deadline on which Rommel had already admitted to his prisoners that he would be forced to negotiate a surrender. After 10 desperate days, in which the last British reserves of armour were progressively squandered, the 8th Army had been levered out of the Gazala line. Rommel now flung himself against Tobruk, attacking the sector which had been marked down on the eve of 'Crusader'. The Tobruk defences had deteriorated since the 1941 siege, the garrison was improvised, and the perimeter was pierced with ease. Tobruk surrendered on 21 June. 'Theseus' had been accomplished; the road was clear for 'Hercules'; but now the road to Alexandria and Cairo seemed clearer still. Hitler and Mussolini agreed to give Rommel his head and invade Egypt – a move which Rommel himself later admitted to be a 'try-on'.

■ Savage riposte

In the first two weeks of July 1942 Rommel was fought to a standstill at El Alamein by Auchinleck, who employed the disorganised components of the 8th Army with very great skill. The pursuit effectively ended on 1/2 July, when Rommel repeated his old mistake of attacking the first defences he came to and slowing himself down. Auchinleck riposted by savaging the Italian divisions of the *Panzerarmee* and forcing the *Afrika Korps* to wear itself out by doing all the work. By 5 June the tank strength of the *Afrika Korps* was down to 26. By the end of the month the situation was deadlocked. Now it was Rommel who was out on a limb and the 8th Army which had been backed up against its source of supply.

There were factors other than desperation behind Rommel's 'last throw' to break through at El Alamein via the Alam Halfa ridge (31 August–1 September 1942). Like Paulus at Stalingrad, he had been promised supplies which never turned up. German intelligence was faulty and produced a wildly optimistic plan (obliging the *Afrika Korps* to cover 30 miles in seven hours over difficult terrain and through uncleared minefields). But it was a costly failure. Rommel was a sick man; and his new opponent, Montgomery, refused to fritter away the British armour as his predecessors had done, and so won a heartening victory for the 8th Army.

After Alam Halfa Rommel could only prepare for Montgomery's inevitable offensive, which broke on 23 October. It was the most unbalanced line-up of the entire desert war: 96,000 Germans and Italians faced 150,000 men of the 8th Army; 756 Axis tanks were confronted by 1,348 Allied. Such odds were decisive enough for the battle of attrition which Montgomery wanted; the *Panzerarmee*'s fuel shortage made them doubly so. Nevertheless Rommel kept the *Panzerarmee* in position despite Montgomery's grinding attacks until 3 November. He then seized upon Montgomery's caution to make good a staged withdrawal from Egypt which took the *Panzerarmee* clear across Libya to the Tunisian frontier without having to fight another set-piece battle.

This gruelling retreat was forced on him by the Allied landings in Morocco and Tunisia (Operation 'Torch') on 8 November. That the *Panzerarmee* was not cut off and annihilated by this crushing blow was due entirely to the vigilance of Kesselring, who had expected such a move and earmarked troops for a swift airlift across the Sicilian narrows to hold Tunis and Bizerta. The spirited counterattacks launched by Kesselring's blocking force raised faint hopes that it would after all be possible to hold a 'Tunisian bridgehead' which, in conjunction with Sicily, would still deny the Allies free passage through the central Mediterranean. On 23 January 1943, after the *Panzerarmee* had reached the comparative safety of the Tunisian frontier defences, the Mareth line *Armeegruppe 'Afrika'* (Army Group 'Africa') was set up with Rommel as C-in-C, General von Arnim commanding the 5th *Panzerarmee* and the Italian General Messe commanding the 1st Army. It was all a far cry from Rommel's original tiny force of February–March 1941. But Rommel and Arnim planned two offensive moves to jam the Allied vice closing round the 'bridgehead'.

■ **End in Africa**

First came *Fruehlingswind* or 'Spring Breeze' (14–24 February) which was aimed at the green American II Corps and caused considerable initial havoc before it ran out of steam. This was followed by Rommel's last battle in Africa: a costly armoured assault on the 8th Army's prepared positions at Medenine which was a total failure. After Rommel's departure on 9 March Arnim took over Army Group 'Africa'. His contribution – the last Axis offensive on anything like a large scale in Tunisia – was *Ochsenkopf* ('Oxhead') between 26 February and 2 March, on the northern sector. All were fruitless, for with the forcing of the Mareth line (20–28 March) and the Wadi Akarit line (5–6 April), the 8th Army finally 'turned the corner' northward into Tunisia and left Arnim no further room in which to manoeuvre. Despite desperate resistance in the last weeks, the Axis collapse came suddenly on 6 May. Tunis and Bizerta fell simultaneously on the 8th; and by the 13th it was all over. In their leaderless and disorganised masses the men of Army Group 'Africa' were surrendering in their thousands – over a quarter of a million of them. At the most, 800 survivors escaped to Sicily.

For the British, North Africa was the only theatre where an initial decisive blow could be dealt at the Axis; for the German high command, it was a sideshow – especially after the invasion of Russia. Only Kesselring, on the spot, sensed the practical possibilities, and most of his energies were devoted to getting the best out of the Italians. 'Torch' turned the whole scene upside-down and made the eventual reinforcements a waste. The *Wehrmacht* lost more men in Tunisia than it did at Stalingrad.

Tactically, Rommel's troubles stemmed from the fact that he had too few German troops – and when Auchinleck concentrated on the Italian units at Alamein the result was near disaster. Rommel was without doubt a master of mobile warfare with small units; it has been said of him that his 'ceiling' was a division, or at best a corps, and that he lacked the more placid qualities needed for commanding a full army. Certainly the brilliant successes won by his flair for improvisation amounted to a string of empty victories. Only the legend remained.

The disaster at Tunis could not have been worse timed, for coming as it did on the eve of the last German summer offensive in Russia it dashed all hopes of transferring large bodies of troops to Kesselring's southern command – and thus providing at least a chance of preventing the Allies from gaining a foothold in Sicily and southern Italy.

Kesselring was determined to make a fight for Sicily, but he only had the bare bones with which to do the fighting. It was a predominantly Italian defence, with Italian forces manning the obvious invasion beaches at the southern corner of the island and only two German divisions – 15th Panzer (reconstituted) and the 'Hermann Goering' – inland. (The German 1st Parachute Division was dropped into Sicily after the Allied landings went in on 10 July.) But there was no chance of 'Dunkirking' the assault forced on the beaches; the Italian coastal defences collapsed on the first impact; and the British and American forces seized the opportunity to push inland and deploy for the overrunning of the island. The German troops used the natural defences of Sicily's terrain to full advantage and retreated in good order, but Kesselring had no intention of sacrificing them, as Army Group 'Africa' had been sacrificed, in a futile defence, and shipped them across to the Italian mainland before the Americans entered Messina on 17 August.

■ Combined landings

Italy was altogether different. The German high command got early intelligence that its erstwhile Italian allies were negotiating an armistice, and was determined to prevent the Allies from being presented with Italy at a single stroke. Initially, however, Kesselring was alone in wishing to try to keep the Allies as far south as possible; and even Rommel, appointed to the temporary command of Army Group 'B' in northern Italy, believed that the decisive stand should be made along the heights of the northern Apennines to defend the valley of the Po. Further confusion was caused by uncertainty as to whether the Allies would go straight for Rome with an airborne landing, push for Naples by landing in the Gulf of Salerno, or content themselves by crossing the Straits of Messina and advancing methodically up the 'leg' of the Italian 'boot'.

Moreover, when the Allies combined the latter two alternatives (3–8 September 1943) all German forces in Italy were fully engaged in disarming the adjacent Italian troops. Kesselring's genius for improvisation showed itself in the speed in which he drew the hodge-podge of airborne and armoured German units in Italy into a cohesive form (10th Army, commanded by General von Vietinghoff-Scheel), and fed in enough powerful forces at Salerno to bring the British and Americans who landed there to the brink of disaster (8–17 September). Cutting his losses on realising that the invaders were there to stay, and that Naples was therefore lost, Kesselring then supervised a fighting retreat to the superb natural defences across the narrowest neck of the Italian peninsula: the 'Gustav Line', centred on the Monte Cassino massif commanding the direct route to Rome.

Every stream and river, every ridge of high ground, favoured the retreating Germans – and so too did the foul weather and mud of the Italian autumn. By the middle of November the US 5th Army (General Clark) and the British 8th Army (General Montgomery, soon to be replaced by General Leese) were bogged down for the winter facing the Gustav Line. At its heart, Monte Cassino dominated Highway No. 6 and the Liri valley – the road to Rome.

The Allied attempt to lever the Germans out of the Gustav Line by landing at Anzio and Nettuno, far behind the front, failed completely (21 January). The landing, which was concerted with an all-out assault at Cassino, gained initial surprise but was contained by hastily flung-in forces, which were speedily reinforced from the German 14th Army (General von Mackensen) which Kesselring had formed in central Italy. While the Cassino attack was repulsed, the beach-head at Anzio was all but captured by energetic German counterattacks and reduced to a state of siege. Meanwhile, Monte Cassino monastery was bombed by the Allies, giving the Germans the excuse to occupy the ruins and so command the crest of the mountain – leaving the German front stronger than it had been before the attack began.

■ Cassino falls

The second battle for Cassino was fought between 15 and 23 March. Cassino itself was battered beyond recognition, but the German 1st Parachute Division under General Heidrich, holding Cassino town and abbey, held on against all odds. The Allies gained only vestigial advances and the German ring around the Anzio beach-head remained unbroken. Alexander, Allied supreme commander, decided to regroup for a decisive assault in April; but delays in redeploying the troops forced a postponement until May.

On 11 May the last Cassino battle began in the same way as its predecessors, with the Allied attacks blunted by a superb resistance. But the rapid penetration of the

Aurunci mountains by French colonial troops unhinged the Cassino line in three days, and Kesselring had to agree to a withdrawal. The next three weeks were chaotic in both sides. The British and Americans had the chance of splitting the 10th Army and the 14th Army apart and destroying them piecemeal, but despite heavy and irreplaceable German losses Vietinghoff and Lemelsen (Mackensen's successor as commander of the 14th Army) managed to join up and pull right back to the 'Gothic Line' across the northern Apennines, where Kesselring had his best remaining line of fixed defences. By mid-August the Allies had closed up to the line and another temporary stalemate settled over the Italian front.

Alexander now lost four French and three US divisions, earmarked for the landings in southern France. He made a desperate effort to unhinge the Gothic Line on the Adriatic sector, but failed to score a decisive breakthrough before the autumn rains came. Inch-by-inch progress during October and November took the 8th Army as far as Ravenna; on the left flank Clark's Americans were stopped short of Bologna. It was another strategic triumph for Kesselring, preventing the Allies from any chance of reaching the Alps until the spring of 1945.

■ The end in Italy

After a second miserable winter in the Italian mountains, Alexander's two armies prepared for the decisive breakthrough in April 1945. By this time the Allies were across the Rhine and the Red Army was preparing for its final assault on Berlin. But Kesselring had quitted Italy, appointed to the thankless task of presiding over the chaos in the West. He had been replaced as C-in-C Army Group 'C' (the 10th and 14th Armies) by Vietinghoff.

The final Allied push in Italy lasted just 17 days. It opened with an amphibious assault across Lake Comacchio on 9 April. This completely unseamed the German left flank. By the time Vietinghoff finally ordered a staged withdrawal to the River Po, his last possible defence line, the British were already across (20 April). Secret negotiations between Allen Dulles of the CIA and the SS supreme commander in the south, Karl Wolff, accelerated the surrender of nearly a million men on April 29 (the German forces in Austria were included in the surrender). American forces had meanwhile raced north to join hands with their compatriots on the Brenner Pass – 12 months too late to have any effect on the Soviet domination of eastern and central Europe.

FIELD-MARSHAL ERWIN ROMMEL

Gazala is justly hailed as Rommel's greatest victory in North Africa. It ended a three-month period of deadlock in Cyrenaica; it destroyed the cohesion of the British 8th Army and forced it into headlong retreat; it gave Rommel Tobruk and his field-marshal's baton; and it cleared the way for the invasion of Egypt. None of this can be contested. But it is also true that although he retained the initiative throughout the battle, Rommel had set himself an impossibly optimistic schedule. He brought his army to the brink of destruction through rashness, as he had done during 'Crusader' six months before. He won his battle with his flexibility and determination – but only by the narrowest of margins.

Rommel attacked at Gazala on 26 May to forestall the offensive which his opposite number, General Ritchie of the 8th Army, was obviously planning. It had always been fairly clear what Rommel would do – he had very little choice. The chain of 8th Army defences running south from Gazala on the coast ended in the open desert at Bir Hakeim (or Hacheim), a series of wired and mined defences known as 'boxes', each manned by a brigade. Behind the boxes and their connecting minefields was the killing-ground where the British and Axis armour would settle the final outcome of the battle.

Rommel's initial error was to assume that he could arrive in the 8th Army's rear completely by surprise and then fight the sort of battle he wanted. But the big wheel of the *Afrika Korps* southward round Bir Hakeim on the night of 26/27 May was spotted and observed. By nightfall on the 27th he had to accept that he had not gained surprise – and that he had also underestimated two other vital factors: the disruptive rôle of the boxes, which jeopardised his supplies; and the basic strength of the British armoured divisions. What saved him was the tactical adolescence of the British in tank warfare. Although Auchinleck had warned Ritchie 'you should not break up the organisation of either of the armoured divisions. They have been trained to fight as divisions, I hope, and fight as divisions they should', they never did. And this saved Rommel from his initial errors.

The British armour had a superb chance on the 28th, but was repeatedly committed to battle in brigade packets. By the end of the day the *Afrika Korps*, the German 90th Light Division and the Italian '*Ariete*' Armoured Division were concentrated but running dangerously short on fuel and ammunition. Attempts to solve the problem by running supplies past the Bir Hakeim box on the 29th proved inadequate and far too dangerous; and Rommel was forced to think again.

He decided to punch a hole through the Gazala line by reducing the British 150th Brigade Box at Sidi Muftah, which would give him a direct supply-line through the heart of the British defences, and shifted the *Afrika Korps* westward to a fine defensive position which was soon to earn the nickname of 'The Cauldron'. Rommel then fell upon the 150th Brigade Box, where after desperate fighting British resistance ended on 1 June. Once again, Ritchie made no move to intervene.

Although he had taken the first step necessary to compensate for his initial overeagerness, Rommel was still in a most dangerous position. The *Panzerarmee* was split, with the *Afrika Korps* and '*Ariete*' Division east of the Gazala line and the remaining Axis divisions – predominantly Italian – west of it. The obvious move for the British was to exploit this situation, but the next phase of the battle – a concentric attack on Rommel in the 'Cauldron' – failed to use the intact reserves still at Ritchie's disposal. Rommel's forces survived the attacks of 5 June with ease, and flung in a superb counterattack which resulted in the wiping-out of 10th Indian Brigade on 6 June.

During the 'Crusader' fighting the previous November, Rommel had thrown away the methodical and damaging defensive tactics being waged by *Afrika Korps* by making his rash 'Dash to the Wire'. He did not make a similar mistake now. Having restored the dangerous situation created by his own misconception of the 8th Army's position, he now turned south to eliminate the terminal defences of the Gazala line: the Free French box at Bir-Hakeim. Here he found that he had caught a tartar: the French troops under General Koenig held out against merciless Stuka attacks until, on 9 June, infantry units from 15th Panzer Division forced their way on to 'Point 186' – all-important high ground which commanded the main French position. The Bir Hakeim Box held out on the 10th but its days were clearly numbered; and the garrison broke out through the German lines on the night of 10/11 June.

■ Preliminaries over

But all these events were nothing more than the preliminary to the decisive phase of the battle: breaking the 8th Army's main strength in the field. The northern positions of the Gazala line were still intact, and a screen of defensive positions – of which the two most important were boxes at 'Knightsbridge' (201st Guards Brigade) and El

Adem (29th Indian Brigade) – barred the approaches to Tobruk to the north-east. Moreover, Ritchie still had the advantage in armour: 330 cruiser and infantry tanks against 160 German and about 70 Italian machines.

To cope with this problem Rommel reverted to his original idea of a fan-shaped advance across the 8th Army's flank. This sacrifice of concentration was more than justified, and compensated for, by the failure of Ritchie's generals to concentrate their own armour. Rommel's new advance began on the 11th and had taken him up to the region of El Adem by the evening. Then came 12 June, a black day for the 8th Army, with the 21st and 15th Panzer Divisions hammering the separated 2nd, 4th and 22nd Armoured Brigades and wiping out 120 tanks. The armoured balance had now swung dramatically and decisively in Rommel's favour. And with the *Afrika Korps* effectively dominating the desert 'no-man's land', the British did not even have the chance of salvaging their many tanks which had run out of fuel or suffered repairable damage.

Tactically, Rommel had reversed the 8th Army's initial tank advantage by his old trick of luring small British tank units on to the German anti-tank batteries and then scattering the survivors with well-timed tank attacks of his own. This was now the only tactic which offered the 8th Army the chance of fighting a draw at Gazala. But it would only have worked if a clearly-defined objective had been defined at once and the ensuing defensive battle fought by a single commander co-ordinating the efforts of what was left of the 8th Army's original strength. General Ritchie, the 8th Army commander, was constantly looking over his shoulder to the Middle East supreme commander, General Auchinleck, back in Egypt. Auchinleck himself was plagued by a series of constant queries from Churchill in Whitehall – and so, for that matter, was Ritchie. There was total confusion as to what was to be done with Tobruk. Should the perimeter be manned for another siege or not? Snap decisions and counter-orders in the heat of a fluid, armoured battle, especially when made by commanders not on the spot, are a sure recipe for defeat – and at Gazala they were a golden gift for Rommel.

On 13 June the main obstacle to Rommel's attacks during the tank battles of the previous 48 hours – the Guards at 'Knightsbridge', who had offered a fixed rallying-point throughout – was removed by their withdrawal. By the evening the British armour had been given an inevitable additional beating and Rommel now had a tank superiority of two to one – an advantage which was still further increased by field repairs to retrieved tanks.

Then came 14 June, the day that dissolved the 8th Army. Ritchie announced his decision to pull out from Gazala and 'occupy the frontier defences', which meant accepting the investment of Tobruk, if only temporarily. Auchinleck's order that 'our forces will not be invested in Tobruk, and your army is to remain a mobile field army', was not much help. Their opponent, speaking from his front-line perspective, saw things clearest of all: 'Full speed ahead was ordered, as British vehicles were now streaming east in their thousands.' On the 15th he felt free to write to his wife: 'The battle has been won and the enemy is breaking up. We're now mopping up encircled remnants of their army . . .'

Three more days sufficed to make certain of Tobruk. The 29th Indian Brigade was forced off El Adem airfield on the 16th; the 4th Armoured Brigade, the last effective force which the 8th Army could field in the Tobruk area, was smashed on the 17th; and on the following day Rommel, hounding his own exhausted troops like a slave-driver, pushed 20 miles east to Gambut while Tobruk itself was invested from the east. By keeping up this merciless pressure he had prevented Ritchie from making an effective stand west of the Egyptian frontier. Much more important. Tobruk itself, with its run-down defences and polyglot garrison, now lay at the mercy of the *Afrika Korps*. By nightfall on the 19th Rommel had put the 15th Panzer, 21st Panzer and '*Ariete*' Divisions into position at the south-eastern corner of the Tobruk perimeter – the assault sector he had marked down for the previous November, when Auchinleck's 'Crusader' attack had forestalled him.

■ Tobruk falls

Twenty-four hours sufficed to shatter the defenders of Tobruk and take the town, which had been an obsession of Rommel's since April 1941. He held all the cards – total air and armour superiority and artillery support – and he made no errors. General Klopper, commanding the garrison, made his formal surrender to Rommel in person at about 0940 hours on the 21st. In just under four weeks, Rommel had completed the task laid down for him by the Axis high command. He had beaten the 8th Army out of its defences and disrupted it as an organised fighting entity, leaving it with no alternative but precipitate retreat. He had captured the declared objective of the *Panzerarmee*'s offensive: Tobruk. With the surviving elements of the 8th Army retreating at full speed into Egypt, it seemed that the decisive battle of the desert war had been won.

Rommel's Gazala triumph had been nearly wrecked at the outset by bad intelligence and over-confidence. Of the all-important 150th Brigade Box at Sidi Muftah, General Bayerlein has stated: 'We never knew that it was there. Our first attacks on it failed. If we had not taken it on 1 June, you would have captured the whole of the *Afrika Korps*.' And this would have been the result of Rommel's under-estimation of the inhibiting effect of fixed defences and minefields, which left the *Afrika Korps* out on a limb behind the Gazala line after the big encircling wheel on the night of 26/27 May. On 1 June, while putting out all his strength to smash the 150th Brigade, Rommel admitted to a British POW that 'we cannot go on like this. If we don't get a convoy through tonight I shall have to ask General Ritchie for terms.'

Rommel's measures to put matters to rights – moving the *Afrika Korps* into the 'Cauldron' and grinding down the Sidi Muftah and Bir Hakeim boxes – took 10 days to achieve but left him in the position he had wanted for the second day of his original offensive: soundly established in the base positions of the Gazala line, ready for the decisive clash with the British armour. In this ensuing phase he was helped immeasurably by the persistent small-scale armoured attacks which Ritchie's subordinates carried out. This is particularly noteworthy because the British in the Western Desert had been fighting Rommel for 14 months and had been repeatedly discomfited by the concentrated power of the *Afrika Korps* under Rommel's hand: the 15th and 21st Panzer Divisions acting as a single unit.

Moving to the subject of the art of generalship, Gazala saw Rommel adopting the plot of dividing his army in order to fix his enemy's attention with the weaker half and strike the enemy's weakest point with as much force as possible. Until Bir Hakeim fell, this meant that his *Panzerarmee* was effectively partitioned by the Gazala line and that Ritchie had been deliberately offered the initiative. And as far as tank tactics were concerned this was the *Afrika Korps'* favourite trick: luring British tanks against anti-tank guns as a prelude to a decisive counterattack. As General Bayerlein admitted, Rommel's initial leap behind the Gazala line's defences nearly proved fatal. But the assault on the *Afrika Korps*, when it came, was repulsed with ease because the defenders were concentrated and the attackers were not.

Another definite item in Rommel's favour was his leadership from the front line, which the 8th Army never had. Rommel was everywhere the crucial action happened to be, supervising minefield clearance, bringing through supply convoys and pressing home the pursuit. By the time Tobruk was cut off, the men of the *Panzerarmee* were as exhausted as their opponents in the 8th Army. Only Rommel's merciless hounding of his own men prevented stalemate by mutual fatigue on the Egyptian frontier.

Brilliant though it was, however, Gazala remained a Dead Sea fruit. It was not that classic military dream, a 'battle without a morrow'. Gazala was certainly Rommel's Austerlitz; but the sequel to his triumph was the Waterloo of El Alamein.

COLONEL-GENERAL JUERGEN VON ARNIM

Operation 'Torch' – the Allied landings in Morocco and Algeria in early November 1942 – should have spelled doom to Rommel's *Panzerarmee*, which had just begun its long retreat from the battlefield of El Alamein. That this fate was averted was due entirely to the prescience of Field-Marshal Kesselring, who had feared such a move and earmarked a scratch collection of airborne units, plus the transport planes to airlift them to Tunis from Sicily. On hearing of the 'Torch' landings, Kesselring shot these forces across to secure Tunis and Bizerta, and the subsequent reinforcement of the 'Tunisian bridgehead' was swift and effective. Between 10 and 20 November both sides in Tunisia were pegging out claims as far forward as possible; and in the last week of the month the first head-on clashes occurred, between Sedjenane and Mateur, at Sidi Nsir and at Medjez-el-Bab. In this fighting the Germans in Tunisia won a clear first round, halting the British and American probe towards Tunis and Bizerta and throwing the Allies on to the defensive.

At this stage, with Rommel still retreating across Libya, it was vital to win enough time for the battered *Panzerarmee* to pull back into Tunisia itself; and the result was a series of spoiling attacks to make this possible. German troops continued to pour into Tunisia, the most important reinforcement being the 10th Panzer Division, whose advance units on 1 December began a series of successful probes which continued until the 6th, when Colonel-General Juergen von Arnim arrived in Tunisia to take command of the newly-formed 5th *Panzerarmee*, ultimately intended to hold Tunisia together with Rommel's *Panzerarmee Afrika*.

Arnim's first move, naturally enough, was to keep up the existing pressure. Repeated attacks towards Medjez were held, but in Christmas week the Germans successfully recovered the strategic heights of 'Longstop Hill', key to the Medjerda valley

223

leading down to the sea between Tunis and Bizerta. Further to the south, attacks against the French-held sector of the Allied front won the Pichon pass, 75 miles south of Tunis. It was of vital importance to gain Rommel as much room as possible in the southern sector and for this Armin wanted all key passes across the range known as the Eastern Dorsale. A further series of limited attacks in January was completely successful, securing not only the Pichon pass (3 January) but Pont-du-Fahs (18 January) and the Faid pass (30 January). By this series of small offensives in his first month of command in Tunisia, Arnim had deepened and strengthened the Tunisian bridgehead just in time for Rommel's arrival in the Mareth line with the 8th Army at his heels.

By this time Arnim's reinforcements had raised the total German and Italian strength in Tunisia to about 100,000, and to this figure were now added the surviving 70,000 of Rommel's *Panzerarmee*. This gave the Axis forces in Tunisia a splendid chance to counterattack, first against the strung-out British, French and Americans in Tunisia, then against Montgomery in front of the Mareth line. But now the muddled set-up created by the *Commando Supremo*, the Italian high command in Rome, ruined all real hope for concerted and decisive action. Rommel had already been told he was to quit the *Panzerarmee* after reaching the Mareth line: newly entitled the 1st Army, it would be taken over by the Italian General Messe. But Rommel was left to decide when he should actually go. The decision had been taken to create an Army Group 'Africa' to combine the operations of the 1st Army and the 5th *Panzerarmee* in the bridgehead – but no C-in-C had yet been designated. In the meantime friction was rapidly growing between Rommel and Arnim. The former wanted to tear open the Allied right flank by an armoured smash through the Western Dorsale, with the faint possibility of capturing Bône on the coast if the Allied flank could be rolled up. The Axis forces could then turn about and fall on Montgomery. Arnim saw his rôle as purely defensive. The result was the compromise plan which unleashed the Kasserine offensive on 14 February. This hammered an ominous dent in the American positions. The plan came to nothing because of Arnim's caution – he withdrew the 10th Panzer Division at the crucial moment, leaving Rommel facing stiffening Allied resistance at the tip of the salient. By the end of the month the Germans were back at their start-line, having achieved little else but giving a sobering lesson to American troops about coping with Panzer attacks.

■ Timing essential

Before the Kasserine attack petered out, Army Group 'Africa' had been brought into being and Rommel had accepted the command. Messe took over the 1st Army, and Rommel prepared for his 'back-hand' punch at the 8th Army. But Arnim's excessive care for the strength of his own front in keeping a tight hold over the 10th Panzer Division meant that the new attack on the 8th Army could not be dealt with the speed originally envisaged by Rommel. Montgomery had a full week to prepare for

Rommel's attack against the 8th Army's positions at Medenine; and the ensuing battle saw the British make excellent use of the time-tested methods of the *Afrika Korps*. On 6 March 1943 Rommel's armour was allowed to crucify itself on a dense shield of anti-tank guns. The attack was a total failure – and Rommel's last battle in Africa. A sick man, he quitted Tunisia on 9 March; and the command of Army Group 'Africa' passed to Arnim.

Whatever chances of success existed for Rommel's double-blow plan, time was the vital factor. Pinpoint timing was required for the shuttling of the armoured forces between the Kasserine and Mareth fronts, which was not achieved. This was largely due to the half-baked Axis command structure in Africa, which left Arnim outside Rommel's sphere of command. Not only did Arnim deny Rommel the total cooper-ation of the 5th *Panzerarmee* necessary to make the Kasserine attack a success: his own offensive in the northern sector came to nothing. This was the aptly-named *Ochsenkopf* ('Oxhead'), which had as its objective the Allied bases of Béja and Medjez, and was scheduled for 26 February. Other attacks were to be made at Abiod on the extreme Allied left. The best that can be said for Arnim's idea of attack was that it did follow the pattern which he had so successfully set in December and January. But the arrival of Rommel's *Panzerarmee* had transformed the whole situation; and after the failure at Kasserine, Arnim's scheme for the other end of the Allied line was strategi-cally wasteful. None of the *Ochsenkopf* attacks attained their objectives, and all of them had been soundly repulsed by 1 March. As Rommel was soon to find at Medenine, a notable feature of the British defence was the furious and accurate con-centration of artillery.

Rommel had spent much of his remaining time in Tunisia in vainly trying to get the *Commando Supremo* to tell him what the overall strategy for the theatre might be. He pressed for a shortening of the line in Tunisia, abandoning the Mareth line, pulling Messe's 1st Army north to Enfidaville for a higher concentration of the two armies. When Arnim took over as army group commander, his opponent General Alexander sharpened the Axis dilemma by launching attacks on the Gafsa sector. Thus Arnim was never certain whether the next main Allied attack was going to be at Mareth or Gafsa; and by keeping Messe's 1st Army exposed at Mareth he risked its destruction. Arnim's limited determination to hold as much of the original bridge-head as possible was totally unrealistic and certainly helped to accelerate the pace of the Allied advance.

In March, Montgomery squared up to the Mareth line, in blissful ignorance of the fact that Rommel had actually left Tunisia. Messe, facing the oncoming attack, was deceived by American attacks on the Gafsa sector into holding back the 10th Panzer Division from the Mareth front. The actual battle of Mareth lasted from 20 to 28 March and was a fine achievement for the 8th Army, the 1st Army being forced out of the Mareth line. Montgomery, however, had promised his men before the battle that they would destroy their enemy; and that this was not achieved was largely due to a legacy of Rommel. Although the latter had accepted the fact that an Italian general would take out his old *Panzerarmee*, Rommel had provided that General Bayerlein should remain as liaison officer – in effective command of the German forces of the 1st Army. As the Axis hold on the Mareth line was prised away, the surviving German forces conducted their own brand of fighting retreat. It was a paradoxical situation, again created by the muddled and bi-national chain of command. Mareth should have destroyed the 1st Army, but the professional insubordination of its German components kept it in being. Yet the Axis losses were serious. Never again would the 1st Army be able to launch a counterblow of the weight which Rommel had unleashed at Medenine.

Thus it is clear that the turning-point of the battle for Tunisia was in fact Medenine on 6 March. This was the last time that the Axis defenders of the bridgehead had the luxury of the initiative, turning from the Allied 1st Army to Montgomery's 8th Army with separate, heavy counterattacks. Conversely, Medenine was the last battle which saw the 1st and 8th Armies fighting separately. From Mareth onwards, the two armies would be advancing in close co-ordination.

This was proved by the immediate postscript to Mareth: the 8th Army's head-on penetration of the 'Gabes Gap' across the Wadi Akarit (5/6 April). Once again, Messe escaped total destruction, but this time pressures from both Allied armies caused a minor Axis landslide. American forces from Gafsa joined hands with 8th Army forces on 7 April, and on the same day a 1st Army assault on the Fondouk Pass began to batter open the door to Kairouan from the west. Sfax fell to the 8th Army on 10 April, and on the following day British troops from the 1st and 8th Armies met in Kairouan. Sousse was added to the 8th Army's bag on 12 April. But then the pace of events slowed and halted. Army Group 'Africa' had been driven back in to the Tunis-Bizerta litoral, and its line was now correspondingly easier to defend. Once again, Alexander had to sit down before the enemy lines and plan a set-piece attack.

■ No evacuation

Now the total failure of the Axis high command to take the North African theatre seriously came home to roost with a vengeance. Army Group 'Africa', a quarter of a million strong, had been created two years too late to have any strategic vitality as an offensive weapon. It now lacked so much as an inch of spare ground in which it could manoeuvre against its enemies; and its leader, Arnim, was a wooden and limited commander who never realised that his short-sightedness in the vital month of February had brought him and his armies into this deadly trap. With the small-scale attacks of December and January, Arnim had done very well. But that was his limit. His mind recoiled from the daring opportunism which alone could have transformed the Kasserine attacks into one of the most daring Panzer operations of World War II. Nor was Arnim the man to accept the strategic enormity which alone made sense after Kasserine: getting as many men as possible out of North Africa to fight again.

The men of Army Group 'Africa' did all that fighting men could do, when the Allied attack was resumed on 22 April, to hold their last perimeter. Continuing until the end of the month, these attacks battered the German and Italians out of their front-line positions on the vital heights. The final assault on 6 May shattered Army Group 'Africa' like a glass block hit with a hammer. Arnim's insistence on commanding by the book totally deprived his men of any meaningful order after Tunis and Bizerta fell on the 7th, rupturing the chain of command. The hundreds and thousands of milling Axis troops, well armed and supplied, never even received an order to take to the hills and carry on guerrilla warfare from there, which they could easily have done for months. The formal surrenders of Arnim and Messe – on 12 and 13 May respectively – were accompanied by the usual punctilio. They set the seal on what can most accurately be described as a colossal piece of waste – of strategic opportunity, of *matériel* and, most important of all, of men.

FIELD-MARSHAL ALBERT KESSELRING

A natural comparison can be drawn between the attempt of Rommel and Arnim to defend Tunisia after El Alamein, and the attempt of Kesselring to halt the Allies at Monte Cassino after the invasion of Italy in September 1943. Both episodes lasted about the same time: seven months. Both episodes saw periods of marked German success; and both episodes helped prolong the life of the Third Reich and thus inhibit the Allied planning for final victory. As we have seen, however, the Axis position in Tunisia was basically hopeless. This was not the case in Italy, where every feature of the peninsula was ideally suited to a planned defence. Much more important, the defenders in Italy had a clear brief and a simple and effective chain of command. Thanks to Field-Marshal Albert Kesselring and his dogged defence at Cassino, the Allies were kept out of Rome for seven months. This took the victors past the spring of 1944 – the deadline when the armies in Italy must yield their strategic precedence to the forces preparing for the cross-Channel invasion of France – and ended all hopes of a runaway Allied victory in Italy.

Such in essence was the nature of Kesselring's achievement at Cassino. The battle itself tends to overshadow the fact that he had been on the verge of being overruled in his demands to hold central Italy, that Rommel himself, commanding in the Po valley, had believed that the only chance would be to make a decisive stand along the northern Apennines – in short, that there might never have been a stand-up fight at Cassino at all. Kesselring had had to right for his strategy, which was basically to keep the Allied bomber bases as far away from the Reich as possible. Originally, Hitler backed Rommel. But although the *Fuehrer's* lack of interest in the southern theatre had never really been modified since Rommel's first victories in Africa back in the early part of 1941, two concurrent events in the autumn of 1943 caught his imagination. They were the battle of Salerno, in which Kesselring's miscellany of German troops nearly succeeded in forcing the invading Allies back into the sea, and the rescue of Mussolini from his mountain-top prison by Otto Skorzeny's paratroops. These were heartening achievements against which Kesselring's optimistic strategy looked well; and in November 1943 Kesselring was appointed C-in-C of Army Group 'C', responsible for the defence of central and southern Italy.

By this time the Allies had survived the traumatic shock of Salerno, had taken Naples and were inching painfully through one of the foulest Italian autumns for years along the road to Rome. But although his appointment came late, Kesselring did not have to start from scratch. His foresight a year before had enabled him to save Tunisia from the Allies; and during the fight for Sicily in the high summer of 1943 he had taken steps to counter the next obvious Allied move against southern Italy. The narrowest section of the Italian peninsula between Naples and Rome was only 85 miles wide and was studded with perfect natural defences. South of this line, rivers and other suitable ridges of high ground offered the defenders parallel outer lines of defence. Throughout November 1943 the German troops fell slowly back towards the main line of defence, which had been code-named the 'Gustav Line' and whose main features were the Garigliano and Rapido rivers on the right, the Sangro river on the left and in the centre, commanding Route No. 6 and the road to Rome, the *massif* of Cassino itself.

■ 1st Cassino

The defence of the Gustav Line was entrusted to the 10th Army under General von Vietinghoff-Scheel, and it was composed of superb if polyglot troops under equally good commanders: Hube and von Senger of XIV Panzer Corps, Heidrich of the 1st Parachute Division, Fries of the 29th *Panzergrenadier* Division and Ringel of the 5th Mountain Division. But the 10th Army did not wait for the advancing US 5th and British 8th Armies behind static defences. The opening phase of the Cassino campaign was in fact a fighting retreat from the Volturno river (crossed by the 5th Army in mid-October) to the outer bastion of the Gustav Line proper. This was the 'Reinhard Line', a miniature Cassino, with the formidable heights of Monte Maggiore and Monte Sammucro commanding Route No. 6; it took the 5th Army the whole of December and the first fortnight of January 1944 to batter through the Reinhard Line and close up to the Garigliano and Rapido, under the heights of Cassino. Meanwhile, on the Allied right flank, Montgomery's 8th Army (taken over on 30 December by General Leese) struggled forwards across the Sangro river, painfully taking Ortona after a set-piece assault before being halted short of the Arielli river. But Kesselring could afford to give ground on the Sangro front. The decisive fight had to be made at Cassino, against the 5th Army.

What became known as the first battle of Cassino opened up well for the Allies, with the German right flank on the lower Garigliano rapidly losing ground. The

Allied attack at Cassino was co-ordinated with the celebrated landing at Anzio-Nettuno, deep behind the Gustav Line and posing a direct threat to Rome. Although Kesselring had his hands full at Cassino, and was totally taken by surprise by the Anzio stroke, he managed to contain the latter danger without withdrawing any troops from the Cassino front, where his reserves had already been committed on the lower Garigliano. Once again his foresight saved the day. Rome had always been an obvious goal for a surprise Allied attempt, and Kesselring had earmarked nucleus units to stand in readiness to enter the battle if need be. Thus he managed to seal off the beachhead with an extraordinary collection of battle-groups and special detachments from just about every German division in Italy. Another invaluable factor was the caution of the first Allied commander at Anzio, General Lucas, whose road to Rome was wide open on 22/23 January. By the time he started probing cautiously inland it was too late. The ring round the beach-head was secure.

At this point it is necessary to state that the Allies had attached a secondary purpose to the Italian theatre, apart from the obvious advantages of closing in on the Reich from the south. This was to compel the Germans to feed in as many troop reinforcements as possible – troops which would otherwise be sent to France to defend the Channel coast against invasion. Kesselring's improvisations had been made without such a reinforcement – but once again the shadow of Salerno touched the scene. Hitler and OKW wanted a counterattack that would succeed where that at Salerno had failed, and packed four divisions off to Italy, thus indirectly aiding Allied strategy. This fact was certainly not apparent to the wretched troops in the beach-head, who had to fight for their lives to maintain their position and then endure over three months of siege warfare worthy of the trenches in World War I.

Despite the initial danger on the lower Garigliano, the German positions along the Rapido held well and inflicted heavy losses on the Allied attacks during January. During a three-day battle (20/22 January) the US II Corps, and in particular the 36th 'Texas' Division, suffered bloody losses in its attempts to burst through the Gustav Line across the Rapido, and the attacks had to be called off.

Although the fighting on the Rapido was fierce, it was nothing to that seen during the third phase which now ensued: the attempt to force the Germans out of their positions on the heights of Monte Cassino itself. Ten days of intense fighting carried the troops of the US 34th Division to the verge of success on Monte Cassino before desperate counterattacks by German paratroops drove them off. This was a two-level fight, waged with equal intensity up on the heights and down in the shattered ruins of Cassino town.

■ **To bomb or not?**

Meanwhile, Alexander had pulled three of the best 8th Army units out of the line on the Adriatic sector and formed them into a special shock corps under the command of the famous New Zealander, General Freyberg. Final-gasp attacks by the US II

Corps on 11 and 12 February petered out just over a mile away from Highway No. 6 in a welter of persistent counterattacks. The Americans had fought themselves out; and Freyberg's newly-formed New Zealand Corps took over the job of pressing home the offensive.

There now followed one of the most controversial events of the war: the decision to bomb the venerable Abbey on the crest of Mont Cassino. This was a definite Allied miscalculation. There were in fact no German troops in the monastery, for all Freyberg's protestations to the contrary. Indeed the Germans, fearing for the safety of the priceless objects of art and devotion in the monastery, had evacuated the latter to the safety of the San Paolo monastery in Rome, after which Kesselring had drawn a 400-yard perimeter around the abbey precincts at Monte Cassino and issued the strictest orders that no German troops were to violate it. Freyberg's refusal to assault the heights until the monastery had been razed by bombers was an act of military short-sightedness, to say the least. Apart from being mistaken, he should have known that a heap of ruins is far easier for infantry to defend than an undamaged building. It is, after all, impossible to construct an invisible machine gun nest in a smooth and unbroken wall. And the bombing of the abbey on 15 February merely gave the Germans the excuse to move into the ruins and defend them in earnest. Even the pulverising effect of the bombardment was wasted, for Freyberg did not send in a heavy attack until 18 hours after the bombardment. It was handled roughly by a spirited German counterattack; and on 18 February a temporary silence settled on the Cassino battlefield. Kesselring's defenders, although frequently brought to the brink of defeat, had won a resounding victory; and the Allied attempt to dislodge them by the Anzio stroke had also failed.

The second battle of Cassino lasted from 15 to 23 March, and in it the Allies repeated every mistake they had previously made. The assault on Cassino town and abbey was preceded by the biggest air bombardment ever seen in the Mediterranean theatre, with 575 heavy and medium bombers taking part. Manning the crucial eight-mile Cassino sector of the Gustav Line were the crack paratroops of 1st Division under General Heidrich. Like the men of the German army on the Western Front in World War I, they once again proved that heavy bombardments do not mean that every soldier in the target area is killed. The heaped ruins acted as perfect anti-tank traps for the Allied armour, and also slowed the advance of Freyberg's infantrymen to a crawl. It was another sobering defeat for the Allied armies at Cassino.

The keynote of the month and a half after the second clash at Cassino was a regrouping on both sides, and an Allied air bombing offensive – Operation 'Strangle' – aimed at a total disruption of Kesselring's supply-lines in Italy. The latter aim was never achieved, although the repeated raids got a good deal of optimistic press coverage – 'Bombs blast enemy HQ', and so forth. Essentially Kesselring's dilemma remained unchanged. The Allied armies had the choice of making their main attack at Cassino, from the Anzio beach-head, or by means of yet another seaborne hook further north up the Italian coast. In fact Alexander planned for a decisive break-through at Cassino, having decided that the forces of the US 5th Army alone were inadequate. Massive reinforcements were brought across from the 8th Army; and by the opening of the third and final battle of Cassino at 2300 hours on 11 May, 21 Allied divisions faced 14 German divisions.

The story of the third battle is soon told. It was won by the magnificent French colonial mountain troops of General Juin's French Expeditionary Corps, who swarmed through the hills and took the Monte Maio *massif*, opening the Liri valley from the south. The Germans held on at Monte Cassino for four days, but the unin-terrupted advance of the French to the south unseamed the entire Gustav Line posi-tion, and the monastery was finally evacuated on the night of the 17th. When the breakout from Anzio was launched on 22 May it seemed that nothing could prevent the destruction of the retreating German 10th Army, but Allied failure to co-operate – and, some have said with justice, General Mark Clark's anxiety to be first into Rome – served as an unbelievable reprieve for Kesselring. On the very eve of the invasion of Normandy, the Allied armies at last entered Rome after seven months of frustration before the Gustav Line. But Alexander's objective of 'destroying the enemy south of Rome' had not been achieved.

Very few commanders have ever been as well served by their officers and men as was Kesselring at Cassino, yet the credit for that amazing defensive battle remains his. Never was Alexander's verdict on the man – that he could be easily out-thought, but only with the greatest difficulty be out-fought – so emphatically proven.

COLONEL-GENERAL HEINRICH VON VIETINGHOFF

When the Allies entered Rome on 4 June 1944, the German 10th and 14th Armies were still conducting so chaotic a retreat that there seemed every likelihood of cutting them off and destroying them before they could re-form and establish another defensive front. That this was not achieved was due to the magnetic influence of the Italian capital, which had come to obsess the 5th Army ever since the Allies had been fought to a halt at Cassino the previous November. Kesselring's shaken forces were given just enough time to get clear of the trap which never closed.

When Kesselring ordered the retreat to the northern Apennine *Gruen-Linie* (or Gothic Line, as it was more familiarly called) he was in a unique position. He had to retreat fast enough to prevent a débâcle in the Rome area, but not so fast that his armies got to the Gothic Line before its defences were ready. (This was scheduled for the autumn of 1944.) He was helped that he still had the terrain on his side as he retreated along the line of the Apennines, Italy's spine; and on either side of Lake Trasimene he had drawn the 'Albert Line', where he intended to make another stand.

Kesselring was also helped by a dramatic switch in the balance of forces in Italy. His opponent, General Alexander, was about to lose 97,000 men – the US VI Corps and the French Expeditionary Corps – which were required for the 'Dragoon' landings in southern France. This meant that Kesselring would not only be spared from having to face the markedly superior masses which had assailed him in the third battle of Cassino: he would also no longer have to worry about the best troops to serve on the Allied side in the Italian theatre. At the same time, OKW was sending him reinforcements: a paper strength of eight divisions in all, of which the most bizarre were the mounted Cossacks of the 162nd Turkestan Division. The first Allied withdrawals of troops came just in time to take the pressure off the 14th Army, on the German right flank, and enable it to reach the Albert Line in safety (20/23 June).

During the Cassino fighting, Vietinghoff's 10th Army had borne the brunt, drawing on reinforcements from 14th Army. The keynote of operations between 20 June and 3 August reversed this pattern, for Alexander's objective was a powerful thrust up the western side of the Apennines with Florence as its first objective. This was the 14th Army's front, and it was now the 10th Army's turn to do the reinforcing. While Vietinghoff had Lemelsen handled the operations of the 10th and 14th Armies, Kesselring presided like an anxious chef who knows that he is short of ingredients, doling out the appropriate reinforcements as required. The assault on the Albert Line commenced on 20 June, and by 2 July the Allies were through to Foiana, north of Lake Trasimene, and Cecina on the west coast. The Albert Line was breached.

During the next 14 days Lemelsen and Kesselring were helped by the constant withdrawal and replacement of Allied troops for the 'Dragoon' venture, but the 5th Army and its attached 8th Army divisions continued their northward crawl against stubborn resistance. Leghorn fell on 19 July; Pisa on the 23rd. On the night of 2/3 August the Germans evacuated Florence without a fight, and the city was entered by the British on the following day. By the end of the first week of August, the Allied armies had closed up to the approaches to the Gothic Line.

■ No 'Blitz attack'

Alexander knew that there could be no question of a 'Blitz attack' on this new and formidable belt of German defences. For his initial attack on the line he planned for nothing less than a complete switch of mass across to the Adriatic sector and the British 8th Army/German 10th Army front. His first attack would be launched here, and much was expected from it; but if it got bogged down Alexander planned to unleash his 5th Army against the 14th Army and tie down all Kesselring's reserves.

The Allied redeployment was a godsend for Kesselring as many of the key defence positions in the line were still not ready. To make matters worse, the German 71st Division was pulling back from the Metauro river to the Foglia when Alexander's attack opened on the night of 25/26 August, and at first both Vietinghoff and Kesselring believed that the 8th Army's attack was only a limited follow-up. Their disillusionment was rapid and appalling. By the last day of the month the 8th Army was battering at the Adriatic sector of the Gothic Line, capturing German troops who were in the process of occupying their positions. By 3 September the leading 8th Army forces were across the Conca river, over 10 miles to the rear of the Gothic Line.

Kesselring hauled three divisions across from 14th Army to take the sting out of the Allied offensive. Two factors alone saved the 10th Army: the difficulty of getting Allied tanks through the gap won by the infantry, and the eternally fickle Italian weather, which broke on the night of 4 September. The 8th Army's advance faltered and died; and Alexander promptly ordered the 5th Army to push into the mountains and come to grips with Lemelsen's 14th Army, weakened as it now was by the reinforcements drawn off for Vietinghoff. Clark opened his attack on the Imola axis on 12 September, and after a superb initial defence by the green young troops of the 4th Parachute Division, the 5th Army began to make ground. By 27 September the 5th Army forward positions were within 10 miles of Imola, and Kesselring, aware that he had yet another crisis on his hands, threw in units from four German divisions on both sides of the Allied salient. After a week of desperate fighting, Clark accepted the position and began to plan a new thrust in the direction of Bologna.

Back on the 8th Army sector, a new attack opened on 12 September along the lowland coastal strip. A rapid advance was out of the question as the attacking forces were now entering the Romagna plain, which is basically an enormous reclaimed swamp watered by innumerable parallel water-courses. On 20 September Rimini fell and the Marecchia river was crossed on the following day, but ceaseless rain throughout the last week of the month brought the advance to another halt.

Further desperate efforts in October and November halted the 5th Army nine miles short of Bologna and the 8th Army south of Ravenna. Never had the foul winter weather of Italy been of such help to Kesselring: at one stage floods carried away ever Bailey bridge carrying 8th Army supplies across the swollen rivers of the Romagna. A series of limited attacks in late December and early January carried the 8th Army to the southern tip of Lake Comacchio and forced the Germans back behind the Senio river, losing Ravenna in the process; but Kesselring's obstinacy allied to the adverse weather forced the Allies to contemplate another winter south of the line of the River Po.

The remaining months of the winter of 1944–45 were months of preparation on both sides for the final campaign in Italy. There were command charges all round. McCreery had already replaced Leese as commander of the 8th Army; Alexander moved to the post of Supreme Commander, Mediterranean, and Clark took over the Allied 15th Army Group; Truscott, who had saved the day at Anzio, took over the 5th Army from Clark. On the German side, Kesselring finally left Italy in March to try to sort out some order from the hopeless situation in western Germany, and was replaced by Vietinghoff. General Herr took over the 10th Army, while Lemelsen stayed on with the 14th Army. Before he left, Kesselring had been doing the only thing he could: setting his forces to create as many defences as they could on the river lines of the Po valley, the last natural defences left to Army Group 'C' between the northern Apennines and the Alps. Clark's army group, on the other hand, teemed with preparations for the coming offensive. There were lavish supplies of amphibious armoured transports and 'Kangaroos' – turretless tanks to serve as armoured troop-carriers. Allied training stressed the need for complete teamwork between infantry and armour. The lessons taught by the experiences before the Gothic Line last August had been well learned, and there was certainly no underestimating the gravity of the task which lay ahead.

The new German army group commander, Vietinghoff, was an old 'Italy hand', but his character was strikingly – and depressingly – similar to Arnim of Tunisia. He was a dour and methodical ex-Prussian guardsman who fought his battles by the book. He was precisely the sort of German general who could be guaranteed to produce an early defeat by sticking to the letter of Hitler's orders not to retreat an inch – and that was what happened in the campaign of April 1945.

■ Standard tactics

The pattern of the last Allied attack contained many elements which had been familiar throughout the Italian campaign. Vietinghoff was led to expect another Allied amphibious landing in his rear, this time in the Venice area. In fact, the 8th Army would attack across the Senio around Lugo before the 5th Army resumed its drive towards Bologna. Then the 8th Army would switch direction, sending an amphibious push across Lake Comacchio and striking north through the 'Argenta Gap' to pen Vietinghoff's force in the central Po valley.

On 9 April Alexander and Clark opened their offensive. At first definite progress was achieved only slowly, with Truscott's US II Corps managing to advance a mere two miles in three days – but between 15 and 20 April Vietinghoff's defences cracked. The 8th Army's attack poured through the Argenta Gap and closed to within 15 miles of Ferrara. Bologna fell at last on 21 April. Vietinghoff, who had struggled manfully, if myopically, to keep to Hitler's 'no retreat' order, accepted the inevitable on the 20th and ordered a general retreat to the Po, but by now it was too late. In the Gothic Line fighting of the previous autumn, Kesselring had managed to delay until the last minute before giving ground because the difficulties of the terrain prevented the Allies from moving fast enough, but matters were very different down in the Po valley. And this time dominant Allied air power, unhampered by weather, struck at the German bridges across the Po and wrecked them, keeping up constant air strikes, as in Normandy, and making the German withdrawal across the Po a near-suicidal operation by day.

The pursuit was mercilessly pressed and the leading 8th Army troops were up to the Po by the 23rd. On 24 April three British divisions got across. Foremost in the pursuit was the US 10th Mountain Division, which had leaped forward 55 miles in two days to reach the Po. It pounced forward to seize Verona on the 25th and headed up Lake Garda towards Trento and the Alps. Meanwhile, on the extreme left and right of the shattered German front, the Allies fanned out to the north-west and north-east with a relentless symmetry. Genoa fell on the 27th, Turin and Milan on 2 May; the 8th Army took Venice on 28 April and had reached Trieste on 2 May.

Vietinghoff's forces had lost nearly all of their artillery, armour and transport in the retreat across the Po, and there was not even a chance of making any kind of last stand on the north bank. Individual units had already begun to surrender when weeks of undercover negotiations between the SS in Italy and CIA virtuoso Allen Dulles in Switzerland bore fruit. The great fear in the Allied supreme command had been the mythical *Alpenfestung* – a non-existent bastion in the Alps and southern Bavaria and Austria where the last stand of the Third Reich would be fought. The Dulles negotiations, however, provided for the surrender of all German forces in Italy and Austria, and the capitulation came into force on 2 May, the day Turin, Milan and Trieste fell. It involved nearly a million men and is generally agreed to have shortened the course of the war by weeks. As it was, the surrender in Italy was made only six days before the European war came to an end.

Yet at one stage it had seemed most likely that the Italian campaign would have Allied troops knocking at the door of Austria by the summer of 1944 at the latest. That this was thwarted was due primarily to the energy and skill of Kesselring, whose achievements in 1943 and 1944 need little further comment. He was admirably served by competent subordinates – Vietinghoff, Mackensen, Lemelsen, Herr, von Senger, Fries and Heidrich. He had all the luck any general could ever hope to have: repeated mistakes made by his enemy and foul weather practically on order to slow him up. Kesselring's own mistakes were many, and led him repeatedly to the edge of disaster. But his true greatness lay in his talent for repairing them and looking to the next battle, the next day.

ANALYSIS – GERMAN GENERALSHIP IN NORTH AFRICA AND ITALY

In the high summer of 1942, with Kleist's Panzers advancing towards the Caucasus in southern Russia and Rommel in Egypt menacing Alexandria and Cairo, it was easy to imagine that the German 'master war plan' for the conquest of the Middle East was on the verge of realisation. Of course, no such plan existed. The German army in World War II tackled its successive enemies according to the whims of Hitler, not according to an army blueprint. And it would probably never have got involved in North Africa at all had it not been for the military uselessness of Germany's partner in the 'Pact of Steel': Italy.

Mussolini's ignominious defeats in Greece, Albania, Egypt and Libya created a situation which not even Hitler dare ignore. The original *Afrika Korps* was not, as was widely believed, an élite force seasoned for desert warfare by months of training in hot-houses and synthetic sandstorms: it was a scratch force of armour and infantry to save Tripoli for Mussolini. There was a strong parallel between the formation of *Afrika Korps* and the formation of the expeditionary force which took Denmark and Norway in April 1940. Both were maddening distractions for OKH, which in 1940 was concentrating on the imminent assault on the West and in 1941 was concentrating on the imminent invasion of Soviet Russia.

Rommel's thoroughly insubordinate reconquest of eastern Libya for the Axis created far more problems than it solved. It still comes as a surprise to many that Brauchitsch and Halder sent out Paulus to keep Rommel under control, not to help him, in April 1941. North Africa was still irrelevant to OKH and OKW. Not so to the British. It was the only possible land theatre where they could actually fight the Germans.

*

■ OKW obligation

For OKW, Rommel's victories in Libya created the obligation to keep him supplied, to reinforce success despite themselves – an obligation which was never honoured. The 'parallel war' mushroomed in the Mediterranean, with convoy routes, shipping tonnage and the vexing question of Malta nagging at the planners of OKW and OKH as they struggled to get on with destroying the Red Army in Russia.

Even when a compromise was reached – that Rommel should attack at Gazala, take Tobruk, then wait for the conquest of Malta – the unpredictable, off-the-cuff nature of the desert war triumphed in the end with Rommel's invasion of Egypt. Rommel went so far that he put himself beyond the reach even of basic supplies, out on a limb where one slip would leave him hanging. He had made mistakes before, and he made one of the most disastrous mistakes in history when he made his initial heads-down rush at the strongest nuclei of the El Alamein defences in early July 1942. Rommel found himself, moreover, faced by Auchinleck, who actually wrested the initiative from him against all expectations.

Once halted at El Alamein, Rommel's every prospect depended on supply. He was not the first German general who was promised supplies which never turned up, and he found himself trapped by the results of his own successes earlier in the year. He had to attempt a breakthrough at Alam Halfa; he had no choice but to await the inevitable from Montgomery at El Alamein.

Rommel's defeat at El Alamein, and the Allied landings in Algeria, finally woke OKW up to what was going on in North Africa. On his own initiative, Kesselring had prevented the likelihood of Rommel's *Panzerarmee* being destroyed simultaneously with the 6th Army in Stalingrad. OKW decided to reinforce the initial small-scale successes won in Tunisia. Now, far too late, they came – Tiger tanks, *Nebelwerfer*, and above all, manpower. It was all for nothing; it was all wasted. Once they were penned into the Tunisian bridgehead there was nothing that the generals could do.

A very good nickname for Kesselring would be 'the great delayer of defeat'. His lightning seizure of Tunisia had staved off the end in Africa. His stiffening of the Italian garrison of Sicily delayed the Allied conquest of the island. And his equally brilliant takeover of the strategic centres of the Italian mainland when Italy quit the 'Pact of Steel' in September 1943 was the fitting prelude to the long ordeal of the Italian campaign – the protraction of which was Kesselring's finest achievement.

■ Extemporised units

From a scatter of miscellaneous units dotted all over Italy to forestall a variety of possible Allied moves, Kesselring welded a solid and formidable defensive front. His deployment, apparently haphazard, dealt out an initial shock to the Allies at Salerno, where Kesselring pushed home the attack on the Allied beach-head until he saw that there was no point in trying further. Nor was Kesselring remotely interested in defending Naples, the first major Axis city on the European continent to fall to the Allies. He ordered a fighting retreat back to the Reinhard and Gustav Lines, where he intended to hold for as long as he could.

His best ally during the winter fighting at Cassino was the terrain, which not only favoured the defenders but made it impossible for the Allied armies to move fast. Indeed, Alexander had only one unit which worried Kesselring: Juin's French colonials, the men who finally cracked open the Cassino front in May. And he had the best possible troops to hold the town of Cassino and the monastery heights: paratroops. They were not soldiers who depended on orthodox supply-lines and command echelons: they were superbly-trained individual fighting men, used to working in small units virtually on their own.

The controversial Anzio stroke was only a surprise for Kesselring in that he had no way of knowing where and when the landing would be made. The Allies gained total surprise, only to waste it by excessive caution. Kesselring's ingenuity in sealing off the beach-head without fatally weakening the Cassino front was an altogether admirable feat. But he was unable to prevent the Allies from building up the beach-head force and making it a miniature 'second front' against Kesselring when the big push went in at Cassino in May.

When the French swarmed through the mountains and shattered the Cassino front, the 10th Army teetered on the verge of total dissolution. Here again, as in the initial stages of the Anzio landing, Kesselring was lucky in the mistakes made by his opponents. Rome, not the destruction of the German forces which had held up the Allies for so long, was the chief 5th Army objective. This alone enabled Kesselring to pull his 10th and 14th Armies together again and take them north to the last natural defence-line in the mountains of Italy; the 'Gothic Line' across the northern Apennines. Had Alexander been left with the full strength with which he had broken through at Cassino, the story of the August fighting along the Gothic Line would have been very different. As it was, Kesselring was able to fight the Allies to another muddy standstill in the autumn of 1944, while invaluable French and American units fought their way up to the Rhône valley in southern France to form Eisenhower's right-wing army group.

This halting of the Allies along the Gothic Line was Kesselring's last major achievement in Italy. It coincided with the halting of the Red Army along the Vistula and with the petering-out of Eisenhower's advance on the Western Front. For the last time, Hitler's high command had time to take stock behind fronts which were everywhere stable. This respite only produced the Ardennes gamble of December 1944 and the subsequent acceleration of the Allied advance, but set against the overall disasters of 1944 the stabilisation of the Italian front was a notable success.

In a way, the Sicilian and Italian campaigns, twin sequences to the collapse in Africa, were the disastrous fruits of Hitler's decision to make an ally out of Fascist Italy. For over four and a half years German forces fought on the 'southern front', first

240

shoring up the inadequacies of their Italian ally and then holding the breach left by Italy's surrender. Territorially speaking, however, the whole story – Africa, Sicily and Italy – amounts to the defence of the biggest outer bastion by which any nation at war has ever sought to keep the enemy from her gates. The biggest, that is, apart from German-occupied Russia, to which Africa, Sicily and Italy remained of secondary importance in any case.

THE EASTERN FRONT, FEBRUARY 1943–MAY 1945

THE CAMPAIGN AGAINST RUSSIA, FROM KURSK TO BERLIN

O n 12 January 1943, as the grim battle for Stalingrad was drawing towards its conclusion, the Russian armies on the southern front took the offensive against the German, Italian, Hungarian and Rumanian forces of Weichs' Army Group 'B' and Manstein's Army Group 'Don', driving them back from the River Don near Voronezh to a line along the central Donets and Oskol. The Bryansk, Voronezh, South-West and South Fronts resumed their offensive on 2 February, driving the Germans back to a line between Kursk in the north and Kharkov in the centre, and in a great salient towards Dnepropetrovsk in the south.

Manstein decided on a bold counter-offensive to throw back the Russians. In the centre Corps 'Raus' of *Gruppe* 'Kempf' counterattacked on 18 February and on 14 March retook Kharkov, whilst in the south II SS Panzer corps of *Gruppe* 'Kempf', acting in concert with the 1st and 4th *Panzerarmee* from the south, wiped out the salient towards Dnepropetrovsk, restoring the front to the line of the Donets. In the north the battle swayed to and fro for some time before the spring thaw settled matters, leaving the Russians in control of the great salient to the west of Kursk after 20 March. Manstein's forces, although outnumbered by about seven to one, had halted the powerful Russian thrusts, and had even thrown back a considerable portion of the central and southern ones with great losses. It was a quite remarkable feat, and perhaps the crowning glory of Manstein's distinguished career. Nevertheless, the Russian drive and the German riposte had hurt the German cause very considerably. Communist estimates put the German casualties at over one million, together with 5,000 aircraft, 9,000 tracked vehicles and 20,000 guns. Russian losses have never been revealed, but must have been in the same order of magnitude, if not greater.

Manstein's losses had been so great that a major German offensive in the summer of 1943 was completely out of the question. All that could be attempted was a limited offensive to put the Russians off their balance and iron out the salient around Kursk left by the cessation of hostilities with the spring thaw. The offensive, known to history as the Battle of Kursk, was a disaster for the Germans. They had delayed too long so as to introduce significant numbers of their latest armoured fighting vehicles, and the Russians, whom agents had warned of the exact time and location of the German pincer offensive (by the 4th *Panzerarmee* of Army Group 'South' and the 9th Army Group 'Centre'), had prepared formidable defences. The German offensive went in on 4 July, and resulted in the greatest tank battle of history. The Germans made virtually no progress, and lost 70,000 men, 5,000 vehicles, 3,000 tanks, 1,400 aircraft and 1,000 guns, according to the Russians.

As their forces in the salient were halting the German offensive, the Russians launched the fronts holding the German salients around Orel and Kharkov, to the north and south of the Russian salient of Kursk respectively, in a counter-offensive. Despite strenuous German efforts to stem the Russian offensives, both the Orel and Kharkov salients had been overrun by 23 August. Manstein had been ordered by Hitler to hold on to Kharkov at any cost, but refused to do so, conducting a masterly retreat back to the line of the River Dniepr.

■ Manstein retreats

Manstein found it necessary to pull back so far because the local Russian offensives for Orel and Kharkov had on 23 August been joined by a general Russian summer offensive by all the fronts west and south of Moscow – the Kalinin, West Bryansk, Central (later Belorussian), Voronezh (later 1st Ukrainian), Steppe (later 2nd Ukrainian), South-West (later 3rd Ukrainian), South (later 4th Ukrainian) and North Caucasus Fronts. By 16 September the Russians had advanced an average of 50 miles all along the front, the Central Front under Rokossovsky doing best in reaching Nezhin, only some 60 miles from the Ukrainian capital Kiev after an advance of 100 miles. By the end of September the Russian armies had pressed on yet further, retaking Smolensk in the north on 25 September and reaching the line of the Rivers Sozh and Dniepr as far south as Zaporozhye, the front running down to the Sea of Azov from there. In fact bridgeheads over the Dniepr had been gained downstream from Kremenchug, between Bukin and Kanev, and in two places upstream from Kiev. Between the beginning of November and 23 December the Russians continued to advance, recapturing the key city of Kiev on 6 November, encircling Vitebsk in the north, driving Army Group 'Centre' back to the Pripet marshes, and cutting off the 17th Army in the Crimea. This last had evacuated its beach-head in the Kuban by 9 October, but Hitler would not hear of its leaving the Crimea as this would provide a good jumping-off point for another attempt in the Caucasus when the German armies recaptured southern Russia! By the end of December the 17th Army was completely cut off, the 4th Ukrainian Front having advanced to Kherson at the mouth of the Dniepr.

As with all previous Russian offensives, German casualties in men and *matériel* had been extremely heavy, and the Third Reich was finding it increasingly difficult, if not impossible, to find replacements. Even when the required replacements were forthcoming, they were far inferior in quality to the troops who had played so important a part in gaining Germany's victories up to the end of 1941. The Russians, however, were in a far better situation. Although they were still suffering very heavy casualties, they were still able to replace them, to a great extent with conscripts from the liberated areas. *Matériel* was also in better supply, both from the factories behind the Urals and from Lend-Lease from Great Britain and the United States. Of Lend-Lease supplies, perhaps the most important items were the 80,000 trucks supplied by the United States. These gave the Russians a far greater degree of mobility than they had possessed previously, and permitted their commanders to employ more daring tactics. The skill of the Russian commanders continued to improve rapidly with their growing combat experience.

■ Leningrad freed

In the north Leningrad, which had been under German siege since October 1941, was finally freed from German threats in January 1944. A corridor had been driven through to the city along the southern shore of Lake Ladoga in January 1943, but it was not until the concerted drive by Govorov's Leningrad Front and Meretskov's Volkhov Front between 14 and 31 January 1944 that the citizens of Leningrad could be sure that they would not come under German shelling or bombing attacks. Popov's 2nd Baltic Front, which had played a minor part in the first stage of the offensive, played a more prominent part in later stages, which only ended when Model, who had taken over Army Group 'North' from Kuechler on 29 January, halted the Russian advance along the line of the River Narva, Lake Peipus and River Velikaya by 1 March. The spring thaws now intervened to prevent any further movement.

In the Ukraine the Russians had launched another winter offensive on 29 January. The major early event was the trapping of two German corps at Korsun-Shevchenkovsky by the 1st and 2nd Ukrainian Fronts. The weather prevented any success by the relief force and also the breakout by the trapped forces, and Manstein lost another 100,000 men when the pocket was overrun on 17 February. It was now the turn of the 1st *Panzerarmee* to receive the Russians' attentions. Under the command of General H. V. Hube, the 1st *Panzerarmee* was cut off, but on instructions from Manstein and supplied from the air by the *Luftwaffe* (which was making one of its few significant contributions since its losses in the Battle of Kursk), it operated behind the Russian lines, severely hampering Russian supply and communication lines. With the aid of the 4th *Panzerarmee*, the 1st *Panzerarmee* finally broke out to the west on 10 April, with its forces intact. It had played an important part in slowing down the Russian offensive. Along the north coast of the Black Sea Army Group 'A' was having a bad time of it at the hands of Konev's 2nd, Malinovsky's 3rd and

Tolbukhin's 4th Ukrainian Fronts. Odessa had to be given up on 10 April. Hitler was so infuriated by these constant retreats in the south that he sacked both Manstein and Kleist, replacing them with Model and General F. Schoerner respectively. The two army groups involved were renamed Army Groups 'North Ukraine' and 'South Ukraine'. The whole of the western part of the Ukraine had now been liberated from the Germans, and Konev's forces were almost in a position to threaten eastern Hungary. It is worth noting here how the Russians had by now developed their offensive tactics into a fine art. Using their massive numerical and *matériel* superiority, and closely controlled by the *Stavka* or high command in Moscow, the Russians steam-rollered the Germans, accepting heavy losses, but feeding fresh troops into the battle as quickly as possible. Against such tactics the Germans found that there was little that they could do except attempt to slow down the Russian advance.

■ Disastrous tactics

Such was Hitler's preoccupation with holding ground and thinking of offensive action that when the Russian summer offensive of 1944 broke upon the hapless Axis forces in Russia, there was no way to halt the Russian tide. No defensive positions had been chosen or prepared, and German troops were deployed as far forward as possible, with no thought for the expediency of the positions. Thus Zhukov's offensive in Belorussia, and thence into Poland, was a total disaster for the Germans.

Zhukov, now deputy supreme Russian commander, had prepared his plans carefully, with even more massive concentrations of tanks, artillery and aircraft than was usual. The offensive, directed in a south-westerly direction from Smolensk towards Warsaw in Poland, opened in fine weather on 22 June against Colonel-General E. Busch's Army Group 'Centre'. Busch's communications had been cut by partisans, and his air units had been removed to the West to help in the struggle against the Western Allies, who had just landed in Normandy. Busch's forces had not a chance against the Russians, and a 250-mile gap was ripped through the German defences. Zhukov's armour pressed on, leaving the encircled towns of Vitebsk, Bobruysk and Minsk to be overrun by the infantry on 25 June, 27 June and 3 July respectively. Army Group 'Centre' was in ruins, with three-quarters of its 33 divisions destroyed or cut off. German losses totalled 381,000 killed, 158,000 captured, and 2,000 armoured vehicles, 10,000 guns and nearly 60,000 vehicles lost. Busch was immediately replaced by Model. By 10 July Zhukov's forces had cleared Belorussia, and were preparing to debouch into Poland and the Baltic states. Lvov fell on 27 July, Brest Litovsk on the 28th and Vilnyus on the 13th. Rokossovsky's 1st Belorussian Front threatened Warsaw until a desperate counter-attack by Model's forces halted it, leaving the Polish insurgents in Warsaw to be crushed by the SS in a heroic two-month struggle in August and September. By 7 August Zhukov's forces had pushed on some 450 miles and were exhausted; the summer offensive was over. Later in the year Germany suffered another shock when Finland dropped out of the war as a result of a truce with Russia on 4 September. Another near disaster for German arms was the Russian autumn offensive into the Baltic states. Schoerner's Army Group 'North' had nearly been cut off in Latvia by the advance of Chernyakovsky's 3rd Belorussian Front at the end of July. It was in fact cut off in the autumn offensive, in which the Russians retook all the Baltic states with the exception of the Kurland peninsula in Latvia, held by Schoerner's army group. Although fighting continued until 15 December, the Russians made no important gains after the end of October. An offensive into East Prussia was repulsed. The 20 divisions of Army Group 'North', trapped in Kurland, are a good example of Hitler's strategic stupidity. By refusing to allow them to pull back in good time, Hitler condemned these good divisions to a type of captivity, and one in which they could play no further part in the attempt to rescue Germany's fortunes.

■ Balkan fiasco

Back in the south, the Crimea had been cleared between 8 April and 9 May by Tolbukhin's 4th Ukrainian Front. Most of the 17th Army, however, managed to get away from Sevastopol by sea. The 2nd and 3rd Ukrainian Fronts now attacked across the River Prut into Rumania, which was defended by General J. Friessner's Army Group 'South Ukraine'. The offensive started on 20 August, and when Rumania threw in her lot with Russia on the 25th, the Rumanian 3rd and 4th Armies, part of Friessner's command, went over to the Russians, trapping most of the German 6th and 8th Armies. The Russians reached the River Danube south of Bucharest on 1 September, completely outflanking the German defence and causing considerable losses in men and *matériel*. When Bulgaria also defected to the Russian side on 4 September, the whole of the German flank in the Balkans was exposed. The Russians rushed on towards Belgrade, which fell on 19 October, in an effort to cut off the retreat of Army Groups 'E' and 'F' from Greece and southern Yugoslavia respectively. The two army groups managed to escape, however, by veering to the west, and linked up with Friessner's forces, now designated Army Group 'South'. The Russians got a bridgehead over the Danube on 24 December, and invested Budapest on 24 December. The Hungarian capital, however, fell only on 14 February 1945. But Hitler's unwillingness to allow retreat had very nearly lost him his forces in the southern Balkans.

12 January 1945 witnessed the penultimate act in Germany's defeat, when the Russian armies from the Danube valley in the south to the Baltic in the north once again went over to the offensive. In the north Chernyakovsky's 3rd Belorussian and Rokossovsky's 2nd Belorussian Fronts pressed into East Prussia and pushed back Army Group 'Centre' (redesignated Army Group 'North' on 25 January) to the Baltic. The Germans put up a brave defence, but as usual in this late stage of the war, there was nothing the Germans could do but attempt to delay the Russian advances. Koenigsberg and several other isolated beach-heads held out until the end of the war.

Further south, the left flank of Rokossovsky's 2nd Belorussian Front drove to the north-west after capturing Warsaw, whilst Zhukov's 1st Belorussian Front attacked due west, and after an advance of some 300 miles reached the River Oder, only about 40 miles from Berlin, on 31 January. Further south again, Konev's 1st Ukrainian Front advanced from the River Vistula line to the River Oder–Neisse line by 15 February. At this point the portion of the winter offensive north of the Carpathian mountains halted, Russian logistics being unable to supply front-line units any further from their supply bases.

South of the Carpathians, the Russian advance had been checked by the splendid defence of Budapest, which fell only on 14 February. After the vain attempt to secure the Hungarian oilfields in the Battle of Lake Balaton in March, the Germans were unceremoniously bundled out of Hungary into Austria, whose capital, Vienna, fell to troops of Tolbukhin's 3rd Ukrainian Front on 14 April.

■ Germany invaded

Meanwhile, in the north the 1st and 2nd Belorussian Fronts cleared Germany's Baltic coast, which had been left in the Russian advance to the River Oder. The defence of the coastal strip was entrusted to the so-called Army Group 'Vistula', a hotch-potch collection of *Volkssturm*, SS units, police and military remnants under the command of *Reichsfuehrer*-SS Heinrich Himmler, then of General G. Heinrici, and finally of General K. Student. The 1st Belorussian Front attacked northwards towards Kolberg on 16 February, as did the 2nd Belorussian Front towards Gdynia and Danzig. The coast, with the exception of some pockets, had been cleared by 15 April, leaving the northern group of Russian armies free to launch their final offensive – on Berlin.

■ The last act

This final offensive began on 16 April, with advances by Konev's 1st Ukrainian Front and Zhukov's 1st Belorussian Front, commanded in this last offensive by General V. Sokolovsky, allowing Zhukov to co-ordinate the whole offensive. Rokossovsky's 2nd Belorussian Front went over to the offensive on 20 April. The German defence was desperate, but ill co-ordinated, and the Russians reached Berlin on 22 April and invested the city on the 25th. In the north men of Rokossovsky's front had come into contact with troops of the British 21st Army Group in Wismar on 3 May, and in the south contact was made between Konev's front and men of the US 12th Army Group in Torgau on 25 April. Hitler, after appointing Doenitz his successor, committed suicide on the 30th. Meanwhile the Russians were fighting a savage battle for Berlin, which finally capitulated on 2 May.

The last actions of the war against Germany were fought in Czechoslovakia, where Schoerner's Army Group 'Centre' was putting up a final, defiant resistance. Completely surrounded, and attacked by Konev's 1st Ukrainian Front, Petrov's 4th Ukrainian Front, Malinovsky's 2nd Ukrainian Front, the US 1st Army and the US

3rd Army, Schoerner finally called it a day in a pocket between Prague and Pardubice on 11 May 1945.

According to Russian sources, in all probability correct, the last three months fighting had cost Germany at least one million dead and 800,000 prisoners, together with 12,000 AFVs, 6,000 aircraft and 23,000 guns. Hitler's folly had bled Germany white. What was all the most distressing from the German point of view was that given the situation at the beginning of 1943, the Germans could have fought their war far more efficiently with a supreme leader other than Hitler, and even had the war still been lost, as was entirely probably, casualties would have been far less.

FIELD-MARSHAL ERIC VON MANSTEIN

In March 1943, the Germans needed a spectacular victory in the East to make up for the defeat at Stalingrad.

Manstein's plan for such a victory was presented to Hitler as early as February 1943. He believed there was much to be gained from a strategy of manoeuvre and he thought the Germans should await the expected Russian offensive to recover the Donets basin and then hit them hard. He envisaged surrendering the whole Donets basin and luring the Russians as far as the lower Dniepr. The whole weight of the German Panzer force would then strike south-east at lightning speed from Kharkov and pin the attackers against the Sea of Azov. For Manstein, mobile defence was very important. Static defence was useless in his opinion as the Germans had too few troops to defend such an enormous front.

This sound plan was rejected by Hitler on vague political grounds, although the real reason lay in the fact that he would never consider giving up territory.

Others, including Zeitzler, thought that a limited offensive should be waged against Kursk, which would be less risky than simply waiting for the Russians to attack and did not contain a preliminary sacrifice of land.

■ Dangerous salient

The Kursk salient was a huge and menacing-looking bulge 9,000 square miles in area, lying between Orel in the north and Belgorod in the south. It had been captured by the Russians the previous winter. Geographically, it was a far-flung plain, broken by valleys, copses, villages, rivers and streams. Fields of corn made visibility difficult and the ground rose to the north, a fact which was to favour the defenders. Roads were simply tracks through the sand, which became channels of mud when it rained and were thus impassable for motor vehicles. The Russians had large troop concentrations here.

To the Germans, Kursk was a suitable target because simultaneous attacks from north and south could be made, thus trapping large numbers of Russians, including reserve formations.

The plan was that the Colonel-General Walther Model's 9th Army of Army Group 'Centre' should attack southwards towards Kursk from Orel while Colonel-General Hoth's 4th *Panzerarmee* and *Gruppe* 'Kempf' of Army Group 'South' should attack northwards from Kharkov to meet Model at Kursk. The enemy encircled in the Kursk salient was then to be destroyed. This was to be Operation '*Zitadelle*' (Citadel) and Zeitzler was the main architect of the plan. Detailed planning began in March, but delays blighted the operation from the start. Manstein urged the attack be made straight after Kharkov in March, but it was delayed by the difficulties in assembling the necessary troops. D-day was then fixed for mid-April, but by now Model, who approved the plan in principle, had doubts about the adequacy of his resources, and asked Hitler for a post-ponement until reinforcements arrived. Guderian had recently been recalled from retire-ment to take up the post of Inspector General of Mobile Troops. He opposed '*Zitadelle*', anticipating heavy tank losses when tanks were desperately needed on the Western Front. Guderian's task was to invigorate the Panzer forces, and prepare them to break through the Russian numerical superiority. Field-Marshal von Kluge, commander of Army Group 'Centre', and Manstein, commander of Army Group 'South', were both in favour of the plan, but Manstein soon became wary of the delays. Hitler could not make up his mind what to do, and so the weeks passed. The new Panther tanks were beset with tech-nical difficulties and only about 12 were being produced each week.

With time, the concept of Operation '*Zitadelle*' changed from a short, sharp, sur-prise blow to a head-on trial of strength, for the Russians had not been idle while the *Fuehrer* vacillated.

The Russian defences had been organised with the utmost speed. To co-ordinate the arrangements, *Stavka* (the Russian high command) sent Marshals Vasilevsky and Zhukov to Kursk at the end of April. The northern part of the Kursk salient was held by General Rokossovsky's Central Front with the 48th, 13th, 70th, 65th and 60th Armies deployed from north to south; the 2nd Tank Army and three corps lay in reserve. The southern (Voronezh) front was commanded by the General Vatutin with the 6th and 7th Guards Armies, with the 38th and 40th Armies under orders and the 1st Tank Army and the 69th Army in reserve.

The Russians fully expected the attack against Kursk. They received accurate information from a spy in OKW and decided to postpone their own planned offen-sive and await that of the Germans.

■ Good planning

Rokossovsky recommended that their main reserve strength be centrally deployed east of Kursk, from where it could counter the thrusts of Manstein and Model, but where it was unlikely to be cut off. The reserve became known as the Steppe Front, and it was placed under the command of Colonel-General Konev. It comprised five armies, including one tank army and one tank, one mechanised and three cavalry corps. The Steppe Front was also to provide fresh troops for a counter-offensive. And should the battle take a turn for the worse, it was to establish a line across the neck of the salient, so that the attacking Germans would again have to rupture the Soviet line.

Earthworks and parallel trenches made up an important part of the Soviet defences. The main forward defensive zone was three miles deep with at least five lines of trenches, one behind the other, interlinking and containing shelters. The second zone was seven miles further back; the third line lay 20 miles behind the second – and so on. Trenches stretched for hundreds of miles. Anti-tank defences were formidable. Large areas were mined and anti-tank strongpoints were set up. Half a million mines were laid on the Central Front alone – 2,400 anti-tank and 2,700 anti-personnel mines per square mile. The Artillery Reserve of the High Command was in support, and the two fronts had 13,000 guns, 6,000 anti-tank guns and 1,000 Katyusha multiple rocket-launchers. All defending units were subjected to an intensive and repetitive course of training.

The Russian armour comprised mostly T-34s, but the KV tanks available now mounted the 85-mm gun. Also in service were the new tank destroyers – the self-propelled SU assault gun. The 2nd and 16th Air Armies provided 2,500 planes for support.

D-day for '*Zitadelle*' was eventually fixed for the beginning of July. Manstein felt that it was too late, and that the operation was no longer feasible. Model urged that the operation be abandoned because he felt the Russians expected the offensive, but Hitler had now decided to go ahead, even though he confided to Guderian that the thought of '*Zitadelle*' made him feel sick.

The northern pincer movement was to be executed by Model's 9th Army with three Panzer corps, two army corps and supporting infantry. The southern pincer, under Manstein's command, had the 4th *Panzerarmee* (Colonel-General Hoth) with Hausser's II SS Panzer Corps (including the divisions '*Leibstandarte*', '*Das Reich*' and '*Totenkopf*'), and Knobelsdorff's XLVIII Panzer Corps (including the army's '*Grossdeutschland*' division); Ott's LII Corps and also *Gruppe* 'Kempf', whose task it was to guard the eastern flank of the 4th *Panzerarmee* as it moved northwards. Thus some of the finest divisions of the Reich lay shoulder to shoulder within a 30-mile front.

This southern arm alone had 1,500 tanks and self-propelled guns (including 94 Tigers and 200 Panthers) and 2,500 guns and mortars. Model had approximately 900 tanks. In all, the Germans had 70 divisions, totalling almost one million men, and 1,800 aircraft, under command of the 4th and 6th Air Fleets, for the battle of Kursk. Aerial photographs were available of the whole salient. Troops were carefully briefed and rested. The Germans, however, did not have precise knowledge of the weather or the location and strength of the Russian reserves.

Model was to use the traditional method of using the infantry to achieve penetration for the armour – but to Manstein, this seemed too costly and time-consuming, because of the extent of the front in the south and also because of the depth of the Soviet defences. Tactically, therefore, Manstein decided the rapid breakthrough should be made by armoured formations.

The battle commenced at 1500 hours on 4 July, a hot, sultry afternoon with thunder threatening. The 4th *Panzerarmee* manoeuvred to gain possession of the hills in front of the German lines. Probes by Ott's LII Corps and Knobelsdorff's XLVIII Panzer Corps directly south of Oboyan pushed home attacks despite resistance by Chistyakov's 6th Guards Army.

The Russians, however, were waiting with their reserves behind the 6th Guards Army, having realised the German initial thrust would be made at this point. At 2230 hours Soviet artillery opened up heavy firing all over the area. Rain fell during the night, too, and the roads and tracks turned into mud sloughs, which delayed the German tanks.

At 0500 hours on 5 July the German attack was resumed by XLVIII and II SS Panzer Corps. XLVIII Corps broke through the first line of the Soviet defences with little trouble. The Germans had to watch out for mines, however, and the Russian artillery kept up a constant barrage – Luftwaffe attacks on enemy gun emplacements not having much effect.

By nightfall on 5 July, Hausser's SS divisions had also breached the Soviet lines, but nowhere were the penetrations deeper than six or seven miles. Where their lines were breached, the Russians simply moved men and equipment back to behind the second line of defence.

Manstein's instructions said he should achieve the link-up with the 9th Army at Kursk by direct penetration via Oboyan. General Hoth and he agreed, however, that the Russians would expect this and so they decided to meet the expected counter-attack at Prokhorovka before continuing north to Kursk. This was a good decision and, to a certain extent, upset the Russian defensive plans.

German tactics involved thrusts by a succession of armoured wedges (*Panzerkeil*) with Tiger tanks at the tip of the wedges and Panthers and Pzkw IVs fanning out behind. Light infantry followed the tanks and the heavier forces with mortars followed at the rear in personnel carriers.

Russian fire control was in the form of *Pakfronts* – groups of up to 10 anti-tank guns under one commander concentrating on one particular target at a time. The Germans underestimated the number of *Pakfronts* and found the Russian guns difficult to knock out, as they were protected by machine gun and mortar nests. Manstein found that his guns were unable to saturate the Russian defences, nor were they able to clear a safe route through the minefields. German tank crews were instructed not to stop to help disabled tanks, which the Russians picked off without difficulty. By the evening of 5 July, the nature of the Soviet defences was alarmingly obvious and the German tactics were in disarray.

■ Worn out

On 6 July, 4th *Panzerarmee*'s attack in the general direction of Oboyan continued. Katukov's 1st Tank Army was now behind the Soviet 6th Guards Army in the second defence zone, dug in amongst the latter's rifle divisions to thicken up the artillery and anti-tank fire. Hausser's II SS Panzer Corps had now advanced about 20 miles into Chistyakov's front. Hausser continued this drive with great dash, and on 7 July, the situation looked a little alarming for the Russians on the Voronezh Front. More artillery was therefore transferred to it, and Rotmistrov's 5th Guards Tank Army and Zhadov's 5th Guards Army from the Steppe Front also moved in to the Voronezh Front. *Gruppe* 'Kempf' was able to harass the reinforcements.

By 8 July, the ground had dried out considerably and the German armour continued to make good, though slow, progress, with individual divisions making their own dents in the Russian line.

By 9 July, Hoth's forces had been in continuous action for five days, and their ammunition and supplies were running out. A rectangular salient, approximately nine miles deep by 15 miles across, had been driven into Vatutin's front. This was not much after nearly a week of armoured warfare. By 11 July, after establishing a bridgehead on the River Psel and getting close to Oboyan, the 4th *Panzerarmee* had advanced 18 to 20 miles through the Soviet lines.

Meanwhile, in the north, Model had fared much worse. The 9th Army had made some progress on 5 July, but by 6 July the Russians had moved up more tanks and the Germans found it impossible to make any headway against the Soviet artillery. On 7 July, Model switched his attack from the Orel-Kursk road to the area of Ponyri village, further east. Here, for three days, the Germans pounded away without result. By 10 July, Model was on the defensive. Obviously, he was not going to formulate the northern pincer movement on Kursk. In this short time, he had suffered tremendous losses – 50,000 men, 400 tanks and guns and 500 aircraft. To add to his troubles, the Russians were preparing to counterattack around Orel on 12 July.

Back in the south, on the night of 11/12 July, the Russian reserve armour was moved forward towards Prokhorovka to check the German easterly drive. Consequently, the two armoured forces clashed on the afternoon of 12 July, during intense, stifling heat and under an enormous cloud which greatly hindered air operations. This was the greatest tank battle of World War II.

The opponents were roughly equal in numbers – but the Russians were fresh, their machines unworn and with the full complement of ammunition. They had the new SU-85, a self-propelled 85-mm gun mounted on a T-34 chassis as an answer to the Panthers and Tigers.

In contrast, the Germans had just come from fierce fighting with patched up tanks. The new armour – the Panther, the Tiger and the Ferdinand (or *Elefant*) assault gun – all proved disappointing to the Germans at Kursk. The Tiger and Ferdinand had no machine gun and were therefore unable to provide their own short-range defensive fire. There was a shortage of ammunition for both Panther tanks and Ferdinand main-calibre guns. Also, the tactical employment of the large new tanks was at fault. The Germans failed to exploit their long-range guns and stationed the tanks in the foreground of the battle. At close range a T-34 could hole a Tiger as effectively as a Tiger could destroy a T-34.

On 10 July, the Allies landed in Sicily. This introduced a new element into the *Fuehrer*'s thinking. On 13 July, Manstein and Kluge were summoned to East Prussia to hear Hitler's decision to break off Operation '*Zitadelle*' immediately and to redirect a large number of troops to Western Europe to contain the Allies.

Manstein, however, believing that the Red Army's armoured reserves were quickly running out, thought it essential that the offensive be continued and the Russians be defeated. Manstein still believed victory was possible, and he proposed to Hitler that Model should retain sufficient troops in the north to tie the Russians down, and that the offensive should continue in the south. In effect, this would complete half the '*Zitadelle*' plan. Hitler agreed that Hoth and Kempf could continue, but he would not sanction Model retaining a large force. Despite heavy rain, further successes were gained in the south by Manstein's group, resulting in the Soviet 69th Army and two tank corps being trapped between Rzhavets, Belenikhino and Gotishchevo. Hitler then decided to call a complete halt to '*Zitadelle*'; II SS Panzer Corps was transferred to Italy and two Panzer divisions were dispatched to Army Group 'Centre' in view of the worsening situation at Orel. Manstein could not now hold his position and a general withdrawal began at the beginning of August. He had had tactical success and since D-day had taken 24,000 prisoners and destroyed or captured 1,000 tanks and over 100 anti-tank guns.

Manstein's insistence on continuing with the offensive may well have been right, for the Voronezh Front was certainly not very secure, and the whole of the Steppe Front was committed to its support.

With '*Zitadelle*' the Germans lost the initiative in the East and were never to regain it. They had used up all their armoured reserves. With the German retreat, the threatening Russian defeat turned to victory as they vigorously pursued the retreating Germans.

FIELD-MARSHAL WALTHER MODEL

On 22 June 1944 Stalin launched an all-out offensive against Army Group 'Centre'. The commander of 'Centre', Field-Marshal Busch, had four armies holding a salient which stretched from Vitebsk to Mozyr; the 3rd *Panzerarmee* under Colonel-General Reinhardt; the 4th Army under General von Tippelskirch; the 9th Army under General Jordan; and the 2nd Army led by Colonel-General Weiss. However, there were only 38 front-line divisions and the majority of these were understrength. There were three Panzer and two infantry divisions in reserve, and three Hungarian and five special service divisions at the rear.

By contrast, the Russians had amassed 14 armies, amounting to nearly 200 divisions, which gave them a numerical superiority of six to one. They also had the advantage in weaponry in a ratio of 10 to one, and overwhelming air superiority. The Germans could not hope to hold an attack of this magnitude.

The 1st Baltic and 3rd Belorussian Fronts opened the offensive with a pincer attack either side of Vitebsk, taking 3rd *Panzerarmee* completely by surprise. The Russians stormed through, and with the help of the 6th Guards Army closed in on the town. On 23 June, the 2nd and 3rd Belorussian Fronts moved toward Orsha and Mogilev, almost breaking the 4th Army. On the following day, the 1st Belorussian Front smashed into the 9th Army and penetrated its northern and southern boundaries. Busch tried to uphold Hitler's policy of inflexible defence and fortress-holding. But it was the wrong strategy. By the fifth day of fighting, Army Group 'Centre' had used up its reserve forces without stopping the Soviet advance. The fortresses of Vitebsk, Orsha, Mogilev and Bobruysk were soon encircled by pincer movements while the mass of Russian armour swept on westward towards Minsk. Hitler's 'fortified locality' policy had failed. Field-Marshal Busch received all the blame.

On 28 June, Hitler and OKH finally admitted that the Belorussian offensive was more serious than they had previously thought. But they still felt that an attack against Army Group 'North Ukraine' was imminent. So Hitler sacked the loyal Busch and appointed Field-Marshal Model to the command of Army Group 'Centre', whilst at the same time retaining him as commander of 'North Ukraine'. It was hoped that this dual command would facilitate troop movement between the two groups. Model was probably the best tactician apart from Rundstedt in active service at the time, and he was still in favour with Hitler after his successful improvisations at Orel, Rzhev and Leningrad. But the task of limiting the disaster facing Army Group 'Centre' was surely one of his greatest tests.

Army Group 'North', despite being in a desperate position itself, was ordered by Hitler to hand over three divisions to Model. But the new commander-in-chief was unwilling simply to wait for these reinforcements and himself order the transfer of ten divisions, including four Panzer divisions, from Army Group 'North Ukraine' to 'Centre'. On assuming command, Model changed the rigid policies of Busch in favour of a more elastic system of defence. His only hope was to plug the most dangerous holes in his lines, try to re-establish contact with the 4th and 9th Armies and generally stiffen the overstretched front.

But for all this new-found aggression and flexibility, the Russians advanced relentlessly. Perhaps Model's appointment had been made too late. Whatever the case, his actions were all in vain. He could not hold the Polotsk-Berezina-Slutsk line and by 2 July he admitted that he had lost the bulk of the 4th and 9th Armies, trapped by Russian pincers between Minsk and the Berezina. It was estimated that 100,000 men had been cut off.

Part of the 9th Army managed to escape to the west, but most of the 4th Army was truly trapped in a pocket between the Berezina and the Volma rivers. The latter pocket was split into two groups, one under Lieutenant-General Traut and the other under Lieutenant-General Mueller. Marshall Zhukov ordered a colossal bombardment of the 4th Army with rockets, shells and bombs. German resistance was short-lived, and Mueller surrendered to the 2nd Belorussian front. The 57,000 prisoners were paraded through the streets of Moscow on 17 July. Minsk itself, the Belorussian capital, fell on 3 July to Chernyakhovsky's and Rokossovsky's troops. In 12 days, Army Group 'Centre' had lost the most part of 25 divisions.

■ Defeat at Minsk

In order to salvage what he could, Model proposed to halt the enemy along a new front some way behind Minsk, west of the Molodechno-Baranovichi line. This could only be done with new formations plus those Model had obtained from Army Groups 'North' and 'North Ukraine'. He urged OKH to send more reserves from Army Group 'North' to defend Molodechno. These were not forthcoming as Army Group 'North' was also in a desperate situation. Its right flank was held at Polotsk, another of Hitler's fortified areas. Between it and the left flank of the 3rd *Panzerarmee* northeast of Minsk there was a gap of 50 miles. A similar gap opened between the *Panzerarmee*'s right flank and Molodechno. The *Panzerarmee* could be pincered at any time the Russians wanted, and the road to Riga would be opened. But Hitler insisted that Army Group 'North' continue to hold Polotsk, despite Model calling it a 'futile experiment' and urging the *Fuehrer* to withdraw Army Group 'North' to Riga itself. As a result of this policy – and despite the dangers facing the 3rd *Panzerarmee* – no forces could be released to Model to form a new front.

Defeat at Minsk meant that only the flanks of Army Group 'Centre' remained. (According to Guderian the defeat signified the end of Army Group 'Centre'.) A 200-mile break in the German line opened up the Soviets' way to the Baltic states and East Prussia.

Stavka was determined to exploit this opportunity, and so the Russian tank formations moved rapidly westwards from Minsk on a broad front and harried the sparse German forces before the defence could be organised properly.

The Russian strategy was for the 1st Baltic Front under Bagramyan to advance through Dvinsk and on to Lithuania and Latvia after crossing the Dvina river. Chernyakhovsky's 3rd Belorussian Front was to develop a two-pronged attack, one from Molodechno through Vilnyus to Kaunas in Lithuania, and the second to the border of East Prussia via the River Niemen. The 1st Belorussian Front under Rokossovsky was to push through Baranovichi to the River Bug, north-east of Warsaw. Here he was to meet the 2nd Belorussian Front, which was to arrive by way of Bialystok and Grodno.

■ Hopeless situation

Those divisions that Model had managed to scrape together, for example the 14th and 95th Infantry Divisions, were unable to alter the depressing situation. Russian troops were east of Molodechno by 6 July and the way was open to Vilynus. Under the tireless command of Marshal Zhukov, General Batov's 65th Army reached the rail junction of Baranovichi the following day, and despite resistance by the German 2nd Army, the town was liberated. On the 8th, the town of Lida also fell. The German front joining Baranovichi and Molodechno had vanished.

Model faced a hopeless situation. The Russians for the next 20 days covered 10-15 miles per day, often side-stepping the depleted units which Model threw in to plug his broken lines. Model's task was now to try to harass the enemy in order that the necessary time might become available for OKH to form a new and continuous line strong enough to turn back the Russian offensive. One significant success he did achieve at this stage was to persuade Hitler to order the evacuation of a whole series of fortified areas which otherwise would have become death-traps to the encapsulated German defenders.

By 8 July, Model reported that the line Vilnyus-Lida-Baranovichi had also been broken. All three towns were taken. Without reinforcements, he could not stop the Russians anywhere, and had no choice but to sacrifice considerable areas of territory.

The implications of the Soviet successes were not confined to the central area. The German retreat enabled the Russian high command to extend operations to the north and south flanks, against the German Army Groups 'North', and 'North Ukraine' and 'South Ukraine' respectively. On 9 July, Model accompanied the new commander of Army Group 'North', General Friessner, for an interview with Hitler. They tried to persuade him to withdraw from Estonia and so provide badly needed reinforcements. Hitler refused this suggestion although he did promise to give Model two divisions from Army Group 'North'. For the next few days, the position of Army Group 'Centre' continued to deteriorate as the front drifted west to Kaunas, the Niemen and Bialystok. The divisions which Model expected from Army Group 'North' did not arrive, as Friessner was himself threatened with imminent encirclement should the Red Army break through the gap between Army Group 'Centre' and Army Group 'North', to the Gulf of Riga.

Model's Army Group 'North Ukraine' also retreated westward in the face of Russian pressure. On 14 July, Rokossovsky enveloped Pinsk and then moved on to Kovel and over the River Bug. He took the Polish town of Lublin on 24 July. Part of this force turned toward Brest Litovsk while the remainder pushed on to the Vistula, which they reached on 2 August. On 27 July, the Russians took Lvov, but the Germans retreated safely to the Carpathians and the Vistula. The situation facing Army Group 'Centre', and to a lesser extent, Army Group 'North Ukraine', began to improve as the tempo of the Russian attack slowed down. Having advanced so far so quickly, the Russians were outreaching their supplies. Their artillery and supply depots were far from the new front lines and the advance guard lacked petrol and munitions. At the same time, Model had managed to obtain reinforcements including 10 new Panzer divisions to bolster the 'North Ukraine' front. He also received another six battle-proven armoured divisions, including the 'Hermann Goering' Division. Model's forces were gaining strength and the possibility soon arose of initiating small-scale counterattacks.

■ Short-term safety

By 3 August, Model was able to send Hitler a relatively good situation report. He confirmed that a continuous front had been established from Siauliai in the north to the Vistula at Pulawy in the south. The 420-mile stretch was covered by only about 40 German divisions, but nevertheless it seemed that it could be held for the time being and some room for light offensive manoeuvring made available, particularly the relief of Army Group 'North'. Model had fulfilled the job of repairing the situation in the East even if the repairs were only temporary. On 16 August, he was appointed to the command of the Western theatre.

Model was one of a new breed of German general, blindly loyal to Hitler, seldom disputing his orders and appearing to have the happy knack of minimising the catastrophic effects of the *Fuehrer*'s policies. He did not possess the strategic genius of Manstein, but had well-earned his reputation as being a highly competent tactician in defensive situations prior to his appointment to Army Group 'Centre'. Mellenthin considered that he was too prone to interfere in matters of detail, and tell his corps and army commanders exactly where they should deploy their troops. Even so, in the face of the Russian offensive he clearly adopted the correct tactics and his eye for detail, his efficiency and hard work surely contributed to his military efficacy.

He had little option but to withdraw and one of his successes was to convince Hitler of the futility of defending fortified areas as the Russians would simply bypass them. One of his strengths was his ability to stand up to Hitler. During the withdrawal of Army Group 'Centre' his deployment of those forces and reserves at his disposal was of sufficient quality not to tarnish his reputation as the master of flexible defence. He created and stabilised a new Eastern Front and was then whisked away to deal with the crisis in the West.

COLONEL-GENERAL GEORG-HANS REINHARDT

A t the end of 1944, the Russians were planning the winter offensive in which they intended to drive on from Warsaw, which they had reached but not taken in August of that year, to the River Oder, only some 40 miles from Berlin. Whilst Marshal of the Soviet Union G. K. Zhukov's 1st Belorussian Front drove straight on in the centre, and Marshal of the Soviet Union I. S. Konev's 1st Ukrainian Front pushed on from the upper reaches of the River Vistula into the German industrial region of Upper Silesia, Marshal of the Soviet Union K. K. Rokossovsky's 2nd Belorussian Front was to take Warsaw and then drive up to the Baltic Sea, splitting Germany in two. East Prussia was then to be crushed by the combined forces of the 2nd and 3rd Belorussian Fronts, the latter commanded by General I. D. Chernyakovsky, with help from General I. Kh. Bagramyan's 1st Baltic Front along the river Niemen.

The German defence of East Prussia was entrusted to Army Group 'Centre', commanded by Colonel-General Georg-Hans Reinhardt. The army group consisted of three armies: the 2nd Army (Colonel-General W. Weiss) in the sector north of Warsaw; the 4th Army (General F. Hossbach) in the centre east of the Masurian Lakes; and the 3rd *Panzerarmee* (Colonel-General E. Raus) in the northern sector. As usual with German formations of the time, the armies had a fair number of divisions, but these were all at low strength, and the fuel, ammunition and *matériel* available to them was very limited. Reinhardt also had the uncertain help of some 200,000 police and *Volkssturm* units. In the event, the latter were to fight with great stubbornness until demoralised by the desertion of various non-German units serving in the area. Reinhardt had realised early in 1945 that the area with whose defence he was entrusted was far too great for the weak forces under his command, and begged Hitler to allow the evacuation of Army Group 'North' from its bridgehead in Kurland, these forces to be added to those of Army Group 'Centre' for the defence of East Prussia. At the same time Reinhardt noted that the mobility enjoyed by the Russians, combined with the geographical situation of East Prussia (defended in the centre by the Masurian lakes) meant that the Russians would almost certainly launch a huge pincer attack aimed from the south at Elbing, and from the east at Koenigsberg. Such an attack would leave the 4th Army out in a salient in front of the Masurian lakes, where it could not contribute to the defence battle and where it could be mopped up at leisure by the Russians. Reinhardt therefore urged Hitler to allow him to pull the 4th Army back into East Prussia itself. Hitler refused both the request to evacuate Kurland and the plan to pull back the 4th Army.

■ Growing forces

As noted above, the Russian forces by this stage of the war had a considerable quantity of motor transport, and could therefore employ their forces to take full advantage of their mobility. The Soviet armour and artillery was also well up to strength, and had sufficient ammunition to fight a large-scale offensive. Rokossovsky's one real worry was his lack of infantry. This arm, as was often the case with the Russians in World War II, had been used with little imagination or thought for casualties, and had suffered very heavy losses against stubborn German defence. However, the 2nd Belorussian Front received some 125,000 reinforcements in infantry at this time. These were Russians returning from hospital or combed out of the rear echelons, together with some 10,000 recaptured prisoners-of-war and 53,000 Polish, Ukrainian and Balt men forcibly conscripted into the Red Army.

The Russian plan was a large-scale one: while the 47th Army captured Warsaw (which it did on 17 January), the 70th and 65th Armies, with an attached tank corps, were to drive towards Pomerania via Torun, and the bulk of the 2nd Belorussian Front (2nd Shock, 48th, 3rd, 49th and 5th Guards Tank Armies) were to press on towards Elbing via Mlawa, Deutsch Eylau and Osterode. In the east, Chernyakovsky's 3rd Belorussian Front (using principally the 39th, 5th, 28th and 2nd Guards Armies, together with two attached tank corps) was to attack along the line of the River Pregolya towards Koenigsberg. With the help of the 43rd Army from the 1st Baltic Front, this second thrust was intended to destroy the German forces along the River Niemen.

The southern arm of the pincer moved in to the attack on 14 January in appalling weather. In fact the snow was to thick that the Russians advanced on an unsuspecting enemy, and did not need the planned artillery barrage. Once the initial shock had been overcome, however, the Germans began to fight back in their usual determined way, causing the Russians very heavy losses, and slowing down the pace of Rokossovsky's advance very considerably. With the commital to the battle on 15 January of the army group reserves, the 7th Panzer and *'Grossdeutschland'*

261

Panzergrenadier Divisions, the Russian advance was slowed to a snail's pace. Reinhardt might indeed have completely halted the Russians had not Hitler seen fit to remove the '*Grossdeutschland*' Panzer Corps for service with Army Group 'A' in an effort to stem the advance of Zhukov's 1st Belorussian Front past Lodz. But as Hitler removed Reinhardt's last hope, the Russian commander committed another two tank corps, and this enabled the Russians to start moving forward again. The bad weather also lifted at this juncture, allowing Colonel-General K. A. Vershinin's 4th Air Army to fly some 2,500 missions in support of the ground forces. By the 19th the Russians had broken through on a wide front, and had crossed the East Prussian frontier. The German 2nd Army was retreating in considerable disarray, and was close to breaking point. Rokossovsky continued to press on, his forces reaching the outskirts of Elbing on 23 January, and the Baltic Sea north of this town on the 26th. East Prussia was now cut off from the rest of the Third Reich. Further to the south, the left wing of Rokossovsky's pincer had also made good progress along the north bank of the River Vistula, capturing Torun and pressing on towards Grudziadz.

To the north-east, Chernyakovsky's forces had attacked on 13 January, the day before Rokossovsky's front. The Russians used a variety of deceptive measures to fool the Germans as to the true nature of their intentions, but progress was slow, the Germans fighting with great courage and determination. Tilsit was not taken until the fifth day after the start of the offensive. Unlike the 2nd Army to the south, the 3rd *Panzerarmee* fell back in good order. Reinhardt had pressed for the 4th Army to be allowed to pull back right from the moment the Russian offensive broke, but Hitler refused to sanction the move until the 21st, when Hossbach was ordered to pull back his army to Loetzen on the Masurian lakes and form a defence line facing westwards, to cover the gap left by the destruction and disintegration of the 2nd Army. The position of Army Group 'Centre' was by now so desperate, however, that even the 4th Army's new positions would be untenable, and Reinhardt pressed for the evacuation of the military and civilian population of East Prussia. Had this been started early enough, Reinhardt thought, most of the Germans in East Prussia might have escaped to the west before Rokossovsky's troops cut off the province. Hossbach also thought this the only possible course, and pulled back behind the Masurian lakes to prepare to fight his way out towards northern Pomerania. Hitler, who had expressly forbidden any attempts at an exodus, grew suspicious, and on 26 January dismissed Reinhardt and Hossbach, replacing them with Colonel-General L. Rendulic (late commander of Army Group 'North' in Kurland) and General F. W. Mueller respectively. Rendulic's place in Kurland was taken by W. Weiss, lately C-in-C 2nd Army. Hitler ordered that Koenigsberg and as much of East Prussia's north coast as possible be held at any costs; this task Rendulic achieved under Germany's capitulation in May. In the meantime, some 500,000 Germans were evacuated from the various beach-heads by the *Kriegsmarine* in a quite remarkably able rescue operation.

The task that Hitler had entrusted to Reinhardt had been an impossible one made even more difficult by Hitler's complete intransigence about sensible defence measures. Yet Reinhardt fought an able defensive battle, and had it not been for the disintegration of the 2nd Army, he might have inflicted even more grievous losses on Rokossovsky's forces than he did. In the north the 3rd *Panzerarmee* had handled the 3rd Belorussian Front very hard whilst retaining its cohesion.

GENERAL OTTO WOEHLER

By the end of February 1945, the Russian armies were poised in two major groupings for the final destruction of the Third Reich. In Germany herself, along the line formed by the Rivers Oder and Neisse, were the 2nd Belorussian Front, 1st Belorussian Front and 1st Ukrainian Front, whilst further south, in Czechoslovakia and Hungary, were the 4th, 2nd and 1st Ukrainian Fronts. These last three fronts had advanced from the Carpathian mountains–River Dniestr line on 20 August 1944, and having swept south and then north-west through Rumania, destroying Army Group 'South Ukraine' *en route*, reached a line half-way through Hungary by 31 January 1945. Here the Russian forces had halted to rest and redeploy before pushing on into the rest of Hungary, Austria and Czechoslovakia.

Guderian, now OKH chief-of-staff, warned Hitler that the Russians' main thrust, once they resumed their offensive, must come in the northern sector, aimed at Berlin itself. Therefore all the available resources and reserves should be deployed to counter this threat. Hitler, however, with his constant preoccupation with oil, saw a chance for a major counterstroke in Hungary. Army Group 'South', commanded by General Otto Woehler, was to strike through the gap between Lakes Balaton and Velencei with the aim of cutting off the part of the 3rd Ukrainian Front between the Rivers Danube and Drava, destroying it, and then swinging north to retake Budapest, cross the River Danube and recapture eastern Hungary.

Further to the south, pinning attacks on the cut-off portion of Marshal of the Soviet Union F. I. Tolbukhin's 3rd Ukrainian Front were to be made by General M. De Angelis' 2nd *Panzerarmee* of Army Group 'South' and a corps of three divisions from Colonel-General A. Loehr's Army Group 'E' in Yugoslavia. The success of the whole operation, Hitler was convinced, would safeguard the vital oil supplies

Germany was getting from Hungary and Austria. These by now made up some 80 percent of Germany's oil.

The major element of the offensive, code-named '*Fruehlingserwachen*' or 'Spring awakening', was to be the drive to the Danube from the Lake Balaton–Lake Velencei gap. This was to be the task of a formidable strike force, formed against the strongest protestations from Guderian, who felt that these forces should be deployed against the Russian threat against Berlin. Some 10 Panzer and five infantry divisions from the 6th SS *Panzerarmee* (*Oberstgruppenfuehrer* Sepp Dietrich), 6th Army (General H. Balck) and the Hungarian VIII Corps were to drive to the River Danube between Dunapentele in the north and Baja in the south.

Although the German force, totalling 10 Panzer and 12 infantry divisions, appeared strong on paper, its real strength in men and tanks was low. Dietrich's force, in particular, had been severely handled in the 'Battle of the Bulge'. The Russian forces, however, were truly formidable. Tolbukhin's 3rd Ukrainian Front consisted of five armies, with one cavalry, one mechanised and two tank corps, together with 37 Russian and six Bulgarian rifle divisions. In all, Tolbukhin had at his disposal more than 400,000 men, 400 tanks and self-propelled guns, and 1,000 aircraft. The Yugoslav 3rd Army was also co-operating on the Russian's left flank.

■ Attack essential

Hitler was so insistent on the offensive that considerations of terrain and weather were not allowed to intervene. The area over which the 6th Army and 6th SS *Panzerarmee* were to advance was low-lying, swampy and criss-crossed by a multitude of canals and small watercourses. These made progress for the infantry difficult, and for the armoured forces all but impossible. These conditions also made life difficult for the Russians. Although they greatly helped in front-line defence, they made the problem of supply and communications very difficult. The Russians' problems were exacerbated by the fact that ice flows were still coming down the Danube, threatening to sweep away the pontoon bridges so vital for Russian supplies. The construction of an overhead wire track across the Danube was of great use, as was the pipeline for fuel, the first used by the Russians. Finally the weather, with extremely heavy rain and low temperatures, further reduced the Germans' chances of success.

The German build-up had not gone unnoticed by the Russians. As the latter were planning a major offensive, Tolbukhin decided not to deploy his forces so as to be able to launch a counterattack, but instead to deploy in depth, allow the Germans to advance, hold them and then launch his own offensive once all his preparations were complete. Confirmation of the German intentions was supplied by deserting Hungarians.

The German offensive opened on 5 March, when Angelis' four divisions advanced against Lieutenant-General M. N. Sharokhin's 57th Army, and Loehr's three divisions against the Bulgarian 1st and Yugoslav 3rd Armies. By the 15th of the month, none of these thrusts had advanced more than 10 miles. Loehr's and Angelis' drives were subsidiary, and the main German offensive started on 6 March.

After a 30-minute artillery bombardment, the main German forces pushed forward, the 6th Army on the left against Lieutenant-General N. D. Zakhvataev's 4th Guards Army, and the 6th SS *Panzerarmee* on the right against Lieutenant-General N. A. Gagen's 26th Army. The one factor that might have given the Germans a greater chance of success, tactical air support, was limited by the small number of aircraft available and the appalling weather. Nevertheless the Germans drove forward slowly, making nearly five miles in the first two days and just over 15 by the end of the fourth day. But the German advance was gradually slowed and stopped as Tolbukhin sent in his artillery reserves (Colonel-General N. I. Nedelin) and the 27th Army (Colonel-General S. G. Trofimenko) to plug the gap between the 4th Guards and 26th Armies. Tolbukhin was refused further reinforcements, and when Woehler committed his one reserve Panzer division, the 6th, with some 200 tanks and self-propelled guns, on the 14th, the Russian situation began to look serious. But losses on both sides had been extremely heavy, and the Germans were running out of fuel and momentum. On the 15th they were forced to a halt.

Now it was the turn of the Russians, who planned a general counter-offensive by the 2nd Ukrainian Front (Marshal of the Soviet Union R. Ya. Malinovsky) as well as the 3rd Ukrainian Front. But instead of the drive on Vienna originally envisaged, Marshal of the Soviet Union S. K. Timoshenko, who was co-ordinating the offensive for the *Stavka*, decided that the 9th Guards Army (Colonel-General V. V. Glagolev) and 6th Guards Tank Army (Colonel-General A. G. Kravchenko) should be allocated to Tolbukhin to cut off and destroy the 6th Army and 6th SS Panzerarmee. The Russian counter-offensive was launched on 16 March, from positions north-west of Lake Velencei. At first all went the Russians' way, Hitler refusing to sanction the abandonment of *Fruehlingserwachen* in favour of a flank attack on the Russian advance until it was too late. By the time the *Fuehrer* consented on the 19th, the German escape corridor to the north-west was narrowing hourly. In some of the bitterest fighting of the war, most of the men of 6th SS *Panzerarmee* managed to escape. Many retreated without orders, and most of the 6th Army and all the two armies' heavy equipment was lost. Hitler was infuriated, and ordered that all SS units in the rout be stripped of their armbands. As no defensive preparations behind Lake Balaton had been set in hand, the Germans were unable to make another stand, and fell back in complete disorder. The Battle of Lake Balaton can be said to have ended on 25 March with the fall to the Russians of Papa. Woehler was dismissed from his command, being replaced by Colonel-General L. Rendulic. Meanwhile, the Russian offensive had been extended in the north and south, and by 4 April most of Hungary had been cleared, and the Russians were advancing into Austria.

What of Woehler's performance? It has to be admitted that he had been presented with an impossible task right from the outset, and that his mission had been made even harder by his lack of resources and the nature of the terrain and weather. Nevertheless, he had fought his offensive battle with considerable skill. Only when the Russians themselves went over to the offensive did his lack of forethought reveal itself in the lack of defensive positions in his rear.

FIELD-MARSHAL FERDINAND SCHOERNER

B y the end of 1944 it was obvious to almost everyone that Germany would lose the war before the Western Allies and Russia would cease to be on friendly terms. However, Hitler and a small element of his entourage still hoped that they might cause a split between the two Allied groups, or by such firm resistance produce a casualty rate which was unacceptable to an attacker and so force him to negotiate with Germany.

But by the end of 1944 Germany had lost 106 divisions in the East, destroyed or disbanded, in a mere 12 months. She was cut off from her supplies of oil in Rumania, her armaments industry and communications were crippled and she had few generals whom Hitler regarded as sufficiently loyal by his deranged standards. As one general failed to hold back the Russians he would be replaced by another who would receive fantastic promises of new troops and arms and who under pressure from Hitler would give equally fantastic promises – although neither could keep their word. By adjusting the age of entry and period of service Hitler had been able to rebuild his armies with 16-year-old boys and men in their late middle age. Now he looked for generals with fanatical wills to match his own.

One such general, Ferdinand Schoerner, seemed an unlikely man to fulfil this rôle. A heavily-built, bespectacled man, he had served with distinction in World War I and was a specialist in mountain warfare. Devoted to Hitler, he had proved a tough defensive fighter in the East and had risen rapidly, so that by the end of the war he held the rank of Field-Marshal.

Hitler, as always obsessed with oil, considered that it was vital to hold the oil shale areas of Hungary and the Vienna basin. Thus a major portion of the German army was deployed south-east of Berlin, covering Prague and the approaches to Austria. In the recently renamed Army Group 'Centre' which covered Czechoslovakia with its armament industries, some 20 infantry divisions, eight Panzer and *Panzergrenadier* divisions were faced by the 1st, 4th and 2nd Fronts. If the German units had been up to their paper strength, they could have made a coherent and effective defence, but now it was a game of fitting an impressive name to a nondescript unit – so that a party of middle-aged men on bicycles with *Panzerfaust* hollow-charge projectiles slung from the handle bars became a tank-destroyer unit.

■ No real army

On 16 January it was time for a change and Colonel-General Schoerner was ordered to leave his command in Army Group 'North' and take over Army Group 'A' or 'Centre' as it was renamed on the 26th. The promised reinforcements he received from the Replacement Army now under the command of *Reichsfuehrer* Himmler were a few poorly trained and equipped *Volksgrenadier* divisions, the staff and students from military schools and some policemen. With such men he was to cover Saxony, Sudetenland and the whole of Czechoslovakia. In fact for three days the army was without a commander, for it was difficult for Schoerner to quit his previous command in Army Group 'North'.

When he arrived he found that there seemed little for him to command: the staff of the 4th *Panzerarmee* had disappeared, for as far as anyone knew, it was fighting its own war somewhere beyond their front. The 17th Army and the 1st *Panzerarmee* were retreating from Konev's 1st Ukrainian Front in the area of the upper Vistula east of Krakow and in Czechoslovakia. Despite this pressure they had maintained their cohesion. Schoerner therefore sent the dubious reinforcements he had received to bolster the 4th *Panzerarmee*. During the withdrawal he lost the 1st Hungarian Army – it disbanded itself.

The army group stopped on a 300-mile front covering the Oder, and leaving his excellent subordinates, General Schulz of the 17th Army, General Heinrici of the 1st *Panzerarmee* and General Graeser of the 4th *Panzerarmee* to watch their fronts, Schoerner looked to the rear areas. He was a believer in the 'Will to Win' and 'The Fight to the Last Breath' and was well-known as a National-Socialist officer.

Adopting a motto of 'Strength through Fear' he succeeded in making many officers think that the punishment for retreat was more dreadful than the prospect of death in battle facing the Russians. He could still count on the faith of the soldiers and younger officers whom he wooed, portraying the *Fuehrer* as a common man much like themselves.

On 23 January the 1st Ukrainian Front reached the Oder and crossed it at two points near Brieg and in the area of Steinau. With no reserves available, Schoerner ordered the exhausted and understrength XXIV Panzer Corps and the Panzer Corps '*Grossdeutschland*' to destroy the bridgeheads. They tried and failed.

On 8 February Konev broke out from the Steinau bridgehead and punched a gap

40 miles deep and 95 miles wide, getting close to the Neisse and encircling 18,000 troops in the German fortress of Glogau. A week later the 5th Guards drove northwest from the Brieg bridgehead and in conjunction with the 6th Army moving from the Steinau bridgehead surrounded Breslau.

The defence of Breslau stands out as an epic in the defeat and disorder of the last days of the Reich. Two regular army infantry divisions were ordered to break out of the city when it was surrounded and so its garrison was merely the 609th Infantry Division – which had itself only been raised in Dresden a few weeks earlier from stragglers, *Volkssturm* soldiers and SS men. It had no tanks, but did possess 32 batteries of guns, captured in earlier campaigns in Russia, Poland, Yugoslavia and Italy. Under the professional leadership of General Hermann von Ahlfen und Niehoff and the political exhortations of Doctor Goebbels and *Gauleiter* Hanke, the city was still fighting when Berlin surrendered.

Schoerner ordered the 4th *Panzerarmee* to counterattack to clear the Berlin-Silesia railway and relieve the Glogau garrison. It failed to reach Glogau and the city capitulated on 18 March. After warding off this counterattack Konev paused, and then with ponderous strength moved again. On 15 March he attacked on both sides of the town of Oppeln, intending to clear Upper Silesia up to the Czechoslovakia border. By the end of the month he had fulfilled his intention.

On 6 April Schoerner received reinforcements. Three *Panzergrenadier* divisions were switched from Army Group 'Vistula', despite the protests of General Heinrici. The *Fuehrer* had an intuition that the Soviet offensive would not be directed against Berlin, but at Czechoslovakia.

On 15 April Hitler sent out his order of the day. It was to be his last, and reflected the way his brain had deteriorated. He told his men: 'For the last time, the deadly Jewish-Bolshevik enemy had started a mass attack. He is trying to reduce Germany to rubble and to exterminate our people. Soldiers of the East! You are already fully aware now of the fate that threatens German women and children. Whilst men, children and old people will be murdered, women and girls will be reduced to the rôle of barrack-room whores. The rest will be marched off to Siberia.' Now he was speaking the coarse parade ground language of an army corporal.

On 16 April the Russians launched their assault on Berlin and by the 18th, despite determined resistance and counterattacks by the 4th *Panzerarmee*, Konev reached the strongpoints of Cottbus and Spremberg. He was unable to take them, and pouring past Spremberg to the north and south he cut off Schoerner's Army Group 'Centre' from its northern neighbours, Army Group 'Vistula'.

In the midst of this crisis Hitler's 56th birthday dawned on 20 April and Schoerner called at the *Fuehrer* headquarters to congratulate his leader. It was a game of bluff, and Hitler appeared cheerful after the visit. Schoerner had assured him that counterattacks by the 4th *Panzerarmee* were being launched on the Russian breakthrough on the Oder. Hitler pressed that the Oder line be defended, though by now it was, to misquote him, 'merely a geographical concept'.

By the end of April Konev began to withdraw units from the Berlin front and direct them towards the south. On the 26th an excited Hitler telephoned Schoerner and urged his chief-of-staff Natzmer 'to bring the battle for the capital to a victorious end'. He dismissed the protests that there was neither the fuel nor the ammunition to attack over 125 miles: 'that is of no importance. Shortages must be filled, the battle for Berlin must be won.'

■ No surrender

On 7 May OKW contacted Schoerner's headquarters and ordered Army Group 'Centre' to cease fighting at midnight on 9 May. General von Natzmer realised that this meant he would be unable to save his troops from Russian prisoner-of-war camps, for it would be impossible to disengage from the front in the time allowed. Schoerner shouted that he would not obey the order and demanded that his commanding officers submit their opinions by nightfall.

They were rational men, however, and saw that continued resistance would put them beyond the law and make American commanders far less sympathetic to their surrender pleas. Their decision shocked Schoerner, who realised that he was in danger of being captured by the Russians – who had marked his name down on their wanted lists.

Natzmer suggested that the northern wing of the 4th *Panzerarmee* should be ordered to resist so that other units could then set in motion an 'organized flight to the west'. Inevitably men would be captured by the Russians, but the majority, particularly those with vehicles, would be able make their escape.

On 8 May a small convoy set off from Schoerner's headquarters. The Field-Marshal intended to escape westward by light aircraft, and after some near brushes with advancing Russian troops he located the aircraft near Podersham. Here he summoned the local party chief and ordered some civilian clothes. To the consternation of a small crowd that had gathered he appeared in the green jacket and leather shorts of Bavarian traditional costume.

To the disgust of his chief-of-staff, Schoerner made his escape and crash-landed in Austria. As he fled westwards Schoerner did not hear that even in death the *Fuehrer* rewarded his loyal soldiers. In the Doenitz government the Field-Marshal was to head the army. He would be part of an executive which included men like Goebbels, Bormann and Seyss-Inquart. It was another promise that Hitler could never keep. Around 15 May he reported to the staff of the German 1st Army who, though prisoners, were now engaged in the dismissal of low-ranking German troops. The Americans handed him over to the Russians, as they did many of the men of his army group who reached the Allied lines.

ANALYSIS – GENERALSHIP AGAINST RUSSIA

The story of Germany's war in the East is one of missed opportunities and, predictably, of Hitler's interference and indecision. Even before *Barbarossa* was launched there were three plans, and when the operation was under way Hitler changed the priority of Moscow making it as the main objective in the autumn of 1941. When the Germans fell back in the winter counter-offensive before Moscow they made sure that they would not win the war with Russia, and at Stalingrad in the following winter and Kursk in 1943 they made certain their defeat.

Whereas in their attacks in the West the Germans had faced enemies who had been reluctant to incur heavy casualties, the Russians had little compunction about the ruthless use of their manpower. The casualties in prisoners, dead and wounded suffered in the opening months of the war would have crippled any Western nation, but the Russians were prepared to trade not only space for time, but men as well. The shape of western Russia, which tapers from a narrow border to a broad interior, meant that the German and Axis forces were forced to thin their units to cover the whole front as they advanced eastwards. In an attempt to cover the front, satellite armies from Italy, Rumania, Bulgaria and Hungary were moved forward from their rear-area responsibilities. These units became the proverbial weak link in the chain of defences, and were singled out by the Russians for attack. There was, moreover, intense suspicion and ill feeling between Rumanian and Hungarian troops, engendered by prewar land-snatching by Hungary.

Russian tactics, like their men and equipment, were robust and simple, but very effective. They aimed to achieve a massive local superiority before an attack, and when they attacked it was pressed home with a fanaticism second only to that of the Japanese. Surrender was not regarded with the religious horror of the Japanese, but avoided by many men because by Soviet lights it constituted desertion, and action was taken by the authorities against the relatives of those surrendered.

Besides this human enemy, the Germans faced many physical hazards in the East. The severe winter is well known, but the poor roads, broad-gauge railways, river barriers, woods and swamps made communications and logistic support extremely difficult. Most of the highly-bred European horses that the Germans employed for transportation died in the hard winters, and they were forced to use the smaller, but hardier Russian ponies.

However, besides these hazards and their enemy at the front, the Germans were increasingly troubled by partisans in their rear. Their long and ill-guarded communications made an easy target and many small groups of Axis troops were killed even before they reached the front.

The Germans were partly to blame for this because of their genocide policy in the East and because they regarded the Russians as 'Slavic sub-humans' fit only to be serfs. In 1941 many of the inhabitants of the Ukraine had welcomed the Germans as liberators from Stalin's centralised dictatorship, but the Germans tried to harness this good will only when the war had turned against them, and by then it was too late.

Undoubtedly, however, the chief contributor to Germany's loss of the war in the East was the men who originated *Barbarossa*. Hitler, who had saved the army from rout in front of Moscow with his 'Stand and fight, no retreat' order, now saw this as the panacea against all Russian offensives. At Stalingrad he urged the 6th Army to hold on and await relief. It is interesting to note that at the time some Western observers thought that the Russians had committed a blunder and that the Germans would be able to hang on and tie up Soviet forces. After the Stalingrad defeat Hitler was shaken, but this did not last long and he was back to the old formula when the Russians launched their summer counter-offensive after Kursk. It was this desire to hold ground just for the sake of prestige that had produced the earlier massive Russian losses in 1941 and 1942. Now the rôle was reversed and German and Axis troops were being encircled because they could not retreat. Hitler's hatred of the thought of retreat, 'defeatism' in his vocabulary, meant that there could be no reasonable contingency planning and nor could work be done on fortifications in the rear because he said that his generals would simply wish to withdraw to these lines.

■ Spying the key

Mention should be made here of the Soviet use of spy rings in Germany. They employed two varieties, professional spies they had trained and introduced into occupied Europe and Germany, and amateur rings composed of anti-Nazi Germans. From these sources the Russians were able to build up a clear and very detailed picture of German plans and also of their economic and manpower strength. The Kursk attack (Operation '*Zitadelle*') was lost even before the first tank rumbled off or shell was fired, for the Russians had been provided with details of units, objectives and routes, and lacked only the exact date and time. They received this in time, however, to fire a counter-battery shoot at German emplacements – before the German guns had begun to fire.

The Russians must have had an agent placed somewhere very high in the German command structure, because they were kept informed of policy decisions taken by Hitler and his immediate circle. It is interesting that the third battle of Kharkov was fought by Manstein without direction from Hitler, and the German moves remained unknown to the Russians until the trap had been sprung on their two armoured groups. It was the information from Richard Sorge in Japan which enabled the Russians to move their Siberian troops from the Russo-Japanese border in time to launch the winter counter-offensive at Moscow. Moreover, the assurance that Japan would not attack Russia allowed Russia to draw on her vast pool of manpower in the Far East.

Training was not as long or thorough as Western nations and this also enabled Russia to use men from recently liberated areas of her western territories – they might have been peasants or partisans, but if they could use a rifle they were fit to be soldiers.

This crude system of training even extended to tanks. The Germans once destroyed a group of British-made Valentine tanks crewed by industrial workers – operating instructions had been chalked in Russian on the inside of the fighting compartment.

Russian tanks and assault-guns, though poorly finished and without the elaborate optical equipment of western vehicles, were some of the best armoured vehicles to be produced in the war. The T-34 had thicker armour than any of the tanks with which Germany begun the war in the East, a maximum of 47-mm and a minimum of 20-mm, a speed of 32 mph and a 76.2-mm gun. Its broad tracks enabled it to travel over soft ground and snow despite its weight of 26 tons, while its well-sloped hull and turret presented fewer shot-traps for anti-tank shells. Having produced a war-winner the Russians concentrated on its mass production. The plants which produced this tank were situated beyond the Urals, far out of range of any German bomber. This meant that the Germans were confronted with hundreds of tanks which they had to destroy on the battlefield, rather than at their source in a factory.

In the battles of encirclement in 1941 and 1942 the Germans captured or destroyed vast quantities of Russian tanks, guns and trucks. In doing this, however, they assisted the Russians, for the Soviet high command was in the process of re-equipping its forces and the Germans had simply disposed of the obsolescent or obsolete weapons. The Russians produced their own tanks and most of their aircraft, but received a number of these from Britain and the United States. American trucks were an important asset when Russia moved onto the offensive since they enabled her to sustain the momentum of attack by allowing support and re-supply vehicles to keep up.

On 22 June 1941 Germany attacked an enigma. Soviet Russia had built a surprisingly effective security screen between herself and the west and the Germans had calculated that she possessed 155 divisions. In fact she had 230, and of these 170 were within striking distance of her western front. The Germans had based their analysis of Russian forces on the disastrous war with Finland in which the Soviet losses were about 200,000 killed, with 1,600 tanks destroyed. They also thought that the 1937 purges had destroyed the brains of the Red Army. A war in the East, according to Hitler's assessment, could be successfully concluded before winter. The Germans underestimated the courage of the average Russian, and they were unaware of the new industrial power of the Soviet Union. Combined with Stalin's ruthlessness and Zhukov's forceful leadership these elements produced an unbeatable enemy.

THE POLITICAL FRONT
HITLER AND HIS HIGH COMMAND

D uring the war years, and ever since then, the most famous German military word has also suffered misunderstanding and misuse: *Wehrmacht*. It has become popularly identified as the expression of German might and efficiency. It has been used as an alternative description of the German army. It has been wildly over-praised, and as hysterically vilified. But whenever it has been thus misused, the *Wehrmacht* has always been generally understood: powerful, competent, the military weapon for the realisation of the ambitions of Adolf Hitler.

In fact *Wehrmacht*, pure and simple, was the word used for the armed forces – nothing more or less. It was composed of the Army (*Heer*), the Navy (*Kriegsmarine*) and the Air Force (*Luftwaffe*), each of which had a commander-in-chief of its own. The obvious problem in war was the co-ordination of these three entities into the achievement of a common strategy. All combatant nations of World War II had to solve this problem in one way or another; the Allied solution, by no means invariably successful, was the Joint Chiefs-of-Staff Committee. Hitler's version, however, had first come into being as a result of his extension of his personal authority over the German military. Thus it never became a team of professionals working to get the cumulative best out of the three services in the field: it always remained a small military court, on the loyalty of whose permanent members Hitler could always depend.

In the early days of the Third Reich, the forces were the preserve of the Defence Minister, General von Blomberg. How Hitler engineered Blomberg's removal has been described elsewhere. In February 1938 a new command set-up was announced. This was the *Oberkommando der Wehrmacht* (OKW) or 'Supreme Command of the Armed Forces'. Hitler stood at its head, exercising the immediate command. Chief-of-Staff was the former chief of the armed forces office under Blomberg, General

Wilhelm Keitel. Chief of Operations was General Alfred Jodl. These two men remained in their posts until the German collapse of 1945 – a remarkable fact in itself, when the ups and downs of other German generals are considered.

■ Hitler in command

This was Hitler's basic team. It was no part of Hitler's plan to have Keitel act as the chairman of an armed forces committee, in constant touch with the three services on all matters of joint concern. Keitel was in fact technically junior to the three forces commanders. It is essential to grasp the incredible fact that the chiefs of the German army, navy and air force hardly ever met in conference, and when they did it was in Hitler's presence. Rivalry among them was intense, particularly between the navy (Raeder) and the air force (Goering). The latter rivalry was the prime reason why the Third Reich never had a navy with an operational fleet air arm, mercifully for the British. The best co-operation between the services was to be found between the army and the air force, and then it was established at a lower level, between army group/army commanders and air fleet/air corps commanders.

This personal rivalry among the three leaders of the *Wehrmacht* lasted right through the war. It was not changed by Admiral Doenitz's replacement of Raeder at the end of 1942; it was not changed by Hitler's personal assumption of control over the army in the winter fighting of 1941–42, for even then he needed an army chief-of-staff and spent the rest of the war trying to find a suitably pliant candidate. (He never did.) But it was mirrored by an equally serious lack of understanding within OKW itself.

For the fullest details of this posterity is indebted to the evidence of General Walter Warlimont, Jodl's deputy. His main burden of complaint has been the total lack of mutual understanding between himself and Jodl. Warlimont is a lucky man: he has survived Keitel and Jodl, both of whom were hanged by sentence of the Nuremberg Tribunal after the war. He has himself admitted that had he not suffered severe injuries in the bomb attempt on Hitler's life in July 1944, he would have remained with the OKW entourage at Hitler's elbow and would almost certainly have ended up in the Berlin *Fuehrerbunker* in 1945. A good example of the sort of work Warlimont did during the war was his memorandum of what should be done with Leningrad. (His recommended solution was to seal off the city, let as many of its inhabitants starve as possible, evacuate the survivors after the winter, and raze the city to the ground.) Callous though it sounds, this aspect of OKW's work is not relevant. Warlimont's evidence makes it clear that after the first three campaigns fought by the *Wehrmacht* in World War II – Poland, Scandinavia and the West – OKW lost any semblance of being a 'think-tank' of ideas for future operations. The idea of junior officers wilted under the indifference of Jodl, who after the fall of France deliberately kept his better judgement subordinate to his faith in Hitler's genius.

An example of how the hero-worship of Hitler by both Keitel and Jodl sometimes did not matter was provided at the end of January 1940. Hitler's personal aide was Colonel (later General) Rudolf Schmundt, who was frequently entrusted with reporting missions to the army headquarters at the front. Personal reports direct to Hitler would then bypass both the army high command (*Oberkommando des Heeres* or OKH) and OKW. At the HQ of Army Group 'A' in Koblenz, Schmundt heard of the novel operational plan of the army group commander's chief-of-staff – a plan which had been repeatedly sat on by Brauchitsch and Halder at the head of the army, and which had never been submitted to OKW. This plan was enthusiastically adopted by Hitler as the *Fuehrer*'s own, and in due course was triumphantly revealed to OKW and the army. It was, of course, Manstein's 'Sickle' plan for the severance and destruction of the Allied armies in Flanders.

The whole mess reached its most confused state in the Dunkirk fiasco, another major controversy of World War II. By this stage Hitler, encouraged by success, was being tempted to meddle increasingly in the day-to-day conduct of operations, and Keitel and Jodl made no move to discourage him. As a result the army's decision to crash on to Dunkirk and destroy the trapped Allies there before they could get away was reversed, and a priceless opportunity lost.

One of the greatest criticisms levelled at OKW was that as the armed forces high command it should have prepared plans for the eventuality of Britain's continuing the war alone – in other words, a blueprint for invasion. Hitler had already had this done without consulting either the army or the *Luftwaffe* when he made his decision to invade Scandinavia. The real reason why the possibility of an invasion of Britain was not seriously considered until July 1940 was quite simple: Hitler did not consider it necessary, and he was not alone. Jodl did not. Halder, who would have to work out the assault details and bear the direct responsibility for failure, certainly did not. It took six weeks of indecision before Hitler issued his famous 'Directive No. 16' for Operation 'Sealion' and the great inter-services wrangle began. From start to finish of the debate, OKW never acted as a co-ordinating influence. In fact the fear of Raeder, whose navy (what was left of it after the punishing battles off Norway) would have the job of putting the troops ashore in Britain, sufficiently impressed Jodl for the latter to inhibit any tendency towards an early concrete decision. The army passed the responsibility to the navy and the navy to the airforce, and all were happy when the blame finally settled on the failure of Goering's 'eagles' to make the invasion possible.

A definite achievement on the part of Keitel and Jodl was made when they argued Hitler out of an autumn campaign against Russia should the plan to invade Britain come to nothing. This won the approval of OKH and the planning for '*Barbarossa*' proceeded with unaccustomed harmony. Before the offensive could begin on schedule, however, OKW had to issue snap orders for the reduction of Yugoslavia and Greece.

On 13 May 1941, Keitel issued one of the most notorious directives of the war – a limitation of the normal jurisdiction of army courts-martial with regard to the civilian population of Russia after the invasion, providing for draconian maintenance of order in the occupied areas. This was one of the murkiest tasks of OKW, whose planners – men like Warlimont – never showed the slightest reluctance to work out the details of atrocity and submit them in memorandum form.

The blind faith of the top OKW officers in Hitler remained unshaken during the first year of campaigning in Soviet Russia, but there were plenty of fundamental disagreements between Hitler and OKH. Brauchitsch, army C-in-C, was a morally-broken man, as was proved by his order to Guderian not to bring up the subject of a drive on Moscow at the conference of 23 August. (Guderian ignored Brauchitsch, and Hitler turned down Guderian's representations.) Any signs of sympathy on the part of Keitel and Jodl with the increasingly depressing reports from the front were crushed by contemptuous tongue-lashings from Hitler.

■ Obsequious toady

By 1942, the year of the great turning-point for the Axis war effort, the rôle of OKW was firmly defined and never really showed any signs of modification. Keitel, the dim, obsequious toady kept his place as the nominal head of OKW because of his readiness with the right comment at *Fuehrer* conferences and also because he did not tell Hitler 'unpleasant things'. Jodl was the dominant partner. Unshakably loyal to Hitler, he was the man who mattered in OKW. Jodl suffered a traumatic shock in September 1942 when Hitler sent him down to the Kuban to find out why Army Group 'A' was being so slow. When Jodl came back and told Hitler that Army Group 'A' was doing all that could be done, Hitler raged and screamed and ordered Jodl's dismissal. This was never implemented, but Jodl never forgot the lesson. (He so far unbent as to tell Warlimont that 'a dictator, as a matter of psychological necessity, must never be reminded of his own errors'.)

■ Rubber stamp

Thus OKW remained as the official stamp on Hitler's military decrees. The direct control of operations was denied it; this control was exercised by Hitler himself. Keitel, Jodl and Warlimont, however, remained the trio who relayed the orders for atrocity to the fighting forces. Yet OKW was a large, if securely trussed, body. From the original four basic departments – operational orders, foreign intelligence, supply and general purposes – a forest of industrious sub-departments grew. Staffed by professional officers, its work was nevertheless largely nullified by Hitler's increasing lack of touch with reality.

It must also be remembered that OKW, unlike OKH, was mobile. It had to be: it was an extension of Hitler's personal authority, and where Hitler was, there also were OKW headquarters. OKW had started its existence as a revamped war office, centralised on Hitler's orders: it ended the war as a travelling military court.

■ Genuine respect

Jodl undoubtedly deserves credit as the most able of the 'political generals' and was certainly the man for whom Hitler had the most genuine respect. It was no accident that Jodl's ascendancy made him the natural choice to sign the instrument of surrender in May 1945, rather than Doenitz, Hitler's designated successor. But apart from Keitel, Jodl, Warlimont and Schmundt other generals deserve the description of 'political'. Among that handful without hope who committed suicide in the Berlin *Fuehrerbunker* in 1945 there was General Wilhelm Burgdorf. He was head of the army personnel department and armed forces adjutant at OKW HQ; and it was Burgdorf who carried the ultimatum of suicide or disgrace to Rommel in October 1944. General Hans Krebs, a shrewd and adaptable character cast in the same mould as Jodl but without the signs of the latter's ability, became Hitler's last chief of the army general staff and surrendered Berlin. The *Luftwaffe*, too, produced its own 'political' generals, men such as General Korten (chief of the *Luftwaffe* general staff, and killed by the 'July Plot' bomb), and Koller, who replaced him. Then there was the confirmed Nazi, General Ritter von Greim, who was summoned into the hell of Berlin to be promoted field-marshal and be appointed commander-in-chief of the *Luftwaffe* by the crazed *Fuehrer* in 1945.

Throughout the disastrous months of 1943 and 1944, the pattern of OKW remained much the same in defeat as it had done in victory, with the small, permanent group of trusties manning the key posts. Forming an 'outer circle' were a group of equally obsequious generals who had found out how to keep in Hitler's good books. It was left to the last campaign of the war in Europe, the battle of Berlin, for Hitler to do the one thing he had never brought himself to do: unite OKW with OKH. It was in any event an acknowledgement of hard facts, for the tiny compressed pocket of German soil left to the German armed forces was now so small that the two headquarters had been intermingled anyway. It was a symbolic gesture which gave Keitel, for a few meaningless hours, the latitude to exercise, as far as he was able, the actual powers of command which Hitler had always denied him before the inevitable end.

The depressing story of OKW and the 'political generals' reveals not the strength but the basic internal weaknesses of the Third Reich. The 'political generals' were professional officers who had pinned their faith, and their personal careers, on one man: Hitler. They were a unique body of men in that all their training and background before the advent of Hitler went by the board. Closest of all to the core of Hitler's magnetism, they genuinely felt that they were doing their duty as best they could in assisting the German war effort. Labouring under this delusion, they out of all the men of the German officer corps shouldered the most opprobium and blame for the evil which Hitler's Germany unleashed on Europe. They proved that to get on in the Third Reich it was advisable to adapt. But whatever condemnation they merited for their toadying to Hitler and their delinquencies as officers – let alone as human beings

– their main defence at Nuremberg still merits consideration. Even if they had been advisers, instead of opting to become courtiers and sycophants; even if they had spoken out against the wrongdoing they helped to implement, it would have made little difference. They of all people in the Third Reich knew how easily they could be replaced. It was so much easier for them to convince themselves that they would do more good by staying.

FIELD-MARSHAL WILHELM KEITEL

In 1940 the soldiers came home from France, and the Germans thought they had won the war. Britain would come to terms, indeed the *Fuehrer* had offered them a 'Final Appeal to Reason' and translated versions of his speech had been dropped from aircraft over England. It was a time for self-congratulation and promotions.

Hitler made up nine of his generals to the rank of Field-Marshal, and after the ceremony they posed for a photograph in the Reich Chancellery with the *Fuehrer* and *Reichsmarschall* Goering. All of them had proved their worth in the battle of France, except one man who stood a little apart from the group. The photographer caught the look of withering disdain on the face of Field-Marshal von Rundstedt as he glanced with disgust at the chief of the OKW, Wilhelm Keitel.

In his rôle of head of the High Command of the Armed Forces, Keitel was a party to all the major decisions taken by Hitler in the prosecution of the war, yet he exercised no real influence in the planning or choice of these operations. Guderian commented after the war that Keitel 'soon fell under the sway of Hitler's personality and, as time went on, became less and less able to shake off the hypnosis of which he was a victim. He preserved his Lower Saxon loyalty until the day of his death. Hitler knew that he could place unlimited confidence in the man; for that reason he allowed him to retain his position even when he no longer had any illusion about his talents as a strategist. The Field-Marshal exerted no influence on the course of operations.' Guderian is generous to his former colleagues. Indeed, after listing the faults and failings of Keitel and Jodl he adds: 'For all that – they were my comrades.'

Keitel is described as 'lacking the strength to resist Hitler's orders when such orders ran contrary to international law and to accepted morality. It was only this weakness on his part that permitted the issuing to the troops of the so-called "Commissar Order" and other notorious decrees.' Once more Guderian is generous. Keitel was not weak; he was totally subservient to Hitler and served only to put the military rubber stamp on the *Fuehrer*'s dreams and plans. There is no record that he attempted to divert Hitler from the invasions and expropriations which the Germans made throughout Europe.

Keitel fell under Hitler's spell in 1938. On 27 January, after Field-Marshal von Blomberg had departed in disgrace for Italy, Hitler summoned Keitel. At that time Hitler did not know his new Chief of the *Wehrmachtamt* and addressed him as 'General von Keitel', which aristocratic appellation must have delighted the middle-class soldier. The *Fuehrer* complained that he was becoming ever lonelier and that Keitel would have to endure with him the changes which were taking place in the armed forces. Keitel, uncomplicated, found himself touched by this confidence and from that moment was Hitler's man.

■ Intermediary

As head of OKW his signature ratified Hitler's orders and instructions. He was under the *Fuehrer*'s spell and a scribbled 'Keitel' at the foot of some sheets of typescript seemed nothing. He signed for the destruction of Poland, Denmark and Norway, France and the Low Countries, much as a soldier signs for the kit with which he is issued as a recruit. He even signed for the destruction of Britain, but at the end of 1940 OKW informed units on the Channel in the autumn of 1940 that the '*Fuehrer* has decided that from now on until the spring, preparations for landing in England will be maintained purely as a military and political threat.'

It was a meaningless gesture, for on 18 December 1940 Keitel initiated a document of fatal importance. Nine secret copies of *Fall Barbarossa* had been circulated among the heads of the services; Germany would invade Russia and defeat her before she had finished with Britain.

■ Low intelligence

Hitler imagined that Russia would be torn apart by political upheavals when Germany attacked and Keitel supported his master's view. 'The war has been won already; it has only to be terminated,' he told diplomats in Italy and Finland. It sounded like the brave words he had uttered before the attack on Poland in 1939. Hitler had told him: 'We cannot expect a repetition of the Czech affair. There will be war. Our task is to isolate Poland.' Thrilled by the prospect of a real war he told the doubters at OKW, who prophesied that this would lead to a world war for which Germany was ill-equipped: 'France is too degenerate, Britain too decadent and America too uninterested to fight for Poland.'

Yet he had his doubts. Beck had told him that the new army Germany was building would not be a reliable military instrument before 1942 or 1943. Keitel even reached the point of offering his resignation to Hitler, but as usual the *Fuehrer* refused to accept it.

To the surprise of the general staff, the campaigns in Poland and in the West went well and it was not until the halt before Moscow that Keitel began to feel uneasy again. On 1 December Bock reported that the troops were exhausted and would need to go onto the defensive for the winter. In the discussion which followed Keitel suggested that it might be better that the troops withdraw to a winter line.

Hitler turned on him and dismissed the suggestion as one coming from a '*Strohkopf*', crude slang for a man with a low IQ. Deeply hurt, Keitel turned and left the room. Jodl found him in his quarters writing out his resignation with a pistol on his desk. Jodl quietly took the pistol away and tried to persuade Keitel to remain. He gave in and stayed in service.

This reputation of being the servant of Hitler, his military showpiece, had now become public knowledge. Keitel was always hovering near his master on public occasions and the Berliners with their sharp humour dubbed him '*Lakaitel*' or 'little lackey'. It was not far from the truth. Keitel had begun to climb the back stairs to promotion before he met Hitler. In 1937 he married the youngest daughter of Field-Marshal von Blomberg. Three years later he showed off his talents for gross flattery at the *Fuehrer*'s headquarters. Hitler had paid tribute to OKW for its training and leadership, for the Battle of France was clearly going Germany's way and her troops had just captured Abbeville. In front of a large gathering of generals Keitel begged to differ: 'No, no, my *Fuehrer*, to you alone are due these magnificent achievements.'

He backed Hitler even when his judgements seemed to others to be at fault. When the Canadians suffered their disastrous defeat at Dieppe, Keitel saw this as an immediate threat to France. Even though there were protests from Halder and Jodl two divisions, the '*Leibstandarte Adolf Hitler*' and '*Grossdeutschland*', were withdrawn from the Eastern Front, although fortunately the latter unit was still at its railheads when the Russians attacked. Liddell Hart thinks that if both these divisions had been employed they might have turned the scales at Stalingrad.

Understandably a man who did so little to further the war, and who in the pre-Nazi era would never have risen above his majority, earned a name in the army. He was 'knick-Keitel', 'nodding Keitel', the *Fuehrer*'s yes-man. The contempt in which he was held extended, perhaps unjustly, to Jodl. Speaking to Liddell Hart after the war, General Hasso von Manteuffel was more generous: 'Keitel, Jodl and Warlimont had never been in the war. At the same time their lack of fighting experience tended to make them underrate practical difficulties, and encourage Hitler to believe that things could be done that were quite impossible.'

But just as he despised Keitel in 1940, Field-Marshal von Rundstedt, the aristocratic professional still loathed him at the end of the war. In 1944, in a telephone conversation from the Normandy front, Keitel had a gloomy report from Rundstedt. It was uncommon for Rundstedt to speak direct to the head of OKW. Such was his dislike he normally arranged for Blumentritt, his chief-of-staff, to undertake the unpleasant duty. Keitel complained about the way the fighting was going, and Rundstedt snarled over the line: 'If you think you can do any better you had better come down here and lead this filth yourself.' A few days later there was a similar exchange. Cherbourg was about to fall and Keitel was on the line again: 'What shall we do? What shall we do?' This time the answer came in a cool, impassive voice: 'What shall we do? Make peace you idiots! What else can you do?' The line went dead as Rundstedt quietly hung up.

Keitel's tragedy was that despite such epithets as 'the brains of a cinema usher' he was not without intelligence. Free of Hitler's spell, he saw Germany's mistakes quite clearly in his postwar interrogation. Recalling the interview, Milton Shulman writes: 'Second guessing, after it was all over, Field-Marshal Wilhelm Keitel nodded in agreement with history's verdict.

'"Instead of attacking Russia," he said, "we should have strangled the British Empire by closing the Mediterranean. The first step would have been the conquest of Gibraltar."'

Expanding on this theme he said: 'One of the biggest occasions we passed by was El Alamein. I would say that, at that climax of the war, we were nearer to victory than at any time before or after.'

Wilhelm Keitel never had a moment which was truly his own. He won no battles and took no momentous decisions. After five years of service to Hitler he was left by the *Fuehrer* to tidy up the mess that remained in 1945. Despite his protests that he alone enjoyed the right to lead, Hitler evaded the responsibility of ending the war when he committed suicide. On 8 May 1945, at the headquarters of the Russian 1st Belorussian Front with Admiral Friedeburg and Colonel-General Stumpff, Keitel ratified the unconditional surrender of the Third Reich. Impeccably dressed, with his cap, gloves and marshal's *Interimstab* baton, this was Keitel's finest moment. This time his signature marked the end of a war.

COLONEL-GENERAL FRANZ HALDER

On 1 September 1938, Halder replaced Beck as Chief of the Army General Staff. He was then aged 54, a man of wide intellectual interests including botany and mathematics, and the first Bavarian to hold the position.

Beck, who opposed Hitler's policy of aggression, had recommended Halder as his successor when he resigned because he was convinced Halder shared his views and would act with those who sought to overthrow the Nazi régime. The Chief of the Army General Staff was a key figure for the conspirators to have on their side, but Halder soon found himself in a dilemma. He was a devout Catholic and consequently suffered crises of conscience over supporting Beck and the conspirators – which he felt was the right course of action – and his oath of allegiance to the *Fuehrer*, his supreme commander. His first orders were to hasten the preparations for the invasion of Czechoslovakia, whereas Beck had operated a go-slow policy. Halder therefore vacillated and made excuses to the conspirators, saying that nothing could be done against Hitler whilst he was so popular, and that they must wait until the Nazis suffered a defeat. On one occasion, Halder made the tenuous distinction that the could support an assassination attempt, for one could not be loyal to a dead *Fuehrer*, but that he could not support a coup at time of war.

He did nothing more than warn Hitler of the folly of his aggression.

Together, Halder and Field-Marshal Walther Brauchitsch, commander-in-chief of the army, worked on the plans for the invasion of Poland, and pondered on the forces the British and French could muster if they decided to support Poland. There is no record – even in the invaluable diary kept by Halder – of anyone questioning Hitler on the rationale behind the proposed attack. Halder did not speak out against Hitler and in later years he claimed he never believed Hitler would actually go to war, and he certainly did not believe that Great Britain would fight. Only one voice was raised in protest at the military conference at Obersalzburg on 14 August 1939, and that belonged to General Thomas, head of the economics and armaments branch of OKW, who said that Hitler's attack on Poland would start a world war. At a further conference on 22 August, Hitler adopted an arrogant and uncompromising attitude which made it impossible for those present to challenge his statements. In his monologue, he assured them that conflict with Poland was inevitable, that Germany had nothing to lose and must act immediately. Whether Britain fought or not, he said, was irrelevant – 'our enemies are little worms'. Halder knew well enough what Hitler was up to over the negotiations with Poland, but he did nothing. He knew that Hitler would 'raise a barrage of demographic and democratic demands . . . The Poles will come to Berlin on 30 August; on 31 August, the negotiations will blow up; on 1 September, Germany will use force.'

Halder also knew the implications of Hitler's 'final solution' for the Jews in Poland. Hitler had instructed his generals to confine themselves to military matters only. SS commissars would be stationed in each military district and would carry out the required exterminations. Halder accepted that there would have to be these commissars, in order to keep the army out of the exterminations. He also knew of Hitler's plans to drive the Poles from their territory, but he still could not find the strength to join the conspirators.

Warsaw fell after 17 days of siege. Hitler immediately requested plans for continuing the war in the West. Halder told him that only defensive plans existed. Hitler, inflamed by his Polish victory, thought that France would fall just as easily and took no notice of Halder, who commented that the techniques of the Polish campaign were no recipe for war in the West, against a well-knit army. Hitler wanted a lightning strike through Holland and Belgium on a very wide front that Britain and France would not be able to stop. Halder, Brauchitsch and several other generals attempted to prove to Hitler that an offensive was impossible, that it would take many months to equip the army appropriately. But Hitler was longing for battle, and his Directive No. 6 showed an amazing grasp of history, strategy and tactics. Halder and Brauchitsch saw three courses of action open to them: first, go ahead with the attack in the West; second, wait and see; and third, remove Hitler. Brauchitsch did not care for option three (a 'man of straw', Hitler called Brauchitsch) and they decided to try to work further on changing Hitler's mind, although now after Poland, Halder must have known there was little hope of this. But he could not bring himself to act against Hitler without superior orders, and Brauchitsch was not given any.

On 27 October, Hitler told his generals in no uncertain terms that the attack in the West would definitely take place, so they should plan accordingly and stop arguing. Halder felt quite battered after Hitler's tirade and from then on showed dutiful enthusiasm for the offensive whilst, inside, he was filled with gloom. Politically and militarily, he was a defeatist. On 5 November, Brauchitsch complained to Hitler of his interference in the Polish campaign and requested that OKH should be solely responsible for any future campaign. Hitler went into a fury. This was the first occasion on which he truly abused his generals, calling them disloyal, cowardly and defeatist.

On 20 November, Hitler issued Directive No. 8 for the conduct of the war, ordering maintenance of an alert to 'exploit favourable weather conditions immediately'. Fed up with the criticism of the generals, and with what he regarded as the 'stiff-necked attitude' of the general staff, Hitler again addressed them on 23 August, telling them his plans were unchangeable. No one, he said, had ever achieved what he was about to achieve: 'I will shrink at nothing . . . I shall annihilate anyone opposed to me.' There is no record of any general expressing the doubts most of them felt at this time, or questioning the immorality of attacking through Holland and Belgium. From this point on, Hitler considered his political and military judgement to be superior to that of the generals, and henceforth would hardly ever listen to advice, let alone allow criticism. His outburst put a real damper on any thoughts the generals might have had for overthrowing him, and Halder was certainly not the man to stand up to the threat of being 'annihilated'. He was fast losing independent thought.

After the fall of France and the evacuation of the BEF from Dunkirk, Hitler declared 'England's situation is hopeless. The war has been won by us.' In July 1940, planning began in earnest for the invasion of Britain – Operation 'Sealion'. Hitler, however, had decided on the invasion before he knew the inherent difficulties of an overseas landing and at a time when he was also beginning to concentrate on his proposed attack on Russia.

OKH looked forward to a war of movement on the island and Halder, always methodical and meticulous, concerned himself with details such as the difficulties of landing troops where they were supposed to be, and how to convey enough horses for the offensive on limited means of transport. The navy soon revealed the wide margin that existed between the army's requirements for the land war and its own capabilities of conveying these requirements. Halder remarked that if this was so, planning might as well cease, but of course he did not tell Hitler this, and work on the plans continued even though fresh drawbacks were discovered almost daily. Irreconcilable differences arose between the army and navy concerning the length of the front. The army wanted a wide landing front so that it could secure a number of beach heads at an early stage, while the navy felt itself capable of landing troops only on a narrow front. This seemed to Halder like 'feeding the troops into a sausage machine'. Originally, Hitler had stated that he intended hurling 40 divisions across the Channel, but detailed planning showed that only nine could be sent in the first wave with two airborne divisions in support, and that it would take 11 days to land them. Reinforcements would only arrive at the rate of two divisions every four days.

As the dangers and difficulties of an amphibious operation became obvious to

Hitler – Admiral Raeder did his best to persuade the army that 'Sealion' was out of the question, at least in 1940 – he began to hesitate, and it seems that his interest waned, probably because of his concentration on Russia. At the same time, however, he continued to hope that something would turn up to make the invasion possible before the bad weather. With all the delay, Halder requested that the forces concentrated on the Channel coast be dispersed as they presented a sitting target to the RAF. Hitler allowed this and then called the operation off in October.

In this instance, everyone concerned had been loathe to tell Hitler that his ambitions were not possible and so they continued planning regardless. Hitler was then at his zenith.

Hitler intended to attack Russia in the spring of 1941 – 'The sooner Russia is smashed, the better.' Halder and his staff went to work on the plans in August 1940. Halder's diary reveals that he was full of enthusiasm for the task. The German army, with the successes in Poland, Norway, Denmark, Holland, Belgium and France behind it, appeared invincible.

Planning for the invasion of Russia – Operation 'Barbarossa' – had to take careful note of the climate: the short, hot summers and long, extremely cold winters, which necessitated a German victory within a single summer offensive not more than five months in duration. The Germans were not equipped for winter warfare. The spring thaw and autumn rains which turned the roads into impassable quagmires added a further limitation to the timetable.

Hitler and his generals agreed to trap and destroy the main Soviet forces as near to the border as possible, but Halder and Brauchitsch disagreed with Hitler over the means for the final Soviet defeat. They favoured a march on Moscow, where the roads were best and where they believed Russia would commit its last strength to defend the capital. Hitler retorted 'Moscow is not important', and in his directive of 18 December 1940, he provided for simultaneous advances towards Leningrad, Moscow and Kiev.

Then came Hitler's decision to invade Yugoslavia, which meant that 'Barbarossa' had to be put back four weeks. Hitler did not consult OKH, and this decision later meant that deep snow and sub-zero temperatures hit German troops three or four weeks short of what they needed for victory.

Right from the beginning of the German invasion of Russia, OKH underestimated Russian ability and overestimated their own. During the first weeks, Hitler meddled nervously with the plans and attempted to impose on the battlefield his own tactical conceptions.

When the Germans reached Minsk, Halder hoped that the front would become so fluid that it would outrun Hitler's ability as a tactician – but no, Hitler was about to take over completely. Now the row about whether the German advance should be to Moscow blew up again. On 19 July, Hitler completed a directive about which OKH had not been consulted, restating that Moscow was not the primary target.

Army Group 'Centre', the strongest of the three army groups in Russia, was to continue towards Moscow with its infantry alone and was to divert its armour to help the Army Group 'North' thrust towards Leningrad and the Army Group 'South' conquest of the Ukraine. Hitler overruled many generals over this, including Guderian. Halder noted that Hitler was obsessed with the capture of Leningrad and Stalingrad. Hitler called Halder and OKH 'men with minds fossilised in out of date theories' when Halder vainly pointed out that in accordance with Clausewitz, Moscow should be the main aim.

The march on Moscow restarted on 2 October, but it was too late. Victory appeared within Germany's grasp, and then the autumn rains started at the end of October. The army was 50 miles from Moscow, halted by oozing, muddy roads. It moved off again in mid-November but ground to a halt within sight of Moscow, where the Russians counterattacked throughout the winter.

■ Halder lingers on

In December, Brauchitsch retired and Hitler took over as commander-in-chief himself. He had always longed to be a general and to show off his military genius properly. Halder stayed on, but the army's last vestige of existence as an independent service was wiped out. Hitler ignored Halder's advice and ordered the armies in Russia to stand fast. There would be no retreats. Halder observed that the generals were now merely Hitler's postmen, conveying his orders, based on his own conception of strategy. The winter crisis of 1941–42, however, gave Hitler a personal triumph. Against the generals' advice and entreaties, he had ordered the armies to remain where they were, and they had done so. His confidence in his own military ability was further enhanced.

Plans for Operation 'Blau' – the 1942 summer offensive – were drafted by Halder and his staff in accordance with Hitler's detailed instructions. Hitler was now in complete command. The directive called for a full scale offensive on the southern flank of the Eastern Front, towards the River Don, Stalingrad and the Caucasus oilfields. Hitler's fanatical determination to take both Stalingrad and the oilfields was a bad mistake. In the end, he gained neither objective and suffered a humiliating defeat. Halder tried in vain to warn him of the danger of leaving the northern flank of the 6th Army so dangerously exposed along the line of the upper Don for 350 miles from Stalingrad to Voronezh, where only three, weak satellite armies were thinly deployed. Hitler, however, was convinced the Russians were finished and paid no attention, although the Don flank was the key to maintaining the 4th and 6th *Panzerarmee* at Stalingrad and Army Group 'A' in the Caucasus. Should this flank collapse, the troops at Stalingrad would be threatened with encirclement and those in the Caucasus cut off.

Halder then suggested that the offensive against Stalingrad be called off, as it was losing its momentum. Hitler flew into a blind fury and dismissed Halder on 24

September 1942, saying he was no longer up to the 'psychic demands of his position'.

Halder commented in his diary that Hitler's decisions 'have ceased to have anything in common with the principles of strategy . . . They are the product of a violent nature following its momentary impulses which recognise no limits to possibility and which makes its daydreams the father of its acts.'

By the sum of 1942, the chief-of-staff had no power or authority. Hitler was in absolute control of the war in the East. Even the day-to-day battle moves were controlled from his desk. Halder merely had the task of presenting the *Fuehrer*'s requirements in a logical and rational way.

Halder's mind was often confused, and his will to action paralysed. He could not bring himself to take risks. He stood up to Hitler in the early days to a certain extent, then went along with him, always hoping (vainly) he could prevent things becoming too terrible. His main trouble was he could not choose between his duty as a soldier and his patriotic and moral convictions.

COLONEL-GENERAL ALFRED JODL

When Hitler decided to invade Russia he had a special headquarters built in the woods of East Prussia. With his peculiar Gothic imagination he called it the '*Wolfsschanze*' – the Wolf's Lair. In the permanent shadow of the woods and camouflage nets, and confined to log huts and concrete bunkers behind belts of barbed wire and minefields, the staff and aides soon developed a prison psychology. Some visitors landing at the special airfield or coming in on the secret railway branch-line felt the place was like something out of a fairy tale from Grimm or some peculiar Wagnerian opera – with Hitler as the king of a Nazi court.

Among the courtiers who had fallen under Hitler's spell was the chief-of-staff of OKW, Colonel-General Alfred Jodl. Liddell Hart dismisses him as the able clerk to the chief clerk, Keitel. But since Keitel exercised little real control over the prosecution of the war, it was up to Jodl to see that Hitler's ideas and dreams were transformed into some sort of order and instructions for the men on the ground. Guderian, who had little love for restrictive superiors or incompetent subordinates, does not treat Jodl so harshly. Jodl 'had in fact controlled the operations of the combined armed forces ever since the Norwegian Campaign of April, 1940 . . . originally he too had fallen under Hitler's spell, but he had never been so hypnotised as was Keitel and therefore never became so uncritical.'

In 1935 Jodl had been made head of the Department of National Defence, and had worked hard to build it into what was really an operations department of the Reich War Ministry. General von Fritsch regarded him as an exceptionally able officer, but also noted that he suffered from almost pathological personal ambition. It may have been this characteristic that attracted Hitler. Although Jodl admired Hitler, he did have reservations, however, unlike his superior Keitel. After the war Jodl explained to an American doctor at Nuremberg that as the son of a middle-class military family he found Hitler's outbursts against the officer corps and middle-class rather offensive. There were moments during the campaigns in the West when Jodl doubted the *Fuehrer's* judgements of the situation, and there were also times when he imposed considerable burdens on OKW, calling on them to change plans and operations at very short notice. At the operational conferences there was the carping tone of the south German corporal who had made good teaching the German professionals how to make war. It was not until the war with Russia, however, that this behaviour became so intolerable for Jodl that he clashed with his master.

In 1942, after their defeat before Moscow, the Germans struck in southern Russia. Hitler told his generals that it was for economic reasons, and baffled them with talk of the coal and iron of the Donets basin and the oil of the Caucasus. Oil had always been an obsession with Hitler, and he had pressed for the capture of the Crimea so that its air bases could be eliminated as a threat to the Rumanian oilfields. Hitler's Directive No. 41 stated that after Rostov had been secured Stalingrad would be the main objective, but then Hitler changed his mind. He would not merely cut off Russia from her oilfields in the south – he would capture them. Halder noted bitterly in his diary: 'His persistent underestimation of the enemy's potential is gradually taking on grotesque forms and is beginning to be dangerous.'

In Directive No. 45, transmitted to Army Group 'A' under Field-Marshal List, he stated that 'following the annihilation of the enemy force south of the Don the main task of Army Group 'A' is the seizing of the entire eastern coast of the Black Sea, with a view to eliminating the enemy's Black Sea ports and Black Sea Fleet . . .

'Another force, to be formed by the concentration of all remaining mountain and *Jaeger* divisions, will force a crossing of the Kuban and seize the high ground of Maykop and Armavir . . .'

But in addition Operation '*Edelweiss*' called for fast formations from the army group to cut the Ossetian and Georgian Military Highways and drive along the Caspian to Baku. One of these objectives alone would have been enough for List, and he admitted afterwards that he could only assume that OKW had secret information to indicate that enemy forces in that region were severely weakened or under strength.

Assuming that OKW had this information, List set about allocating his forces for their objectives. One of his problems was that his *Jaeger* troops had not seen action in mountains, and had been employed in conventional fighting in the steppes of Russia – they were out of training for their specialised rôle. More disturbing was the fact that the Russians were no longer allowing themselves to be cut off and encircled. Instead they were withdrawing into the vast plains south of the Don.

The steppe south of the Don is rather like the desert in North Africa. Split up by watercourses which made excellent stop lines that could be held by light forces, it is 300 miles deep. To the south-east the River Manych forms the border between Europe and Asia. The Germans were not only in a new territory – they were in a new continent.

Stalin was a Georgian and the area had seen considerable improvements in farming and irrigation. Dams and canals added to the natural obstacles which confronted the invaders. The Manych had been dammed at several points to form lakes, which were in some cases over a mile wide. In addition to these obvious barriers, the Russians exploited the terrain. The vast sunflower fields, which seemed to stretch like a sea of gold as far as the horizon, offered excellent cover for small groups to ambush despatch riders and patrols.

On 28 July the Germans scored their first major victory over their elusive enemy. At Martynovka on the River Sal the 3rd Panzer Division fought a confused short-range duel with a Soviet motorised corps. At the end of the fighting the Germans had destroyed 77 tanks, a mere handful compared with their earlier victories.

A month after the start of operations, Army Group 'A' and the 4th *Panzerarmee* had driven a deep wedge into the Caucasus and by 29 July were within 70 miles of the Caspian Sea. Now Hitler transferred the 4th *Panzerarmee* to Stalingrad to assist the 6th Army – but he still expected Army Group 'A' to reach its objectives. On 9 August they captured the oil wells at Maykop, but only after the Russians had set them on fire.

With the thermometer at 55 degrees centigrade, the Germans advanced through clouds of white dust. On 12 August they captured Elista, the only important town in the Kalmyk steppes and the same day men of the 3rd and 23rd Panzer Divisions caught their first glimpse of the Caucasus. These mountains abut onto the Middle East and Hitler's long-term plans envisaged a link up with the *Afrika Korps* and the capture of the Arabian oilfields which supplied Britain. But it was from this area that the Russians were now drawing their supplies. American trucks loaded with rations and equipment were being driven overland from Persia. Along with Jeeps and scout cars, they would give Russian troops a new mobility. Meanwhile, at the end of a supply line which stretched for over 1,000 miles, the Germans were being forced to use the local dromedaries pulling requisitioned peasant carts.

By 1 September Army Group 'A' had crossed the River Terek and even reached the highest peak of the Caucasus, Mount Elbrus; but it had run out of energy and run into increased opposition. The advance was almost at a halt and the Germans had neither cleared the Black Sea, nor captured the oilfields of the Caspian.

On 7 September Hitler ordered that Jodl should visit List at his headquarters at Stalino and find out why Army Group 'A' was making no progress. He was to discover why the port of Tuapse on the Black Sea had not been taken, though it was less than 50 miles away, and to re-emphasise Hitler's orders.

Away from the claustrophobic atmosphere of Hitler's new Russian HQ near Vinnitsa in the Ukraine, Jodl met the soldiers who were doing the fighting. General Walther Warlimont described to Liddell Hart after the war what happened when Jodl returned that evening to report.

'Jodl reported to Hitler that List had acted exactly in conformity to Hitler's orders, but that Russian resistance was equally strong everywhere, supported by a most diffi-cult terrain. Hitler, however, kept on reproaching List with having split up his forces instead of breaking through with concentrated power.'

■ Hitler's anger

List had in fact been wanting to regroup his forces, but was carrying out his orders as best he could. Enraged by Hitler's implications that he had been duped by List, Jodl repeated in a loud voice the very orders that Hitler had given, which had forced List to advance on so wide a front.

It triggered the biggest crisis that the German high command had suffered since the beginning of the war. With his face discoloured by rage, Hitler rounded on Jodl: 'You're lying, I never issued such orders – never!' He stormed out of the meeting and it was some hours before he returned to his quarters, still clearly suffering from shock.

The truth had hurt. This time there was no one to blame for the failure. Hitler was not the genius he thought he was, and his grand strategy was not invincible. However, Hitler had to shift the blame and so he sacked Colonel-General Halder, his chief-of-staff, and List. There were indeed also rumours that he would dismiss Keitel and Jodl and replace them with Field-Marshal Kesselring and General Paulus – which would have meant that men with active service experience would have been in command and might have been able to avoid the disaster of Stalingrad.

Keitel and Jodl did not go, but instead a stenographer was added to the staff. Every word uttered in conference with his generals was now to be recorded. There were other changes: the *Fuehrer* no longer ate lunch and dinner with his entourage but dined alone in his quarters with the sole company of Blondi, his Alsatian bitch; and he never left his hut in daytime, not even for the daily briefings on the military situa-tion, which were now delivered to him in his own hut with a small circle of friends and aides.

Warlimont said that Jodl reached the conclusion that these changes were attribut-able to the special character of a dictator. By a process of spurious logic he decided that the dictator must never be reminded of his own errors 'in order to keep up his self-confidence, the ultimate source of his dictatorial force'. In other words he must be treated to the lies and flattery once the preserve of an 18th century monarch.

Warlimont came to a more reasonable conclusion that 'Hitler, when confronted with the actual situation at the end of the second offensive against Russia, suddenly grasped that he would never reach his goal in the East and that the war would even-tually be lost.' So, like a spoilt child which is denied its wishes, he had a good howl and went out to sulk, and like indulgent parents Keitel and Jodl made sure that they did not pain him with further direct statements but tried instead to plead or persuade.

COLONEL-GENERAL KURT ZEITZLER

O n 2 September 1942, Kurt Zeitzler, who had been a general officer less than a year, replaced Halder as chief-of-staff at OKH. This promotion astonished everybody. Although the new man had earned the reputation of being alert, energetic and physically active while the chief-of-staff of Army Group 'D' in the Low Countries, it was widely felt that his lack of status, seniority and experience, particularly on the Eastern Front, would rule out his candidature for the post. But apparently Hitler decided that he preferred more hustle and bustle in OKH in contrast with the supposedly woolly intellectualism of Halder. As a result of this appointment, Zeitzler in theory assumed control of the most powerful section of the army, the Army General Staff. Despite his inexperience, Zeitzler soon demonstrated that he was not prepared to be the yes-man that Hitler might have assumed. During the first few weeks of his appointment he successfully engineered a realignment in the structure of power and authority in the German high command, which was to produce significant effects on the future of campaign planning.

The army had, for a long time, been disgruntled at the influence of the Operations Staff at OKW (Jodl) over the formation of *Fuehrer* directives, many of which dealt with tactical aspects of the campaigns on the Eastern Front and had little strategic content. This annoyance had intensified after Hitler became Commander-in-Chief of the Army as it had the effect of reducing the army staff to the position of a second personal staff.

Almost immediately after his appointment Zeitzler approached Hitler and demanded that OKH should assume responsibility for Hitler's campaign directives applicable to the Eastern Front, to the exclusion of the meddling Jodl and his Operations Staff at OKW. His demand was finely timed, for Jodl had recently incurred the displeasure of Hitler by his support for the apparently incompetent List. Hitler agreed to Zeitzler's request and henceforth the former's directives were issued as 'operations orders' through OKH. Subsequently Zeitzler was able to prevent OKW gaining access to detailed information about Eastern Front affairs.

But how far did the change in general staffs alter the situation facing the German armies, and to what extent was Zeitzler able to influence Hitler in the formation of policy? These two interrelated questions will be examined by reference to the events on the Eastern Front in general and at Stalingrad in particular.

Hitler's plans for the summer of 1942 included the taking of the Caucasus oil-fields, the Donets industrial basin and Stalingrad on the Volga. On 23 August, before Zeitzler was appointed, the 6th Army under Paulus reached the Volga just north of Stalingrad. By 4 October, much of this strategic goal had been achieved. The Volga was closed and half of the town was under German control. The rest of Stalingrad was under fire. But Russian resistance was total and the German advance halted. At this stage, it would have been wise to consolidate the position. Yet Hitler was furious at the breakdown of the offensive, and despite vociferous criticism from Zeitzler and others at supreme headquarters, he was determined to occupy the rest of Stalingrad, taking it, if necessary, street by street and building by building. The 6th Army commander had no choice but to continue the bloody battle.

Zeitzler took it upon himself to prepare a long and detailed report on the situation in the hope that a factual and statistical analysis might make Hitler realise the futility of the continued offensive. The Germans simply did not possess the men, arms, ammunition, tanks or transport to achieve their objectives. The Russian resources were superior in all departments. Zeitzler concluded his report with four basic postulates which had to be acted upon if the Germans were not to be routed. These he formulated as follows:

'1. Owing to the summer offensive, the territory to be occupied in the East no longer corresponds to the size of the occupying army. In a word, there are too few soldiers for too much ground. Unless this is adjusted, a catastrophe must occur.

'2. The most perilous sector . . . is undoubtedly the long, thinly-held flank stretching from Stalingrad to the right boundary of Army Group "Centre". Furthermore, this sector is held by the weakest and least reliable of our troops, Rumanians, Italians and Hungarians. This danger must be eliminated.

'3. The flow of men, equipment, weapons and ammunition to the Eastern Front is entirely insufficient. Each month losses exceed replacements. This must have disastrous consequences.

'4. The Russians are both better trained and better led in 1942 than they were in 1941. This fact should be realised and taken in to account.'

Hitler received the report with uncharacteristic patience, and gently chastised his chief-of-staff for being too pessimistic. He minimised the conclusions almost to the point of insignificance. Zeitzler's only recourse was to reiterate his remarks over and over again in the hope that some of them might stick in the *Fuehrer's* mind. He continually impressed upon Hitler that a withdrawal westwards from Stalingrad was the only option open. In this he had the support of both Paulus and his own chief-of-staff. But Zeitzler found himself in the awful situation where he could envisage impending disaster but do absolutely nothing about it. Hitler would not withdraw from Stalingrad; his frustration had overcome his reason. Zeitzler's war of words with the *Fuehrer* had begun in earnest, but time was of the essence.

The Russians had considerable offensive potential. The problems for German intelligence was to predict where the counterattack would occur. It was not long before they found out. In freezing conditions, the Soviet attack, which combined the 5th Tank Army and the 21st Army, was launched on 19 November. It hammered the whole of the Rumanian 3rd Army front north-west of Stalingrad. Zeitzler succeeded in convincing Hitler that the reserve, Panzer Corps H (XLVIII Panzer Corps), must be released and sent to Army Group 'B'. The Russians meanwhile had broken the Rumanian front at two points and the Panzer Corps was sent to counterattack these advanced units. Zeitzler kept Hitler constantly informed about the situation and urged him to withdraw from Stalingrad before the 6th Army became encircled. An irate *Fuehrer* took no notice.

The situation continued to deteriorate s the Panzer Corps itself was attacked by the advancing Russian armour. The possibility of a successful counterattack quickly diminished. Again Zeitzler recommended that the 6th Army should break out and establish a solid front to the west and attack the Russians who had broken through the Rumanian position. Hitler rejected this situation out of hand. Disaster became increasingly inevitable. Two conferences were held at which Zeitzler put forward the views of the general staff, Army Group 'B' and the 6th Army. Again he urged a withdrawal. Hitler lost all self-control and thundered 'I won't leave the Volga! I won't go back from the Volga!'

On 20 November the Russian 57th and 51st Armies launched the second attack, on the Rumanian VI Corps south of Stalingrad. They broke through very rapidly, and the Rumanian Corps disintegrated. The 6th Army was now faced with the almost inevitable prospect of encirclement from both flanks. It was only a question of time before the Russian pincers met and the Germans' escape route became blocked. A message was sent by General Paulus on 22 November informing the high command that his army had been cut off. The worst fears of Zeitzler and the army commanders had been realised. Some 250,000 troops were isolated in 'Fortress Stalingrad'.

Hitler's decision to keep the 6th Army in the city was based on two dubious assumptions: firstly that an operation could be planned to relieve the German forces, and secondly, that the army itself could be effectively maintained by air supply. Zeitzler was not deceived by either assumption and in his daily meetings with Hitler urged, vainly, that the order be given to the 6th Army to carry out a fighting withdrawal.

Despite the bombastic assurances of *Reichsmarschall* Goering, the air-supply failed. The required tonnages of supplies to meet the needs of 250,000 men could not be delivered. Meanwhile, Manstein was appointed to the command of Army Group 'Don' with orders to co-ordinate the counterattack for the relief of Stalingrad with General Hoth and the 4th *Panzerarmee*. Manstein, like Zeitzler, protested vigorously to Hitler that the 6th Army should break out to meet his own relief army and form a new front further to the west. But Hitler remained adamant and stuck to his original scheme for the relief of the 'fortress'.

The attack commenced on 12 December. By the 21st, Hoth's troops were only 30 miles from Stalingrad. But here, the offensive ground to a halt as the exhausted 4th *Panzerarmee* met an unbreachable Russian front. The very last chance of saving the 6th Army had vanished.

Manstein and Zeitzler once again did all that was possible to convince Hitler that he should sign the directive to break out. Zeitzler in particular spent several hours every night trying to make the *Fuehrer* see reason, but to no avail. However, on 26 December, Paulus reported that the cold weather, hunger and the large number of casualties meant that his army could not break out unless a supply corridor was opened. By now this was also impossible.

At the beginning of the new year, the 6th Army was starved and exhausted. Relief supplies were totally inadequate. The final Soviet offensive aimed at destroying the 'fortress' began on 10 January after General Paulus, on the orders of Hitler, had rejected a Russian ultimatum to surrender. After suffering fierce bombardment, Paulus sent a message on 20 January stating that he could not hold Stalingrad for more than a few days. The tragedy was drawing to its close. On 24 January, the Russians again demanded surrender. Zeitzler, despite presenting Hitler with the cold facts of the numbers of dead and wounded, could not persuade him to order a capitulation. Paulus was to continue.

■ Stalingrad falls

On 28 January, the 6th Army commander stopped issuing rations to the wounded in order to maintain the troops still capable of fighting. The final collapse came early on 2 February when the remnants of XI Corps surrendered.

The horrific battle had ended. But it is easy to imagine a much less fateful finale had the 6th Army been allowed to withdraw its 20 divisions from Stalingrad, as advised by Manstein and Zeitzler. The colossal defeat was due more to Hitler's incompetence and refusal to listen to reason than to Russian tactical awareness.

The chances of Zeitzler significantly influencing the course of the war in the West were never very great. Hitler probably wanted a man who would be subservient and unquestioning. With that aim, he appointed Zeitzler, a very junior general, to a very senior position, which had the effect of down-grading the post to an executive level. As a result, Hitler gained tighter control of the command apparatus of the army.

Zeitzler was also handicapped in the early stages by a lack of knowledge of the situation in the East. But he quickly mastered his subject and refused blindly to follow the whims of the *Fuehrer*. Hitler's aim for an acquiescent chief-of-staff did not materialise – instead he ignored Zeitzler's advice.

So Zeitzler' rôle in the Stalingrad débâcle was not one noted for its conspicuous success or great achievements. Although he had ability, worked with great energy, fought hard in the defence of his opinions and was not afraid to stand up to Hitler, he did not wield inordinate influence through his staff office. He was unable to persuade the *Fuehrer* to change his attitude over Stalingrad, but on the other hand, it is unlikely that any man could have done so. Russian victory was facilitated by Hitler's obstinate policy of 'fortress-building' – a policy which Zeitzler could not reverse. During the course of his appointment he offered his resignation five times and on each occasion it was refused. He was finally dismissed in July 1944 after the plot to assassinate Hitler.

ANALYSIS – HITLER AND HIS HIGH COMMAND

The rôle in which Adolf Hitler always fancied himself most was that of supreme commander and omniscient warlord, a fact that bedevilled the professional officers at the head of the German army throughout the short life of the 'Thousand-Year Reich'. As an embittered ex-infantryman from the trenches of World War I, Hitler retained a lasting contempt for 'these stuffed-shirt gentlemen in their red-striped trousers', as he called the generals. Nevertheless he needed them to fight his wars for him. For their part, the generals were not averse to fighting a war, but they wanted to do it their way – and this Hitler never tolerated. In the beginning, of course, he had a very good argument in his favour: every time the generals had prophesied disaster between 1935 and 1939, Hitler had been right and they wrong. The *Fuehrer* found it very convenient to give his generals an inferiority complex about their real abilities and thus get them to try all the harder to prove their worth. But this discounting of professional ability, although justified in the short run, led him to disaster in the end.

The war opened with a lopsided chain of command. At the top, commanding the operations of all three arms, was OKW, presided over by Hitler with the obsequious Keitel and Jodl as his chief executives. The army case was pleaded by the C-in-C, Brauchitsch, and the Chief-of-Staff, Halder, the service chiefs of OKH.

The Polish campaign of September 1939 went smoothly enough, but the real troubled started when Hitler subsequently told OKH that he wanted to attack in the West that November. Brauchitsch failed completely to get an assurance from Hitler that OKH would be allowed to direct land operations in future campaigns. They fell back on delaying tactics for the Western campaign, obstructing Manstein's suggestions for a concentrated drive through the Ardennes. They knew that this campaign would almost certainly win the war and they did not want it launched prematurely.

■ Great annoyance

Hence their fury when Hitler sprang the news of the Scandinavian campaign on them. This was planned rapidly and secretly, with neither the army nor the *Luftwaffe* being informed. Although the army added to its laurels with its speedy victory in Denmark and Norway, it did the army leaders little good in the long run, confirming Hitler's belief that he was a natural general.

The campaign in the West of May–June 1940 proved that neither OKH nor OKW had fully grasped the tactical truth that armour, having broken through, must not wait for the infantry to close up before pushing on. OKH ordered such a halt after Guderian's brilliant crossing of the Meuse; Hitler, on the other hand, temporarily lost his nerve and 'raged and screamed' about a non-existent French threat to the southern flank of the 'Panzer corridor'. Neither lapse was serious because Guderian, the Panzer commander on the spot, ignored the restrictive orders he got from his superiors and drove through to the Channel anyway. Then came Dunkirk. Who was right? There were two logics behind the decision to halt the armour on 24 May. The decisive battle against the French army certainly still had to be fought; on the other hand, the victory in Flanders would be a hollow one if the British army escaped. The resulting compromise allowed the British to escape but did not save the French army. Brauchitsch's order for Rundstedt rather than Bock to administer the hammerblow at Dunkirk had been the correct one as far as the envisaged destruction of the encircled British was concerned.

It was after the battle of France that the total failure of OKW to plan ahead stood revealed, for no detailed plans to invade and conquer Britain had been prepared. This, the ultimate in all-forces operations, was an astonishing oversight. It was easy enough for OKH to do their part: all Halder had to do was to insist on having the assault troops land on as wide a front as possible, as Montgomery did when he saw the first tentative plans for the invasion of Normandy in 1944. The fact that the navy and *Luftwaffe* could not guarantee an unopposed passage was not the army's fault. What was amazing was the speed in which Operation 'Sealion', the final invasion plan, came into being in July and August. It showed what Hitler's military experts could do when they had to.

Now came the awesome revelation that the next victim would be Soviet Russia – and for this, the decisive land operation of the war, OKH gave its full and detailed attention. But the operative word was detailed. Operation '*Barbarossa*' was an open-ended lunge into the void, with no definitive halt-line, relying entirely on the destruction of the Red Army in the initial battles. Brauchitsch and Halder set their team of planners to work on the details of maintaining the advance with their eyes, as ever, fixed on the short-term problems. It was all that they could do in any case. Hitler simply refused to believe such army warnings that the Red Army was armed with a tank superior to the battle-tested Panzers of the German army.

Against this background, the refusal of OKH and OKW to concentrate on North

Africa after Rommel's bewildering first success against the British was hardly surprising. Nor, in view of the Russians' winter counterattack and the near-total collapse of the Eastern Front, was it any more surprising that Rommel got little attention until the summer of 1942. By that time, what remained of the withered authority of OKH had vanished. Hitler had assumed personal command of the army during the Moscow counter-offensive and had overridden all advice from his generals to retreat – a decision which events proved entirely correct. Brauchitsch went; Halder stayed on as chief-of-staff until Hitler replaced him with Zeitzler in September 1942. This was the final turning-point in the day-by-day conduct of the German war effort on land. Down to the battle of Moscow the campaign had been conducted largely in the old style, with OKH carrying out orders from OKW. From Zeitzler's appointment onwards, the army chief-of-staff got his orders at daily conferences at OKW. Zeitzler lasted until July 1944, when he was replaced by Guderian, the one man in the German army, perhaps, who was never afraid to bellow back at Hitler when the *Fuehrer* went into one of his rages. Hitler never did get what he wanted as chief of the army general staff – a yes-man who did not tell him unpleasant truths – until General Krebs took over from Guderian at the close of March 1945, when the war was lost.

■ No central command

With Hitler determined to run the war himself, and totally unpredictable as to when he was prepared to listen to reason, it is hard to see how the staff generals in the army and *Wehrmacht* high commands could have done a proper job. Keitel, Jodl and Krebs were certainly pliant toadies, but they were professionals; and they, too, often felt the rough edge of Hitler's tongue for that very reason. Hitler's obsessive belief that all staff generals were hidebound fogies never weakened, although his sanity and his grip on reality did. The whole story, in fact, might very well be summed up as the struggle of the professionals to do their job. They were certainly capable enough, yet constantly reduced to impotence. What, for example, was the value of the excellent work done by General Gehlen's intelligence staff, when Hitler refused to believe the real figures of the Red Army's strength right from the beginning of the campaign in Russia?

The one thing Hitler could never bring himself to do was to scrap the former system of an independent army command and centralise the whole *Wehrmacht* command set-up. At the very least this would have accelerated the flow of orders. But another of the 'unpleasant things' which he could never bear to accept was that he was not '*der groesster Feldherr aller Zeiten*' – 'the greatest commander of all time'. He needed his staff generals to do the work for him – but the only leeway he would allow them was the short-term resolution of details. At the top of the pyramid, the leadership of the German war machine was carried out in a stifling atmosphere caused by the reaction of megalomania against professionalism. The real victims were the commanders and troops in the field.

GERMAN GENERALSHIP IN WORLD WAR II

For an overall assessment of the standard of German generalship between 1939 and 1945, it is necessary to grasp the fact that right down to the autumn of 1941 the men of the German army and their commanders were learning the technique of modern mechanised warfare. This considerable period – from the invasion of Poland to the commencement of the giant pincer movement of Kiev – taught many lessons which could be learned in no other way by the generals in the field.

The question 'Who was the best German general of World War II?' is a meaningless one, and the only possibly reply is 'Best at what?' The basic building-block of the German army, as with every other, was the division. Above that came the corps, above that the army, and above that the army group. All these levels were commanded by generals and a further basic distinction must be made between infantry and armoured troops, the command of which required very different qualities.

The Panzer tactics as brought to perfection by the German army in World War II were the vital ingredient of success. Two names automatically stand out as brilliant Panzer divisional commanders: Rommel, for his superb performance with the 7th Panzer Division in the Western campaign of 1940; and General Hermann Balck, a veteran Panzer general who served on all fronts apart from North Africa and Italy, eventually rising to the command of Army Group 'G' in the West. Perhaps Balck's finest hour was his counterattack with the 11th Panzer Division in the winter of 1942–43, after the Soviet encirclement of the 6th Army at Stalingrad, when his division broke the Soviet drive towards Rostov.

■ Corps commanders

Moving up the chain of command to the level of Panzer corps commander, it is easy to pick out Guderian, Kleist, Reinhardt and Hoepner, all of whom rose to higher commands. It is almost certainly true to state that Rommel's true operational 'ceiling' was that of a Panzer corps commander, a rôle in which he could still exercise his brilliance as a front-line leader. In addition, Rommel was well served in Africa by a series of able commanders for the *Afrika Korps*, the most famous Panzer corps of World War II. These included Cruewell, Nehring and Bayerlein.

In the first two years of the war, the Panzer divisions went into action as *Panzergruppen* (Panzer Groups), upgraded to the status of *Panzerarmee* (Panzer Army) in the winter of 1941. As a *Panzergruppe* commander, Rommel's record was patchy. He got himself defeated in his first set-piece battle in the 'Crusader' fighting of November–December 1941, bounced back brilliantly to recover Benghazi in January 1942, and won his greatest victory at Gazala and Tobruk in May. He then failed to keep the initiative at El Alamein and was forced to fight against hopeless odds there in October and November. His withdrawal of the survivors of *Panzerarmee Afrika* to Mareth was masterly, and so was the strategy behind his attack at Kasserine in February 1943. Both of the latter two operations, however, were fought with considerably depleted forces and were offset by his resounding defeat at Medenine on 6 March 1943.

By contrast, there was genuine brilliance behind the partnership of Hoth and Guderian during the invasion of Russia, with Hoth going on from strength to strength with the 4th *Panzerarmee* whilst Guderian went into the eclipse of temporary disgrace. Kleist, too, did well with the 1st *Panzerarmee*, most notably in the spectacular advances across the Kuban steppe in 1942.

The infantry were the unsung heroes of the German army in World War II, and their story is summed up by General Heinrici, an unglamorous master of defensive infantry tactics who rose to army command and was entrusted with the thankless job of defending the Oder front in March–April 1945. The top infantry generals at the close of World War II had one thing in common: they had spent years of trying to do the impossible in Russia, holding out against impossible odds when any defence seemed out of the question. One of the most notable defensive feats occurred during the Soviet winter offensive of 1941–42, when 100,000 men of II Corps, 16th Army, commanded by General Graf von Brockdorff-Ahlefeldt, survived complete encirclement from 8 February to 21 April. Further to the south, a combat group under Major General Scherer, around 5,000 strong, held out from 28 January to 5 May, by which date Scherer's effective combat strength was down to 1,200 men.

The name which always hit the headlines were those of the army group commanders, and of these it is fair to say that the most able men did get to the top in the end. These were the dour, hard-core professionals whom Hitler could never really do without – men like Bock, Leeb and Rundstedt, Busch and Kuechler, Weichs and List. For sheer longevity – not to mention the number of times Hitler sacked and reinstated him – the prize must go to Rundstedt. But two army group commanders stand out above the rest: Manstein and Kesselring.

A sound Panzer corps commander in his own right, as he proved with Army Group 'North' during the opening stages of 'Barbarossa', Manstein was the man who had originated the revolutionary 'Sickle' plan which sliced open the Allied front in the West. As an army commander in the Crimea, he earned his field-marshal's baton by taking Sevastopol in July 1942. But his chief claim to fame was the discovery of the only form of strategy which gave the German army a chance in Russia: yielding the initiative to the Red Army and then slicing decisively at the tentacles that broke through the German front. His finest hour was certainly the retrieval of the near-catastrophic situation created by the Stalingrad breakthrough in the winter of 1942–43, when he not only halted the German retreat but launched a breath-taking counter-offensive which was halted only by the spring mud. All his gains were then jeopardised, despite his pleadings, by the ill-advised offensive against the Kursk salient in July 1943. In 1940 the adoption of Manstein's thinking had led to one of the greatest victories in German history. Had his strategy for the Eastern Front been adopted, the German army would almost certainly have been able to hold its gains in Russia west of the Dniepr river line.

Kesselring was unique in that he was the only *Luftwaffe* general who was entrusted with extensive land operations. Down to the end of 1941 he had been commanding his *Luftflotte* (Air Fleet) in support of army groups. His rôle in the Mediterranean started as air commander and chief supply officer to support Rommel in Africa. In this capacity he was able to secure Tunisia for Rommel's retreat, and build up a complete army there in the winter of 1942–43. He refused to throw away German troops in a futile defence of Sicily; and his success in defending southern and central Italy kept the Allies out of the Po valley for 19 months. Kesselring's war ended in chaos: Hitler pulled him out of Italy and made him Commander-in-Chief West, when the Allied rampage across western Germany had already broken loose. But he had certainly earned full respect for his initiative and flexibility in apparently desperate situations.

Model was another remarkable army group commander in that he was one of the few generals whom Hitler trusted. his nickname was 'the *Fuehrer's* fireman' because of the number of appalling situations, from the battle of Moscow onwards, which he managed to retrieve. A typical case was the speed with which he reacted to Operation 'Market Garden', the airborne attack on Arnhem, in September 1944. Model's end was sad: trapped in the vast Ruhr pocket in April 1945, he shot himself rather than surrender.

Against all this professionalism, however, there were many cases where key field appointments were placed disastrously in the wrong hands. Perhaps the most notorious had to be Paulus, the commander of the 6th Army, who surrendered at Stalingrad. Paulus had proved himself a capable staff officer and his spell of field command was only intended as a prelude to an even more senior staff command. His appointment to the 6th Army for the Stalingrad offensive gave him the strongest command on the Eastern Front, which he thoroughly misused. Paulus was by no means the only general in modern warfare to be foxed by the problem of taking a city street by street, but he had plenty of capable subordinate commanders who told him where he was going wrong. He may also be excused for taking at face value the promise that the encircled 6th Army would be adequately supplied. But nothing can excuse his shilly-shallying, his refusal to accept that the 6th Army was not going to get the supplies so lavishly promised, and not making the decision to fight his way out before it was too late. Desperately, Hitler made Paulus a field-marshal, clinging to the historic fact that no German field-marshal had ever surrendered; but Paulus made his inevitable capitulation within 48 hours of his last promotion.

Nazi court politics were responsible for the most disastrous – not to say ludicrous – appointment of the war: *Reichsfuehrer*-SS Henrich Himmler to command the optimistically-named Army Group 'Vistula' holding the Oder front in March 1945. Himmler was totally unfitted for military command on all counts, and his mismanagement of the front was retrieved in the nick of time only by Heinrici with a brave but doomed defence on the Oder when Zhukov and Konev attacked on 16 April.

Mention must also be made of the youngest and most specialised army of the *Wehrmacht*: the airborne forces. These forces, whether landed by transport plane or glider, or dropped by parachute, ended the war with an impressive record of aggressive dash. In General Kurt Student (who also collaborated with Model to win the battle of Arnhem) the German airborne arm had a decisive and forceful leader who understood his job and did it well. Outstanding among the divisional commanders of the airborne arm was General Heidrich, whose paratroops did so well in the long defence of Monte Cassino. And another general of the highest calibre was the German army's top mountain-warfare specialist, Colonel-General Dietl, victor at Narvik in 1940. Dietl spent his war well out of the limelight, commanding the German troops in the Far North. This was a decided oversight on the part of OKW. Dietl's talents would have been put to far better uses in the Caucasus or in Tunisia, while Kesselring would have found him invaluable in Italy.

Napoleon was wont to complain that having raised his marshals to the peak of their profession they were more concerned with their new-found riches than with serving the French Empire. In general, Hitler could not have levelled this accusation against his generals in World War II but there was certainly one glaring exception: Field-Marshal von Kluge, a sound enough army commander who rose to army group command. A touchy and pompous man, Kluge was not above accepting substantial monetary rewards from Hitler – a fact which the members of the anti-Hitler conspirators on his staff used to jog his conscience as they tried unsuccessfully to get Kluge to help them. After the failure of the 'July Plot' of 1944, Kluge committed suicide after penning a note, protesting his loyalty, to Hitler. By this time he had already fallen from favour because of his inability to check the Allied break-out from

Normandy, and he knew full well that the Gestapo would be on his trail once they started rounding up others in the conspiracy. A strange, complex man, Kluge stands apart from the other generals who secretly favoured the idea of getting rid of Hitler but refused to act against the *Fuehrer*.

■ Hitler's rage

All the names mentioned above, and every single general on the active list right down to divisional level, knew that they all had one thing in common. None of them was exempt from the nerve-cracking insults with which Hitler constantly belaboured the German officer corps. This could take the form of a face-to-face screaming-match, a contemptuous dressing-down, or even dismissal by telegram. There were no exceptions.

Another devastating weapon which Hitler used against his generals without any scruple was his fantastic memory. This gift extended to the most remote levels. If a general protested that such-and-such a task was impossible, Hitler would retort by asking him what his shell stocks or fuel supplies were – something detailed, which any general would normally leave to his staff to worry about. Hitler would then produce the actual figure out of his memory and usually, by the implication that the general was not up to his job, get his way.

In general, Hitler's generals tried hard to serve their country well and loyally. This caused constant trouble for the anti-Hitler conspirators, who knew that they would stand no chance without the backing of the field commanders. Most generals genuinely believed that it would be disloyal to act against Hitler, not so much because of the 1934 oath of loyalty but because the enemies of Germany were still in arms – and, after the Casablanca Conference of January 1943, holding out for 'unconditional surrender'. Thus Hitler's sneers and contemptuous insinuations that the army did not want to fight, and that the generals were a pack of contemptible cowards, were particularly unfounded. 'Loyalty up' from the generals to Hitler therefore left little that could be desired; but the fate of Rommel showed how even a general who was a national hero could be driven to his death by the *Fuehrer*.

Rommel was no Nazi; before the war he had had to give up the job of supervising the military training of the Hitler Youth because of his inability to work with the Hitler Youth leader, the arrogant and foolish Baldur von Schirach. But when war came he served his country well. During the Polish campaign he commanded Hitler's bodyguard, and then moved on to command the 7th Panzer Division (an interesting commentary, incidentally, on Panzer appointments in the early months of the war, since Rommel's World War I experience had been with the infantry). By July 1942, newly-promoted Field-Marshal, he could do no wrong in Hitler's eyes. No wrong, that is, until he tried to point out the hopeless case of the *Panzerarmee* at El Alamein. Hitler sent Rommel a 'stand fast' order concluding: 'As to your troops, you can show them no other road than that to victory or death.' After the initial shock of this callous blow, Rommel then experienced 18 months of increasing disillusionment which did not prevent him giving his all, and suffering a near-fatal wound, in the fruitless defence of Normandy. Implicated in the 'July Plot', Rommel was brought Hitler's offer of honourable suicide and a state funeral rather than a public trial by two brother generals, Burgdorf and Maisl. He chose to take poison. It was announced that he had died of the wounds suffered in Normandy.

A famous axiom of generalship holds that 'no commander can be considered a great general who has not had to conduct a dangerous retreat'. The turning of the tide certainly gave Hitler's generals plenty of opportunity to display their skill in that direction after 1942. Rommel's retreat from El Alamein to Mareth remains a classic; so does Kesselring's steady withdrawal up the Italian peninsula. But Hitler tended to give his generals little or no chance to act correctly in the face of hopeless situations. Carried away by the success of his 'stand fast' order during the battle of Moscow, which alone kept the Eastern Front in being, he tended more and more to the hysterical belief that the panacea for avoiding defeat was never to retreat. Thus in November 1941 he sacked Rundstedt for pulling out of Rostov to the Mius river line and replaced him with Bock, who promptly completed the withdrawal. The 18 surviving divisions of Army Group 'North', retreating through the Baltic States on their long retreat from Leningrad, were badly needed on the Oder front; Hitler refused to bring them out by sea when they got cut off in Kurland. The most latitude he ever allowed was to the favoured few such as Model or Manstein on their sudden appointment to 'disaster fronts' – sectors which would never have been in such a serious state if Hitler had let the original commanders use their initiative. Hundreds of thousands of irreplaceable troops were thrown away between the summer of 1943 and the end of the war, hopelessly cut off in surrounded pockets or what Hitler loved to call 'fortress' positions (the latter being towns which Hitler could not bear the thought of losing without a fight).

How did Hitler's generals, gifted as they were in their individual ways, work as a team? Personality had a lot to do with it. Lasting enmities were made by the friction of the early campaigns between the Panzer generals, who chafed at being tied to the infantry, and the infantry generals, who resented being left to do all the heavy fighting while the Panzers dashed on into the blue. The enmity between Guderian and Kluge was a case in point. Kluge's abrasive personality also offended Rommel in the summer of 1944 when the former took over as C-in-C West, fresh from Russia, and breezed into the latter's HQ in the middle of the battle of Normandy saying that now Rommel would have to get used to taking orders. But Kluge was, as we have seen, an exceptionally complex character. In general the system worked well enough. The top generals – Manstein, Model, Rundstedt and Kesselring – never had any trouble in holding the professional respect and loyalty of their subordinates. And all field commanders had a common bond of sympathetic loyalty against the toadies at OKW, which also helped.

In the last analysis it is safe to say that the combined armies of Great Britain, the British Dominions and Empire, the United States and the Soviet Union put together failed to produce so rich a crop of highly talented generals as boasted by the German army alone. The achievements of Hitler's generals in the field were formidable enough. That they managed to achieve anything in the face of Hitler's megalomania was positively astonishing.

PART 3
HITLER'S LUFTWAFFE

A PHOENIX FROM THE ASHES

■ The reconstitution of the German Air Force, 1920–32

The economic bankruptcy to which the might of Imperial Germany was reduced over four years of bloody fighting forced her to sue for peace and to accept cruel Armistice terms signed in November 1918. Within the borders of Germany, the political and social structures were in ruins; her population subsisted at starvation level, yet the armed might of her Army, Navy and Flying Corps was still considerable, notwithstanding the low morale of her fighting men. The rapidity with which World War I came to an end was a prime reason for the ineptitude subsequently displayed by the victorious Allies when it came to convening an international body to decide the future of Germany. Born of the spirit of vindictiveness and war-weariness, the Treaty of Versailles, signed in June 1919, was aimed at the total dismemberment of Germany's economic and military powers.

The Treaty of Versailles contained Air Clauses intended to end military aviation in Germany and preclude resurrection of the German Flying Corps. Under the supervision of an Allied Control Commission, Germany was obliged, in 1920, to surrender all aeronautical material to the governments of the Allied and associated powers. At the end of World War I Germany had possessed approximately 20,000 military aircraft, of which some 2,400 were bomber, fighter and reconnaissance aircraft with front-line combat units. In accordance with the Treaty, over 15,000 aircraft and 27,000 aero engines were surrendered. So far the Treaty was effective. The Achilles Heal of the Treaty with regards to aviation matters, however, lay in the exclusion of any long-term clause prohibiting manufacture and mass production of civil aircraft. Such was the state of infancy of civil aviation in 1919 that the Allies overlooked its potential importance. It is true that, by 1922, there were some limitations on the actual size of civil aircraft that could be built, but the Paris Air Agreement of 1926 withdrew even these restrictions.

The Germans seized upon the opportunity proffered by this lack of restriction for expansion in the civil sphere, and began an unprecedented expansion of commercial aviation; airlines, flying clubs and aviation training establishments. The design and development of new aircraft, and the training of pilots and crews now went ahead virtually unhindered. Under this mantle of pacific respectability the foundations of the new German Air Force were clandestinely laid.

The widespread subsequent belief that Adolf Hitler and Hermann Göring were the founders of the new German Air Force had no basis in fact. As early as 1920 General Hans von Seeckt, then Chief of the Army Command at the Defence Ministry, was convinced that military aviation would some day be revived in Germany. To this end he secreted a small group of regular officers, in the sections of his ministry clandestinely dealing wholly and exclusively with aviation affairs. The fact that some of these officers, notably Felmy, Sperrle, Wever, Kesslering and Stumpff, became high-ranking commanders in the Luftwaffe was to reveal clearly von Seeckt's foresight and the profound mistake on the part of the victors of the 1914–18 war in allowing this military nucleus to be maintained in Germany. Once the statutory six-month standstill expired following the signing of the Treaty of Versailles, German aircraft manufacturers resumed operations. Tempo was slow at first, being dictated by the stagnant economic situation then prevailing, but natural commercial enterprise rather than leanings of a quasi-militaristic nature soon raised momentum. Germany was not short of brilliant and energetic aircraft designers and engineers.

Early in 1920, Professor Hugo Junkers formed an aircraft company at Dessau producing the Junkers F 13 all-metal transport. Later this concern, named the Junkers Flugzeug und Motorenwerk, was to expand into one of Germany's largest aircraft and aero engine manufacturers, with branches at Aschersleben, Bernburg, Halberstadt and Leopoldshall. In 1922, Ernst Heinkel formed his company at Warnemünde, on the Baltic coast, and in that same year Dr. Ing. Claudius Dornier formed his company from the old Zeppelin-Werke Lindau at Friedrichshafen. Two years later, Heinrich Focke and Georg Wulf founded the Focke-Wulf Flugzeugbau at Bremen and, in 1926, the Bayerische Flugzeugwerke was founded at Augsburg from the remnants of the Udet-Flugzeugbau. This concern, eventually to be led by Professor Willy Messerschmitt, was to change its name to that of Messerschmitt A.G. in 1938.

By 1926, when the Paris Air Agreement loosened the last fetters that bound the German aircraft industry, the firms of Junkers, Heinkel, Focke-Wulf and Messerschmitt, along with several others, were keeping pace with the rest of the world, both in terms of quantitative production and technical development. But, hand in hand with the production of airframes and aero engines, ostensibly for civil application, went training and organisation of manpower; tasks achieved through the medium of civil airline companies and numerous flying and gliding clubs.

Two small air transport companies had been operating in Germany from 1920 onwards. In 1924, General von Seeckt had made the astute move of securing the appointment of his nominee, a Captain Brandenburg from the old German Flying Corps, as head of the Civil Aviation Department of the Ministry of Transport. Co-operation between this department and von Seeckt's Defence Ministry was thus assured, and thenceforward the development of civil aviation came under clandestine military control. When the State airline, the Deutsche Lufthansa, was formed in 1926, one more stage in the growth of the new German Air Force had been reached. Lufthansa proceeded to encourage construction of large airfields. It began to exercise considerable influence in the aircraft industry itself, simultaneously experimenting with and improving flying instrumentation and radio aids to navigation. Under its Chairman, Erhard Milch, Lufthansa rapidly became the best equipped and operated airline in Europe, with its experienced pilots, navigators and crews later to provide the nucleus of the training organisation of the embryonic Luftwaffe.

In addition to Lufthansa, Germany could call upon the membership of its main air society, the Deutscher Luftsportverband, for her future aircrews. Within ten years of its foundation in 1920, this society had a membership of over 50,000. The source of this encouragement in gliding and sports flying came from Seeckt's Defence Ministry which saw this as another way to circumvent the strangleholds of the Versailles Treaty. By 1926, the Luftsportverband was already returning rich dividends; while the rest of Europe slept, Germany was becoming the most air-minded nation on earth.

A complication was provided by a clause in the 1926 Paris Air Agreement that severely limited the number of German service personnel allowed to fly. Von Seeckt, however, evaded such restrictions, drawing his nucleus of military aircrews primarily from Lufthansa, wherein they were perforce obliged to operate as ordinary airline crews, but through a clandestine agreement with the Soviet Union he was also able to send service personnel to Lipetz. This was a military flying training centre for German officers which had been established under a blanket of secrecy.

Such were the foundations in men and machines on which the Germans were able to build up their new Air Force. That they were able to do so with such rapidity was due to the short-sightedness of the Versailles Treaty and to the energy and skill of a few regular officers. The advent in power of Adolf Hitler and the Nazi party in 1933 merely provided the political background for which the regular officers had been waiting; they were glad to become fellow-travellers of the Nazis and thus further their aeronautical aspirations.

■ **From the creation of the Third Reich to the outbreak of war, 1933–9**
The disillusion and discontent fostered by world economic depression proffered a rich harvest for Adolf Hitler and his Nazi Party (NSDAP); Germany could only survive

through renewed vigour in industry and commerce and the Nazis seemed to offer the panacea. In July 1932, a general election in Germany returned the NSDAP as the strongest single party in the Reichstag, so that Hitler became Chancellor on 30 January in the following year. For the armed services the first change occurred in 1934, when conscription was introduced and the title of Defence Minister was change to Minister of War and Commander-in-Chief of the Armed Forces – perhaps two of the first tangible pieces of evidence of the new aggressive military thinking within Germany.

In August 1934, von Hindenburg, the old Chancellor, died and Hitler thus gained complete control of Germany. Henceforward the oath of allegiance to the law and people of Germany, taken by men entering the new Armed Forces, was to be made to Hitler personally. Hitler still remained in the background in military matters, however, and it was not until February 1938 that he assumed the title and powers of Supreme Commander. His Chief of the High Command (Oberkommando der Wehrmacht – OKW), von Blomberg, was dismissed and his place taken by General Keitel who was to hold the post until the German surrender in May 1945.

The support given to Hitler early in his career stood Hermann Göring in good stead. He had served in World War I as a pilot, finally commanding in the prestigious 'Richthofen Jagdgeschwader', although his career had not been outstandingly auspicious. When, in 1933, Hitler came to power, he saw in Göring his perfect collaborator and a man to whom was attached enough of the glory of the by now almost legendary 'Richthofen days' to appeal to the popular imagination. Honours and high administrative posts were showered upon Göring and, in April 1933, he became the Air Minister. His deputy was Erhard Milch who accepted the post while still retaining his Chairmanship of Lufthansa, and it was Milch, by reason of Göring's preoccupation with politics, who found himself virtually head of the Air Ministry.

Under Milch's able direction, Lufthansa was enlarged while at the same time the aircraft industry underwent expansion. By 1933, the aircraft industry had for long been experimenting with specifically military types, some being built in relatively limited quantities; in 1934 new types began to appear in really substantial numbers, including the Heinkel He 51 biplane fighter with two 7.9-mm machine guns and a top speed of 210mph (338km/h), comparing with the best fighters extant. Reconnaissance types included the Heinkel He 45 and He 46 with speeds of the order of 150mph (242km/h). Main emphasis at this time, however, was upon trainers, such as the Arado Ar 66 and Focke-Wulf Fw 44, and the trimotor Junkers Ju 52/3m, being produced for Lufthansa as a transport, was also being manufactured in bomber form, whilst the Ju 86 and He 111 were in their early experimental stages. These were to be delivered to Lufthansa as airliners, but were, in fact, designed from the outset primarily for the bombing rôle.

In the political sphere, Hitler's foreign policy was beginning to assume progressively more aggressive form, and through Göring, Milch was ordered to make preparations to meet possible consequences of this changing policy. Milch was already busily expanding the existing resources of the aircraft industry: locomotive firms such as Henschel, rolling stock manufacturers such as Gotha and ATG, and ship-builders such as Blohm und Voss, were instructed to expand into the production of aircraft and aircraft components. By January 1935, Milch was ready to embark upon a new and ambitious plan for the modernisation and expansion of the Luftwaffe, as the new German Air Force had already come to be known to the more perceptive elsewhere in the world, although *officially* it did not yet exist.

In March 1935, Hitler and Göring felt sufficiently secure to proclaim the existence and true nature of the new Luftwaffe – the air arm of Germany's military forces. Hermann Göring was appointed Commander-in-Chief of the new force, which became an independent part of the Armed Forces subordinated to the Chief of OKW (Oberkommando der Wehrmacht, or High Command of the Armed Forces), General Keitel. Milch, as Secretary of State for Air, was still largely in control of the new Luftwaffe; General Wever was appointed as the first Chief of Air Staff. Other staff posts were given by Göring largely to ex-flying officers and particularly those who had served under him in the old 'Richthofen Jagdgeschwader'. Units that had disguised their existence in flying clubs or as SA units were incorporated into the Luftwaffe as regular squadrons. An Air Staff College was set up and the year also saw the development of an anti-aircraft or Flak arm – which was subordinated to the Luftwaffe – and a Signals Service. In its organisation, the Luftwaffe was divided into four main Regional Groups (Gruppenkommandos), centred at Berlin, Konigsberg, Brunswick and Munich. Administration, supply and maintenance, airfield staffing, certain signals functions, recruiting and training, were all controlled by ten Air Districts.

By the time that its existence was publicly revealed, the Luftwaffe's strength stood at 1,888 aircraft of all types with some 20,000 officers and men. With this considerable nucleus of men and machines, and with the support of between 30 and 40 airframe and engine manufacturers, the new Luftwaffe began to organise itself upon the lines which were to continue up to and after the outbreak of war in 1939. Meanwhile, Milch's long term plans for the expansion and modernisation of the Luftwaffe gained momentum: The first six months of 1935 saw a monthly delivery total of 180–200 aircraft which increased during the latter half of that year to an average of 300 aircraft. The accent on modernisation can be gauged by the fact that the Erprobungsstelle (Test Centre) at Rechlin was completing the service trials of 11 new types in March of 1936. These included the Messerschmitt Bf 109 and Bf 110 fighters, the Junkers Ju 88, Dornier Do 17 and Heinkel He 111 bombers, and the Junkers Ju 87 and Henschel Hs 123 dive-bombers.

Milch had been transferred to the Luftwaffe as a General in 1936, and his undeniable brilliance in the fields of planning and organisation soon aroused Göring's jealousy and enmity. It was not to be long before Milch was to feel the baleful influence of Göring's efforts to have him replaced in the various posts that he held. In June

1936, Ernst Udet, a World War I fighter ace with 62 'kills' to his credit and the doyen of German inter-war aviation circles, became the Director of the all-important Technisches Amt (Technical Office) at the Air Ministry – a position previously held by Milch. Ernst Udet continued to profit at the expense of Milch's waning influence, and, by February 1939, had become the General-Luftzeugmeister of the Luftwaffe – a position that offered him omnipotent influence in the design and production of all Air Force equipment. And in this capacity, Udet – the popular 'fighter pilot's man' – was to prove to be a disaster. He was not alone in his belief in the concept of a short war, possibly lasting as little as eighteen months in which the Luftwaffe's prime rôle would be support of the Army. Two major results of his policy were to be the abandonment of the relatively orthodox long-range strategic bomber designs, such as the Do 19 and Ju 89, in favour of the much longer-term development of the very much more advanced He 177 and a grossly under-estimated rate of aircraft production.

It was the Luftwaffe's involvement in the Spanish Civil War of 1936–39 that was largely instrumental in fostering the belief that the prime rôle of the German Air Force in war was the support of ground forces – to the detriment of all other considerations. Hitler was quick to side with the Nationalist forces of General Franco in the fight against the Republicans: In August 1936, six He 51B fighters and 20 Ju 52/3m transports were despatched to Spain, along with 85 volunteer air and groundcrews. This small force was to expand into a powerful, semi-autonomous air component known as the Legion Condor, led at first by Generalmajor Hugo Sperrle and later by General Wolfram von Richthofen.

The Legion Condor achieved little until the early summer of 1937, when it began to receive the latest Messerschmitt Bf 109B fighters, and Heinkel He 111 and Dornier Do 17 bombers. One event which was to shape future German policy of air strategy occurred at the end of March 1937. In an attack on the northern Republican front, He 51s equipped as fighter-bombers, and each carrying six 10-kg bombs were employed in low-level attack on fortified positions with astonishing success. This attack marked the true beginnings of close-support operations which were to contribute substantially to Germany's lightning military successes of 1939 and 1940. The bombs were released by formations of nine He 51s from a height of 500 feet (152m) and up to seven sorties a day were made. Subsequently, three Staffeln of close-support He 51s were organised and were usually to operate with a Staffel of Bf 109s acting as top-cover. Later in 1937, the Junkers Ju 87A and Henschel Hs 123 dive-bombers made their appearance and close-support operations began to increase in efficacy as more experience was gained. These operations were the work of Wolfram von Richthofen, later to command the formidable Fliegerkorps VIII ground-attack formation, who also developed the close co-operation between ground and air forces by R/T link.

The air fighting over Spain offered front-line combat experience of incalculable value to the Luftwaffe. German pilots and crews receive short tours of duty in Spain before returning to Germany where they were immediately posted to schools and conversion units. Fighter tactics, themselves, underwent a revolution. The orderly, set-piece fighter-formation exploded into a medley of individual pilots, each fighting his own battle as soon as combat was joined with enemy forces: this was now replaced by small highly flexible formations with the accent on tactical manoeuvering rather than neat formation flying. The basic format was the Rotte (pair) consisting of two aircraft, with the leader responsible for attack, navigation and fuel surveillance while his wingman covered his tail at all times; the two aircraft flew sufficiently far apart to enable both pilots to give mutual cross-cover while, at the same time, the No 2 man was close enough to his leader to follow his violent turns, barrel-rolls and loops. The process was enlarged to enable two Rotten to fly together, thus producing the Schwarm. Henceforth, German fighter formations of any strength were separated into individual Schwarme and Rotten. To the untrained eye it may have appeared untidy but in the cut-and-thrust of aerial combat the system worked with deadly effect. Other nations ignored this revolution in fighter tactics to their eventual cost.

Far removed from Spain, the year 1938 began as one of great agitation in Europe. Since 1935 Germany had already gained the Saar through a plebiscite and had marched into the Rhineland. Now she was to annexe Austria and occupy the Sudeten borders of Czechoslovakia. The Spanish Civil War was to reach its climax and the postponement of a war in Europe was to be assured by the agreement between Chamberlain and Hitler at Munich on 29 September. Hitler's political successes in the Saar and the Rhineland confirmed his belief in his own infallibility; the pace was beginning to quicken. The Luftwaffe was gaining in strength and deliveries of new types to the combat units were accelerating.

The Munich agreement of September 1938 gave a breathing space to Europe, though by now a major war was viewed by the knowledgeable as inevitable. The Luftwaffe, itself, was no less relieved at this postponement; it was, in fact, in the middle of a period of transition and was not yet ready for a major war. Full production of the latest aircraft types had still to be attained, but it was anticipated that another year would see substantial improvement in the situation. Indeed one year later, at the end of August 1939, Luftwaffe strength stood at 3,750 aircraft as against 2,928 a year previously. Of this figure 1,270 were twin-engined bombers, mostly He 111s and Do 17s, but with a few of the new Ju 88As which had entered production earlier in the year. Behind this first-line strength there was but a small reserve, varying between 10–25 per cent of the first-line strength according to individual types. Added to this strength and its reserve was the training organisation with between 2,500 and 3,000 training aircraft, as well as some 500 operational type used for conversion training.

German aircraft equipment at this time was in some respects superior to that of potential European opponents. The one and only possible exception, and one which could only be proved by operational usage, was the combat performance of the

Messerschmitt Bf 109E vis-a-vis that of the Supermarine Spitfire Mk. I of the Royal Air Force. Both were to prove outstanding; each was to enjoy certain advantages over the other, but the British warplane was in strictly limited supply. The Kampfgruppen (bomber groups) were equipped mainly with the He 111P and Do 17P-1 and Z-2 twin-engined bombers. The Junkers Ju 88A-1 was just entering service with the Staffeln, while the Heinkel units had begun to receive the latest He 111H-1 bomber which was eventually to supplant the P-version. There was still one Gruppe of the obsolescent Ju 86G bomber which was soon to join other variants of this warplane in transport, training and other second-line rôles. The dive-bomber force was by now equipped with the Ju 87B-1 'Stuka'* which could carry up to 1,500lb (850kg) of external stores. The advantage of this sturdy dive-bomber lay not so much in its speed or range but in its ability to place its bombs with great accuracy.

The single-engined Jagdgruppen (each equivalent to an RAF wing) were now almost totally equipped with the latest marks of the Messerschmitt Bf 109, the E-1 and E-3 versions which carried two Rheinmetall MG FF 20-mm cannon and two MG 17 7.9-mm machine guns. Of Swiss Oerlikon design, the 20-mm cannon was a formidable weapon and its widespread installation in both the Bf 109 and the Bf 110 was a measure of its reliability and efficiency. Whereas the Bf109 was undoubtedly superior to any fighter produced by the Allies, with the exception of the Spitfire, the heavy Bf 110C-1 fighters of the strategic fighter element, the Zerstörergruppen, were unable to match the single-engined fighter in terms of manoeuvrability, lack of appreciation of the significance of this fact in the initial operation of this strategic fighter later costing the Luftwaffe dear. For reconnaissance and army co-operation the Luftwaffe employed the Henschel 126, while the transportation of troops and supplies was mainly the task of a considerable force of Ju 52/3m aircraft.

If its equipment was for the most part superb, so was the quality of the Luftwaffe's aircrew and groundcrew. In the summer of 1939 manpower had increased to 1½ million men (of which nearly two-thirds were Flak** personnel). Göring had done his utmost to ensure that his Luftwaffe was the élite arm of the Wehrmacht. The career structure in the Luftwaffe was an attractive proposition along with all the kudos of belonging to a new service equipped with the most advanced weapons that science and technology could devise; little wonder that the Luftwaffe attracted the cream of German youth to its battalions.

The slide to war now accelerated. In May 1939, Germany and Italy signed the 'Pact of Steel', ostensibly welding Europe's strongest Fascist dictatorships. The summer was preoccupied by the question of Danzig and the Polish corridor, to which Hitler's eyes had now turned. As early as March 1939, Britain and France had announced a joint guarantee to Poland and Rumania to intercede in the event of aggression from outside and, on 25 August, the Anglo-Polish Mutual Assistance Pact

---

*Sturzkampfflugzeug. **Fliegerabwehrkanone.*

further reinforced this guarantee. Two days prior to signing of this last pact, Ribbentrop and Molotov signed a non-aggression pact between Germany and the Soviet Union – a political bombshell that decided the fate of Poland. Hitler could not believe that the Western Powers would go to war over Poland and pressed his demands for a solution to the Danzig question. But to no avail; the Poles remained adamant in their insistence on Polish administration of Danzig. It was enough for Hitler. In the early hours of 1 September 1939, without declaring war, he ordered his armies across the Polish frontier. The following day Chamberlain sent his ultimatum to Hitler: If Germany did not withdraw her troops immediately she must consider herself at war with Britain. On 3 September, Hitler received and ignored the ultimatum, and at 11.00hrs on that day the ultimatum expired. Britain and France were at war with Germany.

THE ONSLAUGHT

■ Poland, 1939

At 04.43 hours on 1 September 1939, high above the Vistula River, three Junkers Ju 87B-1 dive-bombers of 3./StG 1 swung into echelon formation on the hand signal of the leader, Oberleutnant Bruno Dilley. The target, the Dirschau bridge, lay 12,000 feet below, half hidden in the early morning mist as each pilot hurriedly completed his vital actions prior to the plummeting dive. First the pitch control set to 2,250rpm, then the supercharger control to 'automatic'; arm the Lärmgerät (screamer siren) and throttle back to 0.8 Ata boost pressure; close the radiator flaps, deploy the dive-brakes and finally open the small ventilation window.

Dilley was already on his way down, an angular pale blue undersurface surmounted by huge black crosses highlighted by the rising sun, and then he was gone. The other pilots half-rolled and aileron-turned into a near vertical dive, eyes alternating between the red lines painted on windscreen, to check the dive-angle, and the bridge – steadily increasing in size beyond the strobing arc of the propeller. At 3,000 feet, still almost vertical, each Stuka released its bombs and pulled out of the dive, its crew crushed into their seats by the acceleration force of over 5 'g' as the horizon swung down from the canopy roof to hover athwart the gunsight.

Dilley's attack occurred eleven minutes before the might of the Wehrmacht, consisting of eleven Panzer divisions and 40 infantry divisions, poured on to the Polish plains under cover of smoke screens and morning mist, bringing with it a new term, 'Blitzkrieg' (Lightning War), and plunging the world into an agony of chaos that was to last for six years.

The possibility of British and French intervention resulting from the German invasion of Poland forced the Oberkommando der Luftwaffe (OKL) to keep a considerable number of combat units in the West, thus limiting the forces earmarked for the attack; nevertheless the 1,550–1,600 aircraft of Kesselring's Luftflotte 4 and Löhr's Luftflotte 1 were considered sufficient for the task. The Kampfgruppen consisted of KG 2, KG 3, KG 76 and KG 77 with Do 17Z-1, Z-2 and Do 17M-1 types, and LG 1, KG 4, KG 26 and KG 27 with Heinkel He 111P-1 and H-1 types. The Stukagruppen (384 on strength: 300 operational) consisted of IV(Stuka)/LG 1, I/StG 1, II and III/StG 2 and 4.(Stuka)/Trägergruppe 186 under Luftflotte 1, and I/StG 2, III/StG 51, I/StG 76, I and II/StG 77 under Luftflotte 4. The single ground-attack unit, II(Schlacht)/LG 2, operated Henschel Hs 123A biplanes. Escort and support missions were flown by Bf 109B-2s and E-1s of I(Jagd)/LG 2, JGr 101, JGr 102, I/JG 1 and I/JG 21. This list does not include a powerful reconnaissance force.

On the morning of 1 September, fog hampered air operations initially, but after widespread reconnaissance of the main Polish airfields, a massive air strike was mounted with complete surprise against these objectives. At the same time Generaloberst von Bock's Army Group North (III and IV Armies) struck south-east from Pomerania and East Prussia, while von Rundstedt's Army Group South (VIII, X and XIV Armies) thrust eastwards towards Krakow and Lodz. On the first day of the campaign, the Luftwaffe followed its primary task – the widespread destruction both on the ground and in the air of the Polish Air Force. Kattowitz, Krakow, Lodz, Radom, Lublin, Wilna, Lida Grodno and Warsaw airbases were bombed by He 111s and Do 17s, while strafing attacks were made by the Bf 109s. The destruction was total and the obsolete Polish PZL P.7 and P.11c fighters that took to the air stood no chance against the fast Messerschmitts. Only 67 Bf 109s were lost throughout the campaign, and these succumbed mostly to ground fire; of the Ju 87B units, only 31 aircraft were lost to enemy action. By 3 September, the destruction of the Polish Air Force was considered complete and some diversion in direct support of the army was considered feasible.

The impetus of the German advance had left numerous nests of resistance in the rear, and it was to the reduction of these that the diversion of effort was now turned. In this phase the major part was played by the Stukagruppen of Fliegerkorps VIII and II, commanded by Generalmajor Wolfram Fr. von Richthofen and General Bruno Lörzer respectively. The Ju 87s offered direct support to the army by bombing strongpoints, artillery batteries and troop concentrations whenever and wherever the Poles chose to offer resistance. It was here that the legend, however spurious, of the Stuka dive-bomber was born. Operating under conditions of total air superiority the weight and accuracy of its attacks were demoralising and devastating. It was a sturdy close-support dive-bomber, capable of sustaining severe damage and of carrying useful ordnance, and while it operated under fighter cover, it was to be the workhorse of the Blitzkrieg until 1943.

The rapidity with which the objectives of the Polish campaign were achieved staggered even the Germans. By 9 September, the IV Panzer Division had reached the outskirts of Warsaw and a few days later the last Polish counteroffensive on the Buzra river had been halted and turned to rout. On 17 September, the Russians invaded Poland from the East, capturing Lwow a week later. Warsaw still held out, but, on 25 September, the city came under heavy artillery bombardment accompanied by large-scale bombing by the Kampfgruppen; the final assault on Warsaw started and, by 27 September, the city had surrendered. The lightning campaign was over.

The success of the campaign was overwhelming. The contribution of the Luftwaffe had been outstanding, and credence was given to the wildest claims concerning the potentialities of German air power. Later, Albert Kesselring was to write: 'Beyond all other military arms, the Luftwaffe, by virtue of its mobility in space, accomplished tasks which in former times had been inconceivable . . . The Polish campaign was the touchstone of the potentialities of the Luftwaffe and an apprenticeship of special significance. In this campaign the Luftwaffe learned many lessons . . . and prepared itself for a second, more strenuous and decisive clash of arms.'

■ The Scandinavian interlude – Denmark and Norway, 1940

Little operational activity save for reconnaissance took place in the West during the bitterly cold winter of 1939–40, while the Luftwaffe faced the Armée de l'Air and the RAF Advanced Air Striking Force. The air defence of Kriegsmarine naval installations and shipping was efficiently executed by the Jagdgruppen; RAF Bomber Command received an early rebuff to its daylight bombing theories on 18 December 1939, when Bf 109E-1s and Bf 110C-1s of 10.(Nacht)/JG 26, II/JG 77, JGr 101 and I/ZG 76 despatched 12 Wellingtons in the Schillig Roads.

Meanwhile the planning staffs of the Luftwaffengeneralstab were far from idle. The projected campaign for early 1940 called for the invasion of France and an advance to the Channel coast, but first it was essential that Germany's northern flank be secured against possible invasion by the British; the deep-water harbours of Norway were particularly required if an effective offensive was to be mounted against Britain's vital sea communications.

The simultaneous invasion of Denmark and Norway, Operation Weserübung, demanded considerable support from the Luftwaffe. However, in addition to its role of tactical and strategic support, the Luftwaffe was required to provide a large transport force to air-lift paratroops, infantry, supplies and fuel in keeping with the air-sea nature of Weserübung.

Fliegerkorps X, commanded by Generalleutnant Hans Geisler, was earmarked for the Weserübung operations; the prime rôle of this formation was anti-shipping strikes, and its selection for this task was in anticipation of strong intervention by the Royal Navy. The force of 290 He 111H-1s and Ju 88A-1s was drawn from KG 4, KG 26, Kampfgruppe 100 and KG 30, the last-mentioned based at Westerland with 47 Ju 88s. Scant resistance on the ground was anticipated and for this reason only one Gruppe of Ju 87R-1 dive-bombers was assigned, this being the I/StG 1. The fighter force consisted of II/JG 77 with Bf 109E-1s and I/ZG 1 and I/ZG 76 with Bf 110C-1s. The transport force, consisting primarily of 571 Ju 52/3m aircraft, was drawn from KGzbV 1, KGzbV 2, KGzbV 101 to 104, KGzbV 106 and 107, and I, II and III/KGzbV 108(See). In the course of the initial campaign, the Ju 52s were to ferry 29,280 men, 2,376 tons of supplies and 259,300 gallons of aviation and M/T fuel in 3,018 sorties. Reconnaissance was the task of Aufklärungsgruppen 22, 120 and 121, while coastal reconnaissance was provided by Kü.Fl.Gr 106 and 506.

Weserübung demanded the closest possible co-operation between the land, sea and air components, and provided for surprise seaborne and airborne landings at Oslo, Arendal, Kristiansand, Egersund, Stavanger, Bergen, Trondheim and Narvik. At exactly the same time, the occupation of Denmark was to be accomplished by a border crossing by German troops timed to coincide with seaborne landings.

After extensive reconnaissance of Scapa Flow and other Royal Navy bases for two days prior to Weserübung, at 05.00 hours on 9 April 1940, German forces crossed the Danish frontier without a shot being fired. By 08.30hrs, the Bf 110s of I/ZG 1 and I/ZG 76 had completed the virtual neutralisation of the tiny Norwegian Air Force at Oslo-Fornebu and Stavanger-Sola, and the first paratroops had dropped on their allotted objectives from Ju52s. By mid-day transport aircraft were disgorging troops and supplies at Fornebu and Oslo-Kjeller, wherein I/StG 1 and I/ZG 76 were shortly installed, II/JG 77 flying to Kristiansand on the following day. Air opposition from the remnants of the Norwegian Air Force and from the RAF was negligible.

The British landings at Narvik on 15 April resulted in its re-capture, but in the isolated campaign that followed the joint British, French and Norwegian force withdrew on 10 June, effectively bringing to an end the fighting in Norway. During this period FlKps X concentrated its effort on Allied landing points at Narvik, Andalasnes and Namsos, while diverting KG 26 and KG 30 against the Royal Navy. At the peak of the fighting the strength of FlKps X rose to 710 combat aircraft, and on 24 April, this command was subordinated to Luftflotte 5 under Generaloberst Hans-Jurgen Stumpff, with Headquarters at Stavanger.

■ The battle for France, 1940

Three days after Hitler had made a disarming declaration of friendship to Holland and Belgium on 6 October 1939, he issued his secret Directive No. 6 to OKH Generalstabes ordering preparations to begin for an offensive in the West against Holland, Belgium, France and eventually Britain. While stressing that the prerequisite for such an operation would be the securing the northern flank, i.e., Holland and Belgium, he stated that the primary task of the Wehrmacht would be 'to destroy as many French and Allied forces as possible, to overrun the bases necessary for an aerial and naval assault on Great Britain, and to secure the vital Ruhr area'.

The planning of this ambitious programme, code-named 'Fall Gelbe' (Plan Yellow), was the task of Generaloberst Erich von Manstein and his staff at OKH.

After several amendments and alterations, the plan called for the primary offensive in the Sedan-Namur area of the rugged Ardennes, followed by a rapid exploitation to the north. The armies of the French and Gort's British Expeditionary Force were expected to rush into the northern sector and then be effectively cut off by a strong Panzer advance from the Meuse to the Channel coast at Abbeville. Having isolated and surrounded the Allies in the north, the second phase was to consist of an offensive striking southwards from the Somme, coupled with another offensive against the rear of the Maginot Line.

'Fall Gelbe' possessed a considerable element of risk, but by powerful and direct air support by the most concentrated air forces yet employed in war, acting in close co-operation with swiftly advancing columns of armour, the offensive was believed capable of succeeding. As in Poland, the Luftwaffe was required to offer massive and overwhelming support of the ground forces – but on an unprecedented scale.

Luftflotte 2 (Kesselring), with FlKps I and IV subordinated and including the sea-mining Fliegerdivision 9, supported Army Group B under Generaloberst von Bock to the North. Von Rundstedt's Army Group A, in the Ardennes sector, was supported by Luftflotte 3 (Sperrle) consisting of von Richthofen's FlKps VIII and Lörzer's FlKps II. Against the defences of the Maginot Line, to the south, Army Group C was supported by Ritter von Greim's FlKps V, operating under Luftflotte 3 control.

Luftwaffe units ranged in the West for 'Fall Gelbe' consisted of 1,120 bombers, half of which were He 111s, drawn from KG 1, KG 2, KG 3, KG 4, KG 26, KG 27, KG 51, KG 53, KG 54, KG 55, Kampfgruppe 100 and LG 1, KG 76 and KG 77, and the mine-laying unit KGr 126. The Ju 87B-1 and B-2 dive-bombers were concentrated within Fliegerkorps VIII, and consisted of Stab, I, II, III/StG 2 with I/StG 76, and Stab, I, II/StG 77 with IV (Stuka)/LG 1 numbering some 380 aircraft; also within this command was II(Schlacht)/LG 2 with Hs 123As. The single-engined fighter force was drawn from Gruppen of JG 1, JG 2, JG 3, JG 21, JG 26, JG 27, JG 51, JG 52, JG 53 and JG 54 numbering some 860 Bf 109E-1s and E-3s. The Zerstörer Gruppen were I and II/ZG 2, I/ZG 1, I and II/ZG 26 and I(Zerst)/LG 1 with 355 Bf 110C-1s and C-2s. The long- and short-range Aufklärungsgruppen had a total strength of 640 aircraft. For supply and paratroop operations there were 475 Ju 52/3m transports and 45 DFS 230 gliders subordinated to Fliegerkorps zbV (General Putzier), drawn from four Gruppen of KGzbV 1 and four Gruppen of KGzbV2, with KGzbV 101, 104 and 106.

At first light on 10 May 1940, this massive force struck without warning. The attacks on airfields proceeded in what was to become a familiar pattern, with strikes by He 111s and Do 17s on Dutch and Belgian air bases, as well as those of the AASF and the Armée de l'Air. At the same time, the Kampfgruppen ranged deep into enemy territory, striking at rail and transportation centres at Metz, Dijon, Romilly-sur-Seine and Lyon. Following the large-scale dawn attacks on airfields in Belgium and Holland, the first of a series of airborne landings took place after 05.00 hours; not all the troop landings and parachute drops at Dordrecht, Moerdijk and Delft, Waalhaven, Valkenburg and Ockenburg were entirely successful, however, due to stiff resistance, and attrition amongst the Ju 52 transport units was as high as 40 per cent. The glider assaults on the key fortress at Eben Emael and the bridges at Kanne, Veldwezelt and Vroenhoven were carried out with dash and efficiency, the men of Hptm. Koch's I/FJR 1 and Oblt. Witzig's Parachute Engineer Battalion being conveyed to their objectives in DFS 230 gliders of I/Luftlandgeschwader 1 towed by Ju 52s.

By 12 May, Guderian's I and X Panzer Divisionen had pushed their way through the wooded Ardennes country to reach the River Meuse at Sedan, the Army being assisted throughout by day and night reconnaissance by the Luftwaffe that secured a continuous picture of enemy positions, movements and weaknesses. On the following day, the main armoured spearhead of Army Group A debouched across the Meuse, between Charleville and Sedan, and struck West. The Luftwaffe quickly assured air superiority over the entire front, and whenever enemy resistance was encountered Richthofen's FlKps VIII was called in to eliminate opposition. The Stukas inflicted a paralysis on the French and British armies that was a revelation to even the Germans themselves; some Stukagruppen flew up to nine sorties per serviceable aircraft during periods of intensive operations, losing only four Ju 87B-2s on the first four days of the campaign. Once again they were permitted to fly in conditions of total air superiority and thus the legend of the Stuka dive-bomber continued to flourish.

Such was the numerical and technical superiority of the Bf 109E fighter over those of the RAF and the Armée de l'Air that the Allied fighters were never in a position to interfere seriously with the Luftwaffe's tactical operations. By 18 May, the German armoured thrusts in the centre had reached Peronne and Cambrai; two days later Amiens fell and by that evening the leading elements of II PzDiv had reached Abbeville on the Channel coast, splitting the Allied armies in two.

After an unsuccessful Allied counter-attack at Arras, the Germans swung north, up the Channel coast, taking Boulogne and investing Calais by 24 May. At the same time, von Bock's forces in the north had reached Ghent, setting in motion the final stages of a massive pincer movement that was to make the position of the Allied armies untenable. On the evening of 26 May, the first elements of Lord Gort's British Expeditionary Force were evacuated from the beaches at Dunkirk and De Panne, and over the next ten days of the evacuation the Luftwaffe made a determined effort to sink shipping in the Channel and bomb the beleaguered forces on the beaches. The whole weight of Fliegerkorps I, II, IV and VIII was committed to frustrating the evacuation attempt, and for the first time met more resilient air opposition from Air Chief Marshal H. C. T. Dowding's RAF Fighter Command.

It was over Dunkirk that the Messerschmitts first encountered the Spitfire Mk I, flown by resolute and skilful pilots; in combat with this nimble RAF fighter, the

German pilots found that their own aircraft could be out-turned and out-climbed, and for the first time were forced to fly their Bf 109Es to the limits of their performance. While the Jagdgruppen were now operating from airfields close to the Dunkirk sector, the RAF fighter squadrons fought at a distinct disadvantage, far from their bases and beyond the range of effective radar control. The German fighters frequently found themselves engaged in dogfights with Spitfires and Hurricanes so that they missed the rendezvous for the escort of their bomber forces. The bombers suffered considerably in consequence, as also did the Stukas, and Luftwaffe losses over Dunkirk were heavy. For the first time the Luftwaffe had met an opponent of equal fighting capabilities in the air and failed to prevent the Dunkirk evacuation in consequence, this operation being completed at 02.23hrs of 4 June 1940.

Freed of its commitment in the north, the Luftwaffe now turned to support the sporadic fighting which culminated in the German occupation of Paris on 14 June, and by 25 June, the campaign in France was over. The Luftwaffe was now withdrawn for rest and re-fit for the next and expected final phase of the war in the West, the invasion of the British Isles. As yet, however, the Luftwaffe had only had a foretaste of effective and determined fighter opposition, but in the flush of victory neither Göring nor his senior commanders had yet recognised its implications.

THE BATTLE OF BRITAIN

The conclusion of the lightning German campaign in Belgium, the Netherlands and France, on 25 June 1940, left the German General Staff with the enormous task of preparing and executing an invasion of Great Britain within the three months of good weather to be expected before the autumn gales would render such a task impossible. The plan for invasion, code-named 'Seelöwe' (Sealion), had been initiated as early as 1939, but had since suffered serious set-back by disagreement between rival army and naval factions. One aspect, however, was agreed to the effect that it would be better to plan an assault by land forces on the United Kingdom rather than face months, possibly years, in a slow campaign of economic strangulation, with its inevitable attrition, by sea and air forces.

Admiral Raeder, C-in-C of the Kreigsmarine, raised the question of invasion with Hitler on 21 May, but largely because of diplomatic peace moves then being made, it was not until 2 July that the Führer finally ordered preparations for Sealion to be made. The plan appeared simple enough and was a projection of the Blitzkrieg theory that had stood the test so well in Poland and France. The assault would be made across the English Channel and would represent little more than a large-scale river crossing, with the RAF and the Royal Navy engaged and destroyed by the Luftwaffe. Firstly, the plan called for the establishment of a bridgehead in Kent and Sussex; this would be followed by other landings in the west culminating in a drive northwards to the line Gloucester-St Albans-Maldon. Subsequent to this no further serious opposition by the British was expected.

The first condition before such a crossing could take place was the defeat of the Royal Air Force so that the essential prerequisite of German air supremacy would be assured. Thus, the German High Command, in regarding the whole undertaking in the same light as a large-scale crossing of a river such as the Meuse, allotted to the Luftwaffe its normal preliminary task – the neutralisation of enemy air opposition and the destruction of its ground installations.

After the cessation of fighting in France, most Luftwaffe units were withdrawn for rest and refit while preparations for the assault were made within the commands. Both Luftflotte 2 and 3 merely extended their bases into France and took over existing airfields. Their common boundary on the Channel coast, at the estuary of the Seine, was extended northwards through the centre of England so that each was allotted its own sphere of operations. Fliegerkorps I, II and IX were subordinated to Kesselring's Luftflotte 2, while FlKps IV, V and VIII were under Sperrle's Luftflotte 3 to the west. During July 1940, the combat units were gradually deployed to airfields between Hamburg and Brest, and by 17 July, when the order for full readiness was given, the striking force had been built up to its intended strength. The actual strength of the forces controlled by Luftflotte 2 and 3 for the assault on southern England and the Midlands comprised:

Bombers (He 111, Do 17 and Ju 88)	1,200*
Dive-bombers (Ju 87B)	280
Single-engined fighters (Bf 109E)	760
Twin-engined fighters (Bf 110)	220
Long-range Recce (Do 17, Bf 110, Ju 88)	50
Short-range Recce (Hs 126, Do 17, Bf 110)	90
	————
	2,600

In addition to the above, Luftflotte 5, with FlKps X subordinated, retained a force of 130 He 111s and Ju 88s, 30 Bf 110 long-range fighters, and 30 long-range reconnaissance aircraft. While this force played little part in the subsequent fighting, it offered a valuable diversionary rôle, forcing the RAF to retain fighter defences in the north of England.

While this massive strike force was gathering on the airfields in France and Belgium, the intervening weeks before the start of large-scale operations were used by RAF Fighter Command to restore its depleted squadrons and build up its reserves. After the Dunkirk fighting, the position of the Command had been desperate and its operational strength had sunk to the lowest level of 1940, notwithstanding the subsequent Battle of Britain. During the operations covering the Dunkirk evacuation alone, RAF Fighter Command had lost over 100 fighters and 80 pilots killed or missing. This baleful episode had been the culmination of a month's air fighting in which, during the period 10 May-20 June, RAF combat units based in France and Britain

Serviceability on 20 July 1940 stood at 69 per cent of this figure.

had lost 944 aircraft, including 386 Hurricanes and 67 Spitfires. On the morning of 5 June, there were a mere 331 Hurricanes and Spitfires, with a further 36 on immediate reserve, available for operations in RAF Fighter Command. However, these figures were soon to improve as a result of the growing inflow of fighter aircraft from the production lines. Whereas RAF Fighter Command could rely on a steady replacement rate of its aircraft the same could not be said of aircrew; trained pilots were already in short supply and a critical shortage was to come.

While the Spitfire had already demonstrated that it was the equal of the Messerschmitt Bf 109E, the majority of Fighter Command's squadrons were equipped with the Hurricane I. This type had proved inferior to the Bf 109E but was of rugged construction, highly manoeuvrable and destined to be the mainstay of the RAF's strength in the crucial weeks that were to follow. These prime weapons were of limited use without proper fighter control, but due to enlightened thinking during the pre-war years, the RAF had a Ground Controller Interception (GCI) system that was without parallel. The radar stations that were position around the coasts of Britain were backed by a highly efficient system whereby the information was analysed, passed to the controlling stations and, through the medium of a Fighter Controller, relayed via R/T to airborne squadrons. There was to be no element of surprise to the advantage of the enemy and no fuel-wasting standing patrols for the defender, at this point in time the GCI system was untried. It remained to be seen how it would operate in the face of unrelenting enemy air attack by day and night.

Within the compass of Operation Sealion the task of the Luftwaffe as detailed to the respective Luftflotten in the middle of July, was twofold:

(a) The elimination of the RAF, both as a fighting force and in its ground organisation.

(b) The strangulation of the supply of Great Britain by attacks on its ports and shipping.

The elimination of the RAF was to be accomplished in two stages. In the first place, the fighter defences located to the south of a line between London and Gloucester were to be beaten down and, secondly, the Luftwaffe air offensive was to be covered northwards by stages until RAF bases throughout England were covered by daylight bombing attacks. Meanwhile, as part of the plan, a day and night bombing offensive was to be directed against the British aircraft industry.

The all-out offensive to eliminate the RAF and lay waste the British aircraft industry was code-named 'Adlerangriff' (Eagle Attack) and the day of its launching, known as Adler Tag (Eagle Day), was originally fixed for 10 August 1940. German Air Intelligence estimated that four days would be needed to effectively neutralise the RAF fighter defences in the South, with a further four weeks required to eradicate the entire RAF as a fighting entity. With the RAF effectively out of action, it was anticipated that Sealion could go ahead as planned in the first two weeks of September.

After the initial skirmishing over the Channel and South Coast during the first week of July, Luftflotte 2 and 3 were deemed fit to increase the tempo and scale of their operations. Although historically there were no fixed delineations in the various phases of the conflict, it is, however, convenient for reasons of clarity to enumerate the differing objectives to which the Luftwaffe found itself committed in relation to periods in time.

■ Phase 1: Testing of Fighter Command, 10 July–7 August 1940

In order to test the mettle of RAF Fighter Command before commencing the assault, it was decided to launch a limited campaign on the periphery of Fighter Command's sphere of influence rather than a direct confrontation over its own bases. Accordingly Fliegerkorps II (Lörzer), based in the Pas de Calais, and Fliegerkorps VIII (von Richthofen), based in Normandy, were assigned the twin tasks of gaining local air superiority over the Channel and closing the same to British convoys. In addition to these formations, a battlegroup consisting of KG 2, II/StG 1, IV (Stuka)/LG 1 and various Jagdgruppen were concentrated into a shipping strike force under Oberst Johannes Fink.

On 10 July, the first large attack came at 13.35hrs when some twenty-six Do 17Z-2s of I/KG 2, escorted by the Bf 110s of I/ZG 26 and Bf 109Es of I/JG 3, attacked the convoy BREAD off North Foreland. The raid was intercepted by Nos. 32, 74 and 111 Squadrons, and a fierce dogfight involving over a hundred aircraft ensued off Dover. From this day onwards, the German bomber forces began to show themselves in greater strength over the Channel, Straits of Dover and South-East coast areas of England by daylight. Their activities were still, however, mainly confined to the ports and shipping, and occasionally to coastal airfields.

At the same time, large formations of Bf 109Es began to trail their coats at medium and high altitudes over Southern England. These sweeps, or Frei Jagd (Free Chase) missions, were designed to draw RAF fighters into combat. At first, Fighter Command obliged; Spitfires and Hurricanes suffered tactical disadvantage while climbing for altitude, being bounced by the 109s and suffering accordingly. RAF fighter tactics, consisting of rigid 'Fighting Area Attacks', 'vic' formations in which only the leader could maintain an adequate look-out and line-astern manoeuvering, could not maintain the balance in face of the fluid German fighter formations. But the lessons were quickly learned and digested with pure fighter-versus-fighter confrontations being avoided and by the adoption of the German Rotte and Schwarm.

■ Phase 2: The assault, 8 August–23 August 1940

The losses sustained by the Luftwaffe during the initial stage had been bearable: 192 combat aircraft were destroyed and a further 77 damaged to varying degrees. But it was clear that the RAF was still an effective force and was not suffering sufficiently heavy casualties in the actions on the coastal fringe. It now became necessary for the Kampfgruppen to penetrate further inland in order that the Messerschmitts could engage and destroy a higher proportion of RAF fighters than hitherto. The initial phase had also highlighted serious shortcomings in both quality and quantity in the German fighter arm. Such was the aggressiveness of RAF fighter pilots that up to three times the number of escorting Germany fighters over the figure originally estimated were found to be needed to provide adequate support for the bomber formations. In addition, the Bf 110C-4 fighter, vitally required for long-range escorted penetrations, was found to be completely out-classed by the Spitfire and Hurricane in fighter-versus-fighter combat. When attacked the Bf 110s were forced into defensive circles and, in the more extreme cases, needed the protection of the 109s.

A new and serious phase of the battle opened on 8 August when bombing was intensified. Fierce air fighting developed with higher losses to both sides and a month of attrition began when the RAF was strained to the utmost. On this day there were three major Luftwaffe attacks on convoys with the Stukas of FlKps VIII bearing the brunt of the action. Over the next ten days the Stuka legend was finally destroyed. In the face of determined enemy fighter attack, the Ju 87 was proved a costly liability, and after the slaughter of StG 77 which lost sixteen Ju 87B-1s on 18 August, the type was withdrawn from the battle.

Bad weather dictated postponement of Adler Tag until 13 August, and even then it was not until the afternoon that the Luftwaffe appeared in force to start the sustained offensive on the RAF's air and ground forces. Portland and Southampton were bombed, in addition to the airfields at Eastchurch, Detling and Middle Wallop. The Luftwaffe flew 1,485 sorties for the loss of 46 aircraft, but the general lack of cohesion and poor bombing results provided a dismaying start to the offensive.

If Adler Tag had misfired then a serious effort was made to redress the situation on 15 August when the Luftwaffe put up no fewer than 1,786 sorties – of which 520 were by bombers – during the 24-hour period. It was a decisive day in which no effort was spared in the attempt to smother RAF air opposition and wreck airfields and radar stations. At mid-day, after Hawkinge and Lympne airfields had been attacked, Luftflotte 5 attempted raids in the north-east of England. Sixty-five He 111s of I and III/KG 26 escorted by I/ZG 76 attacked Newcastle and Sunderland, while 50 Ju 88s of KG 30 raided Driffield aerodrome. The raids were intercepted and the RAF shot down 16 bombers and seven Bf 110s, and largely on account of its poor showing Luftflotte 5 was to take no further part in the battle. Raids by formations of 100–150 German aircraft continued throughout the day, these suffering the shattering loss of 75 of their number.

During the succeeding week, the scale of attack on airfields of all types in southern England was of the heaviest and great air battles were continuously fought over Kent, Sussex and Hampshire. Meanwhile, the day and night attacks on shipping continued, and special targets of the aircraft industry were singled out for bombing. Losses of both bombers and fighters increased. By comparison with RAF claims of 755 German aircraft destroyed, the Luftwaffe actually lost 403 with a further 127 damaged throughout this period, and if somewhat less than was claimed, these figures were nevertheless extremely serious. But RAF Fighter Command's casualties were equally grievous with 94 pilots killed or missing and 60 wounded between 8–19 August and the losses in aircraft amounting to 54 Spitfires and 121 Hurricanes.

■ Phase 3: The tactical revision, 24 August–6 September 1940

In a directive issued by Göring on 20 August, the prime task of the Luftwaffe remained the destruction of the Royal Air Force in the air and on the ground. But time for the establishment of air superiority over England was running out and its achievement now called for the most desperate measures. During this phase, the Luftwaffe's major effort was devoted to the attack on RAF airfields and installations in the extreme south and south-east of England, with emphasis laid on the RAF fighter concentrations deployed around London.

To provide 'overwhelming' escorts of Bf 109s, it was decided to transfer most of the single-engined fighter strength of Luftflotte 3 to Luftflotte 2, and in the following days the bulk of Jafü 3 was transferred to bases in the Pas de Calais. Poor as the combat radius of the Bf 109E was without the much-needed jettisonable fuel tank, operations from the Pas de Calais bases enabled the fighter to penetrate deeper into RAF airspace, but because of mounting bomber losses the German fighter leaders were now ordered to stay close to the bombers – a complete negation of all the design advantages inherent in the Bf 109E.

In addition to the bomber raids aimed at specific targets, this phase of the battle was characterised by extensive employment by Luftflotte 2 and 3 of diversionary feints by bombers and reconnaissance aircraft, and intricate fighter sweeps primarily aimed at catching Fighter Command's squadrons on the ground refuelling.

Perhaps this phase was the most crucial for Fighter Command. By devoting all efforts against the RAF in the south of England to the almost complete dereliction of everything else, the Luftwaffe might have succeeded in its primary aim. On 31 August, Fighter Command's casualties were the highest of the battle – 39 aircraft destroyed in combat and 14 pilots killed. By now the aircrew situation within Fighter Command was approaching crisis level. On paper the numbers appeared sufficient for the task, but in reality it was the loss of experienced Squadron and Flight commanders that was causing intense concern. The major share of the fighting was born by a fast-diminishing band of battle-tried pilots in squadrons that were flying up to 50 hours per day, while fresh units – lacking combat experience – were being decimated by the 109s within one or two weeks.

Throughout this period Fighter Command suffered 295 fighters destroyed and 171 damaged, but far more serious was the loss of 103 pilots killed or missing and a further 128 withdrawn from combat because of injuries. The Luftwaffe's losses amounted to 378 aircraft with a further 115 damaged.

■ Phase 4: The bombing of London, 7 September–30 September 1940

The conditions necessary for the launching of Sealion had not been attained and possibly could never have been achieved by adherence to the original two-fold plan. On the night of 25 August, RAF Bomber Command launched a retaliatory raid on Berlin, and Hitler, in a speech on 4 September, seized upon this attack as an excuse for announcing his intention of a revenge bombing of London. The bombing of Warsaw and Rotterdam had been partly instrumental in causing the respective governments to sue for peace, and to Hitler there seemed no reason to suppose that a similar tactic could fail against the British. Two days before his speech, Hitler directed that the Luftwaffe should carry out attacks on the populations and defences of large cities, particularly London, by day and night.

This decision was in part an admission of defeat by the Luftwaffe, but at the same time Göring still hoped that the RAF fighter arm might be finally exhausted and that a turn of fortune would produce victory at the last moment. It was a fatal blunder, and from thence onwards RAF Fighter Command was able to operate in the air and on the ground with an impunity that it had not experienced since the start of Adlerangriff.

On the afternoon of 7 September, the Luftwaffe flew 372 bomber and 642 fighter sorties against targets in East London starting large fires and causing considerable damage. That night a further 255 bomber sorties were directed to the same area. During the succeeding days and nights, forces of similar strength – although never exceeding the effort of 7 September – were in operation, but extended their target area to Central London generally. Again Luftwaffe casualties mounted on a scale that far exceeded the results achieved; recrimination within the Luftwaffe bomber and fighter arms followed, each sharply criticising the other for its apparent shortcomings. Even the use of fast Ju 88s escorted by large numbers of Bf 109s failed to stem the attrition and loss of 60 German aircraft on 15 September was further proof that the goal of air superiority was as far away as ever. Two days later, Hitler ordered Seelöwe to be postponed indefinitely, but the invasion fleet was nevertheless to remain on readiness until the second week of October.

■ Phase 5: The fighter bombers, 1 October–31 October 1940

Three months less ten days had elapsed since the start of the intensive air battles of July, but for all the Luftwaffe effort there was little to set against the loss of 1,653 aircraft. In order to avoid further bomber losses by day, Göring resorted to the use of fighter-bombers operating at high-altitude.

Specialist fighter-bomber units (Epr.Gr 210, I and II(Schlacht)/LG 2) were bolstered by the addition of a Staffel from each Jagdgruppe which hastily fitted its Bf 109Es with a bomb-rack capable of carrying a 550-lb (250kg) bomb. No formal fighter-bomber training was given to the pilots of these units and as a result the accuracy achieved was poor. Nevertheless the speed and altitude (generally above

25,000ft) at which the fighter-bombers operated rendered their interception extremely difficult. Despite widespread use of bomb-carrying Bf 109s and Bf 110s, and single Ju 88s using weather as cover, RAF Fighter Command continued on its course of recovery. The main Luftwaffe effort was directed now to night attacks which the RAF was woefully unable to counter, but to all intents and purposes the threat by day had been neutralised. The crisis was over.

By the end of October, the Luftwaffe was glad to call a halt to daylight operations due to the deterioration in weather. It was Göring himself who took the decision. The Battle of Britain had been a failure for the Luftwaffe, although none overtly admitted the fact, and it was still hoped to wear Britain down to the point of capitulation by massed night attacks on industrial cities, by making seaborne supply impossible through the destruction of the main ports, and by sea-mining and shipping attacks.

Combined losses of Luftflotten 2, 3 and 5, from 10 July until 31 October 1940, amounted to 1,733 aircraft destroyed compared with 915 aircraft lost (415 pilots killed or missing) by the RAF.

THE NIGHT BLITZ

From September 1940 onwards, Göring's daylight offensive against RAF Fighter Command continued on a gradually reducing scale, with heavy bomber attacks giving way to raids by escorted fighter-bombers. During the same period, attempts to reduce the morale of the civilian population and force the British Government to surrender were made through the medium of heavy raids on London followed by a maximum-effort nocturnal assault on the capital. In November, this assault was expanded to other British cities and centres of industry, alternating between deliberate attempts to wreck civil morale and carefully planned attacks on Britain's supply and production centres. These phases of the German night bombe offensive, beginning with the raid on London on 7 September and dragging on through the winter to cease finally in May 1941, became known in Britain as the Blitz.

The main reasons why the Luftwaffe turned to night attacks lay in the alarming rate of attrition suffered by the Kampfgruppen in their attacks by day. Within the RAF at this time night fighting techniques relying on visual contact assisted by searchlights and the well-proven GCI system achieved few successes. Until the availability of efficient Airborne Interception (AI) radar, the German night bomber was to come and go with little hindrance. The first operational radar set, the AI Mk IV, was about to enter service but only on a very limited scale and was still highly experimental.

The adoption of night bombing also presented problems to the Luftwaffe. There were those of accurate night navigation and bombing, and these were compounded by an overall reduction in efficiency of bomber crews owing to the massive loss of experienced men during the Battle of Britain. The Germans, however, considered that any deficiencies in night operational training would be compensated by the use of radio aids to navigation that were in the hands of a few specialised bomber units.

The Germans had been far ahead of any other combatant power in the design and development of such aids, but by using the various types of equipment prematurely they allowed their secrets to be compromised and effective jamming by the enemy to be initiated. To summarise, the three principal aids to blind-bombing and navigation then in use were as follows:

1. 'Knickebein' (Bent Leg): This relatively unsophisticated equipment could be used by bombers equipped with the Lorenz blind-approach aid. The pilot flew his aircraft along an approach radio beam to the target, the bomb aimer releasing his bombs on receipt of a second radio signal beamed to traverse the approach beam at a particular point. The aid was easily jammed and could even be 'bent', and its only advantage lay in its ability to be used by a considerable number of aircraft.

2. X-Gerät (X-Equipment): Specialised aid to blind-bombing installed only in the He 111H-4s of Kampfgruppe 100 (Maj. Friedrich Aschenbrenner) operating from Vannes and Chartres. It consisted of one approach beam traversed in the vicinity of the target of three others. When the pilot received the first signal 31 miles (50km) short of the target, he lined up accurately on the approach beam, compensating for drift. The second and third signals occurred at 12 miles (20km) and 3 miles (5km) respectively. A computer calculated the aircraft's groundspeed and utilising this information automatic bomb release followed pressing a button on receipt of the third signal. X-Gerät was very accurate but could be effectively jammed.

3. Y-Gerät (Y-Equipment): Specialised aid installed only in the He 111H-4s of III/KG 26 (Maj. Victor von Lossberg) based at Poix-Nord. Once again an accurate target approach beam was used, but in this case bomb release was made at an accurately-measured range along the beam. This range was computed automatically by the associated ground radar station. The station sent an interrogator pulse. After a set interval special equipment in the bomber returned an answering pulse. Range was then deduced by the time signal (a matter of milli-seconds). At the correct range, the ground station relayed a bomb release signal. Y-Gerät was another very accurate system but again one that could be jammed effectively.

■ The night blitz, 7 September–31 May 1941

The Kampfgruppen engaged in the Blitz comprised the same units that had participated in the Battle of Britain under Luftflotten 2, 3 and 5, with the addition of some 90 bombers that had been held in Germany. Some 1,300 bombers were available for operations, but low serviceability kept the maximum effective strength to about 700 of these. After the mass daylight attack on London docks on 7 September, raids by 60 to 260 bombers took place after dusk during every night of the month. The effective jamming of Knickebein by No. 80 Signals Wing of the RAF rendered this equipment useless and throughout October the Luftwaffe had to make use of bright moonlight for navigation and bombing. During the early part of that month, London suffered a nightly assault by an average of 200 bombers. On 9

October, the Luftflotten were ordered to increase the effort, and that night London received 386 tons of HE and some 70,000 1-kg incendiary bombs in the course of 487 bomber sorties: on succeeding nights the attack was repeated by forces mounting 307, 150, 303 and 320 sorties. The Germans anticipated that the civil population would panic and force a surrender, but they, and in turn the Allies, underestimated the resilience of civilian morale in the face of indiscriminate heavy bombing.

Early in November, Göring decided to extend the Luftwaffe effort to a long-term attrition against the whole British industrial effort. Parallel with this new plan came the decision to use KGr 100 and the X-Gerät system as target finders. On locating the target KGr 100 was to drop incendiary bombs as target-markers for the follow-up force of bombers. The new plan as set out for the Luftflotten by Göring was as shown in the accompanying table.

On the night of 14/15 November, the target was Coventry. Using X-Gerät, twelve He 111s of KGr 100 crossed Lyme Bay, Dorset, at 18.17hrs heading north-east. At 20.15hrs, the Gruppe dropped over 1,000 incendiaries on the city starting numerous conflagrations, and as they droned away into the clear night, three separate bomber streams converged on Coventry from the Wash, Dungeness and Portland. Throughout the night successive waves of KG 1, KG 26, KG 27, KG 55, LG 1 and Kü.Fl.Gr 606 flew in to add to the devastation, and in the course of 469 sorties, the Luftwaffe delivered 394 tons of HE bombs, 56 tons of incendiaries and 127 parachute LMB 5 sea-mines; the latter caused considerable blast damage. Air defences were minimal and most of the bombers returned to base unscathed.

Birmingham came under heavy attack on the night of 19 November. Once again the now-established pattern was followed, with KGr 100 leading KG 26, KG 54, KG 55 and Kü.Fl.Gr 606. This time five bombers were brought down by the defences, one, a Ju 88A-4, was shot down over Dorset by Flt. Lt. J. Cunningham and Sgt. J. Phillipson, flying a Beaufighter IF of No. 604 Squadron and using the new AI Mk IV radar. This was the first radar kill of the war, but many months of experiment and disappointment lay ahead for the RAF night-fighter crews before their airborne radar equipment was to bring consistent results. The onus of night fighting still lay on Hurricane, Defiants and Blenheims, their crews relying on visual contact to achieve indifferent success. The Birmingham attack was followed during the remainder of that month and December by a succession of large-scale raids on London, Bristol, Plymouth, Liverpool, Southampton and Sheffield.

The year closed with a sharp attack on London in the evening of 29 December 1940. The raid was abandoned by the Luftwaffe some two hours after its commencement owing to deteriorating weather conditions. Only about 130 bomber sorties were mounted in the event, all aircraft carrying incendiaries, but by the time the weather closed in after 22.00hrs, the City of London was suffering its worst ordeal by fire since the Great Fire of 1666! Contrary to belief, this attack was a routine one and not a deliberate attack to wreck the City. That evening, the X-Gerät approach beam was actually laid in a SE–NW direction over the Charing Cross and Tottenham Court Roads. A fresh wind was blowing from the south-west and insufficient allowance for this wind was made by KGr 100 whose incendiaries fell about one mile to the East and immediately to the North-West of St Paul's Cathedral. The aircraft of the main bomber force, seeing the resultant fires, contributed their loads of HE and incendiaries.

In January 1941, the Luftwaffe still maintained a considerable force of bombers in the West: Fliegerkorps I, IV and V mustered 26 Kampfgruppen based in France and Belgium for attacks on Great Britain. By this time, however, a general lack of confidence in the blind-bombing aids was apparent, owing primarily to British mastery of the X-Gerät and to the widespread use of decoy fires. The Kampfgruppen turned once again to moonlight raids, concentrating on British seaports over which minimum interference to the radio beams could be expected. Accordingly ports such as Plymouth, Bristol, Swansea, Cardiff and Hull came under night attack.

In April, the German campaigns in the Balkans and Greece were already underway. Several fighter, dive-bomber and reconnaissance units had been detached from Luftflotte 3 in Northern France and deployed to the south during the winter and early spring. The anti-shipping force, Fliegerkorps X, had been transferred from Norway to the Mediterranean at the end of 1940. During May 1941, Luftflotte 2 left France for the East, along with KG 1, KG 27, KG 51, KG 54, KG 55, KG 76, KG 77 and I/LG 1. The moves were made under a cloak of secrecy, and as a cover to these movements, bomber raids on Britain were accompanied by false radio traffic to simulate larger forces. To maintain the semblance of a large force in being, the Luftwaffe executed the heaviest raid of the entire Blitz against London on the night of 10 May, crews flying two and even three sorties and 708 tons of HE and 87,000 incendiaries were dropped, causing great damage to greater London in the course of 550 sorties. Three nights later the raid was repeated in similar strength.

By the end of May 1941, Kesselring had moved with the whole of Luftflotte 2, along with the bomber units of FlKps IV and V, to the attack on the Soviet Union, leaving in the West the anti-shipping units of Fliegerkorps IX and Fliegerführer Atlantik, and a mixed force of bombers and single-engined fighters under Luftflotte 3.

In time, these units were to be whittled away by the more important commitments in the Soviet Union and the Mediterranean, leaving only a small force of mine-laying and anti-shipping units in the West. The Blitz was over. The programme for the subjugation of Britain had overrun its time, and although a considerable damage had been wrought to British cities and industries, the time for the hoped-for collapse had passed. The Luftwaffe had had every opportunity to bring Britain to her knees but failed because there had been no firm and continuous policy of attack: a shortcoming compounded by the manifest unsuitability of much of the equipment of the Luftwaffe for the task with which the service had been presented. Lack of coherent policy from OKL had all too frequently allowed hard-pressed cities to recover from large-scale raids where one more raid could have produced complete breakdown. The only solution now lay in the starving of Britain of food and supplies by air and sea attacks on her shipping, and awaiting or forcing surrender after the expected defeat of Russia in the autumn of 1941.

THE LUFTWAFFE STRIKES SOUTH

■ The Luftwaffe strikes south, January–May 1941

While the Battle of Britain was being fought German eyes were already turned towards the Soviet Union, the ultimate goal, but Italy's prevarications in North Africa and the Mediterranean forced German commitment in this theatre before any major assault could be made in the East. Although the Luftwaffe was well equipped for additional commitments in the Balkans, the Mediterranean and North Africa throughout the Spring of 1941, and was to achieve brilliant victories in the course of its campaigns, its involvement on two war fronts came at a time when all effort should have been made to conserve its strength. When, finally, the main weight of the Luftwaffe was to be turned against the Soviet Union in June 1941, a considerable proportion of its strength was already diverted elsewhere.

By December 1940, Italian plans in the Mediterranean had begun to go seriously awry. The invasion of Greece had met with stiff resistance, had ground to a halt, and had resulted in Commonwealth forces establishing themselves in Greece and on Crete. In North Africa, Mussolini's forces, after initial successes, had been thrown back to Bardia with massive losses in men and material. In addition, the Regia Aeronautica and the Italian Navy had proved incapable of stopping British convoys supplying Egypt, and their own convoys were losing heavily in the face of joint RN/RAF strikes from Malta.

These reverses promised to complicate the forthcoming assault against the Soviet Union, and Hitler decided to intervene in order to secure his southern flank before committing himself in the East. This intervention was incidentally, against the advice of the Oberkommando der Wehrmacht, and the ensuing commitments which resulted in a widespread diversification of Luftwaffe effort can be summarised as follows:

1. The First Assault on Malta, from January to March 1941, by Fliegerkorps X partly against the island but primarily against British shipping routes from Gibraltar to Egypt.

2. The establishment of Fliegerführer Afrika in Cyrenaica for the support of Generalfeldmarschall Erwin Rommel's Afrika Korps in early February 1941, resulting in the recapture of El Agheila and the subsequent advance to Sollum, on the Egyptian frontier, in April 1941.

3. The commitment of Luftflotte 4 to the Balkans for Operation Marita, the invasion of Yugoslavia and Greece on 6 April 1941, culminating in the campaign in Crete of 20–30 May 1941.

The Luftwaffe presence in Italy was established as early as June 1940, when Mussolini declared war, in the form of 'Italuft', a liaison mission under General Ritter von Pohl. At first the Luftwaffe's effort was restricted to ferrying Italian troops from Foggia to Albania by Junkers 52/3m transports, and the first combat units did not appear until the arrival of Generalmajor Hans Geisler's Fliegerkorps X in Sicily in December 1940. The operational area of FlKps X was extensive and included the Central Mediterranean, Sicily, Southern Italy and parts of Sardinia and North Africa. By mid-January 1941, FlKps X could muster about 330 aircraft and by March this figure had risen to 450, including 200 under the subordinated Fl.Fü. Afrika. Transport aircraft made up the bulk of these numbers, but the combat units available for operations, primarily against Malta and the shipping routes, were as shown in the accompanying table.

The first action came on 7 January, when a British convoy was sighted off Bougie consisting of four merchantmen under strong naval escort, including the aircraft carriers HMS *Ark Royal* and *Illustrious*. Fliegerkorps X attacked with about 40 Ju 88s, Ju 87s and He 111s in company with SM 79s of the Regia Aeronautica. The *Illustrious* suffered heavily from dive-bomber attacks when about 120 miles off Malta on 10 January, Stukas of I/StG 1 and II/StG 2 achieved four direct hits with 1,100-lb (500kg) armour-piercing bombs, leaving the carrier almost sinking. On 15 January, however, Luftwaffe reconnaissance noted that *Illustrious* had docked in Valetta harbour, Malta. The following day the 'Illustrious Blitz' started. After early morning reconnaissance flights by 1.(F)/121, the carrier once again came under attack from successive waves of Ju 87s of Fliegerkorps X. These concentrated on Valetta harbour in general but the *Illustrious* in particular, with the pilots of I/StG 1 (Hptm. Werner Hözzel) pressing home their attacks with great courage. In fact they achieved only one hit on the carrier, also damaging the supply ship *Essex*, owing to the violent AA fire and continuous opposition from RAF Hurricanes and RN Fulmars. The price was heavy – 2./StG 1 being wiped out with the sole exception of its Staffelkapitän.

Two days later, the airfields at Luqa and Hal Far came under heavy attack, while, on 19 January, Stukas managed to hit the *Illustrious* once again, but makeshift repairs were by now well underway and, on 23 January, the vessel set sail, albeit in parlous condition, for Alexandria. Against almost daily Luftwaffe raids on Malta, the RAF and RN never succeeded in putting more than three Fulmars, six Hurricanes and a single Gladiator into the air to face the onslaught which varied between 40 and 80 sorties per day.

Throughout February and March, Fliegerkorps X hammered at Valetta, and the three Maltese airfields – Luqa, Hal Far and Takali. The raids usually took the form of dive-bombing attacks, low-level fighter-bomber attacks by Bf 110s of III/ZG 26 (Maj. Schülze-Dickow) and medium level raids by Ju 88s and He 111s. Escort was provided by 7./JG 26 (Oblt. Müncheberg), which was joined later in March by I/JG 27 (Hptm. Edu Neumann). Both units flew the Bf 109E-7 capable of carrying a 66-gallon (300-litre) drop-tank. March also saw the arrival of a Gruppe of Ju 88A-6s (III/KG 30) at Gerbini, and II and III/StG 1 replacing I/StG 1 and II/StG 2, which were transferred to Cyrenaica.

The supply position on Malta fell to a critical level until the alleviated by the arrival of a small convoy from Alexandria which reached Valetta on 23 March 1941; a prompt strike by Fliegerkorps X in the form of 30 Ju 87s escorted by 20 Bf 109s damaged two merchantmen at anchor in the harbour. Fourteen RAF Hurricanes sent up to intercept managed to claim seven Stukas, while Valetta's increasingly efficient AA accounted for four. Owing to its commitment in support of the forthcoming Balkan campaign, this attack was to be the last by Fliegerkorps X against Malta for some time, although small-scale harassing raids and anti-shipping strikes continued.

By mid-March 1941, some 400 German aircraft, under General Alois Löhr's Luftflotte 4, were concentrated on the Bulgarian airfields at Sofia, Plovdiv, Krumovo, Krainitzi and Belitza for the proposed invasion of northern Greece in support of the Italians. Neighbouring Yugoslavia was expected to co-operate in this venture but a revolution in Belgrade against the pro-Nazi government of Prince Paul forced Hitler to act quickly. Orders were given on 26 March for the rapid transfer of some 600 combat aircraft from France, Germany and the Mediterranean to bases in Bulgaria and Rumania. These included KG 2, III/KG 3 and II/KG 26 for the establishment of a long-range bomber force. Stukagruppen consisted of I and III/StG 2 'Immelmann', which were joined by II/StG 2 from El Machina in North Africa; one Zerstörergruppe, the II/ZG 26, was posted from Germany to Turnu Sverin, and Messerschmitt Bf 109E-4 and E-7 fighters of I/JG 27,* Stab, I and III/JG 77, I(Jagd)/LG 2 and I (Schlacht)/LG 2 were posted from France and Germany to supplement the already established II and III/JG 27 at airfields in the Deta/Arad sector.

Tactical control of all close-support aircraft was placed under the command of Gen. Wolfram von Richthofen, whose Fliegerkorps VIII was to be enabled once again – after the drubbing in the Battle of Britain – to launch its own pattern of warfare on the classic Blitzkrieg style, unmolested by effective fighter opposition.

*In transit to North Africa.

The simultaneous assaults on Yugoslavia and Greece, code-named Operation 'Marita', started on 6 April 1941 with a massive Stuka attack on Belgrade and heavy bomber raids on the Piraeus. The city of Zagreb fell on 10 April, and seven days later the Yugoslav army capitulated. In the south, resistance by valiant Greek forces, supported by the Imperial Expeditionary Force under General Wilson, was reduced to a withdrawal accompanied by stubborn rearguard actions in the face of List's XII Army. The Greek army surrendered on 20 April, and one week later the fall of Athens brought the campaign to a conclusion. Within the space of less than one year, the British and Commonwealth armies had again been forced to evacuate the Continent in extremis.

■ Crete – Operation 'Merkur', 1941

The decision to invade Crete was an opportunist one. After the rapid success of the Wehrmacht in Greece, the German General Staff had initially considered no further action in the direction of Crete. It was largely the brainchild of Generaloberst Kurt Student, the commander of Fliegerkorps XI, who conceived the idea of an airborne landing on the island. He ventured to Göring that Crete, besides being a vital operational base, would be a useful stepping-stone for a similar invasion of Cyprus with the further possibility of linking up with the Axis in North Africa on the Suez Canal. Göring gained Hitler's permission for the undertaking with the proviso that it took place within the shortest possible space of time, and the decision was taken in late April to launch the airborne invasion on 16 May 1941. The whole operation, code-named 'Merkur' (Operation Mercury) was in Luftwaffe hands and the Army General Staff was not consulted.

Student's newly formed Fliegerkorps XI, a specialised paratroop and air-landing organisation, comprised a large force of Ju 52/3m transport units and the Fliegerdivision 7, wherein were concentrated three parachute regiments (Fallschirmjäger Regiment: FJR) with subordinated flak and engineering battalions. For 'Merkur', Fliegerkorps XI mustered 493 Ju 52s and 80 DFS 230 gliders of KGzbV 1, 101, 102 105, 106, the specially formed KGzbV 40 and 60, and Luftlandegeschwader 1. These units were deployed to Eleusis Tatoi, Megara and Corinth, while the troops of Fliegerdivision 7 made their way by road, rail and air from Germany to the Athens area.

Air support for the operation was to be provided by Fliegerkorps VIII. Long-range bombers based at Eleusis, Salonica, Sofia and Plovdiv consisted primarily of I and III/KG 2 and III/KG 3, but were bolstered by the addition of LG 1, II/KG 26 and III/KG 30 under Fliegerkorps X, which flew operations from Foggia, Brindisi and other bases in Apulia. In all, 280 bombers were available. For close support, all three Gruppen of Obstlt. Oscar Dinort's StG 2 'Immelmann' Geschwader were distributed between Molaoi, Melos and the island of Scarpanto. These bases were also shared by the Bf 109E-7s of Stab II and III/JG 77 and I(Jagd)/LG 2, and lay within 100–120 miles of the northern coast of Crete. The remainder of the strike force was made up of 40 reconnaissance aircraft and the Bf 110s of II/ZG 26 based at Argos and Corinth.

The plan for 'Merkur' called for the seizure of the three main airfields on Crete – Maleme, Retimo and Heraklion – and the capture of Canea town and the important harbour at Suda Bay. These objectives were to be taken on the first day by airborne assault, followed by the landing of troops by Ju 52 and then by sea. It was proposed that 750 troops be landed from gliders, some 10,000 by parachute, 5,000 from relays of Ju 52s and 7,000 from small ships. German military intelligence, which had marred many an operation by its ineptitude, estimated that not more than 15,000 British and Commonwealth troops were stationed on Crete; the actual figure was double this, and did not include some 11,000 Greek troops. Arms and equipment, however, were in woefully short supply.

In the meantime, the Luftwaffe pursued its campaign of softening up the defences of Crete which suffered attacks by Ju 88s, He 111s and Dorniers, and considerable strafing by Messerschmitts. The original date set for 'Merkur' was postponed due to transportation difficulties. In the event, the attack opened at 07.00hrs on 20 May 1941, in moderate visibility but with heavy ground haze. Very heavy attacks by bombers, dive-bombers and fighters were launched on British positions at Maleme and Canea, the objective being primarily gun positions and particularly AA batteries. Then there was a short lull before the first airborne attack materialised at 08.00 hours. In the course of the morning and afternoon the assaults were executed as follows:

Maleme Airfield:
Under the command of Gen. Meindl (Group West), 500 troops consisting of part I and elements of III/Sturm FJR landed from DFS 230 gliders at 08.00hrs in the vicinity of Maleme airfield. These consisted of three separate detachments: the task of Major Braun's detachment was to take the bridge over the Tavronitis river; Lt. Plessen's unit was to storm the AA batteries at the mouth of the Tavronitis and then make its way to the airfield, while Major Koch's men were to storm Hill 107 which dominated the airfield to the south. At the same time 1,860 paratroops, the remainder of Sturm FJR, dropped from Ju 52s along the Tavronitis and around the airfield.

Canea and Suda Bay:
Under the command of Oberst Heidrich (Group Centre: 1st Wave), the landings from gliders and by paratroops started shortly after 08.00 hours. Gliders carrying 270 men of the Sturm FJR landed on the Akrotiri peninsula, overlooking Suda Bay, and to the south-west of Canea to neutralise the AA batteries. At the same time paratroops of I and II/FJR 3 dropped astride the Canea-Alikianou road, while III/FJR 3 was dropped to the east of Galatas village. All assaults suffered heavily, and by the evening

most units were pinned down in small defensive positions. This force consisted of 2,460 men.

Retimo Airfield:
This was the objective of Oberst Sturm (Group Centre: 2nd Wave) whose force of 1,380 paratroops dropped during the afternoon. Starting at 16.15hrs, the drop lasted almost an hour due the congestion of traffic at the Ju 52 bases. Fallschirmjäger Regt 2 was split into two groups under Hptm. Weidemann and Major Kroh after landing, but met stiff resistance from the defenders.

Heraklion Airfield:
Under the command of General Ringel (Group East), the first paratroops arrived at 14.30hrs, but on account of the havoc wrought to the timing by congestion, the last elements of Oberst Brauer's FJR 1 and a battalion of FJR 2 did not arrive until 19.30hrs. Casualties among the 2,360 men dropped were extremely heavy.

By the evening of 20 May, the position of the German airborne troops was critical. At first the very nature of their attack, its terrifying unfamiliarity, had thrown the defenders off balance. But within minutes of the first landings, successive drops by paratroops were met by a hail of smallarms fire. That night, however, the lynchpin of Maleme's defence – Hill 107 – was abandoned by the defenders owing to confusion and misunderstanding, and from 16.00hrs on the following day, German troops began to land by Ju 52s on the newly-captured airfield. Desperate fighting followed, particularly around Galatas and Canea, but by 27 May, the Germans were in control of Canea and Suda Bay. That day General Freyberg's force was authorised by Wavell to commence a withdrawal to Sfakia in the south for eventual evacuation. A day later Heraklion fell, but 4,000 of its defenders had been evacuated by the Royal Navy. By 31 May, the whole of Crete was in German hands.

Brilliant in its conception and an airborne operation of a scale never before attempted, the German invasion of Crete nevertheless suffered the heaviest of casualties. With airborne forces of Fliegerdivision 7 bearing the heaviest losses, German casualties in Crete amounted to 1,990 men killed, 1,955 missing presumed killed and a further 327 drowned at sea. In addition, the wastage in aircraft, principally Ju 52s, amounted to 220 destroyed and 148 damaged in the course of the campaign. Due to the confused nature of the fighting, the Luftwaffe was unable to take any further part in support of the ground forces after the initial parachute landings. However, its bombers and in particular the Ju 87s of StG 2 achieved considerable success in actions against the Royal Navy, which remained heavily committed in the seas around Crete without having any effective air cover.

After bombing Scarpanto airfield, HMS *Juno* was attacked and sunk by StG 2 on the early morning of 21 May. On the following day, StG 2, II/KG 26 and KG 2 sank the cruisers HMS *Gloucester* and HMS *Fiji*, the destroyer HMS *Greyhound* and sustained hits on the battleships *Warspite* and *Valiant*. On 23 May, the 5th Destroyer Flotilla suffered the loss of HMS *Kelly* and HMS *Kashmir*, both being sunk by Dinort's StG 2 dive-bombers. Kampfgeschwader 2 damaged the battleship HMS *Barham* on 27 May, and on the next day high-level attacks and dive-bombing accounted for the destroyers *Hereward* and *Imperial* while damaging the cruisers *Dido* and *Orion*. The Navy's agony was not yet over, for on the final day of the Cretan evacuation, the Luftwaffe attacked and sank HMS *Calcutta* when a mere 100 miles off Alexandria.

■ North Africa, 1941

While the Germans pursued their campaigns in Greece and Crete, Axis fortunes in Cyrenaica and Libya had taken a turn for the better due to the intervention of Rommel's Afrika Korps. When Rommel arrived with the nucleus of his Korps at Tripoli on 12 February 1941, the British headlong advance had reached El Agheila, but its lines of supply and communications were stretched to the limit. Rommel was quick to profit from this weakness and by 24 March had re-taken El Agheila and launched an offensive of his own. Over the succeeding weeks, Wavell's forces were withdrawn in good order to Marsa Brega, Agedabia and Benghazi, and, by 15 April, Rommel had encircled the Tobruk garrison.

Rommel achieved this advance with little air support. However, as early as March, Fliegerkorps X had detached some reconnaissance aircraft and a strike force consisting of 7. and 8./ZG 26 and I/StG 1 and II/StG 2 to bases in Libya. These units, joined on 20 April by the Bf 109E-7/Trop fighters of I/JG 27 and 7./JG 26 based at Gazala, were to increase the tempo of air operations in attacks on Tobruk and with close-support sorties in the line of the German advance. By 25 April, Rommel had taken Halfaya Pass and pushed the British back to Mersa Matruh on the borders of Egypt.

The arrival of 238 tanks in the Tiger convoy on 12 May, enabled the British 8th Army to launch a counter-offensive, Operation Brevity, three days later. The objective was the reparation of the British position on the Egyptian frontier, but after initial successes, including the re-capture of Halfaya Pass, the British withdrew to Sollum and Capuzzo. A counter-attack by Rommel re-captured Halfaya Pass on 27 May. On 14 June, the 8th Army again went over to the offensive in an attempt to relieve the Tobruk garrison (Operation Battleaxe), but its Crusaders and Valentine tanks were decimated by 88.mm anti-tank fire and, by 17 June, the British had withdrawn to the borders of Egypt to consolidate.

Despite its numerical inferiority, the Luftwaffe was able to gain a measure of air superiority over the battle areas. Hauptmann Eduard Neumann's I/JG 27 was an experienced and battle-tried unit, and the Messerschmitt Bf 109E-7 fighter was vastly superior to the Hurricane Is and Curtiss Tomahawk IIs of the RAF Desert Air Force, whose fighter units composed Nos. 2 SAAF, 3 RAAF, 4 SAAF, 33, 73, 94, 112, 213 and 250 Squadrons. I/JG 27 fought numerous dogfights with these units in the course of daily escort missions for the Stukagruppen and the Ju 88A-4/Trop bombers of III/LG 1. Several of its pilots, notably Oblt. Ludwig Franzisket, Homuth, Wolfgang Redlich, Lt. Stahlschmidt, Lt. Körner, Lt. von Lieres, and Ofw. Espenlaub, were to achieve numerous combat 'kills' over Libya during that summer. The most outstanding, however, was to be Oberfahnrich Hans-Joachim Marseille of 3. Staffel. He gained his 11th 'kill' over Acroma on 30 April, after a career that had been marred by instances of indiscipline and clashes with his superiors, but the campaigns in North Africa and the combat successes he was to achieve during them were to make him a legend in his own time.

Following the failure of 'Battleaxe', both opponents in North Africa regrouped to await supplies of men and material, and the situation on the ground remained relatively static. The Luftwaffe command in the Mediterranean, Fliegerkorps X, was compelled to devote most of its effort to the supply and support of the Axis forces in North Africa. By late June 1941, all units were withdrawn from Sicily and distributed to either the newly-constituted Fliegerführer Afrika (Gen. Maj. Fröhlich) or to bases in Greece and Crete. On the eve of Operation 'Barbarossa', Hitler's invasion of the Soviet Union, Fliegerkorps X had 240 combat aircraft based in Southern Greece, Crete and on Rhodes, while a further 150 were in North Africa. The components of Fl.Fü. Afrika on 21 June 1941 were as shown in the accompanying table.

FROM BARBAROSSA TO STALINGRAD

■ The Luftwaffe in Russia, 1941–3

Shortly after 03.00hrs on Sunday, 22 June 1941, 117 German infantry and armoured Divisions, supported by 14 Divisions of the 3rd and 4th Rumanian Army and the Hungarian Army Corps, rolled forward on a 1,200-mile (1930km) battle-front into the Soviet Union. The greatest clash of arms in the history of mankind had begun. The reasons behind Hitler's decision to attack the Soviet Union lie outside the scope of this chapter, but it is reasonable to assume that all Hitler's peacetime preparations and subsequent war aims were levelled at the eventual conquest of Soviet territory and the acquisition of the Lebensraum (living space) so dear to Nazi ideology. As early as June 1940, after the fall of France, both OKH and OKL were informed of the plan, and although several senior staff officers voiced misgivings, even Hermann Göring was unable to sway Hitler. To many the prospect of committing Germany to a war on two fronts was appalling and in their view was inevitably to lead to the loss of the war, just as it had done in the Great War of 1914–18. The Führer believed that Britain was beaten, however, and that a massive campaign against the demoralised facade of bolshevist Russia would lead to its collapse in as little as six weeks. In the light of the Wehrmacht's brilliant and precipitate triumphs, few had had the temerity to oppose this view.

For the Luftwaffe, preparations for the war in the East had started as early as October 1940; the 'Ostbauprogramm' (Eastern Construction Programme) was already projected and from then on until the end of the year Luftwaffe works units and construction material were steadily moved into newly-occupied Polish territories. By early spring, the construction of airbases, the establishing of fuel dumps and the deployment of Flak units were well under way, but it was not until April and May

1941 that preparations to receive combat units were started. By mid-June, the Luftwaffe had moved 2,770 front-line aircraft to the East from France, Germany and the Mediterranean, this force included 775 bombers, 310 Stukas, 830 Bf 109s, 90 Bf 110s and 765 reconnaissance and coastal types, out of a total Luftwaffe first-line inventory of 4,300 aircraft.

Four Luftflotten in all were engaged at the opening of the campaign against the Soviet Union, code-named 'Barbarossa', and these were disposed as the table shows.

In addition to the powerful reconnaissance arm, the long-range bomber units were KG 1, KG 3, KG 4, 6./KG 30, KG 51, KG 53, KG 54, KG 55, III/KG 76 and KGr 806. Now operating the Ju 88A-4 and He 111H-6, these units were mostly concentrated in FlKps II in support of the centre thrust. Zerstörergruppen and fighter-bombers consisted of I and II/ZG 26 and Schnelleskampfgeschwader 210.

While several Jagdgruppen were still using the Bf 109E-4 and E-7 fighter, the majority now based in the East were mounted on the new Messerschmitt Bf 109F-2. Powered by a Daimler-Benz DB 601N-1 engine but relatively lightly armed with two 7.9-mm MG 17 machine guns and a single 15-mm MG 151 cannon, this model added a dazzling high-altitude performance to the already sound attributes of the basic design. With the arrival of the Bf 109F-4 in August 1941, the Luftwaffe could count on a fighter that possessed an overwhelming degree of performance in comparison to anything that the Soviet Air Forces could put into the air. Indeed, if General Josef 'Beppo' Schmidt's Air Intelligence 1C department of the RLM could be believed, Soviet Air technology bordered on the mediaeval, and although quantitively the V-VS was the equal of the Luftwaffe, qualitively its equipment, aircraft and aircrew were of very low standard.

During the Spring of 1941, a German Industrial Commission brought back favourable reports concerning Russian productive capacity and in particular, the appearance of new aircraft designs based on sound technology, but all had been largely ignored by the Luftwaffe hierarchy. Schmidt's 1C department dismissed the report as an elaborate bluff and there was much evidence to support this view.

On the morning of 22 June 1941, the Luftwaffe unleashed its forces. Fliegerkorps II and VIII were heavily committed in support of Army Group Centre with Stuka and bomber attacks on Soviet troop concentrations and communications. Due to widespread aerial reconnaissance, principally by Oberst Rowehl's Aufklärungsgruppe Ob.d.L., during the preceding months, every forward V-VS airbase had been pinpointed. These now came under sustained attacks by Ju 88s and He 111s, while low-level strikes were made by Bf 110s and bomb-carrying Bf 109s. The few Soviet fighters that got airborne were mostly despatched with ease. On this day, for the loss of a mere 32 aircraft, the Luftwaffe destroyed 1,811 Soviet aircraft, all but 322 of these being destroyed on the ground.

After a month of scorching advance, Army Group North halted west of Lake

Ilmen to regroup its exhausted forces. To add impetus to the drive on Leningrad, Richthofen's FlKps VIII transferred its 400 Stukas from Luftflotte 2 to Luftflotte 1 at the end of July. In the centre, von Bock's armies had encountered stiff Soviet resistance but, on 5 August, completed the encirclement and destruction of the Soviet forces in the Smolensk pocket. In the south, the drive to the Ukraine resulted in the fall of Tarnopol and Zhitomir, the encirclement of the Soviet armies in the Uman pocket, and the capture of Odessa and Nikolaev, and had reached Kiev by 19 September. By the end of that month, Leningrad was under siege, Army Group Centre was within 290 miles of Moscow, Kiev had fallen and the southern groups of the Wehrmacht had advanced to a 300-mile front from Konotop, through Zaporozhe to the Crimea. In the annihilation battles of Uman and Kiev, 665,000 Russian troops were either killed or captured – nearly one-third of the entire strength of the Soviet Armies at the outbreak of 'Barbarossa'.

Throughout these advances the Luftwaffe retained almost total air superiority, although the strong reaction by Il-2s and Pe-2s, covered by MiG-3 and Yak-1 fighters, during the Kiev fighting came as something of a surprise to the Germans. The scale of Soviet losses during the first months of Barbarossa can be shown by the claims of the Luftwaffe: totals of 1,570 and 1,360 Soviet aircraft were destroyed by combat units on the Central and Southern fronts respectively, from 22 June to 28 June, while Luftflotte 1 claimed 1,211 in the air and 487 on the ground from 22 June to 13 July 1941. These claims were undoubtedly exaggerated but there was no gainsaying that Soviet losses were enormous.

The claims of the Jagdgruppen were colossal. On 30 June alone, they claimed to have destroyed in combat no fewer than 114 Soviet aircraft. Commanded by the brilliant Obstlt. Werner Mölders, JG 51 was the first Luftwaffe fighter unit to achieve 1,000 combat 'kills' in the war; JG 53, under Major Günther Fr. von Maltzahn, was next to achieve the one thousand mark, followed by Major Hannes Trautloft's JG 54, and Obstlt. Günther Lützow's Jagdgeschwader 3. These achievements came within six weeks of the start of the Soviet Campaign. Several of the Jagdgeschwader were destined to see action on the Soviet Front throughout the remainder of the war, the principal being JG 51, JG 52 and JG 54, while JG 3, JG 53 and JG 77 all saw extensive action until redeployed to the Reich and the Mediterranean in 1943. Jagdgeschwader 5 also fought a gruelling campaign in northern Norway and on the Soviet-Finnish Front.

That the air fighting over the Soviet Union was 'easy' is a matter of considerable conjecture, particularly when the massive combat scores of individual German fighter pilots, operating in the Soviet Union, are compared with those fighting in the Channel Front, over Germany and in the Mediterranean theatre. There is no doubt, however, that, for the first two years, the German fighter pilots held complete hegemony in Soviet skies, and only after 1943 did they finally meet a foe who fought on relatively equal terms. Their combat claims, large though they were to be, possessed the same measure of credence as was attached to those of Luftwaffe fighter pilots fighting elsewhere. Nowhere is the scale and nature of air combat over the Soviet Union revealed more clearly than by the career of Lt. Günther Scheel of 3./JG 54 'Grünherz'. Lt. Scheel joined his unit in the Spring of 1943, and before his death near Orel on 16 July 1943, he had shot down 71 Soviet aircraft in 70 sorties! The first pilot to score 150 victories was Major Gordon M. Gollob, Kommodore of JG 77, in August 1941; Hptm. Hermann Graf of 9./JG 52 was the first with 200 'kills', this score being attained on 2 October 1942; Hptm. Walter Nowotny, Kommandeur of I/JG 54, was first to achieve 250 'kills' on 14 October 1943, but the greatest eastern 'Expert' was Major Erich Hartmann of JG 52 who claimed 352 'kills' between 1943 and 1945.

■ Operation Typhoon and the first Russian offensive, 1941

Code-named Operation 'Taifun' (Typhoon), the German drive on Moscow started on 1 October 1941, but due to Hitler's pre-occupation with the campaigns in the Ukraine, this assault was too late in being launched. Prior to operations in support of II, IV and IX Armies, the III and IV Panzergruppen and the II Panzer Army of Army Group Centre, a force of 1,320 combat aircraft was concentrated in Luftflotte 2. This was achieved by transferring FlKps VIII along with the entire bomber and fighter force of FlKps I from Luftflotte 1 in the north, in addition to Jagdgruppen transferred from Luftflotte 4. As a result, the strength of Kesselring's Luftwaffe 2 rose to almost 50 per cent of the total Luftwaffe strength in the Soviet Union. The close-support forces within Luftflotte 2 were assembled in the Konotop sector and SE of Smolensk, extending towards Roslavl.

The offensive started in ideal weather conditions and, by 7 October, the Panzergruppen had sealed off massive troop concentrations in the Bryansk and Vyasma pockets. On the following day, it rained heavily and in the days that followed roads and airfields were transformed into morasses. By 25 October the impetus of Typhoon had been halted by over-stretched lines of supply and increasing Russian resistance. For a time, the Wehrmacht consolidated its gains, but when the second phase was launched the drive became paralysed in 20° of frost and even stronger resistance. On 27 November, the Panzers were within 19 miles of the suburbs of Moscow, but this was destined to be the limit of the German advance.

For the first time, the Germans realised that their equipment was not capable of withstanding the sub-zero temperatures. By November, airfield conditions had become exceedingly difficult, alternating between mud in which aircraft became bogged and hard frozen surfaces that caused damage to undercarriages. Heating equipment for early morning starts was non-existent, forcing tired groundcrews to run-up engines during the night and even light open fires under the aircraft. On the other hand the Soviet Air Forces showed that they were largely unaffected by the weather, operating as they did from permanent airfields around Moscow.

After days of furious argument between Hitler and his generals in the field, the

Moscow offensive was finally abandoned on 5 December, but on the following day the Russians went over to the offensive. To the Germans, it seemed impossible that the Soviet Army and Air Forces could be capable of sustaining a large-scale offensive: German military intelligence estimated that the Russian attrition in men had been 300,000 at Minsk, 650,000 in the Kiev pocket and another 663,000 in the Vyasma-Bryansk debacle, and added to this was the claim by the Luftwaffe of 15,877 soviet aircraft destroyed from 'Barbarossa' to 20 November (although the Russians later put this number at 6,300). But over the next three months the Soviet Army managed to push the Germans back to Cholm and Smolensk in the centre, while in the south threatened the important centres at Kharkov and Kursk.

The Luftwaffe was already weakened by the transfer, in December 1941, of Kesselring's Luftflotte 2 and Fliegerkorps II which had been redeployed to Sicily. This decision had been taken as early as October, when Axis fortunes in North Africa had worsened. Among the units that left the Soviet Union for the Mediterranean were II/JG 3, III/JG 27 and three Gruppen of JG 53 with Bf 109F-4s, and elements of KG 54, LG 1 and KGr 806 with Ju 88A-4s. While these did not amount to a serious weakening of the Russian Front, the transfer came at a time when several combat units were in Germany re-fitting. Thus, the Luftwaffe in the Soviet Union was reduced to some 1,700 aircraft. In the north, Luftflotte 1 and FlKps I remained, with FlKps VIII alone in the centre engaged on a 400-mile front. In December, Fliegerkorps V, which had been engaged in the assault on Kharkov in the Kursk-Stalino sector under Luftflotte 4, was withdrawn. Later it was to be used, in part at least, as Sonderstab Krim (Special Staff Crimea) in support of Fliegerkorps IV in neutralising the bastions in the Crimea in June 1942.

Throughout the first six months of the Russian campaign, the Luftwaffe had operated perforce in all weather conditions, averaging 1,200 sorties per day, with peaks at 2,000 during high-intensity periods, for its establishment of some 2,500 aircraft. Particularly in winter, the rate of attrition had been high due to operation from poor airfields and the extremely efficient Russian AA fire. The wastage in the Soviet Union caused a reversal in the expansion of Luftwaffe first-line strength, reducing it to about 4,300 aircraft by December 1941, and for the first time it became apparent that the production of aircraft was inadequate to sustain a long period of heavy air operations. It was primarily this, coupled with his failures elsewhere, that forced the Generalluftzeugmeister, Ernst Udet, to take his life in November 1941. His place passed to the able Erhard Milch.

■ The Road to Stalingrad, 1942

The original Barbarossa plan to knock out the Soviet Union in a gigantic, three-pronged invasion had failed on account of the winter, over-stretched resources and the Soviet offensive, which finally petered out in March 1942. Hitler still believed, however, that the Wehrmacht could bring the war on the Eastern Front to a victorious conclusion. But with the summer now approaching, German strategy in the Soviet Union had undergone a complete change: the axis of all German efforts would now be in the South. The new offensives would thrust south-east to the Volga, to Stalingrad and down to the oil-rich foothills of the Caucasus mountains.

The great offensive in the South, with the prime objective being the Caucasus, was planned to develop in four stages.

1. The II Army and IV Panzer Army were to break through to Voronezh on the river Don; VI Army was to break out of the area west of Kharkov and smash the Soviet armies west of the Don in co-operation with IV Panzer Army which would turn southwards along the Don in order to encircle the enemy there.

2. After this move, IV Panzer and VI Army (Army Group B) would co-operate with I Panzer Army and XVII Army (Army Group A) to encircle Stalingrad, on the river Volga.

3. Army Group B was to push down the Don in a south-easterly direction, while Army Group A thrust eastwards to the river Donets.

4. The fourth phase of the summer offensive was to be the southward push to the Caucasus.

As a preliminary to the plan, it was necessary to cover the southern flank by the German occupation of the Crimea. This task was given to Gen. Erich von Manstein's XI Army. By April 1942, the Germans had occupied the Kerch peninsula, thus effectively isolating the Crimean fortresses, and for the offensive which started on 8 May, Luftflotte 4 mustered some 600 aircraft. Tactical control of air operations in support of XI Army was in the hands of FlKps VIII (von Richthofen) which had been sent to the Crimea from the central front, its place in that sector being taken over by FlKps V – now re-named Luftwaffenkommando Ost. Fliegerkorps IV was still under Luftflotte 4, but was heavily committed against Soviet pressure in the Volchansk and Krasnograd sectors, to the north and south of Kharkov.

The attack on Sebastopol, the key to the Crimea, started on 2 June, with sorties by FlKps VIII averaging 600 per day, and rising to a peak of 700 sorties on 6 June, when the city finally fell. Some 2,500 tons of HE bombs were dropped – some being the heavy SC 1000 type (2,200-lb) – by StG 1, StG 2 and StG 77, by now re-equipped with the improved Junkers Ju 87D. With the fall of Sebastopol, FlKps VIII was rushed to the Kharkov area to support the German offensive aimed at relieving the pressure on Kharkov and encircling the 6th, 9th and 57th Soviet armies in the Barenkovo salient, and by mid-June, Richthofen's command was in the Kursk sector in preparation for the massive German drive on Voronezh and the Don.

In the Mediterranean, the improved situation in the desert and the ending of FlKps II's second air assault on Malta, enabled the Luftwaffe to redeploy units from this theatre to the Soviet Union, along with refurbished units from Germany. By the start of the German summer offensive there were thus 2,750 combat aircraft on the Russian Front – a situation similar to that at the start of 'Barbarossa'. Of these, 1,500 were in the crucial Don-Caucasus sector of Luftflotte 4, 600 were in the centre under Luftwaffenkommando Ost, 375 under Luftflotte 1 were in the Leningrad sector and 200 under Luftflotte 5 were in the far north. On 20 June 1942, these units were composed of: JG 3, II/JG 5 and 7. and 8./JG 5, JG 51, JG 52, JG 54 and JG 77 with Bf 109F-4 fighters; twin-engined and ground-attack – ZG 1, ZG 2, I and II/Sch.G 1, 13(Zerst)/JG 5; Stukas – StG 1; III/StG 2 and StG 77; Long-range bombers – KG 1, III/LG 1, KG 3, I and II/KG 4, II/KG 26, KG 27, KG 30, KG 51, KG 53, II/KG 54, KG 55, I and III/KG 76, I/KG 77 and KG 100.

That the Wehrmacht would succeed in its second attempt to crush the Soviet Army was uppermost in the minds of German soldiers and commanders alike, but no amount of contingency planning and talk of 'stop-lines' could shroud the fact that this was also to be the last attempt. Another winter on the frozen Russian Steppes was unthinkable. When, on 28 June 1942, Army Groups A and B launched their all-out offensive, the Luftwaffe went over to the attack on the dreaded Blitzkrieg pattern. Supported by the Stukas and ground-attack aircraft of FlKps VIII, General Hoth's IV Panzer Army fanned out over hundreds of miles of rolling corn towards Voronezh and the Don. Opposition was scant with the Soviet Army trading ground for time.

At first the offensive went brilliantly. In the south, Army Group A crossed the river Donets and then swung south to Rostov, took Proletarskaya on 29 July, Stavropol on 5 August and reached the blazing oilfields at Maikop four days later. Within a week, Kleist's I Panzer Army was in sight of Mount Elburz and was thrusting east towards the Caspian Sea.

In the northern sector the plan also went well. Hoth's IV Panzer and VI Army (Gen. Paulus) followed the line of the Don to the south-east smashing all resistance, but on 23 July the first flaw in the plan appeared. The twin-thrust was split as Hoth was ordered to drive south to assist Army Group A, while Paulus's VI Army swung east to reach Stalingrad on 10 August, where, for the first time, serious Soviet resistance was encountered. Paulus now had to wait another ten days before Hoth would arrive. Meanwhile, it became apparent through the large Soviet reinforcements flooding into the area that the Soviet Army intended to make Stalingrad the crucible of the battle.

The first German attempt to storm Stalingrad, on 19 August, failed, largely due to mishandling by Paulus, and even the massive air support by FlKps VIII, now operating from the Morozovsk airfield complex, failed to alter the situation on the ground. The air attacks of the night of 23/24 August by FlKps I, IV and VIII reduced the city to ruins by high-explosive and incendiary bombing. But the stubbornness of the Soviet defence of Stalingrad baffled the Wehrmacht – and as it became tied down in savage hand-to-hand fighting, it chose to regard it as a battle of attrition in which the Soviet Army would be bled white. But it was the Wehrmacht which failed to understand the tactical as well as strategic reality; it was the Wehrmacht which was to become exhausted and be forced to throw in all its reserves, while the Russians built up their strength, committing only enough troops to stop the Germans from breaking through. Stalingrad, and the series of battles that raged around it, became the cemetery of the German VI Army and turning point of the war.

On 23 November, the Soviet armies linked up and completely cut-off the VI Army fighting in Stalingrad. Frantic German counterattacks aimed at its relief failed. On 31 January 1943, Paulus surrendered with the southern group of his beleaguered VI Army and, on 2 February, Gen. Schreck capitulated in the northern sector. At the cost of 120,000 men killed or missing and with the capture of 91,000 men, including 24 generals and 2,500 other officers, it was the most catastrophic defeat of German arms in the Second World War.

Throughout the six months of the Stalingrad battles, the Luftwaffe's strength in Russia had remained at the remarkably consistent figure of 2,450–2,500 aircraft. In the north, the Soviet offensives on Lake Ilmen and in the vicinity of Leningrad necessitated combat units being moved from the Stalingrad Front to bolster Luftflotte 1's strength to 550–600 aircraft, but with the worsening situation at Stalingrad in October, some 300 aircraft were hastily transferred back to this front from Luftflotte 1. At this time, Luftflotte 1 was also forced to release FlKps I which was sent south to the Voronezh area and was re-named Luftwaffenkommando Don.

Despite the crucial campaign in the Don Basin and the Kuban district of Russia, the Luftwaffe was once more forced to relinquish vital combat units to the Mediterranean. As early as September 1942, I/JG 53 'Pik-As', III/ZG 1 'Wespen' and 6./KG 26 were transferred from the Eastern Front to Luftflotte 2 in Sicily. The Axis reverse at El Alamein, followed on 8 November by the Allied landings in French North Africa, served to accelerate the out-flow from the East. By late December the following units had been posted; Stab, II and III/JG 77 and II/JG 51 'Mölders' with Bf 109s, and III/KG 4, II and III/KG 26, Stab and III/KG 30, II/KG 54 Stab, I, II, III/KG 76 and Stab KG 100 with Ju 88A-4s and He 111H-6s. The Ju 52 transport units, I/KGzbV I and KGzbV 102, were also sent, but had returned by early December. The total transfers from the Soviet Union and Northern Norway totalled almost 400 combat aircraft, bringing down the Luftwaffe's strength in Russia to about 2,000 aircraft, reducing the strike forces of FlKps I and VIII in the Don sector to 600–750 aircraft (the normal establishment was over 1,000), and weakening the complement of German single-engined fighters to a mere 375 over the entire Soviet Front.

The Jagdgruppen had received the first Bf 109Gs in August 1942. That superlative fighter, the Focke-Wulf Fw 190A, had first appeared in Soviet skies after I/JG 51's conversion at Jesau in mid-August, and during the autumn both III and IV/JG 51 'Mölders' converted. A fourth Gruppe, I/JG 54 'Grünherz', was operating over Leningrad front by February 1943. But this injection of Germany's finest fighters to the Soviet Front coincided with the influx of new Soviet aircraft types. The Lavochkin La-5 was powered by the Shevtsov M-82 radial engine developing 1,570bhp at 6,656ft (2050m) and was capable of matching the Bf 109Gs and Fw 190s when flown by a competent pilot. Its introduction in late-1942 was accompanied by the debut of the Yak-9. The La-5 and Yak-9 first saw large-scale action against German fighters over Stalingrad in November.

As the situation grew more critical in Stalingrad, the Luftwaffe was forced to divert a considerable portion of its strength to the supply of the VI Army, and also to support the XI Army in the Kuban. At the turn of the year, the Ju 52 units were joined in their task by He 111 bombers of KG 27, KG 55 and I/KG 100; these were augmented in January by He 177s under I(Erganzungsgruppe)/KG 50 and the Fw 200C-4s of 1. and 3./KG 40 – the latter operating under a specially formed unit known as KGzbV 200, first based at Stalino and later Zaporozhe. When the main airfield at Pitomnik was captured by Soviet forces on 16 January, supplies could no longer be landed and had to be dropped by parachute. The entire area was ringed by Soviet AA batteries which caused the Luftwaffe severe losses and, despite the gallantry of the transport pilots, the situation soon became hopeless.

The campaign in the Soviet Union leading to the German defeat at Stalingrad demonstrated that the Luftwaffe still adhered to the battle tactics of Blitzkrieg in close support of ground forces and armour. These tactics, so brilliantly successful in Poland, France and the Balkans, had demonstrably failed to achieve the desired results in the great battles of attrition in 1942. This was due not only to the immense length of the Soviet Front, which meant that every concentration for an impending offensive left the German flanks exposed, but also to the depth of the battlefield. The Soviet Army exploited these circumstances to the full by withdrawals which extended the German lines of communication until the combat units of the Luftwaffe, drawn far forward away from their supply bases, were weakened and hampered by supply and maintenance difficulties. Thus, the peculiar warfare conditions in the Soviet Union never enabled the carefully-conceived and well-tried Luftwaffe air strategy of combining the heaviest possible close-support with massive bombing attacks on factories and rear supply areas to result in final victory in spite of great initial successes.

THE STRUGGLE IN THE MEDITERRANEAN

The operational strength of General Hoffman von Waldau's Fliegerführer Afrika stood at 190 aircraft at the start of the long-awaited British counteroffensive, Operation Crusader, on 18 November 1941. Of these, some 70 were Ju 87B-2/Trop dive-bombers of Stab StG 3, I/StG 1 and II/StG 2, which represented the main striking force pitted against Auchinleck's tank squadrons. The remainder of Fl.Fü. Afrika comprised Stab, I and II/JG 27 with approximately 50 Bf 109E-7 and F-4/Trop fighters, a tactical reconnaissance unit, 2.(H)/14, a Staffel of long-range Bf 110D-3s of 8./ZG 26 and III/LG 1 whose Junkers 88A-4/Trop bombers suffered a high rate of unserviceability on account of the spartan desert conditions. However, von Waldau's small force was bolstered by some 320 aircraft of the Regia Aeronautica, of which half were single-engined Macchi C.200s and C.202s.

On 19 November, the 8th Army, bypassing Sollum and Halfaya Pass, commenced an all-out drive towards Tobruk but was checked by Rommel at Sidi Rezegh and Bir El Gubi. The subsequent tank and artillery battles of Sidi Rezegh were followed, on 7 December, by the relief of the garrison in Tobruk and, by 16 December, Rommel was forced to retire from Gazala to the west. Auchinleck triumphed and followed hard on the heels of the Afrika Korps and, by 6 January 1942, Rommel had retreated to the El Agheila defensive lines from which he had launched his first attack one year previously.

Throughout the short campaign, the Luftwaffe averaged 100 sorties per day, with peaks of 200, this low-key effort being due primarily to a critical fuel shortage brought about by shipping losses at the hands of the RAF and Royal Navy strike forces based on Malta. In December 1941, Kesselring's Luftflotte 2 arrived in Sicily with Fliegerkorps II from the Central Russian Front, but the addition of some 400 combat

358

aircraft in the Mediterranean theatre could not help Rommel's position in the desert at this time, due to the shortage of airfields in the Gulf of Sirte. The single-engined fighter units in Africa were stiffened by the addition of III/JG 27 (Hptm. Erhard Braune) and III/JG 53 (Hptm. Franz Götz), but the latter returned to Sicily on 26 December.

By January 1942, Luftflotte 2 was fully established at its Headquarters at Taormina, Sicily, with Generalfeldmarschall Albert Kesselring exercising full command over Fliegerkorps II (Sicily), Fliegerkorps X (Greece and Crete) and Fliegerführer Afrika. With almost 650 combat aircraft at his disposal, his task was to finally dispose of Malta and thus secure Axis sea communications in the Mediterranean as a whole and to North Africa in particular. With the failure to secure a quick victory in the Soviet Union, German attention was now turned to Southern Russia and North Africa from whence final victory could be achieved by the conquest of the Middle East oilfields from the Caucasus in the north and from Suez in the south.

While Kesselring made preparations for the assault on Malta, Rommel's counteroffensive from El Agheila started on 19 January 1942. Once again it was the problem of supply over the long desert routes that accorded either success or failure. The British lines of supply were stretched whereas Rommel had received fuel, men and material with the arrival of a large convoy in Tripoli and by air transport. The forces of Fliegerführer Afrika at the time of Rommel's offensive were: 2.(H)/14, three Gruppen of JG 27 with the Bf 109F-4/Trop, Jabostaffel/JG 53 with Bf 109E-7/Bs. 7./ZG 26 with Bf 110D-3s, Geschwaderstab StG 3 (Major Walter Sigel), I and II/StG 3 and Erg.Staffel StG 1. The serviceability status of these units was consistently low and, on 17 January, JG 27 mustered only 24 aircraft while, out of a strength of 69 Ju 87B-2/Trop dive-bombers, only 54 were fit for action. In the event, this force played little part in Rommel's counteroffensive, save for about 250 sorties on 21 and 22 January. Due to the poor condition of forward airfields, this sortie fell to about half during the proceeding weeks, and Rommel's drive to Benghazi and thence Gazala was all the more remarkable in view of the virtual absence of Luftwaffe support. In the ensuing three months, until May 1942, the situation in the desert remained static. Stukageschwader 3 was committed to harassing Tobruk, while JG 27 continued to profit from the superiority of the Bf 109F-4 over the Hurricanes, Kittyhawks and Tomahawks of the Desert Air Force.

In the Mediterranean, all eyes were turned upon Malta. Since April 1941, when the bulk of Fliegerkorps X retired from Sicily, RAF aircraft based in Malta had been able to inflict considerable damage on the ports through which passed the supply of materials for Rommel's Afrika Korps, and Maltese-based reconnaissance aircraft had been able to observe the traffic pattern to North Africa, enabling the RAF and the Royal Navy to reap valuable rewards from their attacks. To avoid the Malta-based aircraft, Axis convoys had to make large detours almost doubling the sea distance from Messina to Tripoli.

In January 1942, the fighter defence of Malta consisted of three Hurricane squadrons – Nos 126, 185 and 249 – based at Hal Far and Takali, while the Navy provided a flight of Fulmar Is under No 201 Group, Royal Air Force. On 17 January, the forces of Fliegerkorps II earmarked for operations against Malta were composed as the accompanying table shows.

The Luftwaffe air offensive on Malta was resumed in mid-January 1942 on a relatively modest scale, with some 65 sorties being flown every day, of which 40–50 sorties were flown by the Ju 88s. The pace continued at this level, amounting to little more than harassing attacks until the middle of March. On 7 March, fifteen Spitfire VCs were flown off HMS *Eagle* and arrived safely due to the efforts of the Hurricanes which successfully engaged a reception committee provided by 44 Messerschmitts of Major Günther Fr. von Maltzahn's JG 53. The Spitfires first saw action on 10 March, but further operations were halted by a period of bad weather.

The Luftwaffe launched a major assault on 21 March, and was to maintain a level of effort for the rest of the month and throughout the following April that was without parallel. At this time Fliegerkorps II was strengthened by 1. and 2.(F)/122 deployed to Gerbini and Trapani, II/JG 3 to San Pietro, III/JG 53 to Gela, 8. and 9./ZG 26 to Trapani, II/LG 1 to Catania and III/Stukageschwader 3 to San Pietro.

On 23 March, a determined effort was made to destroy the Vian convoy from Alexandria. The *Breconshire* was hit by Bf 109F-4/Bs of Jabostaffel/JG 3 at 09.20hrs when she lay off Valetta, the *Clan Campbell* was sunk south of Malta at 10.40hrs, and the remainder of the convoy came under heavy attack. This marked the start of the Luftwaffe's all-out attack on shipping and supplies, and from 24 March to 12 April, Fliegerkorps II flew 2,159 bomber sorties, sinking ships, devastating docks and installations, blocking quays and roadways, and cutting off power, water and communications.

During April 1942, 6,728 tons of bombs were dropped by the Luftwaffe on Malta. Valetta absorbed 3,156 tons, with the remainder aimed at the airfields of Takali, Luqa and Hal Far, the Luftwaffe attacking in force and with persistent regularity on every day but three when inclement weather prevailed. The crews of the Ju 88s flew three to four sorties a day for four days a week against spirited but totally inadequate RAF opposition. On 20 April, the USS *Wasp* flew off 45 Spitfire VCs manned by pilots of Nos. 601 and 603 Squadrons. As they completed the 600-mile flight to Malta, they were met by a few Hurricanes and Spitfires, but the Bf 109s reported their arrival and after 325 sorties by Ju 88s and Ju 87s against their bases half of the newly-delivered Spitfires had been destroyed.

As April drew to a close, the situation on Malta grew desperate; the RAF was virtually grounded, while the anti-aircraft batteries were critically short of ammunition. Throughout the month Nos. 126, 185 and 249 squadrons, along with the amalgamated units at Luqa and Takali, claimed over 200 enemy aircraft destroyed, but in relation, their own losses were far more serious: 23 Spitfires and 18 Hurricanes destroyed and 87 more in various states of damage.

The next reinforcement of Malta's beleagured fighter force came on 9 May, when the US *Wasp* and HMS *Eagle* flew off 64 more Spitfires which landed at Takali and Luqa at 10.30hrs. The Luftwaffe mounted some nine separate raids during that day in attempts to destroy these aircraft. At 05.25hrs on the following morning, HMS *Welshman* arrived in Grand Harbour, Valetta, with supplies of fuel and ammunition, and when the Luftwaffe struck at 10.20hrs with 20 Ju 87D-1s of III/StG 3 and 10 Ju 88A-4s of KGr 806, it was met by the largest fighter force ever mounted by the RAF over Malta. Thirty-seven Spitfires and 13 Hurricanes were scrambled, and in combats over the harbour these shot down four of III/StG 3's Stukas. In addition to these casualties, Fliegerkorps II lost four Ju 88A-4s and three Bf 109F-4s in the course of the day's fighting.

During May 1942, RAF fighters claimed 122 Axis aircraft destroyed, while the AA shot down a further 15; the cost was 23 Spitfires and two Hurricanes. In mid-May, Luftflotte 2's offensive on Malta was called off due to the now-active campaigns in North Africa, and to the fact that campaigns were to be resumed in the Soviet Union in the near future, the aircraft engaged against Malta now being needed elsewhere. It was becoming increasingly apparent that the Luftwaffe was becoming over-taxed and that major operations in one theatre could now only be mounted at the expense of another. The operations against Malta were not without their effect on the Luftwaffe. Some 300–400 had been kept heavily engaged from January to May, when they might have been conserved for efforts elsewhere. Moreover, the wastage rate had been high; about 250–300 German aircraft having been lost during April, with some 500 aircraft lost or severely damaged during the entire period.

Malta's ordeal was by no means over, however, and the island was kept in a state of semi-starvation throughout the summer, when desperate attempts were made to send convoys to the island from Gibraltar and Alexandria. The convoys 'Harpoon' and 'Vigorous' suffered near annihilation at the hands of Fliegerkorps II and X and the torpedo-bombers of the Regia Aeronautica's Aerosiluranti on 14 June. The great 'Pedestal' convoy sailed from Gibraltar bound for Malta on 10 August 1942, and on that day, II Fliegerkorps received reinforcements: 20 Ju 88A-4s came in from Fliegerkorps X in Crete, the Torpedo School at Grosseto supplied 10 He 111H-6s and Ju 88A-17s, and a Staffel of StG 3, resting in Sicily, was rapidly made ready. The Luftwaffe and the Regia Aeronautica mustered some 700 aircraft to attack the 'Pedestal' convoy and major actions were subsequently fought between 10–15 August 1942. The losses to both sides were appalling, but a few ships, including the vital tanker *Ohio*, managed to reach Malta with enough supplies and fuel to sustain the island until December.

In North Africa, the lull in fighting, which had enabled the British and Rommel's Afrika Korps to renew their resources, came to an end on 26 May 1942. It was Rommel who struck first and opened an offensive from Gazala which was to carry the Afrika Korps into the depths of Egypt – to El Alamein. At first it seemed as if Rommel had miscalculated; that shortages of fuel and water would destroy the Afrika Korps. However, Rommel was saved by his willingness to improvise and by the slow reaction of the British commanders. All German efforts were now concentrated upon the land battle in Libya, with a Blitzkrieg through the Nile Valley and on to Suez. In support of Generaloberst Erwin Rommel's Panzerarmee were 312 Luftwaffe and 392 Regia Aeronautica combat aircraft and transports. At the start of the offensive, III/JG 53 and Jabostaffel/JG 53 with 42 Bf 109F-4s joined Neumann's JG 27, while Major Sigel's Stukageschwader 3 was brought to full strength by the arrival of II and III/StG 3. Additional support was provided by the Ju 88s based on Crete and Sicily. The strength of the Desert Air Force opposing the Germans consisted of 320 aircraft, of which about 190 were combat ready.

Such was the diminishing importance of Malta that Kesselring transferred his headquarters to Africa from Taormina at the start of Rommel's offensive. The immediate aim was the seizure of Tobruk by a swift thrust through the Gazala- Bir Hacheim line. In this Rommel failed initially, becoming entangled in the fierce fighting around Bir Hacheim and the 'Knightsbridge' sector. During the first week of the offensive, Luftwaffe air effort was to be the greatest achieved throughout the whole North African campaign – no less than 300–350 sorties per day with the Stukagruppen contributing 100 of these and the fighters flying 150–200 sorties per day, representing 2.5 sorties per serviceable aircraft. Although this effort fell by about a third during the second week, the third week saw a new peak of intensity led by the assault on Bir Hacheim, which managed to hold out for nine days. With JG 27 and III/JG 53 flying escort, the effort of the Stukagruppen was reinforced by 30–40 daily sorties by the Ju 88s of LG 1 based on Crete. More than 1,400 bomber and dive-bomber sorties were flown against Bir Hacheim until its fall on 11 June.

Ten days later Tobruk fell. This was a terrific blow to Allied morale and as Lt.Gen. Ritchie's 8th Army retired to its defensive positions at El Alamein, for Rommel the road to Egypt and Suez now seemed open. JG 27 and III/JG 53 were constantly in the air, escorting Ju 88s and Ju 87s, and flying Frei Jagd missions over the British lines. Oberleutnant Hans-Joachim Marseille, Staffelkapitän of 3./JG 27, had reached the zenith of a brilliant combat career in North Africa. Since his arrival in Libya, he had scored consistently: his 50th 'kill' had been achieved on 22 February 1942, his 75th on 6 June, and on 18 June, Marseille was awarded the Schwertern (Swords) to the Ritterkreuz for his 101st kill! His rise to fame had been meteoric and he was hailed as 'the unrivalled virtuoso of German fighter pilots'. His greatest achievement came on 1 September when he shot down 17 enemy aircraft in the Imayid sector during Rommel's offensive at Alam Halfa. He received the Brillanten (Diamonds) – as the fourth fighter pilot after Mölders, Galland and Gordon Gollob – on the following day. On 30 September, however, while returning from a Stuka-escort, the engine of his Bf 109G-2 caught fire. Marseille jettisoned the canopy, half-rolled his machine and baled out, but, knocked unconscious by the tailplane, he never pulled the rip-cord of his parachute and was killed. His final score was 158 kills – all but 7 were shot down in North Africa – in the course of 382 operational flights.

Having failed to make any further progress after the battles of Alam Halfa in September, Rommel was forced hereafter to hold on to his positions west of El Alamein and endeavour to consolidate his forces in the face of growing strangulation imposed by interference with his lines of sea supply. Fuel, little as it was, was passed to the XV and XXI Panzer Divisions at the expense of the Luftwaffe. Thus, although on the eve of the British offensive at El Alamein, the operational strength of the Luftwaffe amounted to only 290 aircraft, it being impossible for logistic reasons to maintain a stronger force in Africa at this crucial time.

When the El Alamein battle started, on 24 October, both I/JG 27 and II/StG 3 had been posted back to Sicily for a renewed bombing assault against Malta. The sole addition to Fliegerführer Afrika prior to El Alamein comprised I/Sch.G 2 (ex-III/ZG 1), based at Bir El Abd with 35 ground-attack Bf 109F-4/Bs.

On the eve of Montgomery's great counteroffensive the strength of the Allied air forces had been boosted to some 750 aircraft, of which 530 were combat ready, and this numerical superiority over the limited and fuel-starved Luftwaffe proved decisive. The constant RAF and US air attacks on the main German air-bases at Fuka, Qotaifiya, Daba, Qasaba and Sidi Haneish seriously impaired the effectiveness of the Luftwaffe, and during the first week of the battle combat operations by JG 27 and StG 3 diminished to almost nothing. Following a week of bitter and confused fighting, Rommel's Panzerarmee retired to the Fuka positions on 2 November, and two days later was forced into a fighting retreat along the Via Balbia to the West.

By 15 November, Fliegerführer Afrika was operating from airfields in the Benghazi area, its Stuka strength having fallen to about 30 Ju 87D-3s, while no more than 80–100 Bf 109G-1/Trop and G-2 fighters of Stab, I and III/JG 77 and II/JG 27 remained, and these were further reduced to about 60 with the retreat to Arco and Nofilia, in the Gulf of Sirte. These forces moreover, were in no position to continue operations in the absence of appreciable supplies and ground organisation, and in the prevailing confusion and demoralisation of retreat. Such was the situation of the remnants of Fliegerführer Afrika's forces at the moment when the Allies landed in French North Africa on 8 November 1942.

■ The Allied landings to the German defeat in Tunisia, 8 November–12 May 1942–3

Secure in the knowledge that the Allies would open a second front in the Mediterranean in the Autumn of 1942, German reinforcements started to flow into that theatre as early as October, but there still remained the question of where the Allied landings would be made. Prior to the Allied landings at Oran, Algiers and Casablanca on 8 November, Kesselring's Luftflotte 2 received the following combat units from the Soviet Union, France and the Eastern Mediterranean. From 31 August to 31 October: 11./JG 2, 11./JG 26, II/JG 2, I/JG 53, Stab and III/JG 77, with Fw 190A-4s equipping Hptm. Adolf Dickfeld's II/JG 2 'Richthofen' and the rest with Bf 109Gs; II and III/ZG 1 with Bf 110G-2s and a staffel of Me 210A-1s; and 1. and 2./KG 60, III/KG 30, 9./KG 40, II/KG 54, II/KG 6, II and III/KG 26, III/KG 4 and Stab/KG 100.

During the four weeks following the landings, strong Luftwaffe reinforcements continued to flow into Luftflotte 2, and by 12 December, the Mediterranean theatre contained a peak strength of 1,220 combat aircraft, of which some 850 were based in Sicily, Sardinia and Tunisia. Of particular importance was the denuding of a large force of Ju 88A-17 and He 111H-6 torpedo-bombers from Luftflotte 5, in Norway, that had been committed against the vital PQ convoys to northern Russia. And the transfer of 120 Ju 88s and He 111s, along with a similar number of Bf 109Gs, from the Southern and Central Fronts in the Soviet Union coincided with the Soviet Army's new offensive on the Don.

Notwithstanding the surprise caused by the landings, German reactions to the threat were prompt. By 9 November, a number of Bf 109G and Stuka units were sent to Bizerta, Tunis-El Aounia and Souk El Arba in Tunisia from Sicily and Sardinia. These moves were accompanied by the air-lifting of supplies by Ju 52s, Me 323s and Go 242s, and by the end of the second week the Luftwaffe had occupied the airfields at Gabes and Dejedeida. A new command, Fliegerführer Tunisien, under Generalmajor Harlinghausen, was formed. On 10 January 1943, this command comprised the following units – 2.(H)/14, II/JG 2, Stab, I and II/JG 53, III/SKG 10 and one staffel of II/StG 3. Due to the shortage of suitable airfields, Luftflotte 2 did not commit any Kampfgruppen to Tunisia, and Harlinghausen's command was destined to be essentially a close-support and tactical organisation. Fliegerführer Tunisien was soon to be in the remarkable position of being able to maintain an equality with numerically superior Allied air forces, owing to the even greater problems of forward supply with which the Allies were faced.

When Montgomery re-opened his offensive against Rommel's defensive position at Beurat, in Tripolitania, on 15 January, the Luftwaffe units in that sector were subordinated to Oberbefehlshaber Süd, and consisted of 4.(H)/12, 1.(F)/121, Major Jochen Müncheberg's JG 77 'Herzas', I Gruppe plus 4./Sch.G 2 and III/StG 3. In addition to the Fl.Fü Tunisien, a Kommando Roth at Gabes consisted of elements of 2.(H)/14, II/JG 51 'Mölders' and a staffel of II/StG 3.

Tripoli fell on 23 January, and the 8th Army pushed forward to Mareth on the Tunisian border, while from the West, the Germans were threatened by the Allied offensive into Tunisia. On 14 February, the Germans launched a counteroffensive against the two Allied thrusts that threatened the armies of Rommel and von Arnim. On this day, the Ju 87s, Hs 129B-2s, Fw 190s and Bf 109Gs of Fliegerführer Tunisien flew 360–375 sorties in support of the successful German thrust to Feriana and Sbeitla, reducing this effort to 250 sorties per day until bad weather intervened. The strength of Fl.Fü Tunisien remained around 300 first-line aircraft throughout this campaign, and this number was maintained during the subsequent offensive by the 8th Army from Mareth to 19 March 1943. The II/JG 2 achieved considerable success in Tunisia; Oblt. Kurt Bühligen claimed 40 'kills' during the campaign, while Oblt. Erich Rudorffer shot down 26 Allied aircraft including eight 'kills' on 9 February and seven on 15 February. However, attrition among experienced fighter pilots was high. For example, Major Joachim Müncheberg of JG 77 was killed on his 500th operational flight in combat with Spitfires of the US 52nd Fighter Group on 23 March, and Hptm. Wolfgang Tonne, Staffelkapitän of 3./JG 53, was killed in an accident on 20 April, his score being 122 victories.

As the German situation in Tunisia deteriorated, so the gradual transfer of Luftwaffe units to Sicily took place. By the beginning of May, only 200 aircraft of Fliegerführer Tunisien remained in Africa, these withdrawing to Sicily in total by 12 May 1943. In the last days of the North African battle, the Luftwaffe in the Mediterranean, although still comprising over 800 aircraft, was an effete force, completely unable to achieve effective intervention. Its influence in the last days of the Tunisian campaign was nil, and Allied aircraft and naval forces were able to counter the frantic German evacuation effort and thus translate defeat in North Africa into a disastrous rout.

THE HOLDING CAMPAIGN IN THE WEST

■ The night fighters, 1940–43

At the beginning of the war German defence against nocturnal air attack was almost wholly dependent on flak and searchlights. Indeed, the Flak regiments of the Luftwaffe were considered to be the élite arm, and the efficiency of their weapons, searchlights and prediction equipment was of a very high standard. But the limitations of anti-aircraft artillery were soon to become painfully obvious. On the night of 15/16 May 1940, Royal Air Force Bomber Command was authorised to launch an attack on German industrial targets in the Ruhr for the first time, after months of needless restrictions on its operation. The strategic bombing of Germany had commenced, although it was to be another two years before RAF Bomber Command was in a position to achieve worthwhile results. That night, however, heavy ground haze in the Ruhr robbed the Flak of the possibility of effective action.

Apart from a small number of Staffeln practising a rudimentary form of night fighting with obsolescent Bf 109Ds, no attempt was made to form a realistic nocturnal fighter force until early June 1940, when elements of ZG 1 were sent to Düsseldorf to form the Nacht und Versuchs Staffel (Night and Experimental Unit) under Hptm. Wolfgang Falck. On 17 July 1940, a further development in the creation of a night-fighter force took place when Göring entrusted Josef Kammhuber, ex-Geschwaderkommodore of KG 51, with organisation and formation of Nachtjagddivision 1. Although Kammhuber had no previous experience in night fighting, he applied himself to the task of equipping and expanding his Division with energy and skill.

Promoted to Major, Wolfgang Falck formed his Geschwaderstab NJG 1 at Düsseldorf on 20 July. On that day also, two Gruppen were formed from existing units: I/NJG 1 was formed from two Staffeln of I/ZG 1 and the remnants of IV/JG 2 and equipped with Messerschmitt Bf 110C-2s, and II/NJG 1 was formed from the Zerstörer Staffel/KG 30 with Junkers Ju 88C-2 fighters issued to two Staffeln, while 4./NJG 1 of the same Gruppe was equipped with the Dornier Do 17Z-10 (Kauz II). Within weeks, III/NJG 1 had been formed from a nucleus of pilots from IV/JG 2. During September, a specialist night intruder Gruppe was also formed. This, the II/NJG 1, had been termed a 'Fernnachtjagd Gruppe' (Long-range night fighter unit), and it was redesignated I/NJG 2 and based at Gilze-Rijn in Holland. To replace the old unit, a new II/NJG 1 was formed from I/ZG 76 and equipped with Bf 110D-1/U1 night-fighters at Deelen-Arnhem. By the Autumn of 1940, the three Gruppen of NJG 1 were operational and based at Venlo, Leeuwarden and St Trond Deelen for specialist night fighter work, while II/NJG 2 embarked on a series of successful night intruder missions across the North Sea against RAF Bomber Command airfields. At this time, NJG 3 was formed on Bf 110s but, by December 1940, the I Gruppe had been posted to FlKps X in Sicily.

Generalmajor Kammhuber had himself no knowledge of radar and his ground organisation, largely drawn from the Flak, had as yet no awareness of its possible application. In Autumn 1940, the Würzburg A, a parabolic reflector ground radar unit, was introduced, but was largely seized upon by the Flak Command as an aid to fire and searchlight prediction. General Martini, the Luftwaffe Signals chief, however, assigned to Kammhuber six trained signals companies equipped with Würzburg A, and, in co-operation with his staff, Kammhuber evolved a night fighting tactical procedure called Helle Nachtjagd (Illuminated Night Fighting). In October 1940, the first Helle Nachtjagd sector was established astride the main RAF Bomber Command route to the Ruhr. This area measured 90km in length and 20km in width, and was split into three sectors. Each sector contained a searchlight battalion, two Würzburg A radar units and attendant night fighters. While one Würzburg radar controlled a master searchlight, the other tracked the movements of the night fighters; the two sources of information were correlated by a ground controller who, in turn, passed R/T instructions to the night-fighter pilots. In good weather conditions the system worked well; the three night fighters in the sector could be vectored simultaneously by the controller, with each pilot attacking his target while it remained in the searchlight.

Kammhuber fully appreciated the limitations imposed on Helle Nachtjagd by bad weather or cloud conditions; even 6/10th cloud cover created considerable difficulties. He therefore concentrated wholly on the perfection of ground control interception based on radar. At this early stage, German night fighters did not carry airborne interception radar, but the new control procedure, known as Himmelbett (Four-poster Bed), enabled a good fighter controller to vector the night fighter to within 400 yards of its quarry. At that stage, the pilot was able to see the bomber's exhaust flashes and carry out a visual attack.

The Himmelbett system relied on two different types of radar equipment, each having advantages over the other. Firstly the Freya radar (manufactured by Gema GmbH and working on 118–130Mcs) offered long-range target location, normally – with a maximum of 60–75 miles – the first Freya to be discovered by the British was at Auderville on the Cap de la Hague in February 1941, and by October of that year the RAF had located a line of Freyas stretching from Bödo in Norway to Bordeaux in the Bay of Biscay. Freya could plot range and azimuth but not the altitude of the target. Produced by Telefunken and working on the 545–570Mcs band, the Würzburg Reise was limited to about 30 miles in range but worked to very fine limits and could produce an estimation of target height. In the Himmelbett system two Würzburgs worked in conjunction with a Freya and a number of night-fighters that 'stacked' over a radio beacon. Freya provided the early warning and the Würzburgs plotted the target and the selected night fighter for a ground controlled interception.

What was to be known later as the 'Kammhuber Line' was a series of GCI Himmelbett sectors located at first in the immediate approaches to the Ruhr and then extended, by March 1941, from Antwerp to Sylt, on the Danish border. The Himmelbett system worked well and achieved results, but RAF bombers soon started to fly detours around the searchlight and night fighter zones on their way into Germany, dictating the continual lengthening of the defence line.

Air Marshal Sir Richard Peirse, the AOC Bomber Command, was also encountering problems at this time. Firstly, there was the lack of a clear strategic policy. The original bombing directive called for an offensive against the German synthetic oil industry when weather conditions were suitable, and for raids on large cities (area attacks) for the purpose of 'undermining civilian morale' when bad weather precluded 'precision' attacks. However, RAF Bomber Command was unable to achieve anything approaching a precision night-bombing attack due to the absence of any suitable radio aids to navigation. In March 1941, the Command was forced to concentrate on naval targets due to the escalating losses in British shipping in the Atlantic that were causing great concern. In good weather, coastal targets were easy to locate at night, and Hamburg, Bremen and Kiel were frequently subjected to area attacks. In June and July 1941, the main effort was directed at Brest and the vessels *Scharnhorst, Gneisenau* and *Prinz Eugen*. Meanwhile, the oil plan had cooled and, at the end of July, Bomber Command was left without a concrete bombing strategy, switching from attacks on the oil industry to transportation. The bombing directive of 8 July earmarked nine important rail centres, mainly in the Ruhr, for subsequent attack.

In April 1941, Kammhuber's Nachtjagddivision 1, previously subordinated to Luftflotte 2, came under the newly-formed Luftwaffenbefehlshaber Mitte (Air Command Centre), which controlled all day and night fighter operations over Germany, Denmark and Holland. As of 1 August 1941, Nachtjagddivision 1 became Fliegerkorps XII, with its Headquarters at Zeist, in Holland. The establishment of

Stab, I, II and III/NJG 1 and Stab and I/NJG 2 on 31 May was 188 aircraft of which 140 were serviceable.

By late summer 1941, RAF Bomber Command was beginning to suffer consistent losses to German night fighters and flak, culminating in 37 aircraft being lost on the night of 7 November, which represented 10 per cent of the force despatched. The only way in which Bomber Command could achieve reasonable bombing accuracy was by operation in clear weather and preferably on moonlit nights: such offered ideal opportunities for easy 'kills' by the German night fighters, their crews having every reason to regard the Himmelbett system as sufficient for their task. However, Kammhuber considered airborne radar as an aid to final interception as essential to the efficiency of his command. As early as 1940, Kammhuber had submitted a technical requirement for an airborne radar resulting in the installation, in July 1941, of a pre-production FuG 202 Lichtenstein BC airborne radar set in a Do 215B-5 fighter of 4./NJG 1 based at Leeuwarden. Manufactured by Telefunken GmbH, and working on 490Mcs, Lichtenstein BC offered good azimuth presentation with a minimum range of 200 yards and a maximum of 3,000 yards in expert hands.

Several aces, notably Hptm. Helmutt Lent and Oblt. Paul Gildner of NJG 1, would have nothing to do with AI because its cumbersome aerial array caused a reduction in speed of some 15–25mph. This attitude became widespread and prevailed until Oblt. Ludwig Becker of 4./NJG 1 began to achieve positive successes with Lichtenstein BC – his fourth 'kill' using this equipment was picked up at an initial range of 3,060 yards. Although the potential of Lichtenstein BC was now realised and Kammhuber persuaded Hitler to give this apparatus top industrial priority, the loss in aircraft performance that its installation entailed continued to be resisted, and crews often opted to fly aircraft not fitted with radar. By the early months of 1942 FuG 202, was undergoing operational trials in four Bf 110E-1/U1s of I/NJG 2. Despite the high priority, the supply of sets remained slow, and it was not until July 1942 that all II/NJG 1 aircraft were fitted with Lichtenstein, while other units remained partially equipped.

By November 1941, two new Gruppen had been formed – II/NJG 2 and II/NJG 3. During the following month, I/NJG 2 was re-equipped with the Ju 88C-4 fighter and posted to FlKps X in Sicily. The night intruder work of I/NJG 2 had abruptly stopped in October on an express order of Hitler, despite notable successes and enthusiasm of the crews. In March 1942, the first Dornier Do 217J-1s were issued to 4./NJG 1 for combat trials, but the type was considered inferior to the older Do 215B-5.

This period coincided with a time of crisis for RAF Bomber Command in which the lack of a clear-cut bombing policy, the constant diversion of its forces to other tasks and the failure of some of its principal aircraft, had finally come to fruition. The Manchester bomber had been something of a failure owing to the inadequate state of development of its engines, and the Stirling was disappointing primarily as a result of the limitations of the specification to which it had been designed. The bulk of Bomber Command squadrons were equipped with the Wellington, a reliable aircraft but without the range and bomb load to sustain a new offensive. Britain had now entered the phase of the war wherein her fortunes were at their nadir. Something had to be done and the only direct means of attack at her disposal was RAF Bomber Command.

When Air Marshall A. T. Harris assumed command on 22 February 1942, a new directive called for bomber attacks on Germany with the prime objective being the undermining of the morale of the civilian population. Bomber Command was materially assisted at this time by the withdrawal from Brest of the *Scharnhorst* and *Gneisenau*, thus removing an onerous commitment. In addition, the introduction of Gee (TR 1335) in a growing number of bombers enabled a nucleus of the force to locate targets with a modicum of accuracy in all weathers. From this time onwards, all was aimed at trading maximum destructive effort for the minimum of losses. Mass incendiary bombing would achieve the destruction by fire, while the active and passive German defences could be saturated by the concentration of the bomber force over the target in the shortest possible time spread. The navigational aid, Gee, was first used operationally by 22 bombers on 8 March in a raid on Essen. This was followed rapidly by eight other attacks, but despite the assistance given by Gee and the use of marker flares, industrial haze foiled Bomber Command which produced poor results.

Harris next turned to small, easily-identifiable targets to be raided during moonlight periods. These controversial area attacks against mostly civilian targets opened with Lübeck on 28 March, continued with an attack on Rostock a month later and culminated in the first 1,000-bomber raid on 30/31 May 1942 on the city of Cologne and during which 41 RAF bombers were shot down – this representing only 3.8 per cent of the attacking force of 1,046 aircraft. This raid was of propaganda value primarily, and such numbers of aircraft could not be used again until 1944. The political aspect of the Cologne raid was significant and thenceforth RAF Bomber Command underwent expansion and enjoyed high industrial priority. The crisis was over.

To counter this ever-growing threat from RAF Bomber Command, Kammhuber was forced to expand his existing forces. In October 1942, IV/NJG 1 was formed from a nucleus of II/NJG 1, and other Nachtjagdgeschwader underwent expansion. The Messerschmitt Bf 110G, equipped with either FuG 202 Lichtenstein BC or FuG 212 Lichtenstein C-1, appeared in service. Other types, including the Ju 88C-6b and the Dornier Do 217J-2, were also on strength by the end of the year, when Kammhuber's forces consisted of NJG 1, I/NJG 2, NJG 3, NJG 4 and NJG 5. Together, these had inflicted, in conjunction with Flak, a loss rate of 4.1 per cent of Bomber Command's sorties – a figure altogether too high if the offensive was to be maintained and increased. The night fighter crews could be satisfied that their efforts were gaining in momentum, but their real test was yet to come.

■ The day fighters, 1941–3

By November 1940, while the Kampfgruppen of Luftflotte 2 and 3 pounded British cities by night, the Messerschmitt Bf 109Es of the Jagdgruppen were committed to fighter-bomber work and high-altitude Frei Jagd sweeps over the Channel and southern England. Combats with Spitfires and Hurricanes of Fighter Command still raged, although on a much reduced scale than hitherto. The German fighter losses were relatively light, but one of the Luftwaffe's leading 'Experten', Major Helmut Wick, Geschwader Kommodore of JG 2 'Richthofen', was shot down on 28 November by Flt. Lt. J. C. Dundas DFC of No 609 Squadron, in a dogfight off the Isle of Wight.

Rest and re-equipment for the Jagdgruppen was the order of the day throughout the winter; most unit remained at the same airfields from which they had operated during the Battle of Britain under Jafü 2 and Jafü 3. The first unit to be issued with new Messerschmitt Bf 109F-1 was the Geschwaderstab and III/JG 51 at St Omer-Wizernes. Commanded by Major Werner Mölders, the top-scoring German fighter pilot, JG 51 first received the Bf 109F-1 in early February, but its service introduction was marred by structural weaknesses in the tail-plane – on 10 February, Lt. Ralf Steckmayer of 11./JG 51 became the first casualty when his Bf 109F-1 crashed under unknown circumstances at Balinghem. After a temporary grounding of all Bf 109F-1s, flying was resumed but resulted in yet another crash. Suspicion turned from the engine to the unbraced cantilever tail unit which was found to suffer a sympathetic vibration leading eventually to structural failure. Within weeks, all F-1s had been modified, and the problem solved. The introduction of the Bf 109F-2 followed during March and April. This type was on initial issue to JG 51 and II and III/JG 53, but JG 2, JG 3 and JG 26 were partially equipped with it during May.

Royal Air Force fighter pilots first met the Bf109F in combat during March, but it was not until 8 May, when a Bf 109F-2 flown by Lt. Günther Peopel of 1./JG 3 crashed in Kent, that the RAF could confirm the existence of the new Messerschmitt model. With the rapid withdrawal of Luftflotte 2 from France in June 1941, only JG 2, JG 26 and II/JG 52 remained on the Channel Front; in Norway, two Staffeln of I/JG 77 remained, while elements of JG 1 were stationed in Denmark, Germany and Holland. This last mentioned unit consisted of only one Gruppe and was largely occupied on convoy escorts and training duties.

The restoration of RAF Fighter Command's strength during the winter enabled it to pursue a limited offensive against the forces of Jafü 2 and 3 during the Spring. With the opening of the German offensive in the Soviet Union in June, RAF Fighter Command, under Air Marshal William Sholto-Douglas, and No 2 Group Bomber Command opened a limited campaign against the Luftwaffe in northern France with the object of tying down as many fighter units in that theatre at the expense of the Russian Front. For the next two years, JG 2 and JG 26 fought a lone and bitter battle against the RAF over the Channel and northern France. Pitted against Nos 10, 11 and

12 Groups, Fighter Command, these Geschwader inflicted a 2 to 1 ratio of casualties against the RAF despite their numerical inferiority. The operational strength of JG 2 and JG 26 seldom exceeded 240 aircraft, but they were well led, were always equipped with the latest Bf 109s and Fw 190s and fought with all the advantages that had hitherto been the prerogative of RAF Fighter Command during the Battle of Britain.

Initially the RAF fighter tactics were encompassed within an operation known as the 'Circus'. This was a shallow penetration raid accompanied by a mass of escorting fighters, the object being to bring the Luftwaffe to battle and inflict casualties. The 'Circus' was later modified to include fighter-sweeps (Rodeos) acting in conjunction with the main force, or as a diversion. By late-1941, however, German radar coverage of northern France was efficient, the performance of the latest Bf 109F-4 was superior to the Spitfire VB in all but tight turns, and it was the Luftwaffe that began to inflict a prohibitive loss rate upon Fighter Command. During August 1941, JG 2 and JG 26 shot down 98 Spitfires and 10 Hurricanes for the loss of eighteen fighter pilots killed in action.

By November 1941, Fighter Command called a halt to offensive operations and embarked on a winter of conservation. The plan for the new offensive called for nothing new, although the faster Boston III in place of the Blenheim IV promised to make the job of the fighter escorts a little easier. All hopes of an effective and less costly offensive due to the widespread re-equipment with the Spitfire VB were dashed with the entry into combat of the Focke-Wulf Fw 190A fighter. The service introduction of the Fw 190A with II/JG 26 in July 1941 had been marred by numerous teething troubles, mainly associated with the new BMW 801 engine. The RAF encountered the Fw 190s during late-summer and autumn, but the new German fighter was unable to display its full potential until 1942.

Both JG 2 and JG 26 were heavily engaged on 12 February 1942 while providing fighter protection for the *Scharnhorst, Gneisenau* and *Prinz Eugen* during Operation Cerberus-Donnerkeil – the daring Channel passage from Brest to Kiel. Operation Donnerkeil (Thunderbolt) was the task of Oberst Adolf Galland, the General der Jagdflieger, and consisted of the air-phase of the operation. The forces under his control consisted of one Gruppe of ZG 26 with Bf 110D-3s, JG 2 with Bf 109F-2s and F-4s, and Major Gerd Schöpfel's JG 26 with Bf 109F-4s Fw 190A-1s and A-2s. The Fw 190 component consisted of II/JG 26 (Hptm. Joachim Müncheberg) and III/JG 26 (Hptm. Josef Priller), based at Abbeville-Drucat and Coquelles respectively. At the close of day, when the ships were off the Dutch coast, support was to be provided by I/JG 1. The operation was carried out with brilliant results. A number of Bf 109F-4s of JG 2 were damaged as a result of bad weather landings in Holland, while JG 26 suffered 4 pilots killed – 35 RAF aircraft and six Swordfish of No 825 FAA Squadron were shot down by flak and fighters.

In April 1942, Major Walter Oesau's JG 2 received its first Fw 190A-2s while at the same time Hptm. Johannes Seifert's I/JG 26 underwent conversion at St Omer-

Arques. On 18 April 1942, the order of battle of Sperrle's Luftflotte 3 was made up of fighters, reconnaissance units, bombers and coastal aircraft. Their dispositions are shown in the accompanying table.

The Jabostaffeln of JG 2 and JG 26 were formed on 10 March 1942, with the BF 109F-4/B fitted with bomb-racks capable of carrying an SC 250 (550lb) bomb. Operations started in April, and the RAF could offer no positive defence against these fast, low-flying fighter-bombers which achieved an effect out of all proportion to the effort they represented. The Chain-Home and CHL radar stations situated in Britain were unable to plot the movements of the Jabos on account of their low altitude and Fighter Command was forced to mount standing patrols in order to counter the threat. Most targets were situated along the southern coast of England and only on rare occasions did the Jabos penetrate inland. Canterbury suffered a heavy attack by 10.(Jabo)/JG 2 and JG 26 on 31 October 1942, and this was followed by a maximum effort by the Jabos on London on 20 January and 12 March 1943. By this time, a specialist fighter-bomber unit – SKG 10 – had been formed and, in April 1943, JG 2 and JG 26 transferred their Jabostaffeln to IV/SKG 10.

The Jagdgruppen based in northern France continued to inflict prohibitive casualties on Fighter Command's incursions throughout the summer and, despite the slow introduction of the Spitfire IX, the ascendancy of the Fw 190 remained unchallenged. In July 1942, two high-altitude units (Höhenstaffeln) were operational on Bf 109G-1s, these being 11./JG 2 at Ligescourt and 11./JG 26 at Norrent-Fontes. 'Gustav' proffered little performance gain by comparison with the Bf 109F-4 that it succeeded, and 11./JG 2 suffered a setback when its Staffelkapitän, Oblt. Rudolf Pflanz, was killed over Berck-sur-Mer on 31 July 1942.

Fighter Command received an added commitment on 17 August 1942, when the 8th USAAF flew its B-17E Fortresses on an operational mission to Rouen for the first time. At first targets for the USAAF bombers lay within the combat radius of the Spitfire, but by late October, the B-17s and the B-24s that had followed them to the UK were venturing outside this radius to St Nazaire, Lorient and La Pallice. These attacks were usually intercepted by Hptm. Egon Mayer's III/JG 2 based at Vannes. The Gruppe was faced with numerous combat problems in their attacks on the high-flying, well armed and closely-knit formations of bombers. The head-on attacks, first attempted on 23 November 1942 over St Nazaire, solved some of these difficulties, but they lacked cohesion and results were limited.

Luftflotte 3 was forced to relinquish a number of fighter and fighter-bomber units to other theatres during November, and II/JG 2, 11./JG 2 and 11./JG 26 were posted to Luftflotte 2 in the Mediterranean. The Jabostaffeln and I/JG 2 were sent to the South of France in December, while I/JG 26 was transferred to the Soviet Union during the following month.

MARITIME OPERATIONS OF THE LUFTWAFFE 1939-45

Prior to 1939, so powerful was the concept of a Continental strategic war, with emphasis on land operations supported by strong air forces, that little thought had been given to the possibility and potentiality of maritime operations by the Luftwaffe against enemy shipping. This was a naval affair and, in 1939 the few maritime units whose task was mainly reconnaissance were under the command of a Führer der Seeluftstreitkräfte, himself subordinate to the General der Luftwaffe beim Oberkommando der Kriegsmarine (Ob.d.M). The Seeluftstreitkräfte, or Fleet Air Arm, bore no resemblance to the carrier-borne forces of either the Royal Navy or the US Navy and consisted in the main of maritime reconnaissance types such as the Heinkel He 59B, the Heinkel He 115A and the Dornier Do 18D seaplanes and flying boats. Concentrated within a number of Küstenfliegergruppen, these aircraft were stationed at coastal bases in the Baltic and North Sea, and whereas their prime rôle was that of the 'eyes of the Fleet', offensive capability was restricted to mine-laying and torpedo operations on an experimental scale.

Late in the summer of 1939, the Luftwaffengeneralstab became convinced of the necessity of providing a force of modern bombers for offensive operations against enemy naval forces which might attempt to enter German waters. In addition, it was propounded, these could also attack the bases of the Royal Navy. The use of Seeluftstreitkräfte forces for this purpose was out of the question due to inter-service prejudices and the obsolescence of the naval aircraft, with the result that the Luftwaffe went ahead with the formation of a specialised anti-shipping force on its own initiative. Already in April 1939, General Hans Geisler had been appointed as General zur besonderer Verwendung (Gen. z.b.V) and charged with the task of forming the nucleus of an anti-shipping strike force. He and his staff were stationed at Kiel-Holtenau, under control of Luftflotte 2.

With the outbreak of war in September 1939, Geisler's command was up-graded to Fliegerdivision 10, with Major Martin Harlinghausen as Ia Offizier responsible for operations. Harlinghausen's anti-shipping experience dated back to the Spanish Civil War, and the development of the Luftwaffe anti-shipping arm was to owe much to this ex-naval martinet in the ensuing years. At first, the strike force of Fl.Div 10 consisted of elements of two Kampfgeschwader that were built up to full strength over the next six months. These were I and II/KG 26 'Löwengeschwader' and I/KG 30 'Adlergeschwader' equipped with He 111P-2 and Junkers Ju 88A-1 bombers respectively, the latter being activated at Jever on 22 September. These bomber units acted in close co-operation with the reconnaissance units of Ob.d.M, and in the opening weeks of the war made their presence felt over the North Sea and in attacks on RN bases at Scapa Flow and in the Firth of Forth. Operations of a more limited nature were also carried out by Do 18s of 2.Staffeln of Kü.Fl.Gr. 106, 406, 506, 806 and 906, while staffeln of these same units used He 115s.

The crews of KG 26 and KG 30 had little or no previous experience of attacking warships, but a select band of officer pilots, one of whom was Major Werner Baumbach of I/KG 30, evolved and perfected their own methods in operations over Scapa and the North Sea. Much German publicity was given to the alleged sinking of the carrier HMS *Ark Royal* on 26 September by I/KG 30, but in fact the vessel was only lightly damaged. Two Ju 88s, including that flown by the Gruppenkommandeur, Hptm. Pöhle, were shot down by Nos. 602 and 603 Squadrons when I/KG 30 attacked the anchorage at Scapa Flow on 16 October, and during which attack the cruiser HMS *Southampton* was hit by a bomb which failed to explode while damage was suffered by HMS *Edinburgh* and HMS *Mohawk*.

On 1 December, II/KG 30 was activated at Barth, followed one month later by the formation of III/KG 30. In February 1940, Fliegerdivision 10 was again up-graded to the status of Fliegerkorps X, and with the anti-shipping operational experience gained by this command it became the natural choice for Weserübung – the closely co-ordinated land–sea operation for the invasion of Denmark and Norway. Both KG 26 and KG 30 were selected to play a leading part in this operation in which a powerful enemy naval reaction was anticipated, and their operations were to be in conjunction with the mine-laying forces of Ob.d.M.

While the parallel development of maritime bombers was in hand, a small number of enthusiastic officers of the Seeluftstreitkräfte had been successful in evolving tactics for aerial sea mining. General Joachim Coeler became the Führer der Seeluftstreitkräft in April 1939, and as soon as his appointment had been confirmed, he set about the task of forming units as specialists in the work of sea mining. At first he met with considerable opposition from the Kriegsmarine and it was only through continual agitation that he finally gained authority from Ob.d.M to proceed with operations on a limited scale. The early sorties to the Thames Estuary and the coastal regions off

Sheerness each had to carry the explicit permission of the Kriegsmarine, but, in time, Coeler was granted clearance to operate independently; the obsolete He 59s were replaced by Do 17Z-2 and He 111P-4 aircraft, and the selected Küstenfliegergruppen ranged to coastal waters off the Clyde, the Firth of Forth, Plymouth, Liverpool, and the Thames Estuary. Standard parachute sea mines of this period were the LMA (1,102-lb) and the LMB III (2,028-lb).

Growing losses on mining operations attracted the attention of Herman Göring and Coeler was called to give an explanation. This he did with such emphasis on the successes of sea mining operations as opposed to the losses that Göring was convinced of the efficacy of mine-laying and undertook to create a special Luftwaffe command for mine-laying forces; in February 1940, this command was formed and named Fliegerdivision 9. On the formation of this command, the minelaying unit which had been responsible for the development of aircraft and tactics was withdrawn from the influence of the Seeluftstreitkräfte and the Ob.d.M. This move marked the beginning of a disintegration of the Seeluftstreitkräfte, a tendency which became more pronounced as units were seconded to the Luftwaffe proper and then absorbed. In July 1942, the Seeluftstreitkräfte was dissolved.

During the initial phases of Weserübung, KG 26 was deployed at Lübeck-Blankensee and Marx, in Germany, but by 10 April, 1. and 7. Staffeln were installed at Stavanger-Sola and Fornebu. KG 30, at Sylt-Westerland, mustered 84 Ju 88A-1 bombers of which 47 were combat ready on 9 April, the launching day of Weserübung. Elements of this Geschwader were later deployed to Stavanger, Fornebu and Trondheim-Vaernes. The Junkers 88s were heavily committed against the Royal Navy on the first day of Weserübung, flying 47 sorties against British warships. KG 26 also put up 41 sorties, the joint action resulting in damage to the cruisers *Devonshire, Southampton, Glasgow*, and the sinking of the destroyer *Gurkha*.

Prior to Weserübung, extensive sea reconnaissance work was carried out by He 115s of Kü.Fl.Gr. 506 and Major Edgar Petersen's Fernaufklärungsstaffel equipped with Fw 200C-0 Condors, which reconnoitred the sea approaches to Norway up to Lat 63° North. Foreseeing the need for very long range maritime reconnaissance aircraft, Petersen, a navigation specialist on the staff of Fliegerkorps X, had recommended the use of the Fw 200 transport as the only type suitable for adaptation for this work. His efforts resulted in the formation of the Fernaufklärungsstaffel in November 1939, which took on hand six of the ten Fw 200C-0s being built and became operational immediately. On 17 April 1940, this staffel was redesignated 1./KG 40, sent to Aalborg, and then to Copenhagen-Kastrup on 26 April for anti-shipping and supply duties in the Narvik theatre. By late June 1940, the unit had been increased to Gruppe-strength as I/KG 40, and was operational with Fw 200C-1 Condors from Brest and, while administratively it was under Luftflotte 2, it operated under the direct control of the naval command at Lorient, known as Marine Gruppe West.

During the campaign in the Low Countries and France the aircraft of Fliegerkorps X continued their attacks on naval and merchant shipping, and improved their tactics in the bombing of coastal convoys in British waters. The FlKps X was now stationed at bases in Norway and Denmark under Luftflotte 5 and, in addition to reconnaissance units, consisted of KG 26, KG 30 and Kü.Fl.Gr. 506; all other units had been withdrawn to take part in the operations in Holland, Belgium and France. Fliegerdivision 9, on the other hand, was able to increase its minelaying forces after the fall of France by a whole Geschwader of some 100 aircraft. This was KG 4 with I and II Gruppe equipped with He 111Hs and the III Gruppe working up on Ju 88A-1s. The remainder of Fliegerdivision 9's forces consisted of KGr. 126 and Kü.Fl.Gr. 106, the former with He 111s and the latter with He 115B-2 seaplanes. On 17 October 1940, Fliegerdivision 9 was renamed Fliegerkorps IX and, at this time, controlled Stab, I, II and III/KG 4, Geschwaderstab KG 40 which was operational on Ju 88s, Stab, II and III/KG 30, KGr. 126 and Kü.Fl.Gr. 106. The only bomber unit remaining in Fliegerkorps X was II/KG 26, the other Gruppen serving with FlKps I as normal bomber units engaged in operations against England.

With the failure to force a decision against Great Britain during the summer, the task of bringing an eventual surrender was entrusted to the Kriegsmarine. The spearhead of these forces was the U-boat arm commanded by Grossadmiral Karl Dönitz, the Oberbefehlshaber der U-Boote, whose bases were now situated along the western coast of France at Brest, Lorient, La Pallice, St. Nazaire and Bordeaux. The smaller Type IIA U-boat of 303 tons had been supplanted by the 871-ton Type VIIC with ocean-going capability, and its crews ranged far and wide across the North Atlantic, attacking the vital supply convoys from Canada and the United States of America. The amount of shipping sunk by U-boats during the summer of 1940 rose to staggering proportions: in June fifty-eight ships of 284,000 tons, in July thirty-eight ships of 196,000 tons, in August fifty-six ships of 268,000 tons, in September fifty-nine ships of 295,000 tons and in October a peak of 63 ships of 352,000 tons, all with the loss of only six U-boats. Small wonder that the achievements of June to October 1940 were dubbed the 'happy time' by the U-boat commanders and crews.

Allied convoys lacked adequate escort and the merchant vessels, themselves, were pitifully lacking in armament, and these factors were largely instrumental in bringing success to the Condor crews of I/KG 40, by now based at Bordeaux-Mérignac. Throughout August and September 1940 I/KG 40 claimed the destruction of 90,000 BRT, and during the autumn and winter the Condor menace became a baleful factor in the Battle of the Atlantic. To the crews, however, the Condor, despite its 14-hours' endurance, displayed some notable deficiencies due largely to its airliner pedigree. Its relatively light construction was inadequate for the long periods of low level flight over the sea in which turbulence continually put stress on the airframe; evasive manoeuvres had to be performed delicately, while the bomb load with normal fuel amounted to only four SC 250 (550-lb) bombs – less than that of the very much smaller but purpose-designed Junkers 88. Accordingly, the serviceability of the Fw 200 was to remain low throughout its operational career. Despite this, its early operation against Allied shipping was attended with conspicuous success.

Deliveries of the Fw 200C-1 Condor to I/KG 40 were slow, and for this reason, when III/KG 40 was formed in January 1941, it was equipped with He 111H-6 bombers, with the intention of re-equipping with Fw 200s when these became available. The successes against Allied shipping continued with 63,000 BRT claimed in January, and rising to 22 ships of 84,500 BRT claimed during the following month. One notable individual achievement during this period took place on 16 January 1941, when Hptm. Verlohr, the Staffelkapitän of 1./KG 40, sank two ships totalling 10,857 tons. Several Condor sorties at the behest of Marine Gruppe West consisted of a three-day detachment to Trondheim-Vaernes, a patrol being flown from Mérignac to reconnoitre the seas off Ireland and the Fw 200 then making its way to either Trondheim or Stavanger in Norway.

The anti-shipping command, FlKps X, had been transferred in December 1940 to the Mediterranean theatre for operations against Malta and the British convoys sailing between Gibraltar and Egypt. It had now become apparent to the Führungsstab (Operations Staff) of OKL that if a blockade of Britain was to be carried out a more formalised structure of anti-shipping commands would have to be set up as soon as possible, while forces were still available and before the impending commitments in the Balkans and the Soviet Union complicated the situation.

In March 1941, a re-grouping of commands took place whereby the whole European coastline facing Great Britain and the Atlantic was covered by anti-shipping forces. In practice, this reorganisation did little more than take over existing anti-shipping forces, but their strength immediately began to increase, particularly in the area facing the Atlantic and Western Approaches. After the withdrawal of FlKps X from Norway, Luftflotte 5 (Stumpff) created two new subordinate commands. These were Fliegerführer Nord (later split up into Nord and Nord-Ost), and Fliegerführer Lofoten; their duties were anti-shipping operations and reconnaissance for the U-boats and other naval forces to the North of Lat 58°N. The North Sea area from Lat 52°N to 58°N still remained the responsibility, as far as reconnaissance was concerned, of the Führer der Seeluftstreitkräfte, whose Gruppen were based along the western coast of Jutland. Fliegerkorps IX, based in Holland, retained the responsibility for minelaying around the British coasts. To cover the Western Approaches and Atlantic, and South-West coasts of England, the regrouping was completed by the formation of Fliegerführer Atlantik, under Obstlt. Harlinghausen, with Headquarters subordinated to Luftflotte 3 (Sperrle) at Lorient.

The main focus of U-boat and anti-shipping operations by Fl.Fü. Atlantik throughout 1941 was on the Allied convoys to Britain from Gibraltar, the South Atlantic and the United States. The two primary tasks of Harlinghausen's command were therefore divided as follows:

1. Reconnaissance reports to Fliegerführer Atlantik and the Befehlshaber der U-Boote by Fw 200s of KG 40 concerning the position and movements of shipping for subsequent attack by U-boats. In this capacity the Condors acted as Fühlungshalter (shadowing aircraft) for the U-boats by keeping in visual contact with the convoys and enabling German D/F to fix the position by continual radio (W/T) transmissions. This task was in addition to normal bombing attacks on shipping when the opportunity arose.

2. Attacks of coastal shipping around the eastern, southern and western coastlines of Britain, by Ju 88s and He 115 torpedo bombers.

At its inception Fl>Fü. Atlantik's complement of aircraft amounted to 44, but, by April 1941, its establishment consisted of 21 Fw 200C-2 Condors (of which 6–8 were stationed at Trondheim, in Norway) of Obstlt. Petersen's Geschwaderstab and I/KG 40, 26 He 111H-6 bombers of III/KG 40, 24 He 115B-2 torpedo-bombers of Kü.Fl.Gr. 906 and the reconnaissance 3.(F)/123 with 12 Bf 110s and Ju 88D-2s. The serviceability of I/KG 40 was rarely more than 6 to 8 aircraft out of an operational strength of 25 to 30; a frequent cause of unserviceability were failure of the rear spar and breaking of the fuselage just aft of the wing trailing edge. This parlous situation was reduced slightly by the introduction of the strengthened Fw 200C-3 version that came on strength during the summer. The 'happy time' for the Condor crews, if not entirely for the U-boats, was already over and losses suffered during lone shipping attacks grew alarmingly. Allied merchant vessels now carried machine-guns and 20-mm Oerlikon cannon, and could put up a spirited fight, making the low and slow pass of the Condor a hazardous affair. By November 1941, the classic Condor tactics of a mast-height approach from astern or abeam had been rendered virtually impossible due to its inability to take punishment from even relatively small calibre defensive fire.

After the withdrawal of Luftflotte 2 from France to the Soviet Union at the beginning of June 1941, Fliegerführer Atlantik became the primary anti-shipping strike force based in the West; Fliegerkorps IX restricted itself to minelaying and was often used on night bomber operations over England, while Fliegerführer Nord and Fl.Fü. Lofoten were employed on reconnaissance duties. On 16 August 1941, the forces under Fliegerführer Atlantik consisted of I/KG 40 with a strength of 28 Fw 200C-3s, II/KG 40 with 24 Do 217E-2s, III/KG 40 with 20 He 111H-6s, three staffeln of KGr. 606 with 20 Ju 88A-4s, two staffeln of Kü.Fl.Gr. 906 with 9 He 115B-2s, and 5./BFGr. 196 with 26 Ar 196A-2s and He 114A-2s. These anti-shipping and convoy protection forces were also bolstered by Stab, II and III/KG 30 which, with II/KG 2, operated under FlKps IX from bases in Holland and Northern France.

By the end of August, KG 30 had retired to Northern Norway, while Kampfgruppe 606 transferred its Ju 88s from France to the Mediterranean during the early part of autumn, thus seriously depleting the anti-shipping component of Fliegerführer Atlantik. Meanwhile two further Gruppen were formed within KG 40; II/KG 40 was established in August on the Dornier Do 217E-2 and operated from

Soesterberg under FlKps IX in the coastal anti-shipping rôle and IV(Erg.)/KG 40 was established at Bordeaux as a training and replacement unit for the Geschwader.

There was now an increasing tendency to employ the anti-shipping forces equipped with Ju 88s and Do 217s in bombing raids at night and in bad weather against targets in England. This was done to assuage German public opinion in the face of mounting attacks by RAF Bomber Command and vehement protests at the misuse of these forces by Sperrle and Harlinghausen fell upon deaf ears. Indeed, it was apparent that the importance of Fliegerführer Atlantik had waned. Firstly, the force was accorded fewer combat units and, secondly, when Harlinghausen was wounded during an operational mission over the Bristol Channel in October 1941, his post was filled by a deputy only. The officer appointed as Fliegerführer Atlantik early in 1942 was Generalmajor Kessler, one who hitherto had held obscure posts in the Luftwaffe. Battle returns of 1 January 1942 showed Fliegerführer Atlantik's forces as being I/KG 40 with a strength of 18 Fw 200s, 8. and 9./KG 40 with 18 He 111H-6s (7.Staffel was re-equipping with Fw 200s), Kü.Fl.Gr. 106 with 20 Ju 88A-4s, Kü.Fl.Gr. 506 with 23 Ju 88A-4s, and 2./Kü.Fl.Gr.906 with He 115C-1 torpedo-bombers.

■ Torpedo bomber operations, 1942

Since 1932 German torpedo development had been in the hands of the Kriegsmarine which had purchased the Horten naval torpedo patents from Norway in 1933 and the Whitehead Fiume patents from Italy in 1938. Development in the direction of air-launched torpedoes was pursued in a leisurely manner by the Seeluftstreitkräfte, and the results of trials and reports of combat operations were jealously guarded by the naval parties responsible. When the Luftwaffe finally took an interest in torpedo work to reduce losses suffered on anti-shipping sorties, it received scant assistance from the Kriegsmarine.

In 1941, the Luftwaffe decided to pursue its own development trials with the intention of setting up a powerful force of torpedo-bombers. The first torpedo development establishment was formed at Grossenbrode, on the Baltic coast. Several aircraft types were exhaustively tested and it was soon apparent that the He 111 and, in particular, the faster Ju 88 were the most suitable. Kampfgeschwader 26 was to play the leading rôle in this new torpedo plan, with Stab, I and III/KG 26 selected as the specialist torpedo unit while II/KG 26 remained in the bomber rôle, operating under FlKps X in the Mediterranean. The detachment of a few of KG 26's He 111s to FlKps X in the autumn of 1941 for torpedo operations was shortlived due to lack of torpedoes, or, in some cases, the delivery of the same without warheads.

In January 1942, the Luftwaffe's demands for the centralisation and control of all German and Italian torpedo development were granted. Oberst Martin Harlinghausen was appointed as the head of all Luftwaffe torpedo development, supply, training and operational organisations, with the Torpedo Training School established at Grosseto, south of Leghorn in Italy. During the early months of 1942,

I/KG 26 underwent torpedo conversion courses lasting on average between three and four weeks. The Gruppe's He 111H-6s could carry two torpedoes slung on racks beneath the belly; the standard torpedoes used were the German LT F5 and LT F5W, both of 450-mm calibre, with the latter based on the Italian model made by Silurificio Whitehead di Fiume.

While I/KG 26 underwent conversion at Grosseto, its future and the bases from which it would operate had already been decided. With the failure to crush the soviet Union before the winter of 1941–42, the Anglo-American supply convoys that were being sent to Russia via the Arctic route began to assume even greater importance to the Germans. The forces under Luftflotte 5 available for the interception of these convoys were normally engaged in such duties as the protection of the Petsamo nickel mines, shipping attacks in the White Sea and the bombing of Soviet ports and communications in the area, as well as Wehrmacht support operations on the Finnish Front. In February 1942, these forces consisted of 1.(F)/120, Stab JG 5, 3. and 7./JG 5, Einsatzstaffel Trondheim, 2./KG 26, 4. Staffel and III/KG 30, and the coastal forces of Kü.Fl.Gr 706 with Ju 88A-4s, 2./Kü.Fl.Gr. 406 with BV 138B-1s, and 1./Kü.Fl.Gr. 906 with He 115C-4s. In addition, I/StG 5, engaged on the Russo-Finnish Front, was available at short notice for short-range anti-shipping strikes over the White Sea.

In March, Göring ordered Luftflotte 5 to collaborate with the Kriegsmarine whenever the Allied supply convoys should pass through the Arctic area. When such convoys were expected, their progress was to be reported by Fw 200s and BV 138s, while all possible striking forces were to be temporarily withdrawn from the Finnish area to the airfields at Banak, Bardufoss and Kirkenes to supplement existing forces and to attack the convoys as soon as they came within range. Long-range reconnaissance was to be undertaken by the Condors of I/KG 40 operating from Trondheim-Vaernes and northern airfields, and was to cover the area of sea between Iceland, Jan Mayen Island, Bear Island and the North Cape, supplemented by the BV 138s of 2./Kü.Fl.Gr. 406. April 1942 saw 2./KG 40 detached to Rechlin and the reconnaissance duties from Vaernes falling upon 1. and 3.Staffeln and III/KG 40, which alternated between Bordeaux and Trondheim. At this time, Petersen had been succeeded by Oberst Pasewaldt as Kommodore. Within I/KG 26, based at Banak and Bardufoss, there were now 12 crews available for torpedo operations with the Heinkel He 111H-6 (Torp).

During March and April, the convoys PQ 13, 14 and 15 sailed for the Soviet ports of Archangel and Murmansk. I/KG 40 located these supply convoys and attacks by I/KG 26 and KG 30 followed in which the collective Allied losses amounted to two cruisers and 15 merchant vessels – seven of the latter being claimed by the Luftwaffe. While convoy PQ 16 set out from Iceland on 21 May 1942, the returning empty convoy, QP 12, left Murmansk on the home run. The escorting ships and the 35 merchantmen of PQ 16 were sighted by KG 40 which sent back position reports to

Luftflotte 5's operational headquarters at Banak. The first torpedo attacks by I/KG 26 and high level bombing attacks by the Ju 88A-4s of KG 30 commenced on 25 May, and lasted for five days, with the Stukas of I/StG 5 joining in when the convoy entered the final leg into the White Sea area. Seven vessels were sunk, but the Luftwaffe claimed the destruction of the entire convoy.

After this action the Luftwaffe forces once more retired to their duties on the Finnish Front. I/KG 26 remained at Banak, however, to await the coming of the next convoy. After the passage of PQ 16, new lessons had been learned which were to form the basis of later tactics when greater torpedo forces were expected to be available. It was found that considerable confusion could be sown among the enemy defensive screens by the use of co-ordinated torpedo and bomber attacks. The most favourable time was at dusk, with the torpedo-bombers running in from the darker hemisphere aided by the ships pre-occupied in warding off dive-bombing and level-bombing attacks by the Ju 88s of KG 30, thus affording the low-flying Heinkels an element of surprise. The tactic known as 'Golden Zange' (Golden Comb) consisted of a mass torpedo attack by as many as 12 He 111H-6s flying in wide line-abreast, with a simultaneous release of torpedoes to obtain the maximum spread while dividing defensive fire.

The battle returns of Luftflotte 5 of 20 June show the strike force as consisting of Führer Kette KG 26 and I/KG 26 with an establishment of 53 He 111H-6 (Torp) aircraft and III/KG 30 with 35 Ju 88A-4s. The fighters of 2. and 3./JG 5, along with IV/JG 5, were primarily responsible for the defence of Kriegsmarine units based at Trondheim – at this time the battleship *Tirpitz* was stationed near Trondheim along with the cruisers *Hipper* and *Scheer*.

When warnings of the next convoy, PQ 17, were received in early July, the strength of Luftflotte 5 was bolstered by the arrival of the whole of KG 30 and I/StG 5 to 264 combat and reconnaissance aircraft. At this time of year, daylight conditions prevailed throughout the 24-hour cycle and, on 1 July, the convoy was sighted and remained under continual surveillance by Fühlungshalter aircraft. The Heinkel He 115C torpedo bombers of 1./Kü.Fl.Gr. 406 conducted the first aircraft attack on this luckless convoy, when eight intercepted PQ 17 at 18.00hrs on following day. On 4 July, the torpedo bombers of Major Werner Klümper's I/KG 26 and the Ju 88s of KG 30 sank two merchantmen and damaged two others. The likelihood of naval intervention by *Tirpitz* now caused alarm at the British Admiralty, and that evening the order for the convoy to scatter was sent to the incredulous escort commanders. They acted with immediate effect and from here it was a question of *sauve qui peut*. Throughout the following day, the U-boats and the Luftwaffe fell upon the defenceless and dispersed merchantmen, sinking twelve of their number. Only two vessels reached Archangel on 10 July, but over the next few days the stragglers came limping in. The final count of this disastrous convoy was 23 ships sunk out of the original total of 33 that sailed from Iceland on 27 June. Luftflotte 5 lost five aircraft during the action and sank thirteen merchantmen and one rescue ship.

By the end of July, III/KG 26, under Hptm. Nocken, had completed the course at Grosseto and had transferred its Ju 88A-4 (Torp) bombers to Rennes-St. Jacques in Brittany. The Gruppe carried out its first torpedo operation against a convoy off the Scillies on 3 August, was transferred to Banak for an impending convoy operation on or about 10 August, but when this did not materialise, was sent back to Rennes. On 1 September 1942, the Gruppe was again sent to Banak. The forces under the control of Luftflotte 5 on 10 September 1942 were as follows: 1.(F)/120 with reconnaissance Ju 88D-5s at Banak and Bardufoss; II/JG 5 with 33 Bf 109G-2s at Alta, Altengaard and Petsamo; IV/JG 5 with 24 Fw 190A-3s at Banak and Bodo; the torpedo-bomber units, I and III/KG 26 with 34 and 24 He 111H-6 and Ju 88A-4 aircraft respectively at Banak; the Geschwaderstab and three Gruppen of KG 30, including the Epr.Staffel KG 30, mustering a strength of 113 Ju 88A-4s, A-6/Us and A-14s, were also stationed within the Banak airfield complex, and elements of Kü.Fl.Gr. 406, 706 and 906 forming the seaborne component. A formidable anti-shipping force indeed.

The Convoy PQ 18, which came under attack by German aircraft and U-boats between 11–18 September 1942, differed from previous Arctic convoys in that its anti-aircraft defences, which included an aircraft carrier, were incomparably stronger. Thirteen merchantmen out of a total of 40 were sunk from PQ 18 and three out of 15 were lost on a returning QP convoy that came under attack at the same time, in addition to a tanker, a destroyer, a minesweeper and four aircraft of the Fleet Air Arm. Four U-boats were destroyed and in marked contrast to PQ 17, Luftflotte 5 admitted the loss of no fewer than 41 of its bombers.

The torpedo attacks by I and III/KG 26 were usually timed to follow immediately after the high-level bombing attacks by KG 30. Owing to bad weather, however, III/KG 26 carried out only four torpedo attacks on PQ 18, and the cloud base (never more than 1,000ft) prevented any attempts at the synchronised torpedo and bombing attacks that had hitherto been so successful. The ring of escorting vessels and the presence of RN Hurricanes and Wildcats rendered the torpedo attacks particularly vulnerable, with I/KG 26's slow Heinkels taking much punishment. Hauptmann Nocken's III/KG 26 attacked PQ 18 off Spitzbergen on the 11th losing two Ju 88s; an attack on the aircraft carrier on the following day cost the Gruppe three or four torpedo-bombers. These were long and strenuous flights, lasting in some cases as long as seven hours. The AA fire was described as horrific; the chances of rescue for a downed crew were nil and, besides, in the freezing waters so far north of the Arctic Circle life was measured in minutes only.

The III/KG 26 employed the 'Golden Zange' tactic during their attacks in which the Ju 88s, flying at sea-level, extended into line abreast when about 20kms from the convoy, a distance of 200–300 metres separating each aircraft. The pilots then approached the convoy from directly abeam and, flying in this fashion, it was relatively easy to slip between the escorting vessels. The formation's spacing prevented individual pilots from selecting the same target, and such was the spread of the convoy that the entire Gruppe flying in line abreast could only 'comb' part of the convoy at a time with its torpedoes. Both LT F5b and Italian LT F5W torpedoes were used; the F5W was preferred as the F5b's whisker type detonating pistol seldom operated when the target was hit at an acute angle.

The attack itself was launched amidships, with the approaching aircraft at exactly 90° to the course of the ship. The torpedoes were launched at a range of 1,000 metres, and usually from a height of 40 metres (125 feet), the aircraft then pulling up over the nose of the ship. The aircraft had to be flown dead straight and level in order for the weapon to enter the water at the stipulated 12°, and this was considered the time at which the crew was in the greatest danger. Anti-aircraft fire, and in particular 20-mm Oerlikon fire, was considered a greater threat than escorting RN fighters. Owing to the time lag there was seldom any opportunity to observe either the track of the torpedo or the possibility of an eventual strike, and every attempt was made to execute violent evasive action. In the final analysis I/KG 26 claimed ten vessels. KG 30's attempts were recognised as poor and lacking in determination for only 13 per cent of the sinkings were accorded to the Geschwader with the lion's share of 87 per cent being attributed to the torpedo-bombers of KG 26.

The Convoy PQ 18 saw the last of the massed torpedo attacks by the Luftwaffe and never again were the concentration and results achieved in subsequent actions in the Mediterranean and elsewhere. With the Allied landings in North Africa, the Mediterranean became the pivot of anti-shipping operations by the Luftwaffe. During October and November 1942, the Stab, I and III/KG 26 were sent to Grosseto for re-fit, joining II/KG 26. The I and II Gruppen resumed operations from Elmas under FlKps II, while III/KG 26 went to Heraklion under FlKps X. KG 30 was also posted to FlKps II in Sicily, with the exception of the I Gruppe. Subsequent operations saw the anti-shipping forces taking massive casualties in the face of growing Allied air superiority and the negative results achieved were attributed largely to the inexperience of replacement torpedo-bomber crews.

■ The Atlantic and the Bay, 1942–3

The anti-shipping forces under Fliegerführer Atlantik had been reduced still further by the end of May 1942. They consisted of 3.(F)/123 at Lannion, Stab and III/KG 40 with 19 Fw 200C-4s at Mérignac, Stab KG 6 and Kü.Fl.Gr. 106 with 19 Ju 88A-4s at Dinard and coastal reconnaissance units Stab/Kü.Fl.Gr. 406 and 5./BFGr. 196 at Brest. The Dornier Do 217E-4 bombers were concentrated under FlKps IX, with KG 2 and II/KG 40 based in Holland.

Kampfgeschwader 40 had been relegated to reconnaissance duties for the Befehlshaber der U-boote, while forced at the same time to detach its units to Luftflotte 5; the 1.Staffel was undergoing He 177 conversion at Fassberg, in Germany. The Condors now carried the Rostock ASV radar for shipping search, and the later FuG Hohentwiel radar was also appearing as standard equipment. The III/KG 40's normal patrols at this time were termed the grosse and kleine Aufklärung; the patrols were divided by Lat 45°N with the westerly limit extending to Long 19°W, or on occasions to 25°W. On grosse Aufklärung the northerly limit was Lat 50°N, beyond which there was a grave risk of interception by RAF Beaufighters and Mosquitoes. The Facher (Fan) method of search was a form of 'creeping line-ahead' in which the Condor started from 15°W, for example, flew West for 3 degrees of longitude, turned South for 30 miles and then turned East for another 3 degrees.

The axis of U-boat operations was now centred in mid-Atlantic, with a growing tendency by U-boat commanders to venture far south into the Caribbean and the Gulf of Mexico. Through the Bay of Biscay there passed, on numerous occasions, damaged U-boats returning from their patrols, and these were frequently subjected to attack from RAF Coastal Command. At the time U-boat sinkings in these circumstances were not serious, but there now arose the need for some form of long-ranger fighter cover to reduce the threat of attack. In July 1942, III/KG 40 took charge of a small number of Ju 88C-6 fighters for duties over the Bay of Biscay; by September, with the activation of V/KG 40,* the Ju 88s were concentrated in the 13.Staffel with the Gruppe made up to the full strength of four staffeln by December. The formation and conversion took place at Mérignac and when operational the staffeln were sent to Kerlin-Bastard, near Lorient.

It was not until the spring of 1943 that operations for V/KG 40 took on a more serious nature. Five out of every six U-boats made passage through the Bay of Biscay for operations in the Atlantic and the Caribbean, and this small area of sea, only 300 miles in length and 120 miles in width, became the chosen killing ground. Hitherto, Air Vice Marshal G. R. Bromet's 19 Group, RAF Coastal Command, had reaped little success in this area for which it was responsible – seven U-boats had been sunk in the Bay in 1942, with two more added by February 1943. The introduction in March of ASV Mk. III and the American ASV Mk. IV radars, both working, on the 10-centimetre band, radically altered the situation. The U-boats carried a radar location aid called Metox 600 which gave range (up to 40 miles) and bearing of the ASV Mk. II (1½-metre band) radar, carried as standard on Coastal Command's patrol aircraft, and this allowed the commander to submerge in good time. With ASV Mk. III, however, there was no such aid to location, and losses in the Bay started to mount. To counter this, the U-boats were fitted with Flakvierling 20-mm and Flak 18 37-mm guns and their crews were encouraged to fight it out on the surface.

In May 1943, V/KG 40's strength averaged some 45 Ju 88C-6s. The Gruppe's HG was at Kerlin-Bastard, but staffeln were always detached to Mérignac and Cognac. Reinforcement crews were trained in the 10.Staffel of IV/KG 40 at Chateaudun, where new Ju 88C-6s and R-1s were received for allocation. The normal

Formed from elements of KG6.

duties of V/KG 40 consisted of U-boat escort and sweeps over the Bay to counter RAF Coastal Command anti-submarine aircraft. Normal patrols, when engaged on counter sweeps, extended to Lat 8–10°W with a northern boundary fixed at Lat 45°N, but on occasions patrols went as far as 15°W. At first, the Ju 88s operated in Schwarme (four aircraft) but in face of increasing Beaufighter opposition, it was common procedure to operate at least eight, or even 16 aircraft in one formation; normal formation was an extended echelon port or starboard. Of all the Allied aircraft frequently encountered over the Bay, the Sunderland was considered the most difficult to shoot down. One example of this occurred on 2 June when a Sunderland of No. 461 RAAF Squadron fought a running battle with V/KG 40s Ju 88s in which the Gruppe lost three without being able to destroy the flying boat. The Ju 88 crews preferred to attack Sunderlands either from head-on or directly abeam in order to avoid the potent rear armament.

At one time, during the summer of 1943, Coastal Command was losing one aircraft per day to V/KG 40 in battles over the Bay of Biscay. The courier service between Portugal and Britain also suffered from the attentions of the Gruppe. The 14.Staffel was on patrol between 12° and 13° West on 2 June 1943 when it intercepted the DC-3 transport carrying Leslie Howard, a well known British actor who lost his life when the aircraft was shot into the sea. However, the losses of V/KG 40 were consistently high, one crew captured by the British in July 1943 estimated that some 37 crews had been lost since it had joined the Gruppe in November 1942.

Such was the high level of RAF activity in the Bay during the late summer that additional Luftwaffe fighter units were drafted at the urgent request of Dönitz. The II/ZG 1, under Hptm. Karl-Heinz Matern, was transferred with its Bf 110G-2 fighters from Pratica de Mare to Kerlin-Bastard on 5 August, and a week later the Gruppe was operating patrols from Lanvéoc-Poulmic, near Brest. The forces under Fl.Fü. Atlantik on 30 September 1943 consisted of the fighters of Jagd Kommando Brest with five Fw 190A-4s, 1./SAGr. 128 with 17 Fw 190s and Ar 196s, and 2./SAGr. 128 with six Ar 196A-3s. The V/KG 40 had 44 Ju 88C-6s and II/ZG 1 had 39 Bf 110G-2s on strength. The 2./KG 40 had nine He 177A-5 bombers while 7. and 9.Staffel of KG 40 operated the Condor with the former at Cognac and the latter at Mérignac.

■ New weapons and new tactics, 1943–4

By the late summer of 1943, two of Germany's air-launched guided weapons were ready for action in the anti-shipping rôle. The first was the Ruhrstahl FX 1400 (Fritz-X) stand-off bomb. Carrying a 3,300-lb warhead, Fritz-X was released by its parent aircraft from 16,000–20,000 feet and fell at a terminal velocity approaching the speed of sound. It carried no propulsive motor, but was guided by a bomb aimer in the parent aircraft who was aided by a bright flare mounted in the tail of the bomb. The first unit to use Fritz-X was III/KG 100, formed from Lehr and Erprobungskommando 21, with Do 217K-2s which each carried two such bombs on ETC

2000/XII racks. The second new weapon was the Henschel Hs 293 glider-bomb which carried a 1,100-lb warhead. A small rocket motor accelerated the glider-bomb to 370mph, cutting out after a period of 12 seconds and allowing the weapon to coast in a shallow glide. Once again a flare mounted on the fuselage assisted the bomb aimer in its guidance, flight being controlled by use of a small joystick. This weapon was first issued to II/KG 100 equipped with Do 217E-5s which could carry two Hs 293s under the wings outboard of each engine.

Both units were under the overall command of Major Bernhard Jope, and commenced operations from Marseilles-Istres under Fliegerdivision 2 in late August 1943. The first missions of these Gruppen were attended with some success; a notable achievement occurred on 9 September when III/KG 100 sank the *Roma* and severely damaged the *Italia* battleships. During the following months both II and III/KG 100 were in actions against Allied supply convoys in the Mediterranean and flew missions during the Salerno and Anzio landings. The torpedo bomber units, I and III/KG 26, also operated from bases in Southern France under Fl.Div 2 with tangible results achieved on all their missions, but at an appreciable cost which rose, on one occasion, to 20 per cent of the force involved. Rest and replacement took place of necessity, and after four further missions, in October and November, the anti-shipping units in the Mediterranean remained inactive until 10 January 1944, when an Allied convoy was attacked off Oran.

During the autumn, III/KG 40 started receiving Hs 293 glider-bombs which were fitted to Fw 200s which each carried two of the new weapons and desultory operations with these were commenced on 28 December. The Heinkel He 177, upon which so much reliance had been placed, was also now finally reaching operational units, both as a bomber and an anti-shipping aircraft. The dismal story of its development and operational debut are beyond the bounds of this chapter, but, during late 1943, two Gruppen of KG 40 were undergoing conversion to the He 177A-5. The 1./KG 40 was sent from Fassberg to Chateaudun along with half of 2.Staffel on 19 December, and here joined I/KG 100, also equipped with the He 177. These units were not connected with anti-shipping operations and were earmarked for Operation Steinbock, the retaliatory attacks against Britain, under Fliegerkorps IX. The II/KG 40, however, was intended as an anti-shipping force from the outset. Formed from I/KG 50 (the original Dornier 217-equipped II/KG 40 was redesignated V/KG 2), II/KG 40 was transferred to Bordeaux-Mérignac and flew its first operation on 21 November, when its He 177A-5s attacked a convoy. Twenty Heinkels, each carrying two Hs 293s, were despatched to intercept Convoy SL139/MKS 230, outbound from Britain to ports in North Africa and Sierra Leone. Despite bad weather, Fliegerführer Atlantik insisted on the attack which resulted in one straggler being disabled for the loss of three of II/KG 40's bombers. A disastrous mission was flown against a convoy off Bougie on 26 November, four He 177A-5s being shot down, three crashing in France and casualties included the Gruppenkommandeur, Major Mons. This operation and that preceding it left II/KG 40 with only seven serviceable aircraft. The Gruppe now turned to night operations in which a Kette would drop flares while another launched its Hs 293s from a range of 6–9 miles; this had the salutory effect of reducing losses to a bearable level.

By December 1943, long-range reconnaissance work was conducted by FAGr. 5 which maintained a small force of Ju 290A-5s at Mont de Marsan, in Southern France. The heavy fighter unit, V/KG 40, was incorporated into Stab, I and III/ZG 1 which operated Ju 88C-6s from Kerlin-Bastard and Vannes. In March 1944, Fliegerführer Atlantik was disbanded and all anti-shipping forces came under the command of FlKps X with Fl.Div 2 subordinated. Grandiose plans calling for an anti-shipping force of major proportions with which to oppose the long-awaited Allied invasion of France all came to nought as units were diverted from their intended tasks and relegated to bombing attacks under the auspices of Operation 'Steinbock'.

Immediately prior to the invasion of Normandy, in June 1944, the anti-shipping forces of Fliegerkorps X consisted of Stab, II and III/KG 40, and III/KG 100 with the torpedo-bomber units of Stab, II and III/KG 26 and Geschwaderstab KG 30 making up the components of Fliegerdivision 2. In all, these amounted to some 200 aircraft, a potentially formidable force, but suffering from a deep-seated weakness in that it contained a high proportion of inexperienced crews. From 6 June until 1 July 1944, the anti-shipping elements of Luftflotte 3 were active over the beachheads during the hours of darkness. In mining operations, 1,906 mines of the BM 1000 and LMB types were laid from the mouth of the River Orne to Courseulles. Within Fliegerdivision 2, the torpedo-bombers flew a total of 384 sorties, with I and III/KG 26 claiming 60,000 BRT sunk for the loss of no aircraft. Weather minima for torpedo operations required a cloud base of 600–900 feet and a visibility of 10–15 miles during the approach flight, which was increased to a base of 900–1,200 feet and a visibility of 15–20 miles in the attack area itself; cloud cover needed was at least 5/10ths. In view of overwhelming Allied air superiority, torpedo attacks were made by night only with – on average – one major operation being flown per week. Loaded with two LT F5b torpedoes, the Ju 88s made and intermediate stop at Dijon or Chalon-sur-Saône before flying on to the combat area. After the attack a direct flight was made back to bases in Southern France.

Despite the mass of Allied shipping traversing the Channel and lying off the Normandy coast, only five ships were sunk by air attack during the first ten days of the invasion. Mining achieved better results in the sinking of nine warships and 17 auxiliary vessels and merchantmen. By mid-July, the growing losses coupled with the start of the fuel famine enforced termination of large-scale attempts at anti-shipping attack, and the remnants of Fliegerkorps X and Fl.Div 2 retired to bases in Norway and Germany. The eclipse of the once-powerful anti-shipping forces of the Luftwaffe was now complete, and only in Norway was a powerful force maintained in the form of KG 26 with Ju 88A-4 and A-17 torpedo-bombers, which were supplemented later by the new Ju 188E-2. This force, numbering about 110 aircraft, remained dormant until 6 February 1945, when a major attack was made on a convoy bound for the Soviet Union. In the next four days, over 200 torpedo missions were flown, but the attacks proved totally unsuccessful. Further operations were undertaken between 18–23 February, during which some 60 aircraft of KG 26 engaged in a returning convoy wherein one vessel was sunk. Thereafter KG 26 relapsed into inactivity from which it was for the final time to emerge only in the last days of the war.

THE PROSPECT OF A LONG WAR

The reverses suffered by the Wehrmacht at Stalingrad and El Alamein finally disposed of any German illusions of a swift victory. Some considered the war already lost when the Soviet Union was invaded, and some could see the final outcome with the entry of the United States of America. But, for the majority of Germans, the defeats in the winter of 1942–3 indicated not so much that the war would one day be lost; rather the inescapable fact that Ende Siege would take not months but possibly years to achieve. The Luftwaffe had prepared itself for a short war. And with the Soviet Army on the offensive when, to all intents and purposes, its recent losses should have ensured its virtual defeat; with Germany facing two closing battlefronts in Tunisia and with the day and night bombing of Germany becoming an increasing significant factor, it was not surprising to find the Luftwaffe in a state of crisis.

The barometer of battle capability of any military force is its morale coupled with its numerical strength. While there was no cause for concern for the fighting spirit of the Luftwaffe's airmen, there most certainly was for the service's diminishing strength, both in manpower and material. From July to December 1942, the Luftwaffe's first-line strength fell from 4,000 to 3,850 aircraft, the lowest since August 1939, due to wastage in the Soviet Union and the Mediterranean theatre. In manpower, the Luftwaffe had grown from 600,000 at the beginning of the war to 1,100,000 men by late 1942, but now the diversion of manpower to the Felddivisionen for ground fighting had started to erode this figure; while recruitment was later to restore strength, the strength reduction was serious at this critical time of change in Germany's fortunes.

Coupled with this manpower drain was the special problem of aircrew training. Like aircraft production, this had been organised upon the assumption of a short war.

The Luftwaffe started the war with a large body of fully-trained aircrew, but the first year of the Soviet campaign ate deeply into this force which had already sustained the losses of the Battle of Britain. In the Jagdgruppen, in particular, the reservoir of older experienced pilots was all but exhausted, and the flow from the Jagdschulen was no longer sufficient to replace losses. The result, already evident by the summer of 1942, was contraction and, in consequence, standard deterioration in the training of pilots and crews. At about this time, the IV Gruppe, or Ergänzungsgruppe, of each Geschwader, which hitherto had provided valuable *ab initio* operational experience for freshmen crews, was largely disbanded, its place being taken by Fighter Pools situated at Mannheim, Krakow and Cazaux. This situation applied also to the bomber and close-support arms. It was inevitable, therefore, that crews now suffered some loss of pre-operational experience before reaching the frontline.

The expectation of a short war had manifested itself in Germany's policies in aircraft production and aircraft development. In the first two years of the war, no less than sixteen different aircraft production programmes were started: none lasted longer than six to eight weeks before being shelved or amalgamated to form yet another programme. Under Generalluftzeugmeister Ernst Udet, German aircraft production rose only by 5–10 per cent, despite the pressures and wastage of two years of continuous air fighting. But so long as a strong reserve could be maintained, the pinch was not felt. However, the battles of attrition in the East now coupled with the entry into the war of the USA, the most highly industrialised nation in the world, had changed the situation dramatically. If Schmid's 1C Intelligence Staff was to be believed, the combined Anglo-American air forces were estimated to be capable of fielding 10–20,000 bombers by the end of 1943! To this threat Udet had no answer.

After his decrease, Udet's place was taken by Erhard Milch, who thus regained the position he had lost in 1938. This remarkable man was aware of the need for a thorough overhaul of the whole production situation in order to counter the growing strength of the RAF and the manufacturing potential of the Soviet and American aircraft industries. Milch's first production programme, authorised in March 1942, was only a modest instalment towards fulfilling the requirements of the Luftwaffe and was deliberately scaled down in order to forestall the objections of Hitler and the Generalstabes of OKW.

Under Milch's direction, German aircraft production rose from just under 1,000 aircraft per month at the end of 1941 to 1,650 per month by the end of 1942; these aircraft included 500 Fw 190s and Bf 109s, 500 He 111s, Ju 88s and Do 217s, 100 Ju 87Ds and 150 Bf 110s. With Germany now on the defensive, fighters assumed highest priority for Milch, and despite much opposition, he managed to boost the output of fighters to over 1,000 per month by June 1943 – 800 of these being Bf 109Gs and Fw 190As. By this time, Allied bombing had underlined the need for priority in fighter production, but much effort was still diverted to the production of bombers and Stukas, and it was not to be until July 1944, when the Luftwaffe's situation was beyond recovery, that all emphasis was laid on the production of fighters. That the Luftwaffe was able to defend Germany with such resilience during 1943 and 1944 was totally due to Milch's first programme, which laid the foundations for a second calling for 2,000 fighters per month by January 1944 and up to 3,000 fighters monthly by July 1944!

At first, the massive scale of the impending Allied bombing offensive was not foreseen. Part of Milch's re-organisation called for the centralisation of aircraft factories to boost production. Thus, for example, production of the Bf 109G was centred at Erla-Leipzig, Regensburg and Wiener Neustadt, the Ju 88 at Bernberg, Oschersleben and Halberstadt, and the Bf 110G at Brunswick. This was to prove a costly mistake and, when these centres were virtually wiped-out by bombing, it was only the most energetic programme of de-centralisation that was to prevent production grinding to a standstill.

If quantitative production could be maintained, there still remained the problem of quality. German aeronautical research had been, and still was, capable of indisputable brilliance in the design of airframes and engines, but the few aircraft earmarked for the re-equipment of the Luftwaffe in place of older types had failed to come up to standard. Notably these were the Me 210, the He 177, the Hs 129 and the Ju 288, which had either failed to meet operational requirements or, in the case of the last-mentioned type, had never left the research establishments. No priority whatsoever was assigned to the turbine-engined Me 262 and He 280 and, while these remarkably innovatory fighters were allowed to remain the playthings of the aircraft industry and test centres, the Luftwaffe was forced to soldier on with the established types. Of these, 80 per cent consisted of Bf 109Gs, Fw 190As, Ju 88s, He 111s, Bf 110s and Ju 87Ds, the last three being obsolescent by then current standards. In mitigation, however, the fighter types – the Bf 109G-6, the Fw 190A-6 and the Ju 88C-6 of 1943 – were efficient, high-performance aircraft each possessing formidable capabilities.

The early months of 1943, therefore, were a period of crisis in Luftwaffe dispositions, resources and manpower. In the Soviet Union, the last great Wehrmacht offensives in the Ukraine and the Caucasus had foundered at Stalingrad, and now the Russians were gathering their strength for the summer campaigns. In the Mediterranean, where even the transfer of over 400 combat aircraft from the Soviet Union had failed to restore the balance, the situation was one of impending defeat in North Africa. And now there was added a third commitment: that of defending Germany and the occupied territories in the West against Anglo-American bombing by day and night.

For the Luftwaffe, the first priority lay in the stabilisation of the situation in the Soviet Union and the Mediterranean. From the point of view of Hitler and the OKW, the first necessity was to bring the Russian advance to a halt, and by reason of this the Soviet Union had the first claim on the Luftwaffe in the Spring of 1943.

RUSSIA 1943–4

T he opening of year 1943 saw the Red Army taking advantage of the massive Wehrmacht concentration in the Stalingrad sector, and going over to the offensive along the entire Eastern Front. The siege of Leningrad was raised on 18 January 1943; in the centre the Soviet armies on the Moscow Front recaptured Rzhev and Vyasma before the completion of their winter campaign, while further south, on the Upper Don, Voronezh was recaptured on 26 January.

It was in the south that the progress of the Soviet Army was most rapid. Bypassing Stalingrad, the southern Soviet thrust reached the Donetz river, taking Rostov, Voroshilovgrad and Kharkov by mid-February, at the same time covering the northern flank by recapturing Kursk on 8 February. Meanwhile, the Wehrmacht was forced to make a precipitate retreat from the Caucasus. Mozdok, three-quarters of the way between the Caspian and the Sea of Azov, was retaken by the Russians at the beginning of January and only five weeks later Krasnodar changed hands, leaving the Germans to defend the narrow bridgehead in the Kuban peninsula.

Throughout this period the Luftwaffe concentrated on Stalingrad, continuously transferring units to that sector at the expense of others, so that by January 1943, out of a total front-line strength of 1,715 aircraft, 900 were concentrated in the Don sector under Luftflotte 4 (FlKps VIII) and Luftwaffenkommando Don (FlKps I); 240 were under Fliegerkorps IV in the Crimea and Caucasus; 380 were on the Moscow Front under Luftwaffenkommando Ost (FlKps V) and 195 were on the Leningrad Front under Luftflotte 1.

These forces consisted of the following units as of 20 February 1943: Single-engined fighters (Fw 190A-4 and Bf 109G-4): II and III/JG 3, Stab, II and III/JG 5, I/JG 26, Stab, I, III and 15.(Span)/JG 51, Stab, I and II/JG 52, Stab, I and II/JG 54;

ground-attack (Fw 190A-4, Bf 110G-2, Hs 129B-1): II/ZG 1, 13.(Zerst)/JG 5, Pz. Jäger Staffel JG 51, I and II/SchG 1; dive-bombers (Ju 87D-3): Stab I, II and III/StG 1, Stab, I, II and III/StG 2, I/StG 5, Stab and I/StG 77; long-range bombers (He 111H-16 and Ju 88A-4): Stab, I and III/KG 1, Stab, I and III/KG 3, Stab, II and III/KG 4, I and III/KG 27, I/KG 30, Stab, I and III/KG 51, Stab, II, III and 15./KG 53, and Stab, I and III/KG 55.

The preponderance of Soviet tank and troop concentrations called for an increase in the number of specialised close-support and ground-attack aircraft and by way of expedience, the Luftwaffe formed Störkampfstaffeln (Harassing bomber units) and Nachtschlachtgruppen (Night ground-attack units) in the spring of 1943, equipped with obsolescent He 46C, He 45C and Ar 66 aircraft. The anti-tank element was now under a Führer der Panzerjäger, who conducted combat operations for I and II/SchG 1 (Bf 109, Hs 123 and Hs 129), Pz.Jäger St./JG 51, Pz.Jäger St. Ju 87, I/ZG 1 (Bf 110) and later Staffel 92 equipped with the Ju 88P-1. With the exception of the Ju 88P-1, which carried a 75-mm cannon, the heaviest tank-busting weapon was the Rheinmetall Flak 18 (BK 3.7) 37-mm cannon installed in the Ju 87G-1 and the Hs 129B-2/R3. While incapable of piercing the armour of the T-34 and KV-1 tanks, the 37mm weapon was capable of immobilising the T-34 by blowing off a track. A further expedient taken at this time was the formation of specialised train-busting units equipped with Ju 88C-6 heavy fighters, and these consisted initially of 9./KG 3, 14./KG 27, 9./KG 55 and 4./KG 76.

None of these measures, however, could do anything to stem the tide of the Soviet advance which had been carried across the Donetz by mid-February. But by now the momentum of the Soviet Army's offensive had slowed in order to consolidate its position; lines of supply and communication were fully stretched and a number of Soviet Air Force units were grounded due to lack of fuel. It was in these circumstances that the Wehrmacht was able to launch a counteroffensive, on 20 February, that culminated in Manstein's capture of Kharkov and Belgorod between 15–18 March 1943. The offensive saw the reappearance of the classical Blitzkrieg advance, with the armoured spearheads of 2nd SS 'Das Reich' Panzer Division advancing under overwhelming air support from von Richthofen's Luftflotte 4. Fliegerkorps IV bore the main weight of the assault in support of I and IV Panzer Armies in the drive to the Donetz and onwards to the south and south-eastern sectors of Kharkov. At the same time, Fliegerkorps I supported the assault on the north and north-western sectors, while Fliegerdivision Donetz was assigned a defensive battle on the eastern flank of I Panzer Army, where it was essential to hold the Russians back while the Kharkov attack was in progress. As soon as its task was completed Fl.Div. Donetz took its powerful ground-attack forces away from the Stalino area to support Fliegerkorps IV.

Combat sorties by Richthofen's pilots averaged 1,000 per day, rising to a crescendo, on 23 February, with 1,250 and maintaining the pace until the capture of Belgorod, which effectively re-established the German hold on the Donetz line. By the end of March, the Spring thaw slowed the advance and saw a slackening in Luftwaffe activity, but the limited aims of Manstein's offensive had been achieved. This remarkable recovery undoubtedly saved the Wehrmacht from being overwhelmed after the Stalingrad disaster, and now the dominant feature on the Soviet Front was the huge Orel-Kursk salient that was destined to be the graveyard for either the Wehrmacht or the Soviet Army in the summer of 1943.

When, at the beginning of April 1943, weather conditions made a continuation of intensive operations on the Donetz front impossible, renewed Soviet pressure in the Kuban, to the East of the Crimea, compelled the Luftwaffe to redispose its forces in this new theatre. Some 550–600 strike aircraft, under FlKps VIII, were sent to bases in the Crimea and commenced intensive operations from 17 April onwards. The Russians did not allow the Luftwaffe to relax its effort, and a daily rate of 400 sorties was perforce, maintained at the very time that rest and re-equipment was required. This concentration was reduced, however, at the beginning of May, and redistributed fairly evenly over all sectors from Smolensk southwards. By June, the preparations for the Kursk offensive were in progress, and Fliegerkorps VIII was posted to the Kharkov-Belgorod sector facing the southern Kursk salient, while a new command, Luftflotte 6, formed from Luftwaffenkommando Ost, took up position in the Smolensk-Orel sector in the north. This command was led by Generaloberst Robert Ritter von Greim.

Another important change, which met with violent opposition from von Manstein, the Army commander, was the transfer of Wolfram von Richthofen from Luftflotte 4 to officer-commanding Luftflotte 2 in the Mediterranean. After the disaster at Tunis, there had been an increasing tendency to reinforce the Mediterranean at the expense of the Soviet Front. General Dessloch succeeded Richthofen as commander of Luftflotte 4.

Luftwaffe first-line strength in the Soviet Union rose from 2,100 aircraft after the abortive Kuban offensive to approximately 2,500 in June 1943; this figure was achieved by bringing back units from rest and re-equipment. The Luftwaffe's ability to mount a force of this size for the third consecutive summer's operations in the Soviet Union, despite its increased commitments in the Mediterranean and over the Reich, was possible as a result of the remarkable recovery in total first-line strength which took place in the first six months of 1943. At the end of 1942, the total Luftwaffe strength hovered below 4,000, but by June 1943 this figure had increased to almost exactly 6,000 aircraft – a total never again to be achieved throughout the remained of the war.

■ Operation Zitadelle – the battle for Kursk, 1943

Aimed at wresting the strategic initiative from the Russians and ultimately turning the course of the war, the planning and preparation of Operation Zitadelle were carried out with·unparalleled thoroughness by the Germans. The offensive called for two simultaneous assaults on the northern and southern sectors of the Kursk salient to destroy the Soviet armies, straighten the frontline and, in the event of success, exploit the situation by a plunging advance to the Don river. No effort was to be spared, and among the 2,700 German tanks assembled for the offensive were the latest PzKw V Panthers and PzKw VI Tigers which were to spearhead the assault. The Soviet Army had, however, had adequate time in which to prepare its defences and build up its resources. Anti-tank ditches had been dug along the entire perimeter of the salient and in depth, while 1,300,000 troops supported by 3,600 tanks and 2,400 aircraft, including the latest La-5 and Yak-9 fighters, were deployed to counter the German attacks.

The Luftwaffe fielded at least 1,000 aircraft in direct support of Zitadelle, representing 50 per cent of the total forces available for the whole Soviet Front, from Murmansk to the Sea of Azov. While including several Kampfgruppen with He 111s and Ju 88s, these forces comprised primarily II and III/JG 3, I, III and IV/JG 51, I and III/JG 52 and II/JG 54 with Fw 190A-5 and Bf 109G-6 fighters; the ground-attack units were Stab, I and II/SchG 1 and 4./SchG 2, Stab and I/ZG 1. and Pz.Jäg/JG 51, and the Stukagruppen available were I, II and III/StG 1, I, II and III/StG 2, III/StG 3, and I, II and III/StG 77 equipped with Ju 87D-5s.

At 04.30hrs on 5 July 1943, after a preliminary bombardment, III Panzer Corps and IV Panzer Army of Manstein's Army Group South struck northwards from Belgorod, while IX Army and II Panzer Army under Mödel's Army Group Centre attacked the northern flank of the Kursk salient from Orel. Both assaults quickly became bogged down in bitter fire-fights with dug-in Soviet troops and armour. Such was the strength of Soviet resistance that Mödel had committed all his reserves to the battle by 9 July, but to no avail. The greatest tank battle in history took place on 12 July, when IV Pz. Army, III Pz. Corps and Einsatzgruppe Kempff lost 350 tanks in combat around Prokhorovka, some 25 miles north of Belgorod. On this day, while the Soviet Army fought the Wehrmacht to a standstill in the Kursk salient, the Russians opened an offensive in the north, threatening the German rear at Orel. Other Soviet counteroffensives followed, and by 23 July both Army Group South and Army Group Centre had been pushed back to their starting lines, thus committing Zitadelle to crushing defeat.

During the opening phases of Zitadelle, the Luftwaffe flew over 3,000 sorties a day, with each serviceable Ju 87D flying up to 5–6 missions per day. This effort decreased to around 1,500 sorties per day after the first week, and then averaged 1,000 per day for the remainder of July. The Jagdgruppen claimed 432 'kills' on the first day, of which II/JG 3 claimed 77 'kills', including 62 bombers, and III/JG 52 shot down 38 Soviet aircraft. German losses on the first day of Zitadelle amounted to only 26 aircraft. In total, the Luftwaffe flew 37,421 sorties throughout the battle, destroying 1,735 enemy aircraft for the loss of 64. Twenty thousand tons of bombs were dropped and Fliegerkorps I alone claimed 1,100 tanks and 1,300 vehicles.

While these impressive figures applied to the battles in the Kursk salient, elsewhere the situation gave cause for concern. German aircraft losses, which in June had totalled 487, rose to 911 in July, and in August were 785 over the entire Eastern Front. By 5 August, the Soviet Army had captured Orel and Belgorod, opening the way for the great autumn offensive, while the entire German position in the south was put at risk by the Soviet re-capture of Kharkov on 23 August.

For the Luftwaffe, the failure of Operation Zitadelle was to have widespread repercussions. Generaloberst Hans Jeschonnek, the Chief of Air Staff, had been the apostle of tactical air power in support of the Army, and had staked his reputation on a decisive and quick victory in the Soviet Union. The failure at Kursk, allied with the inability of the Luftwaffe to alter the disastrous situation first in North Africa and now in Sicily, rendered his policies bankrupt. He committed suicide. The Soviet Front, the cornerstone of his policies, was no longer afforded top priority by the Luftwaffe.

■ The Russians assume the offensive, August–May 1943–4

Generaloberst Korten, the ex-commander of Luftflotte 1, was Jeschonnek's successor as Chief of the Air Staff. His views differed radically from those of his predecessor in that he favoured increased emphasis on fighter defence of the homeland, and on the belated constitution of a strategic bomber force. In compliance with these objectives, the Luftwaffe, in his opinion, was henceforth to accord only the minimum amount of tactical support to the Army. His views, allied with the growing weight of the Allied bombing offensive against Germany, were to result in a marked reduction in German fighter units on the Soviet Front and the withdrawal, in December 1943, of the whole of Fliegerkorps IV from its tactical support duties and its redeployment for strategic bombing.

As early as June 1943, Major Johannes Seifert's I/JG 26, which had exchanged duties with III/JG 54, returned to Northern France; the 7./JG 26, also based in the Soviet Union, returned to the West in mid-July. This month also saw the transfer of Geschwaderstab and I/JG 3 'Udet' from Luftflotte 4, and I/JG 5 'Eismeer' from Luftflotte 5 to the defence of the Reich, while the II and III/JG 3 were both installed at bases in Holland by the end of September. Significantly, no Jagdgruppen were returned from other fronts to Russia to fill this vacuum.

However, the transfer of bomber and single-engined fighter units was balanced, in part, by the strengthening of the ground-attack forces now controlled by the General der Schlachtflieger, Oberst Hubertus Hitschold. The appellation Stukageschwader (StG) was dropped and became Schlachtgeschwader (SG); the old SchG 1, SchG 2 and SKG 10 being re-organised into the new SG 4, SG9 and SG 10, and the five anti-tank Hs 129 staffeln became IV(Panzer)/SG 9. In addition, the Gruppen of Ju 87Ds were converted on to Fw 190Fs and Gs at the rate of two Gruppen every six weeks.

When the Soviet offensive to liberate the Eastern Ukraine and establish bridgeheads on the Dneiper river opened on 26 August, Fliegerkorps I in the Stalino-

Taganrog area and Fliegerkorps VIII in the Poltava-Kharkov area could only muster some 900 first-line aircraft. They were unable to stem the tide of Soviet advance which, by 23 December, had isolated the XVII German Army in the Crimea, had retaken Smolensk, Bryansk, Gomel and Chernikov in the northern sector, and had taken Kiev, Kremenchug and Zaporozhe, pushing the entire German line to the east of the Dneiper.

This time there was to be no German counter-offensive, and such was the numerical strength of the Soviet Army and air forces that, without their pausing for breath, the entire Soviet Front erupted in December 1943, when the Soviet winter offensive got underway. In comparison with a total strength of 2,500 aircraft in July, the Luftwaffe's resources amounted to 1,710 combat aircraft on 1 January 1944. The bulk of these were concentrated in the South, resulting in only minimal opposition from the Luftwaffe on the Leningrad Front. In the Ukraine, the Soviet Army drove full tilt for the Dneister river, the Carpathians and to the borders of Rumania, beyond which lay the vital oilfields of Ploesti.

In the face of this advance, Fliegerkorps I and VIII managed to fly only 300–350 sorties per day, due to appalling weather, bad airfield conditions, and low serviceability. On 29 February 1944, of the 377 German fighters on the Eastern Front, only 265 were serviceable. These consisted of Bf 109G-6s of Stab, I and III/JG 5, Stab, I, III, IV and 15.(Span)/JG 51, Stab, I, II, III and 15.(Kroat)/JG 52 and I/JG 302, with the Fw 190A-5 units being Stab, I, II and IV/JG 54. The close-support elements consisted of 653 aircraft of which 483 were serviceable for combat. These were Stab, I, II and III/SG 1, Stab and I/SG 2, 10.(Pz)/SG 1, 10.(Pz)/SG 2, Stab, I, II and III/SG 3, 1. and 4./SG 5, Stab, I and III/SG 77 with Ju 87D-5 and Ju 87G-1 types, and II and III/SG 2, Stab, I and II/SG 10, and II/SG 77 with Fw 190Fs and Gs. The Henschel 129 units was the IV(Pz)/SG 9 with 62 aircraft. This was the strike force, extending from Finland to Nikolaev on the Black Sea, in addition to a force of reconnaissance, night-harassing, and long-range bomber units that made up Luftflotten 1, 4 and 6.

By mid-April 1944, the frontline stretched in the south from Kovel (50 miles SE of Brest-Litovsk), across the Dneister to the Carpathians, and down to Jassy on the Rumanian border. In May 1944, Fliegerkorps VIII and Fliegerkorps I had 750 aircraft (40 per cent of the strength on the Soviet Front) stationed in Rumania and Bessarabia in anticipation of the next Soviet offensive that threatened the Rumanian oilfields and the resources of the Balkans. On 9 May, the XVII Army capitulated in the Crimea, but for a while the situation remained static as the Russians brought up their reserves, giving the Germans two months in which to consolidate their defences before the next Soviet offensive.

The history of the Soviet campaigns of 1943 and 1943–44 was the clearest tribute to the tactical skill with which the Soviet Air Forces exploited their numerical air superiority, extending the weakened Luftwaffe opposed to it by constant and ever-shifting pressure up and down the front. But without the pressure exerted in the West by the RAF and USAAF, and in the Mediterranean, the balance in the East would perforce have been radically different, just as the Wehrmacht's opposition in Sicily and Italy would have been radically different if the bulk of its divisions had not been tied down by the struggle in the Soviet Union.

THE MEDITERRANEAN 1943–4

■ The invasion of Sicily, 1943

The collapse of Axis resistance in Tunisia, on 13 May 1943, left the Luftwaffe faced with a multiplicity of problems which absorbed its attention, to the detriment of other commitments, throughout May and June. First in importance was the rest and refit of the shattered units withdrawn from North Africa, and next was the need to reinforce the Mediterranean theatre, in view of the proved inadequacy of the forces allocated in the early months of the year. In addition, there was the strategic problem of deploying forces to meet the multiple threats of Allied landings. Allied security had been extremely good and the Germans had no means of knowing where the next blow would fall: Sicily, Greece, Crete, Sardinia, and possibly the Italian mainland were all feasible possibilities.

To meet the new situation, a reorganisation and strengthening of the Luftwaffe operational commands was put into effect without delay. The operational area of Luftflotte 2, hitherto encompassing the whole of the Mediterranean, was restricted to Sicily, Sardinia and Italy, while a new command called Luftwaffenkommando Süd-Ost, with Luftflotte status, was established in the Balkans, Greece and Crete. Generalfeldmarschall Albert Kesselring became the supremo of all military forces in the Mediterranean, and his successor as OC Luftflotte 2 was Generaloberst Wolfram von Richthofen. Further changes brought about by the lamentable inefficiency of the Headquarters staff of Luftflotte 2 included the posting in of Gen.Lt. Alfred Bülowius as the commander of Fliegerkorps II and Gen.Lt. Mahncke as chief of tactical operations. Apart from these and other staff officers from the Soviet Union, Gen.Maj. Harlinghausen was relieved of command of the Mediterranean bomber units and replaced by Oberst Pelz, previously of I/KG 60. At the same time, Gen.Maj. Adolf

Galland, the General der Jagdflieger, was despatched on an extended tour of duty in the Mediterranean with the task of restoring morale and efficiency.

At the end of the Tunisian campaign, the total strength of Luftflotte 2 was 880 aircraft of all categories, based in the Central and Eastern Mediterranean. In one and a half months this figure rose to 1,280 (as of 3 July 1943) and of these 440 additional aircraft, 260 were Bf 109G-4 and G-6 fighters – an indication of German concern at growing Allied air superiority. On 10 July 1943, the day of the Allied invasion of Sicily, the overall strength had dropped to 1,150 aircraft, of which 885 were under Luftflotte 2 and 265 were under Luftwaffenkommando Süd-Ost, and of these a mere 175 were stationed in Sicily, indicating the total ignorance of where the actual landings would occur. On the day of the Allied invasion the dispositions and locations of Luftflotte 2 were as shown in the accompanying table.

The units based in Sardinia consisted of 4.(H)/12 with Bf 109F-5 reconnaissance fighters at Decimommanu; and II/JG 51 and III/JG 77 with Bf 109G-6 fighters at Casa Zeppara and Chilivani respectively. On the Italian mainland, IV/JG 3 at Lecce, II/JG 27 and I/JG 53 at Vibo Valentia equipped with Bf 109G-6s were within close proximity to battle area. Elements of II and III/SKG 10 with Fw 190 fighter-bombers were stationed at Montecorvino, which also housed II/ZG 1 with Bf 110G-2 fighters. Twin-engined fighter units consisted of Stab ZG 26 at Naple-Camoldoli, III/ZG 26 at Rome-Ciampino and Pisa, and 10./ZG 26 with Ju 88C-6s at Pratica de Mare.

Widespread Allied bombing of airfields in Sardinia, Sicily and Southern Italy had forced Luftflotte 2 to withdraw its Kampfgruppen to the Foggia area, although a number of units were further north at Piacenza, Viterbo and Airasca. This force consisted of I/LG 1, Stab, I and III/KG 1, Stab, I and III/KG 6, III/KG 30, III/KG 54, Stab, I and II/KG 76 and III/KG 77, and the Geschwaderstab KG 100, equipped with Ju 88A-4, A-14 and A-17 bombers, Stab, I and III/KG 26 at Grosseto with He 111H-6 torpedo-bombers, and II and III/KG 100 at Foggia-Morin with Do 217E-5 and K-2 bombers and in progress of working up to operational standard with the Hs 293 glider-bomb and the FX 1400 (Fritz X) stand-off bomb.

In the early hours of 10 July, the 7th US Army under Patton and the 8th British Army under Montgomery landed on the Sicilian coast in the Liccata-Gela and Avola-Pachino sectors. The resistance from Italian defences was stiff at first, but by the end of the first day the Allies had managed to secure their respective beachheads. For a week prior to the invasion, the Allied air forces had pursued an all-out bombing offensive against Axis airfields in Sardinia, Sicily and on the mainland, and this was largely instrumental in reducing the Luftwaffe's scale of effort to 275–300 sorties between 10–12 July, with 50 per cent of these operations being flown at night. In the face of overwhelming Allied air superiority, even this mediocre reaction was not maintained and, thereafter, the average effort fell to about 150 sorties per day, including fighters and fighter-bombers based in Sardinia and southern Italy which moved forward daily to landing grounds in Sicily. By 19 July, Allied bombing had effectively reduced the serviceability of Luftwaffe units to about 35 per cent of actual strength, leaving only 25 aircraft capable of operations based in Sicily.

Combat operations by German fighter and fighter-bomber units continued with negligible effect from bases in Calabria, but the dogged rearguard actions by XV Panzer and Hermann Göring Panzer Divisions were notable for their total lack of air support from the Luftwaffe. The most demonstrable failure of the Luftwaffe was the level of impotence to which the Kampfgruppen had been reduced. At no time did the number of Ju 88s, He 111s and Do 217s fall below 250–300, but this considerable force was hamstrung by low serviceability and a chronic shortage of fully-trained crews, the latter factor now being endemic within the Luftwaffe as a whole. The Kampfgruppen failed to intervene during the Allied build-up for the invasion and their scale of effort during and after the landings was negligible.

The fighting in Sicily finally ceased when Patton's troops entered Messina on 17 August. For four days prior to this event the Jagdgruppen raised their total effort from 60 to 150 sorties per day while covering the evacuation of the remnants of the German forces from Sicily. With the Luftwaffe's defeat over Sicily, out of 1,250 combat aircraft available in July, only approximately 625 remained, covering the whole of the central and western Mediterranean areas, including southern France, Sardinia, Corsica and Italy. This decline marked the end of the Luftwaffe's attempt to contest Allied air superiority in the Mediterranean, but a second factor had by now come into play. During August 1943, 210 aircraft were withdrawn from the Mediterranean, and all but one unit were transferred to the Western Front. The fighter units included II/JG 51, II/JG 27, I/ZG 1 and III/ZG 26 for daylight interception duties over the Reich.

The defeat of the Luftwaffe over Sicily had been total. After the decisive German defeat at Kursk in July, the priority had passed to the Mediterranean, but within two months this pre-eminence had been finally and irrevocably lost.

■ The Allied invasion of Italy, 1943

At 04.30hrs on 3 September 1943, the first echelons of the British 8th Army waded ashore from their landing craft on to beaches north of Reggio. The landings were virtually unopposed with the XXVI Pz. and XXIX Pz. Grenadier Division electing to pull back when it became apparent that the difficult terrain was enough to slow the British advance.

The Germans realised that this landing was a diversionary feint to be followed by another, more significant Allied invasion. Opinions differed as to where the next blow would fall. Hitler expected an assault in Yugoslavia, Kesselring anticipated a decisive fight near Rome and Vietinghoff, the commander of X Army, expected a landing in the Gulf of Salerno. The Gulf of Salerno proved correct, but, in the meantime, Badoglio's interim government, that had followed the fall of Mussolini, surrendered to the Allies. While militarily this was not too important, the political implications caused grave concern to the Germans, for the surrender put the entire German southern flank in the Central and Eastern Mediterranean at risk. On learning of the Italian surrender, Kesselring stated: 'If we retain our fighting spirit and remain calm, I am confident that we will continue to perform the tasks entrusted to us by the Führer.' The German naval command in Italy was more blunt: 'Italian armistice does not apply to us. The fight continues.'

The Wehrmacht stationed in Southern Italy, composed of crack divisions, immediately disarmed the Italians and took over the defences. Militarily their dispositions consisted of the XXVI and XXIX Pz. Divisions, under 87 Pz. Corps, in the toe of Italy, the Hermann Göring Pz. and XV Pz. Divisions in the Gaeta-Salerno sector under XIV Pz. Corps, the I Fallschirm Division at Foggia under Vietinghoff's control, and II Pz. Grenadier and II Fallschirm Division in the Rome area under Kesselring's direct control.

On 9 September 1943, the day of the Allied invasion in the Gulf of Salerno, the Luftwaffe's forces consisted of the following: IV/JG 3 at Foggia, I, II and III/JG 53 'Pik-As' at Grazzanise and Cancello-Arnone, and Stab and I/JG 77 'Herzas' at Crotone. The III/JG 77 was at Chilivani in Sardinia and the entire force, equipped with Bf 109G-5 and G-6 fighters, numbered 51 serviceable aircraft out of a strength of 96. The ground-attack and fighter-bomber element, which played an important part in opposing the Salerno landings, comprised II and III/SKG 10 with 68 (41) Fw 190A-5/U3s at Crotone and Montecorvino, and two staffeln of II/SchG 2 with 28 (10) Fw 190F-2s at Ottana.

There is no doubt that the Luftwaffe made an all-out effort to liquidate the Allied bridgehead at Salerno, and Allied forces were not afforded adequate fighter protection. The airfields in Sicily were in a deplorable state and the Allied fighter squadrons based there found their 'loiter' time over Salerno severely limited due to the distance involved. For the first ten days, the Luftwaffe close-support forces maintained the high average of two sorties per serviceable aircraft, beginning with some 170 sorties on 8 September, and rising to a peak effort on 13 September when the German counterattack threatened to drive the Allies back into the sea. The Fw 190 fighter-bombers, which operated effectively against shipping and landing craft, were supported by IV/JG 3's Bf 109G-5/R2 fighters using the Wfr.Gr 21 rocket mortars, while top-cover was flown by Major Johannes Steinhoff's JG 77 and Obstlt. Günther Maltzahn's JG 53.

Most significant of all, however, was the revival of the long-range bomber force. On the night of 8–9 September, approximately 155 sorties were flown, and further effort of 100 sorties was attained on the night of 10–11 September, the strongest reaction since the Malta battles of March 1942. Conventional bombing sorties were carried out by II/LG 1, I and II/KG 1, Stab, and III/KG 54, Stab, I and II/KG 76 and II/KG 77, operating from Foggia, Piacenza, Airasca and Viterbo. Three Gruppen of KG 30, based at Grosseto, carried out torpedo attacks with Ju 88A-17s, in co-operation with I and II/KG 26 from Marseilles-Istres. Of particular interest was the use, on an intensive scale for the first time, of the Hs 293 glider-bomb and the FX 1400 'Fritz' stand-off bomb, used by II and III/KG 100 from bases in Southern France. The Luftwaffe achieved 85 bomb strikes on Allied vessels lying in the Gulf of Salerno, sinking four transports, a heavy cruiser and seven LSTs.

After 15 September, the Allied foothold at Salerno became less critical, and three days later the Germans carried out a strategic withdrawal to their prepared defensive positions on the Volturno river, named the Gustav Line. Naples was captured on 1 October, and on this day the important airfields at Foggia fell into Allied hands, wherein the southern flank of the Reich, the Balkans and northern Italy came within easy range of Allied bombers. After Salerno, the Luftwaffe in Italy was reduced to a shadow of its former self, the defensive campaigns in this theatre, in themselves ideally suited to the ragged mountainous terrain, were placed firmly into the hands of Kesselring's experienced ground forces. But while the situation remained static in Italy, a new threat had to be faced in the Aegean.

■ Operations in the Eastern Mediterranean, 1943

The large-scale defection by the Italian garrisons in the Eastern Mediterranean compromised the entire German position in the Balkans, Greece and the Aegean, putting the southern flank at risk. However, the German reaction to this threat was systematic, vigorous and effective. Between the Italian capitulation, on 8 September, and 3 October, Luftwaffenkommando Süd-Ost was reinforced by 110 combat aircraft raising its strength to 345 assorted types. Primarily, these included III and IV/JG 27 with Bf 109G-5s, and I and II/StG 3 with Ju 87D-3 dive-bombers, and 11./ZG 26 with Ju 88C-6 heavy-fighters to bolster the elements of LG 1 and SAGr 126 in Crete.

The first objective was the capture of Cephallonia island, covering the entrance to the Gulf of Corinth, which was attacked on 21 September. The Germans then switched to Corfu, the main fortress on the eastern side of the Strait of Otranto, which fell on 24 September, followed by the capture of Split island on the following day. Air operations proceeded unhindered by Allied intervention due to their tardy exploitation of airbases in Apulia, and the Stuka dive-bombers, which played a leading rôle, suffered minimal losses.

Having secured their supply routes through the Adriatic to the bases in Greece and the Aegean, and having forestalled any likelihood of an Allied invasion of the Balkans via the Strait of Otranto, the Germans now turned their attention to the Dodecanese islands in the eastern Aegean.

Here the British had failed to profit from the capitulation of Italian garrisons in the Dodecanese, wherein lay a number of good airfields, and their intervention was inefficient and piecemeal. While they gained Kos, Samos and Leros, they failed lamentably to secure Rhodes, with its airfields at Maritsa and Calato. The island was secured by a small German force on 12 September, and with the conclusion of operations in the Adriatic on 27 September, III/JG 27 and StG 3 were flown in. Other units, including IV/JG 27, were transferred to bases in Crete and southern Greece for support operations.

The Luftwaffe took advantage of the low Allied priority accorded to this theatre, and subsequent operations in securing the southern flank in the Eastern Mediterranean were to prove a model of efficient and resolute action by a small compact force against an undetermined enemy.

As dawn broke on 3 October, some 1,200 German troops under Gen.Lt Müller landed on Kos, supported by Stukas and Bf 109Gs flying top-cover. In the two days that were all that were required to eliminate British resistance, StG 3 put up 140–150 sorties in addition to about 65–70 by III and IV/JG 27. The Luftwaffe, using up to 300 aircraft based in the theatre, started the process of softening up Leros which continued throughout October, with an average of 60 sorties by Ju 87s and Ju 88s per day. At first light on 12 November, 90–95 Ju 52/3m transports dropped 675–700 paratroops on the narrow stretch of land between Gurna and Alinda Bay. During the five days' fighting which culminated in the German capture of Leros, the Luftwaffe flew between 675–700 sorties, and at no time was its air supremacy challenged with any lasting effect. The capture of Leros was followed closely by the British evacuation without a fight of Syros and Samos. The Germans had the encouragement which victory affords, and Turkey, who had been quite clearly shown who was still master in the Aegean, refused to join the Allies and remained neutral until the end of the war.

■ The Italian Front, 1943–4

By December, the Allied 5th and 8th Armies had been halted on the Gustav Line which stretched across the Apennines from Gaeta, through Cassino, to Ortona on the eastern coast. Throughout the following weeks, successive Allied attacks failed to dislodge the 76th and XIV Pz. Corps of Vietinghoff's X Army. In order to counter this enforced stalemate on the Italian Front, the Allies decided to launch a large-scale amphibious landing at Anzio, a distance of 50 miles behind the prepared defences of the Gustav Line.

Such an operation was inconceivable to the Germans, considering it was mid-winter, and the lethargic reconnaissance work carried out by NAGr 11, 2.(F)/122 and 1.(F)/123 failed to note Allied sea and land movements that would have indicated an impending landing. Thus, when Gen. Lucas' 6th US Corps landed astride Anzio and Nettuno on 22 January 1944, the Germans were taken completely by surprise. However, the surprise was not exploited, the Wehrmacht was permitted to recover and the ambitious plan degenerated into a bloody battle of attrition with heavy cost to the Allies.

As always, the German reaction to a major strategic threat was prompt and energetic. By 1 January, the total Luftwaffe strength in the Mediterranean had sunk to 575 aircraft, 307 being under Luftflotte 2 in the Italian theatre, but despite the priority afforded the renewed bombing offensive against the United Kingdom, several bomber units were sent to Italy from France. From 23 January to 3 February, the solitary Geschwaderstab KG 76 in Italy was joined by I and III/LG 1 from the Balkans, I and III/KG 26, part of I and II/KG 30, and I/KG 76 from Luftflotte 3 in France, while Stab KG 100, with He 177A-5 bombers, and II/KG 100 which was transferred to Marseilles-Istres.

The Jagdgruppen under Luftflotte 2 (as of 31 January) consisted of I/JG 4, II/JG 51, I and III/JG 53, and Stab, I and II/JG 77, equipped with Bf 109G-6 fighters. The close-support element consisted of Stab, I and II/SG 4 equipped with Fw 190F-8s, and I/NSGr 9 equipped with Caproni 314s for night ground-attack work. A further 50 single-engined fighters were transferred from Northern Italy to the Anzio area by 23 February, in addition to the crack I/JG 2 'Richthofen', equipped with Fw 190A-6s, under Major Erich Hohagen, which was installed at Canino by the end of the month. Overall the reinforcements to Luftflotte 2 amounted to a rise of 35 per cent, reaching a peak in March 1944 of 600 aircraft, of which 475 were engaged in operations against the Anzio-Nettuno beachhead.

Despite their precarious position at Anzio, the Allies had virtually complete control of the skies, forcing the anti-shipping and bomber units to operate at night. This factor rendered the operations of II and III/KG 100, using the Hs 293 and FX 1400, less effective than they had been at Salerno. By day, the inclement weather curtailed combat operations by the Luftwaffe during the initial phases of the Anzio battle, but in support of the second German counterattack on 16 and 17 February, Fw 190 fighter-bombers flew 160–170 sorties and the Bf 109Gs some 300–350 sorties on each day. This was the peak, however, and such an effort was not again to be mounted for the remainder of the Anzio embroglio.

German fighter pilots were engaged in combat by Spitfires, P-51s, P-47s and P-38s whenever they chose to leave the ground. A Messerschmitt pilot of II/JG 77 'Herzas', who was shot down over Cassino on 27 March, told his captors that the Gruppen strength was never above 20 aircraft, of which an average of 12–15 were serviceable, and 15 pilots had been lost during the previous two months. The normal pilot strength of the Gruppe was 50, but II/JG 77 possessed 20–25, of which only a small proportion had any real combat experience. Thus it was that several Gruppen in Italy had been reduced to Staffel strength.

With deadlock at Anzio, the Allies turned once again to exerting pressure on the Gustav Line at Cassino at the beginning of March. The Germans were, therefore, able to return to the purely defensive policy of the previous winter, radically curtailing the scale of air support and again withdrawing surplus Luftwaffe elements for operations elsewhere.

Of the Luftwaffe's offensive force, almost all bomber and torpedo-bomber units were transferred to the Western Front, leaving I and II/SG 4 to carry out desultory fighter-bomber operations. The strength of the Jagdgruppen was further weakened by the transfer of I/JG 4 to Rumania to join III/JG 77, while I/JG 2 returned to France in April 1944. When the Allies opened their offensive across the Garigliano and Rapido rivers on 11 May, they did so in the total absence of the Luftwaffe and, by 4 June, they had taken Rome. The insignificance to which the priority of the Mediterranean theatre had fallen had already been indicated by the transfer, as early as February 1944, of Fliegerkorps II to Northern France, followed by Fliegerkorps X to SW France as an anti-shipping command. Operations in Italy were reduced to the status of a Jagdfliegerführer within Luftflotte 2, and by July 1944, the total first-line strength in the Mediterranean had sunk to only 300 aircraft.

The Mediterranean campaigns of 1943–44 were a drain on the resources of the Luftwaffe which interfered with its efforts at expansion and recovery, and therefore vitally affected its capacity to counter the RAF/USAAF bombing offensive against Germany, and ultimately to oppose and withstand the Allied invasion of Normandy. It was not only at Stalingrad but in the Mediterranean that the cream of the Luftwaffe's bomber arm perished, and it was the relentless drain on crews and aircraft which, long after Stalingrad, reduced German offensive air power to a nullity.

THE DEFENCE OF THE REICH

■ The Allied bombing offensive against Germany, 1943–4

Before covering the tactical and operational aspects of the Luftwaffe's counter-offensive against the weight of RAF and USAAF bombing throughout 1943 and 1944, it is necessary to outline the general bombing policies carried out by the Allies, and study the changes, successes and failures experienced by these policies, and their ultimate effect on the Luftwaffe's capacity to fight. From July 1943 until the end of the war, the joint RAF and USAAF bombing offensive against Germany was to be the dominating factor in the air.

The Allied conference at Casablanca, in January 1943, met in a spirit of renewed and justified optimism because, for the first time in the course of the war, the tide of Axis victory had been stemmed at Stalingrad, El Alamein and Guadalcanal. Among the revisions of global strategy discussed at Casablanca came the call for the heaviest possible Allied bombing offensive against the German industrial and economic capacity to wage war. RAF Bomber Command, under Air Chief Marshall A. T. Harris, received the following directive: 'Your primary objective will be the progressive destruction and dislocation of the German military, industrial and economic system, and the undermining of the morale of the German people to the point where their capacity for armed resistance is fatally weakened.' The Casablanca directive gave renewed impetus to the Allied air commanders and, from January 1943 onwards, Germany was to suffer raids by RAF bombers by night and by bombers of the 8th USAAF, later joined by the 15th USAAF, by day on an ever increasing scale.

In the final analysis the subsequent Allied strategic bombing offensive failed either to dislocate German war production or to undermine civilian morale. The production of weaponry increased due to energetic dispersal to less threatened areas, the resolve of the German people, if anything, was sharpened to see the war through to the bitter end, and the entire offensive suffered from disagreements in high quarters and a dispersal of bombing effort until the final year of the war. It was only after May 1944, that the USAAF, belatedly joined by RAF Bomber Command, turned its full effort to the destruction of the oil industry – the life blood of Germany's capacity to wage war.

At the beginning of 1943, the main effort of the Luftwaffe's home defence was directed against the night bomber raids of RAF Bomber Command's Lancasters, Halifaxes, Stirlings and Wellingtons, but a new threat appeared on the scene when the 8th USAAF's Boeing B-17 Fortress bombers commenced operations against targets in Germany on 27 January 1943. Their crews had had five months of operations against targets in France and the Low Countries, and although their combat missions were still largely experimental in nature, their close, mutually-protected formations had offered reasonable protection against marauding German fighters. In clear weather and by using the Norden bomb-sight, they were able to bomb with relative accuracy. However, their bombs - 500-lb and 1,000-lb GP high-explosive – were not heavy enough to make any impression on the U-boat pens which had constituted their primary target since November 1942.

After Casablanca, the U-boat bases, repair and construction yards remained the top priority of the 8th USAAF and, between January and April 1943, 63 per cent of its attacks were directed at U-boat targets at Emden, Wilhelmshaven, Kiel, Hamburg, Flensburg, Lubeck and Bremerhaven, in addition to the Kriegsmarine's operational bases at La Pallice, St Nazaire and Brest. Throughout this period, RAF Bomber Command devoted 30 per cent of its attacks to the U-boat priority, while committing its major effort against German industry located in large conurbations. In March 1943, Harris' bombers were engaged in an intensive spate of night operations against targets in the Ruhr, attacking Essen, Duisburg, Wuppertal and other towns situated in this great industrial heartland. By now bombing accuracy by night was being assisted by radio navigational aids, although the RAF found it impossible to bomb nocturnally with the same precision as achieved by the 8th USAAF diurnally.

During RAF Bomber Command's campaign, known as the Battle of the Ruhr, the flak defences and in particular Kammhuber's night fighters imparted an average casualty rate of 3.6 per cent on Harris' squadrons, revised bomber tactics having brought the overall rate of 1942 (4.1 per cent) down to a level that was still prohibitive if a long-term offensive was to be follows. Meanwhile, the losses suffered by the 8th USAAF were even higher, and it soon became clear that a change of target priorities was needed. If a bomber offensive was to succeed, it was concluded, then first the enemy air force must cease to give effective opposition.

The Joint Planning Team, responsible for overall policy and set up in April 1943, was soon urging that the Allied bombing effort be diverted from the U-boat priority to that of the destruction of the German aircraft industry; the airframe, engine and ancilliary plants that were now producing the Bf 109Gs, Fw 190As, Bf 110Gs and Ju 88Cs in alarmingly high quantities. In order of their priorities the new list of bomber targets, as suggested by the Team, was as follows: aircraft industry, ball-bearing industry, synthetic aviation fuel, machine-tool grinding and sharpening plants, non-ferrous industries, synthetic rubber, U-boat production and maintenance, the motor industry and transportation.

On 10 June 1943, the 'Pointblank' directive was issued to the Allied bomber chiefs charging them with the following objectives according to the specialised rôles:

– The 8th USAAF's primary objective was to be the destruction of the Luftwaffe Fighter Arm, and the industries that equipped it, supported it, and enabled it to fly.

– RAF Bomber Command was to be employed in accordance with its main aim in the general destruction and disorganisation of German industry, its operations being designed as far as practicable to be complementary to those of the USAAF.

The directive also charged the bomber chiefs to co-operate and co-ordinate their actions in pursuance of the aims, and to assist them a Joint Operational Planning Committee was constituted. It was now that the first serious disagreement arose between the respective commanders. The 8th USAAF was understandably insistent that all efforts were now diverted to the task of neutralising fighter opposition. Harris thought otherwise. His interpretation of the 'Pointblank' directive was that while the 8th concentrated on the German aircraft industry and its ancillaries, RAF Bomber Command would be sent 'against those industrial towns in which there was the largest number of aircraft component factories.' And to this interpretation Harris adhered.

July 1943 was a milestone in the history of the Allied bombing offensive, in which the 8th USAAF turned from U-boat objectives to those within the 'Pointblank' directive and Bomber Command waged the Battle of Hamburg. It was to be a month of major significance for the Luftwaffe as well. Hitherto the B-17s and B-24s of the 8th USAAF, usually 80–100 strong, had flown unescorted raids against coastal targets but, with the start of 'Blitz Week' in July, forces of 250–300 made for targets deep inside Germany, still without escort, and, moreover, these attacks proved extremely damaging. At the same time, RAF Bomber Command completely neutralised the radar defences of the Kammhuber Line by the first use of 'chaff' – strips of metal foil which obliterated the radar returns of the bombers. The use of 'Window', as this jamming was called, caused considerable scientific and technical problems for the Germans, and Bomber Command's raids were countered only by the reversion to visual night-fighting aided by flares and searchlights. At Hamburg, Harris' bombers carried out the first really devastating area attack, causing damage on an unprecedented scale. Thus, the threat posed by the RAF and USAAF assumed new proportions with the ending of July.

These missions of intent coincided with German crisis on other battlefronts far removed from the skies over Germany. With the German defeat at Kursk and the decimation of the Luftwaffe over Sicily, the priorities accorded by the Luftwaffe to first the Eastern Front and then the Mediterranean passed finally and irrevocably to the air defence of Germany. From July until October 1943, Luftwaffenbefehlshaber Mitte, the command responsible for the defence of the Reich, turned its full attention to countering the 8th USAAF by strengthening existing Jagdgruppen, calling in others from the respective battlefronts, and concentrating its forces in Germany and Holland. Its first offensive was to culminate in the Schweinfurt massacre on 14 October, forcing the USAAF to cease deep penetration unescorted attacks and to reduce its offensive, within the terms of 'Pointblank', to the point of crisis. As such it was a victory for the Luftwaffe's day fighter forces.

The 'Pointblank' offensive, pursued with such determination by the 8th USAAF had ostensibly failed; there were more German fighters in the air than ever before and their attacks had caused a casualty rate that was totally unacceptable. In the altercations that followed between the Allied air chiefs, numerous new proposals were made. The Americans, while maintaining that the prime target remained the German aircraft industry and the defeat of the Luftwaffe, called for greater co-operation between RAF Bomber Command, the 8th USAAF and now the 15th USAAF, which started operations against Southern Germany and Austria from the Foggia bases in October. They also called for a new list of target priorities. To Harris, the reason for the apparent failure of 'Pointblank' was the insufficiency of the forces allocated and the dispersal of effort. Regarding the latter, he indicated the 'abortive' Ploesti raid, in August 1943, when the whole B-24 force had been diverted from the 8th USAAF to bases in North Africa for this purpose. In the end, the Americans decided to proceed with 'Pointblank' but with the proviso that all raids be escorted by long-range fighters and to this they devoted all the resources at their disposal.

In November 1943, RAF Bomber Command turned to a new offensive against industrial areas in Germany that was to last until the end of March 1944. Known as the Battle of Berlin on account of the preponderance of raids against the capital of the Third Reich, this offensive was to culminate in the disastrous Nuremburg raid of 30 March 1944, presenting Harris with a similar crisis to that besetting General Carl Spaatz, the commander of the 8th USAAF, after Schweinfurt. From 10 June 1943 to 25 March 1944, RAF Bomber Command launched 58 major* raids against Germany. With the exceptions of Berlin and Nuremburg, all the targets lay in the western districts of Germany within range of the 'Oboe' navigational aid. Unable to bomb with the same accuracy as the Americans, Harris stuck to his policy of attacking industry that lay within an agglomeration of large towns and cities wherein the 'undermining of German morale' was a consideration. Few targets, with the exception of Kassel, wherein lay the Betthausen Fw 190 plant, came within the terms of the 'Pointblank' directive, although several of the concerns attacked made essential parts of some nature.

*400 or more aircraft.

In the battle against the Allied bombing offensive, the Luftwaffe had reasonable grounds for optimism by the winter of 1943–44. The success of the day fighter force in the Autumn had forced the USAAF to revert to shallow penetration targets and now, having recovered from the effect of 'Window' jamming through the use of new equipment and tactics, the night-fighters were inflicting heavy casualties on RAF Bomber Command. However, these results had been achieved only by the concentration of fighters in the West at the expense of other war fronts. Of the total fighter strength of the Luftwaffe, 68 per cent was concentrated in the West, along with 70 per cent of the Flak personnel in the autumn of 1943. On 1 January 1944, 1,650 single- and twin-engined fighters were based in Germany, France, Southern Norway and the Low Countries, in comparison to 365 in the Mediterranean and the Balkans, and 425 on the Soviet Front. At the beginning of 1944, 75 per cent of the fighters based in the West were concentrated within Germany, leaving only a small force in France to counter the activities of RAF No 2 Group and the 9th USAAF.

Under Milch's programme fighter production had soared to a monthly peak of 1,050 aircraft (725 Bf 109Gs and 325 Fw 190s) in July 1943. The 8th USAAF's raids on Augsburg, Regensburg, Marienburg and Wiener Neustadt had been effective only in so far as they reduced this figure to around 1,000 fighters per month for the remainder of 1943. But energetic dispersal and sub-contracting programmes had restored the production rate, although not to the July record.

The fuel situation was in excellent condition, with the synthetic plants reaching peak production. The crisis in aircrew training had been overcome under the influence of Generalleutnant Werner Kreipe, and pilots and aircrew were being processed from the schools at a high rate, although their flying standards hardly approached those of the US and RAF aircrews.

In terms of equipment, the Fw 190 was steadily replacing the BF 109G in several Jagdgruppen and replacing the Ju 87D in the ranks of the Schlachtgruppen; production of the promising He 219 and Ju 188 was proceeding apace, while the deficiencies in the Me 410 and He 177 were ameliorated, and at last the radical Me 262 jet fighter had been earmarked for mass production in the Spring. But it was at this juncture, in February 1944, that the whole situation violently changed; the 8th USAAF renewed its offensive against the German aircraft industry, but the bombers were now escorted by P-51s, P-38s and P-47s, these providing target cover, approach and withdrawal support throughout. The long-range escort fighter at a stroke capsized German defensive strategy, for the Luftwaffe Planning Staff had been lulled into a false sense of security during the winter of 1943–44, on the assurance of the Research and Development Branch that such an aircraft was, in the short term, a technical impossibility.

By April 1944, the 8th USAAF had gained a measure of air superiority over Germany that enabled it to strike targets without incurring the prohibitive losses of the previous Autumn. For the Luftwaffe, the attrition in aircraft and experienced pilots was appallingly high, and the successes against US bombers correspondingly low, despite the use of Sturmgruppen (Assault Groups) with heavily armed Fw 190s. The main source of US bomber casualties now became Flak.

The heavy attacks carried out in February 1944, which saw the culmination of the 'Pointblank' offensive, devastated three engine plants and 23 airframe factories which threatened to bring German aircraft production to a halt. The situation called for desperate remedy. The entire industry was placed under Albert Speer, the Minister for Armament and War Production and controlled through the Jägerstab (Fighter Staff) under Otto Saur. Full priority was accorded to the production of fighters, principally Bf 109Gs and Fw 190s, while the production of other aircraft types was drastically pruned. However, it was not until July 1944 that Saur was at last able to obtain Hitler's consent to a reduction in bomber output in favour of an all-out drive for fighter production.

The subsequent success of the Jägerstab was staggering and neutralised any further attempts by the Allies to forestall aircraft production, albeit of almost totally fighter types, by bombing. The acceptance of fighters in March 1944 exceeded the figure of 1,300 in January, and by April had increased by another 25 per cent. Thereafter, output continued to mount rapidly until a peak of 2,995 (1,605 Bf 109s and 1,390 Fw 190s) was achieved in September, and, although a decline set in, the level remained at 2,300–2,700 per month until the end of the year.

Despite the undoubted success of Jägerstab in reinforcing the Luftwaffe's fighter arm during the Summer of 1944, its efforts were completely nullified by the belated Allied bombing offensive against German oil targets. On 5 April, the Foggia-based 15th USAAF attacked the Ploesti oilfields, already under threat from the Russians in the north. The 8th USAAF raided oil objectives for the first time on 12 May, and again on 28 and 29 May 1944. But before any major oil offensive could get underway both the 8th USAAF and RAF Bomber Command were diverted to transportation and communications targets prior to OVERLORD, the invasion of Normandy on 6 June 1944.

Since its defeat at the hands of the German night fighter force during the Battle of Berlin phase, RAF Bomber Command had switched to shallow penetration targets and had embarked on the dislocation of the German transportation system with considerable effect. Its Mosquito bombers were, however, in a position to mount an intensive offensive against sundry targets in Germany itself. But it was not until October 1944 that the Lancasters and Halifaxes sought out the oil targets within Germany, being enabled to do so because of the complete dislocation of the German early-warning radar system effected by the Allied advance to the borders of Holland.

After D-Day, the 8th USAAF embarked on the oil offensive proper, attacking the synthetic oil plants at Leuna, Politz, Böhlen, Lutzkendorf, Magdeburg, Zeitz and Ruhland wherein some 40 per cent of German oil needs were provided. German fuel stocks amounted, in September 1943, to 280,000 tons and, by conservation (the Führer Reserve, for example) and added production, this amount had risen to a peak of 574,000 tons in April 1944 – when the Allied oil offensive began the reserves were higher than any time since 1940. While the reserves enabled the Luftwaffe to operate at maximum effort throughout the Normandy battles, the first critical shortage occurred at the end of August 1944. Oil production, which had been 195,000 tons in May, slumped to 52,000 tons in June, to 35,000 tons in July, to 16,000 tons in August and was down to a mere 7,000 tons in September 1944. As the result of the crucial fuel shortage that ensued, the Luftwaffe was in no position to use its vastly increased first-line fighter strength after September. August 1944 also saw a renewal of effort by the 15th USAAF against Ploesti, Brux and other oil plants in the southern sector, and by the end of the month the Russians had overrun the Rumanian oilfields. The crippling of the Luftwaffe had finally been achieved, but on the ground rather than in the air.

Apart from its direct effects on the German war industry, the Anglo-American air offensive in the West, in 1943 and 1944, had the following results applicable to the Luftwaffe's conduct of operations:

– A reduction in the Luftwaffe's strength in the Mediterranean (1,280 aircraft in July 1943 reduced to 475 in July 1944) to a size at which its influence over the course of events was negligible.

– The transfer of first-line fighters from the Soviet Union to Germany at the very moment when the growing numerical superiority of the Soviet Air Forces required strengthening of German fighter opposition.

– The concentration of productive capacity on fighter types brought about the weakening and eventual eclipse of the long-range bomber force. In particular, expansion of the night-fighter arm could only take place at the expense of the bomber arm.

– The exertion of every effort in defence of war industry inflicted a rate of wastage which limited numerical expansion and resulted in a rapid decline in performance and quality: Performance due to the reliance on contemporary aircraft types, at the expense of the development and production of the Focke-Wulf Ta 152, Dornier Do 335 and others, and quality due to the casualties in fighter leaders and experienced pilots.

– The concentration of fighter units in the Reich permitted the Allies to bomb the V-1 launching sites in Northern France with virtual impunity and ultimately facilitated the immediate establishment of Allied air superiority over the beachheads in Normandy at the time of the invasion in June 1944.

HORRIDO!

■ **The defence of Germany by day, 1943–4**

On 1 January 1943, the total strength of the Jagdgruppen in the West was 635 Bf 109Gs and Fw 190s, stationed at airfields that stretched from Banak, in Northern Norway, to Brest-Guipavas on the Atlantic coast in Brittany.

The Geschwaderstab of JG 26, under Major Josef Priller, was at Lille-Vendeville in Northern France, with I/JG 26 at St Omer-Fort Rouge, II/JG 26 at Vitry-en-Artois and III/JG 26 at Wevelghem. Operating under Jafü 2, within Luftflotte 3, the Geschwader was equipped with Fw 190A-4s, with the exception of III/JG 26 and 5./JG 26 which were equipped with Bf 109G-3 and G-4 fighters. By the end of the month, both I/JG 26 and 7.Staffel were in the Soviet Union. In exchange for these units, III/JG 54, under Major Reinhard Seiler, was posted to Vendeville from the Soviet Union for operations in France. By 27 March, however, this Gruppe had been redeployed to Oldenburg, in Germany, under Luftwaffenbefehlshaber Mitte.

The 'Richthofen' Jagdgeschwader (JG 2), based west of the Seine, had been weakened by the transfer of II/JG 2 to Tunisia, but by January, I/JG 27 was working up to operational readiness at Evreux-Fauville after its withdrawal from North Africa. The I/JG 2 was scattered, with individual Staffeln at Triqueville, Beaumont-le-Roger and Evreux wherein the Stab and 12./JG 2 were located. Hauptmann Egon Mayer's III/JG 2, the most experienced unit in combatting the 8th USAAF's B-17s, was based at Vannes-Meuçon, with Staffeln at Brest-Guipavas and Cherbourg. Both Jafü 2 and Jafü 3's fighter forces, therefore, were now up to strength; much of this strength, however, was to be diverted from operations against US bombers to daily combat with RAF Fighter Command and RAF No 2 Group during the Spring, when the 8th USAAF turned to targets in Germany.

The first US raid over German soil, to Wilhelmshaven on 27 January, was intercepted by elements of Obstlt.Dr Erich Mix's JG 1, and the loss of seven of its fighters in return for one B-17 and two B-24s clearly indicated this unit's inexperience in comparison with the battle-hardened pilots of JG 2 and JG 26, that had hitherto opposed the 8th USAAF. Under Luftwaffenbefehlshaber Mitte, the four Gruppen of JG 1 were stationed over a wide area; the Geschwaderstab and II/JG 1 were at Jever, I/JG 1 at Schiphol, Katwijk and Bergen, in Holland, along with elements of IV/JG 1, while the III Gruppe was scattered at airfields from Husum to Aalborg. The remaining Jagdgeschwader in the West and one that was to play little part in the defence of Germany was JG 5. Commanded by Major Günther Scholz, I/JG 5 and elements of IV/JG 5 protected important naval bases in Norway from Banak and Bardufoss.

Between January and the end of March 1943, the activities of JG 1 were limited to the rare occasions when the 8th USAAF raided targets in Germany and Holland – in February, only Emden and Wilhelmshaven were attacked, and in March only Bremen-Vegesack, Wilhelmshaven and Rotterdam. The bulk of 8th USAAF's attacks on Brest, Lorient, St Nazaire, Amiens, Rennes, Rouen and other targets which lay within range of RAF Fighter Command's Spitfire IXs which could keep JG 2 and JG 26 at bay over most of the bombers' route.

In April, the improvement in weather saw an upsurge in the 8th's activity over Germany. On 17 April, during a raid on Bremen, German fighters from I and III/JG 1 and flak brought down 16 B-17s and caused damage to 48 more. The month saw a strengthening of Luftwaffenbefehlshaber Mitte's fighter units: III/JG 54 and 2./JG 27 were installed at Oldenburg and Schiphol respectively, while JG 1 was reinforced and elements diverted to constitute a new unit, JG 11. The command of JG 1 passed to Major Hans Philipp, an ex-JG 54 'experte' with the Schwertern to the Ritterkreuz, while the Kommodore of JG 11 was Major Anton Mader, who had led II/JG 11 in Tunisia. On 10 May 1943, fighters engaged in the defence of the Reich, with Jagddivisionen 1, 2 and 3, consisted of Stab, I and II/JG 1, 2./JG 27, Stab, I and II/JG 11, Jagdstaffel Helgoland and III/JG 54. In France, under Luftflotte 3, were Stab JG 2, I/JG 2 including 11.Staffel, II/JG 2 consisting of 12.Staffel only and III/JG 2; Stab, II and III/JG 26, 1. and 3./JG 27 and 4./JG 54, the total first-line strength being 354 fighters based on the Western Front.

The major problem faced by the Jagdflieger was the breaking up of the tightly packed formations of B-17s and B-24s, each heavily armed with Colt M-2 0.5-inch machine guns. With or without the attendant Spitfires – and the 8th's incursions over Germany were completely devoid of escort – the problem of attacking B-17s and B-24s was great. The immediate step was to increase the armament of the standard Bf 109G and the Fw 190A. Earlier, the Bf 109F-4/R1 had carried two Mauser MG 151/20s in gondolas under the wings in addition to the normal weaponry. In the Bf 109G this modification was standardised as 'Rustsatz 6'. Thus, the Bf 109G-6/R6 carried three MG 151s in addition to the twin fuselage-mounted MG 131 13-mm machine-guns, although much to the detriment of its performance. It was normal, therefore, to equip only a proportion of a Gruppe's 109s with the additional cannon while the remainder were used for fighter-versus-fighter combat. The Fw 190's normal armament for combat in France consisted of twin MG 17s and two MG 151s, but for anti-bomber work the Rheinmetall MG FF-M 20-mm cannon was re-installed in the outer wing bay, outboard of each undercarriage bay.

Late in June 1943, the Fw 190A-6 became operational with the Jagdgruppen, this aircraft having increased firepower by the deletion of the MG FFs and substitution of the more efficient MG 151 20-mm cannon. In an attempt to break up formations of US bombers, aerial bombing had been tried as early as 22 March, when Lt. Heinz Knoke of 5./JG 1 dropped a 250kg bomb, bringing down three B-17s near Wilhelmshaven. The technique was tried by other units, including 10./JG 26, but effective evasive action by wary US crews was to lead to its eventual discontinuation.

As early as June 1942, the Y-Gerät apparatus, which had proved its efficiency during the Blitz against Britain in the winter of 1940–41 as a blind-bombing aid, was used experimentally to guide day fighters to their targets over great distances. The standard Lorenz VHF transmitter/receiver set (FuG 16) could be fitted with blind-homing apparatus (Zielanflug) with a fixed D/F loop, and this equipment was in widespread use in day and night fighters by the summer of 1943. When fitted with a transmitter/receiver that picked up signals from the Y-Gerät ground station and sent modulated carrier wave (MCW) signals back in return, the equipment, now modified to FuG 16zY, enabled the ground station to plot the fighter's range and bearing. Operating on the 38.4-42.4 M/cs frequencies, FuG 16zY was normally installed in one aircraft in a large formation of fighters, nominated the 'Y' aircraft, and this aircraft enabled the ground controller to plot the position of the entire formation between 100km and 200kms with an accuracy of 0.5 per cent.

The 'Y' system thus enabled the controller to vector his formation of fighters to within visual range of the bomber stream in areas that were devoid of radar coverage. His instructions to the 'Y' aircraft were given over the Divisional Commentary (Gemeinschafts Welle), to which wavelength all aircraft of the fighter force were tuned, and could thus be heard by the formation leader and all the fighter pilots, but the 'Y' aircraft's commentary was on a re-transmitted frequency and could only be heard by ground control. Radio silence was observed on pain of subsequent disciplinary action and, in case of the Divisional Commentary being inaudible on account of jamming or because the fighters were out of range, pilots could switch over to the Reichsjägerwelle (Reich Fighter Wave) which broadcast commentaries for the benefit of all fighters operating over Germany – this recourse was seldom used. This was the primary control system used by Reichsverteidigung forces throughout 1943 and 1944.

In June, III/JG 26 was transferred from Wevelghem to Nordholz, near Cuxhaven on the North German coast, to bolster JG 1 and JG 11. On 13 June, during an attack on Kiel and Bremen by the 8th, III/JG 26's Kommandeur, Hptm. Kurt Ruppert, lost his life when his 'chute folded after baling out at excessive speed. It was a bad day for the 4th Bomb Wing of the 8th as well, for the Wing lost 22 B-17Fs out of 26 brought down by flak and fighters. The day was to also see the Thunderbolt cut its teeth, when the 56th Fighter Group bounced 10./JG 26 over Dixmuide shooting down three Fw 190A-4s during a support sweep to Lille. Like the Spitfire, the P-47C was hamstrung by range, and it was not until September 1943 that it was able to furnish continuous escort for the B-17s as far as Emden by using 75 and 108-gallon drop tanks.

On 24 July, the 8th USAAF attacked the nitrate plant at Heroya, in Norway, starting a spate of intensive summer operations within the terms of the 'Pointblank' directive. In what was to be known as 'Blitz Week', Warnemünde, Hamburg, Kiel, Wustrow, Hannover, Kassel and Oschersleben were attacked, while No 2 Group and RAF Fighter Command flew 'Ramrods' to the Luftwaffe airfields at Schiphol, Woensdrecht, Wevelghem, Merville, Triqueville and Abbeville. This immediately prompted the Luftwaffe to increase defences. The Stab and III/JG 26 were sent to Schiphol, I/JG 26 – fresh from Russia - was installed at Grimberghen, while II/JG 26 spent two weeks at Deelen-Arnhem and Volkel before returning to Beauvais on 15 August. By the end of August 1943, JG 3 'Udet', commanded by Obstlt. Wolf-Dietrich Wilcke, was installed at Schiphol, Deelen and Munster-Handorf with three Gruppen of Bf 109G-6s; I/JG 5 had been posted to Germany from Norway at end of July; II/JG 51 (Hptm. Karl Rammelt) arrived at Neubiburg from Sardinia; II/JG 27 (Hptm. Werner Schroer) arrived at Wiesbaden-Erbenheim on 6 August, and while JG 1 and JG 11 were brought up to full Geschwader strength, JGr 25 (Major Herbert Ihlefeld) and JGr 50 (Major Herman Graf) were formed at Neubiburg and Wiesbaden respectively, to combat the fast Mosquitoes which had become a serious menace. Equipped with specially-boosted Bf 109G-6s, the short operational careers of JGr 25 and JGr 50 were to be conspicuous for their lack of success.

The 8th raided Gelsenkirchen on 12 August, losing 25 B-17s despite the efforts of the Thunderbolts which staggered under the load of their long-range tanks. The withdrawal support provided by the Thunderbolts during these missions was growing in efficiency, however. On 17th August, the 8th launched a major attack on the Messerschmitt concern at Regensburg and the VKW ball-bearing works at Schweinfurt. In the first shuttle mission of the war, 147 B-17s made for Regensburg and started suffering fighter attacks at 10.21hrs, after the P-47s departed over Eupen. After bombing Regensburg the force made for bases in North Africa. Flying their second mission of the day, the 56th Fighter Group was over Eupen at 16.20hrs to meet the returning Schweinfurt force. At the time, the B-17s were under attack from 50–60 German fighters – mostly Bf 109Gs and Fw 190s, with some Bf 110s of ZG 26. In the ensuing engagement the 56th FG claimed 17 German fighters. Of these 6 were Fw 190s claimed by Lt. McCauley, Capt. W. Mahurin and Lt. Schultz: one of these was flown by Major Wilhelm-Ferdinand Galland, Kommandeur of II/JG 26, who was killed when his Fw 190A-6 crashed at Hees-Vlytinghen, west of Maastricht.

Sixty B-17s were lost during Mission 84 to Schweinfurt and Regensburg, but the apparently unfavourable results of the bombing did not discourage the US air chiefs. Among the attacking fighters, several were observed carrying rocket-mortars which were fired, albeit with poor accuracy, well outside the range of the US gunners. This weapon, the Wfr.Gr 21, had been fitted experimentally on the previous day to the Bf 109G-6s of 5./JG 11, and was to be liberally used in subsequent battles of the summer and autumn on the Bf 109 G-6/R2 and Fw 190A-4/R2 (carrying two) and the Bf 110G-2/R3 (carrying four).

Until their eventual decimation at the hands of 8th's fighters, the Zerstörergruppen, and to some extent the Nachtjagdgruppen, were to play an important part in breaking up US bomber formations so that the Bf 109s and Fw 190s could attack stragglers and individual formations. On 30 September 1943, the Zerstörer element consisted of Stab and III/ZG 26 and I/ZG 1 with 97 Bf 110G-2s on strength, and III/ZG 1 and I(Jagd)/KG 51 with 58 Me 410A-1 and B-1 heavy fighters.

By October 1943, the combat radius of the P-47D had been markedly increased by the 108-gallon tank, enabling the Thunderbirds to accept combat as far inland as Duren during a mission to Frankfurt on 4 October. But outside the P-47's radius of action, the German fighters reigned supreme. On 8 October, Bremen and Vegesack were the targets and, once again, as soon as the P-47s had departed, the first concentrated attacks by German fighters, began. Thirty B-17s succumbed to flak and fighters, but the 8th won a victory when Thunderbolts tangled with Geschwaderstab JG 1 over Nordhorn killing Obstlt. Philipp.

Mission 115 to the VKW plants at Schweinfurt, on 14 October, resulted in the loss of 60 B-17s over enemy territory, 5 crashed in England, 12 were Cat.3 write-offs, and a further 121 returned with degrees of battle damage that ranged from severe to superficial: 600 crew-men were missing in action, five were dead on arrival at their bases and 43 were wounded. After the P-47 escort had left the force near Aachen, the US bombers came under continuous attack by relays of Bf 109s and Fw 190s, whitepainted Ju 88Cs and Bf 110s of the Nachtjagdgruppen and the Zerstörergruppen's Bf 110G-2s and Me 410s which fired Wfr.Gr 21 rockets, and 30-mm and 37-mm cannon. Fog and other complications prevented the withdrawal cover, by Spitfires and P-47s, from being as efficient as had by now come to be expected, and the US bombers continued to take losses well out over the sea during the return. Luftwaffe losses were approximately 35 out of the 300 day fighters and 40 Zerstörer which took part in the battle. The losses suffered by 8th Bomber Command to flak and fighters was 20.6 per cent of the force, a prohibitive casualty rate.

Schweinfurt was the final proof of the Luftwaffe's ability to inflict consistently high losses on unescorted US bombers, but for the Jagdgruppen revelling in the luxury of unhindered interception, time was running out. The 8th was hard at work, improving the combat radius of the P-47D. The 75- and 108-gallon tanks increased radius to 340 and 375 miles respectively, while new tactics wherein fighters flew to appointed escort areas, throttled back for endurance and held on to their drop tanks until the last minute, allowed this combat radius to be increased. Already moves were afoot to fit a larger drop tank to the P-47. In October, the 55th FG became operational on the Lockheed P-38H Lightning, while the 20th FG was busily working up on the same type. This aircraft had a combat radius of 400 miles, including 15 minute at emergency boost for dog-fighting in the target area. The North American P-51B was first issued to the 9th USAAF n December 1943, and it was inexplicable that this first-rate long-range fighter went to this tactical command instead of the 8th US Fighter Command. By February 1944, however, the 4th FG within the 8th USAAF became fully operational on the Mustang with other Groups following suit shortly after.

In late December 1943, all units operating in the defence of Germany were put under a new command, Luftflotte Reich, led by Generaloberst Hans-Jürgen Stumpff. By March 1944, Jagdkorps I, with Jagddivisionen 1, 2, 3 and 7 subordinated, was responsible for all fighter operations within Germany and the Low Countries, while those in France were controlled by Jagdkorps II with Jagddivisionen 4 and 5 and Jafü Brittany subordinated. On 20 February 1944, the day-fighter units under Luftflotte Reich consisted of the following: Stab, I, II and III/JG 1, Stab, I, II, III and IV(Sturm)/JG 3, I/JG 5, Stab, I, II, III, 10 and 11./JG 11, Einsatzstaffel Erla, Epr.Kdo 25, I and II/JG 27, II/JG 53, III/JG 54, Sturmstaffel 1, Stab, I, II and III/JG 300, Stab, I, II and III/JG 301 (less 10./JG 301) and Stab, I and II/JG 302 (less 1./JG 302). These units were equipped with Bf 109G-6 and Fw 190A-6 and A-7 fighters. The Zerstörer units were: II/ZG 1, Stab, I, II and III/ZG 26, and Stab, I, II and III/ZG 76, equipped with Bf 110Gs and Me 410s. The total strength of Luftflotte Reich's fighters on this day was 863, of which 517 were combat ready. To this was added six Gruppen of JG 2 and JG 26 under Jafü 4 and 5 within Jagdkorps II in France, along with I and III/ZG 1 based in Brittany.

German aircraft production ensured a steady supply of fighters to these units, while they were backed by an excellent ground control system. There was no shortage of aviation fuel. The performance of the ageing Bf 109G-6 was improved by fitting high-altitude DB 605AS, ASCM and D motors, to which GM 1 and MW 50 power-boosting could be fitted. Firepower was increased by the widespread use of the Rheinmetall MK 108 30-mm cannon – the 'pneumatic hammer', as it was called. Its muzzle velocity was only 500m/sec and the rate of fire 600 rounds per minute, but the effect was devastating, with one strike capable of bringing down a fighter and three sufficient to shoot down a B-17 or B-24. The incendiary qualities of 20-mm ammunition were enhanced by the introduction of the Hexogen A-1 round with high phosphorous content.

It was against strong, well-equipped and resolute forces of Luftflotte Reich, that the 8th and 15th USAAFs resumed deep penetration raids in January 1944 – this time with fighter escort. The casualties to 8th bombers remained high, however, sixty bombers were lost on 11 January against Oschersleben and Wallam, largely due to poorly co-ordinated fighter escort, and this once again emphasised the perils of long-range penetration. During 'Big Week' (19–25 February 1944), which saw the ending of the 'Pointblank' offensive, 21 US bombers were lost on 20 February (Leipzig), 41 on the 22nd (Brunswick), 49 on the 24th (Schweinfurt) and 31 on the 25th (Augsburg, Regensburg and Stuttgart).

The 8th USAAF's offensive against Berlin in conjunction with RAF Bomber Command opened in March 1944 with very heavy losses. On 6 March, 68 B-17s and B-24s and 11 US fighters failed to return, and 37 bombers were lost on the 8th, although on the following day only nine failed to return. But in the great aerial battles of attrition throughout March and April, it was the Luftwaffe that was ultimately the loser. Whether taking-off, assembling, intercepting, recovering and landing, the Jagdgruppen suffered great losses at the hands of the aggressive P-51s, P-47s and P-38s. Fighter aircraft could be replaced, pilots could be replaced, albeit by hastily-trained youngsters with as few as 80 hours' flying time, but not the Kommodoren, Gruppenkommandeure or Staffelkapitäne with their years of experience. Killed in the battles of 1943 were Hptm. Heinrich Setz, Hptm. Fritz Geisshardt, Oblt. Horst Hanning, Obstlt. Johannes Seifert, Major Erwin Clausen, Major Kurt Brandle and Hptm. Wilhelm Lemke. Now in the Spring of 1944, JG 2 lost two Kommodoren within weeks – on 2 March. Obstlt. Egon Mayor fell over Montmedy in a dogfight with Colonel H. Coen's 365th Fighter Group and on 27 April, Major Kurt Ubben was shot down by P-47s over Château Thierry. Oberst. Wolf-Dietrich Wilcke was killed over Schoppenstadt on 23 March, and on 11 May, Oberst Walter Oesau, Kommodore JG 1, was shot down by P-38s over St Vith, in the Ardennes. These men were irreplaceable and their loss was to be felt keenly in the battles over Normandy in the months to come.

In April, the General der Jagdflieger, Adolf Galland, reported: 'The ratio in which we fight today is about 1 to 7. The standard of the Americans is extraordinarily high. The day fighters have lost more than 1,000 fighters during the last four months, among them our best officers. These gaps cannot be filled. During each enemy raid we lose about 50 fighters. Things have gone so far that the danger of a collapse of our Fighter Arm exists.'

As a desperate remedy Sturmstaffeln were formed, manned by picked crews inculcated with a spirit of determination and recklessness, and encouraged to ram Allied bombers rather than return to base without a 'kill'. The inception of the scheme dated back to the winter of 1943–44, with the formation of Sturmstaffel 1, and by April 1944, IV(Sturm)/JG 3 'Udet', under Major Wilhelm Moritz, was carrying out 'Company Front' assaults on US bombers. The Sturmstaffeln flew the Fw 190A-8/R7. This aircraft was specially armoured, had the twin MG 131 machine guns removed and carried two MG 151 and two MK 108 cannon. Laden with a 66-gallon

Zusatztank, it was heavy and unwieldy in flight. The IV/JG 3 was joined in the summer of 1944 by II(Sturm)/JG 300 and finally by II(Sturm)/JG 4.

The Sturmgruppen, covered usually by two Gruppen of Bf 109G-10s flying up-sun, attacked the bombers from astern in line-abreast in three waves. The pilots usually opened fire with the MG 151s at about 400 yards, bringing the MK 108s into play at 200 yards. At first, short bursts were directed at the tail gunner, then transferred to either of the inboard engines, with break-off following at point-blank range. The results gained by the Sturmgruppen were good, but US fighters continued to shoot down the heavy Fw 190s.

In accordance with orders from Göring, the weight of German fighter attacks was concentrated on the destruction of bombers throughout March and April 1944, and, partly to conserve forces, German fighters were ordered to avoid combat with US fighters at all costs. The result was, as the Kommodore of JG 6 pungently remarked, that 'the safest flying that was ever possible was that of an American fighter over Germany.' In no way did this denigrate the performance of US fighter pilots, but it imbued them with a spirit of superiority, the German fighter pilot finding himself restricted and acquiring, as a result, a corresponding sense of inferiority.

In May 1944, the 8th USAAF's bombers sought out transportation targets in the campaign of dislocation prior to the D-Day invasion of Normandy, while flying numerous missions over Germany itself. By this time the P-51 had assumed almost total superiority over the Luftwaffe, ranging as far as Berlin, Dresden and Frankfurt.

PAUKE! PAUKE!

■ The night-fighter's war, 1943–5

'Did they realise how small were their chances if once seen by a fighter? I guess that none knew that the exhausts of their Lancasters could be spotted from a mile-and-a-half, and they could be seen as silhouettes against the stars from nearly a mile away, while the fighter could be seen against the ground at only about a hundred yards.' So wrote an experienced RAF night fighter pilot. Indeed, by 1943, through the efforts of science, the night sky offered but a tattered cloak to hide the nocturnal bomber.

By the beginning of 1943, the Kammhuber Line – the areas covered by Himmelbett fighter-control sectors – stretched from Troyes, 80 miles SE of Paris, to the northern tip of Denmark, extending in depth from the coast to 100–150 miles inland, covering the Low Countries, the Ruhr, Westphalia, the Hannover-Hamburg area, and the whole of Denmark. Only by flying several hundreds of miles were RAF bombers able to avoid this defensive area via the Skaggerak or far to the south of Paris. Almost 95 per cent of the five Nachtjagdgeschwader, operating Bf 110F-4, Ju 88C-6 and Do 217N-2 types, were using the Lichtenstein BC or C-1 radar. The German night-fighter crews were now skilled in its use, eager to fly in all weathers and ruthless in their determination to inflict casualties on RAF Bomber Command. Their leading 'experte', Major Helmut Lent of IV/NJG 1, had claimed his 50th 'kill' on 8 January 1943, and others such as Streib, Gildner, Knacke, Becker and Meurer were adding to their growing list of nocturnal victories.

Against this formidable opposition, RAF Bomber Command was also growing more cunning and determined. In March 1943, when Harris committed his forces to the Battle of the Ruhr, Bomber Command consisted of eighteen squadrons of

Lancaster Mk Is, fourteen squadrons of Halifaxes (mostly Mk II Series IIA), seven squadrons of Stirling I bombers and several units with the Wellington III, IV and X. These bomber units were allocated to Nos 1, 3, 4, 5 and 6 Groups, Bomber Command, while No 8 Group (Pathfinder Force), commanded by Gp.Cpt. D. C. T. Bennett, consisted of Nos 7, 35, 83, 109 and 156 Squadrons. The function of this élite force was to locate and mark the target with 250-lb Target Indicator bombs for the following bombers. While 'Gee' (TR 1335) was of little use because of enemy jamming, other aids to navigation had taken its place: 'Oboe' blind-bombing system had first been employed by a No 109 Sqdn Mosquito on Lutterade on 20 December 1942, and H2S radar had first been used to good effect against Hamburg by Nos 7 and 35 Squadrons (No 8 Group PFF) on 30 January 1943. The equipment was sound and other squadrons were receiving it.

All effort was now made to reduce the amount of time over the target, and gone were the great streams of bombers that enabled the Himmelbett operators to direct the night fighters to attack with leisure. Instead of a question of hours, it now took a narrow, compact bomber stream between 30 and 40 minutes to cross the Kammhuber Line. The narrower the width of the stream passing diagonally through the GCI area, the fewer the number of controls that could have bomber aircraft within their range; the shorter the period in which the bombers passed through each GCI area, the fewer the number of possible interceptions which could be effected.

To counter these new tactics, the Himmelbett stations were widened and deep-ened, and the control system was developed so that two or more night fighters could be brought into action simultaneously in any one Himmelbett sector. Even so, the Himmelbett GCI system was particularly susceptible to saturation tactics and was very uneconomical since it necessitated the wide dispersal of fighters over the whole defen-sive belt, of which only a few could be brought into action against any one threat. Hence, already by the early summer of 1943, two measures had been adopted which fell outside the scope of the classic system. These revised night fighting tactics were:

– ZAHME SAU (Tame Sow). This operation, unfettered by the Himmelbett GCI stations, enabled night fighter crews to be directed en masse to the bomber stream by R/T running commentaries from the respective Jagddivision. Once the night fighters had reached the stream, the crews endeavoured to make AI contact with individual targets. Thus, a sortie could start over the North Sea, follow the bomber stream to Mannheim, for example, return with the stream on the out-bound leg and finally land at an airfield far removed from the parent base. In Zahme Sau, the five hours' endurance of the Ju 88C-6b and Ju 88R-1, despite their inferior handling qualities, offered an immediate advantage over the more nimble Bf 110G-4a fighter that became standard equipment for many Nachtjagdgruppen in the late-summer of 1943. Apart from the FuG 212 Lichtenstein C-1 radar, the night-fighter crew was soon able to obtain 'homing' on RAF bombers by additional equipment. Thus, Flensburg (FuG 227/1) could home on the 'Monica' tail-warning device fitted in RAF bombers, while the radar transmissions from H2S could be homed on to by Naxos Z (FuG 350) from a maximum range of 30 miles.

– WILDE SAU (Wild Sow). This was the freelance visual night fighting that dated from before the introduction of Himmelbett, wherein the pilot relied on searchlights and visual contact to make an interception. Wilde Sau fighters operated over the target area, above a flak-free zone, and were aided by searchlights, flares and pyrotechnics. Normally the Flak fire was limited to a certain altitude, say 15,000 feet, above which the Wilde Sau fighters operated. The flares were dropped by special Beleuchter (Illuminator) staffeln, usually Ju 88s.

The reintroduction of visual night fighting was due to the energetic efforts of Obstlt. Hajo Hermann who gained Göring's authority on 27 June 1943 for the formation of a Kommando equipped with twelve Fw 190A-4 fighters fitted with 300 litre (66-gal) drop tanks. The Kommando quickly proved its worth by shooting down 12 RAF bombers over Cologne on the night of 3 July, and, as a result, Göring gave his approval for the formation of further Wilde Sau units. Over the summer months, after the formation of JG 300 (Major Kurt Kettner) at Bonn-Hangelar, both JG 301 (Maj. Helmut Weinreich) and JG 302 (Maj. Manfred Mössinger) were formed at Neubiberg and Döberitz. Only one Gruppe of each Geschwader possessed its own aircraft, the other Gruppen sharing their fighters with a Jagdgruppe based on the same airfield, much to the detriment of serviceability. Later on, the Fw 190A-5/U2N and Bf 109G-6/U4N, equipped with the Naxos Z homer, were added to the inventory of the Wilde Sau units. With the onset of winter, losses rose alarmingly and, although some Wilde Sau elements of JG 300 and JG 301 continued night operations, most were retrained for combat operations against day bombers of the 8th USAAF.

The formation of JG 300 proved fortuitous for the Luftwaffe when, in late-July 1943, RAF Bomber Command commenced the Battle of Hamburg, the second largest city in the Reich. Situated on the coast, Hamburg was an easy target to identify on H2S and, on the night of 24 July, 740 bombers out of a total of 791 despatched dropped 2,396 tons of HE and incendiary on the districts of Barmbeck, Alster, Höheluft and Altona. The raid was completed in two-and-a-half hours, 74 bombers carrying H2S and 'Window' jamming being used for the first time. 'Window' consisted of tinfoil strips cut to a length equivalent to half the wavelength of the Würzburg and Lichtenstein radars, a bundle of 'Window' dropped from an aircraft gave an immediate radar return on the enemy operator's screen. The effect was a catastrophe for the entire Himmelbett GCI control system and for the night-fighters which relied on FuG 202 and FuG 212, with a simultaneous effect on radar searchlights and flak prediction. General Martini, the chief of the Luftwaffe Signals Command, had for long known about the possible use of metallic strips with their jamming potential, but his warnings had fallen upon deaf ears. Characteristically, it was he who had to take the full blame for the 'surprise' of Window!

A total of 3,095 sorties were despatched by RAF Bomber Command and the 8th

USAAF against Hamburg between 24 July and 2 August, 2,630 of these dropping 8,621 tons, including 4,309 tons of incendiaries on this ancient Hanseatic city. Eighty-seven bombers were lost, but the devastation and fire storms killed 41,800 people and injured 37,439 while thousands were missing presumed killed.

While Kammhuber's Fliegerkorps XII recovered from the effects of 'Window', the Wilde Sau units came into their own during the long summer nights. When Bomber Command returned to Berlin, JG 300 claimed 56 RAF bombers on the night of 24 August, operating in good visibility above a flak-free zone designated at 4,500m; 47 were claimed on the night of 1 September and a further 26 on the night of 4 September. The first large-scale Zahme Sau operation was flown on the night of 17 August; 40 Lancasters out of a despatched force of 597 were shot down by flak and night fighters using brilliant moonlight. The pace continued throughout the autumn as RAF Bomber Command sought targets at Mannheim, Hannover and Kassel.

Collisions, bad weather, and return fire were constant threats to the German night fighter pilots. NJG 1 lost Hptm. Reinhold Knacke, Oblt. Paul Gildner and Hptm. Ludwig Becker in February 1943, and on 27 September, Maj. Hans-Dieter Frank, the Kommandeur I/NJG 1 with 55 'kills', was lost in a mid-air collision. Hptm. August Geiger of 7./NJG 1, with 53 'kills', was lost on 29 September. Concerning the tactics and organisation of night fighter units, the evidence given by a crew shown down off Texel on 25 July 1943 during the 8th USAAF raid on Hamburg is of interest. Flying a Bf 110G-4a, this crew belonged to 12. Staffel of IV/NJG 1 based at Leeuwarden. Gruppenstab IV/NJG 1 consisted of three crews, that of the Kommandeur, the Adjutant and the Technical Officer, and the three Staffeln of the Gruppe averaged about ten crews apiece. The Leeuwarden area had been relatively quiet to that time, and this crew had flown 75 operational flights in 21 months. Losses had been low. The whole of NJG 1 was equipped with the Bf 110G. The aircraft was in plentiful supply and there always were more aircraft than crews. Replacements were drawn from Werl and Schöneberg-Diepensee, where calibration of the Lichtenstein BC was carried out. The operational sector of IV/NJG 1 was based on Leeuwarden with the following fighter-control 'boxes': 'Schleier' at Schiermonnikoog, 'Tiger' at Terschelling, 'Lowe' SW of Leeuwarden, 'Hering' at Medemblik, 'Bisbari' on the east side of the Zuider Zee and 'Salzherring' on the North Sea coast, opposite Medemblik. These were M/F radio beacons over which the fighters orbited prior to instructions from the controller.

The pilot expressed a decided preference for attacking four-engined bombers: there was a considerable danger in over-shooting when approaching a slow bomber, such as the Wellington, whereas it was easier to synchronise speeds when dealing with Lancasters and Halifaxes. With the latter it was seldom necessary to lower flap to reduce speed. One form of attack was to approach from astern to within 30–50 yards and silence the rear gunner with the first burst, after which the bomber could be dealt with at leisure. Another form of attack, which the crews of IV/NJG 1 regarded as their speciality, was to make a slow approach until the fighter was about 150 feet vertically below the bomber and then fly along at synchronised speeds until ready to attack. From this position the night fighter was immune from the bomber's lookout and from its MG fire. The actual attack was made by pulling up almost vertically and firing when the bomber's nose met the top of the Revi C.12/D gunsight. Operating within the Himmelbett area, normal interceptions lasted between five and seven minutes from the first vector to the kill.

The introduction of 'Window' failed to reduce RAF bomber losses due to night fighters to any marked extent, although those sustained from flak did decrease. If any-thing, the Wilde Sau and Zahme Sau tactics more than compensated for the set-back in efficient radar control. In September 1943, a new AI radar set, FuG 220 Lichtenstein SN-2, was introduced and units were rapidly re-equipped. SN-2 worked within 73 and 91 M/cs, was unaffected by 'Window' jamming and had a maximum range of 4 miles and a minimum of 400 yards. Its minimum range, therefore, was not as low as FuG 212 Lichtenstein C-1 and for this reason the latter was often retrained to enable the crews to get within 200 yards. This led to a veritable forest of aerials on the noses of the night-fighters, reducing their speed advantage even more. But, by early 1944, SN-2 had been perfected and was giving ranges down to 200 yards. Armament was also increased; the Bf 110G-4b/R3 carrying two Mk 108 30-mm cannon and two MG 151/20s. The so-called 'schräge Musik' (Jazz Music) installation of Bf 110s, Ju 88s and Do 217s enabled crews to attack a bomber from directly below, without having recourse to the hair-raising manoeuvre described earlier by the pilot of IV/NJG 1. Two MG FFs or MG 151/20s were mounted in the cabin or fuselage at between 70–80° from the vertical, and were aimed by a second Revi C.12/D or 16B gunsight mounted on the canopy roof. The so-called 'schräge Musik' was highly efficient and some experienced pilots could stay directly below a cork-screwing bomber while remaining immune from its return fire.

The night war over Germany was becoming increasingly one of radio measure and countermeasure, with each opponent seeking a technological loophole through which to gain an advantage over the other. In November, greater bombing accuracy was attained by the introduction of Gee-H, while the specialist No 100 Group, RAF Bomber Command, was formed under Air Cdr. E. B. Addison. Its rôle was bomber support, and through radio countermeasures (RCM) and the introduction first of Beaufighter VIs and later Mosquitoes for intruder work within the bomber streams and over German night fighter bases, No 100 Group was to provide a valuable service. Bomber Command's first reaction to Wilde Sau was to shorten its attacks to 15–20 minutes' duration, and this was quickly followed by the development of feint or 'spoof' routes and attacks to despatch the German night fighters to the wrong area. The task of the defenders was to be rendered the more difficult by R/T jamming by 'Mandrel' and 'Airborne Cigar', while 'Corona' consisted of further confusion by the broadcast of spurious information.

However, when Harris turned to the Battle of Berlin in November 1943, these measures were in their infancy. This was to be Harris' attempt to end the war by strategic bombing, and it was to end in failure despite the gallantry and determination of his crews. Primarily directed at Berlin, from 18 November 1943 until 31 March 1944, Bomber Command's intensive attacks resulted in the loss of 1,047 bombers with a further 1,682 damaged through enemy action. The offensive was carried out usually in unfavourable weather, with No 8 Group PFF having to sky-mark the target with flares and 'Window' being used extensively.

But the Nachtjagdgruppen had solved the 'Window' problem to a large extent by the introduction of SN-2, while Flensburg and Naxos allowed them to operate with considerable freedom. The situation on the ground was also improving, with the older Freya and Würzburg radars being replaced by Wasserman and Mammuth radars that were unaffected by the then current wave-length jamming. On 31 December 1943, out of a strength of 517 night-fighters, 334 were combat ready. Allotted to the defence of the Reich were Stab, I, II, III and IV/NJG 1, Stab, I, II and III/NJG 2, Stab, I, II, III and IV/NJG 3, Stab, I, II, III and IV/NJG 5 and Stab, I and II/NJG 6, while Stab, I, II and III/NJG 4 were subordinated to Luftflotte 3 in France. Fliegerkorps XII was now disbanded, Kammhuber was replaced by Generalleutnant Josef Schmid in September 1943, and the latter now took over Jagdkorps I under Luftflotte Reich.

The majority of Nachtjagdgruppen was equipped with the Bf 110G-4b/R3, but the Ju 88C-6b was growing in preponderance, while a small number of units used the Dornier 217N-2. Some Gruppen had a few Fw 190A-5/U2Ns on strength. The I/NJG 1, under Hptm. Manfred Meurer, had several Heinkel 219A-2/R1s along with Bf 110Gs and Ju 88Cs. This excellent fighter was destined to see only limited service, despite its fine performance that enabled it to intercept the Mosquito. Meurer was killed on 2 January in a collision. This was followed on 21 January by the loss of Maj. Heinrich Prinz zu Sayn Wittgenstein, the Kommodore NJG 4, who was shot down by return fire during a raid on Magdeburg. Despite the losses, the Luftwaffe's night fighters reaped a grim harvest, as indicated by the growing losses of Bomber Command: 55 bombers failed to return from Magdeburg on 21 January and 43 were lost out of a force of 683 to Berlin on 28 January. Bomber Command's heaviest raid on Berlin (1,066 despatched) saw the loss of 42 on 15 February, and, on 19 February, 78 were lost out of 823 sent. The Kommandeur of IV/NJG 1, Hptm. Heinz-Wolfgang Schnauffer, destined to become the greatest of all night fighter pilots, claimed his 50th 'kill' on 24 March 1944. On this night, 72 RAF bombers were lost out of 811 sent to Berlin. The climax came on the Nuremburg raid on 30 March, when 94 bombers were either lost or damaged beyond repair.

On this night, 795 bombers were despatched to Nuremburg. The weather over the North Sea precluded any attempt at 'spoof' raids. Thickening cloud over Belgium was followed by a brilliant half-moon which made for almost daylight conditions over Germany. The Nachtjagdgruppen were despatched to the Frankfurt and Bonn sectors on Zahme Sau missions. Before the first RAF bombers had reached the coast, the direction of their course was already plotted from their H2S emissions, enabling Jagddivision 3's fighters to position themselves in the path. In brilliant moonlight, with several of the Lancasters and Halifaxes leaving long condensation trails, a running battle commenced over Aachen to the target. Over 200 German night fighters were committed to the battle that was to continue well out over the North Sea, amongst the hail and thunderclouds.

The loss of 11.3 per cent of the force committed was prohibitive and the victory accorded to Schmid's night-fighters was instrumental in the decision to curtail deep-penetration night attacks. The Mosquitoes of RAF Bomber Command, to be joined in the summer by the MK XVI capable of carrying a 4,000-lb bomb, continued their sorties deep into Germany, however, and the heavy bomber element was now turned to transportation and communication targets prior to OVERLORD. Even these raids did not go unscathed – the attack on Mailly-le-Camp, in France, which was the depot for the 21st Pz. Division, resulted in NJG 4 and III/NJG 5 shooting down a considerable number of RAF heavies.

The finest night fighter of the Luftwaffe, the Ju 88G-1, was issued to several Gruppen in early June 1944, and the Allies reaped a windfall when one landed in error at Woodbridge, in Suffolk, at 04.25hrs on 13 July. Carrying the very latest in German avionics this aircraft allowed scientists to modify 'Windows' to jam the Lichtenstein SN-2 and, for the first time, gave positive evidence of German capability to home on to Monica. In addition to FuG 220, FuG 227 and FuG 16zY, the Junkers carried Peilgerät 6 automatic D/F, FuG 10P short-range R/T and long-range W/T, and FuB1 2F blind-approach.

After the German rout of August and September 1944, the Nachtjagdgruppen suffered a catastrophic set-back when the early-warning radar network was overrun by the Allies. This enabled Bomber Command to execute numerous, and extremely intricate operations, backed up by RAF Mosquito night fighters and copious RCM jamming, against the vital oil and transportation targets deep within Germany. Although the German night fighter force continued to operate efficiently, its back was finally broken by fuel shortage.

THE LAST BATTLES

■ **From D-Day to the final defeat of Germany, 1944–5**

On 1 April 1944, out of a total Luftwaffe strength of 1,676 Bf 109Gs and Fw 190As, 850 were committed to the defence of the Reich against the depredations of the 8th and 15th US Air Forces. Only 135 were stationed in Northern France and Belgium facing the might of the 9th USAAF, the 2nd Tactical Air Force, and RAF Fighter Command. In Norway there remained only 40 Fw 190s of IV/JG 5, while in Italy there were 145 Bf 109Gs of JG 53 and JG 77. In the East, on a front of 1,500 miles from the Baltic to the Caspian, only 515 German fighters faced the overwhelming numbers of the Soviet Air Forces now equipped with Yak-9s and the latest La-7 fighters.

An uneasy lull reigned in the East. The Crimea had been lost, the Northern and Central Fronts had stabilised while the Russians consolidated, while in the South the last offensive of spring had brought the Soviet Army to the borders of Rumania. Such were the resources of the Soviet Army that there could be little delay before the summer offensive. In mid-May, the Allies renewed their offensive in Italy to which the Luftwaffe's opposition was negligible. The next Allied blow would fall in the West, at some point along the coast of Northern France, but when the invasion would come was open to conjecture and all the Wehrmacht could do was to wait and strengthen its defences along the Atlantic Wall.

For the Luftwaffe, the preparation for an Allied invasion of France had started early in 1944, with a re-organisation of command and strengthening of bomber and anti-shipping forces. In August 1943, Gen. Maj. Dietrich Pelz had taken over Fliegerkorps IX in France and the Low Countries, and this command had been steadily reinforced by Kampfgruppen drawn from Italy. In February 1944, Gen.Lt.

Alfred Bülowius' Fliegerkorps II arrived in Northern France in name only, with the task of building up the ground-attack and close-support forces. The maritime command, Fliegerführer Atlantik, was absorbed into Fliegerkorps X (Gen.Lt. Holle) with Fliegerdivision 2 subordinated. Based in the extreme south and south-west of France, both organisations consisted of long-range reconnaissance and anti-shipping units. Jagdkorps II, under Gen. Maj. Werner Junck, was responsible for fighter defence over Northern France and Belgium, with Jafü 4 and 5 subordinated. In May, only two Jagdgeschwader were operational under Jagdkorps II, but it was proposed to rush fighter reinforcements in as soon as the Allies invaded.

It was the bomber and anti-shipping forces that were to be the spearhead of the Luftwaffe's offensive operations against the Allied landings, but by the eve of D-Day, Fliegerkorps IX, which had 550 bombers on strength in December 1943, had been reduced to some 170 by April 1944. This was due to Pelz' bomber campaign, the so-called 'Little Blitz', which had opened on 21 January 1944. To meet the invasion it was hoped that Fliegerkorps X would have five Gruppen of torpedo-bombers and a similar number of Gruppen using Fritz X (FX 1400) and the Hs 293 glider-bomb, but owing to the priority afforded fighter production, the force rose to only some 200–250 aircraft, and even this strength could not be maintained, for by early June 1944 it had dwindled to about 190 aircraft and there was a critical shortage of trained crews. On the day prior to D-Day (Operation OVERLORD), Luftflotte 3 (Sperrle) consisted of 815 combat aircraft. These included 170 single-engined fighters based over the entirety of France, 130 bombers of FlKps IX and 200 anti-shipping aircraft of FlKps X and Fliegerdivision 2.

On 31 May, 1944, the forces under Jagdkorps II consisted of Stab and II/JG 2 at Creil with 21 (15) Bf 109G-6s and Fw 190A-8s, and I and III/JG 2 at Cormeilles-en-Vexin with 48 (33) Fw 190A-8s. Geschwaderstab JG 26 was at Lille-Nord. I/JG 26 at Lille-Vendeville and Denain, and III/JG 26 at Nancy-Essay; the total strength of the Geschwader amounting to 75 fighters of which 47 were serviceable. The II/JG 26 was resting at Mont-de-Marsan, south of Bordeaux. Bülowius' FlKps II consisted of III/SG 4 and I/SKG 10 with 73 fighter-bombers; Fliegerkorps IX comprised Stab, I, II and III/KG 2, Stab, I and III/KG 6, 1. and 2./KG 66, II/KG 51, Stab, I and III/KG 54, 6./KG 76 and Stab I and III/KG 77, and under Fliegerführer West were Stab, I and III/ZG 1 with Bf 110G-2 fighters, while the forces of Holle's FlKps X consisted of 1.(F)/SAGr 129, III/KG 26, Stab, KG 30, I/KG 40 and Stab and III/KG 100. The reconnaissance forces subordinated to Luftflotte 3 were FAGr 5, 1.(F)/33, Sonder St.Ob.d.L., 7.(F)/121, Aufkl.Gr 123 and 3.(F)/122.

■ The invasion of Normandy and the retreat to the German border, 1944

On the first day of the invasion, some indication of the disparity between the Luftwaffe and the Allied air forces can be gauged from the fact that by comparison with the 100 fighter and 175 bomber sorties mounted by the Luftwaffe on 6 June no fewer than 14,674 were flown by the Allies. Over the beachheads themselves, the Luftwaffe was noteworthy for its virtual absence. During the day, the RAF flew 5,656 sorties in the face of minimal air opposition. Nevertheless, there was a stiffening of Luftwaffe opposition during the following week. In the 36 hours following the invasion 200 Bf 109Gs and Fw 190s arrived from the Reich, 45 torpedo-bombers were sent to FlKps X from Germany and 90 Ju 88s, Ju 188s and Me 410s reinforced FlKps IX from Germany and Italy. By 13 June, over a thousand aircraft had been rushed to counter the new threat n the West. By 10 June 1944, the following fighter units were based in France and engaged in combat operations against the Allies: Stab, I, II and III/JG 1, II, III and IV(Sturm)/JG 3, I/JG 5, I, II and 10./JG 11, Stab.I, III and IV/JG 27, II/JG 53 and III/JG 54. There was also an autonomous JGr 200, made up of Jagdschule aircraft, based at Avignon, which took no part in the Normandy operations.

By the end of June 1944, Allied air superiority was such that most Luftwaffe units were suffering from depleted strength and low serviceability. Great difficulty was experienced in getting new aircraft to the Jagdgruppen for, with the bombing of Le Bourget and Toul, spare aircraft had to be ferried from as far afield as Mannheim, Wiesbaden and Cologne. Five Jagdgruppen had to be withdrawn to Germany for re-fit after only ten days in Normandy. One example of this was the experience of II/JG 1, under Major Heinz Bär, which operated from a small grass strip near Semalle, 6–7kms north of Alençon. At 13.00hrs on 25 June, II/JG 1's airfield was strafed by 16 P-51 Mustangs. The attack was extremely successful and destroyed 15 out of the Gruppe's 24 Fw 190s, putting II/JG 1 out of action for several days. That night, 20 pilots of the Gruppe flew from Le Mans to Köln-Ostheim by Ju 52 to get replacement aircraft, but it was not until 1 July that these arrived. On 1 July, Bülowius took over Jagdkorps II from Junck, with the staff of Fliegerkorps II withdrawing from Normandy, but this commander could do little to urge his pilots to greater efforts in the face of Allied air superiority. The wastage in machines and pilots was immense; JG 26 alone lost 67 pilots in combat from D-Day to 31 August.

The Allied advance in Normandy had been checked at Caen, but on 1 August, the 3rd US Army attacked the weak front at Avranches and broke out to the West, South and East, encircling the German armies in the Falaise Pocket. In the Mortain-Falaise sector, the Wehrmacht suffered its greatest defeat since Stalingrad, but on the Allied side there was considerable disappointment because more than one-third of the German VII Army had eluded the trap. By 26 August, the British 2nd Army and the 1st Canadian Army had reached the Seine, while the US 1st and 3rd Armies had reached Paris, lunged south and reached Troyes. The air situation in the West by this time could hardly have deteriorated further, and to all purposes the Luftwaffe was a spent and exhausted force with little future prospect of recovery.

After a brief sojourn on the airfields in Belgium, the fighter units that had pro-vided the rearguard for the retreating Wehrmacht, namely, III/JG 1, Stab, I, II and

III/JG 2, Stab, II and III/JG 3, II/JG 6, I and II/JG 11, Stab, I, II and III/JG 26, III/JG 27, Stab and II/JG 53, Stab and III/JG 76 and I/JG 302 (Wilde Sau), were withdrawn to bases in Germany for re-fit. Nachtjagdgeschwader 2, 4 and 5 were likewise transferred, while FlKps IX's bomber force, which had shrunk to 175 aircraft, was pulled back and was to remain largely ineffective due to the increasingly difficult fuel situation. Meanwhile events in the East had given cause for further concern.

■ The Eastern Front, 1944

Contrary to German expectations, the Soviet summer offensive broke initially against the weak Finnish Front in Karelia on 10 June 1944, but this was opposed by the Luftwaffe in numbers far exceeding those committed to countering the Anglo-American invasion in the West. Of the 2,085 combat aircraft based in the East in June 1944, 105 were under Luftflotte 5 in the Gulf of Finland sector, 360 under Luftflotte 1 in the Baltic States and around the Narva area, 775 under Luftflotte 6 in the central sector, covering the Polish approaches where the main Soviet blow was expected to fall, and 845 were under Luftflotte 4 in the Balkans and the Carpathian sector.

When the main Soviet offensive opened on the Central Front, on 23 June, the forces of Luftflotte 6 had already been weakened by the transfer of 50 fighters and close-support aircraft to Finland and a Jagdgruppe to Germany following the large-scale despatch of fighters to the Normandy Front. By 3 July, the Russians had taken Vitebsk, Mogilev and Minsk, and were advancing steadily, forcing the Luftwaffe to throw in every available unit: 40 Bf 109G-6s were brought in from Germany (III/JG 11), III/JG 52 and IV/JG 51 were transferred from Luftflotte 4 in the South, while the need for ground-attack Fw 190s forced the transfer of I and II/SG 4 from the already denuded battlefront in Italy, followed later by III/SG 4 from Normandy. But the reinforced combat units facing the main Soviet assault failed to stem the rout that followed. In the north, Vilna fell on 13 July, followed by Grodno and Pinsk and, in the centre, the Wehrmacht was forced to abandon first Brest-Litovsk, then Lublin and Lwow, and finally Przemsyl on 28 July. By the end of the month, the Luftwaffe's total strength in the East had fallen to 1,750 aircraft, while the average daily effort of 500–600 sorties was inadequate to relieve the hard-pressed ground forces.

It was at this critical moment in time that the Balkan Front suddenly flared up. In Rumania, the Luftwaffe's weakness had already been shown by the paltry effort against the 15th USAAF. During the heavy B-17 and B-24 raids on Ploesti of 9 and 15 July, only 50 sorties (half of which were by Rumanian units) had been put up in defence of the vital oilfields. The fighter units in this sector were elements of JG 77, I/JG 53, II/JG 301 and the night-fighter IV/NJG 6.

All resistance in Rumania came to a precipitate end with the Rumanian *coup d'état* on 23 August 1944, which, in effect, ceded the country's cause to the Soviet Union. The transfer of I/SG 2 and a Rumanian Ju 87D unit to Zilistea was all that the

Luftwaffe could spare in an effort to retrieve the situation, but in the face of the Soviet advance across the Pruth river, all German units were quickly withdrawn to Hungary. By the end of August, Constanza, Ploesti and Bucharest had fallen: Bulgaria turned against Germany on 6 September, and thereafter the situation in the Balkans became untenable, with the Wehrmacht extricating itself to the best of its ability.By October 1944, all Luftwaffe combat operations were drastically curtailed due to the oil shortage. The combat units based in the East, as of 10 October 1944, were as follows:

Reconnaissance: NAGr 2, 4, 5, 8, 10, 2.(H)/12, 1. and 7.(H)/32 and Gruppen (H) 14 and 15; long-range reconnaissance: FAGr 2, Stab FAGr 1, 2.(F)/11, 4.(F)/11, 4.(F)/14, 3.(F)/22, 2.(F)/121, 2.(F)/100, 5.(F)/122 and 1.(F)/124; fighters: Stab, III and IV/JG 5 in Finland, Stab, I, II, III and IV/JG 51, Stab, I, II and III/JG 53, I/JG 53, Stab, I and II/JG 54 and Geschwaderstab JG 76; night-fighters: Stab, I and IV/NJG 5, I and 4./NJG 100, NJG Staffel Finland, Einsatz Staffel NJG 102; Zerstörer: IV/ZG 26 in Finland; Schlachtgeschwader: Stab, I, II, III and 10.(Pz)/SG 1, Stab, I, II, III and 10.(Pz)/SG 2, Stab, II, III and 10.(Pz)/SG 3, Stab, I, II and III/SG 4, IV(Pz)/SG 9, Stab, I and III/SG 10, Stab, I, II and 10.(Pz)/SG 77 and the Kroat Staffel. Bomber and heavy ground-attack units were Stab, II and III/KG 4 and the 14.Staffel of KG 3, KG 27 and KG 55.

By December 1944, Luftflotte 1 was cut-off and isolated in the Courland, Luftflotte 6, under Gen.Oberst Ritter von Greim with FlKps II and VIII subordinated, faced the Soviet armies in Central Poland on the line Königsburg-Warsaw-Krakow, while Luftflotte 4, under Gen. Oberst Dessloch with FlKps I Fl.Div 17 subordinated, occupied the line Krakow-Budapest-Lake Balaton, the latter now joining forces with Luftwaffenkommando Süd-Ost in the Balkans.

■ The closing ring, 1944

By September 1944, the steadily shrinking perimeters of the Third Reich had forced a general re-organisation of the command structure within the Luftwaffe. On 21 September, Luftflotte 3 was degraded to the status of Luftwaffenkommando West – an event already presaged by the replacement of Sperrle by Gen. Oberst Dessloch in August – which became subordinated to Luftflotte Reich. This command was responsible for tactical and close-support operations in conjunction with the air defence of Germany and, under its control were Jagdkorps II and Fliegerdivision 5. The strategic fighter defence of Germany was in the hands of Jagdkorps I, under the overall command of Stumpff's Luftflotte Reich, with HQ at Truenbreitzen. Jagdkorps I controlled Jagddivision 1 (Döberitz), Jagddivision 2 (Stade) with Jagdabschnittführer Denmark subordinated, Jagddivision 3 (Dortmund) with Jagdabschnittführer Mittelrhein, Jagddivision 7 (München) and Jagddivision 8 (Vienna); the Eastern Approaches were covered by Jafü Ost-Preussen and Jafü Ober-Silesien.

At the same time Luftflotte 5, in Norway was down-graded to Luftwaffen-kommando Norwegen and similarly, in Italy, Luftflotte 2 relinquished its functions to Luftwaffengeneral Italien (Gen. Ritter von Pohl). In the Balkans also a general re-shuffle of Commands took place, numerous subsidiary formations being placed under Luftwaffengeneral Nord-Balkan covering Northern Yugoslavia, and Luftwaffen-general Greichenland, both of them being subordinate to Lw.Kdo Süd-Ost. This extensive regrouping resulted in a great concentration of forces which should, theo-retically, have added flexibility and effectiveness to the defence of Germany, but in practice this improvement was offset by the increasingly desperate fuel shortage, the steady decline in the fighting value of crews and pilots, and congestion and increased vulnerability of airfields.

With the resumption of the Allied bombing offensive against the synthetic oil industry, the decision was taken at the end of September 1944 to leave no more than a small force of some 300 Fw 190s and Bf 109Gs to support the Wehrmacht in the West covering the approaches to the Rhine, while no less than 1,260 single-engined day fighters (including some 25 Me 163B-1s of I/JG 400) were allocated to the defence of the Reich, out of a total day fighter strength of 1,975. To provide this accu-mulation of strength for the defence of the oil installations, even the fighter force on the Eastern Front had to be reduced to no more than 375 aircraft. On top of this, 900 Ju 88Gs and Bf 110Gs of the Nachtjagdgruppen were available against the RAF's night bombing offensive, and altogether 70 per cent of the total Luftwaffe fighter strength was now earmarked for the defence of the oil industry.

For Allied pilots and aircrews, nurtured by the Press that stated, on every occasion, that the Luftwaffe was a beaten force as demonstrated by its absence over the Normandy battlefields, this resurgence of strength came as a grim reminder of the resilience of the Luftwaffe so often displayed in the past. True, the pilots of 1944 were not of the calibre of the Jagdflieger of 1940, but, to the end, they displayed an enthusiasm for flying, an aggressive spirit and tenacity and determination comparable with that of RAF fighter pilots during the Battle of Britain, or the US Navy pilots at Midway.

Within the average Jagdgruppe, at this time, only a tiny minority had any opera-tional experience of more than six months duration, with the exception of the Gruppenkommandeure and the Staffelkapitäne; a small percentage of personnel had an average of three months active service, while the majority of pilots had seen as little as two or three weeks. The training schools had emphasized the technicalities of fly-ing to the detriment of gunnery and tactics. This was revealed in all the fatal mistakes of the inexperienced pilot in combat – absurdly inadequate air-search and pre-occu-pation with formation keeping; an inability to fly the aircraft to its limits; a tendency to forget to jettison the drop tank or arm the weapons when joining combat and, finally, an inability to break off combat and escape when warranted by a tactical situ-ation. Equipment was good and the fighters were available in quantity, but their pilots lacked the vital element of quality.

The day fighter units under Jagdkorps I and II, on 10 October 1944, were: Stab, I, II and III/JG 2, Stab, I, II and III/JG 26, III/JG 27, Stab, II, III and IV/JG 53 under Luftwaffenkommando West: Stab, I, II and IV(Sturm)/JG 3, Stab, I, II(Sturm), III and IV/JG 4, I, II and IV/JG 27, IV/JG 54, Stab, I, II(Sturm), III and IV/JG 300, I/JG 400 and Jagdgruppe 10. Jagdgeschwader 1, 6 and 11 were either in process of re-equipping or formation.

In terms of aircraft performance, the pace was being maintained with that of the Allies. The Bf 109G-14 and K-4 were in widespread use, both having first class altitude combat performance, while the Fw 190A-8 and A-9, although much heavier, still displayed the original fighter's formidable qualities in the hands of a good pilot. Hauptmann Robert Weiss's III/JG 54 was the first unit to receive the Fw 190D-9 fighter that restored the performance balance vis-a-vis the Tempest V, the Spitfire XIV and the P-51D Mustang, and on 12 October 1944, 9. and 10./JG 54 were sent to Achmer and Hesepe to provide airfield cover for the Kommando Nowotny. Formed from Epr.Kdo 262 and led by Major Walter Nowotny (ex-Kdr. I/JG 54), this Kommando was the first Me 262 jet fighter interception unit. Its establishment was nominally forty Me 262A-1a fighters, but the strength never exceeded 30 and, during the subsequent operations from Achmer and Hesepe, this strength fell rapidly to no more than three, these losses being compounded by the death of Nowotny on 8 November 1944. The Kommando was subsequently disbanded and provided the nucleus of the similarly equipped III/JG 7 in December.

Fighter operations against the 8th USAAF continued to take a high toll of inexperienced pilots. Seventy pilots were killed and 28 wounded during the Leuna raid on 2 November. The Sturmgruppen, IV/JG 3 and II/JG 300 claimed 30 B-17s, but most of the 500 sorties put up were intercepted by P-51s, with JG 27 alone losing 25 pilots killed in return for seven Mustangs destroyed. Other maximum-effort interceptions on 21 and 26 November resulted in similar losses, but, thereafter, the diversion of fighters to support von Rundstedt's Ardennes offensive prevented further mass interception operations.

Towards the end of October 1944, the operational commands of the Luftwaffe first received warning of a large-scale project in which they were scheduled to play a prominent part. Under a tight cloak of security combat units were concentrated in the Vechta-Twente-Wesel sector during the closing weeks of November for tactical operations in support of the last Wehrmacht offensive in the West. The aim of the offensive was to destroy the Allied forces North of the line Antwerp-Brussels-Luxemburg. The 6th SS Panzer and V Panzer Armies, supported by the VII and XV Armies, were to break through the weak US lines in the Ardennes to the River Meuse under cover of bad weather, and then exploit their position by thrusting north-west to Antwerp and the Scheldt Estuary to cut off all the British forces and the northern flank of the 1st US Army from their sources of supply and destroy them. It was believed that for all practical purposes the British would drop out of the war as military opponents if this ambitious plan succeeded.

The plan was primarily that of Hitler and his subordinate commanders, von Rundstedt and Manteuffel, considered it impossible of fulfilment, accordingly setting themselves the more limited task of reaching the Meuse and wiping out the Aachen salient. The offensive in the Ardennes broke at dawn on 16 December 1944, in weather conditions that kept the opposing air forces grounded. To provide the necessary air support, some 1,200 single-engined fighters had been transferred to Luftwaffenkommando West from units engaged in the defence of the Reich, while about 100 Fw ground attack aircraft were moved in to the area from Luftflotte 6, in the Soviet Union. The total strength of Lw.Kdo West, on 20 December, amounted to 2,360 aircraft, leaving 400 Fw 190s and Bf 109s, and 1,100 night-fighters for the defence of Germany. These units were: Reconnaissance: NAGr 1, NAGr 13, and Einsatz.Kdo Braunegg (Me 262A-1); Fighters: JG 1, JG 2, JG 3, JG 4, JG 6, JG 11, JG 26, JG 27, JG 53, III and IV/JG 54, and JG 77; Ground-attack: Stab, I, II and III/SG 4, and NSGr 1, 2 and 20; Bombers: Stab I and II/LG 1, I/KG 66, Stab, I, II and III/KG 53 (operating under 'Rumpelkammer' and carrying V-1 flying bombs), Stab, I and 6./KG 51 with 42 Me 262A-2 bombers and 7./KG 76 with 10 Arado Ar 234B-1 bombers. The fighter force kept for defensive purposes were JG 300, JG 301 and I/JG 400, with the Nachtjagdgeschwader 1, 2, 3, 4, 5, 6, NJGr 10, I and II/NJG 11 and II/NJG 100. One Kampfgruppe, II/KG 100 with 44 He 177A-5s, was on the strength of Luftflotte Reich in addition to the above.

The force of 1,770 Bf 109s and Fw 190s now under Lw.Kdo West and 400 reserved for strategic defence contrasted sharply with the strength of 300 and 1,300 respectively on 1 October 1944, but, at the same time, indicated the expansion that had taken place in the Luftwaffe's fighter arm.

Prior to the Ardennes offensive Jagdkorps II was taken over by Gen.Maj. Dietrich Pelz, posted from the now moribund bomber forces of Fliegerkorps IX. The thick fog, which had aided the initial phases of the German offensive, lifted only slightly during the next week, in consequence of which both Allied and German air operations were very badly hampered. During 17 December, the Schlachtgruppen flew 600 sorties, whilst during the following night 250–300 sorties were flown against Allied lines of communication. On the ground, the Panzer spearheads by-passed Bastogne and, by 24 December, were in sight of the Meuse at Dinant. But now the PzKw V Panthers and PzKw VI Royal Tigers of II Panzer Division were at the limit of the German advance, awaiting fuel. The fuel was never to arrive. Then the weather improved, enabling the Allied air force to operate over the battlefront and, during the four days that preceded another deterioration in the weather, the RAF 2nd Tactical Air Force and the 9th USAAF were able to wrest the initiative away from the Luftwaffe.

Some 600 sorties per day were flown by the Luftwaffe during this critical period, and night-fighters (equipped with bomb racks), night ground attack aircraft and bombers contributed another 200–250 per night. The Me 262 bombers of KG 51 operated in insufficient numbers to achieve any real effect and their contribution consisted of tip-and-run raids on Liege and forward Allied airfields. The 'Mistel' Ju 88/Bf 109 composites also proved to be a dismal failure. The bad weather which set in again on 28 December gave both the Luftwaffe and the Wehrmacht a badly needed respite, but the damage was done. Bastogne was relieved on 26 December, Rochefort was re-captured on 31 December and the US forces went over to the offensive.

Before day-break on 1 January 1945, some 900 aircraft, mostly Fw 190s and Bf 109s, were being readied by their groundcrews on more than a score of airfields in Western Germany in preparation for the Luftwaffe's final, desperate gamble – Unternehmen Bodenplatte (Operation Baseplate). This was to be a low-level, surprise attack on the Allied airfields in Belgium and Holland; the targets chosen were Eindhoven, St Denis-Westrem, Volkel, Evere, Grimberghen, Melsbroek, Antwerp-Duerne, St Trond, Le Culot, Asch and Metz-Frascaty. The fighter units involved were JG 1, JG 3, JG 6, JG 26 with III/JG 54, JG 27 with IV/JG 54 and JG 77 from Jagddivision 3; JG 2, JG 4, JG 11 and JG 53 from Jagdabschnitt Mittelrhein, supported by JG 104, SG 4, NSGr 20 and I/KG 51. The fighters were led by Ju 88 night fighters from 5, 7, and 9./NJG 1, 4, 9, and 10./NJG 3, and 11./NJG 101 which were to provide navigational assistance to the frontline, and then depart. The time over target was to be 09.20 hours.

The attack achieved almost complete surprise, but whereas results were good at Eindhoven, Evere and Melsbroek, some airfields, such as Volkel which housed the crack No 122 Wing of the 2nd TAF, escaped damage entirely while the attacks on other airfields were not pressed home to advantage. A high proportion of the German fighter losses were inflicted by their own flak. The total casualties of all German units taking part in Bodenplatte amounted to 170 killed or missing in action, 67 taken prisoner, and 18 wounded, as against 144 RAF and 134 USAAF aircraft destroyed and 84 and 62 damaged respectively.

Whatever the motivations behind the Bodenplatte attack, the Luftwaffe was given no respite in the weeks that followed, and in early January 1945, the renewal of Russian pressure in Prussia, Poland and Holland brought about the transfer of combat units from Lw.Kdo West. By 15 January, 300 aircraft had been sent to the Eastern Front to bolster the 1,875 aircraft already there and, by 22 January, another 500 were about to be transferred or already on their way. These units were JG 1, JG 3, JG 4, JG 11, JG 77 and SG 4, consisting of about 650 fighters and 100 ground-attack Fw 190s. Accordingly, the total fighter and close-support strength available for operations in the East rose to 850–900 and 700 respectively.

At this time another re-shuffle of Commands took place. On the Western Front, Jagdkorps II, the tactical fighter command engaged in the northern sector, was disbanded and its place taken by Fliegerdivisionen 14 and 15. At the same time, Jagddivision 5, operating in the southern sector, was renamed Fl.Div 16, all three being subordinated to Luftwaffenkommando West. The strategic air defences of

Germany were similarly reorganised, Jagdkorps I being disbanded and its functions taken over by Fliegerkorps IX(Jagd) commanded by Pelz.

The fighter units remaining in the West were held at maximum strength while a strict policy of conservation was inaugurated. Measures were taken whereby only 50 per cent of the Jagdgruppen remaining was to be employed on operations, the remainder having to rest to conserve fuel. These units were forbidden to operate beyond the frontline; combat, even against heavy bombers, was to be avoided except in the most favourable circumstances. When operations were carried out, formations were to be used in maximum possible strength. Defence of the supply lines was now the first consideration.

By the beginning of February 1945, the Russians had reached the Oder and were advancing northwards into Pomerania while, in the southern sector, were debouching into Silesia, by-passing Breslau. The major Wehrmacht counteroffensive at this time took place in Hungary, when Wöhler's Army Group South made a surprise assault and established a bridgehead across the Hron river. On 6 March 1945, the 6th SS Pz., II Pz., VI and III (Hungarian) Armies launched a major offensive to relieve Budapest, but the part played by the Luftwaffe in support of the drive to the Danube was to be relatively minor. The Soviet counterattack of 16 March put the grandiose aspirations of Operation Frühlingserwachen (Spring Awakening) to rout; by 28 March the Soviet Army had reached the Austrian border in the Köszeg-Szombathely sector and, on 13 April, took Vienna. This was followed by the Soviet breakthrough on the Oder-Neisse line between 16–19 April, and the advance and encirclement of Berlin by the end of the month.

Excluding the reconnaissance units, the Luftwaffe combat units stationed on the Eastern Front on 1 April 1945 were as follows:

Luftflotte 1 (Prussia): Stab, I and III/JG 51 "Molders", and I/SG 3. Isolated in Courland (Latvia): Stab, I and II/JG 54 "Grünherz", III/SG 3 and NSGr 3.

Luftflotte 4 (FlKps I and Fl.Div 17): Stab JG 76, II/JG 52, I/SG 2, 14.(Pz)/SG 9, Stab, I, II and III/SG 10, NSGr 5, NSGr 7, Stab and 1./NSGr 10.

Luftflotte 6 (FlKps II and VIII): Stab, II and III/JG 1, Stab, II, III and IV/JG 3, Stab, I, II, III and IV/JG 4, Stab, I, II and III/JG 6, Stab, I, II and III/JG 11, Stab, I and III/JG 52, III/JG 54, Stab, I, II and III/JG 77, Eins.Kdo II and V/EJG 1, Stab, I, II and III/SG 1 (less 8.Staffel), Stab, II, III and 10.(Pz)/SG 2, Stab and II/SG 3, Stab, I, II and III/SG 4, 1, 2 and 10.(Pz)/SG 9, Stab, I, II, III and 10.(Pz)/SG 77 and 13./SG 151; II/LG 1, Stab, I and 8./KG 4, and 7./KG 53.

The extensive withdrawals to the Soviet Front had, by the middle of March 1945, reduced the strength of the Luftwaffe in the West to some 1,000–1,100 aircraft, of which 80 were Me 262A-2 fighter-bombers and Ar 234 reconnaissance-bombers. A further 1,000 aircraft were available for the strategic defence of NW Germany, divided roughly equally between day fighters and twin-engined night fighters, with some 50 Me 262A-1s operating in the interceptor capacity.

The Allied advance to the Rhine, culminating in the establishment of the Remagen bridgehead, and the piecemeal destruction of the Ruhr airfields, had led to some local redisposition of Luftwaffe forces to bases further removed from the front-line. Some 400 tactical sorties per day were flown by Me 262 and Ar 234 bombers, and Fw 190s against the 1st US Army's forces at Remagen, and these were joined by Ju 87Ds and Fw 190s of NSGr 20 during periods of bad weather and at night. On 23 March, the British 2nd Army crossed the Rhine at Wesel, followed two days later by the 3rd US Army's crossing at Mainz and Oppenheim. No attempt was made to re-inforce the West at the expense of the 2,200 combat aircraft now engaged on the Eastern Front, and, in consequence, Luftwaffe opposition to the Rhine crossings amounted to only 200 fighter sorties flown against the British at Wesel, and 350–400 against the 3rd US Army in the Oppenheim area. Luftwaffe reaction against the lat-ter collapsed after 25 March with the capture of the jet bomber airfields in the Darmstadt and Frankfurt areas.

The fuel situation was as critical as ever and the major Allied air assault on German airfields, that started on 21 March, reduced the Luftwaffe's capacity for operations still further. The major Luftwaffe effort was now committed to the East but, although it was no longer possible to differentiate between airfields holding units engaged on the Soviet Front and those employed at bases against the Western Allies, the Luftwaffe made no effort to use the seasoned ground-attack units facing the Russians in attacks on British and American armour which roamed Germany more or less at will.

The Luftwaffe units based in the West on 12 April 1945 were as follows:

Fliegerkorps IX (J): Stab, II and III/JG 4, Stab, I and III/JG 7 with 71 Me 262A-1s, I/KG(J) 54 and 25 Me 262A-2s, JGr 10, Stab, I and II/JG 301, I/JG 400, Stab, 1, 4, 7 and 10./NJG 1, Stab, I and III/NJG 2, Stab, I, 7 and 10./NJG 3, Stab, I, 4 and 7./NJG 4, Stab, I, 4, 7 and 10./NJG 5, 4, 7 and 10./NJG 11, 1./NJG 100 and Kommando Bonow with Ar 234B-1s. The forces under Fliegerdivision 14 consisted of: 2./NAGr 6, 1.(F)/33, 1.(F)/123, Stab, I, II and IV/JG 26, Stab, 6, and III/KG 76 with Ar 234B-1s, NSGr 20 and III/KG 200. The forces under Fliegerdivision 15 were NAGr 1, Stab, I, II and III/JG 2 and Stab, I, II and III/JG 27.

The third week in April showed a continuing general reduction in strength, though the scale of operations rose to a token 200 sorties per day against the Allied bridgeheads over the Elbe and the US advance on Nuremburg. Effective opposition had by now ceased in the West, while the Luftwaffe effort against the Russian assault against Berlin, which had risen to a peak of 1,100 sorties per day during mid-April, waned as each successive airfield was overrun. Berlin fell on 2 May, and on 8 May 1945, Germany surrendered to the Allies.

INDEX

447